third edition

Leisure

John R. Kelly
University of Illinois

Allyn and Bacon
Boston • London • Toronto • Sydney • Tokyo • Singapore

Senior Series Editor: Suzy Spivey
Vice President, Publisher: Susan Badger
Editorial Assistant: Lisa Davidson
Production Administrator: Joe Sweeney
Editorial-Production Service: Walsh Associates
Cover Administrator: Suzanne Harbison
Composition Buyer: Linda Cox
Manufacturing Buyer: Aloka Rathnam

Library of Congress Cataloging-in-Publication Data

Kelly, John R. (John Robert)
  Leisure / John R. Kelly. – 3rd ed.
    p.   cm.
  Includes bibliographic references and index.
  ISBN 0-13-110561-2
    1. Leisure–United States. 2. Leisure–United States–History.
  I. Title.
  GV53   IN PROCESS
  790′.01′350973–dc20   95-1087
                                                CIP

Printed in the United States of America
10 9 8 7 6 5 4 3 2   00 99 98 97

Part opening photo credits: xii, 204, and 300 © Frank Siteman; 116, Robert Harbison.

Contents

Preface

This book will not answer all your questions about leisure. It is an introduction to the study of leisure, but not an encyclopedia of all we know about the subject. However, it is intended to raise the most important issues. There is much that we don't know about the history of leisure and about its contemporary manifestations. But we are coming to know what the issues are and how we can approach them. New voices raise different issues and offer new perspectives. The primary aim of this book is to bring the reader into an engagement with both the known and the unknown about the human phenomenon we call *leisure*.

Knowledge is always based on some kind of research. Investigation may be formal or informal, systematic or haphazard, cumulative or novel. In the past four decades we have learned a good deal about leisure that was only guessed at before. And every new discovery leads to another set of issues that calls for investigation. We are always in the process of learning.

This book is not a collection of research reports. No attempt is made to summarize or even refer to every worthwhile study in the field. However, it is based on the developing body of knowledge in Leisure Studies. This text demonstrates that Leisure Studies is a field based in research that connects with recognized theory and research in social studies and the humanities and has both significance and integrity. Further, it is an attempt to provide some shape and structure to that knowledge. Historians, philosophers, economists, sociologists, political scientists, and psychologists have applied their scholarly tools to leisure. In Leisure Studies, it is time to try to integrate their discoveries into a coherent approach.

Whenever a new approach to understanding something like leisure is developed, much of the old and accepted "conventional wisdom" is challenged. It is found that some ideas that have been taken for granted do not stand up under new scrutiny or the passage of time. Some of what made sense in 1950 has collapsed under the pressure of unanticipated social change. Nevertheless, we have to do our best to understand every important aspect of our lives in our time.

One way of doing this is to allow people to tell their stories. Considerable material in this book comes from various attempts to encourage, record, and interpret the stories that a wide variety of persons have told about their leisure and its meanings for them. We also have considerable quantitative information gathered in surveys and government reports and computer-analyzed to aid our comprehension. A number of methods have been developed that add to the richness of a class or discussion group by stimulating participants to tell their stories and to gain further understanding from the analysis of experiences available to them. The discussion questions for each chapter are intended to help a group using this book to be knowledge producers as well as learners.

Approach

A comprehensive approach: *Leisure, 3/e* integrates history, current data and trends, a variety of conceptual approaches, critical perspectives to stimulate discussion, and full attention to the kinds of things that people do along with where and how they do them. This text provides a basis for classroom discussion and frees the instructor to concentrate on the issues and materials of greatest interest to the particular class. This inclusion allows the instructor to select emphases and focus on issues. I have made no attempt to disguise the premises that have guided my own study of leisure. Among them are some assumptions that are not shared by all interested in leisure. Leisure is understood here as a central element in being human. It is not peripheral or separate from the rest of life's meanings and relationships. In fact, leisure may be crucial to our personal and social development and to our concepts of ourselves and the world around us. Leisure is, after all, learned behavior. Its forms and content are a part of our culture and are transmitted in social contexts. As a consequence, we will have to examine much more than games and activities to begin to comprehend the significance of leisure in contemporary life. Leisure is thoroughly social.

Leisure is not only central and socially learned; it also involves meaning and action. The abiding theme of every leisure philosophy is freedom. Freedom means more than lack of constraint. Freedom is the possibility of self-determining action. In the incredible variety of what people do as leisure, there is a dimension of meaning. Therefore, a recurring question in trying to understand leisure in any culture is Why? How do people make choices, and what seems to be their consequences?

There are several limitations to this book. One, of course, is the author. As a sociologist with some background in philosophy, social psychology, and other social sciences, and with experience as a professional participant-observer in more that a dozen communities from New York to California, my background is broad but still limited. Even though considerable research has been done in Europe that has informed American scholars, for the most part this book concentrates on leisure in North America. Further, although almost every chapter includes several references to sources and publications that deal with the related issues, as an introduction this book is not all-inclusive. Rather, the philosophy and research considered most relevant and productive have been selected as a beginning. Many issues and agendas are suggested for further investigation.

New to this Edition:

- **Gender throughout the text:** Issues related to gender and the meanings and conditions of leisure for women—past and present—are woven through most chapters rather than limited to a single chapter. What does it mean to seek leisure in a sexist society? How has the study of and by women required reformulations of agendas and theoretical approaches? How do women "compose" their lives in the midst of a "stalled revolution"?

- **Leisure diversity in a multicultural society:** The study of leisure is beginning to expand its scope to recognize that "minorities" are becoming majorities in many American social worlds. Issues related to racial, ethnic, and social class diversity are combined with attention to gender and sexual orientation. What are the new agendas and issues provoked by this recognition of diversity? A new chapter (5) focusing on such diversity is augmented by the introduction of such issues throughout the text. The fundamental issue concerns the meaning of leisure in a society that is both inclusive and diverse.
- **Leisure as a political issue:** The thoroughly political nature of leisure is examined in a new chapter (6) as well as in the historical section. The allocation of resources is political as well as economic as demonstrated by debates over the environment. Issues of privilege and social control are balanced with analysis of the taken-for-granted political support and limitations of contemporary leisure and recreation.
- **Leisure in the marketplace:** Expanding on the 2nd edition's chapter on leisure as business, the 3rd edition analyzes what it means for 97 percent of leisure-related spending to be in the market sector. What are the aims of leisure businesses? Is leisure becoming more and more consumption of marketed commodities rather than action and interaction? Are there economic imperatives in a market economy that are shaping the nature of contemporary leisure?
- **Twentieth-century history:** The historical analyses from Greece, Rome, and western history are compressed in order to expand on technological change, the new metropolis and its suburbs, and the impacts of mass media and culture. Roots of social division and sources of contemporary culture are examined more fully.
- **History and contemporary issues:** Still the only text with more than a nod to history, *Leisure, 3/e* recasts the historical chapters to prompt discussion of implications in current leisure practices.
- **Sexuality in society:** The chapter on sexuality (22) is revised to introduce issues beyond sex-role socialization. The significance of sexuality for leisure is approached as pervasive rather than as a separate issue or as limited to sexual identification. The multiple meanings of "family" are placed in a focus on the centrality of primary relationships for leisure.
- **Aging and the life course:** Issues raised by social gerontologists in the author's recent book on activity and aging are used to give greater attention to this growing segment of the population. What are the continuities and changes in later life that impact patterns and meanings of activity? The chapter on the life course (4) now gives aging attention equal to youth and the middle years.
- **Mass media and popular culture:** The chapter on popular culture (16) is revised to give greater attention to the significance of mass media, new electronic developments, and the diversity of cultural styles. The dominance of television in non-work time allocation is central to understanding contemporary leisure styles and meanings.
- **The nature of leisure:** The classic analysis of definitional and theoretical approaches to leisure is revised to include a focus on such concepts as "flow," "creativity," and "existential" life-development. Further, the integrated approach avoids a tedious listing of individual studies, yet is based in research and theory.

Acknowledgments

During the years that the first two editions of *Leisure* have been used by colleges and universities from Maine to California and from Nova Scotia to New South Wales, I have received useful comments and suggestions from many faculty and not a few students. Many have been incorporated into this third edition. Also, I have learned more about leisure through research and exchange with colleagues throughout the world in the fourteen years since the first edition of *Leisure* was written. The content, order, and presentation ought to be considerably improved. I would like to thank and acknowledge those reviewers who provided feedback and suggestions for the 3rd edition. They are: James Bristor, Michigan State University; John R. Brouillette, Colorado State University; Frances C. Cannon, Florida State University; Craig Finney, California State University at Northridge; Donald V. Joyce, retired, Pennsylvania State University; Jean Keller, University of North Texas; Dennis Nelson, Utah State University; Steven Philipp, University of West Florida. I hope that I will continue to receive feedback from those who read and use this third edition.

The intent, then, is to raise important issues rather than to close them. Science, after all, is a process of learning and communication, not a body of facts. In the end, this book is an invitation to join in that process of learning as well as to engage in the full potential of leisure and of life.

Two chapters of the second edition are based on writings that I have published elsewhere. I am grateful to Venture Publishing for permission to use "Sources of Leisure Styles" (Chapter 3), which is revised from Thomas A. Goodale and Peter A. Witt, eds., *Recreation and Leisure: Issues in an Era of Change,* revised edition, 1985. Chapter 24, on theories of leisure, is based on my book *Freedom to Be: A New Sociology of Leisure* (Macmillan, 1987).

Thanks could be given so many colleagues and associates that the list would be almost endless. The Department of Leisure Studies at the University of Illinois has supported my work for more than nineteen years now. My colleagues there have always been a source of understanding and insight. My work with the World Leisure and Recreation Association and the Research Committee on Leisure of the International Sociological Association has brought me into association and exchange with scholars from around the world who have enriched my thinking in countless ways. Any book such as this one is built on the contributions of many others, acknowledged and unacknowledged. To them all I am grateful for the opportunity to join with them in the ongoing development of the important field of Leisure Studies. Finally, I continue to learn from my wife, Ruth, and my daughters and colleagues, Dr. Susan Kelly of Stanford University and Dr. Janice Kelly of Purdue University.

John R. Kelly
Champaign, Illinois

Section *I*

Contemporary Leisure: People and Resources

What do we need to know in order to begin to understand leisure in our world today?

If leisure is personal freedom, expression, and self-development, then we need to know about individual people. We need to have some grasp of how they learn, how they communicate, how they take action, and how they define themselves.

If leisure is social interaction, relationships, and the expression of community, then we need to know about stability and change in social contexts, about groups, normative expectations, self-presentations, the regularities of institutions, and the meanings of life together.

If leisure takes place in time and space, then we need to know about personal timetables, the interrelation of social schedules, and the ecology of leisure behavior, both indoor and outdoor.

If leisure patterns change with the rest of the society, we need to know as much as possible about what is going on in our society—about population shifts, economic and political change and conflicts, value orientations, group identifications, composite life styles, and new technologies.

The intent of this first section of *Leisure* is to bring insights from a variety of sources and disciplines into a focus on leisure. The material is selected to form a coherent introduction to the behavior and meanings that we call *leisure.*

1

Chapter *1*

The World of Leisure

What is leisure?
Why study leisure?
How can leisure fulfill its potential to meet human needs?

The first question is both simple and complex. *Leisure* is defined in this introductory level as *activity chosen in relative freedom for its qualities of satisfaction.* Yet, even with such simplicity, the variety of activity that may be leisure is staggering. There is no list of even a thousand and one activities that encompasses all leisure. It may be that there is no time and no place in which leisure is completely impossible. When leisure is defined as a quality of experience and as the meaning of activity, then it may be almost anything, anywhere, and anytime for someone. The simple definition leads to a vast panorama of human activity.

Reasons for studying leisure may be both qualitative and quantitative. On the one hand, leisure is very important to most people. In fact, there is evidence that leisure may be becoming more and more important in our lives. On the other hand, the scope of leisure is also vast in terms of the use of time, the expenditure of financial resources, and its relationship to home, family, and community.

So the importance of leisure to people and the scope of leisure in the society lead us to the third question about how the potential of leisure can be fulfilled in the lives of human beings. And that is really what this book is all about.

ISSUES

What is the scope of leisure in contemporary society?
What kinds of leisure are most important to people?
Is leisure a set of special activities that fill leftover time?
Is it important to study leisure?

3

✳ The electrician and his wife, a part-time secretary, have the trailer hitched to their pickup, the boat on top, and food and clothing carefully packed. They crisscross the still-dark streets of their community and slip onto the freeway headed north. Both sigh deeply. For the next three weeks they will camp, fish, boat, relax, talk, and visit relatives in the Pacific Northwest. Hot, crowded, and busy Los Angeles is left behind for an interval of carefully numbered days of green forests, cool lakes, struggling fish, and quiet conversation. This trip, like last year's, has been planned and anticipated for eleven months.

✳ Her children in school and outlines made for the afternoon's series of piano lessons with grudging children, the thirty-year-old wife-mother-homemaker-piano teacher sits before the piano. As her fingers quickly and competently trace the counter-melodies of a Bach prelude, her mind recalls with still-warm pleasure the praise of her university teacher when she first played the same piece flawlessly before a class of peers.

✳ Home from the plant where he has put in another eight hours in which his now-automated set of lathes perform the same operation every 6.42 minutes, the machinist hurries through his supper. In the basement is his own lathe—small, simple, and yet precise—at which he hopes to complete the piston rods for a small engine he has been building for almost a month in his free time. When completed, the engine will be run awhile, shown to approving friends, and perhaps placed on a shelf to be given someday to a yet-unborn grandson.

✳ A young art editor hurries from her office an hour before noon. At eleven-thirty she will meet three friends for an hour of doubles in an old armory converted to a downtown tennis club. By one o'clock she will be back at her desk, where she will remain until at least seven to meet another deadline.

✳ With the children departed from the table for their homework hour, two people who have been married to each other for sixteen years are talking for the only time that day. Not just announcements and requests, the morning conversational fare, but feelings and memories fill the half-hour over the last of the coffee.

✳ The noise and dust of the Ford assembly plant are repressed but not forgotten as the worker drops heavily into "his" chair, snaps the remote control of the color television set, and begins to tilt his first can of beer. The yard can wait until the weekend.

✳ Wife, children, and dog are all in the station wagon as the husband-father-bank teller backs out of the driveway. The Wisconsin landscape is not spectacular, but the fields punctuated by white houses and red barns, the spots of woods, and the first hints of fall color will keep all eyes engaged on this Sunday afternoon drive. The power of the car and the two-laned vista of secondary road give them a sense that they are going somewhere together.

✳ In the gray light of early morning, a man and a woman reach toward each other, mold their bodies together, and hold each other in silence. Remembered for the moment is the rush of feeling leading to intercourse the night before. Forgotten for the moment is the quarrel over Friday's party and his promise to usher in church later that morning.

* As the father joins in the cheers for the local high school basketball team—now heading for the bench with a twelve-point, third-quarter lead—he wonders how soon the coach will consider the margin adequate to remove that 6′ 4″ senior forward and put in his 6′ 2″ son.

* Picnics are an old family tradition. Children enjoy the change of environments. Father has an opportunity to focus on the children away from any telephone connection to the office and the unending chores of maintaining a house and yard. The mother, of course, has arranged the time, prepared the food taking into account both tastes and allergies, and managed to get everyone ready. Picnics are fun, but the household manager/provider/counselor cannot leave those roles behind. The event is valued, but is hardly free from responsibility or even conflict.

By most definitions, all of these people are engaged in "leisure." Each such event is a space of leisure in an ongoing journey of life. Performed with a variety of companions or none, strenuously or without effort, frequently or rarely, indoors or outdoors, spontaneously or on schedule—what do these events have in common that permits them to be defined as leisure? The common element is not place, nor is it the nature of the activity, the companions, the time of day or of the week, or even the kind of satisfaction that is gained. The only common element seems to be that each occasion has been chosen with some satisfaction anticipated. None *had* to be done. None was sheer duty.

Is leisure simply any activity that is chosen rather than required from which some satisfaction is expected?

The Variety of Leisure

When asked about their leisure, most Americans respond in terms of particular kinds of activities. If they are young, they may begin listing sports they play, concerts they attend, and whatever they do on Saturday nights. If they are a few years older, they may refer to vacation trips, evenings with friends, and family outings. If they are approaching retirement, they may talk about evenings at home or with friends, trips to see the grandchildren, and development of a yard or a garden. Some are forthright enough to mention television and, once they think about it, most speak of reading for pleasure.

Several studies have produced rankings of the kinds of activity that are significant in people's lives. Some list those kinds of activities that occupy the most time. In modern societies that list is always headed by watching television and informal interaction with others in the household and friendship and work groups. Others list activities in order of frequency of participation. Such lists should add very frequent off-task moments of daydreaming and exchange with others in the work or home environment.

More often such lists include only "official" recreation activities, such as sports, going to concerts, and jogging. As we will see, such lists distort the picture of actual patterns in two ways. First, they usually include those who engage in activities very rarely, sometimes as seldom as once or twice a year. So the number of 18 million tennis players includes many who would have to search for that racquet they last used months ago. Second, such activities are not necessarily at the center of an individual's leisure priorities.

In studies of leisure patterns in three communities in the United States, the activities most often ranked among the most important to participants yielded the following picture:[1]

1. Six of the ten top-ranked were some sort of interaction with family and friends. In order they were
   Affection and intimacy
   Informal conversation
   Activity as a couple: talking, walking, shopping, etc.
   Outings and social events
   Visiting family and friends
   Playing with children
2. Others in the top ten were
   Reading for pleasure
   Watching television
   Outdoor sports: individual or pair such as swimming, racquet sports, etc.
   Eating out
3. Others on the list in order were
   Religious worship
   Short auto trips
   Gardening and yard care
   Home decorating and shop projects
   Arts or crafts such as ceramics, painting, etc.
   Entertaining at home
   Hunting and/or fishing
   Child-centered events such as school events and sports
   Conversations with friends and neighbors
   Walking and/or jogging
   Hobbies such as collecting
   Companionship on the job

Importance is not the same as the amount of time or money spent on an activity. Some activity may be primarily a time-filler such as considerable television watching. Other activity may be quite central to important relationships or to self-development. And a special vacation trip may come only once a year, but be extremely important in its place in the whole scheme of values.

One approach suggests that the wide variety of leisure may be seen as a kind of balance. Some activity is of high intensity, requires considerable effort and discipline, and is quite central to self-definition. For example, a person may be very involved in sports as a player or coach, in the arts as a creator or organizer, or in some particular form of travel. At the other extreme are activities of very low intensity that tend to be oriented toward relaxation and offer

[1] J. R. Kelly, "Leisure Styles and Choices in Three Environments," *Pacific Sociological Review,* 21 (1978), 187–207.

a change from other demanding aspects of life such as employment or child care. In the overall balance, most people have both relatively intense and relaxing engagements.

Another approach suggests that leisure is both personal and social. The primary orientation of some engagement is to be *with* important other people, to develop and express relationships. Other leisure is oriented more to the self in expression, self-development, or emotional release.

The ordinariness of most leisure does not mean that many people would not like to participate more in outdoor sports, visit places of scenic beauty or cultural interest, or engage in recreation at lakes, rivers, or oceans. However, distances and limits on time and financial resources prevent most people from doing many things they would like to do. Most choices are made among relatively accessible and low-demand activities. The available resources of home and neighborhood come first because they are at hand. They also come first because the periods of time available for recreation are almost always limited. Activity has to be fit into the timetables and demands of lives in which there is seldom any totally "free time."

The point is that people do all kinds of things as leisure. While we may be intrigued by accounts of people who step out of airplanes or sail across oceans, most of our leisure is quite ordinary, readily available, and demanding only in that it requires us to get along with our families and friends.

Just as leisure can take place anywhere, it can occur anytime. While some periods—weekends, evenings, and vacations—are most likely to be available for those with regular work or school schedules, people can seek *moments* of leisure at almost any given point within a work schedule.

How Can Leisure Be Identified?

Students have been asked: Is there any activity that is always leisure? Usually no answer is forthcoming that is not quickly retracted when someone else comes up with an exception. Almost anything can be required or done for reasons quite distinct from satisfactions anticipated. The one exception that seems difficult to remove from contention came from a student who frequently practiced what he suggested: daydreaming. By definition, when daydreaming turns to some purpose, it becomes contemplation or planning. Its aimlessness and the freedom of its fantasy may make daydreaming the nearest thing to an activity that is always leisure.

A related question provokes similar hesitation: Is there any setting or time in which leisure always takes place? As already suggested, it seems possible to trade freedom for constraint and satisfaction for duty anywhere at any time.

More provocative questions have to do with associations, modes of participation, and expected benefits. With whom is the activity done? How is it done? Why is it done? Answers to these questions seem more central to leisure than what, where, and when.

According to *Webster's Third International Dictionary,* the word *leisure* is derived from the Latin *licere,* meaning "to be free." Leisure is done in a *leisurely* or relatively unconstrained and uncoerced manner. It is done *freely.* Leisure is freely chosen because the activity or the companions or some combination of the two promises personal satisfaction. It is the personal and social orientation of the participant that makes an activity leisure—or something else. Leisure is defined by the use of the time, not the time itself. It is distinguished by the meaning of the activity, not its form. Aristotle, in Book 8 of his *Politics,* was right in pointing to the intrinsic pleasure or happiness that distinguishes leisure from lesser activity. Leisure is activity that is chosen more for its own sake than for ends related to survival or necessity. There is more to defining leisure, but choice for its own sake is central.

Some would define leisure quite exclusively. For Sebastian deGrazia, leisure is a rare and exotic state, one that may never be achieved by most of us.[2] Any trace of social manipulation or lack of free expression keeps that experience from being defined truly as leisure. The result is that very little remains. After all, everything we do has some elements that limit our freedom. Any activity that involves another person calls for some adjustment to the expectations of that other person in order to meet and communicate.

On the other hand, inclusive definitions run the risk of not distinguishing leisure at all. If leisure is defined as anything done outside of employment, then it may include some of the least free events of our lives, such as taking a test for a driver's license or waiting for a ride to the hospital. However, if most leisure involves other people, and meeting people includes some constraint, then leisure can hardly be completely free in every sense. At this point, an ordinary definition should be adequate. *Leisure is activity chosen in relative freedom for its qualities of satisfaction.*

The Scope of Leisure

Taking the general and inclusive approach just suggested, what is the scope of leisure in people's lives and in society? Or perhaps the question should be, What are people *not* doing as leisure? There may be about 16 million people in the United States who engage in the time-honored hobby of collecting stamps,[3] but it is also possible to fill entire arenas with people trading and selling old beer cans. It is estimated that in 1991 some 18 million seats were occupied at professional football games and attendances of more than 64 million were counted at thoroughbred horse races. Almost 40 million also visited a museum at least once during the year. Up to 10 million people may have investigated their ancestry and genealogical lines, but over three times that many were at home gardening. More than 36 million attendance was recorded at college football games and 33 million at college basketball; estimates of the number who attended high school games, hometown Little League, and softball would be staggering, if rather inaccurate. Tennis may have grown to a high of 30 million players by 1976 before declining to about 17 million by 1991, but either figure is dwarfed by the 40 million who bowled in 1991.

These statistics do not even begin to describe the scope of leisure in contemporary American society. For every one person who attends a cultural or sporting event on a Saturday, there must have been fifty who went to a nearby shopping center to *look around* for a while and perhaps pick up one or two items as a justification for going. The meeting place for teens has become the shopping center, not the gym.

[2] Sebastian deGrazia, *Of Time, Work, and Leisure* (Garden City, NY: Doubleday, 1964).

[3] This and other participation estimates to follow are taken from a variety of sources and published in the *Statistical Abstract of the United States,* 1993 edition. Most are probably accurate within a 10 to 20 percent margin of error.

As shown in studies on adult leisure and outdoor recreation, it is the informal and everyday kinds of things that are the heart of most people's leisure. Events outside the home are special; they heighten and give needed interruption to the ordinary. Vacations are even more special, since they provide a longer break from routine. But for the most part, in their leisure, people talk to each other, watch television, read, do something around the house or garden, play with the kids, go to the store, and fantasize about other things they might be doing if life had no limitations.

The list of activities that are leisure to some people is endless. Even the most prosaic lists prepared by recreation professionals contain hundreds of possibilities. Reports of snake roundups in the Southwest, roping clubs in cattle country, and just whittling in the hills remind us that there is no way we could even begin to think of all the varieties.

The amount of time spent also varies, but it does suggest the importance of leisure in the overall scheme of life. If 56 hours are subtracted for sleep and 50 for work and getting to work from the week's 168 hours, some 62 hours remain. Much of that time is obligated to maintenance of the self and of the household. While younger and older people have more time free from obligations, we can say that generally people have as much as 35 hours a week available for some kind of chosen activity. Measured by time, the potential scope of leisure is considerable.

Leisure Expenditures

Measured by money, leisure has become a leading industry. *Not* including equipment such as automobiles that are used for leisure as much as or more than they are used for necessities, or government spending on recreation programs and facilities, or the incalculable worth of federal land used for recreation, or the cost of space in homes, churches, and schools used for leisure, direct leisure spending in the United States is estimated to exceed $300 billion a year. This amount, adjusted to include inflation, is at least double what it was in 1970. Several estimates suggest that the average household spends about 8 percent of its income directly on leisure.

Of course, such figures do not necessarily represent participation. Some expensive items, such as boats, trailers, and vacations homes, may be used very little. On the other hand, a television set costs only a few cents an hour to watch, including depreciation, electricity, and repairs. At the same time, items such as moving to an expensive house in the suburbs may be in part a leisure expenditure to obtain a safe yard for children to play in and proximity to outdoor opportunities for both children and parents.

The financial scope of leisure is enormous, even when only expenditures that are clearly leisure-related are included. Stadium admissions, equipment, resort and vacation travel costs, and other such items make clear that leisure is big business, even without including the oversized station wagon useful primarily for the vacation trip or the game room, yard, or entertainment space built into a new home.

Values and Leisure

The significance of leisure in the value systems of contemporary adults is less clear. We cannot assume that people invest the most time or money on what they find most important. On the contrary, people appear to value most those relationships and activities that require the least in special equipment or resources. On the other hand, there is evidence that leisure is quite important to many people.

What is most important to people? A study of factory workers in the Midwest found that only 24 percent could be classified as "work-oriented."[4] Three-quarters saw the family, leisure, and their own well-being in some combination as more central to their lives than work. Similar results were obtained in a French study by Joffre Dumazedier. He found that among skilled workers 25 percent found their maximum satisfaction in leisure and 53 percent in family activities.[5] A more recent study of Midwest men and women workers found that most valued their families most followed by leisure and work in that order.[6] Most, however, tried to develop a balance among these elements even when there were conflicts among time allocations or role responsibilities.

On the basis of survey data gathered in the United States and ten West European nations, Ronald Inglehart of Michigan's Institute for Social Research discovered a shift away from material values and physical security (materialism) toward a greater concern with self-expression and the quality of life (postmaterialism).[7] While the rates of change differ from one nation to another, the growth of what might be labeled a *leisure ethic,* stressing the quality of life's experiences and environment rather than possessions and occupational prestige, suggests that a postmaterialist worldview is increasing. Postmaterialists are twice as likely to be university educated as materialists and, depending on the nation, three to five times as likely to be under thirty.

No one can be sure that the "postindustrial" age will also be predominately "postmaterialist." However, this survey of values is only one of several indications that people are tending to take the development of their relationships, their environments, and themselves more seriously.

For some, a higher material "standard of living" comes first. Even leisure may be defined primarily in terms of what is spent to purchase equipment, clothes, environments, and the consumption of entertainment. For others, the leisure element in a total "quality of life" is more a matter of experiences of sharing with others, an immersion in natural environments, and the challenge of action. There is cultural conflict between leisure as what we buy and possess and leisure as what we do and who we become. Is leisure the height of consumption, an add-on after we have achieved a full material package, or essential to a life in which meaning is not lost in possessions?

Leisure in the emerging society may not be as idealistic and person-centered as some would hope. Quality of life can be defined and measured in quite materialistic ways as well as in terms of environment and personal development. Leisure may be viewed as purchased opportunities and possessions as well as nonmaterialist values. Modern societies do, however, seem to be shifting from a focus on production to a multidimensioned valuing of the

[4] Robert Dubin, "Industrial Workers' Worlds: A Study in the 'Central Life Interests' of Industrial Workers," *Social Problems,* 3, 3 (1956).

[5] Joffre Dumazedier, *Toward a Society of Leisure* (New York: Free Press, 1967).

[6] John R. Kelly and Janice R. Kelly, "Multiple Dimensions of Meaning in the Domains of Work, Family, and Leisure," *Journal of Leisure Research* 26, 3, pp. 250–274 (1994).

[7] Ronald Inglehart, *Culture Shift in Advanced Industrial Society* (Princeton, NJ: Princeton University Press, 1990).

quality of life. Within this shift, leisure is emerging as a significant dimension of the over-all values and priorities of those who are moving into the twenty-first century.

Paradoxically, this rise in leisure expectations may be combined with a loss of time for nonobligated activity. *The Overworked American*[8] points to a time scarcity for many in contemporary society. Those vital to the research and development underlying economic productivity, those in service industries with long and irregular hours, and women who come home from employment to primary responsibility for childrearing and household maintenance are not experiencing the dawn of an "age of leisure." Some report time famine while others deal with unemployment and lengthening years of retirement.

The Importance of Leisure

Some indications have been presented that leisure is increasingly important in the value schemes and schedules of modern Western adults.

Leisure and Personal Welfare

What are the common reasons that people seek leisure opportunities and activity? If asked, most respond simply that "I like it." When questioned further as to why they "like it," common responses suggest some of the dimensions of why leisure is valued.

"I like concentrating my mind, emotions, and body on the music," replies the young mother who plays Bach. Leisure integrates the self at the same time that it is expressive of it, especially when the activity requires the bringing together of attention and action. Further, the demonstration of mastery achieved through discipline and practice is found to be satisfying.

The couple described at the beginning of the chapter, who were packing for their annual trip to the lakes and mountains, like the opportunity to get away from the city and its crowded streets and freeways and from the routines of work. Even more, however, they would say that they like it because they have a chance to really be together and to spend some time with their relatives. The travel, camping, and fishing have their freedom and relaxation, but more often they speak enthusiastically about the companionship.

The machinist will refer to the satisfaction of actually making something, of creating by employing his skills. The art editor speaks of the relaxation of tennis in the midst of a harried schedule and of the sport being good for her physical and emotional health. However, given more time to think about it, she will also mention the new friends she is making and the satisfaction of improving her game.

The couple talking over coffee find that the relaxed communication has become almost as much of a need, a craving, as the dinner that goes before. The Ford worker remembers the strain of the factory and speaks of his need to relax. The father at the basketball game hopes for the joy of seeing his son play, but also knows that the boy would be disappointed if Dad were not there. The mother values the family event despite the "work" that makes it possible.

---

[8] Juliet B. Schor, *The Overworked American: The Unexpected Decline of Leisure* (New York: Basic Books, 1991).

What do people find in their leisure? Self-expression, companionship, integration of mind and body or wholeness, physical health, a needed contrast or rhythm in the work-constrained schedule, rest and relaxation, a chance to try something new and to meet new people, to build relationships, to consolidate the family, to get in touch with nature, to test oneself in risk or competition, to meet the expectations of people who are important to them, and to just feel good without analyzing why. All these are among the benefits people find in their leisure.

Leisure and the Society

Of course, if leisure is beneficial to the health of the citizens of a society, it benefits the society in general. That has been the most common argument for the support of leisure programs. The origin of the recreation movement in the United States stemmed from the rise of the industrial cities, their lack of recreation space and opportunity for children and youth, and the quite evident problems of physical and social health.

Today, although there are still many people in the inner cities and rural fringes whose opportunities for leisure are extremely limited, the question of the value of leisure to the society has changed. Some of the urgency felt in the time of the Industrial Revolution, when so many lives were being chewed up in the factories and smothered in the crowded sprawl of the city, has been lost. This loss is due as much to familiarity with old problems as to improved conditions for those still caught in the twin trap of poverty and lack of opportunity. For most Americans, however, recreation has become an accepted public program. As such, it must compete for support and funding with national defense, education, health care, housing, and highways. How can public recreation be supported?

Without anticipating all of the discussion of later chapters, at least four arguments for leisure programs and provisions may be outlined as follows:

1. As suggested, leisure as a part of the rhythm of life, freedom, and self-development is important to the wholeness of human life. Leisure is good for people.
2. There are still several significant kinds of opportunities for leisure that require public provisions. In the city where land is expensive, in the forestland where trees may be used for paper as well as shade, and along the water where wealthy private owners have cut the public off from beaches and shorelines, public action and public funds are required to hold space for recreation. Further, while many can pay to go where they want, others cannot pay for learning opportunities for their children or a trip for themselves.
3. With more than half of American workers engaged in services and with the proportion in manufacturing continuing to decline, many refer to this as a "postindustrial age." Such a turn from production and stress on material goods toward the development of selves and society supports the increasing importance of leisure.
4. Finally, adapting a classic sociological argument, the social nature of much leisure would indicate that leisure has the special function of building community in a society. In the chosen activities and relationships of leisure, the bonding of intimate groups such as the family and larger groups of the community takes place. In short, a society needs leisure so that people can learn to live together.

Why Study Leisure?

In a sense this entire book is an answer to the question "Why study leisure?" A summary of the answer would be simply: *Because it is important to people.* Leisure is important because we need some freedom to become and to be ourselves. Leisure is important because we need to develop and maintain relationships with other persons on more than a *have-to* basis. Leisure is important to most of us as we manage our schedules, develop our priorities, and seek to make our lives as full and rich as possible. Leisure is a major and growing sector of the economy. And leisure is important as a phenomenon in society when measured by time invested, money spent, or values expressed. We need to know as much as possible about anything that important to so many people.

But there is more. If leisure is so very important to people, then we also need to know what kinds of social arrangements facilitate leisure and what kinds of arrangements block participation and satisfaction. The crucial issue around which this book revolves is this: *How can leisure fulfill its potential to meet human needs?* To answer this question, we need to know as much as possible about people, about social contexts, and about the nature of leisure as a human phenomenon. For this reason we will employ the resources of history and philosophy, sociology and psychology, economics and political theory, as well as a fair amount of personal experience and shared understanding, to introduce ourselves to leisure—its potential and limits, its past, present, and future.

A Preview of Coming Attractions

To introduce leisure, this book travels back and forth across traditional academic disciplines in an attempt to develop an integrated approach to the subject. Although many unclear and even blank areas in the overall picture will remain, the premise is that leisure as human activity requires that no useful or relevant source of understanding be omitted simply because the author recognizes that his grasp of the area is incomplete.

The first two chapters of Section I, on contemporary leisure, introduce the topic of leisure. In Chapter 2, contemporary definitions of leisure, recreation, and play are examined for similarities and differences. An inclusive definition of leisure is proposed that is based on the one theme that is central to all definitions and approaches: *freedom.* Recreation as *organized leisure* and play as *leisure in action* encompass the common distinctions.

Chapter 3 examines leisure styles and begins to put leisure in a more systematic social context. Chapter 4 raises issues of social diversity and conflict based on social class, race, ethnicity, gender, and age. In Chapter 5, political dimensions of leisure are explored. In Chapter 6, leisure is placed in the context of the life course. The metaphor of life as a journey with changes and continuities is employed to examine how leisure is based in the social relationships and developmental issues of life. In Chapter 7, the life domains of work and leisure are related to each other and to the framework of time.

In Section II, on the past and future of leisure (Chapters 8 to 12), the narrative interweaves concepts of leisure with their historical contexts. In a rapid transit through Greek, Roman, and Judeo-Christian traditions to past American times and traditions, the discussion focuses on issues that have reemerged in more recent times. Rather than an exhaustive history of leisure, the intent is to provide a historical context for contemporary issues.

Section III is on forms of leisure and recreation. The forms and locales of activity are an important component of their possibilities for action and interaction. Sport, resource-based outdoor activity, the arts, popular culture, mass media, and travel are forms of leisure that receive particular attention in Chapters 13 to 17.

Section IV deals with leisure contexts and resources. First the provisions of the public sector are introduced. Then the significance of education and of market sector provisions are examined. These chapters are followed by consideration of special leisure subcultures, sexuality and leisure, issues related to persons with special participation requirements and limitations, and an outline of eight theoretical metaphors for understanding leisure.

Throughout this book, the aim is to approach leisure as more than a set of activities engaged in when everything important has been completed. Rather, leisure is understood to be human activity that is interconnected with everything important in life. Leisure cannot be understood as a separate realm of life. This requires that attention be given to both the self and society. Leisure is action taken by the person that has meaning for the present and the future. Leisure is also social in being behavior that is learned and acted out in social contexts. The aim, then, is to take what seems most relevant from current knowledge of personality, social interaction, social institutions, and human development to yield a comprehensive basis for understanding. The underlying assumption is that there is now enough known through research in history, psychology, sociology, economics, anthropology, and other disciplines to provide an adequate basis for such a synthesis.

Although the number of pages and chapters ahead may appear formidable, it is important to keep in mind that this is only an introduction. There is a great deal more to know about leisure and even more that remains to be discovered. In one sense, this is an invitation to join in a lifelong exploration of the meanings of leisure.

HIGHLIGHTS

1. Leisure is a vast and varied set of activities incorporating an incalculable range of personal interests, market provisions, and public resources.
2. Although the study of leisure will reveal many exceptions to every generalization, for most people, informal leisure, often social and usually close at hand, is most significant.
3. Leisure is freedom, and as such it is crucial to human and social development. Therefore, leisure cannot be reduced to any list of activities, places, or times.
4. If leisure is important to people and to society, then we need to understand both what it is now and what it might become.

Discussion Questions

1. Why study leisure? How would you respond to the charge that the study of leisure is inherently frivolous?

2. Give examples of activities that are always leisure. What is never leisure?

3. How would you define leisure? Recreation? Play? Fun?

4. How would the leisure most important to students differ from the ranking of their parents? Why?

5. What kinds of activities are most likely to decrease with age? Why?

6. What seems to be missing from the definition of leisure as *activity chosen in relative freedom for its qualities of satisfaction?*

7. Can you cite evidence that many people are finding leisure more central to their lives now than it was a decade ago? Than fifty years ago?

Bibliography

Chubb, Michael, and Holly Chubb, *One Third of Our Time?* New York: John Wiley, 1981.

Godbey, Geoffrey, *Leisure in Your Life: An Exploration.* State College, PA: Venture, 1985.

Goodale, Thomas L., and Peter A. Witt, eds., *Recreation and Leisure: Issues in An Era Of Change,* Third edition. State College, PA: Venture, 1991.

Graefe, Alan, and Stanley Parker, *Recreation and Leisure: An Introductory Handbook.* State College, PA: Venture, 1987.

Kaplan, Max, *Leisure in America: An Overview.* New York: John Wiley, 1960.

Kelly, John R., *Recreation Trends toward the Year 2000.* Champaign, IL: Management Learning Laboratories, 1987.

Kraus, Richard, *Leisure in a Changing America: Multicultural Perspectives.* New York: Macmillan, 1994.

Roberts, Kenneth, *Contemporary Society and the Growth of Leisure.* London: Longman, 1978.

Chapter 2

Leisure, Recreation, and Play

In defining leisure and recreation, the same words have often been used in exactly opposite ways. *Leisure* refers to an experience for some users and to a quantity of time for others. *Recreation* is an emotion to some and institutionalized activity to others. *Play* has been employed to refer both to free expression and to necessary learning. In such a situation, we have to get our terms straight or suffer confusion that will eventually lead to conflict.

Another problem with definitions is that within a field of study the esoteric is often mistaken for the profound. The further away from common usage a definition is, the more impressive it is to some who confuse novelty with originality. A definition has to distinguish what is defined from other similar referents or it is of no use; however, such precision need not produce another jargon.

What, then, do terms like *leisure, recreation,* and *play* mean? In general, does leisure mean "What I choose to do because I enjoy it"? Do most people refer to organized leisure activity as recreation? Is play most often seen as the free and expressive behavior of children? The definitions proposed here attempt to combine such common usage with the history of the terms to produce enough agreement to go on with our enterprise of coming to understand leisure and the people who engage in it.

ISSUES

How are leisure, recreation, and play best defined?

Why have conflicting definitions been proposed for the same phenomenon?

What is the significance of freedom for leisure and play?

Can leisure be defined in a way consistent with ordinary usage, or must a scientific definition be complex and esoteric?

What Is Leisure?

How many ways are there to define leisure? One? Four? Six? Or are there as many ways as there are people working out a pattern of choices satisfying to them at the time?

In 1899, Thorstein Veblen defined leisure as the "nonproductive consumption of time."[1] He stressed that leisure differs in intent from work and is symbolic of high status because it does not produce wealth or income. Since then, definitions have proliferated into complex schemes and lengthy lists.

Max Kaplan proposes six kinds of definitions.[2] He recognizes that they do not all begin with the same premises. For example, the humanistic or classic definition begins with a concept of humanity and requires freedom from necessity. The therapeutic approach assumes that some people are less than healthy and that leisure is good for them. The quantitative model assumes that time can be identified by the way it is used. The institutional concept presupposes a functional division of institutions within a social system in which leisure may stand with the school, the family, the church, the economy, and the state. The epistemological conception is based on the values of a culture. And the sociological approach begins with the belief that leisure and everything else is defined in a social context by social actors who are creating their universe of meaning. Kaplan makes it clear that definitions differ more profoundly than a list of alternatives would suggest. They begin with different views of people and the world.

A somewhat similar array of six kinds of definitions is proposed by James Murphy.[3] His scheme includes concepts of time, work, and leisure in a diagrammatic spectrum of leisure. The basic dimension is the constraint and self-determination continuum. Like Kaplan, he presents a sixth approach that includes salient elements of the other five. Murphy's six types of leisure definitions are

1. *Discretionary time*—Leisure as the time remaining in a work-determined cycle when the requirements of subsistence and work have been met.
2. *Social instrument*—Leisure as a means to social ends such as therapy for the ill, entrance into social participation, skill development, and fulfillment of social functions.
3. *Social class, race, and occupation*—Leisure as determined by social and hereditary factors. This determination model has been the basis of much research into participation prediction and, as such, is not a definition but a sociological assumption.
4. *Classic*—Leisure as a state of freedom, a "condition of the soul," and a seldom achieved goal.
5. *Antiutilitarian*—Leisure as an end in itself, not secondary to work, as self-expression, and as self-fulfilling satisfaction.
6. *Holistic*—Leisure as discoverable in any activity anywhere. The work-leisure distinction is abandoned in favor of definition according to the quality of the experience. Murphy's premise is that true leisure is person-enhancing freedom expressed in activity.

[1] Thorstein Veblen, *The Theory of the Leisure Class,* Second edition. (New York: New American Library, 1953), p. 46.

[2] Max Kaplan, *Leisure: Theory and Policy* (New York: John Wiley, 1975).

[3] James Murphy, *Concepts of Leisure: Philosophical Implications* (Englewood Cliffs, NJ: Prentice-Hall, 1974).

While these lists and schemes may illustrate some of the complexities of defining leisure and delineate critical dimensions of previous attempts, they may also prove more complicated than necessary. The three approaches of viewing leisure as time, activity, or condition appear most useful in sorting out what is peripheral from the necessary defining elements.

Leisure as Time

"Leisure is time beyond that which is required for existence, the things which we must do, biologically, to stay alive . . . and subsistence, the things we must do to make a living. . . . It is *discretionary* time, the time to be used according to our own judgment or choice."[4] Charles Brightbill combined the two common elements of defining leisure as time. Leisure time is residual, leftover from time that is obligated to meet work and self-maintenance requirements. And leisure time is that in which we may choose what we do; it is "free time."

There are several advantages to this approach. Most important, leisure as time is quantifiable. It is possible to answer the question "How much?" with a number. It is then possible to compare the leisure of different people and of different social groups. The method is that of "time-budget" studies. People are asked to record hourly, in blocks of fifteen minutes or so, how they spent their time. Usually they are asked what they were doing, where they were doing it, and whom they were with. Then it is possible to make concrete statements such as "employed women in the United States have about one and a half fewer hours of leisure per day than unemployed women." Or "in southern California youths and people of retirement age have twice as much leisure as those of employment age."

The International Time Budget Study[5] is based on the concept of leftover time. Leisure is defined as *doing things that are not connected with employment or with maintaining home and self.* But is that really possible? Can we know how much time is leisure without knowing something of what the activity means to the participant? Is reading always leisure, yard work always required maintenance, and time at the office always work?

Leisure as a quantity is both simple and useful. Dictionaries usually define leisure as time free from work and other necessities. However, even this is deceptive. Is any time really free from obligation? Any time we are with other people we are under some obligation to either meet or redefine the expectations of the situation. We may choose to join a softball team, but having made that choice we are under considerable obligation to get to practice and games on time. Once there, we are not free to run the bases in either direction or to pitch overhand.

Or is any time really residual or leftover? We may choose to read in the evening, but we know that the car needs an oil change and the kids would like to be driven to the pool. We may decide to take a walk with a friend, but we know that homework is waiting for our return. There is always something that needs to be done that has not been done. We may be free in the sense of being able to delay doing it, but the time for which we choose a book or a walk is seldom "leftover."

---

[4] Charles Brightbill, *The Challenge of Leisure* (Englewood Cliffs, NJ: Prentice-Hall, 1960), p. 4.

[5] A. Szalai and others, eds., *The Uses of Time: Daily Activities of Urban and Suburban Populations in Twelve Countries* (The Hague: Mouton, 1972).

The *discretionary time* concept seems more realistic. Leisure time may not be completely free, but it is time for which we exercise some choice. There are two problems with this idea. One is that those comparative studies with time as a quantity are placed in jeopardy. Only when we know that choice has been exercised can we be sure that the activity was, indeed, leisure. The second problem stems from the first. Only by somehow finding out how a choice was made and how free from constraint the decision was can we know whether time was discretionary. Therefore, it is not time as a quantity that is leisure, but the quality of time. The defining factor is the freedom of choice, not time as a remainder or amount.

The *leisure-as-time* approach is neat and simple—at first glance. It is useful in comparing population groups, different cultures, and various historical eras. Unfortunately, as a definition it breaks down unless it becomes time as defined by the person. But questions such as "How free?" and "How chosen?" lead us to qualities rather than quantity.

Leisure as Activity

Again, defining leisure as certain kinds of activity has considerable appeal. It is neat to be able to say that we are studying leisure when we investigate activities that can be identified by their form. Leisure is games, sports, culture, social interaction, and some activity that looks like work but is not. Already the problems begin. Is basketball leisure after school, but something else when played in a required physical education class? Is chopping wood leisure at the campground but not when a dead limb falls over a sidewalk at home? Is a cocktail party leisure on weekends but not at a sales conference?

Defining leisure simply as specified activities presents a strange paradox; almost no one actually defines leisure that way in theory. There are no lists of activities that are said to encompass leisure. Partly because such a list would be too long to deal with, no theorist has attempted to list activities and then say that when people are doing these things, they are engaging in leisure. The problem is illustrated just by considering such an activity as walking—which may be leisure, work, maintenance, or therapy. Or an event such as a dinner party may be a mixture of arduous preparation and social leisure for those who do the work that makes it possible.

On the other hand, when designing research in leisure, most social scientists do produce some kind of list of activities. They develop lists of twenty common or representative activities and begin their questioning: "Have you been swimming in the past month?" "How far did you go?" "With whom did you swim?" "Why do you like swimming?" Suddenly swimming is assumed to be leisure, as are the other activities on the list. Especially government and community surveys of the use of public recreation provisions assume that the activities on their list represent the leisure they want to know about. And there is some theoretical justification for this. Even though we cannot list the activities that are leisure, we generally think of leisure as doing something. That "something" may be very quiet such as sunbathing or weaving a new fantasy life during a dull lecture, or it may be quite active. It may be primarily athletic or social or cultural, but it is activity in the broadest sense.

The catch is that leisure activity is distinguished by elements other than form or content. Joffre Dumazedier lists four types of activity: remunerative work, family obligations, sociospiritual obligations, and activity oriented toward self-fulfillment or self-expression.[6] He suggests that leisure is only the fourth kind of activity while the obligation element in family and other institutional activities make these "semileisure." This seems consistent with his earlier sociological definition:

> Leisure is activity—apart from the obligations of work, family, and society—to which the individual turns at will, for either relaxation, diversion, or broadening his knowledge and his spontaneous social participation, the free exercise of his creative capacity.[7]

Leisure is activity in the sense of being purposive. It is doing something by choice. However, it is also activity that is chosen, according to Dumazedier, for ends that in some way enhance the self. Leisure is not purposeless, but its purpose has to do with the expression, diversion, or development of the self. According to Dumazedier, leisure excludes meeting the social expectations of family, friends, the state, or the church. For example, reading may be leisure when it is chosen for enjoyment or self-development, but it is not leisure when the book is assigned in school or when attached to a religious duty. Playing with children often mixes parental role expectations with enjoying the shared experience.

Kenneth Roberts, on the other hand, recognizes that leisure is commonly distinguished from work as well as understood as having been chosen. Since some expectations and constraints are found in any social interaction, he identifies leisure as "relatively freely undertaken nonwork activity."[8]

From this revised perspective, then, no activity is always leisure because of its form. Almost anything may be an obligation under some conditions. An activity is leisure, first of all, when it is chosen: The dimension of freedom is primary. It is leisure, second, when there is something about that activity at that time and in that place that will benefit the participant. It is the quality of the experience of doing the activity, not the activity itself, that makes it leisure. Therefore, as with time, we are brought back to the necessity of knowing how and why an activity is chosen and continued in order to distinguish whether or not it is leisure. Leisure is, indeed, activity; but an activity is defined as leisure only according to the freedom perceived and the benefits anticipated by the participant.

Leisure as Experience

John Neulinger suggests that time is an objective definition of leisure and that defining leisure by attitudes is subjective.[9] As already discovered, neither time nor activity provides a clear quantitative definition of leisure. No matter where we begin, we find ourselves dealing with its meanings to people in trying to identify leisure. The third approach to defining leisure begins where the others leave off—with the state of mind, the orientation, the

---

[6] Joffre Dumazedier, *Sociology of Leisure* (New York: Elsevier North-Holland, 1974).

[7] Joffre Dumazedier, *Toward a Society of Leisure* (New York: Free Press, 1967), pp. 16–17.

[8] Kenneth Roberts, *Contemporary Society and the Growth of Leisure* (London: Longman, 1978), p. 3.

[9] John Neulinger, *The Psychology of Leisure* (Springfield, IL: Chas. C Thomas, 1974).

attitudes, the conditions, the experience, or the definition of the leisure actor. Leisure is not in the time or the form of the activity, but in the actor.

Probably the best known of contemporary experiential definitions is that of Sebastian deGrazia in the now-classic book *Of Time, Work, and Leisure:*

> Leisure and free-time live in two different worlds. . . . Anybody can have free time. Not everybody can have leisure. Free time is a realizable idea of democracy. Leisure is not fully realizable, and hence an ideal not alone an idea. Free time refers to a special way of calculating a special kind of time. Leisure refers to a state of being, a condition of man, which few desire and fewer achieve.[10]

It is important to note the difference between deGrazia's understanding of leisure as a "condition" and the simpler suggestion that leisure is just feeling pleasure. "Feeling good" may be part of leisure (we are unlikely to consistently choose to do things that are unpleasant or painful) but many enterprises that we *have to* do can also make us feel quite good. At the same time we may choose to go on a vacation that finds us very cold and wet camping under soggy canvas after three days of rain. It may be leisure, but it's not much fun. deGrazia refers to a quality of life that is more than a fleeting feeling. To have leisure in his classic sense is to be a person who knows and experiences the richness of leisure.

In his more religious approach, Josef Pieper appears to be defining leisure more in attitudinal terms when he says that "leisure, it must be clearly understood, is a mental and spiritual attitude—it is not simply the result of external factors. . . . It is, in the first place, an attitude of mind, a condition of the soul, . . ."[11] However, like deGrazia, Pieper refers to a "condition" of the mind and spirit rather than just a feeling. There is the suggestion of wholeness here despite the references to mind and soul. A person does not just have leisure, certainly not as a possession. Rather, leisure is a state of being, momentary or more lasting as the case may be. Pieper demonstrates his religious orientation by going on to propose that pleasure involves "contemplative celebration" and "affirmation." Again, it is more than doing; it is being.

Neulinger takes a more attitudinal approach to leisure. As a psychologist, he hopes to be able to measure in some way, even though the measurement must be of the perceptions of individuals, rather than that of time or activity. He has developed a paradigm that includes three dimensions: perceived freedom, intrinsic motivation, and noninstrumentality. The leisure actor understands that what he or she is doing has been chosen rather than coerced. Further, the choice is made for reasons intrinsic to the activity rather than as a means to another end. Most simply, leisure is the perception of free choice for the sake of doing or experiencing. The elements are choice and motivation.

Leisure, then, is not distinguished by its form or by its location in time. Rather, from the experiential perspective, leisure is a mental condition that is located in the consciousness of the individual. Two questions follow from this view: First, is leisure detached from activity? If it is only a mental state, then the nature of the stimulus is irrelevant. Drugs are

---

[10] Sebastian deGrazia, *Of Time, Work, and Leisure* (Garden City, NY: Doubleday, 1964), p. 5.

[11] Josef Pieper, *Leisure: The Basis of Culture* (New York: Random House, 1963), p. 40.

as legitimate as contemplation. There is no way of raising questions of authenticity or even of long-term meanings and outcomes. All that is relevant is the mental state of the moment.

The second question is just what perceptions of the actor distinguish leisure from other mental conditions. While a variety of emotions and attitudes may be found in leisure ranging from ecstasy to relaxation, from high to low intensity, three orientations are common to most ancient and modern approaches:

1. Leisure is distinguished from what has to be done. It is not enough to say that leisure is "nonwork." Nevertheless, leisure is consistently differentiated from the realm of necessity, of what has to be done.
2. Most important, leisure is freely chosen. Such freedom may be relative rather than absolute, but at least there is the perception on the part of the participant that the activity could have *not* been done.
3. The motivation is largely intrinsic. Leisure may combine reasons for participation and anticipated benefits, but central is that it is done primarily for the quality of the experience.

The question remains, however, as to whether leisure is the state of mind of the actor or a dimension of the action. The distinction is not trivial. If leisure is the attitude itself, then any stimulus or environment that produces that feeling of relative freedom, however deceptive or spurious, must be said to produce leisure. If, on the other hand, leisur

rather than *feel*. Such activity is distinguished, however, not by its form but by the nature of the experience. It is, at least, activity that involves decision and that is engaged in primarily for the experience.

A somewhat more specific definition than the interim one in Chapter 1 would be: *Leisure is activity that is chosen primarily for its own sake.* What makes an activity leisure is the definition of the action by the participant. It is something more than just a state of mind, however. The freedom may be relative, but it is more than just a feeling. Leisure is directed action in the sense that there is real decision. Further, the focus is on the experience and its outcomes rather than on some external set of aims. The alternatives are displayed in a simple diagram:

LEISURE IS:

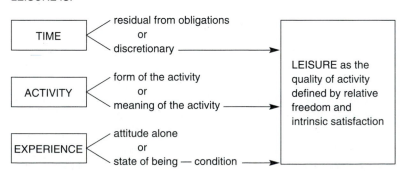

Is leisure, then, just the perception, the definition, or the attitude? When the psychologists begin to study what goes on in the minds of people, they immediately have to find something concrete to ask about. As a result, the research is about perceptions and definitions of activities or kinds of activity. Leisure is not just an attitude or state of mind in general. Rather, it is the attitude toward or definition of activity by a participant. It is, as suggested in the previous section, the quality of activity. This attitudinal approach adds a crucial perspective. The quality that defines activity as leisure or something else is found in the mind of the leisure actor.

Leisure as Action

Leisure as action includes elements of the other three approaches. Leisure takes place in time. It is not defined by time or place, but it does not float off into an unrelated attitude or feeling. It is connected to the realities of identifiable spatial and temporal dimensions. Further, leisure has form. The forms are almost infinite in their variety, but it is possible to identify activity, be it contemplation or competition, in which leisure occurs. It takes place in the "real world" of possibilities and limits, of resources and responsibilities. It is legitimate to study those forms, not as leisure but as events in which leisure happens. Finally, leisure is experience. It involves the perceptions of the actor—going into the experience, during it, and coming out of it. Such perceptions are essential dimensions of the action.

Leisure, however, is realized action, not just a feeling or mood. If freedom is the essential dimension of leisure, then action is implied. Freedom is not the absence of limit or constraint, but involves some element of self-determination.[12] In such action, there is some realization of the freedom to do and to become. Leisure is more than the illusion of freedom. It is more than a drug-induced mood. It is more than buying something on the market that is advertised as leisure. Leisure is taking action that does something and that has outcomes for the actor. Such action creates the experience rather than simply absorbing it.

Leisure, then, is activity in the sense of directed action. It may encompass moments of fantasy and long-term plans of action. It may be simple or complex, relaxed or strenuous. It may have only momentary outcomes or may be central to a plan of development. It may be oriented toward the self or toward social bonding with others. Leisure, from this perspective, is action with the qualities of not being required, of decision, and of focus on the experience. It is the quality of activity for the actor. Such action is related to all of life, not a separated segment with totally different meanings.

All this may seem to be needlessly complicated and argumentative. It might be that it would be better just to say something to the effect that "leisure is what we don't have to do" and go on to try to understand that vast realm of activity that is done primarily because we want to. It might be better to leave the boundaries fuzzy and the definitions general. For the most part, that is the approach of the remainder of this book. Leisure will be defined inclusively as a realm of behavior that is related to work, family, education, the economy, government, religion, personal development, sexuality, and almost everything else. Yet it has those distinguishing dimensions that may be approached in elements of time and place, nature of activity, and orientations of the actor.

[12] John R. Kelly, *Freedom to Be: A New Sociology of Leisure* (New York: Macmillan, 1987).

A Case of Leisure as Meaning

To illustrate this approach to leisure as quality rather than quantity, we may take a trip through the career of one leisure activity, that of dance.

Very young children dance. Even before dancing is demonstrated by older children or adults, they move their bodies in ways that are responsive to music. The rhythm of a band march, a Bach trio, or a rock album may provoke responsive movement of head and feet, of arms and body. Dance is then a free and expressive activity that is responsive to the environment. It is both integrative and spontaneous.

However, parents very quickly express approval or disapproval; older brothers or sisters show the child how to "do it right"; and television provides models. To dancing is added a third component of social learning and sanctions. Dancing may still be expressive, but it is also done with an eye to the audience and a memory of how others do it. In cultures where dance is central to role behavior, children are taught to dance at such a young age that the products of a more restrained socialization may marvel at the "naturalness" of their body movement and freedom.

However, it is in the preteen and teen years that dance in American culture takes on its most social meaning. The forms of dance may change. The staid traditions of ballroom dancing taught to middle-class children of aspiring parents from the 1930s through the 1950s have given way to a series of forms that reached a height of individual expression in the late 1960s and then began to move slowly back to greater concern with form. Such dancing has been very important in the developing sexual exploration and expression of the dancers. The partner, the onlookers, and the pleasures of moving with and sometimes touching another body make the dance a profoundly social experience. Without losing all the expressiveness and spontaneity of the child, the learning has now added the social dimension of sexuality.

There is for some another kind of dance that is oriented toward individual expression, skill development, and performance. In various forms dance is learned as a form of art for which there are performance standards, recruitment and exclusions, and rankings by skill. The blending of gymnastics and ballet is not the only parallel between dance-as-performance and sports. In both there are discipline, rules, training, evaluation, and in the end, winners and losers.

In many cultures dance remains a central form of social expression throughout the life career. In North American cities and suburbs, participation in dancing has generally dwindled until it is a rare experience. Though they may be involved in occasional dance clubs, country club events, and the ubiquitous folk dancing, for the most part "old folks" are a strange sight at a rock club or discotheque. On the other hand, Saturday night dances that mix age groups are still common in some rural areas. In the Appalachian hills, you don't have to be young to "clog" (though it helps). The formal dances central to major cultural celebrations in the cultures of Native Americans and others have no equivalent in our culture, where we seem unable to either disengage dance from sensuality or to accept the sensuality and go on dancing.

However, there are retirement villages where dancing has become a major social attraction. Square dancing, ballroom dancing, and other forms of dance within the tempo aptitudes of the group are the main way in which the community gets together. For the married as well as the formerly married, dancing is a way to reestablish contact with others, to enjoy (like the little child) the responsive integration of body and emotion to music, and to get some exercise as well.

Dance, then, has a kind of social career in which over a life span the free and expressive movement of the small child increasingly becomes channeled and shaped into forms approved in the culture. The sheer expressiveness takes on more of the meaning of skill acquisition and may culminate for some in performance-oriented dancing. For most, that expressiveness becomes interwoven with the developing sexuality of the adolescent. The meaning of dancing is not just in what you do but with whom you do it: it is not just "for its own sake," but also for the sake of relationships. Through the years, without losing the meanings of expression and body-emotion integration entirely, dance may become primarily social in meaning. In many cultures, that social meaning is a central celebration and ritual expression of the social bond.

Where, then, is the meaning of dance as leisure? Is it in the time, the place, the activity, the social context, or the definition of the dancer? The answer appears to be "yes" to all the possibilities, at least at some point in dance's career of meanings. But in the end, it is the meaning to the participant that is crucial. It is that meaning, that definition of the activity for a time and place, which determines whether dancing is primarily expressive leisure, social leisure, or activity that is required by social or professional roles.

What Is Recreation?

Recreation may be defined in the same way as leisure. Many recreation theorists prefer to define it as inclusively as possible. Therefore, one option for defining recreation is as all nonwork activity that is beneficial to the participant. Others define recreation as one kind of leisure with distinct characteristics.

The term *recreation* stems from the Latin *recreatio,* which refers to restoration or recovery. The term implies the re-creation of energy or the restoration of ability to function. Unlike leisure, which has more and more been defined as a human phenomenon in its own right rather than something different from or leftover after work, *recreation* contains the concept of restoration of wholeness of mind, spirit, and body. It presupposes some other activity that depletes, tires, or deteriorates that wholeness.

However, this is not the only difference between recreation and leisure. Although no activity may be any more restorative than daydreaming, few would include that activity in the realm of recreation. Recreation generally refers to more organized activity. Recreation is socially organized for social ends.

Recreation and Leisure as Equivalents

When leisure is defined as *free time,* then recreation may be said to refer to activity carried out within that time. This neat distinction is exemplified in a text by the Neumeyers in which recreation is defined as "any activity pursued during leisure . . . that is free and pleasureful, having its own immediate appeal, not impelled by a delayed reward beyond itself or by any immediate necessity."[13]

In a text on community recreation, George Butler takes the same approach. Recreation is characterized by freedom and "direct satisfaction." "Recreation may be experienced at

[13] M. H. Neumeyer and E. Neumeyer, *Leisure and Recreation* (New York: Ronald Press, 1958), p. 22.

any time and anywhere."[14] It is the experience rather than the activity. Both the Neumeyers and Butler are responding to the unsatisfactory definition of leisure as time by redefining recreation as free and satisfying activity or experience. The problem with this is partly historical. It is *leisure* that has the etymological roots signifying freedom and intrinsic satisfaction and *recreation* that has the restorative and social benefit meanings.

The approach suggested here is that leisure be redefined, as already outlined, in a way consistent with its roots, and that recreation be defined less inclusively. This does not imply that *recreation* is somehow less worthy because it is more specific. Rather, recreation is leisure activity with social purposes and organization. In this sense, while some leisure may be destructive to the self or to the society, recreation—by definition—is always beneficial in intent.

Recreation as a Social Institution

As we will see in Chapter 8, in the Roman state, recreation was intended to be useful to the state. Mass recreation was organized to divert attention from problems of unemployment and social inequalities. Even without such a manipulative aim, recreation has generally been considered to have some purpose that benefits the society. Richard Kraus has argued that too much stress on the intrinsic and self-justifying nature of recreation ignores the fact that public recreation is in competition for financial support, for space, and for attention. Its purpose and results will be evaluated. Recreation is intended to be good for the people of a society in specific ways and is organized and supported with such benefits expected.

There are two elements in this more specific perspective. The first is that of restoration. deGrazia writes: "Recreation is activity that rests men from work, often giving them a change (distraction, diversion), and restores them for work."[15] The references to "work" and to "men" may be too narrow. We may need to be restored or re-created for other ends: to be good citizens, to relate better to our families, to relieve tensions and restore some emotional balance, to study more effectively, or just to feel better. Recreation is intended to restore us to wholeness, to health, for whatever purposes we may have. We do not recreate only to work. We recreate to live. Further, recreation is itself a part of living and has its own value to us. Nevertheless, that element of restoration for whatever we consider important, including ourselves, is one part of recreation.

The second element is that of social organization. Recreation has purposes and is organized for social ends. It is not just "for its own sake." It differs from leisure in that recreation is not likely to be "anything, anytime, anywhere" if only we choose it for some personal satisfactions. Neil Cheek and William Burch have made this distinction central to their approach to leisure and recreation: "Broadly conceived, recreation is rationalized leisure; it is the routinization of enjoyment."[16]

They go on to analyze the rise of recreation in modern society as an institution of the social system required by the loss of time and space in which leisure could be integrated

---

[14] George D. Butler, *Introduction to Community Recreation,* Fifth edition (New York: McGraw-Hill, 1976), p. 8.

[15] deGrazia, *Of Time, Work, and Leisure,* p. 233.

[16] Neil Cheek and William Burch, *The Social Organization of Leisure in Human Society* (New York: Harper & Row, 1976), p. 224.

with the ongoing work and family life. Recreation had to be provided for, organized, and even taught. Recreation as a separate institutional component of the social scene is found for the most part in urbanized societies with a high degree of organizational complexity. Leisure, on the other hand, in some form or forms is universal. Recreation is programmatic; it has organization and goals.

Kraus suggests that various definitions of recreation have contained elements of activity, social acceptability, voluntary choice in participation, intrinsic motivation for the participant, attitudes, and desirable outcomes.[17] While all these elements *may* be present in recreation, those that distinguish it from leisure are those of acceptability, organization, and purpose including restoration. For our purposes, *recreation is defined as voluntary non-work activity that is organized for the attainment of personal and social benefits including restoration and social cohesion.*

A slightly more humanistic and less sociological definition is also possible. This definition stresses value to the individual rather than social aims. Recreation is opportunities provided for the re-creation of the person—mind, body, and emotions—through participation in and appreciation of activities, environments, and associations. Whether the stress is on restoration toward wholeness or on the social provisions and aims, recreation is a functional social institution with goals that benefit individuals and the society.

What Is Play?

Like recreation, play has been defined in ways that make it indistinguishable from definitions of leisure that stress freedom and satisfaction. One of the simplest definitions is that "play is self-expression for its own sake."[18] However, in its usage, one distinction between play and leisure frequently recurs. *Play* is used to refer to such activity by children and *leisure* to adult participation. Most would recognize that adults may play or may engage in playful activity. On the other hand, children are seldom said to have leisure. Therefore, one possibility would be to define play and leisure in essentially the same way—as activity chosen in relative freedom for some intrinsic satisfaction—and then continue to use *play* to refer to children and to especially frolicsome adult occasions and employ *leisure* to refer only to the activity of adults.

However, the history of definitions and theories of play does not allow us to dismiss the matter so quickly. For example, deGrazia begins by appearing to adopt this simple age distinction: "Play is what children do, frolic and sport. . . . Adults play, too, though their games are less muscular and more intricate."[19] However, deGrazia then goes on to suggest that there is a play element in adult recreation. He seems to be suggesting that play is a way of engaging in recreation.

[17] R. Kraus, *Recreation and Leisure in Modern Society,* Second edition (Santa Monica, CA: Goodyear, 1978), pp. 32–37.

[18] A. V. Sapora and E. Mitchell, *The Theory of Play and Recreation* (New York: Ronald Press, 1961), pp. 114–115.

[19] deGrazia, *Of Time, Work, and Leisure,* p. 233.

The approach to play that focuses on the manner of doing the activity is almost as common as the assumed reference to children. The term *play* comes from the Anglo-Saxon *plega* referring to a game, sport, or even a fight. The Latin *plaga* means a blow, thrust, or stroke, as in a ball game or combat. Since many early games were mock combat, the play element may have evolved into stressing the nonserious aspect of the act. Now we say and do things "in play" because they do not signify serious intent. We are "playful" in the sense of acting in a light and limited way, even suggesting that it's "all in fun." We act in a "play" that involves a temporary suspension of our distinction between the real and the unreal, the true and the false. Children "play house" or "play cowboys and Indians" in the confines of a New Jersey backyard.

Play has a certain representative nature in that the game is something like real combat or real life, but is temporary and therefore basically nonserious. We may behave in a "playful" manner in almost any situation, although sometimes the playfulness is not appreciated by others. Play, then, is doing something for its own sake, for the satisfaction of the moment. Like leisure, play is defined by how we do it rather than what we do.

The three elements of play identified thus are

1. Play generally refers to the activity of children or to a "childlike" lightness of behavior in adults.
2. Play is expressive and intrinsic in motivation.
3. Play involves a nonserious suspension of consequences, a temporary creation of its own world of meaning, which often is a shadow of the "real world."

Theories of Play

Michael Ellis has summarized a number of theories about why people play.[20] He reports that there are at least fifteen identifiable play theories. Most are quite old and, according to Ellis, not very useful in guiding contemporary research and practice. Among the most common older theories are the following:

Surplus energy—When the organism has more energy than can be stored, it is expended in play.

Instinct—Whatever people keep on doing from generation to generation must be transmitted by a genetic code.

Preparation—Play is a trying out of actions and responses that the player knows will be useful in a future stage of life.

Recapitulation—Play that appears irrelevant to the child is actually a reenactment of a progression of the development of the entire species.

Relaxation—The opposite of surplus energy; when tired from work, people play.

---

[20] Michael J. Ellis, *Why People Play* (Englewood Cliffs, NJ: Prentice-Hall, 1973).

More recent theories include

Generalization—Play repeats experiences that have been satisfying at work.

Compensation—Play contrasts with experiences that have been unpleasant at work.

Catharsis—Play is a relatively harmless expression of aggression that reduces hostilities.

Psychoanalysis—Play repeats an unpleasant experience to reduce its seriousness or to simulate control over its consequences.

Development—Play is governed by intellectual development and is an expression of the current stage of mental abilities.

Learning—Play is simply a form of learning through maximization of pleasant events and consequences.

Ellis goes on to propose a combination of two more recent theories: arousal-seeking and competence-effectance. The complexity and uncertainty of environmental factors are elements stimulating play in which the satisfaction is gained from demonstrating mastery of the environment. It is a learning theory that stresses the stimulation of the player by environmental factors.

In one sense, it is true that we can never fully explain any human behavior. There is a shifting multiplicity of perspectives, drives, memories, social influences, and anticipations in any set of decisions and actions. However, theories that extract the playfulness from play, that lose sight of the expressive freedom in choosing and in doing the activity, would seem to be dealing with something other than that mode of leisure in which we are interested.

Kinds of Play

There are a number of other ways of understanding play that may be helpful in grasping its scope and meaning. M. I. Csikszentmihalyi has introduced the concept of "flow experience" to suggest the transcendence of some play.[21] *Flow* is the experience of purely intrinsic satisfaction that may accompany familiarity and mastery in participation. Play, then, would have as its essence a heightened experience of doing something entirely for its own sake, for the experience of that moment.

This does not imply that play has no identifiable outcomes. Rather, play is action that may create its own environments. The "play" of the theater is designed to create its own world of action. In such play, the social interaction and communication become for that bounded time and place an event of meaning. In somewhat the same way, an episode of social play creates a symbolic world, however temporary and transitory. What is special about play is that its outcomes are not predefined. In much of productive life, the product is specified at the beginning of the action. In play, the end is not predetermined. Therefore, the possibility of creating something new is always present.

Like leisure, play may be seen as the quality of action. Action is play when it is open, when the action develops its own world. There may be forms and limits. In fact, agreeing

---

[21] Mihaly Csikszentmihalyi, *Beyond Boredom and Anxiety* (San Francisco: Jossey-Bass, 1975).

on those forms may be necessary for the integrated action of a number of players. The world of play may be symbolic with outcomes limited to the play event. And just because of this special world, play may create that which previously did not exist. It is more than repetition; it has the possibility of the novel.

The concept of the transcendence of play is developed in the classic book *Homo Ludens* by Johan Huizinga. Huizinga stresses the enjoyment of play and its consequent intrinsic motivation. However, he adds that play is "out of the ordinary,"[22] a sphere of activity that creates a temporary reality. Due to its temporary nature, play may be disinterested and yet have its own order and beauty. With that created order, play can relate the player to meanings quite beyond the particular time and space. The "theatrical" or "representative" character of play gives it a meaning that is related to the more lasting ideas and structures of a culture.

Play both suspends reality and heightens its meanings. It is like art in being more real, more full of meaning, than the everyday life that so easily passes without its significance being noted. According to Harvey Cox, play contains a refusal to "be bound by the narrow world of fact. . . ."[23] Communal play, the festival, celebrates the meaning of being together—the community, the social order, the culture, and even the universe. The routines of play are like religious rituals that suggest uncommon meanings beyond the repeated activity. From this perspective, then, play and worship are both done for their own sake and yet have meaning that cannot be contained in either the routines or the spontaneity of the action.

Roger Caillois proposes two styles of play at opposite ends of a continuum.[24] The first is *paidia,* or free and spontaneous play. The second is *ludus,* or rule-governed activity. When both the freedom and the representative order of play are recognized, then play becomes a more complex phenomenon than the simple "expression for its own sake" suggests. The forms of play are varied. Play does include both freedom and order. Paradoxically, both the freedom and order point to Huizinga's idea that play is related to the fundamental values, myths, symbols, and meanings of the culture. In play we are free to create a shadow world in which to act out our imagined place in the real world. It is, then, no wonder that the freedom of play may in many instances lead to creation and the self-transcendence of "flow."

Summary of Issues

There are many possible definitions of leisure, recreation, and play. This chapter does not begin to encompass all the possibilities or all the major examples of each. On the other hand, enough sorting should have taken place to provide a framework for understanding. In the later chapters on history and philosophy, contemporary leisure, and public recreation, enough content will be put into the framework to enable students to develop their

---

[22] Johan Huizinga, *Homo Ludens* (Boston: Beacon Press, 1955), p. 4.

[23] Harvey Cox, *The Feast of Fools* (New York: Harper Colophon, 1969), p. 142f.

[24] Roger Caillois, *Man, Play, and Games* (London: Thames and Hudson, 1961).

own concepts and definitions. At this point it is more important to get on with the operation than to run more words through the definitional process.

To begin (and not to close) the examination of leisure, recreation, and play, the following approaches will be used:

Leisure is defined as activity chosen primarily for the experience itself. The dimensions of freedom and intrinsic satisfaction are seen as the central defining elements. A possible integrating perspective is that leisure is action in which the focus on the experience and dimension of determination by the actor creates meaning.

Recreation is held to be leisure activity that is organized for the attainment of personal and social benefits. The re-creative aspect of the activity relates recreation to participation in such social institutions as the family, school, economy, and state.

Play is leisure activity with the childlike characteristics of spontaneity, self-expression, and the creation of its own nonserious realm of meaning. Its satisfaction is concentrated in the experience of doing the activity and accepting the intrinsic meaning of its playful context.

Leisure and *play* refer to qualities of action and meaning rather than to time, activities, or forms. The definitions, therefore, all require reference to the meaning that the activity has for the participant. These are more matters of attitude and definition than of what, when, and where.

HIGHLIGHTS

1. Freedom of self-determination is central to every definition of leisure and play.
2. Both leisure and play incorporate the element of doing something for its own sake, for intrinsic satisfaction in the experience.
3. Recreation is leisure that is organized to pursue personal and social benefits. One such benefit is *re-creation* for more effective participation in the economy, family, state, and community.
4. Conflicting definitions of leisure have different starting points, but may lead to the same question: What does leisure mean to people in a society and a culture?
5. There is no conflict between such definitions and the common "Leisure is doing what I like, what I don't *have* to do."

Discussion Questions

1. What is usually meant by *leisure* in ordinary conversation? Is it different from *not-work?* If so, how?

2. Should leisure be defined in a normative way, that is, with a value standard of what is "true" leisure?

3. What are the strengths and weaknesses of each type of definition of leisure—time, activity, and state of mind? Can these be combined? If so, how?

4. Are there any definitions of leisure that do not include the element of freedom of choice? What does "choice" mean in the midst of real life?

5. What are the dangers of deGrazia's approach to leisure?

6. What would you add to the author's brief definition to make it more adequate or precise?

7. What would be examples of activity that might generally be leisure, but not recreation? Recreation, but not leisure?

8. Is restoration always an element in recreation? Give examples of possible exceptions.

9. How institutionalized must leisure be to be recreation? What about children's games and sports?

10. When would you not want to use *play* to refer to children's activity or *leisure* to refer to adults?

11. Which theories of play, if any, do you find most useful?

12. Just what does it mean to be "playful"?

13. What are the elements that make an activity "play"? Give examples.

Bibliography

Caillois, Roger, *Man, Play, and Games*. London: Thames and Hudson, 1961.

Cheek, N., and W. Burch, *The Social Organization of Leisure in Human Society*. New York: Harper & Row, 1976.

Cox, Harvey, *The Feast of Fools*. New York: Harper Colophon, 1969.

Csikszentmihalyi, Mihaly, *Beyond Boredom and Anxiety*. San Francisco: Jossey-bass, 1975.

Csikszentmihalyi, Mihaly, *Flow—the Psychology of Optimal Experience*. New York: Harper & Row, 1990.

Dumazedier, Joffre, *Sociology of Leisure*. New York: Elsevier, 1974.

Dumazedier, Joffre, *Toward a Society of Leisure*. New York: Free Press, 1967.

Ellis, Michael J., *Why People Play*. Englewood Cliffs, NJ: Prentice-Hall, 1973.

Goodale, Thomas L., and Geoffrey Godbey, *The Evolution of Leisure*. State College, PA: Venture, 1988.

Huizinga, Johan, *Homo Ludens*. Boston: Beacon Press, 1955.

Kaplan, Max, *Leisure: Theory and Policy*. New York: John Wiley, 1975.

Kelly, John R., *Freedom to Be: a New Sociology of Leisure*. New York: Macmillan, 1987.

Murphy, James, *Concepts of Leisure: Philosophical Implications*. Englewood Cliffs, NJ: Prentice-Hall, 1974.

Neulinger, John, *The Psychology of Leisure*. Springfield, IL: Chas. C Thomas, 1974.

Pieper, Josef, *Leisure: The Basis of Culture*. New York: New American Library, 1963.

Roberts, Kenneth, *Contemporary Society and the Growth of Leisure*. London: Longman, 1978.

Smigel, E. O., ed., *Work and Leisure*. New Haven, CT: College and University Press, 1963.

Veblen, Thorstein, *The Theory of the Leisure Class*. New York: Macmillan, 1899.

Chapter 3

Sources of Leisure Styles

The variety of leisure styles is beyond question. We seldom ask why, given a choice, all people do not want much the same kinds of activities and satisfactions. In business terms, the leisure market is highly segmented. Different people seem to want quite different kinds of leisure. Some are deeply involved in strenuous physical activity, but most are not. Some are "party animals" who want active interaction with others at all possible times, but some want to be alone. Some seek the challenge of high-risk activity on the mountain or in the air, but most prefer the comfort and safety of television and the recliner chair.

This evident variety is only the beginning. Individuals also have considerable variety in their leisure engagements. The same person may seek solitude one evening and a crowd on another, run in the morning and read late into the night, fly to China for one vacation and go back to the same lake for another. Further, leisure patterns for individuals change throughout the life course. The same person may be very involved in sports in her twenties, focus on family activity in her thirties, go back to school in her forties, do a lot of traveling in her fifties, take up golf in her sixties, engage in volunteering in her seventies, and concentrate on grandparenting in her eighties. More likely, an individual will have combinations of complementary activities that change through the years.

And different people have different styles of leisure. Some concentrate on one or two activities, and others do a little of fifteen different things. Some do little outside the home, and others are quite involved in many kinds of community activities and organizations. Some are constantly trying to learn and develop, while others prefer to be entertained. "Styles" of leisure refer to these combinations of activity and meaning. It seems possible to characterize such patterns according to a number of dimensions. Some styles are individualistic, and some are more family-oriented. Some exhibit high degrees of engagement, while others are more passive. Some are quite home-centered, while others focus on environments outside the residence.

The first question is whether or not such styles can be characterized in ways that reflect realities of action and orientation. More important, are there consistent ways in which activity patterns are tied to value systems, social relationships, and cultural contexts? Do similarities and differences in leisure styles reflect other factors, such as age, gender, social position, and access to resources? In short, what are the sources of all this variety?

ISSUES

Can the leisure styles of individuals be characterized by useful descriptive labels?

Do leisure styles include both a "core" of similarities and a "balance" of differences?

How do leisure styles and orientations change throughout the life course?

How do the elements of existential becoming and social contexts blend into a leisure style?

Is leisure central or peripheral to who we are?

The observable diversity in leisure is almost beyond description. Let your imagination roam freely enough to picture some of the variety:

> There are countless environments for leisure: natural and constructed, open and confining, quiet and clamorous, inviting and forbidding. . . .

> There are the social contexts of leisure: solitary and intensely interactive, silent and communicative, unstructured and rule-intensive, cooperative and competitive, exploratory and role-rigid, strange and familiar, comfortable and threatening, mass and intimate. . . .

> There are the mental states of leisure: relaxed and tense, detached and intensely involved, preoccupied and exhibitionistic, free and conforming, excited and bored, seeking novelty or defensive, sensual or rational . . .

And then there are the activities themselves: from daydreaming to drag racing, running to reading, contemplation to conversation, gardening to grappling, painting to parading, and devotion to drinking.

Stylistic Variety in Leisure

However, much more significant are the orientations of engagement. Exactly the same activity may have different meanings for participants of the same age depending on how they define themselves. For example, a teen may drink decorously in anticipation of adult status-group behavior or rebelliously in defiance of both law and parental preferences. A woman in midlife may take an evening class as a pastime, an exploration of her potential to begin a career, or hoping to meet interesting others. Retired men and women may have a familial style of nonwork life or be seeking new investments in personal development. The real issue of style is not what people do, but how they do it.

All this suggests that the variety in leisure styles may be even greater than is palpably observable. Not only are there thousands of activities that may be leisure, but there are the different meanings, intensities of engagement, and intentions for any activity. Leisure is "existential" as decision inaugurates action that creates at least part of its own meaning. It is also social in both its aims and its resource contexts.

This chapter explores the seemingly endless diversity of activities that may be leisure and the different meanings, intensities of engagement, and intentions for any activity. Three models depicting ways of viewing people's activity patterns are explored as a way of bringing some order to the diversity. This search for order in what people do is followed by a discussion of why people undertake specific activities or a particular activity in a particular way and what may account for changing patterns over the life span. A role-identity model is used to show that leisure may vary in meanings and environments, in intentions and intensity. And the self we present or hope to become may vary from one context to another. Leisure with its existential element of relative freedom may be that social space for *becoming,* for developing and establishing our personal and social identities. Whether a special event or interstitial in a routine of obligations, leisure has meanings and consequences that are more than the filling of leftover time.

Three Models of Leisure Styles

The *how* of leisure engagement, the style of participation, may be approached in a number of ways. Three basic approaches have emerged in the literature. Each has some basis in research, but each also has the potential to be deceptive and misleading.

The Stereotypes Model

Stereotypes are a form of convenient classification, based on attaching a label according to some simple and generally observable factor. Leisure stereotypes presuppose that individuals are essentially monothematic in their leisure. A leisure style may be multidimensional, but a stereotype is reduced to a single dimension.

The stereotype of the blue-collar male is that he is so stifled by his work routinization that he seeks his only escape in the relatively undemanding leisure of drinking with male companions, watching television (especially contact sports), and occasional masculine excursions into the back country armed to the teeth to slaughter some small animal. The stereotype of the history professor is that he drinks a dry white wine, reads thin books of poetry, listens to string quartets, and carries an umbrella when the sky is clear. Stereotypes of adolescent males focus on sports and sexual aggression, of older widows on loneliness and soap operas, of young mothers on discussing toilet training with other young mothers, and of urban singles on specialized bars and one-night stands.

Of course, we seldom know anyone who fits the stereotype. Further, the support seemingly given by research in the 1960s has largely evaporated. Multivariate analyses of national samples in North America now report that very little variation in frequency of participation in kinds of activities can be accounted for by discriminating variables of sex, age, income, occupation, education, and race.[1] Once the threshold of real poverty is crossed, remaining correlations are largely limited to the masculine dominance of team sports and drinking in bars, decreases in active sport participation with age, a female reluctance to go hunting, and a relationship between education level and certain elite arts interests.

A major justification for presuming the existence of leisure stereotypes has been on-site observation. However, seeing 1,000 teens on a beach does not tell us where the other 100,000 are at the same time. Knowing that 50,000 people went to a rock concert on Friday does not tell us what they will do on Saturday. Most of leisure is not that observable, and the stereotypes tend to be based on the very biased evidence of impressions gained at public events.

This does not mean that there are no single-minded individuals who pursue a high-risk sport, fine arts production, or some social group to the exclusion of almost all else. Nor does it mean that there are no significant differences in leisure styles, in *how* people do what they do. But, for most of the population, stereotypes are blurred by the commonalities of leisure as well as by the relative diversity of interests and commitments.

Styles, more than the activities, differ in significant ways. Eastern dressage and point-to-point horse riders are clearly distinguishable from those in the West who train for cutting-horse contests and run quarterhorses. Drinking in a truckers' bar and an exclusive country club are not much alike, even in the kinds of drinks consumed. How activities are done may be more indicative of social status than the activities themselves. There are, indeed, different cultures of leisure within such survey categories as "entertaining at home," "visiting friends and family," "drinking in bars," and "attending concerts."

Predicting Leisure Participation

Prediction in the social sciences is always a matter of probabilities. We can never predict whether or not John Smith, a junior at Western University, will take a date to the movies next Friday. However, after investigating an adequate sample of students and the opportunities available, we may be able to predict that between 20 and 25 percent of the male juniors at universities with more than 10,000 students will have at least one movie date a month.

It would be quite useful if we were able to take available information and estimate the likely participation in theatergoing, bowling, boating, or downhill skiing in a given area. Then both public and commercial providers would be able to plan their facilities and programs with the least chance of not being used to capacity. The kind of information most available from census sources is the size and distribution of the population by age, gender, income, occupation, race, marital status, family size, and sometimes education level. In such models, however, recreation has been found to be less predictable than was once assumed. Especially when the categories of activity to be predicted are quite general—swimming, reading, or fishing—survey data do not pick up the differences that are based on income or education levels.

---

[1] John R. Kelly, "Outdoor Recreation Participation: A Comparative Analysis," *Leisure Sciences,* 3 (1980), 129–154.

However, careful analysis has yielded some clues for improving the process. For example, it has been found that low income prevents some people from even considering kinds of recreation with high travel or equipment costs. In much the same way, factors of health filter some out of activities that require unusual strength or endurance. The "filtering model" of estimation takes into account those who are eliminated from access to opportunities by costs, distance, or other barriers.

Explanation of differing rates usually involves multiple factors. There are statistical techniques for weighing a number of measures in one process to identify those that are most salient. They still depend, however, on measures that are considered independent: income, race, gender, age, and family composition. In real life, such measures are not independent. Being a white, college-educated male with two school-age children in Scarsdale, New York is a total condition, not a set of numbers. Being a Mexican-American grandmother still doing farm labor in California's San Joaquin Valley is a life, not a list of factors. Some kinds of leisure are possible, and some are not. Some interests and skills have been developed in a personal history. Some values have been learned and some rejected. All make some difference, probably in different ways for sequences of particular decisions. A young mother with two graduate degrees may put going to string quartet concerts on hold for a few years to spend evenings with her children. A construction worker father may give up league softball to coach his son's Little League team. A California teen who loves surfing may go to a Saturday concert instead of Malibu because that's what her friends want to do.

A more complete model of leisure decision making, then, would have to include the following sequence:

1. Factors such as limited resources of time, cost, access, and physical potential filter out many activities from consideration.
2. Socialization history with family and friends influences choices of interests among real possibilities. Such socialization is specific to a family and culture and differs by gender as well as particulars of the environment.
3. Decisions about actual participation are made with consideration of such immediate factors as availability and preferences of possible companions, the fit of schedules, habit, competing possibilities, weather, and other items specific to that decision.[2]

Another problem with predictive models is that they have the wrong outcome variables. Styles of leisure may be more significant than the activities themselves. All sorts of people read; the issue is what they read. All sorts of people travel; the salient question is how they travel, where they go, and, for the tourism industry, what they spend. There are innumerable kinds of bars, parties, restaurants, resorts, sports, and dances. Where, how, and with whom may be more important in understanding a leisure event than the form of the activity itself. Diversity is only superficial when measured by lists of activities. More important are shared meanings, customs, and symbols of group identity. Thorstein Veblen described how individuals display styles of leisure behavior and ownership symbolic of

---

[2] John R. Kelly, "Situational and Social Factors in Leisure Decisions, *Pacific Sociological Review,* 21, (1978), 313–330.

their presumed social status.[3] "Tastes" serve to identify social level and consolidate attachment to social groups.

The Balance Model

The balance model is based on the evident variety of leisure common to most individuals and on the multiplicity of meanings that they find in their activities. The same activity generally has more than one meaning. Those meanings shift from one occurrence to another, depending on a number of social and environmental factors as well as the predisposition of the actor. Further, anticipation and satisfactions often change for the same activity as we move through our life course.

Nor do most persons engage in only one kind of activity. Rather, we do a variety of things, seeking many different outcomes. We seek to make new friends and deepen ongoing intimacies, to learn new skills and enhance old competencies, to relax and discover excitement, to gain interpersonal acceptance and self-development, to express our individuality and strengthen role relationships, to discipline our bodies and free our imaginations, to think quietly and subject our minds to maximum stress, to risk uncertainty and enjoy comfort and security. In our leisure histories, we have found that certain activities, locales, and social contexts are most likely to produce certain combinations of outcomes for us. So we return to such opportunities when we seek the outcomes.

The balance we seek may change through the life course. Opportunity structures are different for children, students, establishment adults, and so on. We are likely to seek to explore sexuality in adolescence, develop intimacy in early adulthood, enhance the nuclear family in child-rearing years, seek personal reintegration in midlife, provide a context for social integration in later years, and employ leisure to begin again when life is disrupted by trauma.

In the balance model, leisure *style* is not a monothematic stereotype. Style is the combination of activities and contexts through which we seek to work out the hierarchy of meanings for leisure at that time in the life course. Leisure style is a pattern, not a label; the shape of a process, not a caricature. Style is the set of investments with the personal and social meanings they have for us. A leisure style may not be a perfect balance. At a given time, it may tilt toward personal expressivity, family solidarity, physical development, or affective involvement. Thus, according to the balance model, style is multidimensioned and changing, with contrast and complexity rather than a single color of unrelieved hue and intensity.

The Core Model

The balance model is a significant step beyond stereotypes. However, there are strong grounds for adding to it. The core model does not deny the diversity and richness of the balance mode. Rather, it adds one simple element: the considerable commonality of adult leisure.

---

[3] Thorstein Veblen, *The Theory of the Leisure Class* (New York: Mentor Books, 1953 [1899]).

In a national sample surveyed in the United States, 91 percent read for pleasure, 58 percent walked for pleasure, 48 percent swam, 88 percent watched television, 62 percent listened to the radio, 83 percent spent evenings with relatives regularly, and 65 to 75 percent engaged in sexual interaction.[4] The point is simply that there are a number of relatively accessible, low-cost, and often home-based activities that most people do a lot. Some involve the media, especially reading and television. Many are social, informal interaction with intimates who most often are those living in the same household. Some are found in the midst of nonleisure settings, a bit of fooling around at work or school or task-inattention almost anywhere.

The best supported model, then, is probably the "core plus balance" model. The core tends to cross social lines, partly because so much is available and resource-free. It continues in some form through most of the life course. As a consequence, comprehensive participation studies do not locate the marked differences in style we think we observe.

The balance part of the model is most likely to change through the life course. As opportunities, developmental orientations, and social roles change, we seek somewhat different satisfactions in our leisure. Further, that balance is not just the same for everyone. I may not be able to imagine my own life without both music and strenuous physical activity. However, the contexts of sport and arts investments have both changed considerably in the last twenty years, and no doubt will change again.

Leisure in the Midst of Life

In the next chapter, we will outline how leisure styles and meanings change through the life course. As roles and relationships change, so leisure styles are responsive to new opportunities, to the expectations of others, and to shifts in resources such as residence, income, and geographical location. The core of leisure may be more stable than the balance for most persons, but neither is untouched by the role changes that are signalled by the passing years. Leaving school and entering the full-time work force presents a quite new set of expectations, limitations, and opportunities. Becoming a parent changes everything—time, space, budgets, and even priorities. Developing an intimate relationship may refocus leisure. Leisure is not a separate sphere of life, but is connected to everything else. Leisure changes as our roles and identities change. Our life situations change, and we change with them as we mature, leave the parental home, live in independent singleness, marry, become parents, divorce, see children gain independence, seek and find significant new relationships, and, if married, either die or are widowed.

Social Role Change

All our roles change through the life course. These changes are not independent, but are combined into a set of life conditions. Life is different in urban centers, suburban devel-

---

[4] John R. Kelly, *Leisure Identities and Interactions* (London and Boston: Allen and Unwin, 1983).

opments, and rural or small town locations. Metropolitan areas offer an almost infinite variety of leisure opportunities, but come with crowds, traffic jams, lines, and high residential costs. Cities have a great variety of leisure styles. Ethnic communities are formed and develop distinct sets of celebrations and events. Differences in sexual orientation lead to particular settings for leisure as well as stylistic variations. On the other hand, smaller communities may be more uniform, but often give a sense of being a known part of a definable society.

In every social setting, gender identity impacts everything we do—how we define and present ourselves, what we wear, what others expect in vocabularies and demeanor, and even the activities that are encouraged and prohibited. Gender roles often interact with ethnicity as expectations and even rules vary among third-generation Irish Catholics in South Boston, first-generation Hmong youth in Los Angeles, and second-generation Cuban professionals in Miami. Life is a negotiation that differs in many interrelated ways. A Mexican American woman finding her way as a student at a California State University is not just female, young, second-generation Mexican American, or in college. She is all those and more in her particular set of circumstances. She relates to other students and faculty in her student identity, to her family as a daughter who has entered a different world, and to peers in her own singular styles of play and work.

As children, we are in the playground, the neighborhood, the home, and the school. We learn who we are in each setting and discover that there are subtle differences that impact how we understand and present ourselves in each setting. Our activities are age-graded throughout life. Behaviors considered cute when we are five are prohibited when we are ten. As we move through the life course, we move from school to workplace to retirement, from parental home to independent residence and often back to being cared for, from being looked after to looking after others, and so on. Every aspect of these changes is played out in our leisure: where we go and with whom, what we want to do and what others expect of us. We play "children's games" that are left behind as we become teens. We fool around as teens in ways that are unacceptable for post-school employed adults.

We are always seeking intimacy, but the forms of relationships change with age. We are always trying to learn and establish competence, but the settings of school, work, and recreation are quite different through the life course. And in the process we change along with our circumstances. Even in the establishment of midlife, there may be significant changes. Mental and physical health problems for the self or those close to us, work crises from dissallusionment to dismissal, geographical relocations, disruptions in central relationships, and other traumas impact leisure in all kinds of ways. On the other hand, we may discover a leisure investment that adds meaning to all the rest of life. The loss of some resources may lead to a discovery of others.

Social roles, then, are not a list of items in computer. They are indices of a total life condition that changes in significant ways as we make the journey of life. We have our own histories that are shaped by gender, education, parental influences, access to resources, cultural values and orientations, and even accidents of particular events and experiences. We become who we are in a unique history that is not quite like any other. At any given time, we are at a particular intersection of life in which leisure styles are integrated into the balances and rhythms of life.

Developmental Changes

Shifts in life circumstances are not the only changes important to understanding leisure styles through the life course. A major contribution of Rhona and Robert Rapoport was to begin to combine attention to leisure with both human development and social roles.[5] In our life journeys, we change not only externally, in roles and environments, but also internally, in our selfhood. We respond to social and biological timetables in how we understand ourselves and who we are in varying circumstances.

Some examples have already been introduced. In early adolescence, the child has to learn to define him- or herself as a sexual and sexually identified being, to become a man among both men and women or a woman among significant same and other-sex others. Later, retirement years usually entail defining the self as one who *was* a contributing worker and who now finds meaning and identity without that ongoing role.

Other illustrations abound: What about the home-and-family-invested woman who finds herself without a life companion? How does she redefine herself when so much had been invested in being a supportive homemaker? What about the woman who chooses to make a work identity primary in her life? What about the man who is told that his skills are redundant in the labor market, the youth who can no longer explain himself as still getting ready for some unspecified future, the professional who "burns out" in his or her vocation?

We are not just units being processed by the computer of life, bytes of information to be sorted by the great machine. We are reflexive, thinking, and self-conscious actors who try to make sense of who we are and what we may become. We are always in the process of becoming. That process involves not only social negotiation over who we are; it involves a process of self-definition and development that is never finally fixed. We are always at work on ourselves, on how we can conceive of ourselves, our competencies, our limitations, and our gifts.

The Career of Leisure

Leisure, then, has a career. Like work and family, there is a line of behaviors and actions undertaken primarily for their own sake that we call *leisure*. In this career, there is both change and continuity. There are evident changes in opportunities and competencies through the years. There are less evident shifts in intentions and identities, in the aims of our lines of action and how we define ourselves within them.

In this career of leisure that intersects with our other life careers, style is not static—learned once in the familial culture and retained rigidly ever after. Leisure careers are not isolated, but develop in our "social convoy"—the cohorts who make the life journey through the same historical events and social changes that affect our lives. Further, there are culture-specific attitudes, values, modes of communication, and learned behaviors that make up part of our life and leisure styles. How we present ourselves to others, communicate who we are, would like to be received, and generally negotiate who we are among

---

[5] Rhona and Robert Rapoport, *Leisure and the Family Life Cycle* (London: Routledge and Kegan Paul, 1975).

others—that is, our public leisure styles—are learned in our social convoy and culture. As a consequence, our leisure styles are not quite like those of any other age group when they were or will become our age; just as our own styles change through our life journeys.

A Pluralistic Approach to Leisure

In brief, a pluralistic approach means that leisure is neither separate from its historical, social, and cultural contexts, nor is it wholly determined by them. Leisure is both social and existential. We do choose something of the shape and content of our leisure styles, but we choose out of the times and places through which we make our way.

From a pluralistic perspective, there are multiple and interrelated sources of leisure styles. Leisure is always *of* the culture, ethnic. It is developed in a social context and responsive to the social structures and role norms of the system. It takes place in varied environments and is influenced by their location, size, shape, and quality. On the other hand, the variety of leisure cannot be explained in any deterministic model. It is not simply the result of one or two variables—social class, status forces, market provisions, marketing, mass media, or childhood socialization. Identifying sources of leisure styles does not lead to the further step of labeling "determinants" of leisure.

The two dimensions of leisure, the social and the existential, are also the two polarities in the dynamic of leisure styles. If leisure is neither totally segmented and separated from other roles and relationships nor fully determined by them, then some sort of dynamic relationship is implied. This relationship may be conceptualized as a dialectic in which the social and the existential in tension, with both synergy and conflict, produce actual leisure choices and investments. The sources of leisure styles are in this dynamic interplay between the structures of society and the existential self-creation of the individual.[6]

Socialization into Leisure

From the social side of the dialectic, leisure is viewed as learned behavior. We learn not only how to engage in activities and interact with others in leisure settings, but we learn culture-specific values and orientations for our leisure. The ethnicity of leisure is evident in its aims as well as contents.

In a differentiated social system, divided by cultural identification as well as by economic position, we make our life journeys with different sets of opportunities for leisure. Further, we do not all learn the same expectations for our roles. What it means to be a father or mother, son or daughter, student or worker, neighbor and citizen, all vary according to just where we are in the society. We learn the same roles in different ways.

Insofar as leisure is connected with those roles, then we can be expected to vary in our leisure behavior. We may party, drink, compete, and travel, but in different ways. We may argue, flirt, play games, inaugurate friendships, and demonstrate our gender identities, but with quite different vocabularies, symbol systems, and presentations. We do not all play

---

[6] John R. Kelly, "Leisure Interaction and the Social Dialectic," *Social Forces,* 60 (1981), 304–332.

our parts in our social dramas alike; and, to a large extent, the differences have been learned in our socialization histories.

Nor do we cease learning at some magic point in our development. Leisure style may be changed, both because of how others define and respond to us and because of how we have come to understand ourselves. Further, what is available to us changes and we learn to adapt to our opportunities.

The Existential Element

Such learning does not negate the existential element in leisure. There is always the "not yet" of life, a looking forward to what we might become. We seldom see ourselves as completed products with nothing more in life than to finish out what is settled and unchangeable. We are always in a process of "becoming," of dreaming, planning, and deciding how we may enact our roles in ways that alter and enhance what we may be in the future. We develop lines of action with at least a direction, if not a clear-cut plan and final goal.

Leisure may, in some periods in the life course, provide the fullest space for such existential operation. If leisure is the most free of life's spaces, the least determined by necessity and structure, then we may use our leisure opportunities, activities, and relationships to explore the potential of tomorrow. In the interplay between what is and what we might become, we try out new portrayals and new parts. We may explore the possibilities of change. In the relative freedom of leisure, we take the first steps toward selfhood and contexts for living that are not quite like the present. Leisure, despite the centrality of the present experience, may also have a decisive openness to the future.

The Role-Identity Model

The crucial issue is just how we bring together these seemingly disparate elements in leisure—the social and the existential, socialization and becoming. What I propose is an approach that combines each side of the dialectic in a "role-identity model." If style refers to *how* we enact our roles, then we need both the role context and the decisive element of enactment in the model. Role identity combines the social context with our self-definition of who we are in taking a role and how we choose to enact it.[7, 8] Style, then, becomes a melding of role content and enactment, a bringing together in the decision process of what we have learned and what we seek to become.

Rather than belabor definitions, we may advance the argument best with three analytical examples:

The Party   If a party can be considered a leisure event, then its taken-for-granted and agreed-on expectations for behavior can be assumed to be leisure roles. Depending on the complexity of the party, there may be roles of being host and hostess, intimate helper, familiar friend, official guest, companion of guest, guest of honor, stranger, and so on. The

[7] George McCall and J. L. Simmons, *Identities and Interactions,* Second edition (New York: Free Press, 1978).

[8] Kelly, *Leisure Identities and Interactions.*

interaction patterns, self-presentations, physical gestures, degree of cooperation, self-placement in a central or peripheral position, and other elements of action are role-related.

However, an individual may be in multiple-role relationships with others at the party—spouse to one, boss or employee to another, colleague, partner, neighbor, schoolmate, lover, political opponent, parent, and others. The reciprocal expectations and mutual histories cause the ways party roles are enacted to change from one grouping to another. We may be in several roles at any given time as people move through our milieu.

As if that were not complex enough, each actor may define him- or herself somewhat differently in each of the roles. Therefore, in a given conversation, there is the delicate negotiation of presenting an identity that is not inconsistent for those familiar with any of the roles and yet furthers the line of action desired at that time and place. We may present a self that is not too assertive for a work superior, affectionate enough for an intimate, aggressive enough to secure a place in the interaction, and reserved enough to allow for redirection. Every shift in composition of our conversation group slightly alters how we play our roles. The process of the interaction may even cause us to redirect our self-portrayal as our identity takes shape in the event. We may become funnier, quieter, more poised, or less passive. We may play scholar in one episode, old buddy in another, sensitive listener in a third, and aloof superior in a fourth. In the role mix, we retune our presentations to offer identities—role portrayals—that fit our aims in that particular situation. As a consequence, the party becomes the social context for an endless variety of role-identity offerings. In fact, the real content of the leisure event is the negotiation of such role identities.

Swimming   As another illustration of how role identities give insight into leisure styles, take the common leisure activity of swimming in a public pool. The various styles of behavior—from lounging near the fence and maintaining consistent distance from the water to exhibitionist diving, a boisterous ball game, or solitary swimming of fifty laps—are more than preferences for different degrees of physical education. Rather, they reflect how identities are presented in that leisure context. Further, the behavior may change if only one new person arrives on the scene. The sequence of life course roles and related identities is demonstrated by the quite different behaviors exhibited by frolicking children, self-conscious and posing teens, caretaking young mothers, cardplaying students, and disciplined length-counting later-life men and women. The leisure environment, the pool, provides a social context for demonstrating and trying out a wide variety of portrayals that are the basis for the different styles.

Daydreaming   Even in the movement-free leisure of daydreaming, we try out identities. We may enter a normally inaccessible environment, acquire previously unattainable skills, and interact with formerly distant others. The leisure of daydreaming may leap all kinds of barriers. However, we are still ourselves in some recognizable form. Even more, we transcend some of our normal limitations to try out identities outside our normal reach, relate to others actually continents away, and develop interaction sequences that may never come to pass. Yet, in all this, we are still acting out who we would like to be—on the stage of the imagination—and often the portrayal is that of a wished-for leisure style and competence.

The Centrality of Leisure

How does all this come together? We began with the variety of leisure. Stereotyping approaches were rejected in favor of a combination of core and balance that together make up an individual's leisure style. The core of accessible and informal engagements seems to change somewhat less than the balance through the life course. However, both are affected by role shifts and developmental needs. Leisure was then analyzed as a pluralistic phenomenon, neither separate from our life conditions and cultures nor wholly determined by them. Leisure is both social and existential, shaped by socialization and yet encompassing future-oriented decision. Leisure is experience, with intrinsic meanings rather than productivity aims; yet it is also a social space in which we may work out meanings of selfhood that are crucial to our identities and our primary relationships.

Leisure styles, then, are not the results of some simple set of determinants that can be run through a computer to produce a profile of predicted styles. Again, style is more a matter of how than what, or who we are than what we do. All approaches and models are faulty when they begin with the assumption that leisure is somehow residual, leftover in time and always secondary in meaning. Leisure may indeed be simple rest, a change from duty and a recuperation from strain. But leisure may at some times and places be at the absolute center of our lives, exactly where we develop our most significant relationships, express our most profound emotions and desires, and portray our most crucial identities.

Leisure, then, requires an existential element, that dimension of freedom that enables us to choose, at least within limits, the contexts of our role portrayals. This relative freedom makes possible the investment of self that leads to the fullest development of ourselves, the richest expression of who we want to become, and the deepest experience of fulfillment. This freedom to choose also enables us to relate most fully and expressively to those intimate others central to our lives, to develop trust and communication, to experience histories of enjoyment, and to weave color and texture into our ongoing relationships. Leisure is freedom—sometimes freedom to fill time aimlessly and retreat from ourselves and others, but also to invest ourselves most fully, to seek to become something more than we have yet become, and to add the reality of joy to our bonds of intimacy.

HIGHLIGHTS

1. Leisure styles are varied and multidimensional rather than simple and monothematic.
2. There is a core of accessible activities that persists through the life course.
3. An individual's leisure style includes both a core and a balance that change as roles and developmental orientations change.
4. Leisure involves a dialectic between the existential element of becoming and the social dimensions of bonding and institutional roles.
5. Leisure may be central to our definitions of who we are and whom we would like to become.

Discussion Questions

1. Can you describe any leisure stereotypes that seem to be accurate? What makes such people different?

2. Are there distinctive styles of leisure among students? How would you label them?

3. How do some people make leisure central to their identities and self-definitions? Give examples.

4. How would you argue against someone who says that studying leisure is frivolous and unimportant?

5. How do the leisure patterns of men and women differ? Why?

6. Which is more significant in shaping leisure styles, cultural background or opportunities?

7. List all the satisfactions from your favorite leisure activity. How many are personal or existential and how many are more social?

8. How do you decide what to do on Saturday night? On a weekday evening? What are the most important determinative factors?

Bibliography

Cheek, Neil H., and William R. Burch, *The Social Organization of Leisure in Human Society.* New York: Harper & Row, 1976.

Kando, Thomas M., *Leisure and Popular Culture in Transition,* Second edition. St. Louis, MO: C.V. Mosby, 1980.

Kelly, John R., *Leisure Identities and Interactions.* London and Boston: Allen and Unwin, 1983.

Kelly, John R., and Geoffrey Godbey. *The Sociology of Leisure.* State College, PA: Venture Publishing, 1992.

McCall, George, and J. Simmons, *Identities and Interactions,* Second edition. New York: Free Press, 1978.

Rapoport, Rhona, and Robert Rapoport, *Leisure and the Family Life Cycle.* London: Routledge and Kegan Paul, 1975.

Chapter 4

Leisure and the Life Course

Is the person who crashes into a wedge of blockers on the high school football field at age sixteen the same person who holds his toddler by both hands at a church picnic at age twenty-eight or who watches someone else crash a wedge on television at age fifty-five? Is the person who asserts his presence with confidence on the soccer field the same person who is afraid to dance at a class party? Is the woman directing a complex agenda at a business meeting Tuesday morning the same person who was sewing doll clothes with her daughter on Saturday?

The focus in this chapter is on leisure roles and identities. How does leisure integrate or conflict with family, work, and community roles? Does leisure provide opportunities for self-expression and community that are blocked in other roles?

First, the family life cycle is introduced to provide a framework for examining continuity and change in leisure as our family roles change.

Then a fuller perspective is added. Work and education, family, community, and leisure are all said to have "careers." The career concept implies that each role includes both critical changes and important continuities. Further, the identities we accept and project in those roles contain elements of both persistence and variation. Each aspect of the life course has transitions that have an impact on all of the elements. As we move through those transitions, we gain new preoccupations that alter the meaning of what we do.

The approach of this chapter is longitudinal. What are the meanings, limitations, and opportunities for leisure through the changing course of our lives? What are the changing agendas of life?

ISSUES

How does leisure change in forms and meanings as we move through the role changes of the life course?

How does the family life cycle shape leisure?

Why is leisure especially significant for students and others in the preparatory stages of life?

How do work and family roles intertwine with leisure in the establishment years?

Is the life course the same for women and men?

Does leisure take on increased significance in later years?

The concept of a life course implies both continuity and change. However, the changes in social roles have gained primary attention. In employment careers there are the transitions from school to job, from job to job, and then to retirement. In family careers, stress is on change related to marriage, parenthood, "launching" children, and widowhood. Leisure careers stress the loss of organized recreation contexts on leaving school, new environmental opportunities accompanying geographic moves, family-related leisure for parents, and the reduction of physical activity with age.

However, some aspects of the life course have considerable continuity. There are persistent identities such as sexual identification, feelings of competence, some modes of relating to others, value orientations, and self-images that may be much the same as we move through various roles and situations. On the other hand, there are also some situations in which we present quite different identities. In a marriage or close friendship we may reveal certain vulnerabilities that we conceal in most roles. In some single-sex contexts we may alter our sex-role self-presentation. In a game or at a party we may "unwind" into a more aggressive or outgoing presentation of self and in the situation actually define ourselves in a different way.

Leisure, then, is only one related element of the full life course. Change in other elements will usually affect leisure. The reading on page 53, based on interviews, will illustrate the interrelationship of the leisure career with family, work, and other elements of the life course.

The Family Life Cycle

There are several different versions of the *family life cycle*. The most simple keys on the presence of children in the parental family. The cycle begins with courtship and is followed by marriage, the preparental dyad, childbearing, child rearing, launching when children are leaving the parental home, the postparental dyad, retirement, and widowhood. Childbearing overlaps with child rearing if more than one child is born. Childbearing begins with the birth of the first child and launching ends when the last leaves.

Some find it useful to break down the cycle further. They would add a "honeymoon" period early in marriage when the excitement of the new relationship tends to obscure the tasks of building a relationship. This period may last from twelve hours to a year. Others find significant differences within the child-rearing period. Especially for the mother, having preschool children is considerably more constraining than having children who are all in school most of the day. Combining mother and work roles doubles pressures on time and energy. Parenthood of younger children may be distinguished from parenthood of emergent teenagers, especially when the teenagers are employed part time and have their own transportation.

Further, the periods are not separate and discrete stages of life. Each period provides some transition opportunities to prepare for the next. Children grow in a continual process, not in three separate leaps. Independence develops gradually, not just on the day a driver's license is received. Older children are out of the home more and more before they leave for college, military service, or their first separate residence. The configuration of work, family, and leisure expectations is constantly shifting with every role change.

The family life cycle provides a useful framework for examining roles closely tied to leisure, despite that most families do not complete a "normal" cycle without disruption. Leisure is also related to life careers of work, community involvement, and environmental resources. However, in concentration on the contexts of leisure and changing social roles, we should not neglect the person who takes roles but retains some consistent identity.

The concept of identity includes both how we define ourselves and how others define us. In ongoing negotiations, we present ourselves to others, interpret responses, and sometimes redefine our self-images based on the perceived definitions of others. We are not just roles—workers, fathers, or sisters—but we are people who take on roles in ways that have some element of individuality.

The lifelong process of finding out who we are is one of social interaction. We pick up images from our social environment and try them out to see how they work. Sometimes we are disappointed, or even somewhat humiliated, when the image is disconfirmed. More often we are able to present a self-portrayal that others find authentic and so come to see ourselves as that kind of person. Further, other people important to us have influenced us in the process of learning who we are by their values and their portrayals. We often want to be a lot like a friend, a parent, or an older brother or sister. Such people provide models of selfhood for us.

Identity formation is not just passive learning. In what we do, how we speak, how we dress, where we go, and how we behave, we present a self to other people. We express who we are in our actions. Therefore, the decisions we make about our leisure are one way in which we present who we are to others. In fact, since leisure can be the most open and expressive aspect of our lives, leisure may be quite central to our identities.

Leisure Roles and Identities

If leisure is a pluralistic phenomenon, neither determined by one social factor nor unrelated to several, then the life course framework provides one way of beginning to understand what leisure is and means in modern life. The approach here is to combine family life cycle and work-education careers into a model with three main divisions: preparation, establishment, and reintegration. Leisure will be examined in this general framework, before going on in later chapters to deal with particular forms and institutional settings.

The Preparation Periods

In Western cultures great stress is placed on the "production" periods of family and work life. As a result a third or more of a seventy-five-year life span may be defined primarily as "preparation" for later family, work, and community roles. The early years are a time of learning, anticipation, and of being evaluated for later opportunities.

For example, early childhood may be structured by adults as primarily socialization— the learning of social expectations, skills, languages, value orientations, and other cultural elements considered essential for later functioning in the society. Some of this socialization is structured in school, but more takes place in the family and among peers in contexts of play. The kinds of games and activities encouraged in children generally reflect later role expectations. We are not only socialized into leisure preferences and values during our childhood experiences, but are socialized by our childhood leisure toward other adult roles.

Preparation and New Identities

The preparatory years can be divided into a number of subperiods. It might be assumed that the preoccupation leading to play in childhood years is for learning and expression. As a consequence, the leisure interests of children seem to be quite varied. At some times children prefer newness and exploration. At others they seek equilibrium and stability in

---

Fun and Games

Seven neighborhood children meet on the comer of a schoolyard on Saturday morning for a game of touch football. Although the time had been set for 10 A.M. at school the day before, at fifteen minutes past the hour, Jimmy is still missing. The complications of choosing teams with an uneven number, three of whom are *girls,* consume another quarter hour. Then boundaries are designated by sidewalks and bushes with two trees in the playing field defined as in-bounds natural hazards. One-hand or two-hand touching, limits on forward passes, and number of other rules are negotiated for another ten minutes. The wisdom of such negotiation is revealed by 10:45 when a seeming touchdown is disputed with claims of holding and returning from out of bounds to catch the pass thrown from too near the line of scrimmage. At 11:05 some eight minutes have been consumed in arguing, fourteen minutes in the construction of elaborate plays, and three minutes in their unsuccessful execution. This "casual" group play of children consists largely of scheduling, waiting, rule negotiating, rule interpretation, and organizing. The vocabulary and models of television football permeate the attempts to construct plays that "flood the zone" to allow for a "look-in" or a "buttonhook." The game itself is a complex social phenomenon without including what appearances, success and failure, and other elements actually mean to the players.

their play and games. The play of children is both preparation for later roles and an expression of the world of the child at that time. Even for young children gender identities are reinforced by the subtle and explicit pressures of adults.

The Rapoports' *Leisure and the Family Life Cycle*[1] begins the analysis of leisure with the preteen and early teen years in which youths are found to be primarily occupied with identity crystallization. Young adults are said to be more preoccupied with social than personal identity. Therefore, the exploration and testing of self is succeeded in later teen years by seeking independence and working out sexual identity.

Seeking Personal Identity

The fundamental question is "Who am I?" In this early teen period, the young person tends to try out many kinds of personal identities, to experiment with different kinds of relationships, and to explore just who he or she is as a being with certain physical, mental, and emotional capacities. Autonomy and independence are basic preoccupations. Others include both stimulation and boredom, work, sociability, physical maturation, mental development, and, in some cases, trying different environments, moral sensitivities, and capacities for living.

It is important to recognize the variety of leisure interests for youth. They have different social arenas in which to try out their emerging selfhood. For some, school activities are central, especially sports for some males and an increasing number of females. For others, the social scene outside school is most important. Some have clearly invested more in being *against* the influence and expectations of their parents than others. Most are attached to some social group with a set of expectations that has considerable power to shape leisure styles. However, just as important as the variety is the significance of leisure in the exploration process. Finding out who we are is very serious business even when it is carried out in the least serious places—the club, the bar, the playing field, the street corner, and the shopping center. The kinds of behaviors that allow youth to "fit in" are specific to each setting as well as to identities that vary by gender and social group.

Developing Social Identity

Identification with social institutions is the central preoccupation of young adults, according to the Rapoports. While the quest for a viable personal identity continues, at the point of leaving school young adults are propelled into more adult roles related to the social institutions of family, the economy, and the community. Discovering which roles are most appealing and how they can be engaged gives a more pronounced social orientation to this period of the life career. In this process, some are quite conventional while a minority try out identities that are in conflict with adult preferences.

Identity Formation and Students

High school and college students are engaged in finding out who they are. Their identities have been molded in their homes and communities in a process that has had considerable consistency and continuity for most. Then several transitions occur in a relatively short span of years. The first is the emergence of focused sexuality as more than a general aware-

---

[1] Rhona and Robert N. Rapoport, *Leisure and the Family Life Cycle* (London: Roudedge and Kegan Paul, 1975).

ness. Sexual identity is more than a recognition of oneself as either male or female and of half the people around as of the other sex. Sexual identity, spurred by both social expectations and physical development, calls for building a new reality of the self in relation to the sexual identity of others. Sexual orientation may be problematic in teen years with some facing the difficulties of acknowledging homosexual identifications.

While sexuality may be seen as the most pressing aspect of identify formation by students, there are other changes taking place at the same time. Some changes may evolve gradually and gracefully. Others involve a crisis or trauma for many. One change is the development of independence from parents, at first while still living with them and later when removed to college or some other residence away from home. Another change in American society is increased mobility afforded by the driver's license and access to the automobile. There is the transition from being economically dependent on parents to the attainment of some economic discretion through part-time employment and looking to a time not far away when economic self-sufficiency will be expected of one. Sexual, social, and economic identities are built into the complex process of growing independence, mobility, and exploration of adult roles. Dilemmas of conflict between desires toward independence and desires for social acceptance, especially by peers, may make this a time of stress as well as critical development.

For students who have enough confidence to welcome change, the later student years may be an exciting time of discovery. These years are a time of trying out new possibilities for life, of testing the responses to new aspects of personal and social identities, and of searching for possible futures. In short, this is a time for learning, exploring, and testing new identities. At the same time, the need to integrate those identities into the coherent public self of full adulthood is still ahead.

However, one problem of this identity-forming period is that much of the "real world" of adult life is still closed to the student. Schools and other institutions provide models of student government, social events, and even work projects in an attempt to simulate the "reality" that still lies ahead. However, students are discouraged and even blocked from entering that adult world of work, marriage, parenthood, and full political participation. They are reminded that this is a time of preparation.

As a result, the nonwork elements of life take on great importance. It is precisely in school, sports, social events, dating, vacation trips, activity groups, clubs, and other "youth" activities that the crucial process takes place. In leisure the new elements of selfhood are presented, new roles tested, and new identities are accepted. For male students, sports have been a major arena of working out aggressive and decisive interaction. In the past, social activities have been a central arena of development for females. Now a more critical attitude toward old sex-differentiated roles suggests a more inclusive set of opportunities for both preparation-period men and women.

Sports not only produce a social status in the entire social network of the school but are a primary field for the establishment of physical and social self-esteem. Various kinds of organizations provide ways of trying out roles of leadership, influence, dissent, and cooperation. And almost every situation of social interaction includes some element of sexuality, from the casual encounter through various levels of intimacy. In general, high school students tend to be dissatisfied with the leisure opportunities for their immediate environ-

Leisure Career Transitions

1. *"Good-bye, Columbus"*   When Jim graduated from a state university, he moved out of the Midwest and into a new environment. Gone were the fraternity parties, the sense of community, the friends on and near the campus with parallel interests, the year-round intramural sports program, the open gymnasiums and outdoor facilities, the packed calendar of cultural events, and the countless campus bars.

Now, after the class-structured schedule of his chemistry major and the interstitial periods of campus interchange and activity breaks, he is eight-thirty to five in a petroleum lab. His new associates are scattered around the expanding city in southern Texas rather than concentrated on a campus. Most are married, many have children, and all have some sets of leisure companions. Now Jim has to create a new leisure balance. He can join the downtown Y to continue his racquetball. He may make the transition to the more formal invitations that seem to be expected by single women in the business atmosphere, or he may think of inviting for a weekend a close friend who has a year left back at the university.

Since three of his new colleagues play golf every weekend and the climate is much warmer in winter, he has already begun the shift from team sports into golf. New friends, new schedules, new expectations, and new opportunities have begun to move him into a new set of activities. Further, with his salary, he is able to consider possibilities he could not afford before. This is a good thing because the low-cost resources of the campus are no longer there. However, he is considering a night course at a local university in which he would hope to meet new people, gain access to the campus resources, and perhaps deal with some of that nostalgia for the old school where it all seemed so easy.

2. *"Hello, Mama!"*   For Karen the change was almost too much to cope with. She and her husband had planned for the baby. They had saved money, moved to a larger house from the apartment, fixed up the bedrooms, and talked a lot about how they would share the experience of being parents. Now most of the day he was at work and she was home.

It had been very different before. They had left together in the morning. She dropped him where he could take the bus to his office because she needed the car in her position in community mental health work. Sometimes they met downtown for dinner during the week. It was easy and they had two incomes. She had friends at work, a feeling of being appreciated and useful, the freedom of her own income and checking account, and very full schedule. They cherished the time they had together and planned their weekends carefully. It was almost permanent courtship without the hassles. There were good reasons for postponing having a child.

Now the weekend was still full, but not as planned. Saturday morning Karen took off and he stayed home with the baby. Saturday afternoon seemed always full of projects. Saturday night was the night out and Sunday had really become the day of rest and preparation for the week. After all, his new work responsibilities and opportunities required much more than a nine to five interest.

She still had a few college friends who met twice a month but now she felt closer to the two other young mothers on the block. They did seem to have a lot to talk about over coffee or on the phone. She had taken tennis lessons in the summer and hoped to start a pottery class soon. But the truth was that she was now a mother first of all. He tried to help, but she was home and the demands and interests of his work were out there.

Much as she loved the baby, she felt that her world had shrunk incredibly. What could she do that was *her* own, that expressed the vital and competent person she had been? Or was it selfish to even think such thoughts? How long could they afford for her to stay out of full-time employment? And what about interrupting her career?

3. ***"Put Out to Pasture in the Concrete City"***   Al had known that it was coming for years, but no one had told him about the realities of retirement. There had been a lot of advice: Take up a new hobby! Move to Arizona! Enjoy yourself for a change!

It wasn't that he had been that excited about his job. For a while it had been interesting, especially as long as he seemed to be moving up in the company. When you start during a depression, just having a job looks good at first. Then the "Big War" came along to interrupt the flow. When he returned, the company had held a slot for him and just getting back to an office, a home, and a family took care of the next few years. Al had been forty-five when he realized that he was now doing about what he would do the rest of his life. In his work career it would be more of the same until retirement a long way off.

However, that wasn't so bad. There were the kids to get through high school. Their activities had given some highlights to the routine. Then remodeling the house and adding the paneled back room for parties and the television had stretched out through three—or was it four?—years. Those two trips West had helped, especially the one for which he had saved an extra two weeks of vacation.

They had friends and took their turn entertaining. Two of the grandchildren were only a half hour away; that meant a lot. The old things were no less appealing than before—reading mysteries, sports on TV, and a garden in the summer until they moved to an apartment.

The shock was how much he must have depended on the routine of the job. It hadn't been exciting, but it was regular. It gave Al a time to get up and a reason to go to bed. It meant that the relative freedom of the weekend was special. Now no time is special because every day is Saturday. . . . except that most of the men around have gone to work.

The grandkids are not children now and have their own busy schedules. There is only so much to do around the house. Fishing is okay in season, but the old knee will only take so much climbing or sitting and a new boat is out on a reduced income. Golf is no more interesting than it ever was and collecting stamps still looks like a bore.

However, a new schedule is beginning to take shape. Al drives his wife to her appointments and events and does most of the shopping. They are playing cards more in impromptu evenings with a couple in the same building. Planning a long auto trip together is engrossing. Church and seeing the kids takes care of Sunday. All in all, the transition to a new routine is well under way. After all, it's not so bad to just take it easy part of the time, too. And it's funny how some things just take longer to do than they used to.

ment. Desires for privacy and community, spontaneity and safe routine, independence and security, risk and safety, and responsibility and freedom are often too inconsistent to be satisfied. However, even the simple desire for space and activity outside the view of adults is seldom granted by school, home, or community. One study found that teens are in the best mood when engaged in social interaction with peers.[2]

Some of a student's life is preparatory. It is aimed at the future. That part of life is of greatest concern to parents, teachers, and others with authority. The rest of the student's

[2] Mihaly Csikszentmihalyi and Reed Larson, *Being Adolescent* (New York: Basic Books, 1984).

life is contemporary. That is the part of life that tends to be most expressive, most shaped by symbols of group identification, and most materialistic since the self is presented in clothing, cars, music, and vocabulary that make a statement about who the student is right now. Preparatory aspects of life tend to be institutionalized and to require deferred gratification. The contemporary elements have their meaning in the group and their gratification in the now. They are leisure. At the same time, it is in this area of immediate meaning and gratification, of symbolism and group identification that the most direct and profound self-definitions may be worked out. Decisions, actions, and responses may have the most profound effects on identity just because they are important at that time rather than oriented to the future. Students are living and learning who they are, whether in the game or in the bleachers, at a party or in a bar, on the street or in a dorm.

Courtship

Most courtship takes place in a context of leisure. Formal dating patterns have given way to more informal, group, mutually initiated activities such as concerts, dancing, sports, outdoor events, and many sorts of informal interactions, including watching television and listening to music at home. The school provides a timetable and a variety of activities for meeting others and developing relationships. Along with a reduction of formal dating, another major change in courting patterns is their common delay and renewal. Those who do not marry while in school or whose marriages dissolve are seeking ways of courting outside the school context. Commercial entrepreneurs and voluntary organizations have begun to recognize this increased population and to make leisure provisions for meeting and cultivating relationships. While most preparation social life is not "courting," it is gendered and has pervasive sexual dimensions.

The Establishment Periods

Establishment years are those of finding and consolidating a position in the social system, of preoccupation with productive roles and related rewards, and of an integration of multiple roles into a coherent life pattern. Family and work careers seem central to this period, and leisure is often valued for its contributions to other life spaces. However, all people do not go consecutively from school to marriage and a job.

Singleness and Life's Investments

More and more, men and women are beginning to take regular work roles while still single. For those with high education levels and clear career aspirations, marriage may be delayed until the first steps of work establishment are behind. Therefore, some singles out of school are primarily interested in finding a marriage partner, others prefer to postpone that commitment, and some choose to remain single.

For those who are seeking to establish such a marriage and family commitment, leisure tends to be preoccupied with meeting interesting others and pursuing relationships. In the first stage, activities and locales may be chosen largely for their potential of introductions. Not only singles bars, clubs, dances, and apartment complexes, but churches, recreation departments, and various community organizations recognize this preoccupation and cater to it. Ski weekends, evenings in the city, theater parties, and weeknight programs maximize access and interaction for those who do not come as couples.

On the other hand, many singles do not consider themselves ready for a marriage commitment. Some prefer to accomplish certain education, work, or leisure objectives before risking derailment by family commitments. Others believe that they ought to learn more about themselves and how they relate to others before taking the risk of long-term commitment. For gay men, lesbian women, and bisexuals, there is the challenge of developing intimate and committed relationships without the support of accepted "family" forms and legal protections.

Those who prefer to postpone marriage or not to marry are still likely to want to have a full social expression of leisure. They generally hope to have opportunity to develop their own selfhood in their leisure and try out and test relationships or friendships in intimacy. As a consequence, the leisure interests of those both seeking and avoiding commitment tend to be social. They hope to meet and develop friendships with persons of both sexes. Especially if they live alone, leisure is expected to keep loneliness at bay. One difference for those preferring not to marry is that they are more likely to be heavily invested in starting their work careers than in leisure interests that are personally fulfilling.

Marriage

More than 80 percent of the population still gets married at some point. However, trends toward later marriage and choosing not to marry are increasing. When couples make the transition from courtship to marriage, the impact of the change on leisure depends on whether residence, employment, and relations with the parental families change as well. When couples live together first and marry later, they may not change greatly what they do for leisure. What does change is the increased likelihood that the activities are done with each other. Some separate activities may decrease when expectations of building the relationship become more of a factor for many in their leisure decisions. The preparental period may combine dyadic activity with considerable flexibility. When there are two incomes, leisure may include more eating out, evenings in town, and weekend trips. On the other hand, the financial requirements of setting up even minimal residence exhaust the resources of many with lower incomes. For most couples, early marriage is a time with high expectations for companionship. It is also a period in which couples have to negotiate conflicting expectations and rights of self-determination.

Preschool Parenting: Scarce Resources

The primary resources of leisure are time, space, skill, companions, equipment, and money. Time, space, and money all tend to be restricted by the birth of children. Further, the demand for care of infants and young children is more or less total. Parents must either care for them or arrange to have someone else do it. As a result, leisure is limited not only by lack of time but by the presence of the children.

The loss of freedom is probably noticed first. The couple cannot just pick up and go—to a show, for a walk, to visit friends, or anywhere else. One consequence is that the husband and wife either do less together or stay home more. Another result for the young mother is that she tends to seek weekday activities where she can take her child and where others are coping with the same limitations. If she leaves employment, she also is cut off for a time from her work companions, from the chance to get out regularly to spend the day with other adults, and from having her own income. If she is among the majority of mothers of preschool children in the paid labor force, she has to manage time and energy to cope with the "second shift" of home and family work.[3]

In the home, preschool children require space for their own living. Further, as they learn to walk they are more likely to interrupt the activity, conversation, and intimacy of the parents. Life becomes more crowded and less free, even at home. If the couple moves to a larger residence, then both the children and the larger housing take more of the available financial resources. Therefore, a second income may seem to be a necessity.

The impacts on leisure are manifold and evident. Companionship for two people living together and doing most of their leisure together may be seriously disrupted. Arrangements to spend much time together away from preschool children are difficult and costly. So much that was so easy before becomes expensive and complicated. The need of a couple to continue to develop its own relationship and to find self-expression may be put off due to all the pressures. Conflicts over the allocation of those scarce resources of time, space, privacy, and money may cause considerable resentment of the "selfishness" and lack of understanding of the marriage partner. In most families, the mother is the "manager" and facilitator, even when the father retains final veto power.

The point is that nothing changes leisure quite so much as parenthood. Further, the most demanding phase of being parents seems to come in those early years. Somehow a pregnancy period is not adequate preparation for this impact, no matter how much parenthood is desired and anticipated. The increase of dual careers and new emphasis on the personal fulfillment and freedom of women would seem to call for considerable skill in marital communication and flexibility in management of resources if the period is to be one of enrichment rather than frustration and resentment. All this takes place in the midst of what Hochschild calls the "stalled revolution" in which neither work nor family have changed to support the employed mother.

One possibility is that leisure simply takes low priority in this period of the life course. Leisure expressions are put off until there is more time and money and until children can participate more fully in family activities. Life satisfactions must then be found in the early stages of the work careers. Responsibility tends to dominate decisions and autonomy to become a shrinking domain to be defended with carefully constructed timetables.

Other life investments may conflict with the centrality of parenthood in this phase. Preschool parenthood may also coincide with getting started in a job or profession that is quite demanding. Working under the direction of others who have the power to make critical decisions about one's retention and advancement may call for extraordinary efforts at work and for more preparation in off hours. Night school and work brought home do not blend well with the needs for moonlighting for extra income or with taking a full share in child care.

This can be a period when pressures from legitimate institutional commitments and the investment goals of work, family, and community not only leave little time for leisure

---

[3] Arlie Hochschild, *The Second Shift: Working Parents and the Revolution at Home* (New York: Viking, 1989).

but are in considerable conflict with life's scarce resources. For those with marginal income, the struggle to cope with multiple demands is compounded by an inability to purchase support resources.

Increasingly common today is the single parent. Most common is the mother who is employed and also the residential parent of children from a marriage that is now dissolved. However, there are also many women who are parents without having been married. The limitations are manifold and profound. In most cases, financial constraints are compounded with extreme pressures on time. Leisure, either for the single parent or for the family, has to be budgeted carefully to cope with the limited resources. Employed mothers have been found to have the least discretionary time. Single-parent employed mothers have the least of all.

Midestablishment and "Doing Well"

According to the Rapoports, the central preoccupation during the fifteen to twenty years that children are in school is with *performance*. Part of that preoccupation is concern with how well the children are doing, in school and elsewhere. However, there is also a central concern for measuring accomplishment in work, community standing, the family, and, perhaps, one's own life.

It is also a time of diffusion. As children move through their school careers, they tend to become more and more involved in relationships and activities outside the home. Partly they simply expand the range of their mobility and society. However, at the same time, they are leisure companions for their parents. Parents schedule their own time around the activities of the children. Vacations now tend to be shared rather than being just a struggle with the logistics of child care. To a large extent, the focus may shift more from care to *nurture*. And the investment in being parents grows larger and larger. In this period, despite good intentions, women continue to carry disproportionate parenting responsibilities.

One major task is the integration of the varied interests and institutional schedules of family members. Different styles of coping with the expressed needs of different family members are demonstrated. One parent, usually the mother, may direct and orchestrate the schedule. A second style is to segregate the individual lives as much as possible, so that there is a minimum of interference. A third style stresses the mutuality of family interests and participation. In the "mother-directed" family, she becomes at once the arbiter and executor of activities, timetables, and resources. In the role-segregated family, each person is expected to work out life's possibilities and limitations. In the mutual family, whenever possible, tasks and leisure are shared and decisions made with others in mind.

In North America, research by the author has found a common "parental package" of leisure. This package includes marital, family, home, and recreational activity in a balance that reflects both personal interests and role expectations. It is not accurate to stereotype those in any life course period. It is true that the parents of preschool children, the mother especially, have entered a time of considerable resource limitation in leisure. It is also true that the parents of school-age children are much more likely to engage in "family leisure" and to take the expectations of their spouse and children into account in their leisure decisions. However, as indicated by the "parental package," there is still variety and personal selection in the overall leisure profile of most parents.

In this "performance period," life may be oriented toward "doing well" in the work roles of parents and the school roles of children. With most mothers employed outside the home, there is considerable negotiation over conflicts between caregiving and work expectations. Who arranges schedules, stays home when children are sick, and has primary responsibility for marriage and family relationships?

The periods of maximum concentration on the children and of maximum effort toward advancement in work often coincide. While the children and their accomplishments are a focus of nonwork attention, the job and possible achievement there are also a focus for many managerial, technical, and professional workers. It would not be surprising, then, to find that leisure is less significant in overall life priorities than at other periods of the life career. Rather, major investments are taken seriously as the foundation of the future as well as for their intrinsic satisfaction.

School-age children more and more have their own schedules. In the typical American community, with its dependence on the automobile for transportation, the logistics of working out the transportation timetable may become quite complex. It is no wonder that parents slip into a leisure pattern built around the scheduled activities of children without really giving it much thought. However, when the subject is discussed, they are quite aware of how many kinds of "adult" activity and interaction are postponed or even given up so that everyone can have opportunities for development, accomplishment, and companionship. It is also no wonder that some mothers find themselves deciding that it will be another year before they will seek full-time employment again.

More than half of the mothers in the United States are back in the work force within a year after the birth of a child, however. The most common pattern is that of the married or single mother coping with the multiple responsibilities of employment and managing a household that includes child rearing. All indications are that time for self and time for

---

Family Schedules

What's on for the Jones family this Wednesday night? First, remember that even this comfortable suburban household has logistical limitations. There are two cars for four people, one of whom is too young to drive. Mr. Jones doesn't get off the commuter train until 6:15—if it's on time and he isn't held up leaving the office—and Sharon has swim team practice from 6:00 to 7:00. So, if Jim is to get to band practice on time he will have to eat between 7:10 and 7:25 or not eat with the rest of the family at all. Further, Mr. Jones will have to take Jim to school if he is to have a car to go to the school budget meeting later, since Mrs. Jones is picking up two friends on the way to her class at the community college. All this juggling is routine and easily managed. The real problem is that Mr. and Mrs. Jones value both the sharing of a family meal and the opportunity to talk over their workdays with each other after dinner. Now for the third evening in a row the late meal due to commuting and Sharon's practice combine with transportation management so that twenty minutes of eating together is bought at the price of foregoing any after-dinner conversation. The multiplicity of familial and extra-familial roles and requirements, together with the externally imposed schedules of work, school, and community, seems to squeeze out just that kind of activity that the Jones and many others value most highly.

family activity are severely affected by such dual roles. Increasingly, leisure programs and providers will have to take account of such constraints on resources and opportunities.

The Family Context of Leisure

The "traditional" two-parent family is now a minority pattern. There is a wide variety of household configurations caused by singleness, divorce, sexual orientations, and other factors. Many adults are in periods of transition in and out of relationships. Families are "blended" and reconstituted following remarriage. Nevertheless, leisure and the family are inseparable in Western cultures. The family provides the first context of leisure learning, the primary socialization about leisure values, the companions for most leisure through the life cycle, and (in the residence) the location of most leisure. In North America, the household is the leisure consumption unit—generally owning a television set, one or more cars, and some sort of leisure equipment. It is the family that usually takes the vacation trip, eats as a group, and goes to church together. Families play games, talk, visit relatives and friends, entertain, and travel together. Everyone may not do exactly the same thing or gain the same satisfactions, but more often than not families partake of most of their leisure together.

Further, most leisure takes place in the home. Though the proportion varies, depending on the number of people in the household, the total space, the arrangement of rooms, leisure equipment available, and life style, the space in and around the residence is the locale of most leisure. Especially the day-to-day, informal activities such as casual conversation, lingering after a meal, spontaneous play with children, expressions of love and affection, reading, and watching television happen at home.

The fact that most adult leisure is familial and home-centered does not require that such activity be the most satisfying. We may do things with others in our household just because they are there; they may be the companions of convenience rather than choice. Further, there may be considerable pressure to do something with spouse and children rather than leave for an activity that might have been preferred.

Leisure activity in the family may be parallel, convenient, relational, or role-determined. For example, watching television may be parallel activity with little interaction or communication; two or more people just happen to be doing the same thing in the same place at the same time. Or household members may play cards together because they are present and convenient and the game requires partners and opponents. On the other hand, relational leisure is chosen primarily because the relationship and the companionship is valued and enjoyed.

One study of the relationship of leisure and marital satisfaction found that couples who spent higher proportions of their time in joint leisure activities were more satisfied with the marriage itself.[4] This was especially true for husbands and wives in the preparental period of marriage and in the time of adjustment to children having left home. On the other hand, those with more solitary pursuits tended to be less satisfied with their marriages. It would seem that leisure is one aspect of marital interaction that can enhance the quality of the re-

---

[4] Dennis Orthner, "Leisure Activity Patterns and Marital Satisfaction over the Marital Career," *Journal of Marriage and the Family,* 37 (1975), 91–102.

lationship. However, leisure can also be an area of conflict when husbands and wives disagree on how they want to spend their time and resources.

With the proportion of adults not in intact first marriages increasing, former assumptions concerning the family basis of relational leisure are in question. What are the leisure opportunities and contexts for those outside families who also seek companionship and sharing in their social experiences? Many adults are premarriage, postmarriage, and unmarried and develop different sets of leisure associations.

Launching and the Second Transition

Most children do not leave home all at once. They develop lives that are more and more independent as they move through the grades into high school. The driver's license, income from a part-time job, and the desire to have a life of their own produce more and more separation in activity, companionship, and often communication between parents and their teenage children. No great break or trauma is necessary for such independence to emerge.

So the launching period often begins before the children actually leave home for college, service, or their first separate residence. It is a time of growing independence for both parents and their teenage children. While the financial expenses of child rearing may reach a peak during this period, financial resources are also generally greater and more flexible.

One critical issue is that of leisure for the marriage dyad. Do the parents tend to turn back to the marriage for leisure companionship and satisfaction, or do they turn outward to seek new friends and associations? No study has yet been complete and thorough enough to begin to estimate the extent of dyadic renewal and of leisure independence. There are several indications of emphasis on leisure companionship in the middle years for couples not willing to settle for a marriage of roles without the personal relationship. On the other hand, there are also many segmented marriages in which the husband and wife employ their emerging freedom in expanding their separate activities and social groups.

A second issue revolves around work. Many women now return to the employment market. If so, how does this affect the rest of the family, the leisure schedule, and the resource base? The time-money trade-off may shift drastically if the resource of a second income brings with it all the demands and constraints of regular employment. Further, women with their own incomes and careers have more independence to determine their life directions, relationships, and investments.

At the same time, many workers are finding that some of the hopes and dreams of their thirties are becoming fainter and more distant in their late forties.[5] The excitement of crossing the threshold into a work context and of early advancement may now give way to a realization that "this is about all there is." Further advancement possibilities are small and not too exciting. The job itself has become more and more routine. And just at this time, the process of launching makes parents realize that their roles are also diminishing.

Launching is, for many, the beginning of a second transition. The first was into parenthood. Now parenthood becomes less demanding and less consuming. If the transition is into greater work engagement, as for many women, then something new takes the place of the parental interests. However, if neither the marriage companionship nor work can ex-

---

[5] Daniel Levinson, *The Seasons of a Man's Life* (New York: Knopf, 1978).

pand to fill the time and imagination, then launching may begin a period of exploration and anticipation in leisure.

Reintegration and the Later Years

The Rapoports refer to the final periods as late establishment with the children out of school and the later years and retirement approaching. Here the period in which adults reevaluate themselves and their lives and begin to wind things up is referred to as the time of *reintegration*. The four subperiods are the postparental, preretirement, retirement, and widowhood.

This seems to be a time in which the meaning and the worth of life's commitments and investments are evaluated. As some of the consuming requirements of earlier parenting and the anticipations of a work career are reduced, a person may take a second look at commitments of marriage, friendships, leisure, community, and work. Are they worth the investment? Are they producing the fulfillment they once promised? If not, is it too late for a change? What opportunities have been ignored in the concentration on conventional investments?

Part of the transition may be impelled by a relaxation of previous commitments and role requirements. Part seems to be a consequence of a sense of time—time that is running out. The sense of how many more years of work, health, relative physical attractiveness and strength, or even life itself becomes more of a conscious issue. What is really important? What is really satisfying? What is being missed?

One response may be to make a radical change such as divorce, a second career, or a move across the country. Another is to engage in a pruning and cultivation operation, in which elements of life that no longer bear fruit are clipped away with care taken not to damage the integrated whole life. Promising new possibilities are grafted onto the main tree. Some life courses are thrust into radical change. Others incorporate change into essential continuity. In either case, the discretionary nature of leisure makes it a prime choice for evaluation and alteration. New leisure can be tried with little disruption to the old family and work investments.

Postparental Leisure and Redefined Roles

In the 1890s there was almost no postparental period for most couples. The longer childbearing and child-rearing periods extended farther into the middle years. More often than not, one parent had died by the time the last child had left home. This was accentuated by the practice of having young adults live with their parents until they married. Also in the 1890s the three-generation home that included a grandparent was not unusual. Now the postparental period prior to retirement is the longest period of the family life cycle. If the marriage remains intact, then the issue of leisure companionship is critical in the twenty or so years most couples have together after their children are raised. In fact, a failure in that companionship is one factor in the rising divorce rates for postparental couples. This is also a time in which persons may take stock of their lives and come to terms with themselves, their work roles, and each other. Leisure may become more important as some early dreams of conquering worlds are laid aside. At this point the development of life patterns that are personally satisfying may become more important in life priorities.

Parents are still parents after their children leave home; they just don't have the daily set of responsibilities and opportunities. In some cases they may have heavy financial commitments for education. In others, independence may have to be postponed. For many the postparental years are also a time of paying off debts that have accumulated, especially if there have been critical health problems in the child-rearing phase. There may be caregiving responsibilities for aging parents or others with health impairments. It is not always a moment of instantaneous freedom.

Nevertheless, there are evident changes. For some middle-class adults there is a shift in leisure toward activities done with others outside the family. For more in intact marriages, the husband or wife is again the chief leisure companion. The dyad is reasserted in place of the family group.

A second change is reflected in an increase in the proportion of activities chosen primarily for their own sake, for intrinsic reasons. Whether the activities change or not, the motivation becomes somewhat more related to self-satisfaction rather than meeting role expectations.

Some of this may be a positive response to negative feelings. The Rapoports suggest that emotions of depression, boredom, isolation, and entrapment may surge to the fore in this late establishment period. The loss of the full parental schedule, of the response and feedback of children, and of the social reinforcement for taking parenthood seriously may leave a void. Some may rush to fill the void with activity—leisure, travel, rebuilding the residence, seeking sexual adventure, a new job, or a lot more of the same things already under way. Others may question what their lives amount to and what can be done about evident meaninglessness.

For leisure, the new needs are related to this time of reevaluation and, it is to be hoped, of reintegration. Couples may seek contexts and opportunities for renewing the intimacy and companionship that was partly dissipated in the fullness of parenting. Both men and women may seek new activities such as learning skills in arts that allow for the fullest creativity and self-expression. Some may desire physical activity to maintain health and self-definitions of competence and bodily control. Some may travel together to renew their own relationship and find new experiences in new environments. And those with few resources will have to depend on familiar opportunities and available programs to find satisfying ways of dealing with this new time of both freedom and emptiness.

The ideal is to discover new challenges and experiences. In creative leisure men and women may rediscover each other and the larger world they live in. They may cultivate interests that had been dormant for years and rediscover enthusiasms from school and preparental times. Evenings and weekends are now more free for events that require leaving the home. It may be a time to resurrect interest in the arts, the city, or the joys of being alone. For those who have no exciting or vital interest in their present or their past, this time may be one of disintegration. Some may feel that real life is about over when they actually have two decades ahead of work and more of companionship and development.

Preretirement and Consolidating the Investments

There is no clear designation of "preretirement" by age. Uncertainty as to actual retirement for many wage workers, changes in health and work capacities, and differential opportunities for those in occupations in which self-employed or self-directed work is possible make this period more one defined by each person than a clear age fifty-five to sixty-four category. The self-definition is one concern with preparation. Preoccupation with personal and social integration and security emerges. Coming to terms with life's possibilities and meanings that take into account the limits of accomplishments and of the future may be quite satisfying for some and frightening for others.

Also, most adults have had zigzag work histories with changes, frustrations, dead ends, and even periods of unemployment. Employment is a series of jobs rather than a career of advancement for most men and women. Workers in their fifties and sixties have usually had to redefine themselves through a variety of work experiences.

Aging is not a valued or desirable state in our culture. We tend to celebrate the accomplishments of the young rather than the fulfillment of the old. We usually shelve rather than honor those of advanced years. Further, in the twenty-first century, decades when up to 20 percent of the population will be over sixty-five, the economic costs of aging may be a major factor in social reorganization. Preparation for retirement may have different meanings and problems in 2020 than in 1990.

The Rapoports report that the underlying preoccupation of this period is anticipation. The anticipation may be positive or the future may be looked upon with dread. Most look forward to retirement, to escaping the routine and the everydayness of the job and to having time for activities not relegated to weekends and vacations. Others are not sure what they will do without the structure or the full income of employment. Questions of housing, relationships with children and grandchildren, health, finances, and use of time are all quite real. And, of course, everyone must face the uncertainty that goes with the fact that no one can fully guarantee the outcome of any of these issues.

Leisure may be partly invested in preparation. Exploring more time-consuming activities, the possibilities of moving to an area with desired leisure facilities, and the hope of travel and visiting family and friends can be tried out in those last years of vacation. Some consolidate their lives by moving into less expensive residences that require less maintenance. Some try to acquire and pay for leisure equipment they plan to use in retirement.

Again, it is a time of transition. For the most part, people continue the leisure, social relationships, and life patterns of previous years. The changes may hardly be noticeable in a time diary or on a social calendar. But there is a difference in the ways men and women define themselves. They know they are about to enter a phase of life in which some old values and routines are turned upside down. If they have fulfilling nonwork lives, it may be a time of excitement and anticipation. If not, it may be a time in which thoughts of the future are deliberately submerged. For those who have been able to integrate identities and roles in work, family, leisure, and community, the adjustments ahead may be seen as opportunities.

Retirement: The Acceptance of Self and Time

When retirement arrives as a sudden event, the impact of the relatively unconstrained schedule, loss of income, and shift in central role may be quite dramatic. Adjustment may be difficult and take time. However, retirement is not that sudden for most people. Many wage workers have already lessened their work time and avoided prolonged weekend or evening hours on the job. Many have had longer vacation periods before final retirement. Psychological adjustment to the lack of further career advancement takes place some years prior to retirement.

More common than a traumatic change is a preparation that includes some psychological disengagement from employment roles and identities and anticipation of retirement possibilities. Trips, projects, and expansion of favored leisure may be planned. Defining oneself as "about-to-retire" makes the new definition of "retired" seem less abrupt. While depression, loneliness, and apathy may characterize some retirees, such persons tend to be those who have not found great satisfaction in their preretirement roles. Those who tend to withdraw from previous associations and activities do so more because of health problems than because of any necessity of age or retirement alone.

In the Scripps Foundation studies of leisure in retirement, it was found that the loss of work identification was not a major factor in adjustment to retirement.[6] Rather, those who had been satisfied with their employment tended to be satisfied with their retirement leisure. Further, leisure identities can provide self-esteem and fulfillment *if* the retiree has adequate resources and a community of leisure companions.

The "identity continuity" approach suggests that, since people were not all that work-oriented before retirement, there is no reason why they cannot continue to find their family, leisure, and community identities central when no longer employed full time. Feelings of competence, social esteem, and community acceptance can be derived from leisure roles before and during retirement. As leisure identities become more important to our selves and more valued in the society, they can continue to provide both a sense of worth and opportunities for fulfillment in later years.

In summary, it would seem that those who have had satisfying family, leisure, and community relationships during their working years can be expected to continue those roles in retirement. When the *quality* of the nonwork aspects of life has been high, retirement may come as an opportunity rather than a loss. After all, most of the satisfactions of work can also be obtained in leisure. Adequate income and health are fundamental requirements for satisfying retirement. Financial security is a central precondition of fulfilling retirement. Reasonable health is a prerequisite of activity. While retirees may expand some leisure activities that require blocks of time and contract others that have costs now difficult to meet, in general, retirement leisure is characterized by continuity with the past.[7]

Case studies suggest that the quality of relationships is the critical issue for those possessing the health and income prerequisites. While leisure opportunities, housing, resources, and previous leisure history are all factors, the most important is whether or not a person has a set of satisfying personal relationships. Spouse, children, kin networks, and friends can make activities worth doing. So much of leisure is informal interaction that the quality of that interaction is the most significant element of the new nonwork life. It is possible to adapt old activities to new conditions, to accept limitations and find new ways to develop an activity balance, and to become more deeply invested in time-intensive leisure

---

[6] Robert C. Atchley, *The Social Factors in Later Life* (Belmont, CA: Wadsworth, 1980).

[7] John R. Kelly, ed., *Activity and Aging* (Newbury Park, CA: Sage, 1993).

that was impossible before. With community, reasonable health, and an adequate financial base, "all is possible" for those who have learned to enjoy their lives, their relationships, and themselves. Their resources and resourcefulness are more than adequate to cope with retirement.

On the other hand, for some, health will deteriorate unless death comes quickly. For most women, the marriage dyad will be broken and succeeded by several years of being a widow. Neither health nor intimate community can be guaranteed indefinitely. Aging does have its discontinuities and traumatic losses as well as continuities and opportunities.

Older persons do not define themselves differently at some designated age. Rather, they tend to see themselves in a somewhat "ageless" way, as essentially the same persons they were in earlier periods of life.[8] Therefore, it should be no surprise that relatively few older adults participate regularly in age-segregated activities in special locations such as senior centers. Rather, they fill in the empty spaces left by retirement with an expansion of the activities and associations of previous times. They deal with life with much the same strategies they have employed before.[9] The life investments they have found satisfying are continued when possible.

New approaches to leisure in later life stress the idea of the "active old." Rather than a withdrawal from engagement, older persons who retain viable health and income are likely to be involved in previous activities up to a time of failing health. Further, there is increasing evidence that those who are most satisfied in their later years are those who are regularly engaged in activity outside the home, especially activity that provides challenge and a context of social integration. Older people want to continue to demonstrate that they are persons of worth and competence. As a result, they are most often attracted to activities with high levels of quality and opportunity for effective action.

Widowhood and Role Renewal

There is a paradox of aging and leisure. Those with a fulfilling marriage relationship possess a retirement resource of infinite value. On the other hand, when that relationship is broken—usually by the death of the husband—the loss is greatest. The companion of most of life, including leisure, is gone.

Again, however, many widows demonstrate great powers of adaptation. While the loss of a spouse creates loneliness in the day-to-day round of life, it also changes the context of leisure. Instead of being a member of a couple doing things with other couples, the widow is alone and begins to shift her associations to others who are also alone. New relationships of trust and intimacy, new friendships and caring groups, are required. A study of widows in Chicago indicates that the helping and caring network of family and friends is crucial in taking on the role of widow.[10]

---

[8] Sharon Kaufman, *The Ageless Self: Sources of Meaning in Later Life* (Madison, WI: University of Wisconsin Press, 1987.)

[9] Robert Atchley, "Continuity Theory and the Evolution of Activity in Later Adulthood," in J. R. Kelly, ed., *Activity and Aging* (Newbury Park, CA: Sage, 1993).

[10] Helena Z. Lopata, *Widowhood in an American City* (Cambridge, MA: Schenkman, 1973).

Of course, along with the loss comes some freedom as well. Sometimes a spouse may not have wanted to travel, so a widow with resources is suddenly free to take trips she could only dream of before. In many cases there has been a period of months or years caring for a spouse in failing health. Now death has removed that consuming responsibility. The loss requires a rebuilding of other roles in community and in leisure expression. For most people, grief over the loss does not permit an exploration and acceptance of the freedom until the process of working through the impact of the death has reached a point of acceptance of the reality of a personal future.

The loss of a life companion may be accompanied by the loss of some financial stability. Adjustments for the widow can involve changes in income, residence, social network roles, and meeting the expectations of a primary "other." The primary task for the widow is to rebuild a meaningful set of relationships. Leisure is a major social area in which old relationships are renewed and new friends made. Groups of widows frequently develop a common set of leisure experiences that include mutual entertaining, exchange of reading, telephone networks, common participation in church and other community organizations, trips together, and regularly scheduled events such as playing cards or eating out. Mobility by private or public transportation is crucial to taking on a new schedule and a revised group of companions.

For the widow the preoccupation is generally role rebuilding and the search for community. Being with people who care, understand, and can be relied on is essential. Enjoying the associations requires that leisure activities themselves be mutually acceptable and, for the most part, enjoyable. Regular groups and close friendships may develop around a common activity just as preestablished groups may seek satisfying activities. In the later years a great deal of time is employed in maintenance of self and residence. The tasks of life loom larger and seem to take more and more time and energy. The issue may not be so much that of filling time as of loss of community.

Some people of retirement age change their residence to communities designed for older people. In some such places there is a climate of leisure participation with clear expectations that draw new residents into activities they had seldom or never tried before. The important factor seems to be the social climate. If the community atmosphere is one conducive to doing things with other people, then leisure pursuits and roles are highly valued and the older person's identity may shift almost entirely to leisure participation and competence.

Leisure and the Search for Identity

Identity formation is not confined to students and the young, but is a lifelong process.

The search for identity is seldom complete. For most of us there is always a something more that we have not yet become. Erik Erikson has suggested that for youth there is a crisis as the family definitions of selfhood are left behind and a young man or woman must find a new self to understand, live with, and present to others.[11] Another approach refers

---

[11] Erik Erikson, *Childhood and Society* (New York: Norton, 1950).

to the "passages" of life in which transitions are made that change both inner understanding and outer relationships.[12] These passages continue to have profound meaning in midlife as well as in adolescence and retirement.

A number of attempts have been made to describe the human needs that underlie this search for identity. It can be argued that beyond the animal needs of shelter, nutrition, and sex and the survival needs of protection and nurture there remain two human needs: for freedom and for community. Freedom is necessary according to an existential view of life that requires decision not only in order to express humanness but to create it. Human life is not closed or predetermined, but is open to be built or torn down by the definitions and decisions of human actors. To be human is to act in ways that have consequences. At the same time, to be human means to be in relationship to other humans. We are social beings and need reliable relationships of communication, trust, and caring. We need both the freedom to decide and reach out to the "not-yet" of life and the community in which to learn and love. The realities of both decisive freedom and community also call for a functioning mind, memory, symbol system, and culture. To be human is to exercise that self-conscious potential of decision and relating.

One of the most popular formulations of human needs is that of Abraham Maslow. He proposed a hierarchy of needs that moves from the foundation of basic physiological needs through security and safety, social needs such as belonging and love, selfhood needs such as self-respect and feelings of success, and on to self-actualization.[13] Self-actualization is a realization of human potential specific to the individual. A person who becomes self-actualized is beyond the striving that characterizes segments of life and is able to pull together a wholeness of acceptance and achievement that is uniquely fulfilling. Such a concept is humanistic in its focus on the realization of human potential by the individual as a legitimate aim of life. Further, each level of need serves as a prerequisite for those above.

In a more social approach, Orrin Klapp has added that this search for identity is a group phenomenon as well as individual.[14] He analyzes various group and mass movements in modern society, including cultural fads and religious cults, as social attempts to find an identity in a culture that offers fewer and fewer opportunities to achieve a recognized individual identity. However, he warns against mass consumption and the temporary feeling of personal meaning through possessing something, wearing something, or displaying something presumed desirable to others. Mass advertising and mass marketing are designed to produce in the consumer an anticipation of person enhancement, of being more of a person, by purchase and possession. The danger is that consumer decisions may be a false freedom, that cults may offer a pseudo-community, and that collective symbols may mask a lack of identity.

What is the place of leisure in this lifelong search for identity? Leisure is, by definition, a life space that maximizes freedom. It is a comprehensive part of life in which our

[10] Gail Sheehy, *Passages* (New York: Bantam, 1976).

[13] Abraham Maslow, *Motivation and Personality* (New York: Harper & Row, 1954).

[14] Orrin E. Klapp, *Collective Search for Identity* (New York: Holt, Rinehart & Winston, 1969).

lives are least constrained by schedules and requirements. Therefore, we would expect that both freedom and community will be sought and exercised in that life space. Leisure provides opportunity to make decisions that may have consequences that are personally fulfilling. It is activity in which we may try out actions and self-presentations that may maximize our self-acceptance and our growth. Leisure is opportunity to explore, build, and express community.

It is, therefore, critical that leisure be real, that it be more than a pretense of freedom and community. Leisure is not peripheral to our being human, constructing identities, and selfhood. If leisure is degraded into relationships that only sham community and decisions that are merely a mindless response to the manipulative efforts of those who would profit from our choices, then the search for identity is likely to lead nowhere.

Summary of Issues

The theme of change and continuity in the leisure aspects of the life course includes social roles, personal identities, and the leisure activities themselves. The role expectations and self-definitions contain considerable stability and regularity in both their cultural contexts and in the person's life career. Not only are the expectations for social positions similar for all in those positions, but we tend to develop ways of self-understanding that persist through changes in roles.

Leisure, as relatively free activity, may be the part of life with the least continuity. New activities and interests emerge as new opportunities are perceived. New companions open our minds to new meanings in old activities as well as to new enterprises. Even people well into retirement may begin square dancing for the first time because they are drawn into a group in which that activity is normative. Also, the same activity may have different meanings and motivations for us in different life circumstances. We may do something for social reasons in our teens, for health reasons in our forties, and for intrinsic pleasure a decade later. We may develop deeper and more diverse appreciation of some experiences or environments as years go by.

If leisure as freedom and meaning is a profoundly human expression rather than a peripheral activity, then it is closely tied to who we are as social beings. Leisure is an integral part of who we believe ourselves to be, how others come to define us, and what we would like to become. These meanings may persist through the life career for some and change for others. In any case, leisure cannot be understood as a phenomenon separate from all that we are, have been, or would like to be. The career of leisure is intertwined with other strands of the life course. When transitions are made in our family, work, or leisure roles, the other roles are affected.

The particular functions of leisure stress freedom to be and become and the intimate bonding of family and friends. Even though freedom may be expressed in any aspect of life and community may be developed in any social space, leisure is central to the building and expression of those two essential elements of being human through the entire life course.

HIGHLIGHTS

1. As central goals and preoccupations shift through the life course, so the contexts and aims of leisure may also change.
2. In preparation periods of the life course, socialization needs of exploration, testing, and the development of personal and social identities are central to leisure.
3. Gender differences in role expectations have profound impact on resources and the power of self-determination throughout the life course.
4. The allocation of resources to life investments, especially those of the family, shape leisure choices in early and middle establishment years.
5. Being a parent reorients leisure aims and reconstitutes the contexts and constraints of leisure decisions.
6. While continuity characterizes much later-life leisure, people may never stop learning new skills, gaining new interests, or finding new meaning in established relationships.
7. Leisure is a significant element of selfhood and social identity through the life course.

Discussion Questions

1. Which predictable life career changes are most restrictive to leisure opportunities and resources? Which are most liberating?

2. Which unpredictable life career changes are most disrupting to leisure? Why?

3. Give examples of how identities differ from one role context to another. How can leisure be an experimental social space for trying out new identities that are not well confirmed? Choose examples from different life career periods.

4. What may be the effects of revised family role expectations on leisure such as dual career marriages and the "second shift," greater sharing of domestic responsibilities by couples, greater income independence of women, and more positive definitions of retirement?

5. What are the varieties of household composition and how do they affect leisure opportunities and constraints?

6. Why may leisure become more important for adults in their forties and fifties than in earlier years? What are factors limiting a greater personal investment in leisure during this period?

7. How is freedom from obligation and family-related scheduling a problem as well as an opportunity in postparental years? What about such freedom associated with broken marriages or other life career traumas?

8. What is needed to prepare for retirement? What critical problems cannot be avoided even with careful preparation?

Bibliography

Carpenter, Gaylene M., and Christine Z. Howe, *Programming Leisure Experiences: A Cyclical Approach*. Englewood Cliffs, NJ: Prentice-Hall, 1985.

Coleman, James, *The Adolescent Society*. New York: Free Press, 1961.

Iso-Ahola, Seppo, *Social Psychological Perspectives on Leisure and Recreation*. Springfield, IL: Chas. C Thomas, 1980.

Kelly, J. R., *Leisure Identities and Interactions*. London: Allen and Unwin, 1983.

Kelly, J. R., *Peoria Winter: Styles and Resources in Later Life*. Lexington, MA: Lexington Books, 1987.

Kelly, J. R., ed., *Activity and Aging*. Newbury Park, CA: Sage, 1993.

Kleiber, Douglas A., and J. R. Kelly, "Leisure Socialization and the Life Cycle," in Seppo Iso-Ahola, *Social Psychological Perspectives on Leisure and Recreation*. Springfield, IL: Chas. C Thomas, 1980.

Orthner, D. K., *Intimate Relationships: An Introduction to Marriage and the Family*. Reading, MA: Addison-Wesley, 1981.

Rapoport, Rhona, and Robert N. Rapoport, *Leisure and the Family Life Cycle*. London: Routledge and Kegan Paul, 1975.

Chapter 5

Leisure in a Diverse Society

Even the common labels have to change. What is a "minority"? Most of the people in the world are nonwhite. African Americans are a minority—less than 50 percent—in most North American suburbs. European Americans are a minority in South and Central American suburbs. They are also moving toward minority status in several North American cities when the suburbs are excluded. To use the term "minority" requires specifying the universe: a city, state, nation, or continent.

What is "race"? There is now no consensus on whether the term has any clear and universal meaning. We use it to designate persons with a set of characteristics that may have to do with skin color, continental origin, or even cultural history. But there are no unambiguous genetic markers. Definitional conventions are quite arbitrary. What shading of color? How many ancestors of a designated origin and how many generations back? Race is a social construction, not a biological category.

What is "ethnicity"? If it has to do with culture in a world of mass culture and the disintegration of traditional boundaries, then again the labels are largely arbitrary. If there are Asian cultures, are there also European cultures? Are Americans three generations removed from Sweden or Italy ethnic? If not, then what about those six generations removed from Nigeria or four from China? If there is a identifiable "counter-culture," is there a national culture from which to deviate? If there is a Southern regional culture, is there also a Midwest one? Is everyone of some culture—or of several—and therefore ethnic? Perhaps the question is, When does ethnicity make a difference? Then, we are all ethnic some of the time, but not all the time.

The real issue, then, is just that question: When does some identification make a difference? Are there practices and social institutions that identify and discriminate? Females may be a majority in this society, but may they also be defined in ways that limit their opportunities? "Minorities" may be a numerical majority in some cities, yet be manipulated by and excluded from the political power structure. There is the fundamental dimension of self-determination. The wealthy in Los Angeles County may segregate themselves into hillside enclaves with walls and barred gates. In Chicago, African Americans are still forced into the segregated ghettos of public housing and slums by a self-perpetuating system that has withdrawn opportunities taken for granted in even those most modest but largely white suburbs. Racial identification has intensified economic stratification, however arbitrary the identification may be. It may not be sound biology or anthropology, but it is a practiced social reality.

Does it make a difference to be female? Does it make more of a difference to be a black female? And what about being a black female in urban public housing or a rural slum? The labels are signs of elements of total lived realities of life, and those realities do make a difference. They are cumulative, not separate. Opportunities and resources are unequal in this society in ways that have little to do with innate abilities. Ideologies define people by categories that have their own histories and their own power to shape lives.

No two people are just alike, and we value personal individuality. In this chapter, four pervasive dimensions of diversity are introduced—social class, race and ethnicity, gender, and age. Various aspects of each are examined in other chapters, especially gender in Chapter 22. The significant dimension of sexual orientation is also given attention in the same chapter. Chapter 23 deals with the importance of opportunity, inclusion, and development for those with specific limiting conditions. Age was given a different kind of approach in Chapter 4. The elements of our lives that make us who we are, unique individuals, also are factors in the diversity of a complex and changing society. On both levels, most of us are still learning to understand, value, and learn from those who are different from us.

On the one hand, we may accept and even celebrate diversity. It is exciting to recognize differences that may contribute to the entire society and enrich our individual limitations and biases. On the other hand, there are social divisions that are taken up by government and the economy in ways that close off crucial avenues of human development. Every life journey does not have the same starting point, the same resources, or the same power of choice. Some roads are arbitrarily closed, by custom and even by law. In the 1980s, while the white population was increasing only 6 percent, those of Asian origin increased 108 percent, Hispanic 53 percent, and African American 38 percent. In a society that is becoming more diverse, that diversity may be appreciated and supported when it opens a variety of mutually enriching expressions. Diversity may also be diabolical when it defines any child as unable or unworthy of every opportunity to become a fully productive and expressive human being.

ISSUES

How is leisure ethnic?
Is the "how" of style more significant than the "what" of activity?
What are the critical dimensions of diversity?
Is it possible to value diversity and at the same time attack discrimination?

Everything is "ethnic"—that is, every human action and interaction is of a specific culture. The values, symbol systems, customs, and histories of everything we do are made up of what we have learned. Even the language through which we communicate and in which we think about what we do is "loaded" by the circumstances of learning it as well as its structures and vocabularies. In some languages, words for leisure connote culture and in others laziness. Even our words are ethnic and make a difference in how we think about things.

The Ethnicity of Leisure

The particular forms and expressions of all human action are learned in particular cultures and subcultures. Therefore, everything we do illustrates ethnicity. Nevertheless, two contrasting synopses illustrate the point:

> In the near westside projects of Chicago, people both adapt space and adapt to space.[1] Rooms are cramped. The hallways are dangerous. The playground with dirt like concrete has nothing, not even backboards and rims, that is unbroken. Bedrooms are small and shared. Family leisure is mostly in front of the television. Boys get out into the streets more than girls to "hang out," play some basketball, and look for ways to make a little money. Mothers try to protect all their children from the rampant violence with rules: Come straight home from school. Get on the hallway floor when you hear gunfire. Stay away from gangs. The "streets"—anywhere out of the apartment—are the only alternative to the tiny apartment, but are exposed to every kind of danger. There is no place to go for a visit, no reliable car to drive, and no extra money just for fun. Children sneak onto the railway tracks for their "adventure playground." Gangs offer social identification, support, opportunity, and usually a track to juvenile court. Drugs are everywhere. For kids and parents who are trying, the dream is just to get out of the projects.

> A family was on their way back from their second western ski trip of the season. They left their large home in a "hunt suburb" of Boston and their own ski lodge in Vermont for a week in the more exciting conditions of the Utah and Wyoming slopes. In Vermont they had purchased not only a lodge for themselves and their friends, but also 100 acres to ensure themselves control over their environment. At home, they and their hunt club colleagues could purchase access to enough meadowland to ride their horses across fields and fences only an hour's drive from the city. At home, of course, there were separate rooms for games, entertaining, and reading as well as the latest in electronics.

Are the differences significant—differences of space, financial resources, control over timetables, and social access? Just as significant may be the views of the world that are taken for granted. In the projects, most of the environment is a threat rather than an op-

---

[1] Alex Kotlowitz, *There Are No Children Here* (New York: Anchor, 1990).

portunity. The leisure world of even the middle mass with their cars, private homes, yards, and discretionary income is out of sight, not even a recognized possibility. The wealthy, on the other hand, can purchase access, privacy, and protection by owning and controlling real estate and casually ordering a set of air tickets and condo reservations.

That's the negative side of diversity: immeasurable differences in every aspect of life including leisure. Some have such surpluses that cost and crowding are just not issues at all. Most make plans and decisions with such limits in mind, but with enough discretion to develop strategies to realize some dreams. And at the bottom are those who see the images of the material "good life" on their television screens and wonder if they will ever have even a taste.

The positive side of ethnicity is also in its diversity. Why, after all, should everyone be alike? Are there not values in every culture, whatever their histories of development and adaptation, that offer possibilities of enrichment for us all?

One problem is that there seems to be only a fine line between valued diversity and cultural stereotypes. One reason may be that there is a fundamental ethnocentrism in most of us. We tacitly assume that our own ways are really better than others, that our cultural expressions are the standard by which others are judged. We fail to recognize that those differences are matters of taste, and that taste is learned. Examples are endless:

> Research has found that the picnicking styles of Hispanic families in National Forests near Los Angeles are different from those of most Anglos and may require different site design. Family groups tend to be larger, mix ages and generations, and develop more group activity. Rules limiting parking, multiple site use, and group activity appear to inhibit the styles of outdoor recreation site use that are grounded in a sense of family solidarity and a culture of shared family interaction.

> A ethnographic study of a now-dispersed Italian community in Boston described a mix of cultural values and traditions that shaped the ways in which families gathered for festivals and common meals in their homes.[2] The culture combined elements of food and drink, sex-role segregation, shared work and play, and a richness of emotional expression that would contrast with either the formal dinner party or the restaurant event of urbanites of Northern European derivation.

> The union of extemporaneous shared musical expression, bodily action, sense of community, and building to an emotional climax of an African-American Baptist church in Georgia also contrasts dramatically with the formal, routinized, and largely emotionless common worship of the segregated upper-middle-class mainline Protestant church of European derivation. Some such standard-brand white churches are now seeking to find ways to incorporate more emotional expression and sense of community into their own cultures of worship.

The challenge and opportunity of diversity is clear enough. In a society in which differences are valued and supported, we may all learn from each other. The problem is also clear enough. Too often we have "committed" ethnocentrism. That is, we have implicitly or explicitly taken our own culture as the standard for all others. We have disvalued dif-

---

[2] Herbert J. Gans, *The Urban Villagers* (New York: Free Press, 1962).

ferences and even taken legal action to suppress them. As will be demonstrated in Chapters 6 and 10, those with political and economic power have often tried to shape the leisure of others according to their own tastes. Really supporting and learning from diversity is more a project for the future than a realized cultural accomplishment. Further, the pervasiveness of the mass media, especially television with its marketed and marketing images of leisure, provides a powerful force behind cultural homogenization.

Elements of Diversity

There is considerable sameness in leisure styles. The poor are cut off from opportunities taken for granted by the majority. The wealthy possess the position and resources that admit them to a private world of leisure that is literally out of the sight of most. In between is the "middle mass" for whom everything is done in a cost-conscious style. They may take a special vacation trip to Disney World or the coast, but on a budget. They may make special leisure-based purchases—sports equipment, a gun for hunting, a video player/recorder, and even a boat or RV for weekend and vacation trips. Like the wealthy, they depend on the market sector for leisure resources, but always at a calculated price. Despite particular preferences and tastes, they watch a lot of television, do things with family and friends, and are consumers of the mass culture. From this perspective, diversity is valued as a sign of individuality and the cultural meanings that enrich life. Diversity is even a resistance to uniformity and conformity rather than a surrender to those who mass market the tours and toys.

Other elements of diversity have two sides. Diversity may be based on limitations, barriers to real choice and human development. There may be hierarchies of opportunity that are based on gender norms, racial exclusions, and economic deprivation. At the same time, there is diversity that is responsive to historic cultural differences and that offers opportunities to learn from those who have come from other backgrounds. Leisure, from this perspective, is not a melting pot of uniformity, but a rich landscape of differences that may be affirmed and valued.

From this dual perspective, then, there are at least four primary elements in social differentiation that have powerful impacts on leisure. In an introductory outline, what are they and how do they both limit and enrich?

Social Class: Economic Stratification

The American society is highly stratified economically. For example, in 1991 the lowest 20 percent of the population received 3.5 percent of total income while the highest 20 percent received 48 percent. When government transfers are excluded the lowest 20 percent of households received about 1 percent of the income. Further, the percentage with incomes under $15,000 was racially and ethnically stratified: white, 22 percent; black, 42 percent; and Hispanic, 33 percent. Continued differences in economic opportunity make it difficult to separate the consequences of racial discrimination from the higher incidence of poverty.[3]

---

[3] 1990 and 1993 *Statistical Abstract of the United States.* Money Income of Households. U. S. Census Population Reports.

TABLE 5–1   Household Income Percent Distribution

Quintile	Percent of Wages and Capital Gains
lowest 20%	1
2nd 20%	8
3rd 20%	15
4th 20%	24
highest 20%	52

(*Source:* 1993 *Statistical Abstract of the United States.* Money Income of Households. U. S. Bureau of the Census.)

Households headed by the old and the young are most likely to have low incomes and least often have high incomes. Education is also a major factor. About 15 percent of those with no high school have incomes less than $5000 compared with 3 percent of those with any college education. At the other end, 20 percent of those with some college make over $50,000, but less than 3 percent of those with no high school approach this figure. In 1992, men age 25–64 had a median income of $22,467 and women the same age only $16,227.

Trends, according to the Congressional Joint Economic Committee, indicate that the middle quintile's share of income has declined as has that of the lowest 40 percent of the population. The upper 20 percent has increased its share of income, while the lowest 20 percent's proportion has decreased. From 1980 to 1992, the number of income tax filers reporting incomes of over $1 million increased 600 percent while the median income increased less than $1300. There are many indications that the *shape* of income stratification is changing. For most of the period since the Industrial Revolution, the society was said to be shaped like a *triangle,* with a small number at the peak of earnings and the largest proportion at the bottom. More recently, that shape was seen as more like a *diamond,* with a small number at the peak and the bottom separated by a large middle class. Now the shape appears to be changing again. There are still the 5 percent at the top who control most of the investment wealth and have extremely high incomes. They are followed by the so-called "new class" of managers, research and development technicians, professionals, and finance managers whose share of the total income is rising. They are followed in turn by the large middle mass, about 50–60 percent of the population who work in factories, offices, retailing, and other services. They are less secure, have a series of jobs rather than a career, and often require two incomes to make house and car payments. The bottom layer, about 15–20 percent, are those who are marginal, in and out of employment, and who are never more than a few weeks from destitution if there are changes in income or expenses. They have part-time or entry level jobs or exist on meager government support programs. The new class, costly to replace in its economic roles, is gaining discretionary income for leisure and comforts. The middle mass, easily replaced and less secure, is falling further behind. Further, they are more likely to suffer unemployment at any age.

Income is an index of economic roles and opportunity. It is related to human capital factors such as education and years of work experience. But it is also tied to a number of other factors. There are *places* such as Northern inner cities[4] and the rural South where op-

---

[4] William J. Wilson, *The Truly Disadvantaged* (Chicago: University of Chicago Press, 1987).

portunities for employment are almost entirely lacking. Households headed by a single parent are more likely to have low incomes. And research demonstrates that women and racial minorities are still denied equal opportunity when education and experience are accounted for in ways that can be explained only as continuing discrimination.

It is no wonder that market-sector providers of leisure resources focus on those with the most discretionary income. Nor is it surprising that those with marginal incomes have little left for leisure spending once food, housing, and clothing are purchased. Economic stratification is at least a filter, with low incomes simply eliminating the majority of the population from cost-intensive activity. Further, Veblen was right in analyzing how the really wealthy develop tastes that demonstrate that they have plenty to spend on leisure. Less clear is how the middle mass with limited incomes and less security develop leisure styles that are within economic possibility and still provide for satisfying expression and engagement. What is clear is that there are vast and significant differences in what individuals and households can afford. Insofar as leisure provisions are more and more provided for a price or a fee, leisure life chances in all societies differ widely by economic position, what we call "social class."

Race and Ethnicity: Discrimination and Deprivation

The history of racial and ethnic identification in the United States is one of exclusion. First, for African Americans, there was chattel slavery followed by laws and practices of segregation and exclusion. Civil rights legislation since the 1950s has made a significant difference in access, including to many leisure resources, but many exclusionary practices continue in the workplace, the segregated neighborhood, and even the school. Other ethnic groups have also been admitted or recruited into the country to take on low-wage and health-threatening work. The history in general is one of starting at the bottom of the economic ladder, living in segregated locations, and having to combat discrimination to improve opportunities generation by generation.

The history of African Americans, who make up about 11 percent of the population, has been one of extreme exclusion: first by the total exploitation of slavery and then by a century of economic and social discrimination. Now the results of that history are found in every aspect of life: residential segregation that perpetuates educational disparities, ghettos without any economic base, economic selection that picks a few for advancement, and institutions that still define their membership in racial terms. All this is intensified for "people of color" who are immediately identified and classified according to visual codes.

All this continues despite the growth of "minority" populations at a rate that will make over half the workforce of non-European derivation by the year 2030. The population of North America is becoming increasingly diverse. Religion now means Buddhism, Islam, and others as well as various branches of Christianity and Judaism. Languages multiply in urban school systems. Generations divide, with children speaking English at school and another language at home. Ethnic enclaves develop as newer arrivals locate near relatives and others from the same culture, and then are reinforced by the economics of housing with neighborhoods clearly separated by price level.

Two elements are related. One is culture in which the customs, norms, values, expressions, symbols, and community practices of ethnic groups differ. These differences may be maintained, sometimes fiercely, not just because they are familiar, but because they provide a sense of identity. Distinctive cultures are not something to be casually discarded, but are important in retaining a sense of pride and identity. Celebrations of ethnic cultures provide an important sense of being a people with a history and identity. All the symbols of being a "people" may be cherished and defended against loss to the mass culture.

The other element is economic. Insofar as ethnic identification is coupled with recent arrival, it often means starting in economic roles that offer low incomes and little security. Insofar as ethnic identity is a way of classifying people, it involves exclusion from many economic and educational opportunities. There may be change, but it tends to be slow, a matter of generations rather than years. Hard work and dreams are not enough, especially in an economy in which the doorways to careers of advancement seem harder to find. Even in recreation, it was only a generation ago that American cities closed swimming pools rather than integrate them. Research attempting to disentangle economic and cultural factors in leisure have resulted in weak relationships.[5] More important, no analysis of current activity participation can deal with generations of exclusion and poverty that are part of African-American history.

As a consequence, racial and ethnic identity has often meant a history of *cumulative deprivation* that has impacted every aspect of life. There is no way of separating out differences in income and economic opportunity, educational quality, residential segregation, and institutional exclusion from elements of culture, preference, and taste. Which differences are a matter of deprivation and marginality and which of ethnic preference? When both values and behavior are learned throughout a lifetime, everything impacts everything else.

There have been a number of studies attempting to identify racial and ethnic similarities and differences and account for those discovered. Most have suffered from the flaw of defining leisure by activity label—swimming or going to parties—rather than by style and meaning. As a result, many of the most significant dimensions of ethnicity are lost. Ethnicity is more a matter of "how" than "what." Only when cultures have been entered and engaged has research even begun to incorporate the symbols and meanings of cultural expression. Clearly needed are studies of those in similar life conditions, such as being an older African-American woman who enters her later years after a lifetime of indignities and deprivations and histories of second-class employment and educational opportunities.[6] Race, ethnicity, income, education, and other variables are not separable items in a computer program, but are compounded elements in the real-life conditions of people trying to make their life journeys in the face of often arbitrary limitations and circumstances.

From this perspective, all leisure is ethnic in expressing particular cultures. The common failure to find great differences in activity choice, especially when the core of accessible activities is included and economic costs are factored in, may be mostly a matter of

[5] S. M. Stamps and M. B. Stamps, "Race, Class, and Leisure Activities of Urban Residents," *Journal of Leisure Research,* 17 (1985), 40–56.

[6] Karen Allen and V. Chin-Sang, "A Lifetime of Work: The Context and Meanings of Leisure for Aging Black Women," *The Gerontologist,* 30 (1990), 734–740.

research that is done from the outside and fails to deal with what is truly ethnic. One study in Chicago[7] of Mexican-American park use in comparison with that of African Americans and Anglos found that the Latins formed larger groups based on extended family ties and engaged in activity with ethnic roots as well as mainstream sports.

Racial and ethnic differences may be based on economic factors, especially in activities with high access and travel costs. But such research does not reveal ways in which those of different cultures eat together, worship, form recreational groups, subdivide in leisure settings by age and gender, choose topics of conversation, and defer according to symbols of status and honor. Ethnicity is a whole way of life, not just a label of difference. Nor do surveys of alleged differences even begin to examine the ways in which ethnic and racial identifications are based on fear and lead to profound and enduring conflict.

On the one hand, the consequences of cumulative deprivation are a loss to the society and may change over time. On the other hand, there are ethnic variations that can be valued and preserved, not only for those within an ethnic tradition, but also by outsiders whose lives may be enriched. Certainly in the arts the standards of Western traditions are being challenged and enriched by art, music, and dance from all over the world. Every culture can be enriched by interaction with others with their own special expressions of humanness and community. Perhaps in leisure more than any other domain of life, ethnic differences may be supported as contributions to the entire social ecology of a society.

The positive side is richness and diversity of expression. The negative side is alienation in which some arbitrarily identified as different are cut off from opportunities for expression, development, and community inclusion.

The Constant Factor of Gender

As presented in Chapter 22, no identification is as powerful and pervasive as gender. We have no recollection of life prior to being identified as male or female. Everything we do and everywhere we go, we are gender-labelled and define ourselves as gendered beings. Even the current recognition of greater diversity in sexual orientation does not cancel the centrality of gender. The difference is that sexuality and gender are related in more complex ways.

Again, there are two sides to the relationship of gender to diversity. The history of Western civilization is that of a male-dominated, that is, sexist, society in which women have generally been dominated by males and have been systematically exploited. This institutionalized sexism is usually referred to as being "patriarchal." Like racism, it is not simply a matter of values and ideologies, but is a thoroughgoing institutionalization of roles, expectations, resources, opportunities, rewards, and, most important, the power of self-determination. Changes in opportunity structures for women's sports and other activities do not in themselves change more fundamental role definitions in regard to family responsibilities and economic potentials and rewards. Historically females have most often been "ornaments" in the leisure of males, secondary rather than being socially defined as

---

[7] Ray Hutchison and K. Fidel, "Mexican-American Recreation Activities: a Reply to McMillan," *Journal of Leisure Research,* 16 (1984), 344–349.

having legitimate leisure of their own. Such cultural norms still discriminate by gender and limit the self-determination of women.

For example, the major change in the work force of Western economies is the entrance of women into paid employment. Now *most* women are employed outside the home. Those who are also wives and mothers are expected in most households to take primary responsibility for home management and child nurture without any accommodating changes in work schedules and supports. Women do most, probably between 70 and 80 percent, of the care and nurturing of children and frail parents without any significant change in economic arrangements. Further, most women's employment is in the services with their common long hours, irregular schedules, and demanding requirements. And, despite this landmark economic change, women are found to be paid less than 70 percent of male income for the same or equivalent work.

The impacts on women's leisure are as constant and pervasive as gender-identification itself.[8] For example, women usually do the work that makes family events such as picnics and holiday celebrations possible. Nothing impacts leisure as much as parenting, especially for the primary caregivers. Added to more traditional role expectations is the increase of parenting households headed by women who are also in the paid labor force. It is evident that women in these circumstances may experience the least "freedom" in either time for leisure or separation from family responsibilities. Again, gender is not just a label. It is what we are, how we are treated, and how we understand ourselves. What we want, as well as who we are, is "gendered."

The other side of gender is that women may also raise a new set of issues for leisure that has been conceptualized in male frameworks. To begin with, leisure for women may be more integrated into the whole fabric of life than has been traditional for men. So much leisure is based at home that a clear separation of workplace and leisure place or even work and leisure activity may be not only be unrealistic, but also miss the complex association of tasks and satisfactions in events such as family dinners.[9] More attention needs to be given to playful action and interaction in the midst of life rather than distinct events. Further, much of the experiential satisfaction for women seems to be in rather than separate from primary relationships. Considerable significant leisure is "relational," with central meanings found in the development and expression of relationships. For example, how is it possible to clearly separate care for children and play with children in a context of caring, sharing, nurturing, and love? What is false is to assign such meaning to only one gender who are expected to discover leisure in the midst of nurture and caregiving. Too often leisure theorists have suggested that responsibilities and relationships are negative, a constraint on leisure, rather than central to life's meanings and satisfactions.

---

[8] There have now been numerous important studies of women and leisure that document the institutional structures, ideologies of gender and family, and specific life conditions of women in different cultures and circumstances. Among the most comprehensive are: Karla Henderson, D. Bialeschki, S. Shaw, and V. Freysinger, *A Leisure of One's Own: A Feminist Perspective on Women's Leisure* (State College, PA: Venture Publishing, 1989); Arlie Hochschild, *The Second Shift* (New York: Viking, 1989); and Erika Wimbush and Margaret Talbot, eds., *Relative Freedom: Women and Leisure* (Philadelphia: Open University Press, 1988). The *Journal of Leisure Research*, 26 (1994), edited by Karla Henderson, includes examinations of ideologies that are repressing and potentially liberating as well as studies for the specific conditions of women's leisure.

[9] Karla A. Henderson, "An Oral Life History Perspective on the Containers in which American Farm Women Experienced Leisure," *Leisure Studies*, 9 (1987), 121–133.

The point is that women's voices and perspectives are beginning to be heard in understanding leisure. Not only will this correct previous male bias, but it is already adding richness and valuable perspectives. Can leisure be more cooperative than competitive? Can there be more focus on shared communication rather than contests with scores and recognized losers? Can leisure be located more in the midst of ongoing life and less as a contrast to segmented work? Can leisure become a reality of freedom against repression, even a locus of social change, rather than a purchased reward for economic activity? And, are some gender distinctions a matter of generational differences that are changing over time?

There is now needed attention being given to the real circumstances of women's lives and the lack of self-determination that characterizes many social situations. Just as social class and race has defined loss and limitation in leisure, so gender has too often meant systematic discrimination and even direct and violent subjugation. Women and men are not totally different in abilities, interests, values, or opportunities. Similarities probably far outweigh differences. Yet in women's leisure there may be found emphases of style and meaning that offer promise of enrichment for all, especially when we recognize that achieving leisure may be something of a struggle, not a reward.

Age as a Condition

As is commonly pointed out, the only alternative to aging is death. It is not a special condition. Nevertheless, our society is stratified by age as well as by economic position, race, ethnicity, and gender. We organize our institutions, admit or deny access, and allocate prestige and other rewards with all these factors at work. We may be too young to be allowed some kinds of activity or roles. At the other end, we may tacitly relegate older persons to nonproductive roles that are regarded as of little worth. We may expect little of the old except decay and obsolescence.

Despite massive evidence that older persons, prior to a final period of frailty, retain all sorts of competencies and are quite able to adapt to their relatively minor decrements in abilities, we tend to rule individuals out of productive activity by age alone. Even in leisure, we may direct older people into programs segregated by age rather than ability by labelling them "senior" or "golden." What is ignored are the evident continuities of life in which there is no magic age at which we become quite different persons with altered abilities or interests.

Nevertheless, we pressure older persons out of economic roles, often more to reduce payrolls than give opportunity to younger workers. We assume that those over 65 have discarded lifelong interests and now will trade in hard-earned skills for undemanding entertainments. We define others by age and fail to recognize that they do not define themselves in the same way.[10] The society frequently discriminates by age, is "ageist," when older people themselves tend to have "ageless" identities.

---

[10] See the analyses of the circumstances, relationships, continuities, and self-definitions of older people as related to leisure in John R. Kelly, ed., *Activity and Aging: Staying Involved in Later Life* (Newbury Park, CA: Sage, 1993).

The other side is that the so-called "mellowing" of older persons involves reassessment of life, values revised on the basis of a life of experience, often a new sense of the centrality of family and friendships, and even a sense that each individual deserves a life of his or her own. Men may become more oriented to relationships and community and less competitive. Women may learn that they have every right to invest themselves in activity that is primarily for their own development and satisfaction. Even the social status that may seem to accompany the consumption of leisure things and leisure places may seem less important.

Alienation and Opportunity

Diversity may be a positive element in a society when it is valued and nurtured. The other side, however, is that diversity may lead to exclusion and alienation. As already suggested, social class, race, ethnicity, gender, and age are more than labels. Together with other factors, they are the conditions of life. All too often some or all of those conditions are used to cut people off from the fullest possible range of opportunities—in leisure, work, and everything else.

The condition of exclusion is called *alienation.* It means being denied the resources needed to develop one's full potential and to be fully a part of human communities. The ideal is that all persons have the opportunity to determine the fundamental directions of their lives—to work productively, bond to others in shared community, and express themselves in a freedom to seek satisfying experiences. We need to relate to each other and to the natural world in which we live. Whenever any arbitrary identification or condition limits those possibilities, then we are alienated, cut off from an element of our humanness.

Too often social class, race, ethnicity, gender, and age have done just that. Doors are closed to classes and categories of people. Some work is so routinized and insecure that it yields no sense of ability or worth. Some life conditions cut off life chances for individuals and families. Everything makes a difference for everything else. Race and ethnicity as well as income determine neighborhood. Neighborhood selects schools and the quality of education. Education opens and closes doors for entry and advancement in work roles. The security and rewards of economic roles shape health care, leisure opportunities, and even what is viewed as possible in life.

Differential access to opportunities and resources, however, are only the most manifest aspect of social stratification. There are also "hidden injuries of class" that take from individuals a fundamental sense of control over their lives.[11] What does it mean to lose a sense that we can determine the basic directions and contexts of our lives? In a study of later-life adults in a Midwest city, many of the life stories told by women and men reflected such limited conditions and consequent views of life. Life for many was

---

[11] Richard Sennett and J. Cobb, *The Hidden Injuries of Class* (New York: Vintage Books, 1973). John R. Kelly, *Peoria Winter: Styles and Resources in Later Life* (Lexington, MA: Lexington Books, The Free Press, 1987).

a struggle to avoid catastrophe. There were women who left school early to help support a family in which the father was shut out of work by illness, injury, or a closed mine or factory. All their lives they worked for others—cleaning, washing, and doing the chores of maintenance—while also maintaining their own families. There were men who had a lifelong series of marginal jobs that offered no security for work, health care, or aging. When life is such a continual struggle, a day-to-day attempt to survive, then leisure becomes moments of joy and community found in the midst of survival demands, not a plan for special expression. "Discretionary income" and "free time" have little meaning to those alienated from even ordinary opportunities. The real lived conditions of life are much more than identifying labels, survey research variables, or romanticized ethnic cultures.

Explaining Diversity

The two sides of leisure diversity call for explanation. There are the choices that express the historical values and customs of cultures that are retained because they are valued. They give a sense of being a member of a special people in a mass society. They are an anchor in what seems to be a limitless sea of change. They are maintained because they are important to selfhood and to community.

The other side recognizes arbitrary discrimination, often based on factors of birth rather than achievement. Men, women, and children are placed in marginal positions from which escape is rendered difficult or even impossible. We do not develop and learn in the same or equal circumstances. We learn who we are and what our chances may be in specific life conditions. In Los Angeles, a Mexican-American young woman, raised in a barrio of poverty, is supported by an affirming family, gives her all to school, and enters the selective University of California system in pre-law. In a Philadelphia ghetto, an African-American young man dreams of getting out even when all his older brothers have succumbed to the allure of gangs and drugs. In a suburb of Atlanta, a teen couple are deciding whether to go to the university together or return to the colleges their families traditionally attend.

From this perspective, there is no way of separating out all those factors: family, neighborhood, schools, and economic opportunity, especially when such life resources differ by social designations of class, gender, race, and ethnicity. None of the either/or arguments hold up. Our potential is not determined either by genetics or by nurture, but by complex interactions of both. Life chances are not produced simply by individual effort and direction or by social circumstances, but by a combination of both. And leisure, like the rest of life, is fully a part of all those elements that make up who we are, where we are, and what we are trying to become.

Is it possible to develop a society in which we value diversity, but do not discriminate? Can we learn to hear and learn from multiple voices? Will we work against entrenched power and privilege to open opportunities for the disinherited and excluded when we benefit from the way things are? Is it possible to have a society that is both inclusive and diverse, that is open many styles of life and affirming of the fundamental value of all life? Only then we can really speak of leisure as freedom.

HIGHLIGHTS

1. Leisure, like all of life, is ethnic, of particular cultures. Diversity, however, has often been joined with discrimination.
2. Ethnicity is more a matter of style than activity differences.
3. Race, ethnicity, gender, and age may arbitrarily limit life chances.
4. Social class, based on economic position, is an index of access to all kinds of resources and opportunities.
5. Gender is more than an identification; it makes a difference in every aspect of life.
6. Social designation involves not only different cultures, but also histories of cumulative deprivation.
7. Cultural diversity can enrich the lives of all in a society that learns to value difference.

Discussion Questions

1. What does "leisure" mean in a condition of deprivation such as an urban ghetto?

2. What values do we associate with ethnic differences in leisure?

3. Is it inevitable that those with greatest power and privilege will suppress the diversity they fear and find threatening?

4. How is race different from ethnicity?

5. Is this still a "patriarchal" society that maintains the priority of male power, even in leisure? Give examples.

6. Are females still "ornaments" to male leisure? Are they the unpaid workers that make male leisure possible?

7. Can we learn to value diversity without exclusion? How?

8. Is our society coming together or maintaining divisions? Why?

Bibliography

Deem, Rosemary, *All Work and No Play? The Sociology of Women and Leisure.* Milton Keynes, UK: Open University Press, 1988.

Henderson, Karla, D. Bialeschski, S. Shaw, and V. Freysinger, *A Leisure of One's Own: A Feminist Perspective on Leisure.* College Park, PA: Venture Publishing, 1989.

Henderson, Karla, ed., *Journal of Leisure Research,* 26, 1 (1994). (Special issue on women's leisure.)

Hutchison, Ray, "A Critique of Race, Ethnicity, and Social Class in Recent Leisure-Recreation Literature," *Journal of Leisure Research,* 20, 10–30 (1988).

Kotlowitz, Alex, *There Are No Children Here.* New York: Anchor Books, 1990.

Lemann, Nicholas, *The Promised Land: The Great Black Migration and How It Changed America.* New York: Alfred Knopf, 1991.

Wilson, William J. *The Truly Disadvantaged.* Chicago: University of Chicago Press, 1987.

Chapter 6

Politics and Policy

We tend to think of leisure as largely an individual concern. Considerable leisure is social in that its action involves other people, their expectations, and behaviors that we learn from others. It is economic in that many opportunities and implements are purchased or rented. It is cultural in its particular forms and expressions. But, how is leisure political?

To begin with, many provisions are offered through public, tax-supported agencies. The direction of those agencies is part of the political process. Conflicts, as between the preservation of a mountainside or developing a ski run, are decided in political forums. If leisure is economic, there are taxation issues to be decided. Some kinds of leisure are considered detrimental to public order or "decency" and are regulated by law. And, the allocation of scarce resources may favor some segments of the population over others—again a political decision.

When political decisions are made and implemented, then the resulting consistencies become "policy." What are settled priorities? What kinds of activity are supported, ignored, or banned? To what extent are public agencies expected to control, manage, and give access to particular kinds of leisure resources: sports venues, natural environments, or arts performances? Decisions become policy. Provisions become taken for granted. Conflicting values are debated and adjudicated.

Who makes the decisions? In a local community an elected or appointed board usually decides on the funding of parks and recreation programs. Whom do those boards represent? What are the special interests, and how are they represented? What is the real power structure of the community? In a diverse society, which interests, styles, cultures, and commitments come to gain public support while others are largely neglected? Leisure is indeed political as well as personal.

ISSUES

How is leisure political?

Which interests are favored in the contemporary political processes?

Is leisure a right or a privilege?

What are the values underlying implicit policies?

Can leisure be supported as a "public good"?

Should national parks be opened for the widest possible use or preserved from visitor impacts? Should national parks and forests, owned by "the people," be free to the tax-paying public or managed on a cost-recovery user-fee basis? Should more community recreation programs be directed toward the poor or toward those who pay the highest taxes? Should leisure goods and services be subjected to a luxury surtax or subsidized with tax breaks and deductions? Is some leisure activity so harmful to health—drugs—or defaming of a class of people—pornography—that it should be regulated or even banned entirely?

All these are political issues, some so contested as to make or break political careers in areas where they are especially visible. The issue is not whether leisure is political. Everything is in some ways and at some levels. The issues are: (1) How is leisure political in contemporary societies? And (2) what kinds of policies, if any, guide leisure in the present and for the future?

How Is Leisure Political?

Leisure is political in a number of explicit and covert ways. Governmental bodies provide leisure resources at federal, state, and local levels. Laws regulate where and when certain kinds of activity may exist. But these are only the most obvious political dimensions of leisure in modern society.

There are innumerable examples of how leisure is political:

- Government agencies own and manage all sorts of leisure spaces. As will be outlined in Chapter 18, the federal government is the major provider of forests, water, mountains, and other recreation resources. Some communities spend millions on programs and facilities for recreation. Yet, there are always possibilities unfulfilled and opportunities unmet. Budgets mean priorities, and priority-setting is a political process.
- The historical chapters sketch many attempts by political bodies to regulate leisure. Bars are licensed and have mandated hours. In colonial New England, many activities, including whistling on the Sabbath, were prohibited by "blue laws." More recently no sports activity could begin before noon on Sunday. And even the video watched in the privacy of one's home is rated for its alleged sexual content.
- Less obvious are questions of taxation. In deference to the real estate lobbies, owners of second homes are allowed to deduct interest payments on their loans from federal

income taxes, an interesting policy in a country in which the housing stock of first homes is seriously inadequate. Conversely, for a time high cost boats were subjected to an inflated "luxury" tax. Higher taxes have been proposed for alcoholic beverages, a tax on drinking, but not on high-fat, low-fiber foods.

- Public funding provides the infrastructure that makes many kinds of leisure possible. Travel is subsidized with the federal interstate highway system and air traffic systems and airport construction grants.
- High-level sports are state-supported in many countries in order to enhance the national image and build a national spirit with success at the Olympics and other international contests. The United States is in a minority by giving tax breaks to corporate sponsors rather than direct support.
- The mass media, and especially television, operate under public licenses that are worth millions and even billions of dollars and are periodically renewed. Despite a small public radio/television subsidy, most content policies are market-determined with relatively minor public regulation or provision.

The point is that leisure is at least as political as education with policies of direct regulation only the tip of the iceberg of direct provision, taxation, licensing, and infrastructure support.

What, Then, Is Politics?

Political processes are all around us, affecting how we move from one place to another, how we educate our children, and how we design our homes. Leisure, in particular, is political in at least three ways:[1]

1. The struggle over scarce resources is political. One critical example is the struggle over the management of old-growth forests in the Pacific Northwest. Ninety percent of these forests have been logged. Now the allocation of the remainder for timber harvest, forest recreation, or ecological habitat is being contested at the highest levels of government. In every community with a public recreation program, budgets are subjected to political decision making. There are within-budget clashes among supporters of particular programs, such as Little League baseball, swimming, and bike paths. There are also contests over total allocations with those representing public health, education, safety, streets, and a host of other programs. Allocations of money and space are made in political forums. What is most important for a city—public housing, prenatal care, Headstart, neighborhood parks, or freeways? What are the criteria of assessment? Who has the power, in public arenas and behind the scenes?

2. The domination of one group by another is political. By law, the owners of professional baseball clubs are exempted from antitrust regulation in ways that give them monopoly over siting franchises. The owners of professional teams are also able to allocate new players to clubs through a draft that limits the players to one team. The system gives owners control over both players and the spectators so that franchises are

[1] John Wilson, *Politics and Leisure* (Boston: Unwin Hyman, 1988).

valued at eight-figure levels. Such control, however, is trivial in comparison with totalitarian states in which the literal power of life and death gives the governing elites
control over every aspect of life. A "police state" is precisely that, controlled by those
who possess the power to arrest and execute. In a market economy, power tends to be
economic when those with financial clout are able to exercise disproportionate influence over the political system.

3. On a more immediate level, surveillance and control of behavior is political. At what
   age may youth drink, drive, marry, or leave school? These are political decisions and
   vary from one state to another. What behaviors are banned in public parks and buildings? When are bars opened and closed? What kinds of sexual behavior are illegal, in
   public and in private? What aggressive behaviors are monitored and suppressed by police and what is permitted? For example, so-called "gay bashing" is ignored in some
   communities and penalized in others. From colonial times on, a variety of leisure activities have been controlled by law and by custom according to values that have
   changed. Even the boundary between public and private has shifted from decade to
   decade.

We recognize what is manifestly political, the decisions and implementations of law,
budgets, and control. What we less often recognize are the underlying political dimensions.
For example, policies of resource allocation, taxation, subsidies, and transfers that determine the distribution of wealth and income have profound impacts on leisure and all the
rest of life. In an inclusive sense, everything is political whenever any two population segments are treated differently.

The Regulation of Time and Space

The responses of public and market-sector recreation to the new industrial city will be introduced in Chapter 10. At this point a few examples of political themes illustrate the issue.
The obvious problem was a lack of space in the crowded cities. Children released from the
factories had no place to play except the muddy and dangerous streets. They swam off piers
and organized sports in the midst of delivery wagons and trolleys. They lived ten to a room
in their tenements. One response was to provide regulated space—parks—and regulated
programs as a context for their "healthy" development.[2] At the same time, streets and other
areas were declared off limits.

Space was equally scarce for adults. In their brief off-hours, men gathered in bars.
Soon those bent on reform required licenses, regulated hours, and even banned various
kinds of activities such as boxing matches and dog fights. The aim was to bring the worker
back to the job rested rather than wrecked by drinking and associated behaviors. For women
workers, the regulations extended to sexual behavior as well as recreation.[3] The lack of
success of such regulation, especially of Sunday activity, was demonstrated by the preva-
lence of "Saint Monday"—factory absenteeism that extended the one-day weekend.

[2] Gary Cross, *A Social History of Leisure since 1600* (College Park, PA: Venture Publishing, 1990).

[3] Kathy Piess, *Cheap Amusements: Working Women and Leisure in New York City* (Philadelphia: Temple University Press, 1986).

In smaller communities, "blue laws" limited behaviors on Sunday, a day protected by religious interests. No public sports, no meetings except in churches, no bars open, no stores open, and no public behavior offensive to the "moral leaders" of the community were allowed. In general, the "moral leaders" were the business class that ruled the mainline Protestant churches and enforced their own practices and standards on everyone. The gradual erosion of such regulation is still incomplete in some areas, especially in the rural "Bible belt."

Both time and space for leisure have been contested arenas. There has been resistance on the part of those the power elites seek to control. In the early days of industrialization, there were the unlicensed "shebeens" for drinking beverages that bore no tax stamps. There were ethnic festivals as European immigrant workers found their own space to recreate celebrations brought over from the old country. There was resistance as laws were tested and violated. There was underground provision for leisure, such as the "speakeasies" during the period of Prohibition. And there has always been at least some tacit permission given to sexual commerce that was legally banned.

During the late nineteenth century, communities began to expand their provisions of space for regulated leisure. This development ran parallel to the gradual shortening of the work week as unions bargained and fought for "eight hours for what we will." In time, the weekday evening and the two-day weekend became standard for most workers, at least until retailing took over the weekend. Schools and communities offered "healthy" recreation opportunities for children and youth, especially sports. Teams were sponsored and glorified as symbols of community pride and social solidarity. Insofar as recreation required designated time and space, it was fully a matter of political concern. Insofar as it was socially defined as a public good, resources were selectively allocated and controls exercised.

Politics and Leisure in the Future

What is the political future of leisure in North America and areas similar in economic development and political structures? There is a general impression that leisure is gaining prominence in modern societies. France had, for a time, a Minister of Leisure whose mission was to develop policy in this significant part of the society and economy. The allocation of time, including the common European four-week vacation, was given particular attention.

Such an appointment in the United States is about as likely as a citrus crop in Alaska. Despite the vast investment in federal land and water resources, there is no coordinating agency, much less a principal policy-making department. Rather a mob of organizations with special interests—off-road vehicles, camping, or Olympic sports—lobby relevant agencies for allocations of space, subsidy, legal protection, and programmatic support.

It seems unlikely that leisure and recreation will rise to cabinet-level visibility in federal government. States commonly combine recreation interests with land and water conservation as relatively minor parts of their budgets. Only on the local community level can bond issues or the threatened withdrawal of programs mobilize a high level of attention and action. And even there the common trend has been a constriction of resources in response to the drive to limit taxation.

What, then, are persistent issues that give some insight into the political future of leisure and recreation?

1. In general, the political is determined by the economic. Government in the United States has usually been responsive to economic interests. This is not likely to diminish in this emerging period of a world economic system with its borderless competitions for finances and markets.

Among the most clearly identified economic problems are productivity and unemployment. There has been a significant reduction in the rate of productivity increase in the American economy since the boom decades of the 1950s, 1960s, and 1970s. That reduction makes American goods less competitive on world markets. As a consequence, leisure may be justified insofar as it is perceived as contributing to productivity. If recreation is a positive factor in good health and reduces absenteeism, it merits support. Further, the kinds of recreation that return the worker to the workplace more fit, more attentive, and more loyal will gain the fullest support.

Unemployment is always something of an issue in an society that relies on market forces to determine the shape of the workforce. Now there are some factors that raise particular concerns. Inner-city areas are abandoned by economic enterprise to create unemployment rates of youth in excess of 50 percent. Can recreation play a part in maintaining and restoring a viable context of life for those denied entrance into work? The transfer of labor-intensive production to low-wage parts of the world will continue to erode the supply of low-skill jobs in production. Can recreation provide some sense of worth and engagement for those forced out of the workforce or relegated to part-time service jobs? More older workers in their fifties are being retired, voluntarily and involuntarily. What is the place of leisure as older unemployed adults attempt to build a satisfying quality of life?

One other issue that will gain less directed attention is the great issue of consumption. An economic system requires markets for its good and services. As markets for cars and refrigerators level off, economic expansion may be directed more and more to leisure markets. Governmental agencies will be under pressure to provide the time and space to expand those markets. As a consequence, investment in leisure resources and even a consideration of more limited discretionary hours could become more prominent on political agendas.

2. Running counter to an expansion of public investment in leisure and recreation are the American ideologies of individualism and noninterference. Underlying governmental support of recreation and provision of resources is an ethic of the common welfare (See Chapter 18). This collective ethic is in conflict with the more individualist ethic that places primary responsibility for our lives on ourselves and limits government to actions that absolutely must be public. The fact is that the extent of such actions has radically expanded from common defense to schools, highways, health protection, business fraud, and a thousand other areas we now take for granted.

The place of leisure in this scheme remains problematic. Considerable leisure is more or less private, taking place in the home with few or no outside consequences. Despite public softball diamonds and picnic areas, leisure is largely relegated to the private sphere of life. It is a privilege, not a right. Within regulated limits, we are presumed to be responsible for our own leisure and are encouraged to develop our own preferences. Leisure is "privatized" into the locale of the electronic home and the social world of the family.

As a consequence, resources for leisure are seen as an option and even a luxury. They are not an entitlement and subject to standards of equity. Rather, leisure is what we provide for ourselves, largely out of an economic surplus beyond necessity. The basis for public provisions is not equity, providing significant opportunity to all in some measure. It is efficiency, providing only resources for which private provision is too costly per user. Further, economic efficiency may be measured by cost-recovery rather than maximum opportunity. Planning becomes geared to self-sustaining markets rather than access to resources for a full spectrum of a population. Leisure is defined as fundamentally private rather than public.

3. There remains a conflict between leisure as a right and "the right kind of leisure." It is the issue of control. What are the values on which leisure provision is based? Is there a general consensus as to what is good and proper leading to a homogenization of leisure? Or is there a value placed on diversity that fosters a variety of styles, interests, and investments?

Just what kinds of leisure are too immoral, too "blue," or too destructive to be permitted? Is there a standard of common decency, however defined, that outlaws some kinds of behavior or at least forces them into seclusion? Are some kinds of sexual interaction acceptable, even in public, and others subject to arrest and imprisonment? Are some drugs acceptably recreational and others too dangerous to be allowed? Is violence acceptable on the playing field, but not in the bar? There seem to be two mechanisms of control in contemporary society.

The one that may be receding is that of regulation. Many kinds of behaviors that were outlawed even a decade or two ago are permitted today. They include private sexual practices, the almost total disappearance of Sunday prohibitions, and a greater latitude given to the content of public media, especially television.

The one that seems to be gaining ascendency is that of the market. The doctrine is that of the "sovereign consumer." If enough people will pay enough, then the market will provide opportunity. Jump off bridges attached to a nylon tether, watch very large people deliberately destroy the knees of other people, or hunt the reduced stock of some fleet animal—for a price that yields a return on investment, the market will make it available. In one way, this reliance on the market fosters diversity. It supports a wide variety of leisure styles, if they attract a viable paying clientele. Conversely, this mechanism opens opportunity along an income gradient, maximizing resources for the wealthy and closing off the chances of the poor.

4. There are, of course, other factors as well. The entire context of leisure is becoming increasingly international. Not only do new arrivals in a society bring their own cultures and styles of leisure, but through television and travel we become more aware of what other peoples do. There is a new world order of sport as formerly domestic games are exported. There are basketball leagues in Italy and Argentina, and baseball is the Japanese national game.

At the same time, the media bring to mass attention all kinds of leisure activity, styles, symbols, and locales. Again, this constant exposure to expanded leisure possibilities may be a powerful factor in attracting participation in activities that would formerly have been unknown and "foreign" to our interests and tastes.

Does the United States Have a Leisure Policy?

Policy may be stated in public documents that have been produced in the give-and-take of political debate. They may also be implicit, a matter of the taken-for-granted. Such implicit policy is usually based on a set of societal values over which there is little debate.

Clearly in the United States there is no "Declaration of Leisure" or "Constitution of Play." There is no coordinating agency, no unified political force, and no explicit set of values for leisure. Nor is there likely to be. There are, however, fundamental political values on which implicit policy may rest.

Are there such values in our culture? Individualism has already been proposed as a fundamental social value. Productivity is clearly a basic economic value. And, order is central to the polity, to government. Any implicit policy of leisure is likely to rest on the foundations of such consensual values. Economically, such a policy will support or reinforce productivity in a capitalist economy. That is, it will be presumed to increase the return on investment capital. Culturally, an implicit policy of leisure will enhance individualism. Politically, policy will support a sense of order, even at the cost of diversity.

1. The first element of such an implicit policy is a reliance on the market for the primary distribution of leisure goods and services. Some resources can hardly be market-driven and market-provided. They are scarce, if not unique, and economically inefficient for market-based management. When there is a choice, however, the market will be primary. Ski areas on public land will be franchised to businesses. Services in national parks will also be licensed businesses. Most shoreline is privately held. Television and radio channels are operated by slightly regulated businesses. Prime destination resort sites are held by corporations, not the public. Forty aviation businesses fly tourists over the Grand Canyon, and the Park Service licenses those who operate rafting trips for a profit. And even modest public subsidies to the arts are continually attacked as socialism for the elites.

This implicit policy has certain significant consequences. First, there is a fundamental bias toward the affluent. Maximizing profit return directs businesses toward those who can pay the most, the upscale markets. There are businesses that court middle mass markets with their budget motel chains and fast food at the interstate exchange. Most destination resorts, however, compete for the top 20–30 percent of the tourism market and control prime resources, especially shorelines. Billions are spent in advertising brand-name equipment to expand markets for goods with high profit margins.

Relying on market providers to the extent that over 90 percent of leisure spending is in the market rather than public sector leads to a second outcome. There is a seeming imbalance in investment. Hundreds of millions follow the investment trends so that upscale markets are saturated and businesses fail. Capital is wasted and resources misdirected. At the same time, many public resources, especially low-cost ones near urban centers, are jammed. Both the resources and the experiences they provide are degraded. The market provides almost everything for the top ten percent, mass opportunities for mass markets, and little or nothing for the bottom 20 to 30 percent except television. The large numbers who walk, one of the few growing activities, are relegated to hard and dangerous streets, while Euro Disney consumes American capital in its failure and half-empty high-rise condos line the private beaches of the Eastern seaboard. Housing project playgrounds are mangled trash-heaps, and thirty new cruise ships are under construction.

Implicit policies, especially those of taxation, are designed to promote business interests. Tax revenues are used to provide the attraction of public parks for new residential developments. It is no accident that real estate development interests tend to be well-represented on local park boards and councils. Condominiums and even boats are written off as business expenses. Second homes are subsidized by allowing deduction of interest and taxes from total income. Roads, drainage, sewers, water, police and fire protection, and other infrastructure are provided to recreation developments at public expense to support the tourist visits of nonresidents. In this light, the "implicit policy" seems quite evident and directed to benefit particular economic interests.

2. There is a retreat from those presumed to be unproductive. Even within a corporate structure, the research and development, finance, and sales managers presumed to be most central to productivity are offered vacation and weekend flexibility, health and fitness clubs, and special health programs. Those workers considered to be easily replaceable engage in conflicted bargaining for a little control over their hours and reduced health packages, which are often lost when unemployment is high and management puts on the pressure.

At the same time, resources are directed toward those with the greatest market purchase and away from the marginal, the poor, and especially the poor aged. Some kinds of provisions are made for children, especially in communities with relatively high incomes. There is a new recognition of the market power of the most affluent "young old" with peak incomes and reduced family expenses. Especially those with the discretionary wealth to invest in second homes, big-ticket toys, and overseas trips are the prime target markets. But what is the leisure future for those who are being pushed out of production employment in the new global economy?

3. There is a stress on the "benefits" of recreation.[4] How does recreation enhance health that reduces absenteeism and increases productivity on the job? How does leisure support the family, presumed to be the most fundamental context of healthy and productive life? How do vacation destinations reduce stress? How do leisure opportunities, especially those for sale or rent, give a sense of reward to loyal and cooperative workers, and offer a break in environment or activity from the often stressful routines of work? Ideally, it would be possible to put a dollar value on such benefits as they accrue to the corporation or the economy in general.

4. The final policy implication is that efficiency will usually be a greater factor in resource allocation than equity. There may be measured responses to equity, provisions for the poor, those with limiting conditions, and others less able to pay or travel. The fullest attention, however, will be given to those who can pay for the full costs of public programs. In fact, there will be a common argument that public planning is misdirected, that the market should determine allocations. The so-called "sovereign consumer" (who can pay) should determine even public policies and programs. This policy allows elected officials

---

[4] B. L. Driver, Perry Brown, and George Peterson, *The Benefits of Leisure* (College Park, PA: Venture Publishing, 1991).

to support that much-desired political goal of tax limits or reductions. Especially leisure and recreation, defined as a matter of individual choice and taste, can then be left to profit-making and breakeven operations.

Critical Arguments

There are a number of critiques that can be lodged against such an implicit policy:

First, reliance on the market fails to recognize a full spectrum of the population. As suggested, market sector investment is biased toward the upscale markets, those who can and do pay the most for their pleasure. Further, there are a variety of leisure styles that may be ignored in mass marketing. Also, those with acute limitations may not be enough of a market to attract costly opportunities. In a society with vast differences in incomes and wealth, those at the lower ends are systematically underserved by a policy that directs most resources toward investment return and economic efficiency.

Second, the market has its own peculiar costs. Resources are expended in creating markets for products that are not immediately perceived as useful or satisfying. Further, profit-seeking interests tend to follow the models of what "works." As a consequence, markets, especially upscale ones, are almost always saturated. Hundreds of millions are lost when too many destination resorts are built, too many cruise ships are launched, and too many high-end restaurants are opened. Expensive condominiums close off beaches to local residents and fall into bankruptcy when the investors assume that there will always be a market for "one more."

Third, there is the more philosophical issue of whether leisure is a human right and a public good. Or, is leisure a privilege purchased by productive economic participation and defined as a reward? The first position does not imply that everyone has a fundamental lifetime right to one cruise up the coast to Alaska, two trips to Europe and a trip to Disney every five years. It does imply that there are human meanings in leisure—in play, creative action, emotional and physical expression, and experiencing special environments—that are not just luxuries. Experience-seeking for its own sake is more than an add-on to the "real" material concerns of life. Leisure is, from this perspective, not just time and toys to be purchased by the real value of work. It is a part of the wholeness of life, of its balance and rhythms. It so, then the politics and policies of leisure are a matter worthy of public debate, dialogue, and decision.

HIGHLIGHTS

1. Leisure is political in the allocation of scarce resources, unequal powers of self-determination, and many aspects of surveillance and control.
2. The history of leisure presents many kinds of regulation of time and space through "blue laws," licensing, and direct control.
3. Indirect policies promote particular kinds of leisure through taxation and the provision of infrastructure.
4. Policies of reliance on the market for most provisions bias opportunities and investments toward the affluent and to principles of economic efficiency over equity.
5. Decisions based on marketing and the "sovereign consumer" have their own costs and consequences.

Discussion Questions

1. Are there still various kinds of leisure regulation and even "blue laws"? What are their social and political aims?

2. Should there be a public bias toward toward the poor, the disabled, and others with limited opportunities to balance the biases of market provisions?

3. What leisure interests are best represented in community public debate? Which ones are represented poorly or not at all? What can be done to change this condition?

4. Should public provisions for recreation be justified entirely by their contributions to the economy and public order? If so, how do we defend national parks that most people will never see?

5. Is leisure fundamentally a private concern, or is it also a public good? What are the arguments for each position?

6. Give examples of "implicit" policy in the politics of leisure.

Bibliography

Clarke, John and Chas Critcher, *The Devil Makes Work: Leisure in Capitalist Britain.* Champaign, IL: University of Illinois Press, 1985.

Cross, Gary, *The Social History of Leisure since 1600.* College Park, PA: Venture Publishing, 1988.

Driver, B. L., Perry Brown, and George Peterson, eds., *The Benefits of Leisure.* College Park, PA: Venture Publishing, 1991.

Hargreaves, Jenny, *Sport, Power, and Culture.* New York: St. Martin's Press, 1986.

Hunnicutt, Benjamin, *Work without End.* Philadelphia: Temple University Press, 1988.

Piess, Kathy, *Cheap Amusements: Working Women and Leisure in New York City.* Philadelphia: Temple University Press, 1986.

Rojek, Chris, *Capitalism and Leisure Theory.* New York: Tavistock, 1985.

Wilson, John, *Politics and Leisure.* Boston: Unwin Hyman, 1988.

Chapter 7

Work, Leisure, and Time

Many of the stereotypes of leisure assume that people's occupations determine their leisure. The factory worker is pictured as stopping off at a blue-collar bar after his shift to hoist a few and engage in a discussion of football before shifting his relaxation to home, a soft chair, and the incessant television set. If he has a special interest, it is likely to be something like stock car or motorcycle racing in which he may be a participant if under forty and a spectator if older.

Of course, we all know of exceptions—the factory hand who does fine metal sculpture and the professor who takes his modified bike to the motocross course on Saturday. But in general we suspect that the stereotypes exist because they are often true. Even recognizing that a great many blue-collar workers are camping regularly and lawyers are playing in local softball leagues, that housewives are playing soccer and secretaries are backpacking, we retain the lingering feeling that leisure is secondary to work and the type of work tends to determine types of leisure.

If so, there are a number of factors we should remember:

Home and family tend to be central to most adults so that mill worker and professor alike are frequently found working in the yard or fixing something at home on Saturday. Further, they both are likely to engage in various family activities on weekends and to take their vacations with spouse and children.

Most American adults watch a considerable amount of television, spend the majority of their leisure hours at home, and often come home tired and anticipating some rest and relaxation. While educational experiences and developed tastes may influence which programs are watched, what material is read, and which beverage is consumed, informal activity is characteristic of most leisure profiles.

Even when there are correlations between type of work and type of leisure, there is no reason to assume that the work determines the leisure. Other factors such as educational experiences, neighborhood friendships, leisure socialization habits inherited from the parental family, community opportunities, costs and income, and a host of personal elements enter into leisure decisions.

In general, the relationship of work and leisure cannot be summed up in any stereotypes. Rather, since both work and leisure are complex phenomena, there are conflicting models of the relationships between them. Among the issues that will be explored in this chapter are

Various meanings of work
The alleged centrality of work to life
The myth of the declining workweek
Models of the relations of work and leisure
The time versus income trade-off and its implications for leisure
The possibility of an emerging consensus on work and leisure values

---

ISSUES

Are there striking differences between the leisure behavior of wage workers and professionals?

Is work central to the lives of most employed Americans?

Are work hours still declining while time for leisure is increasing?

Just how are work and leisure related?

Work and Employment

What is work? Is it the drudgery required by a society to maintain its existence, that which has to be done for survival and for the maintenance of a certain standard of living? The dimension of necessity has usually been associated with definitions of work along with some concept of effort, purposeful activity, and production. Work is doing or accomplishing something that needs to be done.

But that is not definition enough. Work may be necessary from a social perspective; however, is all activity that we would call work really necessary for survival? Are there not many work activities that are desirable or that have some market value, but that are not definitely needed? Also, what about human services such as counseling or education that may be needed, but have no product that can be easily identified? Further, work would seem to have personal as well as social meanings. Many people choose to work, even though they do not have to in order to maintain themselves or their household. Volunteers work. Some people choose to add to their work responsibilities without likelihood of gain. Work is more than "what has to be done" and "what we have to do."

Is this because we are, in part at least, *Homo faber*—man the worker? Work is more than necessity. Work has meaning, satisfaction, and excitement when it is more than drudgery and routine. Work is making, fabricating, and producing—not just market items and necessities but also ideas, works of art, and new possibilities in human relationships. Work is making something that did not exist before. Work is creating, and it is an investment of the self in that creative and productive activity. Work is nurturing and caregiving essential to the society, although often not paid activity. Work, then, may have to be done.

It has an importance beyond the experience of doing it. But it may also be meaningful, fulfilling, and satisfying. In some forms, it transcends sheer necessity to become "something more" that no institution could require.

Labor, the work that people do, is a social contribution, but it is also a part of the self. The term *labor* is used more or less interchangeably here with *work* to signify that process of engagement with production. Thinkers as different as Martin Luther and Karl Marx have agreed that worthwhile, productive labor is essential to being human. It is central to human fulfillment. As people need freedom and community, they also need some engagement, some sense of being needed and of doing something that matters. Work in the fullest sense is that personal engagement with significance which transcends the self.

On the other hand, everything that people get paid for doing is not work in this sense. *Employment* is the specific job that a person does and for which he or she receives some reward. Employment may yield little or no sense of satisfaction, meaning, doing something that is needed, or accomplishment. Some employment so alienates the worker from the end product, from control over his or her activity, and from any meaning that it is really not work at all. For this perspective, all paid employment is not work, and all work is not economically paid.

When we refer to employment, we mean here the job that a person does in a given setting and on a prescribed schedule. *Occupation,* on the other hand, refers to the type or classification of employment. Where a person's occupation might be as a welder, that person's employment would be in a particular machine shop. Someone with an occupation of playground director may be employed by a city recreation department. One may work for many reasons, but employment has a designated price.

The distinction is similar to that between leisure and nonwork. If leisure is defined by the meaning and quality of the experience with elements of freedom and personal satisfaction, then much nonwork activity is not leisure. Activity may be outside employment hours and without a prespecified end product and yet lack the freedom and experiential focus of leisure. We seldom refer to carrying out the garbage or driving to the dentist as leisure.

The distinguishing factor is not time or place. Nor is it the production of something of value. The outcome of a leisure engagement may be a performance or artifact of high quality. Activity may, on the other hand, be work in the sense of contributing to the society and be highly satisfying and fulfilling. Further, leisure may take place in playful interludes at the office and work at home on weekends. What is it, then, that differentiates work and leisure if both may be creative or routine, exciting or boring?

One difference seems to be that most work has a product that is predetermined. Whether in the research laboratory or the factory, the school or the hospital, work is to produce an outcome that the society needs and values. That outcome may be an invention, a machine tool, learning, or healing. The end in any case is prespecified before the work begins. Leisure, however, is playful in that there is no predetermined product or outcome. Leisure may be demanding and strenuous, but its outcomes are open. It is chosen and valued primarily for the experience, not the result.

The definitional distinctions may be somewhat fuzzy. Clearly, raising wheat, however satisfying, is work, and backpacking, however strenuous, is leisure. But what about the playful elements of developing a new design or the useful idea that emerges during a vacation conversation? What about the creative flash in the midst of home chores? Again, both work and leisure may be best understood as dimensions of activity: Work is productive and goal-oriented and leisure is free and experience-oriented. Some activity may combine work and leisure dimensions with time segments of each difficult to distinguish. In fact, some of the most fulfilling activity may incorporate both work and leisure dimensions.

Both work and leisure, then, may be satisfying, expressive, and unifying rather than alienating from the self and community. Employment may or may not contain elements of both work and leisure. Both work and leisure are profoundly human activities that may occur at almost any time and place. They may even be mixed together. Further, all nonwork is not leisure nor is all nonleisure work. Here is a general summary of terms:

Work —Productive activity with outcomes of economic or social value

Nonwork—Activity outside the employment schedule and obligations that includes leisure, required activity of maintenance, and residual time

Employment—A job with specified responsibilities and rewards

Why People Work

There are really two questions here: Why do people work? and Why are people employed?

People work because they want to. They want to work because it is satisfying and fulfilling to be productive, to do something that has meaning and value to oneself and others. Work is necessary, in some form, if life is to go on. Some members of any community must be productive for food, shelter, protection, and various kinds of human enrichment to exist. There is satisfaction in knowing that something important—tangible or intangible—now exists because you did it. In this sense, work is important to individual meaning and identity as well as to the society.

However, that does not mean that all employment is satisfying work. In the sense of employment, most people do not "live to work." They are more likely to "work (be employed) to live." At best, they live for work, leisure, relationships of family and community, and for everything that they find has meaning to them. In actuality, most adults who are employed find some satisfactions in their employment, are quite concerned about the monetary rewards, and have a clear sense of the relationship of employment to home, security, and the future of their families.

In national polls, about three workers in four usually respond that they are generally satisfied with their work. That seems to mean that the worker is willing to choose his or her employment out of the kinds of opportunities that might be realistically considered. Also, the proportion satisfied or very satisfied does vary with the type of occupation. Among professionals or managers, 80 percent or more are satisfied as compared to about 60 percent of clerical workers and 65 percent of unskilled workers. However, although about 40 percent of professionals and managers are "very satisfied," only 22 percent of clerical, 22 percent of skilled, and 13 percent of unskilled workers respond so positively. Further, while 80 to 90 percent of professors, scientists, and lawyers would choose the same occupation again, the percentage of unskilled auto workers is 16 percent, of textile workers 31 percent, and of white-collar workers 43 percent.[1]

---

[1] Robert L. Kahn, "The Meaning of Work," in A. C. Campbell and P. E. Converse, *The Human Meaning of Change* (New York: Russell Sage Foundation, 1972), p. 182.

Perhaps more important than the levels of perceived satisfaction are those factors most important to satisfaction in employment. A wide range of research provides evidence that income is still an important factor in job satisfaction. Not only the issues central to strikes and labor disputes but also surveys of workers demonstrate the relationship of income to satisfaction.

However, there are other elements in job satisfaction. Among the most obvious are the physical conditions of the work locale, some sense of contribution and autonomy in the job, companionship of workers, time spent getting to and from the workplace, and symbols of prestige and appreciation. There is evidence that job satisfaction can be raised measurably by improvement of such conditions. In one important line of research, the central element of work satisfaction, however, was found to be self-determination.[2] Employment without some freedom of action is just drudgery.

On the other hand, there is also evidence that the rewards *and* the meaning of those rewards are still central. In his study of factory workers, Eli Chinoy found that an adequate level of security provided by employment was enhanced by the dream of the workers that their children would have opportunities to do better than they. Their income provided a base of home, nurture, and education for a better future for their children.[3] When Bennett Berger studied the lives of California factory workers living in a new suburb, he found no great enjoyment or excitement about their employment. Rather, their employment made having a home, a family, security, and some time for pleasurable activity possible.[4] There is an atmosphere of acceptance in the description of working-class life.

The Work Ethic Revisited

This suggests that we cannot totally discard the concept of the work ethic. In real work there are elements of human meaning and fulfillment related to producing, creating, fabricating, and developing that may be quite central to life. At least as an ideal, the ethic of work as meaningful and productive remains. Further, for some, high levels of work satisfaction suggest that they do find work in their employment, that there is meaning for them in the job. They tend to be those with the greatest freedom to develop their own contexts of work and choose the kinds of results they want to produce.

There is still the worker who with hands or mind or skill in interpersonal relationships brings about a result, a product, that is new and valuable. The question is *Who is the craftsman today?* Which jobs provide opportunity to choose and develop and produce? How many employment situations are perceived as free, important, and productive?

There are those for whom a work ethic attitude among workers would be useful. They are the employers who desire the greatest possible reliability, effort, and productivity for their employees. They are the business people who work long and hard themselves and believe that everyone should hold the same values they do.

But for the most part, there is little more evidence of an active and operative work ethic among American wage earners today than there was in the days of child labor, the sweat-

---

[2] Mel Kohn, "Unresolved Issues in Work/Personality," in K. Erikson and S. Vallas, eds., *The Nature of Work* (New Haven, CT: Yale University Press, 1990).

[3] Eli Chinoy, *Automobile Workers and the American Dream* (New York: Doubleday, 1955).

[4] Bennett Berger, *Working-Class Suburb* (Berkeley: University of California Press, 1969).

shop, and the seventy- to eighty-hour workweek. Just the scale of modern industry would seem to make such personal investment and satisfaction for the mass of workers unlikely.

Work, Satisfaction, and Leisure

Does employment that is enjoyable and satisfying become leisure? The fact that there may be elements or occasions of leisure during employment times and at workplaces has led some to suggest that any satisfaction in those contexts is leisure. They go on to propose that work and leisure thus become merged and indistinguishable. Such an approach may be somewhat "imperialistic" when advocated by those interested primarily in leisure. It makes any activity that is satisfying "leisure."

More common use of the terms would keep work and leisure distinct. Either may be enjoyable, satisfying, and even central to a person's life. And neither is distinguished by when and where it takes place. Rather, the critical difference is that work contributes to the survival and well-being of the society. Work is, in this sense, productive. Leisure, on the other hand, is the free expression of the self and of satisfying relationships *for their own sake*. In leisure even the act of producing something finds its meaning in the act rather than in the product. Real leisure and real work are both satisfying, fulfilling, and profoundly human. That, however, does not make them identical.

The Alleged Centrality of Work

After all, why should we expect a person who spends most working hours keypunching payment records into the accounting program of the telephone company to find the work exciting and fulfilling? Is there any reason for a steel mill worker whose station is on the floor where it is hot, noisy, and dangerous not to feel relieved when his shift is over? So much of employment is routinized, segmented from the whole process of production, with few opportunities for personal interaction, and paced by machines or quotas that any intrinsic interest would be hard to find. It is no wonder that many workers do no more than is required and are primarily interested in the paycheck.

However, the kind of work and how it is defined do make some difference. Robert Dubin developed the concept of "central life interest." He first published in 1956 the results of a study of 1,200 workers in three midwestern factories.[5] He found that 90 percent of those workers preferred that their friendships be off the job and away from the workplace. Only 24 percent of the workers could be defined as job-oriented in their life interests. Three out of four preferred their associations and activities outside employment. Meaningful human relationships, feelings of worth, and enjoyment were sought outside the job. Employment was a means to a greater end.

Further research on this question indicates that interest varies with the type of job. In a study of managers and upper-level employees, their orientation toward their employment was more important. Those with a "career" orientation, who connected their level of work with possible future advancement, were twice as likely as the rest of the sample of man-

[5] Robert Dubin, "Industrial Workers' Worlds: A Study in the 'Central Life Interests' of Industrial Workers," in E. Smigel, ed., *Work and Leisure* (New Haven, CT: College and University Press, 1963), pp. 53–72.

agers and specialists to have their job as their central life interest.[6] Two-thirds of the 14 percent with career orientations had work as a central life interest as opposed to less than 40 percent of those who were ambivalent or not seeking advancement. In general, it was also found that work orientation decreased between the ages of thirty-six and forty-five for those ambivalent about their careers.

Studying a variety of occupations in England, Stanley Parker asked simply, "What is your main interest in life?" Of those employed in business, 11 percent replied "work" as compared to 29 percent of those in human services.[7] Childcare, mental health, teaching, and public welfare work showed the greatest degree of work involvement; banking, insurance, advertising, and retail selling showed the least.

More recently, levels of commitment and satisfaction were found to be highest for the family/community domain of life, followed by leisure and work in that order.[8] Further, dimensions of meaning such as expression, personal development, social interaction, and a sense of productivity and worth were experienced in all three domains.

Part of the problem is that many jobs provide little opportunity for social interaction, innovation, variety, or the satisfaction of seeing the end product emerge. Whether the worker is feeding a large computer in another building, taking a vast sales inventory, or involved in a production process in which final assembly takes place out of sight and out of mind, feeling deep fulfillment and investment in many jobs is unlikely. Ours is, after all, a large and complex industrial economy in which the scale of production, distribution, and consumption is beyond easy grasp. This massive scale creates a certain separation for workers so that they are more likely to come to see the job in terms of personal meanings and rewards than of contribution to the necessary work of the society. Both control and creativity are lost to computerized efficiency and standardization. And much of the employment growth is in routinized, large-scale enterprises in which the worker is a replaceable unit.

What Is Central?

For American adults, as already suggested, their central interests are neither their work nor their leisure as such. Rather, their central life interests are their stable and immediate communities—their families and homes if they are married adults. For others, such as students, that immediate community may include peer friendship groups, living groups, and the family in a significant but less day-to-day way. In fact, emotional depression and dissatisfaction with life, including leisure, seem to be primarily related to a lack of such an immediate community.

Of course, the three life spaces of work, family/community, and leisure cannot be strictly separated. Much of the interaction of family and friends at home is leisure activity. It would be more accurate to say that interaction with our immediate communities, which gives us the satisfaction of engaging in relationships of stability, trust, communication, and intimacy, is primary. Those communities interact in a variety of contexts many of which include forms of leisure.

[6] Daniel R. Goldman, "Managerial Mobility Motivations and Central Life Interests," *American Sociological Review,* 38 (1973), 119–126.

[7] J. Stanley Parker, *The Future of Work and Leisure* (New York: Praeger, 1971), p. 78.

[8] John R. Kelly and Janice R. Kelly, "Dimensions of Centrality and Meaning in the Domains of Work, Family, and Leisure," *Journal of Leisure Research,* 26, 9 (1994), 250–275.

In a study of adults over age forty in Peoria, Illinois, the three life domains of work, family, and leisure were designated as the primary orientations of *life investments.*[9] These are the areas of life in which persons direct their resources in anticipation of receiving a return of satisfaction and meaning for their lives. The largest number were found to be "balanced investors" with at least two of the three domains—work, family, and leisure—given investments that yielded a significant sense of worth and meaning. About half as many were "family-focused," with their resources devoted primarily to that set of relationships and their life satisfactions derived primarily from the family. Very few invested primarily and exclusively in either work or leisure.

Work and the Structure of Life

The failure of work to provide the central life interest for most of those who are employed does not mean that work is at the periphery of their lives. As the nature of the factory gave shape to the geography and the timetable of the industrial city, so the world of work continues to determine much of the shape of the nonwork world.

It is still useful as a general rule to divide the weekday into an eight-eight-eight format. Eight hours are given to employment and about eight to sleep. The eight hours remaining include time for travel to and from the job, eating, care of the self, and numerous maintenance tasks. Women tend to devote a much higher percentage of this time to cooking and home chores than do men. Both, on the average, watch more than two hours of television, do some reading, and engage in some conversation and interaction around the house. On weekdays, that pretty well takes up the third eight hours.

However, the timing of the third eight hours is not discretionary. Employment hours are fixed by the work institution. While some greater flexibility in beginning and ending hours is being tried in some offices and laboratories, the coordination of work usually requires that a large proportion of the workday be synchronized. Sales, production, planning, management, support staff such as secretaries and computer operators, and other sections of a business need to coordinate their work even when they seldom see each other face to face.

Some economic processes require shift work. It may be necessary to keep steel furnaces operating twenty-four hours a day. Some machines may be too expensive to run only forty hours a week. Operating one expensive or exotic press for twenty-four hours six or seven days a week then requires shift work for many others in related functions. Some services such as fire or police protection must operate day and night. The timetable of most workers is not flexible; they must schedule all their lives to meet the rigid requirements of their jobs. With most new jobs in services such as health care and retailing, more and more employment requires some to be at work weekends and evenings. Further, such jobs are disproportionately held by women.

The old single-shift factory schedule, however, is still the basis of the overall societal timetable. Public schools, restaurants, public transportation, human services, and public recreation for the most part open up in the morning either between eight and nine o'clock or at a time coordinated to serve those who do begin work then. The same is true in the afternoon and evening in which noon lunch, 6 P.M. dinner, and evening events in the community presuppose the "normal" work schedule. Five evenings a week we are conscious that we should be in bed at an hour that will allow us to "get up and get to work in the morning."

---

[9] John R. Kelly, *Peoria Winter: Styles and Resources in Later Life* (Lexington, MA: Lexington Books, 1987).

Robert Blauner proposed that although work may not be central to the interests and values of most modern Americans, it is still central to their time and energy.[10] Meeting employment schedules, recuperating from work demands, and preparing for the next day on the job are a regular part of the lives of most adults. The requirements of the job take priority even for those who are primarily interested in the paycheck.

David Riesman added that not only does the old industrial schedule still shape the society's timetable, but the work world also is the basis of the general timing structure of individual lives.[11] Even those with considerable freedom to determine the hours they work still order their priorities with work responsibilities at the center of their decision process. So much of the rest of life is structured around work that leisure and family events may be seen as punctuations or highlights in a work-ordered life. The work-maintenance-leisure rhythm of life is dominated by work time even when the job is found quite unsatisfying.

With over half of employment now in the service sector, which includes retailing, schedules are increasingly varied. Weekends, evenings, and even twenty-four-hour operations require employees to be on the job at all sorts of hours. Fewer and fewer workers are on Monday through Friday nine-to-five schedules. As a consequence, services and opportunities for nonwork activity are also being rescheduled into periods formerly reserved for work or sleep. For employed women, irregular employment schedules are often combined with the conflicting demands of the "second shift" at home.

The Myth of the Declining Workweek

A decade or so ago it was the "common wisdom" of leisure studies that the long-term decline of the average workweek would continue. Predictions of thirty-two-hour and fourday workweeks abounded in both popular and scholarly literature. The presumed consequence was that people would have so much more free time that demands on leisure services would be overwhelming. It was predicted that leisure would be the major growth industry. Some, who were uneasy about common people having more time to do what they wanted, referred to the "problem of leisure." For some, the increased nonwork time that was predicted was seen as a personal opportunity; for those concerned about moralism and order it was seen as a social problem; and for recreation professionals it was seen as a challenge.

The Case for Less Work

Part of the argument between those who forecast a decline in work hours and those who do not is a matter of time perspective. When the early sweatshop hours were soon reduced from eighty to seventy hours a week, the reduction was only the beginning of a long trend. Estimates of average weekly hours of employment in all industries in the United States are seventy in 1850, sixty-five in 1870, sixty-two in 1890, fifty-five in 1910, and forty-five in 1930—a 35 percent reduction in eighty years.[12] A continuation of that proportional trend

---

[10] Robert Blauner, *Alienation and Freedom: The Factory Worker and His Industry* (Chicago: University of Chicago Press, 1964), p. 183.

[11] David Riesman, "Leisure and Work in Postindustriral Society," in E. Larrabee and R. Meyersohn, eds., *Mass Leisure* (New York: Free Press, 1958).

[12] Sebastian deGrazia, *Of Time, Work, and Leisure* (Garden City, NY: Doubleday, 1964), p. 419.

would bring us to forty-two hours by 1950, forty by 1970, and thirty-seven by 2000. If, on the other hand, the steady rate of a five-hour reduction every two decades were to continue from 1930, the average would be forty hours by 1950, thirty-five by 1970, and thirty or less by 2000.

Another aspect of the predicted increase in nonwork time is related to life expectancy. Life expectations after age fourteen have increased by more than ten years for men since 1900 and by more than sixteen years for women. That increase yields more than twelve years outside the labor force for most men and seventeen years for women employed to age sixty-five. As the population bulge of the post-World War II babies moves into retirement, the total nonwork hours available to adults will take a marked, if temporary, leap after 2010. Changes in retirement age in either direction will alter that retirement leisure projection. Current indications are that retirement between ages 55 and 60, voluntary or involuntary, is increasing, especially for males.

Other projections are based on the changing nature of work. Production industries and offices are being invaded by the computer. As automated assembly, accounting, and record-keeping machines are replacing many assembly-line hands, office bookkeepers, and clerks, drastic reductions in those segments of the work force have been predicted. Estimates are that it would be technologically possible to replace 70 to 90 percent of workers in some factories and offices through automation. The issue is between what is technologically possible and what is economically and socially feasible. We do not do everything that is possible technologically. Thus far, the predictions of mass technological unemployment have not come true. However, selective unemployment in some industries due to market pressures for cost efficiency is very much a part of the current employment picture.

The entire Western world is undergoing far-reaching economic change. In what is now truly a world economy rather than a collection of national economies, significant shifts are taking place. Labor-intensive production is being moved to low-cost locations. Formerly strong industries are unable to meet international competition and are being phased out in countries where they had been central to the economic structure. The result is massive unemployment in formerly prosperous areas. Rather than a reduction in average employment hours, the pattern is one of selective unemployment with little change in the work schedules of those who are employed.

The Case for Stability

The main argument against an increase in nonwork time is based on the recent leveling off of the decline in work hours. The U.S. Department of Labor reports a reduction at a declining rate. The average workweek was down to forty-four hours in 1940 and then jumped to forty-six hours due to the pressures of World War II production. Since that war, the average was a little under forty-two hours average in the 1950s, forty and one-half hours in the 1960s, and just about forty hours in the 1970s and 1980s. The slight decrease is due more to timetable changes than reductions in the hours worked most weeks. Paid vacations and holidays have increased along with the number of workers in services whose hours do not total forty for all weeks.

The "average weekly hours" figure is probably more misleading than revealing in any case. While nine out of ten men age twenty-five to fifty-four are in the work force, the rate falls to fewer than three out of four of those age fifty-five to sixty-four. More workers are being retired, by choice or fiat, before reaching the age of sixty-five. Industrial shifts in the world economy have led to more men and women of traditional employment age being out of the labor force. Only an analysis that examined work schedules for both men and women in different economic sectors would give an accurate picture of the changes of the last decades. Overall averages obscure the real changes that are taking place.

For example, most women—married or single, childless or mothers—are now in the paid work force. Conversely, there are fewer employment opportunities for men to take second or "moonlighting" jobs. The second income for most households is now gained from the employment of women. This results in men having somewhat more time outside employment and women having considerably less. Further, as already indicated, those jobs are more and more likely to be in services that maintain long hours of operation and require irregular work schedules. All growth in employment since 1960 has been in services such as government, education, health care, retailing, finance, and recreation rather than in production. Precisely the jobs that require the longest hours are those that now employ most American workers. There is considerable evidence that workers most crucial to productivity are actually working longer hours.[13] This trend, however, is partly balanced by the shift to temporary and part-time employees, especially in retailing and some offices.

Also, the long hours of those professionals, managers, and technical personnel who carry high responsibilities and have a career orientation of expected advancement are unlikely to decline. On the one hand, there are replaceable workers in jobs that require little special preparation or skill whose hours are irregular but may be limited by corporate aims to keep wages and benefit costs low. On the other hand, there are workers with hard-to-replace technical skills who may be pressured to work longer hours for employers striving for a competitive edge in the world markets. The outcome is likely to be considerable variation in workweeks with some production industries remaining stable, some professionals and managers working longer hours, some replaceables being limited to irregular timetables, and many having periods of unemployment ending with early retirement.

Other Recent Changes

Although overall unemployment rates in the United States vary with the economy—high in periods of recession and lower in times of prosperity—a current pattern is one of localization of unemployment. When a dominant industry in a city or region is unable to compete in world markets, its cutback or closure produces very high rates of local unemployment. Again, the average unemployment rates for the country or even for a state or region may obscure virtual collapses of the economic structure of a particular mill town.

Perhaps even more serious is the concentration of joblessness among inner-city youth.[14] Jobless rates of 50 to 80 percent are found among those out of school and under the age of twenty-five in many American cities. The underlying problem is that the former employment opportunities in those areas have moved out of the inner cities, leaving behind

---

[13] Juliet B. Schor, *The Overworked American* (New York: Basic Books, 1992).

[14] William J. Wilson, *The Truly Disadvantaged: The Inner City, the Underclass, and Public Policy* (Chicago: University of Chicago Press, 1987).

populations, largely black and Hispanic, who are cut off from most opportunities. Just at the age when most younger people are finishing school and getting started in work roles, a growing segment of the population is prevented from finding even entry-level employment with any stability and future.

The other two major contemporary trends in employment have already been introduced. The first is the shift toward service sector employment. With all the increase in jobs in services and job losses in production not balanced by opportunities in newer industries such as electronics, productivity in the remaining industries must increase enough to support the greater proportion of workers in services.

The second trend is related to the first. The growth in service employment has been one factor in the increase of women in the work force. This trend is long term.[15] Female employment has increased from 15 percent of women age twenty-five to forty-four in 1890 to 60 percent in 1980. The trend is also related to such factors as the rising divorce rate and the need for more women to be self-supporting. Greater attention to opportunities for women in the women's movement has been concurrent with increased requirements for women's income to support households and with shifts in the kinds of employment available.

Projections for households headed by two adults are that dual incomes have risen from 45 percent in 1980 to 65 percent in 1990 and more than 80 percent by the turn of the century. This change will have great impacts on the distribution of discretionary time in the society. Insofar as women continue to have primary responsibility for child rearing and the home, their discretionary time will be reduced. Currently, the population group with the least leisure time is the employed woman single parent followed by women parents in dual income households. The trend is toward time scarcity rather than increase for many.

Time diary research in the 1960s and 1970s has indicated some redistribution of time away from family care and toward "free time."[16] This was due to the trend toward smaller families and a shortening of the parenting period in the life course. Families are having fewer children closer together. Therefore, the period of extreme demand before children enter school is shorter for most families. This trend may in part mitigate the greater likelihood that mothers of preschool children are in the work force with greatly constrained schedules. There may also be a change in values that has brought people to give priority to time for leisure. Duties related to home and family may be compressed to allow for more opportunity for satisfying activity.

Is time a scarce resource? Increases in television watching suggest a reallocation would solve the problem for many. Others, however, experience pressures at the workplace and at home. Further, success in world markets may put even more pressure on workers most critical to productivity. Juliet Schor argues that capitalism produces such a stress on work and work hours.[17]

There is also the issue of time for consumption. A Swedish economist, Steffan B. Linder, has argued that ours is a "time-famine culture.[18] The great shortage for the affluent middle and upper class who are now the new "leisure class" in Western culture is time

---

[15] Victor R. Fuchs, *How We Live: An Economic Perspective on Americans from Birth to Death* (Cambridge, MA: Harvard University Press, 1983).

[16] John P. Robinson, "Time for Work," *American Demographics* (April 1989), 68–70.

[17] Juliet B. Schor. *The Overworked American,* ibid.

[18] Steffan B. Linder, *The Harried Leisure Class* (New York: Columbia University Press, 1969).

rather than money. The really scarce resource is time to do what one wants to do. Considerable research has found that those who would like to do more of a favorite leisure activity find the major shortage to be time rather than money. As a consequence, in leisure as in work, there is pressure to get as much done as possible in the time available. Leisure may become less "leisurely" as people try to pack as much experience, activity, and enjoyment as possible into the scarce time. Recreation equipment and programs and vacation packages that promise the most leisure experience for the least time investment prosper as people are ready to trade more of their consumer dollars for a promised saving in time.

Add to this a possible rediscovery of leisure consumption as status symbolism. Thorstein Veblen proposed that at the end of the nineteenth century it was the conspicuous consumption of leisure that distinguished the upper class.[19] Today it may be that boat, second home, recreation vehicle in the driveway, vacation trip to Europe, or lavish entertainment that yields community status in the suburb which most people leave when they work and where homes look very much alike. Leisure consumption may symbolize having more than enough to get by in a world where cars, houses, and jobs tend to be almost indistinguishable.

Finally, employment is beginning to be rescheduled to provide larger blocks of time for leisure. Three-day weekends and four-day workweeks allow for activities that require longer periods of time for travel or preparation. Workers seem to prefer having more of their free time gathered in such blocks on weekends and in longer vacations to shortening the workday. The higher value being placed on leisure activities that require some considerable investment of time is suggested in the preferences.

Such shifts in time use, schedule preferences, and values indicate that leisure may increasingly be a factor in determining the social timetable rather than being residual. If so, then knowing the averages of hours spent on the job and maintenance will not tell us much about leisure. Leisure may be a priority that shapes the work and family schedule as more people order their lives to maximize those opportunities to do what they find most satisfying.

Does Work Determine Leisure?

As suggested at the beginning of the chapter, there have been many stereotypes that describe the alleged determination of leisure by work. In some cases the relationship has been seen as very simple and direct. For example, men in high-status jobs would be expected to join country clubs and play games like golf and tennis considered appropriate to that status. They would drink Scotch in the best private clubs, send their children to private schools, and take vacations in exclusive resorts or long trips abroad. On the other hand, the greasy-handed mill worker would be expected to join his buddies at a neighborhood bar, bowl and play cards, drink Blue Ribbon from the bottle, enforce obedience in his family, and grudgingly drive to visit relatives for a week in the summer.

Even if the stereotypes have often been accurate, they have offered no explanations. In general, the opportunities, resources, educational background, and associations are so different for those with "old wealth" and those drawing an hourly wage in an old factory that no direct relationship between the nature of work and the nature of leisure can be demonstrated. However, a number of models have been proposed to attempt just that.

[19] Thorstein Veblen, *The Theory of the Leisure Class,* Second edition (New York: New American Library, 1953).

The process goes back to Veblen's conspicuous consumption, to the studies of "Middletown"[20] and other communities that found that leisure styles are partly based on status groups, and even to the concern of Karl Marx and Friedrich Engels for the Saturday night explosion of the factory worker in the early industrial period. More recently, Harold Wilensky proposed that for those with higher satisfaction in their work, leisure may be a "spillover" in skills, interests, and associations. On the other hand, those highly constrained in their employment may seek an escape in leisure that is a "compensation" for work limitations.[21]

Various attempts have been made to validate and refine Wilensky's model. One study found some spillover in intellectuality and complexity from job to leisure when controlling for possible intervening factors.[22] Another study discovered that although difference or escape from work conditions was seldom cited as a primary reason for selecting leisure activities, it was a secondary factor in choosing up to 25 percent of activities among Wisconsin adults.[23] This supports the commonsense understanding that some who work indoors want leisure outdoors, some who get little exercise on the job want to be active, some who are very tired from their jobs want rest, and some who take orders all day prefer to have some activities that are under their own control. On the other hand, a scholar may choose more reading, a musician more music, and a toolmaker handwork on a home lathe. It is largely a matter of remembered and anticipated satisfaction. Both spillover and compensation exist, but only as one element in the leisure decision process and usually not the primary element.

Stanley Parker developed a model that begins with relative freedom and constraint as the critical dimension of understanding the work-leisure relationship.[24] At the high constraint end of the continuum are work and meeting physiological needs, while at the high freedom end is leisure, whether it takes place in work or nonwork time. In between are various work and nonwork obligations that need to be done at some time and in some way but that are not rigidly prescribed.

Parker goes on to propose three types of relationship between leisure and work. The first, *identity,* describes a relationship in which the meanings, forms, associations, and satisfactions of work and leisure are the same. At the other extreme is a *contrast* between work and leisure in which leisure is different in order to make up for the deficiencies of work. The third possibility is that the two are essentially unrelated. It is a *separateness* that describes minimal contact or influence and in which each is an arena of life with its own integrity.

This model provides another approach to variety. No simple explanation of work determination of leisure is seen as adequate. Rather, for some, work and career are primary and all the rest of life is ordered to contribute to or at least not interfere with that career. For some at the other extreme, devotion to a leisure style or enterprise is so consuming that it becomes the central interest in life and takes priority in scheduling, relationships,

[20] Robert Lynd and H. Lynd, *Middletown* (New York: Harcourt Brace Jovanovich, 1956).

[21] Harold Wilensky, "Work, Careers, and Social Integration," *International Social Science Journal,* 12 (1960), 543–560.

[22] Karen Miller and M. Kohn, "The Reciprocal Effects of Job Conditions and Leisure-Time Activities," paper presented at the Tenth World Congress of Sociology, Mexico City, 1982.

[23] John R. Kelly, "Leisure as Compensation for Work Constraint," *Society and Leisure,* 8, 3 (1976), 73–82.

[24] Stanley R. Parker, *Future of Work and Leisure* (New York: Praeger, 1971).

and values. However, for most people nonwork is one life space in which they find enduring and valued satisfactions, relationships, and enjoyment. Nevertheless, there is some satisfaction, intrinsic and extrinsic, in work just as there is some obligation in home and family. In fact, a clear division of work and leisure may not represent the reality of many lives at all, especially for those whose productive activity is not limited to the workplace.

Dualism, Holism, or Pluralism?

From one perspective the issue is whether we are optimistic about work *and* leisure, pessimistic about work and optimistic about leisure, or have mixed evaluations of both.

The *holistic* perspective has been proposed by James Murphy and others who see meaning and satisfaction in both work and leisure.[25] The holistic model cannot separate the two activities because there is human fulfillment to be found in each. The freedom, relationships, and satisfactions that develop and express our humanity cannot be allocated exclusively to either work or leisure time. Rather, each may be designed and developed to maximize the realization of the fullest human values. Therefore, the holistic model tends to be optimistic about the integration of life through the humane ordering of both work and leisure in a unified human life space.

On the other hand, the *dualistic* perspective is pessimistic about most work and finds attempts to enrich the meaning of work for the worker to be dangerously naive. According to those who take this point of view, much work that has to be done is routine, dull, and personally unrewarding. While every effort should be made to improve work conditions and satisfactions, the effort will not turn every clerk into a free professional. Rather, the "leisure solution to work" is proposed in which the two are seen as separate and leisure as that life space in which personal satisfaction, fulfillment, meaning, expression, and humane relationships can be maximized. Intrinsic satisfaction will be centered in the leisure-family world for most adults and work will have largely extrinsic meaning. This pessimism about work recognizes that there may be occasions of leisure and enjoyment on the job, but finds overall work conditions too constraining to be generally satisfying.

A third approach, the *pluralistic,* tends to agree with some elements in the other two, but finds each too one-sided. Certainly there is leisure to be found on the job in conversations, friendships, accomplishments, and even daydreaming. On the other hand, the requirements of most employment severely limit any intrinsic satisfaction to be found *in* the work itself. Evaluation, cost efficiency, routinization, supervision, the dominance of the machine—mechanical or electronic—and the sheer drudgery of repetition even in human services place limits on finding the central meaning of life in most employment.

Further, leisure is not some kind of one-dimensional area of activity that can be packaged, neatly characterized, determined, or even accurately predicted. One person will decide to devote almost all time and energy to one consuming passion, be it rockhounding, choral music, or motorcycle racing; another from the same office and community will choose a wide variety of indoor and outdoor activities that change with the seasons and op-

[25] James Murphy, *Recreation and Leisure Service* (Dubuque, IA: Wm. C. Brown, 1975).

portunities. One family will drive all night to the ski slopes while a stack of skis gathers dust in their neighbor's basement.

Some of the meanings and satisfactions that are associated with leisure may be found in work as well. For example, a mastery and accomplishment associated with an art or sport, self-enhancement, personal growth, self-expression, physical activity, a sense of belonging or being of service, and even excitement are present in some leisure and some work. Even though the work and leisure locales are separated in most urban settings, some of the same satisfactions are possible.

Therefore, it may be most accurate to understand the relation of leisure to work, family, and community as neither holistic nor dualistic. Rather, leisure is pluralistic in its varied and combined meanings, its forms, its locales, and, to a lesser extent, its associations. Leisure's many forms and orientations are not determined wholly by any other institutional position—in work, education, family, or religion.

Pluralism implies variety without complete separation, multiple forms and meanings without necessary conflict, and real choice without chaotic unpredictability. Pluralism accepts the social, cultural, and environmental contexts of leisure that limit and shape participation, but still allows for a rich variety of outward expressions and inward satisfactions. Holism tends to lose sight of what is distinctive about leisure—its freedom and intrinsically nonproductive aims. Dualism cuts leisure off from social fabric meanings and relationships and may lead to a definition of leisure as simply feelings of pleasure. Pluralism, on the other hand, implies a variety of opportunity and meaning that is necessary for leisure to retain its defining dimension of freedom.

Time, Income, and Leisure Values

It is increasingly evident that we cannot deal with the relationship between work and leisure only in terms of time. While average workweeks, industrial schedules, requirements of getting to and from the job in today's decentralized city, and the effects of unemployment on leisure are all important, the values and priorities of those who engage in both work and leisure may be more important. To understand work and leisure today or to predict the future requires some knowledge of the meanings of work and leisure to people.

One issue in addition to those already sketched is the relative priority of time and income. Another related issue is possible conflict or consensus in work and leisure values.

The Time-Income Trade-Off

If those who describe ours as a "time-famine culture" are correct, then the scarcity of time should make it more valuable. Economists have suggested that in general most people will give up free time for the income rewards of longer work hours. However, there is a point at which the value of the income declines because there is not enough time remaining to use it. Therefore, as time becomes more scarce and income more abundant, time becomes more valued.

That point of income saturation has not been reached by many, especially in a consumption-oriented society. Affluence in the sense of having more than enough for everything important to a household is hardly a widespread condition in any industrial society. Yet there may be a change on the horizon.

That change is not due to universal abundance. Most of the world is still quite poor. The change is among those with enough material security to begin to redefine their priorities. The change may be reflected in new patterns of time as well as financial allocation. Placing a high value on one or more aspects of leisure—exercise, sport, the arts, travel, or intimate social involvement—can reshape the social timetable to give priority to time for leisure.[26]

The change may also be reflected in economic allocations. A family may decide that they have enough of the goods of the world. A bigger house, third car, or even expensive leisure toys may be seen as of less value than more time for fulfilling activity and relationships. The choice may even be for lower fixed obligations that yield greater discretion over time and energy. The trade-off still operates. However, the saturation effect of lacking time for further consumption in the old model may be replaced by the value choices of many who decide that nonconsumption leisure is more important than a bigger house, a new stock issue, or even an expensive ski trip to Austria.

If leisure is defined as doing, relating, and responding rather than consuming, then income is less necessary for leisure. How much house is needed to entertain? It depends on how and whom we entertain. How much equipment is needed to spend a week in the mountains? It depends on our style of travel and camping. How much does friendship cost? It depends on how we define the relationship.

For many, employment will continue to be instrumental. These people will work under conditions of constraint for enough security and financial resources to develop their life style. Insofar as that life style emphasizes freedom, expression, the love of family and friends, and a communion with the environment—the values of a humanistic leisure ethic—then work may be less rather than more central for many people.

There are just so many built-in conflicts that the integration of work and leisure seems difficult for most people. How can we reconcile a switch to nonconsumptive life styles with our dependence on automobiles to get to work, to a food supplier, or to the outdoors? How can we reconcile the idea of leisure as community with those close to us with the increased costs of housing, education, and everything else that families seem to require for full (but not luxurious) living? How can we reconcile pursuit of personal fulfillment in employment with the fundamental lack of freedom to shape work conditions?

If leisure is freedom, then is it not likely to be more a carving out of some life space in which to do as we please than an integration of all the major elements of life—work, community, and leisure? The union of work and leisure in an ethic of human fulfillment is surely worth retaining as a dream for all and a goal for a fortunate few. But it is neither realistic nor helpful to degrade those who have to settle for real leisure and community here and there rather than everywhere. They need help to maximize both their opportunities and their satisfaction in what is possible for them. Leisure is freedom; but it is also actual experience, not just a utopian dream.

[26] Fred Best, P. Bosserman, and B. Stern, "Income—Free Time Trade-off Preferences of U.S. Workers," *Leisure Sciences,* 2 (1979), 119–142.

Summary of Issues

The differences in the meaning of work and leisure are not found in where or when they occur. Free, expressive, and relational activity does happen during the week and at the office or factory. Socially valuable and productive activity and interchange can take place on Sunday afternoon in the home or yard. In fact, both leisure and work are often mixed together at the shopping center on Saturday or the summer trip to the lake. Further, the form of much leisure is worklike, and quiet contemplation may prove extremely productive.

On the other hand, schedule and geographic separation of the workplace from the home and from leisure locales have tended to yield a fragmented view of life. The parallel satisfactions found in activity that is defined as socially useful and productive and activity that is enjoyed strictly for its own sake have often been obscured by separation of employment from the rest of life.

The anticipated "leisure age," in which employment hours are further reduced, has not arrived on schedule. One factor is a complex of economic changes related to service employment, the world market, women in the labor force, and the relation of production to prices and resources. Also, the consequences of technological developments in communications, information processing, and energy are yet to be worked out. The influence of the economic sector of the society on leisure and the family has remained significant in setting the structure of social timetables and urban ecology. To assert that work is distinct from leisure does not suggest that they are unrelated or that leisure does not still have an economic base.

Further, the complex factors in trade-off decisions between time and income suggest that work and leisure are neither unified nor separate, but retain a pluralistic relationship of mutual influence and limitation.

HIGHLIGHTS

1. Both work and leisure may yield intrinsic and social satisfactions important to a full life. The difference is that work is socially necessary productivity while leisure may be an end in itself.
2. Although most employment has primarily extrinsic meaning for workers, the work schedule and social identification are significant factors in shaping life patterns.
3. Average workweek hours seem to have leveled off. However, employment schedules are more varied, especially for service workers; and unemployment is a serious problem, especially in the inner city.
4. The trade-off between income and time reflects both personal economic goals for housing and family and also the desire for more time free for leisure.
5. Work and leisure are neither opposite nor fused in meaning, but have a pluralistic relationship that incorporates variety in meaning and contexts as well as mutual influences and multiple links.

Discussion Questions

1. In your experience, are occupational stereotypes about leisure behavior common? Is the leisure of managers and professionals more creative and expressive than that of factory hands and clerks? Why?

2. Is real work necessary for a fulfilling life? Real leisure? Can one substitute for the other?

3. Is unpaid work less valued than paid? Why? Is it because so much unpaid work is done by women?

4. What evidence is there for a continuation of a work ethic among Americans? Of changes toward a "leisure ethic"? Of value-orientations that are neither leisure- nor work-oriented?

5. In the next decade, is work for most people likely to become more free and satisfying? Why or why not?

6. Does a shorter workweek necessarily mean more time for leisure? For whom? If not, why not?

7. Which of Parker's models of the work-leisure relationship best describes people you know? Give examples.

8. Which view of work and leisure is most realistic—holism, dualism, or pluralism?

9. What evidence is there of a greater tendency to trade income for time? What factors are emerging that are likely to keep many workers choosing income rather than free time?

Bibliography

Braverman, Harry, *Labor and Monopoly Capital.* New York: Monthly Review of Books, 1974.

Clarke, John, and Chas Critcher, *The Devil Makes Work: Leisure in Capitalist Britain.* Champaign: University of Illinois Press, 1985.

Erikson, Kai and S. Vallas, eds., *The Nature of Work.* New Haven, CT: Yale University Press, 1990.

Kelly, John R. and Geoffrey Godbey, *The Sociology of Leisure.* College Park, PA: Venture Publishing, 1992.

Levitan, Sar, and W. Johnson, *Work Is Here to Stay, Alas.* Salt Lake City, UT: Olympus, 1973.

Linder, Steffan, *The Harried Leisure Class.* New York: Columbia University Press, 1969.

MacKenzie, Gavin, *The Aristocracy of Labor: Skilled Craftsmen in the American Class Structure.* New York: Columbia University Press, 1973.

Parker, Stanley, *The Future of Work and Leisure.* New York: Praeger, 1971.

Parker, Stanley, *Leisure and Work.* London: Allen and Unwin, 1983.

Rubin, Lillian, *Worlds of Pain: Life in the Working Class Family.* New York: Basic Books, 1976.

Schor, Juliet B. *The Overworked American.* New York: Basic Books, 1992.

Sennett, Richard, and J. Cobb, *The Hidden Injuries of Class.* New York: Knopf, 1972.

Smigal, Erwin, ed., *Work and Leisure.* New Haven, CT: College and University Press, 1963.

Veblen, Thorstein, *The Theory of the Leisure Class,* Second edition. New York: New American Library, 1953.

Zuzanek, Jiri, and R. Mannell, "Work-Leisure Relationships from a Sociological and Social Psychological Perspective," *Leisure Studies,* 2 (1983), 327–344.

Leisure: Past and Future

If leisure is a human phenomenon, then it should be found in all human cultures and societies. We would not expect to find organized recreation in simple and highly integrated societies. However, leisure and play in the nature of freedom, expression, change, and personal bonding would be part of the lives of children and adults in any time and place. The forms and types of activity might be very dissimilar, but their meanings would be profoundly human.

By examining leisure in the various forms it has taken in different times, places, and cultures, we may be able to sort out some of the enduring meanings. It is, of course, impossible to encompass the full history of leisure in Western civilization in four chapters. Thus, the chapters that follow present sketches in the history and philosophy of leisure chosen on the basis of contemporary relevance.

Our approach is to deal with ideas and practices in their historical contexts rather than to separate history and philosophy and to answer such questions as

What are the recurrent issues in the relationship of leisure to its cultural and historical setting?

What themes of leisure philosophy are persistent through history?

What historical developments have been critical in shaping leisure in our time and place?

No claim is made for completeness. The bibliographies, however, do suggest some of the increasing number of historical studies of leisure and common life.

Nevertheless, a number of issues and ideas with long histories are very much alive today. Introducing them in the context of other epochs will, it is hoped, enable us to understand them as something more than passing fads.

Then there is the future. Analysis of themes and trends in the past leads past the present to the future. As the social, economic, political, and cultural dimensions of society change, what can be expected for leisure? Will dramatic changes overcome the continuities, or will stability outweigh the forces of change? The past is prologue and a new century begins.

Chapter 8

The Ancient Heritage

Civilizations have not all developed at the same rate. A simple culture with the mobility required to hunt small game for food may be found in a jungle enclave at the same time that the people of North America and Europe are exploring the meaning of the postindustrial age. Relatively sophisticated cultures developed in China and the Nile Valley while the ancestors of the current postindustrial Europeans were wearing skins and fighting tribal wars with clubs and spears. There is no way that a world chronology of cultures can be presented that highlights the place of leisure in each. Development has not been synchronized, continuous, or even-paced. Change has come slowly and gradually as well as quickly and cataclysmically. Some sophisticated cultures have risen and disappeared while others have left their mark on succeeding peoples.

Neither are we now as sure as we once were that large and complex cultures are really more "advanced" than simpler social groups. The ideas that progress has only one direction and that material goods can define the success of a social system are under considerable attack.

What we do know is that leisure is profoundly cultural. That is, leisure takes the forms and meanings appropriate to its social setting. Leisure varies from one historical setting to another in resources, value systems, and spirit just as it varies from one climate to another. Therefore, to understand leisure it is necessary to do a kind of mental balancing act: with one hand grasping the cultural materials of a particular time and place and the other reaching for the meanings that transcend the culture and persist from one setting to another.

In this chapter, we begin by sketching some generalities about simple or "primitive" societies and about the more complex but still preindustrial societies of Western civilization. The generalizations provide a base from which to launch more concentrated, if still superficial, analyses of leisure in the ancient Greek and Roman states. Subsequent chapters follow some of the themes through major transitions in European history, antecedents of New World culture, and major epochs of North American development.

ISSUES

Is there a human phenomenon, "leisure," that has existed in some form in all cultures, both pre- and postindustrial?

How can the forms of leisure be quite different in cultures with different value systems, histories, and economic conditions?

What are the philosophical roots of understanding leisure as freedom and intrinsic meaning?

Can the freedom of leisure become a political instrument of tyranny and control?

Are religion and leisure always in conflict?

Is there a fundamental antileisure bias in the Judeo-Christian religious heritage?

Leisure in Simple Cultures

Since all simple cultures have not developed into complex ones, the progression to modernity suggested by the term *primitive* may be misleading. Nevertheless, many social groups have been identified that are small and have relatively little social organization or differentiation. Those studied in the last half century have usually been secluded on islands or in isolated valleys, forests, or deserts.

Such simple cultures are not all alike. After all, some are in very cold or arid regions. The romanticism of ascribing trust, joy, cooperation, and health to such a group tends also to place them on warm islands with abundant fruit and sparkling beaches. In fact, one of the main issues in understanding leisure in such societies revolves around the relative abundance or scarcity of resources. The entire social shape of a group confident of having ample food and shelter is quite different from one always aware of the possibility of famine and death. "Primitive" does not always mean well-fed, warm, and colorful. It refers to Africa's Sahil desert as well as to the legendary South Sea Islands.

Four issues illustrate the basic fact that leisure is deeply a part of the particular cultural and economic structure of the society.

Work and Leisure

In simple social systems, the separation of work and leisure that is characteristic of industrial societies is almost totally lacking. *Modern* means complex and differentiated. In a simple society, life appears to flow without clear boundaries among such activities as production of goods, family life, child rearing, music and dance, affective expression of relationships, and maintenance of social order. In the primary or "face-to-face" community, life seems relatively seamless or undifferentiated.

Margaret Mead's description of a day in Samoa gives an overall impression of tidal ebb and flow as opposed to separated segments of life.[1] Adults and children gather, enter into the work and play that custom has assigned them, and in time retreat before the hot

---

[1] Margaret Mead, *Coming of Age in Samoa* (New York: Morrow, 1928), chap. 2.

sun. In the early evening the community begins to gather again, the fishermen return from the sea, and the activity flows into eating, drinking, circle games for children, courting, community councils, plans for tomorrow, and often music and dancing. Expectations for males and females are related to their age and capabilities. Some do hard work such as fishing all day in the hot sun. Special occasions of festivity and community celebrate some aspects of life together. But time is a matter of the rhythm of climate, harvest, and mythology rather than the clock and the calendar.

There is a kind of rhythmic flow of life in which elements of the necessity we call work and the freedom we call leisure are integrated rather than segmented. In time, place, mode of behavior, companions, and even mood, the clear divisions between work and play, home and workplace, duty and choice almost disappear. There is still necessity. Social requirements for behavior in a simple society may be pervasive and minute. Independence gained from privacy or anonymity are unknown. Life is regulated, but not segregated.

An Economic Base

The economic base of such social integration may create great contrasts. For example, the Pygmies of Africa's Ituri forest were found to have an integrated life similar to that of the Samoans despite the differences in food harvesting and locale.[2] However, Colin Turnbull found on the same continent among the Ik of Uganda a simple people who seemed apathetic, joyless, conflict-ridden, and almost without the "human" qualities that maintain community.[3] The evident difference is that the Samoans and Pygmies live in at least relative abundance. The Ik, on the other hand, are always on the edge of starvation. Their life is not segmented, but neither does it contain the expressiveness, joy, and sense of community we associate with simplicity. Survival is all-encompassing. Freedom to engage in anything for its own sake seems meaningless.

The unity of family, workplace, residence, and community means quite different things for the stable Samoans and the mobile Pygmies. But the differences between them are nothing when compared to the breakdown of community in a Sahil famine or the total preoccupation with individual survival among the Ik. Here an issue is raised that will recur: What kind of economic base is necessary for leisure? In a simple society, no matter how much it is integrated into the social fabric of the community, leisure would appear to require at least the relative abundance that permits looking beyond the next mouthful and the next day. The economic base has to be adequate to allow for some choice, some relaxation of necessity, and some of the sharing of community.

Leisure as Culture

We have already suggested that the variety of forms that leisure may take in modern society is almost infinite. Within simpler cultures, that variety is considerably limited both by available resources and by the culture itself. However, among such cultures, leisure is highly varied. The reason is not hard to discover. Leisure is so much a part of the culture that the same integration that may be exalted from one perspective becomes a narrowing

[2] Colin Turnbull, *The Forest People* (New York: Simon & Schuster, 1962).

[3] Colin Turnbull, *The Mountain People* (New York: Simon & Schuster, 1972).

factor from another. Simple societies do not tend to allow for a great deal of individual difference in values, beliefs, or practices.

This narrowness is illustrated by the relationship between sex roles and leisure in three
cultures. Margaret Mead studied three peoples in New Guinea and found great contrasts in
the kind of behavior acceptable for males and females.[4] Among the mountain dwelling
Arapesh both males and females are expected to be passive, cooperative, peaceful, and
nourishing. Games and cultural celebrations are appropriate to these roles. Less than 100
miles away are the Mundugumol, where for both males and females the role ideal is sexually aggressive, belligerent, and competitive. Games tend to be violent and to mirror the
fighting basis of the culture. The third group, the Tchambuli, have quite different expectations for males and for females. The males, with their delicate hairdos and ornamental apparel, live mainly for their art, dancing, flute playing, and creating costumes. Females, on
the other hand, are practical, efficient, dominating, and sexually aggressive. Games are segregated and appropriate to the roles.

The point is that such a central part of the culture as the role taking expected of each
sex has a dramatic effect on leisure. Aggressive roles lead to competitive activities, whereas
roles of passivity and expressiveness lead to activities of display and artistic development.
Just as children's games in any society tend to prepare them for later adult roles, so the
play of adults is very much a part of the whole cultural system. Note that, as a consequence,
the kind of games and activities we tend to associate with males or females may be reversed in a culture with sex-role expectations quite different from ours.

Leisure and War

Another theme that recurs through history is the relationship of leisure and war. In simple
and complex cultures, games are often the shadow of warfare. Games like the form of
lacrosse played by North American Choctaws were not only practice for battle but a means
of testing and preparation for the next war. Cross-cultural studies of various tribes and cultures have produced an almost limitless series of games that are warlike in their form and
implements and that have manifest training functions. Games in such cultures are much
more than dancing and gentle music; they may be harsh, cruel, and fierce.

In general, then, such glances at simple societies reveal that leisure in many forms does
exist among those not on the brink of extinction. Further, leisure as the freedom in behavior—whether in separate times and places or woven into the everyday fabric of life—expresses the values of the culture for both individuals and the community. Leisure is, then,
highly ethnic. Its forms are related to the food, family practices, religion, sex, war, socialization, stratification, fashion, and most of all, the economic base of the culture.

Preindustrial Societies

Most societies, both historical and prehistorical, have been "preindustrial" in the usual
sense of the term. They have not made the transition from an agricultural base and the re-

---

[4] Margaret Mead, *Sex and Temperament in Three Primitive Societies* (New York: Dell, 1968).

lated dispersal of population to a machine-based productive economy with the population drawn into cities by the joining of power and materials in the factory. Even today some economies are being industrialized while at the same time Europe and North America are being called "postindustrial."

Looking back in European and American history, the Industrial Revolution appears to have been the great change that created the urban society in which we now live. In focusing on our relatively recent industrialization, we may lose sight of the fact that most of the social epochs leading to our own are preindustrial. The nomadic culture of early Jewish history, the imperialistic empire of Rome, the Greek city-states, the Florence of the Medicis, Luther's Germany and Calvin's Geneva, Shakespeare's England, and colonial America were all preindustrial.

The issue to be addressed in general before looking at those particular times and places is this: Are preindustrial societies different from industrial societies in nature and not just in degree? With all the variations from Greece to Rome to medieval Europe to the New World, are there common elements that set them all apart from every society with an economy based on the machine, the factory, and the city?

Among the features of preindustrial societies are the following:

The economic base of most preindustrial societies is land, water, and produce. An agricultural economy requires a relatively dispersed population to unite the worker to the base of production—the land. Even with a plantation system, there is an integration of the workplace, residence, and the natural environment.

Communities tend to be small. Even the preindustrial city with its concentrated functions of government, culture, and trade was small.

The schedule and rhythm of the seasons, of planting and harvest, ruled the time framework of the culture rather than the production-scheduled machine.

The major uncertainty was related to climate, weather, and harvest rather than to the market.

Even though the political systems of preindustrial societies vary, in general a freeholder land system has been less common than some kind of landlord-serf system. Crucial has been the availability of other land—a frontier not yet under the control of large landholders.

Preindustrial leisure is more limited by isolation than by lack of space. Leisure, therefore, tended to be either integrated into the work and survival patterns of life or to be related to special events. Holidays were, for the most part, "holy days" in which people would gather for whatever celebrations were customary. The gathering itself provided the possibility of games, play, spectacles, and various forms of social interaction that would not be generally possible with the dispersed population. Further, the slack periods of agricultural production allowed for far more holiday periods than is ordinarily permitted by an economy in which production requires that the machines be tended and running.

The size of communities, the barter methods of exchange, the tying of families to one place, and the holidays made the social patterns of preindustrial communities generally personal, informal, and face-to-face. Even children were known by name and family to almost all who would see and communicate with them. In contrast, the impersonal, functional, and anonymous interactions of the industrial city make almost all life outside the home different in kind from the "folk" community of the past.

In general, then, preindustrial societies are not just smaller and undeveloped modern societies. The ecological, economic, and political structures of a nomadic or agrarian society make any kind of easy comparison of leisure, family life, culture, or worldviews between preindustrial and industrial epochs dangerous. Modern societies are profoundly and pervasively different from their preindustrial predecessors. In ways that we will document more fully in Chapter 10, the conditions of life, including leisure, changed dramatically in the nineteenth century. We are not Greeks or Romans or villagers today. Nor can a change in values or in leisure alone move us back through the iron curtain of industrialization to a romanticized utopia of a folk culture and a feeling of oneness with nature.

Greek Civilization

At the height of their philosophical creativity, the Greeks did even more than plan cities, develop the arts, and probe the issues of human knowledge and existence. In the ideas of Plato and Aristotle, the two enduring approaches to human self-understanding through thought rather than through faith were established. The requirements and modes of government were argued and some theories tested by trial in a city-state. And leisure was raised to a place of importance in the value scheme both for the sake of free human beings and of the social order. The high value placed on leisure by this "peak" early civilization makes Greece especially interesting to those who study leisure today.

On the other hand, Greek society was deeply divided between those who were free and those who were slaves. The leisure of the free was purchased at the expense of this underclass who were not free. In Athens there was estimated to be a ratio of four slaves to every free male. Further, among the free, many were poor—so poor that in the *Politics* Aristotle commented that "the only slave a poor man has is his wife."

Therefore, two issues are paramount in understanding the meaning of leisure in ancient Greece. First, how did leisure come to take such an important place in the social system? And, second, does a "leisure class" require a slave class?

The Social Context of Leisure

Aristotle's rough definition of leisure was simply "freedom from the necessity of labor" (*Politics,* Book 2). However, for Greeks leisure was freedom *for* as well as freedom *from.* Certain kinds of activity were considered so beneficial that they merited special planning and provision. Greek towns were not just shapeless growths on the landscape, but were carefully planned to enable free citizens to engage in the physical and cultural activities considered important to growth and development.

Not only did a central area for markets and government provide a forum for discussion and argumentation, but the town plan generally provided parks, baths, theaters, sports arenas, gymnasiums, and exercise grounds. Added to these were the academies for the learning and practicing of the arts and philosophy and music. Stress was placed on the wholeness of the free person who would use his freedom to develop both body and mind. Cultivation of skills in the arts, sports, and intellectual pursuits was expected of free men. Leisure was not only valued, but facilities for the exercise of these leisure pursuits were provided for in the architectural planning of the city.

It is true that in time some of the public opportunities were replaced by private parks, baths, and academies. It is also true that these opportunities were for free men only and were closed to women, to slaves, and, for the most part, to the poor. That is, leisure in this full and rounded sense was for a small minority of population.

Further, there are indications that in time the participatory nature of such leisure lessened as greater stress was placed on the performance of those especially skilled. The great theaters with their dramas by Sophocles, Euripides, and Aristophanes employed professional actors. The famed Olympic Games, which were once open only to free citizens, became more and more spectacles performed by elite athletes. The celebrational character of games and festivals seemed better served by specialization and performing excellence than by wide participation.

Nevertheless, at a dinner of the leisure-class elite, the lyre was passed from person to person and each was expected to sing and even to engage in extemporaneous composition. The exaltation of philosophy, the arts, and sport in the Periclean age led to a richness of leisure and culture with a special place in the history of Western civilization. Further, Greek rulers not only valued such leisure but made political decisions to provide opportunities for its exercise.

An important difference from our own time is that of scale. The largest city, Athens, probably never exceeded a population of 200,000. When a town is planned for 50,000 to 200,000 residents, community gatherings are still possible for celebration and entertainment. The ancient cities were modest-sized towns in comparison to modern metropolitan aggregates.

The Economic Context of Leisure

Our delight in the Greek stress on the importance of leisure tends to be dimmed somewhat by the economic context. The training for cultural, intellectual, and physical expressions of leisure was for the very few. Only ruling class males (and a few specialized female companions called *heterae*) had access to this preparation for adult leisure. The free poor were too occupied with survival and the slaves with doing most of the work that supported the leisure styles of the few. Women were considered to be lesser beings whose functions were largely related to the home and childbearing. The famous wife of Socrates may suggest that some women did exercise some limited power within their small domain of home and family. However, leisure is described in male terms. Being male, however, included a wide range of sexual diversity, especially of practices that would now be referred to as "bisexual." Homosexual activity was an accepted part of the sexual spectrum.

Despite our admiration for the cultivation of leisure in developing skills in music, verse, disputation, and sport, the question of cost must be raised. Is the necessary "cost" of such leisure cultivation the existence of an underclass to carry on the necessary work—the production and services—of the economy? Slaves in the silver mines as well as the shops and schools, farmers and serfs on subsistence-size parcels of land, women preparing food and caring for children, and personal servants who were captives of war in a ratio of ten or twenty to each leisured male is a high price. In this later time, does intense leisure still require an underclass of people with limited opportunities who are defined by race, ethnicity, economic origins, or sex? Has the automated machine become the new servant class, or does leisure require so much personal service and maintenance that time will be in short supply for those who provide it?

Philosophies of Leisure

The two great thinkers of Greece, Plato and Aristotle, each had a significant place for leisure in his scheme of thought. Despite basic differences in perspectives on the sources of knowledge and the good, Plato and Aristotle agreed on the importance of leisure. Although leisure was necessary for the development of those capable of ruling the state, it is more than a means to good government. Leisure is an end in itself and at the heart of what it means to be a free human being.

In Plato's philosophy of culture, being free meant not being a slave. Leisure is time free for self-development and expression. However, leisure is more than freedom *from* necessity. It is freedom for engagement with the culture (*paideia*) most fully found in the arts of music, poetry, and philosophy. By employing leisure to actively pursue *paideia,* freedom becomes a way of sensing the meaning of the beauty and truth of the eternal Forms, or Ideas.

For Plato, true happiness is found in becoming more like what we might be, in fulfilling more and more of our character or selfhood. To move toward that self-perfection, it is necessary to devote oneself to thought and culture. Therefore, time for thought, contemplation, philosophy, and self-development is required for happiness. That time, for Plato, is leisure. The result, however, is not only for the self. Rather, those with leisure are expected accept political responsibility. Those who engage in gymnastics, music, and philosophy are in touch with form, grace, and beauty. Through such activity, qualities for leadership in the state are enhanced (*Republic,* Book 2.)

Aristotle's approach to leisure (*schole*) begins in Book 1 of the *Politics* in which he defines leisure as time free from the necessity to work. He proposes that a leisure class should be supported in order to assure a wise and just government. He contrasts leisure not only with work (*ascholia*) but also with the play of children (*paideia*) and the restoration of recreation (*anapausis*). Leisure is an end in itself, intrinsically good and the highest human activity. Sebastian deGrazia sums up Aristotle's approach as follows:

> Leisure is a state of being in which activity is performed for its own sake or as its own end. . . . And we call final without reservation that which is always desirable in itself and never for the sake of something else. Leisure stands in that last class by itself.[5]

For Aristotle, contemplation is the fullest and most satisfying activity. Its intrinsic value, however, is not its total meaning. Like Plato, Aristotle believes that leisure is necessary for those with political and civil responsibility. In the *Politics,* Book 1, leisure is also time free to govern and prepare to govern. The personal development of leisure has social

[5] Sebastian deGrazia, *Of Time, Work, and Leisure* (Garden City, NY: Doubleday, 1964), p. 13.

purposes. A "good" state like a good life requires more than wealth and freedom. A good state must also have justice and valor. A good life, then, has not only freedom from crushing necessity, but also a realization of engagement in activity that sustains and develops both the self and the society. Leisure is not just intrinsic pleasure, but involves the exercise of choice using rational principles to seek a relative mean between polar excesses (*Nichomachean Ethics,* Book 2). Leisure takes forms of philosophy and the arts as well as physical discipline. It is pleasurable in itself, but also builds virtue and character that is the basis of being a good citizen.

Recapitulation

The two issues, the importance of leisure in Greek culture and the slave basis of the leisure class, are not unrelated to each other. Leisure in the full sense of self-fulfillment through immersion in the production of music, verse, and dance, the development of grace and strength in gymnastics and sport, and the exercise of intellectual powers in the dialogue of philosophy requires considerable freedom from interruption and daily necessity. In the Greek social system this freedom was available to a few free males only because of the economic wealth, food, shelter, and personal service produced by slaves, women, and the poor. The realization of the ideal for a few was purchased at the cost of very limited opportunity for most.

Is it possible to support and pursue the ideas without agreeing to such a cost? Is there so much ongoing routine labor required to maintain a society that a "leisure class" must be supported by a "servant class"? Or is it possible in a modern society to distribute leisure opportunity more widely by placing it in blocks of time and space? Can more people have some leisure if few or none have all leisure?

The humanistic approach to leisure with the final value placed in freedom for human fulfillment is a philosophical understanding of leisure that has had profound influence on contemporary leisure studies. The union of freedom with intrinsic satisfaction is central to many current definitions of leisure. At the same time, the economic provisions, the social freedom, and the cultural value system supporting this ideal in Greece remind us that the achievement of leisure may involve high costs.

Rome: The Politics of Leisure

Like the Greeks, the Romans built and planned for leisure. However, the Roman stress on law and custom rather than learning and exploration gave leisure quite a different cast. Further, the social and economic context of leisure in Rome contrasted with that of Athens in significant ways. The result was that leisure eventually came to be viewed more as consumption than creation and as a political instrument rather than as an instrument for the highest human good.

The Social Context of Leisure

In both Greece and Rome, over a period of centuries leisure became less participatory and more a matter of watching what others did. However, in Rome the trend was accentuated by a series of social changes. The most dramatic was the great increase in the number of people moving to Rome and other cities. With slaves or captives replacing free workers on farms and in shops and wealthy citizens buying up the land of the poorer farmers, displaced farmers and workers moved to the city. Soldiers who were not needed in times of peace and the displaced workers formed a ring of poverty and unemployment around the seat of government.

Like Athens, Rome had developed a tradition of public leisure. Baths, outdoor theaters, stadiums, parks, gymnasiums, playing fields, and some indoor halls and theaters were built. With greater stress on preparation for the warfare that had made Rome a great imperial power, sport and physical skill were emphasized somewhat more than in Greece. Nonetheless, indoor rooms for conversation in the baths and gymnasiums and outdoor forums for gatherings, festivals, and political discussions were part of the plan of any Roman city.

As the empire spread in power and geographic scope, the class of wealthy rulers became more and more distinct from the masses. Their villas on the edge of the city with gardens, pools, entertainment halls, and even hunting preserves separated them from those—employed or not—who were limited to their simple homes and to public facilities for their leisure. With so much of the economy based on the exploitation of conquered lands and with the gains distributed so unequally, Rome became by the first century A.D. a city of about a million people plagued by unemployment and underemployment.

The more than 150 public holidays recorded by the first century grew to as many as 200 by the middle of the third. Entertainment in various forms was provided to fill the time of the masses and to distract them from potential political revolution. The phrase "bread and circuses" summarizes the political intent of the ruling class to blunt dissatisfaction by providing public welfare and entertainment programs.

Leisure, then, for the masses increasingly consisted of the consumption of such provisions. The powerless "plebs" were to be controlled by the mythology of the state religion and distracted by spectacles in the stadiums. The leisure of the wealthy became more and more private and that of the poor more and more public. For the rulers, leisure (*otium*) was held to be necessary for the sake of ruling the empire, which was certainly work (*negotium*). For the plebians, leisure was necessary to fill time and forestall a discontent that might erupt into revolution.

Leisure as Consumption

Forms of mass leisure on a scale and with a variety previously unknown were developed in Rome. The sports and games that had once prepared men for war and conquest become spectacles in stadiums that often held up to half the population of a city. The holidays commemorating historical events as well as celebrating the state religion provided time for such events.

In Rome the more than 800 baths (including the huge Baths of Trajan) were available at small cost for daily use. The emphasis on sport took on more and more of a combative nature with various forms of gladiatorial contests often ending in the death of one or more participants. Chariot races were a feature of the circuses with simulated sea battles and wild animals imported to fight each other or human antagonists. The enormous Circus Maximus could hold 385,000 spectators. Sporadic persecution of Christians before the emperor Constantine made Christianity the state religion added their torture, mutilation, and deaths to the fare of entertainment in some periods.

As with other cultures, we do not know many details about the ongoing, everyday life of the poor, of women, and of slaves. Presumably they engaged in various kinds of informal leisure and found satisfaction in close relationships and in some playful outlets in the midst of their labor, long hours, and struggle for survival. On the other hand, we do know something of the lavish entertainment of the ruling class who had profited from the expansion of the empire. There is evidence that the proud and free citizen of the early periods of Rome was squeezed between the servant classes and the wealthy in the time approaching A.D. 300. Opportunities for political, economic, and social participation were narrowed by concentrations of power and wealth.

In any case, mass leisure was provided for Romans by public events and spectacles. Leisure became increasingly the consumption of those provisions rather than a selection among opportunities for participation and self-development. While accounts of the dissipation and clamor for more exciting violence may be exaggerated and the daily relational interaction neglected, the growth of mass leisure seems well documented.

Leisure as Social Control

Too much emphasis on the details of the chariots, gladiators, and arenas may obscure the political aim of such provisions. Leisure in these mass consumption forms did not just arise as a response to popular demand; mass leisure was a political instrument.

Welfare programs provided some food and shelter for the unemployed. The circus and other spectacles provided distraction. Leisure as mass entertainment was intended to preserve the political structure, the power of the ruling class, by giving the majority something else to do. In time, the spectacles became increasingly violent and colorful and the bloodshed and danger intensified to continue the appeal to a population that had lost meaningful direction and no longer participated in the productive life of the society.

Perennial Issues

Rome is the prime example of the political use of mass leisure consumption. However, it is not the last. The question of the meaning of leisure may be raised about any society in which provision of mass entertainment becomes central to the culture. Is a choice among spectacles to be watched, goods to be purchased, or entertainment to be absorbed adequate for leisure? Or is there a lingering element of self-development, expression, and active participation that is more than a residue of the Greek ideal? Does leisure really involve something more than filling time and entertaining?

Just as important is the possibility that leisure may become politically or economically instrumental rather than being simply a rich opportunity for freedom, expression, and relationships. If mass leisure becomes so easy, so available, and so stimulating that few can resist its appeal, then it may become a distraction from the development of human selfhood and a creative culture. Leisure as consumption may be just one more product to advertise, promote, and market to the extent that some people identify satisfaction with purchasing a product.

The Sacred and the Secular

However, the history of the religion-leisure relationship is not simply one of conflict. The contemplative ideal in Christian mysticism holds that the leisure of meditation on the Divine is the highest good. The creation narrative in the third chapter of Genesis portrays humankind as created for communion with God, nature, and each other and that work is a punishment prescribed for breaking that communion. Further, some religious scholars would end the conflict and return the essential unity of religion and leisure to Christian doctrine.

Although the history of religion and leisure contains periods of cooperation, truce, and temporary victories, in general the distinction between religion as sacred and leisure as secular has characterized the conflict.

The Judeo-Christian Dialectic

In Western civilization, the conflict took shape in the first major division within the emerging Christian movement. Most of the early Christians were Jews who revered the Scriptures of their heritage, attended synagogue, and were culturally a part of that Semitic people. As the new persuasion spread, a major question was whether or not a gentile who became a follower would have to become a Jew in order to become a Christian. The conflict was rendered unimportant in A.D. 70 when the Roman army under Pompey leveled the walls of Jerusalem, destroyed the Jewish Temple, and scattered the Jewish population, including Christian Jews, through the Roman Empire. With the political concentration of the Jewish Christians gone, the Pauline element, influenced by Greek dualism, became ascendent and a theology opposing the pleasures of this world shaped the Christian ethos. When the emperor Constantine declared Christianity the favored religion of the empire in A.D. 325, that understanding of life, although modified, became a central influence in Western civilization.

What does this have to do with leisure? Simply that the Greek dualism of the apostle Paul condemned the "flesh" and especially the body and its pleasures as evil and to be scorned. The body was considered a "tomb" to be escaped through a full devotion to things of the spirit. The earthly world was seen as temporary and a distraction from those occupations that would lead to communion with the eternal. Even such ordinary functions as marriage, reproduction, and child rearing were unworthy of full concentration by those devoted to the life of faith.

As a consequence, the greatest honor was given to those whose bodies were subdued, whose secular lives were abandoned, and whose otherworldly inclinations were intensified. Thus, only the sacred leisure of contemplation and prayer could be praised. The common leisure of physical movement and development, of everyday friendships and occasional celebrations, of food and drink, dance and music, pleasure and game was condemned as unspiritual. The Greek-influenced dualists developed a doctrine that was against bodily and cultural expression, against the pleasures of this world, and against placing high value on even the closest human relationships. While the otherworldly perspective was somewhat mitigated in later centuries, this dominant mode of Christianity was hostile to most common leisure of its time.

The Jewish Christians, on the other hand, had taken this world, its history, and its communities much more seriously. They stressed that they were a people who had worldly and historical responsibilities. The world was affirmed as the arena of God's activity and therefore worthy of human attention. Their perspective valued the ordinary relationships of life, celebrations of community, enjoyment of harvests and their produce, bodily expression in music and dance, and human sexuality as part of a good creation. Work was accepted and required, but the family and community expressions of mutual concern were accepted with joy. Pleasure was not considered evil.

In the great theological and political councils of the church in the fourth and fifth centuries, Pauline dualism was elaborated and became the official doctrine of the church in the East and West. This soon led to many manifestations of avoidance and condemnation of the ordinary pleasures of life in this world. The withdrawal from ordinary community intercourse by clergy and by perfectionists who were the forerunners of later monasticism was a consequence of seeing the body and all material things as a hindrance to spiritual life and generally evil.

Of course, many avenues of accommodation were developed. One route was to accept the "weakness" of the majority and to counsel perfection for a few who were specially chosen. Nevertheless, the generally negative view of so much that we would now call common leisure is a theme that has never been wholly absent from the central religious tradition of Western culture. Leisure, again and again, has been viewed as secular and thus a danger to those who would preserve the sacred.

Dualism and the Rise of the Monasteries

The Pauline dualism that was victorious in the first centuries of the Christian church continued as the dominant point of view in succeeding centuries. The otherworldly was seen as paramount and this world as a dismal testing of the spirit. The sacred vocations of the priest, monk, and nun were contrasted to the secular work of the world. Those with sacred vocations were expected to subjugate their bodies to provide an example of holy living for those unable to reach this level of devotion. In time, the monastic orders—despite their differences in style—were regulated to incorporate prayer, corporate worship, learning, and work in a model of a faithful community.

Ordinary people, on the other hand, were not expected to attain such a level of perfection. Rather they demonstrate the "weakness of the flesh" in their engagement with the worldly matters of work, raising families, and seeking pleasure in drink, song, and dance.

The monasteries not only modeled the ordered life of devotion but are also credited with two gifts of note to Western culture. The first is the preservation of much of the documentation of learning from previous centuries. The walls, libraries, and copying rooms of the monasteries held and reproduced the manuscripts of scripture, philosophy, history, and ancient learning that are indispensable in reconstructing the roots of our civilization.

Along with that cultural transmission, another gift that had a lasting impact on leisure is the clock. The order of St. Benedict is often credited with developing this more precise way of measuring time in order to synchronize their communal life. In the rhythms of their prayer and meditation, corporate worship, meals, and work, it was necessary to gather the community for common activity at several times during the day. The clock was introduced by the Benedictines to give measured regularity to their lives. The kind of regular synchronized social schedule that is so central to understanding work and leisure in modern society was first a product of the monastery rather than of the factory.

The unitized linear view of time, rather than some understanding of time that is based on intensity of experience, the cycles of daylight and seasons, or circular recurrence is so much a part of our worldview that we have difficulty imagining how a day might be ordered without a clock. What did work and leisure mean to the peasant who had no clock, no calendar to read, and no mass media to label the hour and the day? Did hours and days simply flow formlessly into each other, relieved by occasions imposed by an unseen calendar and seasons given by unseen powers? It was, in so many ways, quite a different world from the world of the clock, the schedule, and the requirements of a production economy.

Summary of Issues

In Greek civilization, we have seen a high value placed on leisure and a social structure that supported specialized leisure for an elite few. Such leisure, however, came at the expense of classes of people denied the power of self-determination in either work or leisure—slaves, women, and the poor. As a consequence, some of the lofty pronouncements of philosophers about the pinnacles of leisure are mitigated by the stratified elitism of the society. Leisure is not just an ideal; it is also political and social reality. Can real leisure be purchased at the expense of the freedom of others?

The history of Rome raises another set of recurrent issues. Leisure as mass entertainment and consumption is more than the possibility of pleasure. Leisure can be a political instrument that pacifies masses whose lives are otherwise cut off from a sense of meaning and worth. Yet, in the long term, can such leisure really satisfy? If a society is based on a fundamental alienation from the freedom to develop a full life and full community, then even the most elaborate entertainment may not be enough.

Finally, there has been a long history of conflict between religions and leisure. That history will be drawn out further in the next two chapters. Nevertheless, it is significant to recognize that there are other possibilities in the Judeo-Christian tradition as well as in other religions. Leisure may be the basis for religious expression, for contemplation, and for common celebration. Religion may give direction and standards to leisure without profound conflict. All religion is not other-worldly and dualistic despite the recurrence of this theme in most religions. What are the possibilities of a complementarity rather than conflict between leisure and religious expression?

HIGHLIGHTS

1. Leisure has taken quite different forms in cultures in which there are different values, languages, worldviews, resources, and ways of living.
2. Preindustrial societies are too different in ecology, economy, and polity to permit unqualified comparisons with contemporary society and its problems.
3. Although the slave economy and elitism were fundamental to Greek society, the elevation of leisure to the status of a major goal and the insistence on freedom and self-development have had lasting influence.
4. Rome illustrates a political use of leisure designed to quiet nonproductive masses when consumption replaces real choice and growth.
5. The Judeo-Christian tradition includes elements that affirm ordinary life and expression as well as those that condemn bodily life and leisure.

Discussion Questions

1. What does *leisure* mean in a simple and undifferentiated society? What are the basic social and economic requirements for leisure's existence?

2. What does it mean to say that "leisure is ethnic"? Which is more important in shaping leisure, cultural values or economic structures? Give historical examples.

3. Could the Greek ideal of leisure have been reached in a society without slaves? Can it be reached today? How?

4. Which is the dominant theme in Greek approaches to leisure—leisure as the highest intrinsic value or leisure as important so the elite may govern well?

5. What are the functions of mass spectacles and contests in an urban society? Are they different today from those of ancient Rome? Is leisure ever used as a means of social control in modern times? How?

6. What are the differences between mass consumption leisure as provided by the state and as provided by commercial interests? What are the main problems with each type of leisure? Is the market or the state a better provider of leisure to the masses? Why?

7. What are contemporary examples of both conflict and cooperation between leisure and religion?

Bibliography

Chambers, M., *The Western Experience.* New York: Knopf, 1974.

Dare, Byron, G. Welton, and W. Coe, *Concepts of Leisure in Western Thought.* Dubuque, IA: Kendall/Hunt, 1987.

Davies, W. D., *Christian Origins and Judaism.* Philadelphia: Westminister Press, 1962.

Hemingway, John L., "Leisure and Civility: Reflections on a Greek Ideal," *Leisure Sciences,* 10 (1988), 179–191.

Huizinga, Johan, *Homo Ludens: A Study of the Play Element in Culture.* Boston: Beacon Press, 1950.

Goodale, Thomas, and Geoffrey Godbey. *The Evolution of Leisure.* College Park, PA: Venture Publishing, 1988.

Kelley, J. N. D., *Early Christian Doctrines,* Second edition. New York: Harper & Row, 1960.

Mikalson, J. D., *The Sacred and Civil Calendars of the Athenian Year.* Princeton, NJ: Princeton University Press, 1975.

Pieper, Josef, *Leisure: The Basis of Culture.* New York: New American Library, 1963.

Chapter *9*

Leisure Ideals and
Work Ethics

This is a story of conflict. The Protestant Reformation took a number of twists and turns during the sixteenth and seventeenth centuries. One was its alliance with nationalism and developing business interests in Europe. A second was the emergence of the Puritans as rigorists whose aim was to reform the entire culture according to their standards. As a result, the conflict between Protestant and Catholic became political, economic, and cultural. It had its impact on the play of children and Sunday afternoon frolics on the village green.

On the surface, the modern conflict has appeared to be between the sacred and the secular, between those who would impose a religious stamp on all life and those who resisted in the name of some version of freedom. Modern "blue laws" against certain kinds of behavior and entertainment, especially on Sunday, appear to be a clear attempt to control on the part of religious forces.

However, there is an underlying conflict that has taken on a sacred-secular form in Western history. This fundamental conflict is between those who affirm life and individual freedom and those who would exercise repressive control in the name of a greater good. It is between expression and repression, between affirmations of human value for its own sake and philosophies that value human activity only as instrumental. Whether the greater value is the "glory of God," the state, or the economy, all life, including leisure, is then defined in terms of its contribution to that good rather than as essential human expression. It is an old conflict that has taken many forms. In this chapter, we trace a part of its history.

What is the highest mode of life? Is it work or leisure? Does leisure find its meaning primarily in restoring workers for productivity, or is it an end in itself, perhaps even the highest end? Max Weber assigned to the rise of Protestantism the fostering of a "work ethic" that valued economic productivity over pleasure or expression. Countering this ethic was the emphasis on human achievement and creativity of the Renaissance. Do we live to work or work to live? Or are there other alternative views of human life that do not begin with a conflict between work and leisure? One possibility is that work, leisure, family, community, and other elements of life are complementary rather than in inevitable conflict.

ISSUES

Are religion and leisure always in conflict?

Did the Protestant Reformation create a work ethic that has stifled leisure in Western civilization?

Was the Renaissance a reawakening of a humanistic ethic that was, and has remained, in conflict with the work ethic of productivity?

Is the productivity of work or the expression of leisure more fundamental to life?

Amid conflict and division, the dominant institution in Western Europe from Constantine until the sixteenth century was the Roman Catholic Church. It was a political and cultural force as well as a religious power. Its theology and practices tended to divide followers between elites of priests and those in religious orders who were to strive toward a perfection of discipline and "ordinary people" who were to gain an otherworldly salvation. Adherence to the rituals and rules of the church in this world were to lead to perfection in the next. The stress was not on a comprehensive ethic for ordinary people.

Leisure and the Reformation

One consequence of the Protestant Reformation was to shift the attention of the faithful from the otherworld to this one. However, the shift was not from contemplation and prayer to the freedom and expression of common leisure. Rather, the Reformation is credited with focusing on the work of this world.

Luther and Calvin: The Secular Calling

It was Martin Luther, formerly a monk as well as a scholar, who most vigorously denounced the separate life of the monastic orders. His writings are full of the concept of the secular calling: the idea that God calls people to their work in agriculture and commerce, in marriage and the family, as much as to prayer and holy orders. His antagonism toward monasticism and his stress on "salvation by faith alone" rather than by works of piety led to repeated stress that work and the joys and responsibilities of family life might be done for the glory of God.

In Geneva, Switzerland, John Calvin took up the same themes and intensified certain aspects of them. In building a city government to be ruled by divine law, Calvin added stress on responsibilities of both citizenship and obedience. In dealing with the German princes, Luther seemed to stress obedience over responsibility. Calvin also gave a greater religious motivation for engagement in the commerce of the world.

Many changes were taking place in Europe during the sixteenth century. Nation-states were emerging. The Renaissance, especially in Italy and France, brought a widespread flourishing of the arts, the beginnings of science and technology, and a freedom from the cultural domination of the church. New mercantile interests developed both market and financial structures for their trade. And the cities added commerce to their former functions as religious, cultural, and governing centers.

As commerce became more complex and widespread, the first modes of capitalism began to emerge. Trade and the exchange of crafted and manufactured goods were not new; there had been some limited borrowing of money from the few banking houses then in existence. What was new was a greater stress on money as a medium of investment as well as of exchange. In commerce money could make money. Further, money became a standard of accomplishment that could be measured and compared. The former concentration on titles, influence, and land as measures of status was broken by adding the control of financial resources, not only for spending but for investment as well.

Max Weber: Asceticism and the Rise of Capitalism

Three and one-half centuries later, Max Weber, a German sociologist, sought to counter the Marxist argument that history was essentially determined by the economic or "materialist" structures and forces of the time. Weber desired to demonstrate that ideas, in this case even religious ideas, could be one factor shaping history.[1] In fact, religious ideology might even have an influence on economic arrangements, thus reversing Marx's theory.

Weber chose the phenomenon of the rise of capitalism as the most dramatic example of the importance of ideology. He noted that capitalism had developed most fully in the Protestant-dominated areas of Europe and especially in those where the Calvinist influence was strongest. His analysis can be outlined as follows:

1. The primary requirement for the development of capitalism is the availability of investment capital. The attraction of investment capital requires an acceptance of the idea that money can make money, that investment can be rewarded.
2. There appears to be some relationship between the rise of capitalism and the cultural influence of Protestantism. That influence is the new stress on life in the secular world as a legitimate sphere of faithful activity.
3. Paradoxically, this attention to secular activity is based on the doctrine of the absolute sovereignty of God found most centrally in Calvinism. The comprehensiveness of God's rule encompasses such concerns as salvation and the way in which the faithful order their ordinary lives. Since God's rule is absolute, there can be nothing that people can do to affect the divine decision about salvation. Therefore, prior to birth, some are elected by God to salvation and others to damnation. This doctrine of "predestination" prevents anyone from earning salvation by good works.

[1] Max Weber, *The Protestant Ethic and the Spirit of Capitalism,* trans. T. Parsons (New York: Scribner's, 1958).

4. Since none can know with certainty whether they are among the elect, some reassurance may be sought. Evidence of the likelihood of election may be found in the quality of life in this world. The elect are surely among those who are Godly, righteous, sober, well-disciplined, and faithful and not among those whose lives are characterized by waste, frivolity, and dissipation. Further, the elect are most often rewarded in this world by success in their enterprises. After all, if one works diligently, rationally, and in a disciplined way, then the result is likely to be success.

5. Since the elect are also characterized by refraining from self-indulgent consumption or pleasure-seeking, they will not waste the profits of their successful industry on themselves. Therefore, they possess that essential ingredient of capitalism: investment capital. By reinvesting profits into the business, they multiply their success and expand capitalist enterprise. This careful style of life is called "this-worldly asceticism" by Weber. In this life it is important, not to seek and gain pleasure, but to invest one's life properly in the church, the family, the state, and the work of the world.

Thus, the combination of the religious doctrine of election and the ethic of sober asceticism produces both attention to work and to the profit that may be reinvested to expand business interests. The values placed on work in business and on asceticism, taken together, are called the Protestant work ethic. Weber does not argue that only Protestants possess this attitude but that its historical development was facilitated by European Calvinism. In his study *The Protestant Ethic and the Spirit of Capitalism,* Weber traces the expansion of this orientation into England and the New World, its secularization, and its importance in political conflicts such as that between the followers of Cromwell and the Royalists in England. Weber also illustrates how that conflict affected leisure and sports in England.

A related issue questions the extent to which the Protestant ethic has influenced the values of various groups in our culture. There is little doubt that a serious view of life and work has characterized many of those who gather capital and operate businesses on America's Main Streets or whose financial interests have been enhanced by the hard work of others. Whether work is so central and pleasure so much despised by most of those who have worked for others and who have not benefited when capital investment has been rewarded is quite another matter. Nevertheless, the still-common tendency to justify leisure only as re-creation for renewed attention to work does suggest that such sober asceticism still survives in some form.

The Renaissance and Humanistic Freedom

Despite all the attention given to the Reformation-based work ethic, another theme of continuing importance had been developing in Italy in the fourteenth century and spreading across France and England in the fifteenth. That movement was the cultural revolution called the Renaissance. In a sense, the Renaissance was a movement counter to the Reformation that grew in historical parallel.

The Religious Roots of Humanism

It would be incorrect to place the Renaissance in simple opposition to religion. The painting, sculpture, music, and drama of the Florentines and others sprang from a long artistic tradition that was fostered by the Catholic church. To follow the development of painting techniques, it is necessary to move literally from the walls of churches and monasteries to canvas and the Medici palaces. Not only did techniques change and subjects broaden, but the sponsorship of art became more and more secular. Patrons of the wealthy and noble houses provided a new source of support for painters, musicians, and other artists.

In the arts, no clear division between religion and humanism is possible. In choral music the line from the Catholic Palestrina to the Protestant Bach moves from Italy to central Europe through composers some of whom were deeply religious and others who were more secular. The entire city of Florence became a work of art. Churches and palaces, sacred and secular painting, architecture, and sculpture all displayed a remarkable enrichment in perspectives and techniques. The rich painting of Rembrandt, a Protestant, is unique in execution and mode but not in its combination of texture with the exaltation of the human spirit. In the Renaissance period, artistic development blurred the lines between sacred and secular and between Catholic and Protestant.

The Emergence of the Secular Arts

However, there were significant changes in both the support and the aims of artists. The development of printing made possible the distribution of literature, criticism, drawings, and music on a scale previously impossible. The challenge of the Reformation to the authority of the Catholic church opened possibilities of new ways of thinking, composing, writing, and drawing that might not have gained support previously. But perhaps the greatest change was in the turn to the present moment and to the actualities and the potentialities of human life. Human beings were valued because of what they were and what they could do, not just because of what God had done for them. This humanism is still a significant element of our culture and especially of our leisure.

General participation in the arts increased with special attention given to the nobility and their skills in the dance, music, and theater. At the same time, these cultural forms along with opera, sculpture, and painting were professionalized. The royal courts included their composers, ballet companies, singers, actors, and painters. By 1570, the Drury Lane Theatre in London was opened to provide commercial theater for the commercial classes. The idea spread across Europe.

One persistent Renaissance theme was that of creation. The artist was to make something new with hands, mind, and imagination. More than reflecting the glory of God, the artist demonstrated the wonders of man and of woman. And the works of the artist were to be found on the doors of public buildings, on the walls of churches and palatial dwellings, in public theaters and on marketplace stages, and even in the streets as drama companies traveled from place to place.

In their schemes for development of human beings who would reach toward the full potential of human achievement, many philosophers included leisure activity. Rabelais

(1490–1553) stressed games, physical exercise, singing, dancing, painting, and other skills in the education of the ideal pupil. In France, Montaigne (1533–1592) promoted the humanistic concept of the unity of body, mind, and spirit. The dualism of Pauline Christianity and of traditional church doctrine was replaced with a humanistic wholeness of life. The English philosopher Locke (1632–1704) believed that the play of children should be directed toward learning and the building of good habits. Rousseau (1712–1778), the French romanticist philosopher, defended the freedom of children's play, but also wrote that the group play of children should be structured to promote community and equality.

The humanistic approach to leisure contrasted with Catholic dualism and Calvinist repression in several ways. First, creative human expression was valued in its own right: the products of the hands and minds of men (seldom women as yet) were seen as worthy of praise. Second, although there were still clear divisions in the society and in the kinds of activities that were expected of the different classes of people, expression in play and games, dance and drama, music and art was believed to be good. Mind and body were believed to be parts of a whole person, not enemies dividing the self. Third, the attention to this world, which was shared with the Reformation, was for the Renaissance an affirmation of human life and its potential for creativity, learning, community, and discovery. Therefore, in these affirmations, the groundwork was laid for later theory about the centrality of freedom to leisure and of leisure to human development.

Early Park Provisions

It was during the Renaissance period of European history that cities were planned to include space for parks and festival occasions. Paris still retains some of the design from this period, with wide streets and green space along the river Seine. The elaborate gardens and parks of the royal family were established in the height of the monarchy. As had been the case in Rome, gardens in Paris such as the Tuileries and the Luxembourg were occasionally opened for public display. In London, great parks such as Kensington Gardens had become generally accessible to the public by the eighteenth century.

These parks and gardens varied widely in size and design. The relatively small formal gardens with their intricate walkways and plantings were characteristic of French royal preference. Landscaping was often quite ornate and planned to accommodate strolling and formal parties. At the other extreme were the large hunting preserves, such as the Prater in Vienna, which maintained a more natural mode of landscaping. In the more familiar English style of parks, the aim was to retain a higher degree of the natural growth while providing for access with walkways and open space.

Sources of Information about Leisure

Although there is a great shortage of documentation about most of the leisure activity of most people in the sixteenth, seventeenth, and eighteenth centuries, some sources are available for those periods that were scarce in centuries previous to them. The most important are the circulated writings made possible by the printing press. For example, many of the comedies of Shakespeare are a fascinating source of material on the leisure styles of Elizabethan England. Humor about games, taverns, drinking, gambling, and sexual activity yield insights into nonpublic leisure that may be more accurate than staid histories. Various diaries have provided a picture of the rise of the English coffee houses as places of social gathering. The lesser known plays of any period may be even more useful in reconstructing some of the common life of their time.

The public events of the cities are described in detail by letter writers whose works have been preserved. Even here there is a bias toward the perspectives of the relatively few who were literate and a tendency to look down on the common "rabble" and their lesser pleasures. Also, we know less about those in the smaller villages and rural areas than about people in the major cities. In the early eighteenth century, Paris already housed the Opéra, the Comedie Française, and the Opéra Comique. However, the cultural entertainments of the village dweller are largely lost to view. How feast days and holy days punctuated the routine of the rural area is a matter of speculation rather than knowledge. Stress on the Puritan asceticism may be balanced, at least, by attention to Renaissance humanism and the focus on public events in the cities mitigated by inclusion of a wider set of sources of information.

English Conflict: Reform and Restoration

Perhaps the clearest conflict between Puritan asceticism and a more pleasure-affirming ethic occurred in England during the seventeenth century. The Puritans controlled Parliament in 1640, defeated the Royalist army at Marstan Moor in 1644, and deposed Charles I soon after. However, the forces that favored a restoration of the monarchy overthrew Oliver Cromwell's successor in 1660 and placed Charles II on the throne. In that period of political strife, the sober life style of the Roundhead was vividly contrasted with the display of the Cavalier.

In opposition to the Puritan denunciations of enjoyment of games and entertainment, James I had issued the *Book of Sports* in 1618.[2] It was in the form of laws and was read from all pulpits. This book expressly permitted a number of amusements outside of church hours. Any attack on the legality of those games was prohibited under threat of punishment by the crown. The rationale of the *Book of Sports* was that working people have only limited time for recreation. Since Sundays and other religious holidays made up a large part of that time, reasonable amusements should be permitted when they did not interfere with the hours of worship.

James I added that sport has value to the state in preparing men for military engagement. Archery, bouts with staffs and cudgels, running, and wrestling were among the sports allowed. Dancing for men and women, forms of traveling theater, and other pleasures of gathering outdoors were considered healthier than drinking to excess and consequent quarrelsomeness. Of course, for those who had wealth, horse and coach racing on the open roads or cards and drinking in London's West End alehouses were common Sunday pursuits.

Against such entertainments the Puritans upheld the sanctity of the Sabbath. In an effort that has led to conflicts over time up to this day and to "blue laws" that attempt to regulate the use of "sacred times," the Puritans maintained that any distraction from the seriousness of prayer, worship, and other sober enterprises was evil. All the "Lord's Day" was to be regulated and kept free from frivolity, pleasure-seeking, and dissipation.

[2] Foster Rhea Dulles, *A History of Recreation: America Learns to Play,* Second edition. (Englewood Cliffs, NJ: Prentice-Hall, 1965).

Sport was accepted by the Puritans as discipline and training, but not purely for enjoyment. Impulsive enjoyment of life was considered to be the enemy of work, of religion, and of a rational ordering of life. The Puritan hatred of everything that had roots in either folk religions or in the Catholic church led to a banning of Christmas and of other festivals that had provided an opportunity for family and community expressions of joy and celebration. In general, theater and art were also condemned. Any decorative clothing was to be avoided. Life was, in general, to be sober, ordered, and "purified" from all vanity, waste, pride in consumption, display, and pleasure for its own sake.

The sober sanctification of all life by the Puritans, who believed that all human endeavor should be subject to their version of divine law, was more than a preferred life style. Their attempts to enforce that view of life and its consequences onto the entire society brought them into deadly conflict with those who held different views. When a life style, however based on religious convictions, is held to be mandatory for those who do not share those convictions, then the conflict spills over into every aspect of the culture.

The enforcement of "blue laws," in the time of the Puritan commonwealth or at any other time, signifies that a social consensus does not exist. If there is general agreement about what is right, then informal acceptance and exclusion can keep the few rebels in line. If necessary, persistent violators can be banished entirely. But when a large segment of a community would adopt a life style that is considered wrong and dangerous to the community by those with authority to legislate, then the power of law will be applied to the deviants. When the moral consensus is broken, then laws are written to enforce acceptable behavior from those who would choose to live otherwise.

In the Restoration, not only were the laws banning leisure pursuits repealed, but some positive steps were taken to provide opportunities for recreation. The wealthy strolled Hyde Park and St. James Park. Horse races, military exercises, fireworks, music, theater, and professional sports such as boxing drew crowds of the urban upper classes. In the country, a version of cricket and football were developed along with the old standbys: archery, wrestling, cockfighting, and various races of man and beast. The differences between high society and the poor were, then as later, illustrated more clearly in their leisure than in other activities. Yet, in hunting, fishing, gambling, and other activities, the differences were in style of participation. The wealthy had their hunting preserves while the poor poached. In any event, after the Restoration no attempt to smother recreation expressions has succeeded in the Old World. The Puritan efforts were transferred to the New World and are sketched in the next section.

The Colonies and a New Nation

The Puritan ethos was carried to New England by the dissenters who had found England inhospitable after the restoration of the monarchy. Their aim of "purifying" all of the life of their community by bringing it under divine law as they understood it left little tolerance of diversity. From the very beginning, the "saints" who ruled found it difficult to accommodate the "strangers" who lived among them without sharing the Puritan religious convictions.

The Puritan Tradition

There were two roots of the stress on simplicity and work characteristic of the leaders of the Massachusetts Bay Colony. The most enduring was the attempt to establish a theocracy, a community ruled by the sovereignty of God. In their sureness that this was their divine mission, they could afford little of the toleration known in more diverse colonies. The second root of the emphasis on diligence and work was the precarious economic situation of the settlements. Half the signers of the Mayflower Compact did not survive the first winter. Starvation, aggravated by conflict with natives, posed a threat to the survival of the new settlement that continued for some years. There was no margin of abundance that could allow for nonproductive members of the community. Further, debts were owed the sponsoring company so the economy was required to move beyond subsistence to the production of cash crops.

Nevertheless, restrictions on merriment seem to have been more a matter of religious rigor than community need. To begin with, all amusement and merriment were forbidden on the "Lord's Day." The skirmish over Sabbath observance that still continues in some parts of the country began early. The Massachusetts General Court forbade even walking unless it was necessary. Courting couples were to take no pleasure in each other's company on Sunday. Of course, all games and sports were forbidden as during Puritan rule in England.[3]

Such condemnation of worldly pleasure has been connected with being on the edges of society in status. Those whose economic stability is precarious have frequently made a religious virtue of abstaining from the pleasures of the wealthy. The diversions of well-to-do members of the established Church of England were defined as sinful by the poorer Puritans. Other pleasures, such as gambling and related cruelty to animals such as bearbaiting, were forbidden as wasteful of time and resources.

Further, the proportion of "strangers" who were not baptized and convinced Puritans increased. Only 4,000 of the 16,000 who came to Massachusetts Bay in the migration of the 1630s were church members. Therefore, the regulation of the lives of the majority by the "saints" who believed they knew how a godly commonwealth had to be ruled was an important issue. "Blue laws" of Sabbath observance and public conduct were deemed necessary to shape the common life of both those within the Puritan consensus and those who had come with other purposes and different backgrounds.

We tend to commend the community ethic that established the first public schools in the New World and to criticize that same ethic when the seeking of simple pleasure was forbidden. Actually, the two cannot be separated. The aim of the theocratic mission was to build the "City of God" in which divine rule would result in the best life for all citizens. All were to be included in everything that was considered good: education, religion, work, family, and community. However, since all did not meet the religious prerequisite of full and voluntary participation, those deemed capable of ruling in God's behalf had to legislate for the rest.

"No idle drone" would be allowed to exist without taking a share of the responsibility of work. No member of the community would be allowed to offend others or break community solidarity in religious doctrine, Sabbath observance, public conduct, or lack of

---

[3] Gary Cross, *A Social History of Leisure since 1600* (State College, PA: Venture Publishing, 1990).

responsibility. God might not select all for salvation, but all were to live sober and work-filled lives.

Normative Leisure in Massachusetts

All this regulation did not mean that no pleasure was to be found in the colony. While any kind of game and amusement was banned on Sunday, during other days and on festival occasions various forms of celebration were enhanced by food and drink. All of the rum produced in the colony was not shipped to England.

However, some kinds of activity were generally condemned. Public displays of affection were considered wanton. "Lascivious dancing" by men and women together was condemned by the General Court when it was learned that wedding celebrations sometimes included such an affront to decency.[4] The theater and other such entertainments were banned along with an assortment of games such as dice, cards, and gambling. In Connecticut the ban included bowls, ninepins, and shuffleboard as well as the wasting of time in the public smoking of tobacco.

Other than the long church services with their unison songs and endless sermons, what did the colonists do except work? They ate, especially at such festivals as Thanksgiving. They drank, at home and in the taverns, with such staples as beer and cider augmented by rum. In fact, drunkenness became a public concern and sometimes was punished by confinement in the stocks or whipping. Hunting and fishing combined replenishment of the community larder with some pleasure and diversion from farming or a trade. Occasional fairs with shooting matches and other contests and entertainments provided some relief from the ordinary round of the week. The militia gathered to drill and shoot and often stayed for some conviviality.

As always, people talked, walked, and gossiped. Young people courted in ways somewhat more direct than many of their descendants. A bit of dallying and kissing was not considered to be outside the boundaries of acceptability, and there is some evidence that sexual activity may not have been confined to the purpose of reproduction.

In general, relatively private pleasures were not condemned in the same way that public pleasures were. Drinking at home, the affectionate courting of the widow down the street, and the dalliance of young couples under a protecting tree were accepted as a bit impure but not dangerous. On the other hand, heresy was punished severely. Organized religious dissent called for banishment. Active promotion of any doctrines or activities that might create division or conflict in the community could not be allowed. The "wayward Puritans" were chastised, punished, and, if necessary, banished. The basic unity of the community had to be maintained. Public breaks with law or entrenched custom called for remedial action.

Perhaps the most flagrant break in life style came at Merry Mount where the followers of Thomas Morton set up a may pole, danced, drank, consorted with Indians, and evidently did some heterosexual consorting of their own in a party that ran for a number of days. Governor William Bradford and the other leaders could not allow this kind of overt disruption of the common life of sobriety. The leisure age was still far away.

[4] Ibid., p. 6.

The Splintered Theocracy

However consistent the effort of the Puritans to build their version of the City of God, the proliferation of "strangers" and the rigidity of their desired community style led to change. The theocracy was splintered by diversity and by growth. Attempts to enforce the norms with laws, courts, and public punishment only accentuated the breakdown of moral consensus. In time, the sacred-secular conflict that had divided England proved the undoing of those who tried to make a new theocratic beginning.

The breakdown of the consensus involved theology, morals, norms of behavior, culture, and, in time, the political and economic life of the community. New concepts of democracy arose within the institutions of the new England colonies, including the churches. The town meeting came, in time, to include citizens who were not regenerated members of the church. The diverse backgrounds of those who came for economic and social reasons and who were not willing to surrender their lives to the descendants of the founding Puritans added to the change. While the battleground of Sabbath observance and the emphasis on productive work and community responsibility remained a part of the ethos, the religious hegemony faded into disrepute and neglect. The City of God become simply New England towns in which the godly compromised with the unregenerate and the majority of strangers were no longer totally ruled by the saints. As a result, the games, sports, festivals, and pastimes of old England reemerged in the new. The balance of work and leisure, of discipline and pleasure, began to be restored.

The Southern Colonies and the Leisure Class

The contrast between New England and the South is not as extreme as some might expect. Virginia also had its blue laws related to Sabbath observance. Especially in the hardship of the early Jamestown colony, the pressures of survival augmented by poor judgment in choice of location and about crops made the emphasis on work and the moral judgments on leisure similar to those of Massachusetts Bay.

Landowners and Leisure

However, in colonial Williamsburg and the plantation country of Virginia, the landowners and free craftsmen engaged in a wide range of leisure activities. Games, books, music, cards, dances, and the arts were brought by the immigrants from England. Many of the landowners still visited ancestral homes and sent their sons to England for some schooling. The English country life of the gentry was adapted to the greater distances and new climate to provide a lifestyle that included familiar cultural and sporting activities.

Somewhat more inclusive were the ceremonial and festival occasions when large numbers of people gathered in the capitals and other towns for an election, a meeting, or to bring their harvests to market. The ordinary leisure of the home was accented by occasional public gatherings and familial occasions such as birthdays, births, baptisms, weddings, and the like. Unlike most of New England, folk-religious holidays such as Christmas were also celebrated with family gatherings, feastings, decorations, singing, and games.

Few of the landed gentry were as broad in their interest and intellectual occupations as Thomas Jefferson. A visit to the restored Monticello gives evidence of the study, writing, and invention that were an important part of Jefferson's creative leisure. However, at Monticello there is also evidence that Jefferson engaged in a variety of other leisure activities that may have been more common. Among them were cards, gambling, hunting and fishing, visiting and entertaining, and attending to the nurture of his children and grandchildren. The restored area of Colonial Williamsburg and Monticello reveal more about the leisure of the gentry than can be communicated in books.

The Slave System

Evident especially in the restored plantations is the slave basis of the southern leisure class. Not only the hard labor of the fields but also most personal service on the more wealthy plantations was provided by the permanent servant class of slaves. While some supervision was necessary and the planter's wife might spend considerable time directing the work of the servants, the time-consuming toil that was necessary to undergird the gracious way of life of Thomas Jefferson and the other planters was the work of the slaves. They were property to be used as deemed expedient and to be moved or sold according to the economic convenience or whim of the owner. Debate over the stability of slave families has to be carried on within the context of the right of slave owners to separate fathers, mothers, and children. How often that right was exercised appears to have varied from time to time and place to place. What did not vary was that slaves were property and on their lack of freedom was built the lifestyle of the southern landowners and professionals.

Music and dance forms that survived the uprooting from African cultures and the language mixtures on a given plantation were transformed into the slave culture. While it was frequently employed by owners as a means of control, the adaptation of Christianity to slave life became a central theme of much music and storytelling. However, the theme that permeated all of slave life, while frequently disguised from the masters, was that of freedom. Leisure meant the limited cultural expression of the group and the relationships that were formed in that group. But for so many the meaning of leisure that was kept alive within, however repressed in outward expression, was that of freedom.

It would seem that the slave was allowed some "segmented" leisure when work was done. In fallow seasons the allotment of time might have been considerable while during planting, cultivating, and harvest times the rhythm of slave life was simply work and rest. No doubt there was also some expression of leisure on the job in song and stolen moments of conversation. However, the fundamental freedom to shape the context of life and to choose at least some elements of participation and association was almost totally missing for the slave. Insofar as leisure requires freedom of choice—something more than a little leeway for adaptation—then the slave class created leisure for their owners by being forced to surrender their own.

Asceticism versus Expression

The continuing issue is not really that of the conflict between religion and leisure. That conflict, however fierce at times, has turned to accommodation, reconciliation, and even union, in some periods and places. The continuing conflict is between any set of values that stresses the serious against the pleasurable, the functional against the intrinsic, and the ascetic against the expressive.

The issue can be put in philosophical or theological terms: What is the chief goal of humankind? Is humankind a species whose fulfillment is found in labor (*Homo faber*), in leisure and play (*Homo ludens*), or even in religious duty? In Puritan theology, life is serious and work is of real significance, but even work is secondary to the exaltation of worship and devotion. This world is important, but it is not final. What is unambiguous is that enjoyment for its own sake is seen as unworthy of a creature of God.

The issue can also be approached in terms of social philosophy: What are the requirements of maintaining or creating a good society? If the stress is on the production of economic goods, on order and obedience to authority, and on stability, then *Homo faber* is exalted. Leisure and play may be acceptable as re-creation, but have no intrinsic worth. Work is necessary and good for the sake of the self and others. Leisure is of value only as it contributes to the really important things in life: the economy, the state, the church, the family, and the school.

One difference is in the starting point. Philosophies that exalt work and seriousness at the expense of leisure and enjoyment seem to begin with the fundamental institutions of the society. Economic production, religious devotion, or political stability come first. Anything that detracts from such priorities is condemned, or at best tolerated. Any aspect of life has to be justified in terms of the priority of the economic, religious, family, or political institutions. Therefore, leisure may be accepted as useful for recuperation for labor, as time for contemplation or sacred art and learning, or as a means of building family solidarity.

However, when the philosophy begins with the individual, then leisure may be valued as important to being human. A humanistic perspective, whether Renaissance or contemporary, may exalt leisure because it provides the freedom for self-expression and self-development. Leisure is seen as necessary to achieve full personhood. Human beings, from this point of view, need to express themselves, to create, to respond to their environments, and to relate to each other. The satisfaction from such activity is self-directed and experienced as intrinsic to the participation. The focus is this-worldly but it is not ascetic. Humanism is expressive rather than ascetic, joyous rather than sober, and with a discipline of creation rather than of repression.

Therefore, despite the history of conflict illustrated in this chapter, the basic issue is not religion versus leisure. The issue is affirmation versus denial. It is humanism—religious or secular—versus repression. The basic question is simply: Can the expression and freedom of leisure be affirmed for its own sake or only as instrument? This issue is very much a part of our history.

Summary of Issues

In Western civilization, the frequent conflicts between religious institutions and common expressions of leisure may obscure the more basic issue. In the Judeo-Christian religious tradition there have been themes that deny the wholeness of life and the validity of human expression and those that affirm the body as well as the spirit. Religious elements that have attempted to enforce dualistic and repressive perspectives on entire populations have come into conflict with both ordinary leisure and with cultural elements that exalt freedom and human expression.

The Puritans of Europe and America, with their attempt to enforce their beliefs and practices on entire populations, have exemplified a negative ethic, which denies common aspects of leisure that are not considered "spiritual" and which has often repressed kinds of leisure that are based on an affirmation of human life. The Renaissance has come to be identified as a source of humanistic attitudes toward leisure, just as the Protestant work ethic has been the common label for those value systems that demand a useful product out of all activity.

Despite oversimplification in the identification of the work ethic with the Reformation Protestantism and of humanism with secular movements, the conflict between life-affirming and life-denying value systems is real and continuing. In general, philosophies that divide life into dualisms of good and evil, spirit and matter, or sacred and secular tend to result in attempts to repress freedom and activity that is an end in itself. However, life-affirming movements are found in both the religious and the secular institutions of Western history. The fundamental division is not between religion and leisure but between different worldviews that may take both religious and secular form.

HIGHLIGHTS

1. The Protestant work ethic of ascetic attention to productivity and relegation of leisure to an instrumental social role was only one element of social change among many. However, such asceticism continued to find religious support when it came in conflict with more secular views.
2. The humanism of the Renaissance returned attention to human development as a social goal and to the values of freedom and creativity.
3. The Puritan agenda was to place all of life under a theocratic rule, resulting in a set of repressive rules.
4. The basic value conflict is not between religion and leisure but between ascetic and expressive orientations, between repression and freedom found in both religious and secular forms.

Discussion Questions

1. What have been the "proleisure" elements in Christian practice and doctrine? In other religions? If contemplation is the highest form of leisure, then why has "idleness" so often been condemned by churches?

2. Which has been more influential on modern leisure, the Reformation or the Renaissance? Which emphases of each movement are complementary rather than contradictory?

3. Is Weber's Protestant ethic analysis of the rise of capitalism an argument for the centrality of work in life? What groups in modern society have been most likely to be proponents of such a work ethic? Why?

4. Which definitions of leisure seem most influenced by the Renaissance and humanistic values? How? Which themes are similar and which in conflict?

5. Are there any nonreligious social forces that foster repression? Any religious movements that are supportive of freedom and self-enhancement? What would be the basis of a religious leisure ethic?

Bibliography

Bainton, Roland, *The Age of the Reformation.* New York: Anvil, 1956.

Carson, Jane, *Colonial Virginians at Play.* Williamsburg, VA: Colonial Williamsburg, Inc., 1965.

Clayre, Alasdair, *Work and Play: Ideas and Experience of Work and Leisure.* New York: Harper & Row, 1974.

Cross, Gary, *A Social History of Leisure Since 1600.* College Park, PA: Venture Publishing, 1990.

Dulles, Foster R., *A History of Recreation: America Learns to Play,* Second edition. Englewood Cliffs, NJ: Prentice-Hall, 1965.

Kelly, John R., *Freedom to Be: A New Sociology of Leisure,* chap. 9. New York: Macmillan, 1987.

Walker, Williston, *A History of the Christian Church.* New York: Scribner's, 1950.

Weber, Max, *The Protestant Ethic and the Spirit of Capitalism,* trans. T. Parsons. New York: Scribner's, 1958.

Chapter 10

Industrial America and the City

Change was the order of the day! Like a giant steam engine that took centuries to slowly build up pressure in its boilers and revolve its wheels a quarter-turn at a burst, the train of social change gradually got under way. Then the acceleration became a rush of power, sound, and movement going faster and faster. The acceleration of change in Western societies gathered such momentum by the middle of the nineteenth century that until the first half of the twentieth the movement was all-encompassing.

The spatial and social ordering of life, the security of tradition and the small town, the passing on of trades and land, and the agricultural cycle of seasons and harvests pushed into the background. Now it was the city, the railroad, the factory, and the machine that dominated. The smokestack replaced the steeple on the horizon of people's lives. The density of the city closed in around men, women, and children who had once accepted open space as a natural condition of life.

Out of this rush of change and concern for the people caught in the process came the American recreation movement. It was part of a larger concern about the social consequences of the industrial city. Public recreation was humane in its instigation, political in its implementation, and complex in its development. The Industrial Revolution was a time of conflict between mill and mine owners and wage workers. There was conflict over work conditions and hours, over control of the workplace and the community. The drive for productivity led to programs to control workers' leisure as well as their labor. In the industrial city, everything was changed.

Now the industrial city has turned into the metropolis, most employment is no longer in the factory, and the map of residence and of leisure has expanded along the highways of a mobile people. Nevertheless, we come out of an industrial age that has left its marks on our leisure as well as our economy.

ISSUES

How did the profound and pervasive changes of industrialization and urbanization reshape American leisure?

What were the conditions that brought about the beginning of the public recreation movement in America?

Why was leisure an area of conflict as the economy changed from the farm to the factory?

How have changes in housing, transportation, income distribution, and work conditions altered leisure in the modern city?

The second half of the nineteenth century was a time of intense social change. The Civil War had spurred industrialization in the North and brought an end to the slave-powered agricultural economy of the South. New citizens from Europe entered through the New York gateway and most stayed in the cities of the Northeast. Electricity and the gasoline reciprocating engine began to revolutionize the home and transportation. The day of the gaslight, the horse, and the agricultural society was almost over.

The new industrial city loomed on the horizon and threatened to remake the landscape and the social fabric of a nation. There had been cities before; tame centers of commerce and government, of culture and retailing. The new city demanded power, raw materials, transportation by rail and river, and *people*. It demanded concentrations of investment capital as factories replaced handwork with machines. And the city demanded markets for its products that were manufactured for a nation and a world coming alive to iron, steel, and power.

It is hard to imagine those changes now, to think of cities with mud streets, horse-drawn vehicles, the wealthy and the business classes living near the city centers, and groceries and ice delivered by cart. A technological explosion changed both the face and the structure of a nation.

Factories for textiles were developed in England in the early nineteenth century, and the raw materials and market flow of the British political and economic empire were set into motion.

The steam engine powered ships by 1815 and railways in the United States in 1827. By 1850, the United States had increased its railways from 21,000 to 170,000 miles. Canals were dug to move cargo to and from the cities.

By 1885, Thomas Edison had not only developed electric light with the incandescent carbon filament but had refined the electric generator. By 1890, London had an underground electric railway. The Atlantic Ocean was crossed by radio in 1901. Then, in the twentieth century, the automobile changed from a toy of the wealthy to the mass-produced Model T, and a whole people took to wheels.

In the office, Remington was producing a usable typewriter by 1880, and calculating machines were in common use by the end of the century.

But it was the factory that made the new city. The sewing machine was ready for industrial use by the 1850s. Interchangeable parts and mass production were introduced into gun making, clothing, all kinds of metal products, electric motors, gasoline engines, and eventually the automobile. Steel production rose from less than 100,000 tons in 1870 to 25 million tons by 1910. The 10 million tons of coal produced in the 1850s increased fiftyfold by 1910. Railroads boosted their freight hauling from 10 billion ton-miles in 1870 to 150 billion forty years later.

During the first half of the twentieth century the population of the United States doubled to 150 million, life expectancy increased from fifty to almost seventy years, per capita income went from $231 to $1,870, and the number of automobiles went from 13,000 to 44 million. The 1 million telephones in 1900 rose to 43 million in 1950, and the use of electric energy increased almost 7,000 percent. The workweek declined on the average from eighty-four hours in 1800 to sixty in 1900 and about forty by 1950.

And now there is television, the miniaturized computer, and suggestions that we are entering a "postindustrial society."

With some sense of the radical nature of the changes of industrialization, what were some of the consequences for those who lived in that time of transition?

The New Industrial City

The city of the immediate past was a product of the factory. When the workplace was the home, the field, and the small shop, then people could be dispersed. When the main industry was agriculture, which requires productive land, people were located on or near that land. Prior to industrialization, America was a country of farms and villages. The cities, modest in size by today's standards, were centers of finance, culture, education, and retailing.

The new industrial city was a center of production. The factory requires raw materials to fashion into its products, power to run the machines, and people to operate them. Since the steady influx of materials and outflow of manufactured goods require some means of transportation, most cities were located at harbor sites or where rivers join. In time the railroads would expand city siting to locations near critical raw materials.

Of the three requirements—materials, power, and people—the most mobile was people. So the labor supply was brought to the mushrooming city alongside the harbor or the river. Some workers were recruited and transported by manufacturers. Others left places where they could not find employment to migrate to places where they heard jobs were available or where a relative had already found employment. They came to shacks and slums, to fringe areas, and to crowded tenements. In mining towns they were housed in company barracks and later in company houses. Many came off the boats from Europe. Others left worn-out land or had been displaced by new powered machines on the farm. They came drawn by the factory and often pushed by starvation and persecution. They came because there was work; and work meant food, a roof, a bed, and possibly a better tomorrow.

The shape of the new city tended to push outward from its financial heart. From the financial and retail center there were rings of transportation, factories, warehouses, and residential areas. The old neighborhoods ringing the center of the city with fine town-houses and even mansions of the old aristocracy gradually were displaced. A few pockets of wealthy residence were maintained alongside lakes or on hilltops, but most of those with old wealth or with new high incomes allowed themselves to be pushed to the expanding fringes of the city. In time they moved out again and then again to establish the suburban areas that could be protected from the crowding and pollution of the city.

In the meantime, old buildings were divided and subdivided to provide rooms and apartments for the immigrants. Men, women, and children from Irish and Italian villages and cities came for work with others from the American South. At first the children worked in the factories and mines with their parents. In time child labor laws left only "adults" over twelve and then fifteen with women in the textile mills, men in steel and machines, and mixtures elsewhere. The sixty-hour week with Sunday off became the standard and was gradually reduced during the first half of the twentieth century.

Critical to understanding the industrial city is the issue of space. First, the workplace was separated from the residence. Those with the greatest resources were able to travel farthest to escape the effects of industrial pollution and wastes. Wage workers were clustered around the factory so they could walk in for their long shifts and walk home to sink, exhausted, into some corner of the crowded tenement. The principle of the separation of workplace from residence was compounded by crowding everywhere. Factories were jammed with machines and accidents were commonplace. Residences were jammed with people and were hazardous due to fire and lack of sanitation.

And where was there space for leisure?

Industrialization, Time, and Space

The industrial city gave a new shape to the time and space composition of the Western world. The social timetable was no longer based on the cycles of planting and harvest of crops or the milking of cows. Time was reshaped by the rigid requirements of the machine for attention. Early factories were labor-intensive with hundreds of interrelated jobs feeding and harvesting the machines. The ecology of human settlement was no longer based on tending the land but on getting to the factory. The significant distance was not how far a wagon could travel in a day but how far a factory hand could walk or ride a horse-drawn street car to work.

The Factory and the Work Schedule

The early days of the factory have now passed out of living memory. Children were working six days a week in English factories. Men labored fourteen hours every day but Sunday and then were chastised from middle-class pulpits because they got drunk on Saturday night. Shopgirls in Chicago earned three to five dollars a week in the "best stores" in town and were grateful to escape the lung-destroying air of the mill or sweatshop.

It was the coal mines and the iron and steel mills that destroyed men most quickly. In the mills the drive for production often kept workers at a seven-day-a-week twelve-hour day in the 110-plus degree heat, poisonous fumes, and machine-paced pressure. When the combination took its toll on health, the lucky ones were able to stay on as sweepers at seventy-five cents a day while the "less fortunate" were left destitute. In the mines some lads began to descend the shafts as breaker boys at as young as six years of age.

Young women earned the same three to five dollars a week at their sewing machines, barely enough to purchase a loaf of bread, a cup of tea, and a bed in a tenement attic. In 1842, Massachusetts passed a law that confined the workday of children under twelve to ten hours, but there was no effective enforcement. It was not until the early 1900s that a national movement to control child labor closed the mines and the mills to children. These children were part of families desperate to secure food and shelter on a combined income of a few dollars a week. Illness and accident reduced the income and added to expenses. To the mill owner, workers of any age or sex were replaceable and far less costly than machines.

Of course, there were protests. The Pullman strike in 1893 and the Homestead steel strike in 1892 were only two of the most famous and bitter of more than 2,000 between 1880 and 1900. The Pullman strike was triggered by five cuts in wage rates, the last by 30 percent, when the company was distributing more than $2 million a year in dividends. The Homestead steel strike was crushed by armed militia in the name of keeping order in the society. Twenty workers were killed and 3,000 fired. With few exceptions, the 6 million workers who struck in the twenty years before 1900 were defeated by the united power of the industrialists and the government ready to employ troops to preserve the way things were.

As the unions gradually began to secure improvements in working conditions and wages and reductions in hours, it became economical to expand the proportion of work that could be done by machines. The workday shortened to about ten hours and the workweek to six days by the turn of the century, but the factory still was the basis of the social schedule of the cities. Sunday was *the* day free from the work schedule. The long workweek and overpowering conditions in mines, factories, and most shops dominated nonwork time. Workers were exhausted, frustrated, and, in many cases, ill.

Some of the concern over the activities of those workers expressed by the "leaders" of the society demonstrated their lack of understanding of the work and living conditions of the time. The tensions and fatigue did lead many to use their one weekly break to escape and to try to forget. The neighborhood bar was one place to go, especially when the tenement was crowded. There were, after all, no parks, playing fields, or other recreation areas near those tenements. The saloon was better than the streets, especially in the winter. For women there were few places to go; for the most part, they had to make do with the space of their rooms and front steps.

As children left the factories, they were gradually absorbed into schools that kept them off the streets for a time. The school kept factory hours of starting, and there were usually some older women or mothers of infants at home in the afternoons. Schools took from the factory their opening times, days of operation, and internal timetables of fixed periods of study. But when school was out, where were the children to go? Some would work delivering goods in this time of small shops and personal service. Others cleaned up in stores and mills. For many there was no place but the street and any isolated cellar where a group of peers could gather. The industrial city was built for finance and the factory, but not for the child.

The Ecology of the City

By 1960, city dwellers were more than 70 percent of the population, but occupied less than 1 percent of the land. The ecology of the centralized industrial city has always been characterized by crowding. The city brings together finance with production. At first factories were labor intensive. Women garment workers were tied to sewing machines jammed into airless lofts. Men tended their machines in multifloor factories ringing the heart of the city.

In area the industrial city of the nineteenth century was no more than a tenth the size of the modern city with its modern transportation and communications. The city of the factory had to be highly centralized and concentrated, unlike the metropolitan sprawl of today. Residence and workplace were separated only by distances that could be travelled on foot or by horsedrawn streetcar. The residential areas were immediate slums. Buildings were crowded and unsafe with minimal sanitary facilities, perhaps one toilet per floor of several flats.

The crowding was further intensified by ethnic and racial segregation. Working-class neighborhoods around the mills tended to solidify immigrants from Europe, first from the north and later from the south. Even today there are residual ethnic enclaves in northern cities. Segregation by race, however, has been maintained by combinations of poverty and practices of discrimination. African-American workers were recruited from the South into northern industrial cities during both World Wars to work in war-mobilized factories. At the end of the wars, they were usually the first fired and the last to be rehired. At the same time, mechanization of agriculture in the rural South propelled many left without work to the cities.[1] They were poorly prepared for urban life by a disastrous educational system and lack of skill-developing work opportunities. In Chicago, for example, they were jammed into southside ghettos with 90 percent of Chicago's African-American population concentrated into an area about seven miles long and one and a half miles wide. This was the area that in time was abandoned by all who could leave as well as by the factories. Such racial exclusion and abandonment eventually led to the "projects" of public housing.

Over time the city gradually spread out over wider areas as public and private transportation became more common. At first there were concentric rings of factories, warehouses, and working-class residences around the downtown financial center. In time, railways led to suburbs and then highways to the current sprawl of the metropolis. In the first decades of industrialization, however, the cities were tightly packed with only a few protected areas on hilltops and lakefronts for the wealthy.

The Recreation Response to the New City

The recreation movement in the United States began as an urban phenomenon. It was in part a response to the sight of children being arrested for playing in the streets and youth hauled off to jail for swimming off a New York pier. Public concern for recreation was a response to the evident fact that children in the city had no place to play. First, in 1885

[1] Nicholas Lemann, *The Promised Land: The Great Black Migration and How It Changed America* (New York: Alfred A. Knopf, 1991).

there was a little sand area in a Boston churchyard. Then there were a few playgrounds. About 1900, a few small parks for recreation and play rather than just strolling were established. Just before and after the First World War, provisions of neighborhood recreation centers became part of public programs in many cities. The more than 2 million acres of city parks and more than $900 million in city recreation budgets of the 1970s developed from one sand pile ninety years earlier and a few little parks only seventy years before.

The Early History

The need was plain enough. Crowding at home and rampant disease were compounded by the lack of space for escape. A selection of events as follows may give a sense of the gradual building of momentum in the recreation movement:

1820–40: Some schools and colleges provide outdoor gyms and sport areas.

1853: Land is purchased for Central Park in New York City. The design is for strolling more than games and sports, and it is miles away from the poor.

1885: First sand garden at Parmenter Street Chapel in Boston.

1892: A model playground at Hull House in Chicago.

1905: Opening of ten South Park centers in Chicago.

1906: Playground Association of America organized (recreation added to the title in 1911).

1924: Conference on Outdoor Recreation called by President Calvin Coolidge.

1930: National Recreation Association formed from old PRAA and first National Recreation Congress held two years later.

1933: Expansion of recreation facilities and services through national work programs.

1945: North Carolina establishes first state recreation commission.

1958: Outdoor Recreation Resources Review Commission begins study and reorganization of federal outdoor recreation program with a report submitted in 1962.

1964: National Council on the Arts established.

1965: National Recreation and Park Association created by merging the American Institute of Park Executives, the American Recreation Society, the National Conference of State Parks, and the National Recreation Association.

The early parks were quite different from playgrounds. Central Park, designed by Calvert Vaux and Frederick L. Olmstead, was completely a product of the architects and not a preservation of terrain and natural growth. While some space for riding, boating, skating, and children's play was provided, Central Park was like European gardens and parks in that it was primarily for strolling and appreciation. Golden Gate Park in San Francisco, completed in 1887, was transformed out of marsh and sand dunes into a place for walking, riding, and carriages.

A number of parks were designed more for activity than these classics. As early as 1871 the citizens of Brookline, Massachusetts, authorized the purchase of two pieces of land for parks, but they were not developed. However, by 1892, as many as 100 cities had land designated for parks, but their use was retarded by a lack of design and facilities. Their use by children who played there anyway is not recorded.

Perhaps a ten-acre tract along the river in Boston was the first serious attempt to provide facilities and supervision for games and sports. It was fenced and landscaped for wading, bathing, rowing, gymnastics, and running and had swings, seesaws, and a sand garden for children. Just as significant, the park department hired directors to develop activities in the Charlesbank Outdoor Gymnasium.

After considerable effort by Jacob Riis, an urban reformer, New York City purchased a little more than two and a half acres in a tenement area for $1.8 million and opened Seward Park in 1899. Play apparatus, a wading pool, a gymnasium with changing rooms, game areas, and seats for spectators were included in the design planned as a model. Within a few years, Louisville, Chicago, and Boston had begun to follow this lead.

The $5 million bond issue for ten parks in South Chicago may have been the most dramatic action of all. By 1905, these parks were hailed as a major achievement and established a new standard for such provisions.[2] The parks varied from seven acres to three hundred and included indoor facilities for sports, dramatics, eating, clubs, and reading and outdoor space for games, sports, band concerts, swimming, and a wide variety of programs. They were the launching pad for major municipal entry into modern recreation programs and provisions.

One antecedent of importance was the stress on recreation in the program of the famous Hull House in Chicago. Jane Addams established the settlement house to provide comprehensive services to the poor—especially foreign-born—and to assist their adjustment to the city. Hull House included indoor and outdoor recreation facilities along with several opportunities to learn skills in the arts. It became the model for many other such comprehensive settlement house programs, which provided opportunities for the development of the whole person. Unlike some programs, Hull House took account of the needs of both men and women. It was also a center of political resistance and action.

Other developments of importance were the opening of school buildings with grounds for recreation and the inauguration of organizations dedicated to expanding the recreation movement. As in Boston, when the first play areas were begun as the projects of voluntary associations and religious organizations, the general trend was toward public support. Public agencies began to finance and operate playgrounds and recreation projects by 1900 in many cities. Also, almost from the first, the public schools entered into the provision of recreation opportunities. In 1901, the Boston School Committee operated playgrounds. By 1898, some schools in New York City were opened in the evenings for recreation and nearly thirty schools were being used within a decade. Rochester and Milwaukee were other cities that took an early lead in developing recreation opportunities through their school systems.

It was not until the early twentieth century that people concerned with recreation took the initiative in forming organizations to further the recreation movement. In 1906, with the endorsement of President Theodore Roosevelt, the Playground Association of America was established in Washington, D.C. Roosevelt was elected honorary president and

[2] George D. Butler, *Introduction to Community Recreation,* Fifth edition (New York: McGraw-Hill, 1976).

Jacob Riis, the urban reformer, was honorary vice president. Luther H. Gulick was the first president and Henry S. Curtis the first secretary. In 1910, Joseph Lee, who with Gulick provided much of the early spirit and philosophy of the movement, was elected president. The next year the name of the organization was changed to Playground and Recreation Association of America. Lee served as president until 1937, providing both continuity and wisdom to the new movement.

The Aims of the Recreation Movement

The recreation movement was in its inception a humanitarian response to the city. The appetite of the mills and the mines for cheap labor and the general indifference to the consequences for the men, women, and children working there could not go without protest for long. At first, with others equally destitute waiting to take any job, the protests could not come from the workers themselves. Reformers came, then as later, from the same institutions that supported the economic system and that benefited from it. Some reformers were from the schools and some from the churches. Some were people of considerable personal wealth. They protested child labor, degrading working conditions, endangered health and safety in mill, mine, and tenement, low wages, unemployment, the compliance of government officials in suppressing protests, and the general human costs of the industrial system.

Among the reformers were a few especially concerned with the opportunities denied children and youth to play, to learn, and to develop healthy bodies and minds. They saw children with no place to play. They saw the waste of human lives in the city where space was so costly. They were also concerned that "healthy recreation" replace activities that rendered workers unfit for the factory.

Joseph Lee was probably the most influential pioneer in the early recreation movement. A lawyer from a wealthy Yankee family, Lee participated in a survey of play opportunities for children in Boston in 1882 when he was twenty years old. Shocked at seeing boys hauled off to jail for playing in the streets, he helped organize a playground in a vacant lot. In 1898, he joined in developing a model playground in Boston that included a play area for small children, a larger space for boys and sport, and separated gardens. His speaking and writing in the following years, his inauguration of a training program for recreation leaders, and his direction of services for troops during World War I were major influences on the movement in which he continued to be active until his death in 1937.

In his book *Play and Education,* Lee discussed the channeling of play instincts into constructive activity through leadership and education. Play instincts require direction into games, artistic creation, and social expressions through teaching. Motives for play were not seen as secondary but as focused around the desire to achieve that is found in both work and play. Simply pursuing pleasure was not the end of play:

> Pleasure results from play, and may, in the sophisticated, become a conscious motive, but it is not the play motive. It is extraneous, a by-product; it does not in any way account for the play attitude or the direction of the play instincts. In play the motive of the act is the doing of it.[3]

---

[3] Joseph Lee, *Play and Education,* Second edition (New York: Macmillan, 1929), p. 255.

Play involves both learning and discipline. Because of its expression of social relationships, intrinsic satisfaction, and physical and emotional well-being, play is health-producing. It is one factor in combatting the social and personal ills of the city:

> The battle with the slum is not primarily a battle against the obvious evils of drink, overcrowding, immorality, and bad sanitary arrangements. These are the evidences that the slum exists. . . . The slum is what is left when from an aggregate of people living together you subtract the local personality. . . . Every social environment that is not a neighborhood is essentially a slum.[4]

Lee was expressing a concept that was to reappear a half century later. The urban neighborhood as a social network of human support and cultural expression is more than a political district or church parish. It is the context of life together. When that social context is destroyed by any set of conditions, then isolated programs or provisions cannot make the area capable of sustaining human life. Recreation is only one element, an important one, in the total neighborhood life.

Constructive leisure was for Lee an essential element in re-creating a city that could nurture and enhance human development. Therefore, while play is motivated by the experience of doing it, the provision of opportunities for play and recreation has social purpose. With the mill stifling rather than offering human expression, Lee believed that leisure was necessary if civilization was to advance.

Luther H. Gulick, a physician by training, was a founder of the forerunner of the National Recreation Association and a leader in providing special training for recreation leaders. In 1887, Gulick began the first summer program for the "special training of gymnasium instructors" at the School for Christian Workers (later to become Springfield College) in Massachusetts. He directed all physical education programs for the YMCAs in the United States and Canada and was director of physical education for the New York City school system. He was the first president of the Playground Association of America and the Camp Fire Girls of America.

Gulick's activity and concerns draw together the public, professional, voluntary, educational, and religious elements in the early recreation movement. He saw the need for cooperative approaches to community recreation provision and organization. He believed that much behavior was "degenerative" and led to crime and other unhealthy activity. Recreation provided a positive substitute for such activity and in the long run would be more beneficial than restriction and punishment alone. Despite his humanitarian concerns, he was one of those who feared that too much free time for common laborers would make them less efficient in the mill and mine. In his book *A Philosophy of Play*, Gulick proposed recreation as important to building character in ways that would make people better workers.

On the other hand, play for children was seen by Gulick as "doing what we want to do, . . . simply for the joy of the process.[5] Play for children is important and serious just as work is for adults. Play is engrossing, tiring, and vigorous for children and youth. It is the life space in which they invest themselves and find expression. Unlike recreation for adults,

---

[4] Ibid., p. 385.

[5] Luther H. Gulick, *A Philosophy of Play* (New York: Schirmer, 1920), p. 125.

which Gulick saw as primarily rest and restoration for work, the play of children is essential for their growth and development.

In general, the early recreation leaders were concerned for the play element in life and especially for children and youth. They believed that opportunities for physical and social activity, for expressive and developmental play, were essential to a full life. Seeing clearly that opportunities for such activity were severely limited in the new industrial city, they set out to bring about change through action by governmental bodies, schools, churches, and voluntary organizations. They got the attention of the White House and of mayors, of educators and philanthropists, and even of the political machines of the eastern cities. Their aim was not narrow. Joseph Lee and others like him had no less a vision than to re-create life in the city. Their program was to provide opportunities for play and recreation, for sport and cultural development, where there had been none.

The Struggle for Leisure

Industrialization changed not only the configuration of the city, but also the shape of social life. Workers were now totally dependent on the wage of the factory, shop, and mine with no relation to the land where they produced at least some of their own food and household support. In the early period, everyone—men, women, and children—were in the mills. Families no longer worked together. Work became separated from the life of the family. In time, children were barred from the workplace, and women became less likely to stay in the mills once they married and bore children. The factory not only separated people from the land, but also separated families from each other in the workplace, by gender as well as by age. Employed women were in gender-segregated industries. More and more, men became the "provider" and women focused on home and family. Industrialization in time led to the segregation and division of work by gender. Women were in the paid labor force primarily in conditions of necessity. Work at home was directed to women, unpaid and considered of marginal economic value. Outside the home, women's economic roles were limited primarily to support and caregiving with low wages almost universal.

Recreation programs for wage workers, especially for men, were intended to keep employees fit for productive effort. Especially in the early days of long hours and six-day weeks, there was great concern over the "curse" of drinking and its consequences. Bars and taverns were licensed and limited in hours. Alternative opportunities were offered with the goal of producing workers who were healthier and more productive. Apprehension was expressed from church pulpits and in editorials about the inability of ordinary workers to develop leisure that would contribute to work and to family life.

The work schedule was designed to keep the factory machines operating as long and as fast as possible. In time mill owners discovered that shorter hours and better working conditions increased productivity. The so-called "work ethic" was hardly universal among workers who saw mill owners as ones who exploited "real labor."[6] The workplace was a contested area with unions organized to improve working conditions and reduce hours as well as raise wages.[7] At the same time, there was a struggle for leisure, for time and for

[6] D. T. Rodgers, *The Work Ethic in Industrial America, 1850–1920* (Chicago: University of Chicago Press, 1978).

[7] Roy Rosenzweig, *Eight Hours for What We Will: Workers and Leisure in an Industrial City, 1870–1920* (New York: Columbia University Press, 1983.)

freedom of expression. Industrialists joined with reformers, religious organizations, and political machines to offer alternatives to workers' leisure that was considered dangerous to the social order. At the same time, direct control was exercised over ethnic celebrations imported from the "old country," sports such as prizefighting sponsored by bars, drinking outside licensed establishments, and "street" activity considered disruptive.[8] Gambling was common on boxing, cockfighting, animal combat, horseracing, cards, and other unregulated contests. Alcohol was even more common and restrictions eventually led to an attempt at Prohibition.

Government regulated and even suppressed various kinds of leisure, especially of working males. Other activities were permitted only when local political organizations including the police were paid off with bribes. On the other hand, government bodies eventually joined with voluntary organizations to provide acceptable recreation opportunities in the cities. These efforts were usually promoted as alternatives to license and as ways to create more productive workers and more stable families. In opposition to these efforts, there was a struggle on the side of the workers themselves. First, they sought greater leisure time, "eight hours for what we will." Second, they rebelled against regulation that attempted to limit their freedom. And third, they participated in schemes to subvert the system of control by setting up their own places and buying off the enforcers. Even the young women in the urban shops in Northern cities commonly attended the "immoral" dance halls rather than the programs offered to protect them from temptation and danger.[9]

During this period of privation and attempts to control the lives of workers, there were conflicts over both work and leisure. Hundreds of strikes were directed toward reducing hours and the dangers of work conditions as well as wage increases. Often they were put down when mill owners called in the police, private armies, and even state militia. Less dramatic were the struggles over leisure that took place in the neighborhoods, on the streets, and even in parks. It is now difficult to identify the motivations of early reformers. Their humanitarian values seem to have been mixed with concerns over social order and the aim of creating a more cooperative and productive work force. They were, after all, believers in the system, even in this period of rapid and uneven change.

Leisure in the New City

However, the rise of the new recreation movement was not going on in a vacuum. Not only were there reforms of working conditions and expansion of educational opportunities, but other leisure provisions were being developed. The growing city was also a new market for the providers of commercial entertainment.

Sport as Leisure

Spectator sports emerged before the Civil War as major occasions. In the city, sport was the consumption of entertainment as well as participation. As many as 100,000 people

[8] Gary Cross, *A Social History of Leisure since 1600* (College Park, PA: Venture Publishing, 1990).

[9] Kathy Piess, *Cheap Amusements: Working Women and Leisure in Turn-of-the-Century New York* (Philadelphia: Temple University Press, 1986).

crossed the Hudson River from New York City for horse races. Boxing was generally illegal, but drew crowds in secluded back rooms of saloons or warehouses in the city or outdoors where authorities would not enforce legal prohibitions against "prizefighting." In the 1860s and 1870s, track and field competition was promoted by athletic clubs, gymnastics was imported on the model of the German Turnverein and sponsored by various groups including the YMCA, and colleges began early forms of intercollegiate football.

High society continued horseback sports such as hunting and racing and added polo and coaching. Cycling clubs organized weekend runs on country roads and bicycling grew as a participant sport. Lawn tennis was still primarily a sport of the upper classes, but skating was more available to the less affluent in the northern states. Rowing grew in the East along with other sports imported from England. Lawn bowling and other games increased in popularity after the Civil War.

However, the peculiarly American sport was baseball. By 1845, some men had formed the Knickerbocker Club and adopted rules specifying nine men to a side, three outs to an inning, and twenty-one runs as the winning score. Although the first teams were composed of "gentlemen," baseball could not be confined to one class. The Eckford Club in Brooklyn was formed in 1855 and made up of shipwrights and mechanics. Before long, upper class dominance was at an end.

The sport moved west as well. In 1858, Chicago had four teams and the National Association of Base Ball Players was formed to organize the sport nationally. The same year 2,000 people paid to watch a game at the Fashion Race Course. In 1869, the Cincinnati Red Stockings were formed as professionals and went on tour. In 1871, the amateurs of the National Association lost in an organizational dispute to the professionals. Then, within a few years, the players lost control to the club owners and the present economic basis for professional sport was established.

In the meantime the "trickle-down" pattern of introducing a sport for the wealthy and having it adopted by middle and lower classes after a few years was continued in roller skating. Its introduction at fashionable Newport was followed swiftly by the construction of rinks in towns across the land with immense arenas in the cities. The Olympic Club in San Francisco advertised 5,000 pairs of skates and 69,000 square feet of hardwood floor.

Football had been banned in the eastern colleges due to its danger to participants. The first recorded intercollegiate game between Princeton and Rutgers was in 1869, and Harvard and Yale revived the sport three years later. Four thousand spectators were at the Princeton-Yale game in 1878. In ten years the crowd swelled to almost 40,000. At first an adaptation of English rugby, football was quite a different game when the Intercollegiate Football Association adopted the first rules in 1881.

Commercial Recreation in the New City

Despite the long hours and grinding poverty of the urban factory workers, there was a desire for recreation. Some leisure was rest and an opportunity to talk, listen, and daydream. Some was developed around the ethnic cultures brought to the Italian, Irish, Jewish, and German ghettos of the New World. There was no space or opportunity for many to join in the sports described above, but they did seek some entertainment that could be purchased for pennies, nickels, and dimes.

The new Bowery in New York entertained mill workers with its melodrama and variety acts. The air was blue with smoke and redolent of beer and sweat. The audience might respond to a weak act with catcalls and rotten fruit, but admission was only a dime and the theater had a bar. Melodramas with their treacherous villains, innocent heroines, and valiant heroes were produced by the thousands all across the land. Gentleman Jim Corbett and Buffalo Bill Cody appeared in such theaters to save various young women from several fates. In time, Buffalo Bill organized his Wild West, Rocky Mountain, and Prairie Exhibition that played to more than a million people in one five-month tour. Indians, cowboys, steers, stagecoaches, and even Sitting Bull joined the white-hatted hero in this wide-stage extravaganza.

Burlesque, vaudeville, minstrels, and a wide range of entertainments shared the stage with drama in the growth of theater entertainment, They competed for the dimes with dancehalls, shooting galleries, bowling alleys, pool halls, beer gardens, and countless saloons. Dime museums and their curiosities and "freaks" were less elaborate versions of P. T. Barnum's circus, which was a national institution by the 1840s. By the end of the century, the new electric trolleys were able to transport people to the amusement parks constructed on the outskirts of the cities. Coney Island had its bathhouses, minstrel bands, dance halls, shows, and by 1900 a series of "rides." Chicago's Midway at the World's Fair of 1893 introduced the Ferris wheel, which soon was duplicated by the hundreds in the trolley parks.

Despite efforts at control, the desire for leisure was too powerful to suppress. In the neighborhoods of the cities, most bars were clearly identified as catering to one ethnic group. They became a center of men's recreation, while the women tended to maintain their territory in the flat. But on the festive occasions of family, church, or ethnic celebration, the songs and dances of the culture were revived in parades and large and small gatherings. The front steps and entryways were gathering places for the women and the young in the warmer months, while the males ventured farther out to form groups and seek excitement. All this time their schedules and their energies were still dominated by the factories where the machines ruled and workers were considered replaceable. Alienation from control over the self or the work process combined with poverty, insecurity, and exhaustion to make escape the natural aim of the few hours free from the factory.

In many mill towns, games and entertainments were brought from Europe with the immigrant workers. Ethnic clubs provided organized activity as well as places to meet. Neighborhood saloons in time were licensed and regulated as they moved from tenement basements to established storefronts. In much the same way, penny movies were replaced by the ornate movie palaces, but remained a major leisure resource for the women shop workers. Most communities attempted to organize festivals and other recreation events that could be regulated. For the most part, however, opportunities for dancing, drinking, and other entertainment were provided by local business enterprises. In the midst of crowding and squalor, the men and women of the mills found low-cost escape from the conditions of their work and living conditions.

Even in the city of the nineteenth century, leisure became a significant industry. The film industry was dominated by a few corporations that controlled both production and distribution. Sports were spectacles to be consumed. Entertainment was changed by technologies and designed for mass audiences. Ethnic associations lost influence with the emergence of the car, the radio, and the movie palace. In time, leisure became big business.

Urbanization and Leisure: A Summary

Major sections of this book on contemporary leisure trace the later history of public recreation provisions and the changing geographic contexts of leisure. Historical materials and analysis are found in chapters on government organization, economics, work and leisure, sport and leisure, and others. However, critical issues related to industrialization and urbanization call for some emphasis and analysis before moving to the contemporary era.

In the context of the history of the industrial city, one myth should be put to rest. It is the myth of dominance of the Protestant work ethic in American culture. Accounts of work conditions in the mill and mine of the early period of industrialization do not suggest that work was satisfying, central to life's meaning or personal identities, or an experience to be looked forward to. Rather, in those days not working meant for factory labor an inability to feed, clothe, and house a family. There was no welfare or unemployment insurance. In fact, there was no insurance to protect those crippled in industrial accidents.

The kind of alienation from control over the process of work and of identification with the product of the factory expressed in contemporary interviews would hardly have been an issue in 1880. Not only were hours longer and conditions worse, but voicing such dissatisfaction would have meant instant dismissal with no union to seek redress. It is true that the Andrew Carnegies and some of the pious and protected servants of industry in pulpits and in academic halls spoke of the importance of work and the dangers of indolence. (Indolence was defined as not working sixty hours or more a week.) But the worker was, in most cases, just learning how to fight back out of his powerlessness. He was beginning to risk his little bit of security to organize and to strike. The work ethic was alive in those days, in corporate offices and in Main Street shops, but seldom in the mine, the factory, or the slum. Most worked to live, and did not live to work.

A number of other issues emerge from a consideration of urbanization and leisure. Any ethic, work or leisure, presupposes freedom. An ethic requires that some value or set of values will guide decisions. Without some measure of freedom to decide among alternatives, the ethic and the values are meaningless. Industrialization and urbanization seem to have posed the same kind of threat to that freedom as did slavery and conditions of scarcity in previous eras. Work hours, poverty, lack of space, health conditions, and some loss of old community ties in the industrial city may have left little freedom and few alternatives.

The Industrial Revolution was a time of the profound transformation of a society. Nothing remained the same. The agricultural economy, small towns, direct connection with nature, seasonal cycles, integrated family work, and a sense of being part of a community—all gave way to the industrial city. Space for living became an issue. Work was tied to the machine and the factory. Leisure became less based in natural environments and communities and more on specialized and often commercial environments. Control of leisure in the neighborhood as well as of the workplace created conflicts between workers who sought greater freedom and owners who attempted to maximize the output of their factories. Ethnic celebrations and expressions gave way to mass leisure and consumption. Women were limited, for the most part, to secondary positions in the economy and to segregated lives at home.

In time, work hours were shorter, reduced for most to about 40 hours in a five-day week. Work conditions became safer, if still highly controlled and routinized for many. The incomes of most workers rose to a level permitting home ownership, more education for children, and even some discretionary spending for leisure. Yet, the city is still divided, conflicted, segregated, and crowded. Work roles are still uncertain and often insecure. Technologies have increased the scope and variety of leisure, but considerable time remains devoted to consuming entertainment. The themes of urban and industrial change set the stage for modern society. Even the most recent social transformations are called "post-industrial."

HIGHLIGHTS

1. The new industrial city, built for the factory, did not provide space for living, especially after children were barred from factory and mine.
2. The factory determined the ecology and the timetables of the industrial city.
3. The early public recreation movement was part of a social reform response to urban conditions as well as controlling working-class leisure.
4. Despite elements of elitism and the justification of recreation as necessary to provide health and contentment among workers, the necessity of play and leisure as a free and creative element in human life was basic to early rationales for public recreation.
5. The commercial entertainments of the city were quite different from the leisure of agricultural communities.
6. Just as the early industrial city was dramatically different from the small town, so the modern metropolis is evolving into an environment different from that of the old centralized city.

Discussion Questions

1. Were there alternatives to the establishment of a public recreation program in American cities in the late nineteenth century? Why did schools not become the primary recreation providers? Commercial enterprises?

2. How likely are workers to believe in a work ethic when they find their work exhausting, routine, and unsatisfying?

3. Was the early public recreation movement more a response of social concern or of a desire to control those who were needed in industry? What evidence is there for your position?

4. Was leisure really possible in the early industrial city when so many workers had so little time, space, energy, or financial discretion?

5. Are many of the conditions that stimulated the founding of the American recreation movement still limiting the lives of urban children and youth?

6. How much space is needed for leisure? In the city, is there a basic need for outdoor space, for protected space in severe climates, and for space in the home? Give examples of space-intensive and space-free leisure.

7. Does the forty-hour week alone make leisure possible? What more is needed for leisure to be fulfilling and human? Are there conditions of life in the contemporary city that make leisure difficult or even impossible? What would they be? Are there limits to people's ability to adapt?

Bibliography

Bettman, Otto L., *The Good Old Days—They Were Terrible!* New York: Random House, 1974.

Braden, Donna R., *Leisure and Entertainment in America.* Dearborn, MI: Henry Ford Museum, 1988.

Cross, Gary, *A Social History of Leisure Since 1600.* College Park, PA: Venture Publishing, 1990.

Cumbler, John T., *Working-Class Community in Industrial America.* Westport, CT: Greenwood Press, 1979.

Dulles, Foster R., *A History of Recreation: America Learns to Play,* Second edition. Englewood Cliffs, NJ: Prentice-Hall, 1965.

Hardy, Stephen, *How Boston Played.* Boston: Northeastern University Press, 1982.

Lemann, Nicholas, *The Promised Land: The Great Black Migration and How It Changed America.* New York: Alfred A. Knopf, 1991.

Park, Robert E., and E. W. Burgess, *The City,* Second edition. Chicago: University of Chicago Press, 1967.

Piess, Kathy, *Cheap Amusements: Working Women and Leisure in Turn-of-the-Century New York.* Philadelphia: Temple University Press, 1986.

Rodgers, D. T., *The Work Ethic in Industrial America, 1850–1920.* Chicago: University of Chicago Press, 1978.

Rosenzweig, Roy, *Eight Hours for What We Will: Workers and Leisure in an Industrial City, 1870–1920.* New York: Columbia University Press, 1983.

Ross, Steven J., *Workers On the Edge: Work, Leisure, and Politics in Industrializing Cincinnati, 1788–1890.* New York: Columbia University Press, 1985.

Sennett, Richard, *Families against the City.* New York: Random House, 1974.

Terkel, Studs, *Working: Working People Talk about What They Do All Day and How They Feel about What They Do.* New York: Pantheon, 1974.

Chapter *11*

From Community to Consumption

The great and pervasive social change of industrialization began in the early nineteenth century. The massive shifts, however, took place between the Civil War and World War I. A nation of agriculture, expansion into the open West, small towns, and a close connection with the land and nature became dominated by the rising industrial city, especially in the Northeast. At the same time, however, Midwest farms were becoming mechanized, homesteads were established and abandoned in the Plains, and the economy rose, fell, and rose again. While urban slums jammed immigrants together, troops were still decimating Native American communities. The Gold Rush transformed California while cattle were trailed to Montana. The South remained mainly agricultural as chattel slavery was replaced by sharecropping and the oppression of "Jim Crow."

Away from the cities, leisure was still tied to the land and work. Small communities existed to serve family farmers and revolved around their churches and organizations as well as general stores. Great wars punctuated the flow of years in ways that reshaped where and how people lived as well as economic structures. The boom of the 1920s was followed by the Great Depression that was, in turn, ended by World War II. The city was ringed by suburbs made possible by the private transportation of the car. The mass media of radio and magazine were overturned by television, and the consumer society had its symbolic centerpiece.

For most households, the relative simplicity of the small community was replaced by the complex metropolis. Social networks of family and friends, usually of similar cultural backgrounds, were challenged by urban diversity. Mass culture and entertainment entered into almost every home. And in the boom years of the 1950s and 1960s, all kinds of consumer goods created markets that had as much to do with the symbols of status and lifestyle as with use. The transformations were not as dramatic as those of industrialization, but they also changed everything.

ISSUES

What were the main elements of social change that transformed American leisure?

How did wars, the Great Depression, and the post–World War II economic expansion change the basis of the culture?

What were the most significant "transforming technologies" that changed leisure?

How has contemporary leisure become a part of the "consumer society"?

Divisions and Contrasts

Without exhausting the range of leisure that has characterized different groups from the early colonies through the middle of the nineteenth century, two comparisons will illustrate the variety.

Town and Country

From the late seventeenth century on, some colonists, especially in New England, settled in small towns while others moved out to the fringes of settlement to establish dispersed homes and farms. The patterns varied from region to region with dispersal being more common in the southern colonies, where a more congenial agricultural area beckoned. However, even in New England some moved westward to chance a new life amid the hazards of wilderness, native tribes, and distance from the help of neighbors. In any case, the leisure of those in towns was enriched by the availability of neighbors, regular social interchange on the streets and around school and church, and ease of visiting. Community events were a regular and expected part of the weekly round. On the other hand, those in the country were forced to find most of their leisure within the family and in such survival-related engagements with the natural environment as fishing and hunting.

Landowner and Servant

Throughout the colonial period of American history, there was a considerable proportion of the population that was not free. Some were slaves for life, captured near the African coast and sold as property. In the seventeenth century a larger proportion was indentured servants who were bound for a period of years to pay off previous debts or the cost of their passage to the New World. Even today there are large landholdings on which the manual labor is done by sharecroppers whose livelihood and housing are dependent on doing the bidding of the owner.

It is too limited to characterize the leisure of a town or an area in terms of the written records of the elite, the landowners, and the leading citizens. At the same time, there were those who were directly under the orders of a master, for life or for a fixed period. There were many others who were obliged to work for those who controlled the land. Their schedules, personal resources, and opportunities for leisure were quite different from those who could manage their resources to provide land for hunting, horses for transportation, spacious manors for entertaining, books for reading, time for education, and relative abundance for pleasure. The servant managed his leisure out of a scarcity of time, resources, and autonomy.

Documentation of Leisure Histories

While the reconstruction of towns has yielded some material about the leisure of ordinary free men, women, and children, for the most part documents that allow reconstruction of ordinary life are scarce. George Washington, Thomas Jefferson, James Madison, and others left letters, diaries, and other documents. Intense research has discovered considerable material about slave life. But the life of those who were free but obscure remains in the shadows of history.

Some of the games—shooting, racing, and the like—appear to have been accessible to the poor and the near-poor as well as the gentry. Drinking, talking, gambling, cock-fighting, and other "men's" activities were widespread. Most who were married no doubt did engage in considerable interaction with their families and found pleasure in that. Women combined domestic duties with extra touches of sewing, weaving, food preparation, and decorating that were at least "semileisure." People did gather in twos and twenties to talk and enjoy each other's company.

Westward Expansion and Preindustrial America

Fortunately, in later segments of American history the everyday composition of life is more accessible. At least a few of those who remember are still around to tell us about the Old West and the rural small town. Leisure in these places was that of common people because those were about all who were there. The occasional English lord or eastern investor such as Theodore Roosevelt who lived for a time in cattle country only served to accentuate the ordinary pleasure-seeking of the rancher or farmer who was struggling to establish a viable unit, of the homesteader and of the cowboy, of those who began the services of the towns, of the itinerants, and of the increasing numbers of women and their children.

Space was both the attraction and the enemy. Broad and apparently fertile expanses, plains without even the barrier of forests to remove for farming, and coastal valleys rich in their promise of lush growth drew those hoping to make a new start.

The Old West

In the earlier days of settlement—whether the economic base was ranching, farming, mining, or trading—it was a man's world. The chances of marriage were small for most men; therefore, many of the means of entertainment did not require any companions but other men. Two or three sprees in town per year might be all the social outlet a man would have except for ongoing interaction with workmates. A good deal of the leisure was related to work and involved making some kind of game of the tasks around the ranch. For example, breaking horses was hard and dangerous work, but it could also be a contest.

Of course, there was always town in the distance. A town might be little more than a combined bar and store and eventually a school, but it was someplace to go. In time, however, the real cow towns offered legal and medical services of sorts and some variety of entertainments with drinking and gambling first and prostitution not far behind as a "leisure business." There would also be occasional meetings held by traveling preachers.

Even in homestead areas, the nearest neighbor was usually out of sight. There were dirt trails but no roads, and some homesteaders could not afford to keep even one horse through the winters. Tiny log cabins with dirt floors and roofs and "soddies" that were all dirt but surprisingly warm were all the shelter and space a family would have in the long winter. An oil lamp but little to read, chores outside and each other inside, and hope for a better time in the summer were the only "leisure" resources for so many. They would welcome anything that would break down the loneliness, any excuse for getting together with people, any visitor, any conquest of the distance and the dangers of travel. One ranch wife remembered how it was near Miles City, Montana:

> Parties were held every so often in our countryside by anyone who had a room big enough—and it didn't have to be very big. . . . People would drive to them from miles and miles away, all bundled up in a wagon with babies in their arms. At most of the dances the babies were simply laid on the floor under the benches where the spectators sat. The few women present would be danced half to death. And it lasted until morning, because you couldn't drive home anyway until it was daylight.[1]

Any kind of event—branding, driving cattle to market, a wedding, a funeral, a revival, or a hanging—was a social event. Where both neighbors and opportunities were few and far between, people had to take their leisure where they found it.

Of course, there were also a variety of leisure providers in the Old West. In the larger towns, the three most common might be categorized as shows, sex, and sanctity. Both the saloon and the church were establishments that brought people together. The saloon was there for men to meet, play cards, drink, and, in some, to watch and purchase the favors of "professional" women. The church provided a gathering place for families of "respectable" citizens and for most of the women. Denominational differences were unimportant as women gathered for worship, for sewing, for study, and for all the accompanying informal socializing.

People gathered for revivals and for executions, for celebration and for mourning. And when they gathered, they reached out for whatever companionship was available because it might be a long time and a long way to the next opportunity.

Small Towns in Transition

It is a long jump in years from the eastern seaboard colonies of the 1600s and 1700s to the period of westward expansion that lasted past the Civil War into the late 1800s. The Industrial Revolution was under way before the last tribes of Native Americans were decimated, starved, and finally trapped on reservation lands that no one else wanted. Home-

---

[1] Mark H. Brown and W. R. Felton, *Before Barbed Wire* (New York: Bramhill House, 1956), p. 58.

steading in the West and the rise of factories along the rivers of the eastern and central states went on at the same time. There is no clear linear progression from colony to town to city or from East to West. Settlements and socioeconomic developments overlap and leapfrog across the map.

The isolation of the frontier community gave way slowly to the car and truck and, in time, to paved roads. Electricity and the telephone reached the more sparsely populated agricultural areas as late as the mid-1900s. Now mass media and modern transportation have brought rural areas into constant contact with what is now a predominantly urban culture. Teens in Keokuk dress much the same as those in the Bronx, see the same TV and videos, and dance to the same music.

Small town life, however, retains some characteristics of former years. Smaller communities are still centered around their primary institutions—schools, churches, and community organizations—even when Main Street is losing out to the shopping mall down the interstate highway. The old myth of Americans as joiners is based largely on studies of small towns. Such communities are, like the rest of the society, divided by social class and race. The "other side of the tracks" is still there. Nevertheless, the anonymity of urban life contrasts the small town in which almost everyone knows almost everyone else. The older forms of entertainment, such as cards and attending school events, have been partly replaced by the mass media. Nevertheless, there is a sense of "community" that is lacking in the city and suburb. For teens, the car has become a means to privacy and separation from the social control of adults. Even the smallest towns usually have at least one bar and one gas station. In the Midwest and South, however, churches still provide as much as 60 percent of the group recreation for adults.

As the nation expanded westward, cultural and religious diversity was intensified by geographical dispersion. In time, communities with rigid blue laws and religious codes of conduct had to accommodate to this diversity. The long battle over the Sabbath was reduced to protection of Sunday morning as sacred. Regional differences emerged as the industrial East and open West were less likely to protect "sacred times" than the so-called "Bible belt" of the South and Midwest. The gradual expansion of nonreligious recreation into formerly protected times led to a new form of conflict between religion and leisure. In time, however, mainline Protestant and Catholic churches and Jewish synagogues adapted to the loss by offering their own recreation opportunities. Youth groups, summer camps, music, drama, and sports were added to their religious programs.

Wars and the Great Depression

One series of events had considerable influence in the growth of the city and the mixing of cultures: the wars that uprooted young men from small town and city alike and required greater production from the factories. The Civil War, World War I, and World War II each had many far-reaching effects on the society. While it is not possible to trace them all or to draw out all their implications for leisure and recreation here, there are three major consequences that are highly significant for shaping contemporary leisure.

1. The mobilization of young men for battle brought about a cultural mixing of rural and urban, native and foreign-born, and different regions. While the organizational structure of the Civil War kept units from a state together for the most part, in encampments and sieges they were exposed to different cultures. Songs, games, sports, language, stories, and hopes and dreams for the future were exchanged. Young men saw parts of the country they had never heard of before. Wars have had important effects in widening cultural and geographic horizons.

2. When the men were gathered for training and combat purposes, they required some opportunities for recreation. In the Civil War they had to make those opportunities for themselves. During the world wars various government and voluntary organizations provided entertainment, social outlets, and sport programs. In World War I the Playground and Recreation Association assisted in developing programs for troops. At the same time various kinds of events related to the war effort were developed in the home communities. The War Camp Community Service was reoriented after the war to continue recreation programming.

3. The backbone of each war effort was industrial. Wars, too, now required machines. As a result, each war brought about an expansion of the factories designed for heavy industry and a recruitment of workers into the cities. Especially during the world wars workers were brought to the northern cities to replace drafted workers and to meet the growing labor requirements. Those new workers, usually from rural areas and ill-prepared for life in the city, often remained after the wars were over. In the transition to peacetime economies, they were the most likely to be laid off. If they were black, they were crowded into the poorest areas of the cities with little opportunity to obtain work anywhere. Racism compounded the picture of a surplus of urban labor to create the racial ghettos plagued with massive unemployment. Now the cities had taken another leap forward in population but backward in provisions for housing, work, and leisure.

Between the Wars

Between the two world wars there were two distinct periods. In the 1920s, relative prosperity for the growing middle class and higher income for both salaried people and investors made it a time of optimism. Not only did more people have financial resources for their leisure, but they tended to see their own pleasure and entertainment as worthy of the investment of both time and money. The failure of Prohibition to curtail the consumption of alcohol was a clear sign of the loss of influence of the old moralism and a greater acceptance of pleasure. Music and dance crazes swept the country, and the courting and sexual customs of the country began to be transformed.

But drought and the tragic failures of agriculture in the Great Plains preceded a general economic collapse by only a few years. The stock market crash of 1929 was only a symbol of the trauma. Rising incomes reversed their trend. Investments, even in banks, failed. And hundreds of thousands were unemployed.

The effects of the depression on the minds and emotions of those people who saw their worlds collapse were pervasive and lasting. For the whole generation that experienced that collapse, willingness to join wholeheartedly in pleasure-seeking was tainted by economic insecurity and fear.

However, for recreation there was a paradoxical benefit. Federal efforts to lessen unemployment and stimulate the economy included the development of many outdoor areas for recreation, the construction of halls and community theaters, and the creation of programs that paid artists to write, compose, and perform new works in music, drama, dance, and literature. Almost 50,000 people were employed at one time in the recreation division of the Works Progress Administration, building and operating parks, playgrounds, athletic fields, beaches, and swimming pools. The Federal Art, Theater, and Music projects did live performances for millions and employed more than 30,000 writers, artists, and performers. From 1932 to 1937, the federal government is estimated to have spent about $1.5 billion in developing camps, trails, buildings, and areas for recreation. State park systems were inaugurated with the help of the Civilian Conservation Corps.

The massive unemployment of the 1930s raised grave questions about the nature of the economy. Many questioned whether a capitalist economy could survive such a prolonged period of collapsed financial structure and markets. Two possible solutions to the unemployment dilemma were proposed.[2] The adopted response was to create jobs through government programs including those that built recreation and conservation projects. Those with incomes from such jobs were to create a wide demand for consumer goods and revive the economy. Also considered was a possible "leisure solution" in which work hours would be reduced to make way for more workers. Attacked by moralists who distrusted the ability of workers to use leisure wisely and by economists who questioned how business enterprises could add such labor costs, the reduction of the workweek was rejected by the Roosevelt administration. In the end, only the mobilization demand of the second World War ended the depression.

Strangely, both the wars and the depression had side effects of promoting interest and opportunities in recreation. However, the more direct effect of those events on lives—on attitudes as well as the economy, health, housing, and families—remains as well. Some of the problems of the modern city were intensified by both wartime mobilization and peacetime problems.

Nongovernment Recreation Organizations

Paralleling the development of the recreation movement, government activity, and the growth of commercial leisure was the founding of a number of voluntary efforts to provide recreation opportunities. One of the first was a cooperative effort of the churches to provide healthy and constructive programs under Christian auspices. The Young Men's Christian Association was begun in 1851 and followed fifteen years later by the Young Women's Christian Association. The same concern for young people in the cities and towns led to the founding of the National Association of Boys' Clubs in 1906, the Boy Scouts and Camp Fire Girls in 1910, and the Girl Scouts in 1912. All grew rapidly, so that, by 1926, the Boy Scouts had 625,000 members and 189,000 leaders and officers. The YMCA had almost a million members and the YWCA almost 600,000 members.

Further, Jane Addams's concern for recreation had led to her participation in the early recreation movement as well as to provisions for recreation at Hull House on Chicago's West Side. Settlement houses, community groups, athletic associations, clubs for boys and for girls, and countless groups that had more temporary existence developed ways to meet the needs of children and youth in the cities. Although many abandoned the most deprived areas of the city to serve the young in less severe circumstances, many others did not. The

---

[2] Benjamin K. Hunnicutt, *Work without End* (Philadelphia: Temple University Press, 1988).

heritage of many youth-serving groups is that of attempting to meet the developmental needs of those trapped in the industrial cities.

Transforming Technologies and the Commercialization of Leisure

As already outlined, the city itself altered leisure with its spatial constrictions, masses of people, and commercialization of leisure. The small neighborhood silent film parlor with its piano accompaniment was replaced by the elaborate movie palace. Sport became professional spectacles. The "trolley parks" drew crowds in weekends. Leisure was organized, licensed, and provided by the market as well as by private and public agencies. Even in the nineteenth century, technologies created new opportunities. The electric trolley and train replaced horsedrawn vehicles and widened the geographical scope of leisure in the city. Electricity made theaters safer and enriched home entertainment. "Wireless" transmission of sound led to the radio and the beginning of mass entertainment in the home. Championship prize fights, the baseball World Series, comedy programs and their celebrity personalities, radio music and drama, and even adventure serials for children came into almost every home.

The motion picture industry moved to southern California and was dominated by a few large corporations. Circuses moved across the country by rail. Tourist trains took leisure travellers to cities and even the premier national parks. Owners wrested control of baseball from the players, built ballparks, and established leagues. With financial control and the "reserve clause" that bound players to one club, baseball set the pattern of professional sport as a legally protected business enterprise. Football moved from the campus to the city and became professional. The weekend was institutionalized as a time for leisure, and religious control of the "sacred Sunday" was lost. It was in the twentieth century, however, that the really "transforming technologies" had their impacts on leisure.

Henry Ford and the Expansion of Leisure Space

At first, the automobile was the product of craftsmen, expensive, and owned only by the wealthy. Henry Ford introduced the Model T in 1914, the first mass-produced automobile. Ford had several aims. The first was to bring the cost within range of the middle class and even of the factory worker. The second was to standardize the product ("Any color as long as it's black"). The third was to raise productivity by replacing crafts with standardized production-line tasks. The fourth was to purchase worker loyalty with the unheardof wage of $5 for an eight-hour day. Workers were to become more reliable and efficient and also consumers of the product.

The results were astounding. By 1927, 85 percent of the world's cars were being built in the United States despite their origin in Europe. A new Ford cost about $290. Ford, General Motors, and Chrysler produced multiple lines of cars to attract mass markets. In the process, life in city and country was transformed:

> The metropolis developed outward with rings of suburbs. Life in the suburb required a car to negotiate its sprawling housing and resulting distances.

> Private transportation dominated travel with over 85 percent of trips made by car.

A complex industry developed around the use of the car for recreational travel. At first there were cabins succeeded by motels. Visits to National Parks doubled and redoubled.

Recreation businesses responded with drive-in movies and restaurants. the first shopping center surrounded by parking was opened in Kansas City in 1923.

The car became taken for granted in the location of public parks and recreation areas.

Family vacations and family schedules presupposed private transportation.

The car widened opportunity, altered household timetables, reconfigured retailing locations, shrank the functions of smaller rural communities, led to the demise of the country schoolhouse, scattered second and vacation home sites, and threatened the passenger railways. The car provided privacy and mobility for youth. Cars became status symbols as well as essential transportation. All this was before the development of the interstate limited-access highways, the common multiple-car household, and the internationalization of car production and distribution. It was a truly transforming technology.

Television: the Omnipresent Home Entertainer

The car dispersed leisure. Then television returned it to the home. Television was introduced widely in the 1950s, by 1970 was in 58 percent of American homes, and in almost 90 percent by 1980. No study of leisure, family, time allocations and schedules, or cultural exposure prior to television has any but historical interest. After work and sleep, television consumes the most time every day of the week for most adults. It is central to activity patterns and to learning about the world. Like the automobile, its impacts are profound:

It has brought leisure home as easy, accessible, and inexpensive entertainment.

It has transformed images of play with its depictions of special equipment, dress, and locales that can be purchased in the marketplace of leisure.

It has brought high levels of the arts and sports, distant travel environments, a variety of cultures, and a wealth of information into the home for both children and adults. At the same time, it has brought the most mindless and escapist entertainment.

It has reshaped household timetables with "prime time" programming that conflicts with community organization schedules, religion, family interaction, and other more involving kinds of leisure.

There are countless critiques of television as undemanding entertainment, direct and indirect promotion of all kinds of consumer goods, portrayal of life built on affluence and the possession of material goods, and solutions of real problems with sudden violence. The impacts of such visual images on call in the home are still being measured. What is evident, however, is that television leaves no aspect of life untouched. It is vivid, enchanting, and always there.

Other Leisure Technologies

Technologies are constantly being developed and disseminated that change particular activities. Fiberglass and composite materials have changed boating, racquet sports, and golf. Electronics has had impacts on fishing. Linked computers have transformed the travel industry by worldwide reservation systems for air travel, hotels, rental cars, and other destination resources. The credit card is a travel convenience, but also a convenient way of playing now and paying later. These and other technologies are always being incorporated into the spectrum of leisure marketing. There are, however, three technologies of particular significance:

1. The most important, although the most obscure, are the technologies of contraception. Sexual behavior at all social levels has been radically changed by reducing the likelihood of conception resulting from sexual intercourse. Sexual activity as part of leisure has increased dramatically. Just as important, the size of families has decreased so that a small proportion of adult life is focused on childcare and nurture. Now techniques are also important for their protection against sexually transmitted diseases, especially HIV-AIDS.
2. Perhaps less far-reaching but still important is the jet airplane. Its larger capacities, greater speeds and efficiencies, and vast networks of routes have opened travel opportunities to a wide range of the population. Money and time costs have been cut enormously. Oceans are now effectively bridged. Off-price packages present chances for vacation travel to hundreds of thousands even when close to 90 percent of trips are by car. The modern tourism industry is a product of the jet.
3. Earlier the telephone also had profound impacts on every aspect of business and social life. Talking on the telephone is an important leisure activity in its own right. The phone enables individuals and groups to arrange leisure occasions. Now the telephone is combined with computer systems to make possible all kinds of leisure arrangements across the neighborhood, and continent, and the world, especially with toll-free numbers.

Some technologies are so powerful that they change society. Most are widely adopted only when they fit into established patterns of the social system. Some are specific to an activity, a leisure style, or an age-based culture. Others simply widen or facilitate participation in an activity by lowering costs. When we look back over decades to 1900, however, technological development has transformed the nature of leisure and of social life in general. Now that leisure is more recognized as a major part of the world economy, such impacts are likely to increase. Just try to imagine, for example, how the proliferation of electronic devices will continue to turn the residence into a full-service entertainment center, not in a generation but in a few years. There is one significant warning, nonetheless. Insofar as technologies are developed and marketed by those seeking a profit, they will remain unavailable to the poor. Further, they will be designed disproportionately for those with the discretionary income to buy expensive toys.

The Consumer Society

As early as the 1920s, leisure had been identified with consumption.[3] There were amusement parks, tours, the entertainment of professional sport, movies, and travelling shows,

---

[3] Gary Cross, *A Social History of Leisure since 1600* (College Park, PA: Venture Publishing, 1990).

eating and drinking out, and all the ramifications of style and fashion. The middle class began to spend as well as save, value leisure as well as work. Magazines, billboards, and radio offered a new lifestyle of based on consumption not only of household goods and transportation, but also of leisure experiences. Consumption reflected status, taste, and also individual gratification.

Moving into the post–World War II era, leisure became more privatized as television provided a new level of home entertainment. Now one no longer had to leave the home to obtain a variety of entertainment—sports, the arts, drama, and all kinds of mass culture. The cost, of course, was advertising. Congressional action rejected models of public provision and control of television in favor of a market model. Television gained its economic support from advertising rather than public funding or subscription. As a consequence, that dominant medium entered the home with the purpose of selling goods, of increasing market consumption. The indirect messages of programming reinforced the direct messages of advertising to present a commodified view of "the good life." Individual pleasure was not only legitimized, but presented in attractive visual form for all the hours now devoted to the new medium.

New Markets and New Styles

During World War II, the federal government directed the economy toward the production of the instruments of war. Tanks, airplanes, uniforms, guns, and even food were first of all for the war effort. All "unnecessary" consumer production was put on hold. Even food and gas were rationed as production was redirected. Wages and prices were frozen. Prewar cars and machines were repaired rather than replaced.

Then came the end. The production machine that won the war turned to new markets, those of the consumer. Soldiers and sailors returned home with their bonuses. Factories geared up to make cars, refrigerators, and clothes. Housing starts soared. Electronics turned from radar to television. Incomes rose in conjunction with production. All the pentup consumer demand from the Depression and the war boosted the economy. Productivity rose and purchasing power doubled and redoubled.

There were a number of significant changes that altered the nature of American leisure. First, most of the new homes were built in the new suburbs. Detached homes ate up enormous space. Highways, cars, shopping centers, and dispersed recreation sites added to market demand. New homes had to be equipped and furnished. Delayed marriages and childbearing created more markets. Most young women married, stayed home while their children were young, and became front-line consumers. The gendered separation from the workplace and division of labor was intensified as women were bumped from wartime factory jobs to make way for returning men. The ideology of the "family" idealized the nurturing, managing, and consuming mother at home. The ideology of leisure turned attention to all the wonders offered by the market. Consumption itself became a major leisure occupation as the malls welcomed shoppers who drove cars with plenty of space for purchases.

Second, the growing metropolitan area offered a wide variety of leisure resources. The limitations of the small town and its reliance on community interaction were replaced by everything that could be purchased in the great retail world of the city. Women were still expected to center their leisure around the home and family. The poor, crowded into racially designated ghettos and cut off from the economic opportunities that now followed the highways to the edges of the city, could participate in the new consumer leisure only vicariously on television. For the majority with enough affluence to enter the leisure markets, however, it was a time to buy into lifestyles previously limited to the wealthy. At some level and in some style, just about everything was for sale.

Mass Culture and Mass Leisure

Mass leisure became part of the mass culture. At the high end of the income scale, the wealthy are able to purchase privacy, access, and exclusive leisure that symbolizes their elite social status. At the bottom end, households struggle to survive in hostile environments, and leisure is a combination of low-cost entertainment and seeking possibilities of escape from oppressive conditions. For the middle mass, however, there is mass leisure— the kinds of activities that most people do most of the time. First, of course, is television, the low-cost entertainer designed to sell consumer goods to all levels of markets. Second is shopping itself, trips to retailing centers to view, investigate, dream, and buy. Third are all of the away-from-home entertainments that draw people to shows, restaurants, and other venues in a variety of offerings. Fourth is travel, more and more an industry that sells packages of experiences for all ages and a variety of tastes.

Leisure, from this perspective, is seen as a reward for work that may be less than deeply satisfying. Leisure becomes a separate element of social life with its own budgets, symbol systems, and ascribed meanings. The close connection of work and leisure in preindustrial societies is broken by the segregation of work from both family and leisure. Now leisure is tied more to home and nonwork associations than to work places, skills, or companions. The relationship of leisure to work is instrumental, the things and experiences that can be purchased with discretionary income. Mass leisure is made of up market commodities rather than experiences integrated into the fabric of social life.

Now there are references to "the leisure industry" rather than to leisure as a theme or dimension of life. There are a number of problems with this approach. One, of course, is that the market excludes many who cannot afford what others take for granted. They see the glamorized possibilities on television, but are unable to participate. A second problem is that leisure comes to be identified with the purchase rather than the experience. We may even have an underlying assumption that the more we spend, the better time we will have. A third problem is based on the premise that satisfaction and meaning are not really for sale. Our desires become insatiable if we believe that buying more, buying "better," and buying up the price scale will in the end produce a higher level of satisfaction. A fourth problem is that we come to believe that the fake is real. More and more entertainment becomes a show. Disney builds its own reality and calls it "the world." Las Vegas obscures its casinos behind fake castles, circuses, and pirate sea battles. Even in the local community chain restaurants sell standardized meals behind the facades of ethnic cuisine. All of this and more are promoted by the wizards of advertising that attempt to convince us that leisure experiences are really for sale if only we buy right, dress right, and go to the right place.

It is, after all, much easier to watch others perform than to invest years in acquiring the skills to perform ourselves. It is more convenient to watch the struggles of other families, sometimes funny and sometimes tragic, than to engage ourselves in the give-and-take of real relationships. It is easier to be taken on a cruise with nonstop shows, gambling, food, and drink than to negotiate our way around a real country where we know only a few tourist phrases in the local language. We may not grow or learn much when we just sit back and let others do it for us, but the personal cost of being entertained by mass leisure is relatively low. All it takes is the allocation of some income. And the hope of buying a really pleasurable experience helps us at even the least stimulating or challenging job.

Privatizing Leisure

Another approach to the same set of social changes suggests that leisure is not only more commercialized, but also "privatized." With almost all the growth in housing in the metropolitan suburbs, life at home became more and more cut off from the workplace. The car enabled workers to crisscross the city to get to and from work. Commuting became a way of life, consuming great amounts of time as the more affluent suburbs moved further and further from the urban core. Leisure meant home and household, a segregated locale of the detached home, private yard, and family room as only one site for multiple television sets.

Leisure that is privatized is located more in the home rather than public places. It involves family and familiar friends more and community gatherings less. It is focused on individual fulfillment and development more and serving others less. It consists more of a one-to-one encounter with television and less of encounters with people who make demands as well as offer opportunities for sharing. It depends more on the things we can buy and less on the experiences we create. It is, in short, what passes for leisure for many people most of the time.

Note that everything seems to come together to support such leisure. Commuting is tiring and time-consuming. Families are smaller and less stable. The suburbs are designed for privacy rather than gathering. Work careers are less secure and regular as men and women bounce from one job to another. Home electronics make just sitting there so easy, so inexpensive, and so attractive. The expanding leisure "industry" offers great variety in responding to all sorts of tastes. Households with multiple cars can split off individually in any direction to find entertainment to taste. And, for the majority, there is enough income over and above necessities to buy some more leisure things. All this is not a conspiracy: It is just the way the market operates in an affluent economy, the way the greater city has grown, and the way that we respond to all those opportunities. The market responds to all sorts of preferences as long as the goods and services can be delivered at a profit. Belief in the market is, after all, a fundamental part of American culture . . . and increasingly of the rest of the world.

Leisure takes its functional place in the system. It supports the economy as a reward for work that has little intrinsic appeal and provides expanding markets for consumer goods. Further, a variety of styles and tastes to serve to identify social subgroups as well as diversify demand. All that this requires is that to some extent the "good life" be defined in terms of leisure commodities.[4]

---

[4] Richard Butsch, *For Fun and Profit: The Transformation of Leisure into Profit* (Philadelphia: Temple University Press, 1990); John R. Kelly and Geoffrey Godbey, *The Sociology of Leisure* (College Park, PA: Venture Publishing, 1993), Chapter 25.

There is, on the other hand, a counterargument. It suggests that all that spending on leisure does not necessarily lead to the conclusion that all leisure is commodified. An analysis by the author of a number of trends yields some reservations. First, participation in cost-intensive activities is not increasing faster than in those that are relatively cost-free. Second, activities that people do the most—entertaining friends at home, informal interaction, watching television, walking, listening to music, and reading—are low cost. More adults cook for pleasure than gamble. More garden than go to clubs and shows. Third, expenditure trends indicate that the percentage of household income spent directly on recreation has risen only slightly in the past decades, from 6.5 to about 8 percent. Fourth, those owning leisure equipment who purchased new goods during 1983 ranged from 20 to 50 percent, depending primarily on replacement needs. Fifth, most leisure trips are still by car and on a budget. Sixth, leisure engagement tends to have multiple satisfactions, not just demonstrating taste or status. And, seventh, the kinds of activities that adults value most are those shared with "significant others" and those that call for skill development.

Nevertheless, there is no question that leisure and consumption have become closely related. Further, in a scarcity of time, many may attempt to gain more pleasure by spending more. It is difficult to separate any activity from the consumption of goods and services in a market economy that is always alert for viable new markets. There are concerns about increasingly excluding the poor from leisure resources, about confusing satisfying experience with purchasing, and with the development of a value system that identifies quality of life as consumption.

HIGHLIGHTS

1. Life developed around community in preindustrial societies. The suburb has separated leisure from work, accentuated a sexual division of labor, and privatized leisure.
2. The rise of the city was also the beginning of mass leisure entertainment.
3. The car and television are only the most powerful of the technologies that have transformed leisure.
4. Leisure as the consumption of goods and services ties workers to their economic roles and provides markets in an expanding economy. Such consumption may also identify leisure with market participation rather than the meaning of the experience.

Discussion Questions

1. How has leisure become more individual and less social? In the process, has leisure become more self-centered?

2. What kinds of goods and services are most likely to be supplied by the market rather than by public providers? Why? Does the profit motive direct resources toward particular kinds of leisure?

3. How might the American society be different today if the leisure solution of shorter work hours had been adopted during Depression unemployment?

4. Which technologies have had the most profound impacts on leisure? On the family? On adult life styles? How and why?

5. What evidence can you suggest that contemporary leisure has become quite "commodified"—based on consumption of marketed opportunities? Is this a problem if people are choosing to do what makes them happy?

6. Is leisure more a private than a public matter, something best left to the "sovereign consumer"?

7. Has industrialization so robbed work of meaning that leisure has become more important in the quality of people's lives?

Bibliography

Bellah, Robert, R. Madsen, W. Sullivan, A. Swidler, and S. Tipton, *Habits of the Heart: Individualism and Commitment in American Life.* Berkeley, CA: University of California Press, 1987.

Butsch, Richard, *For Fun and Profit: The Transformation of Leisure into Consumption.* Philadelphia: Temple University Press, 1990.

Cross, Gary, *A Social History of America since 1600.* College Park, PA: Venture Publishing, 1990.

Kelly, John R., and Geoffrey Godbey, *The Sociology of Leisure.* College Park, PA: Venture Publishing, 1993.

Larrabee, Eric, and R. Meyersohn, *Mass Leisure.* Glencoe, IL: The Free Press, 1958.

Marcuse, Herbert, *One-Dimensional Man.* Boston: Beacon Press, 1964.

Rojek, Chris, *Capitalism and Leisure Theory.* London: Tavistock, 1985.

Veblen, Thorstein, *The Theory of the Leisure Class.* New York: The New American Library, 1953 (1899).

Chapter *12*

Leisure and the Future

Utopians foresee the future of leisure in Western civilization transformed by servant technologies. Entertainment is envisioned as available at the touch of a transistorized dial providing wall-sized sports, drama, and variety acts selected by the viewer rather than the sponsor. Travel will be common and inexpensive. Employment will demand less and offer more in the way of satisfaction. Self-cultivation will be valued in an encompassing way that includes body and mind, the physical and aesthetic. In a future world of subdued nature and technology, leisure will have become varied and enriching for all. Since it will be a major element of the consumer economy, leisure will be highly valued rather than excused as just preparation for work.

Prophets of doom point to all the unresolved problems and issues in the world that may well undercut even the current level of comfort. When the majority of the world is still near a bare subsistence level of life, revolution is not an impossibility and the gross discrepancies in distribution of income and resources may well be overturned. The foreseeable end of most fossil fuel energy supplies, continued political turmoil on most continents, population growth that threatens selective mass starvation, massive stockpiling of weapons, social divisions leading to conflict and terror, and other world problems dim the utopian optimism. Add to this domestic problems such as the continued decay of cities, pollution of the ecosystem, economic cycles and inflation, unemployment and poverty, and a disillusionment with the ability of government to solve problems. From such a perspective, cataclysmic social events seem as likely as new worlds of leisure.

It is clear from the previous chapters that leisure is one dimension of life that is related to all others. Economic, cultural, political, and other changes have their impacts on leisure. Both continuity and change are part of the complex and multidimensional contexts of dynamic social systems.

The most likely future is probably somewhere between the utopian new world and disaster. However, even assuming continuity rather than revolution and self-destruction, many profound changes are taking place in American society at this time. Not only will leisure itself be changed, but the environments of leisure are constantly in flux. Developing scenarios of tomorrow's leisure requires interpretation and weighing of many interrelated factors. The future will not be just more of the same; it will be different.

ISSUES

Will leisure in the future be simply an extension of the present, more of the same, or different in significant ways?

What are probable critical limits on technological development?

Which are the most profound trends in the economy, population, family, and other institutions that will have consequences for leisure?

Is there evidence of a new "leisure ethic" in American society?

A number of exotic scenarios for the future of leisure in a technologized tomorrow have been written. All assume that no limits in energy sources, raw materials, and productivity will keep economies from actualizing whatever is technically possible. Such scenarios ignore political and social conflicts and assume that problems such as air, water, and soil pollution are temporary and will be overcome by new technologies. They further project the emergence of a new consciousness that will embrace leisure as worthwhile in its own right. The possible conflict between the production of endless consumer resources for leisure and the reduced productivity of a "leisure age" are seldom mentioned. A composite scenario might be something like that given in the accompanying reading.

Of course, the scenario portrayed in the reading presupposes that whatever can be done technologically *will* be done. As evidenced by the same failure to employ hydrogen bombs in warfare, we often do not do what we are technically capable of doing. Nor does the vision take into account any limits of resources, social organization capabilities, or ideological conflicts. A fundamental consumer orientation is assumed to have led to the utilization of every means of production for the purchase and rent of leisure goods. Nor is the likelihood that some programs and goals may be mutually exclusive taken into account. Questions about how a world economy would support affluence adequate for such leisure in India as well as Los Angeles or who would do the work to provide such an array of leisure opportunities are ignored. No limits on resources or social development are included in the script of a world without conflict.

If such futures scripting is not adequately grounded in the real world, then how can we look ahead? What are more reliable ways of envisioning the future?

A Leisure Fantasy: Technological Wonders

In-home leisure in this future age of technological wonders extends far beyond what is available today. Not only will "telesensing" be wall-sized, offer a fantastic store of programs through its interactive cable system, and instantaneously reproduce any event around the world, but it will have sound and sensual capabilities to provide a total experience far richer than the cool little visual screen of primitive television. Since most housekeeping chores will be automated and even food preparation computerized, much more time will be available for leisure consumption. No mode of transportation can substitute for the immediacy and convenience of in-home leisure products. Electronics will also offer whole libraries of literature and music, a variety of interactive games, and instantaneous visual communication throughout the affluent world. The mushrooming growth of destination leisure in the later twentieth century barely gave a hint of the future. With the off-airport time loss problem solved through a network of satellite vertical-lift stations connecting the major long-distance terminals, it will be possible to be on almost any island, coast, or resort area in a few hours and go from city to city in supersonic minutes.

However, just as significant a change as in the means of transportation will be the revolution in accommodations. Literally everything will be available for rent almost anywhere. Rather than the old rigid tours of the 1970s and 1980s, the leisure travel business will have expanded to prepackage any conceivable combination of activities, meals, social events, and environments on order—at a price. The thirty-hour employment week made necessary by productivity gains in the late twentieth century will have been augmented by the flex-time schedules that allow for blocks of days free for travel at any time of the year. Since everyone will be replaceable on the job, everyone will seek a variety of leisure experiences to express individuality. Of course, technical advances will also have impacts on every other aspect of leisure. A vast spectrum of leisure goods will be available through commercial and public provisions to enable a person to select stimuli, entertainment, food and drink, cultural enrichment, and physical challenge with a speed and convenience that makes the home a leisure center and every community a full-service resort. In fact, only satisfying relationships with other people will be outside the call of the electronic consoles in every "recreation room."

The Nature of Social Change

Social change may be either gradual and evolutionary or sudden and revolutionary. Only one thing is sure: societies do change. They may cease to exist, dissolved by internal conflict or overcome by external forces. Fundamental changes in the institutional structures, locus of power, and value orientations can take place. There are a number of models of social change:

1. A revolutionary model:
   Condition of internal conflict recognized → Organization of the powerless → Revolutionary struggle → Replacement of old power structure → Reorganization of social institutions.

2. A conquest model:

   Conflict of interests with another nation-state → Overt struggle with opposing state → Victory by external force → Replacement of power structure with conquerors → Institutional reorientation.

3. An evolutionary model:

   Continual process of change within social institutions → Strains and inconsistencies develop in the social system → Adjustments in institutional organizations, values, and roles are required → Process of institutional change continues without altering the locus of power.

4. A technological model:

   Technological development requires alteration of the economic mode of production and distribution → Noneconomic social institutions change organization and values to incorporate the new technology and related economic shifts → Pervasive social adjustment moves toward a new equilibrium of institutional structures.

Both the revolutionary and conquest models of social change are always a possibility. However, such change would be so radical and pervasive that predicting the consequences for leisure roles and resources would be an exercise in imaginative construction—intriguing but imprecise. In the following attempt to delineate factors related to the future of leisure in America, the evolutionary and technological models will be combined. However, a number of warnings are necessary:

First, the potential of internal and radical social conflict is real. The present concentration of economic power and reward could lead to revolutionary conflict. At the present time, however, the signs of such an event appear dim. Conflict is more often confined to one locality or region.

Second, external threat to the economy if not the polity of Western nations from the have-not and developing nations is quite real. Despite interconnected production and market networks, the control of key raw materials and labor supplies by the Third World may be employed to diminish the economic hegemony of the developed economies. Now there is a world economy in which finance, production, and marketing are organized on a global scale by multinational corporations

Third, the influence of new technologies is not always easy to predict. As leisure in the past has been radically altered by such developments as the printing press, the automobile, and television, so some powerful technology may produce a similar change. Developments related to energy depletion and new sources may be the next drastic intervention into living environments. What is certain is that some technologies will not be adopted and that others may have unexpected consequences.

Fourth, perspectives on social change are somewhat like waves approaching an ocean beach. Some waves appear to grow, disappear, and never reach the sand at all; others suddenly reach surprising height and power as they approach shore; and some have their small impact and are reabsorbed into the wave cycle. We cannot always tell just which of the factors on the social horizon will have major impact. Some social movements that appear to be growing now will almost disappear in less than a decade.

On the other hand, there are a number of well-established trends that have already begun to require adaptation and are unlikely to recede without impact. There are some institutional changes now under way that appear to have sustaining force because they are consistent with other related changes. We will focus on these ongoing trends, still recalling the warnings about the inadequacy of such conservative forecasting.

Leisure as a Factor in Change

The technological model includes the assumption that other elements of a social system are secondary to the economic. The classic example of this model is that of the massive social changes begun by the introduction of concentrated power into the production process in the factory and into transport by the steam engine. The consequent urbanization transformed every social institution—family, government, education, religion, and leisure. Leisure, then, is viewed as a trailing element in change, that is, an eventual effect and never a cause.

An alternative model would retain the view of a social system of interrelated institutional elements but drop the premise that economic change is always primary. It would adopt the view of Max Weber that change in values and ideologies in church, school, or home might influence the economic structures.[1] It would allow for the possibility that some change in leisure practices or orientations might have an effect on the rest of the social system. For example, were the relative value placed on leisure to gain ascendancy over that on work or social status, then an altered allocation of resources would affect the economy.

An attempt to look ahead, then, calls for more than identifying economic and population trends and tracing their probable effects on leisure. When the society is understood as an interrelated set of institutions, value orientations, cultural elements, and symbol systems in an ongoing process of change, then it becomes more difficult to identify the elements most likely to influence the directions of that process. When it is assumed that leisure may be an element generating change as well as one affected by change, then writing scenarios about the future becomes more complex.

One method is to add to the general analysis of major trends some special attention to leading-edge groups and movements. If it is possible to locate social groups and environments where some parts of the future are already being worked out, then a glimpse of the future may be possible. For example, counterculture movements may anticipate some aspects of future leisure. The technically employed and educated "new class" represents a growing element in the society. Some demographic and economic trends now appear to be well established. All of these trend and leading-edge ingredients will be mixed into the futurizing that follows. The basic assumption is that of gradual and systemic rather than revolutionary change. However, even a gradual process of change could lead to a future for leisure radically different from today's.

Institutional Factors in Leisure Change

Without deciding in advance which factors are most important, we will examine a number of ongoing trends and indications of change.

[1] Max Weber, *The Protestant Ethic and the Spirit of Capitalism,* trans. T. Parsons (New York: Scribner's, 1958).

Economic Factors

While the economy may not totally determine all the social institutions, it is central to social stability and change. Not only is a viable economy necessary for the production and distribution of the necessities of life, but the structure of the economy also is significant for the schedules, ecology, value systems, and social differentiation of the society. Karl Marx argued that control of the means and instruments of production was the determinative element in the social system.[2] Many others have agreed that economic power permeates all other social institutions without accepting Marx's alleged absolutism of determination. In any case, few would disagree that, more often than not, economic change precedes other elements of social change.

A number of economic trends and issues are significant for leisure:

Employment Trends: Who Works and When?

The leveling of the average workweek during the 1970s and 1980s does not mean that this may not be a temporary plateau. Continued advances in the automation of production and microchip utilization in information and clerical processing appear likely to shift employment even further toward the majority in service occupations. At this time, however, most decreases in employment hours have been selective. Shorter hours have been established in some factories. Employment schedules among the human and social services as well as in retailing, financial enterprises, health services, and other occupations have not demonstrated decreases in hours worked. The exception is in retailing such as fast foods in which many employees are on part-time hourly schedules.

Human services and retailing are facing a demand for increased hours of operation. Stores stay open longer, and counseling and health facilities offer evening and weekend appointments. Varied work schedules then call for complementary services to expand their timetables. The old eight-to-five and Monday-through-Friday patterns have lost their rigid shape. A major segment of the labor force now works changing hours with different days of employment from week to week. Employees become more and more interchangeable to keep the enterprises running all week. The family doctor is now a group practice; the client is now a case; and the friendly salesperson is not on duty the next time you go to the store.

Add to this the pressures on many professionals, research and development personnel, and managers to increase their productivity by adding to their weekly hours. In highly competitive markets, the expectations for long hours and high levels of performance place considerable pressure on those who are least replaceable in corporate programs. In many cases, they are working longer rather than shorter hours.[3]

One thing is sure: although additional holidays and vacations may have decreased the overall average work hours for some who are employed, any unqualified predictions of increased free time based on long-term reductions in the workweek are misleading. Work schedules may be more varied and variable, but there is no general trend toward reduced employment schedules. Rather, many factors suggest that free time is likely to become more scarce for many in technical, research and development, managerial, professional,

---

[2] Karl Marx, *Capital: a Critique of Political Economy* (Moscow: Foreign Language Publishing House, 1962).

[3] Juliet Schor, *The Overworked American: The Unexpected Decline of Leisure* (New York: Basic Books, 1991).

and service occupations. The marvels of electronic information processing are as likely to increase expectations as to reduce employment.

Women's Employment

The growing service sector has been more likely than production industry to employ women in positions such as retail clerks, nurses, teachers, and other kinds of direct person-to-person work. The growth in service employment has been one factor in the increase of women in the labor force. Especially in the lower paid occupations, women have been recruited at entry levels, maintained on limited wage levels, and always considered replaceable by the presumed supply of those ready to take employment at income levels that average 60 percent those of men.

The trend toward increased women's employment is now firmly established in economic and social change. It reflects fundamental labor force shifts into services and social change in the family. First, the trend is long term. Female employment increased from 15 percent for those age twenty-five to forty-four in 1890 to 60 percent in 1980 with a steady increase at about 3 percent per decade to 1950 and 9 percent for the 1950s, 1960s, and 1970s.[4] Second, the trend is related to family changes such as the rising divorce rate and the need for more women to support themselves and their households. Since 1950, the greatest increase in women's employment has been among mothers with children living at home. Third, ideologies stressing women's economic opportunities have generally followed rather than led the changes. Fourth, women's service sector employment is often part-time and without security or health and retirement programs.

It is important to recognize that most employed women report that their motivation is primarily economic; they need the income for household support. This is especially the case for single-parent households. However, the proportion of dual incomes in households headed by two adults has risen from 45 percent in 1980 to 65 percent in 1990 and is projected to grow to more than 80 percent by 2000.

Other Employment Trends

Another employment trend is just beginning to emerge. The labor force rates for men age fifty-five to sixty-four are declining. The rate, as high as 85 percent in 1965, has fallen to below 70 percent. Some is due to voluntary retirement. Other reductions are the result of industrial layoffs in "sunset" industries as well as layoffs of managers and others by businesses striving for more cost efficiency. The trend toward joblessness in the former "pre-retirement" age group, sometimes masked as early retirement, is becoming more common.

Still another trend that appears to be increasing is the structuring of employment to allow people greater control over their own schedules. Not only are there occasional three-day weekends and a small number of corporations adopting four-day workweeks, but the more rapidly growing flex-time employment schedules allow workers to select within limits their own hours of arrival, meals, and departure. Such flexibility enables young mothers to adjust to school schedules, fitness buffs to break during the day for exercise, and city-lovers to exploit the downtown area during parts of the workday. It further facilitates

---

[4] Victor Fuchs, *How We Live: An Economic Perspective on Americans from Birth to Death* (Cambridge, MA: Harvard University Press, 1983).

various kinds of continuing education, whether oriented toward work or leisure. Such flexibility, along with the increasing number of workers in services who do not work the traditional eight-to-five hours and the number of unions increasing their efforts to shorten work hours, can both expand the hours of leisure services and lessen the conflict over resources in the evening and weekend periods. It may also have some psychological effects as employment and play are less rigidly compartmentalized into time slots.

Impacts of Employment Trends

One impact is extreme unevenness in work schedules. Average workweeks become more and more misleading as some work schedules expand, some become more irregular, and some are reduced at the convenience of the employer. In general, the variety of schedules will include more "off time" as well as overtime.

A second impact is the scarcity of time for many. All studies show that employed women with children living at home have the least discretionary time of any segment of the population. They must negotiate relatively compact periods for leisure out of the demands of employment, household maintenance, rest, and nurture and child care.

Some households, however, may have a higher level of discretionary income due to dual incomes. Synchronization of schedules for family activity and recreation and the amount of time available may be more of a problem than the financial costs of leisure.

Income and Wealth: Who Has It?

As introduced in Chapter 4, American society is marked by great disparities in income and wealth. Entry-level and low-threshold service sector jobs pay minimum wage. Even for those with year-round employment, income before taxes will total only about $8,000 to $10,000. At the other end are positions in finance, medical specialties, and management with incomes of from $100,000 to $500,000 per year. A great many workers are running short of money for food and rent each month, while others are primarily concerned about investments that minimize taxation rates.

The result is that the lowest end in earnings, up to 20 percent, has no discretionary income at all. At the other end, 10 percent have enough to be able to allocate significant amounts on leisure. In between are the 70 percent who are able to spend modest amounts directly on leisure, $500 to $3,000 per year, but for whom cost is always a major factor in participation.

There are no indications that the overall disparities are changing. Some analysts are suggesting that the shape of the income pyramid is being altered. The upper 20 percent are increasing their share of total income and wealth. Unemployment and minimum wage jobs for the bottom 30 percent suggest that the marginal and submarginal household percentages may also be increasing.

Whatever the more specific shifts, the overall distribution remains one of great differences. Those differences will affect participation in all kinds of recreation that come at high cost, especially those requiring travel or access to expensive resources. Only an overall increase in real income, not likely in the global economy, or a dramatic shift in the pattern of distribution, not likely in the political climate, will alter the significance of income for recreation demand.

Technological Development

Further technological development will have direct and indirect effects on leisure. First, there are the new leisure toys and instruments that diversify leisure opportunities. The transistor has made possible a range of games, communication devices, and entertainment unimaginable a few years ago. Miniaturization has not only brought calculators and computers into the home but devices and games for leisure as well. Music can go anywhere, and complex interactive games are played in the living room rather than the downtown entertainment center. The home video has augmented television with its technology providing greatly increased diversity and choice for the already dominant entertainment. Its success is based on its relatively inexpensive addition to established leisure patterns.

The future of home electronic entertainment is likely to be one of greater opportunity and choice. Cable television offers the possibility of greater convenience in a system in which a metered receiving device will enable the viewer to choose among hundreds of programs and video films on demand. Already technically possible, such a development in the next decade will enhance opportunity for convenient entertainment without requiring changes in activity commitments or timetables.

Other leisure technologies include faster and less expensive travel, information processing allowing advance scheduling of various services and facilities, greater communications capabilities, newly developed games and equipment, and expanded media introduction to leisure opportunities. The availability of such developments is largely through the market and is dependent on economic factors such as discretionary income of the consumers and investment return in the leisure markets.

Indirect effects of new technologies on leisure are even more difficult to predict. If something like television were just over the horizon, then a single technology could transform every current use of time and bring about incalculable changes in social patterns, leisure values, and uses of space. The most likely developments at the present time would seem to be those that enhance the potential for both entertainment and intellectual activity in the home. Miniaturization of electronics is now so far advanced that commercial development for leisure has a vast potential. However, possibilities in personal transportation, chemical induction of feeling-states, and cost reduction in leisure goods are also possible. In the complex network of a world distribution market, all sorts of changes may take place in relatively brief periods.

Resource Limitations

Resource limitations may place profound constraints on the utilization of current and future technological developments. The depletion of known fossil fuel resources will require increased efficiency in power use for transportation. Smaller personal transportation vehicles may be only a step toward filling the need for a greater proportion of travel to be by public means. The current tie between the freedom of leisure and the personal use of an automobile could be severed by rising costs and direct limitations. A turn away from the automobile would alter every element of leisure, not only the traditional vacation and weekend trips but also access within the community.

Use of resources frequently results in degradation of the environment through pollution or direct impacts. Leisure patterns that include more use of outdoor resources such as water are subject to such impacts and may be self-limiting. The quality of the resource may deteriorate and become less attractive or user pressures may bring about rationing of use. Lotteries like those for hunting licenses may be expanded to include camping, wilderness backpacking, and use of forest trails and sailing lakes.

Leisure, especially consumption leisure and travel, does use many kinds of resources. None of these can expand infinitely to meet every possible demand. The hopes and desires of people seeking pleasure and satisfaction may run up against barriers of resource shortages. Space, energy, and other resources are finite. One method of allocation is by pricing so that those with the most discretionary income will retain access to whatever is scarce. Policy for distribution of public resources is more likely to include some elements of nonprice allocation.

The power of the Western economies to command resources may also diminish as economic leverage shifts from Europe and North America to Africa, Asia, and South America. While the speed and manner of such shifts are difficult to predict, both population and natural resource factors make new balances in the world economy likely in the twenty-first century.

Other Economic Trends

A number of other economic factors will have significant effects on recreation participation. While it is impossible to forecast the cycles and waves of economic expansion and recession, to specify the sectors of the economy most likely to prosper during any period, or to project income and inflation trends for the next decade, certain contextual elements seem well established.

First, the scope of economic enterprise and organization is now global more than national. Finance, production, and distribution now involve world more than national markets. Corporations are international even when based in a particular economy. Therefore, the presumed relative strength of the American economy *separate from* world markets, production costs, and capital investments is no longer valid.

Second, the long-term trend for the American economy has witnessed a decline in productivity growth. Formerly dominant positions of major industries such as in automotives, steel, heavy construction equipment, and electric power devices have been lost and are unlikely to be regained. The impacts for the magnitude and distribution of income in the United States have already been significant and promise to continue.

Third, labor-intensive production is being shifted to regions with relatively low wages. This shift, along with the loss of world markets, has moved more and more employment out of production and into the service sectors of the economy. For overall economic health to continue and to support the consumer and service economies, markets for those goods produced by American firms and yielding a return on American investment must be maintained and expanded.

Fourth, through this period of change, the percentage of income directly spent on recreation has increased slightly from 6.1 percent in 1980 to 7.9 percent in 1990. That percentage is higher for those with greater discretionary income and lower for those with less. Therefore, the distribution and the total magnitude of income have impacts on recreation participation that are costly. Much of the expansion in recreation expenditures since 1950 has been correlated with a growing economy. If the world market and productivity factors suggest that the American economy is now in a low-growth period, then the demand for cost-intensive recreation will grow slowly as well. In the past three decades, there has been considerable growth in the leisure sector of the American economy. If the economy can maintain its relative strength in world markets, then such growth may continue. Investments and employment in businesses providing leisure resources will go on increasing as one of the three major sectors of the economy.

There has been a steady growth in efforts to develop and exploit leisure markets. Conglomerate corporations have entered the entertainment and travel businesses and are also taking on satellite companies that specialize in various kinds of leisure equipment. Consideration of such products as activity-specific clothing, schemes for marketing resort real estate, the rise of commercial sport and fitness enterprises in middle-class communities, and various responses to the increased dining and entertainment market supported by employed women indicates that the increase in leisure-related marketing is no minor phenomenon. What will be the impacts on American leisure of this intensified entry into marketing leisure commodities? If supply, properly advertised and promoted, does in part create demand, then it is possible that leisure will increasingly become oriented toward market-distributed goods. In turn, public providers would be under pressure to increase opportunities and facilities for the use of these goods.

Values and Economic Changes

However, as indicated in Chapter 7, the critical issue may be that of values. How highly is leisure valued in the overall scheme of life's possibilities? Will the income-time trade-off gradually shift to a greater value on discretionary time and less on income and buying power? Or will the influence of the media and the market increase the expectations for leisure-related commodities, including space and facilities at home, so that there will be increased pressure to gain income adequate for an expensive leisure style?

One value issue is that of the relative worth of leisure in relation to other elements of life. A second value issue focuses on the kind of leisure that is valued. Will the leisure of freedom and expression, of simplicity and the cultivation of human relationships, be valued more or less? Will personal development and intrinsic satisfaction take a more central place in the value schemes of American youth and adults, or will commodity-intensive rentals and purchases come to define the highest of leisure goals?

There are many conflicting indications. On the one hand, there are individuals and employee organizations striving for contracts and job descriptions that allow for more time, even at the cost of greater income. On the other hand, leisure-related fad items still sweep the country with enormous gross sales figures. Inflation increases pressures to obtain as high an income as possible. Even the ordinary space for leisure activity in homes built twenty or fifty years ago is now out of the reach of most young families. Expectations built on the realities of the past may be so costly to realize that the squeeze on incomes may allow for little discretionary spending.

Political Factors

One possible change is that leisure may become a legitimate political issue. For the most part, when people are freezing, starving, and otherwise dying quick and slow deaths, running for office on a leisure platform would appear frivolous. Unemployment, inflation, international relations, defense, nuclear proliferation, housing, and health are issues that seem serious enough for political exploitation. Leisure is a background concern that might be considered only as part of taken-for-granted services that are best left unmentioned.

What is the political future of leisure? Is there any likelihood that leisure provisions and possibilities will receive greater attention in the political priority-making process in North America? Is there likely to be some massive reallocation of resources to recreation in the foreseeable future? Probably not. However, some political changes may well be among the elements in an altered leisure climate.

The first is a renewed attention to the urban scene. American cities may be in trouble, but they are not about to die. They may be poor, but they are not empty. In fact, the concentration of political power in the cities along with greater attention to people with no choice but to remain there has caught the attention of national legislators and agency decision makers.

Attention to inner city recreation, however, will have to be only a part of an overall program. One alternative is for significant reinvestment to reconstruct schools, housing, and economic opportunities. Recreation can be an important, if not central, element of such programs. The other alternative is to help households leave the destruction and violence of such areas that may be too far gone to rebuild, economically and socially.

The second political theme, as analyzed in Chapter 5, is to continue the implicit policy of reliance on the market to provide most leisure resources. This likelihood will target those markets most able to pay and support a return on investment. Leisure provisions will be skewed toward cost-intensive kinds of activity for those with the discretionary income to make the purchases.

Third, tax policies will continue to support particular leisure resources. Contributions for the fine arts of music, theater, opera, dance, and other arts will provide indirect subsidies for such activities that appeal primarily to those with higher educations and incomes. Nor does it seem likely that there will be any dramatic change in the tax code that allows deductions for taxes and loan interest paid on second homes. By and large, current taxations policies benefit most those in the upper third of income levels.

A fourth political trend is the move toward more comprehensive long-term planning. Government agencies are being required to integrate their plans and programs of resource management and to coordinate with other agencies. Land-use planning has been implemented in many states with a view toward improving the long-term living habitat. In many cases, resources for recreation are being included in the plans. As a result, factors such as distance, accessibility, natural features, residential patterns, population characteristics, and projections of future needs are being considered before land or other resources are committed to any use or combination of uses. Some of the conflicts and resource losses experienced in the past may be partly alleviated by this kind of integrated planning. While leisure may not be viable as a major political issue as yet, it is being considered as one significant element in the quality of life both now and in the future.

The final political trend is toward cost recovery in the administration of public recreation resources. At all levels, from the local community to the federal, there is a systematic effort to incorporate user fees for resources and programs that approach or approximate the costs of operation. In some community recreation programs, the revenues from popular programs are used to subsidize those that cannot be self-supporting. A market price and marketing approach is being explored by many public recreation providers. Even when resources are unique, as with national parks, entry and user fees are being raised to levels that are a contradiction to the former ideology that such opportunities should be available at costs that maintain access to all who come to the site.

Demographic Factors

Recreation participation in types of activities as well as frequency and style, varies by age, gender, education level, ethnicity, and financial resources. Therefore, changes in the composition of a population will have impacts on recreation demand. Demographic trends include shifts important to the identification of recreation markets.

The Graying of America

The long-term trend is toward an older population. At the beginning of the century, less than 4 percent of the population was age sixty-five or older. By 1980, there were more than 11 percent in this "retirement period," with the percentage expected to exceed 20 percent by the year 2030. For most of the century, the increase came from the reduction in death rates in lower age categories. Now the age group with the greatest rate of increase is the "old old," those over age seventy-five.

A second cause of the shift in age-group proportions has been the result of the long-term decline in fertility. Smaller families shift the percentages upward. Now the decline in middle-age and later-age mortality is increasing the absolute members of the over-sixty-five age group. That increase is disproportionately composed of women over age seventy-five.

Fertility and Family Size

The long-term rate of fertility, the number of children per adult woman, has declined for the entire century. Only a brief surge following World War II interrupted this decline. The rate was halved in the nineteenth century and halved again between 1900 and 1980.[5]

Several factors are intensifying that long-term trend. Delayed marriage for women, along with women's rising education levels, labor force participation, and early-marriage divorce rates have reduced the number of children desired. There are fewer husband-wife households, fewer women leaving the work force for childbearing and child rearing, and more women remaining unmarried.[6] The conditions for childbearing combine with the higher costs of child rearing to reduce the number of children desired. Every cohort except the "baby boom" crop from the 1950s is smaller than the one preceding.

---

[5] Ibid.

[6] George Masnick and Mary J. Bane, *The Nation's Families: 1960–1990* (Cambridge, MA: Joint Center for Urban Studies of the Massachusetts Institute of Technology and Harvard University, 1980).

Household Composition

The makeup of households is also changing in consistent ways. Masnick and Bane[7] have projected the trends from 1960 to 1990:

Widow-headed households increased from 9 to 11 percent.

Female-headed households increased from 17 percent to 37 percent; those headed by single women from 3 percent to 8 percent; and by the divorced or separated from 4.7 percent to 11 percent, half of whom will have children living at home.

Households headed by married couples declined from 75 percent to 55 percent.

In brief, about double the proportion of households are headed by single adults. The increases are most dramatic for women, especially the never-married, the formerly married with and without children, and older widows.

This means that in the coming decades, at least half of American children will have some period of childhood in single-parent families. They will have fewer brothers and sisters, usually one or none. The breaking and reconstituting of family units with periods of transition will be a common experience at all levels of society. Further, more and more adults will reach later periods of life without a marriage intact and with a history of family instability and marital dissolution.

Other Demographic Trends

A number of other trends are expected to continue through the twentieth century:

The overall size of the population of the United States will remain relatively stable. The periods of major growth due to immigration and fertility are over.

Half or more of the growth will be due to immigration. Major sources of new citizens are Latin America and southern Asia. While language and other problems appear to slow the rates of assimilation, adoption of majority patterns through school and work force learning requirements are already under way, especially for the second and third generations.

The geographic area of most rapid growth has been the South and Southwest, with 90 percent of the total growth occurring in the 1970s. A reduction of employment opportunity growth in those areas and such factors as water limitations in the Southwest are now slowing this trend.

The "baby boom" cohort now age thirty-five to fifty will continue to age as a population "bulge." In the 1990s, their leading edge is entering the preretirement age period of those who have "launched" their children and who now have maximum discretionary income. They increase the number of persons in their ten-year cohort by more than 6 million and account for more than 40 percent more persons than does the preceding cohort.

Education levels are higher for every succeeding population cohort. Of those entering the work force now, 70 percent have some college education, while the majority of

---

[7] Ibid.

those beginning work a half century ago had nine years or less of schooling. Increasingly, some posthigh school education is a threshold requirement for employment that is not marginal, unstable, or subject to replacement at minimum hourly wages.

Higher education levels will raise the depth and breadth of skill repertoires for a variety of recreation activities. More and more people have had opportunities to gain interests and experience with activities previously reserved for the affluent. This may be a snowballing trend as more such families introduce their children to leisure possibilities and skill acquisition.

Summary

The American population at the turn of the century will consist of smaller families, more households headed by single adults, more unstable marriages, higher education levels, and greater population segments in retirement and "old old" periods of the life course. An anomaly is the "boomer" cohort born between the end of World War II and 1960 when the long-term fertility decline was reestablished. The population of the United States is no longer increasing steadily with each infant and childhood cohort being larger than the one before. Even a temporary increase in childbearing by the "boomers" who delayed starting families will be dampened by marriage instability, women's participation in the labor force, and the desire for fewer children.

Family Factors

Such demographic changes as smaller families, marriage instability, singleness, shorter periods of parenthood, and increased female employment are all significant for leisure because the social spaces of leisure and family are so intertwined. As analyzed earlier, family, home, and leisure merge into one social realm for most adults with economic and political roles somewhat separated.

What is really going on in such changes in the familial institution? Will the predominance of family activities and companions in adult leisure decrease? Do rising divorce rates indicate that the family and marriage are being replaced as the central and stable social unit of bonding, self-development, and community? Will other forms of leisure take on new importance in this social world that is less bound to one spouse, one home, one neighborhood, and one set of children? When commitments to children living at home no longer span over half of preretirement adult years for most adults, what are the alternate intimate communities, schedule determinants, resource uses, and sources of meaning and fulfillment?

One answer is that we really do not know. The changes have been slow enough that no dramatic upsurge in alternate social arrangements has been documented. Attempts to meet the leisure and social needs of single adults are found in almost every community, but few stories of profound success have been told. Divorce rates climb, but most formerly marrieds reenter marriage and form new households. Further, leisure associations frequently are the beginning of the new relationships. The issue is clear: If the family is so central to most adult leisure patterns, then what will be the impacts on leisure of shorter parenting periods, more divorces, and greater involvement of women outside the home?

Most probable consequences are

1. Most adults will continue to find their primary context for leisure in the home and immediate community. While that "immediate community" less commonly will be the childrearing family, regular relationships of some intimacy as well as availability are necessary.

2. There will be, however, greater stress on the marriage dyad in leisure companionship. Expectations that the dyad provides a personally enriching and satisfying experience are likely to be higher. As a result, many divorces may involve a failure in leisure roles rather than in breadwinner, homemaker, or parenting roles.

3. At the same time, women will be less bound to the home and become more involved in work roles. They will then have more control over their financial resources, more regular relationships with men and women away from home and neighborhood, and less time free from extrafamilial obligations. The kind of companionship that many men have enjoyed around the employment site will now be available to more married women. This may reduce some pressure on the marriage to provide so much companionship for women but also will require a new balance of freedom and dependence for many marriages. For many women, however, such opportunity and resources will come with the price of the stress of the "second shift" of household tasks and obligations.

4. Some kinds of leisure opportunities for adult "noncouples," including single parents, will emerge that provide regular companionship as well as activity. Sports, arts, adult education, religion, neighborhood organization, and job-related opportunities will be adjusted to meet the needs of the unmarried, the formerly married, and those hoping to be married again as well as those of homosexual orientations. Companionship styles other than "premarital" and "married" will be accepted and understood as appropriate for people at various times in their life careers. Such changes in social acceptance may be more significant than new programs. The companionship, sexuality, communication, and personal growth of intimacy will not be limited to those choosing one life companion until death.

5. The central implication for leisure in the future may well be in the importance of leisure to many adults. As traditional family roles and responsibilities take less time and offer less pervasive meaning through the life career, then the roles of leisure—in and outside the family—seem likely to take on increased importance. Leisure as opportunity for personal meaning and for fulfilling community will be more and more crucial to the way life is understood and evaluated.

6. For children, the assumption that almost every child has two biological parents jointly engaged in child rearing becomes less viable. Both the freedom and the developmental potential of childhood leisure may be provided more often than not without a mother/caretaker/chauffer available throughout the day and a father offering evening and weekend companionship. Less and less will skills and interests be initiated in the family. The social world of children will be widened by accommodation to two-parent employment, a single parent, and to changes in the nuclear family.

Leisure, then, will undergo some reorientation due to changes in family structures and patterns. However, leisure values will also become more and more a factor in changing family, parenting, and residence expectations and roles.

Value-Orientation Factors

Many kinds of evidence have been presented that leisure is very much a part of its historical and cultural time and place. The work ethic has been alleged to be a major inhibitor of leisure in capitalist societies in which leisure has been seen as of value only when it contributes to economic productivity. Forms of leisure are shaped not only by available resources and technologies but also by cultural values and customs. Worldviews about the nature of humankind, the relation of people to their natural environment, and time and space differ from one civilization to another and produce different modes of both work and leisure. What, then, are the cultural values and views that seem most likely to influence American leisure in the next decades?

1. The diminishing centrality of religion and the church has already affected leisure. Leisure schedules are changed by the loss of control of religious institutions over the "sacred times," especially Sunday. Sunday as a day of leisure rather than of socially expected religious observance has legitimated the use of that nonworkday for a variety of enterprises, both organized and informal.

However, more important in the future may be the loss of the moral influence of organized religion. The social ethics of Western religions have stressed responsibility to the neighbor, community, and common good as well as to the religious institutions themselves. Giving priority to the investment of time and resources primarily for the self, for personal expression and enhancement, and even for pleasure has generally been discouraged. A loss of importance of religion in the culture may raise the likelihood of a leisure ethic that values intrinsic satisfaction, freedom, and expression *for its own sake*. If leisure becomes self-justifying and does not have to be justified by its social worth, then both the whats and whys of leisure will be affected.

2. Both preservation and appreciation of natural environments are emerging as accepted values even when in conflict with economic productivity. Quality of life is now considered vital even when gross national product may be inhibited. As evidence accumulates that leisure is a major component of overall satisfaction with life and that the quality of the environment is significant to the general quality of life, then economic goals will have to compete with other social goals. It may be more and more responsive and responsible politically to measure economic gain by its contributions to the long-term common good rather than to short-term national productivity.

The issues are not simple. Few people are willing to forgo employment, the security of a regular income, or the creature comforts now taken for granted in order to preserve the ecosystem. The greater value placed on leisure is more of an "add-on" after food, housing, education, private transportation, and an accepted standard of living are ensured. Nevertheless, more and more of the products of industry may be valued only when they add more to life's quality than they detract from life's context.

Immediate production is less and less likely to be at the expense of the long-term consideration of watersheds, aquifers, topsoil, various species of plants and animals, arable land, free-running streams, clean air, and food free from dangerous substances. While the special experience of outdoor natural resources recreation is only one kind of leisure, it is one valued too highly to surrender for brief economic gain.

3. Perhaps the value shift more directly related to leisure is the possible replacement of an ethic of extrinsic goals with one of intrinsic meanings. When most people say of their leisure that they do it because they like it, they are probably referring to multiple and mixed satisfactions. Pleasure is seldom pure and unambiguous. Liking an activity is usually more than just a positive emotional response. Nevertheless, investing time, effort, and resources in an activity or relationship need not be based on some economic, social, or even developmental goals. In some cases, the experience itself may be reason enough for the activity.

If pleasure is seldom pure and simple, at least for long, the complex satisfactions of personal expression, freedom, creativity, excitement, and mastery would seem to need no further justification. An action need not be good for the community, family, employment status, or social prestige if it yields a full measure of personal satisfaction. Even the joys of rich or playful human communication need not be designed to have any consequences beyond the moment or event. It is conceivable that we may do many things for their own sake.

The issue is whether or not intrinsic motivations are becoming more and more accepted and valued as distinct from motives of achievement, reward, or status. Are American adults more likely to choose life investments and singular events just because they promise some personal joy or fulfillment and are not likely to harm others?

There is little evidence that most industrial wage workers, the poor and marginally employed, and those caught in labor routines ever unambiguously applied the work ethic to their own situations. On the other hand, there is also little evidence that they have valued leisure for its own sake. Life for most has tended to center around the immediate values of family, home, friends, security, and a few opportunities for enjoyment. What is possible and available is valued without the development of any self-conscious system of values. In general, those who have preached a work ethic are those who have stood to gain by it—investors, entrepreneurs, and the career-oriented.

Now there are hints of change. Workers insist on control over their schedules rather than required overtime despite the extra income. Employed women may give no reason for a regular leisure engagement other than "I like it and it's important to me." Men adjust their job schedules to make time for something totally unrelated that they find satisfying. Students maintain that the purpose of their preparation is employment that will provide an economic base for the style of life they desire rather than for a career of advancement bought at a high personal price.

These hints are not of a return to the woods, a dismissal of the comforts of a well-financed standard of living, or a rejection of most conventional values. The more radical counterculture movements appear to remain marginal in both numbers and influence. Rather, the hints are of a gradual shift in conventional values toward a modest commitment to leisure. Leisure in the sense of autotelic or self-justifying experience may take a larger and more central place in the values and commitments of postindustrial Americans and West Europeans. If this is true, then leisure may be one factor causing social change rather than simply being shaped by other factors.

Some will decry such a shift. They will point to excesses of pleasure-seeking that become dangerous to the self and harmful to others. They will suggest the danger of leisure privatism that discards social concern and concentrates on entertainment. Some will point to the dangers of any leisure that becomes so self-oriented that there is an eventual cost in loss of community. There seems little doubt, however, that more and more leisure entertainment will be promoted and marketed by American and world business.

Nevertheless, whatever the influences, moving beyond struggle and survival to a context of living in which more possessions or income add little to satisfaction with life seems to direct some people toward leisure in the classic sense. Leisure that is free and fulfilling, exciting and creative, and community-building and enriching is the "something more" in life that can be neither bought nor sold. It is, as Aristotle and deGrazia proposed, a condition of life and a state of being that is as much a gift as an achievement.

Continuities and Changes

One further review will offer a more complete background on leisure in general: the continuities and changes in leisure contexts, resources, styles, and meanings.

Continuities in Leisure and Recreation

1. The 7 or even 8 percent rule of leisure expenditures indicates that an infinite expansion of recreation spending cannot be anticipated. Even though the key concept is *discretionary* income—and those who have higher incomes tend to exceed the average—expenditures have consistent limits, especially when the economy is growing slowly.
2. The "core plus balance" model remains valid through the life course. Special recreation activities are part of more comprehensive leisure and lifestyles that include regular participation by most adults in accessible activity, especially at home.
3. Leisure is embedded in the life course with its continuities and changes. As a consequence, both meanings and activities shift somewhat as individuals age, take up and drop various family and work roles, and change in interests and self-definitions.
4. Time remains scarce for most adults. The time costs of recreation participation may be a greater constraint than financial costs, especially for dual-income households with children and for single parents.
5. The one really profound social revolution of our era is in the sexual realm. Major behavioral changes since the 1950s permeate every aspect of the society, including leisure. Sexual expression is accepted, diversity is legitimized, and sexuality is presumed as a dimension of activity. Recreation meanings and choices have recognized sexual dimensions even when focused on a specific activity or environment. Intimate relationships will continue in diverse contexts as well as those of marriage and the family.
6. Considerable recreation involves self-display and style. How participants manage impressions to gain approval and acceptance involves styles of participation, clothing, equipment, and being with the "right" companions. Impression management may be more important than the game for some leisure events.
7. The distance costs of recreation continue to mount in growing urban areas. Distance is translated into time costs increased by crowding and "rush hour" timetables that affect leisure as well as work. Private transportation may be a recreation necessity for time efficiency.

8. Race-intensified poverty, especially in urban ghettos and rural fringes, is set against the affluent life and leisure styles portrayed on television. Anger and alienation may focus on leisure as much as on economic rewards and opportunity.

9. Shopping continues as a central leisure activity for American adults, both in the home community and while traveling. Shopping malls and boutique boulevards are major leisure environments.

10. Travel remains important for adults even when styles and costs vary widely. In 1991, 1.3 billion Americans took trips, over 80 percent by car. Styles, however, are very different for the rich in comparison to the middle mass or for parents in comparison to the retired.

11. Leisure and recreation investments are an important component of marriage and family life. For both intact and serial marriages, recreation choices can be conflict-ridden at the same time that they are contexts for expressing and developing relationships. Disappointment in leisure companionship and support can be a major factor in marriage dissolution.

12. Developmental aims for families with children will be important in selecting recreation investments. Parents, perhaps especially those with only one or two children, will seek recreation that will improve their children's chances to compete in the worlds of school and work.

13. Every younger cohort has had a higher level of education with consequent variety of leisure interests and experiences.

14. The quality of relationships remains central to satisfaction with most recreation experiences.

15. Concerns over the environment will continue to be balanced against development for recreation and other uses.

16. The trend toward securing blocks of time—long weekends as well as vacations—for leisure engagements will also continue. Travel-based activity will remain special, but somewhat more frequent.

17. The trend toward more independence and self-reliance for women will also continue. This means that women's interests will become more and more important in determining patterns and resource allocation.

Changes in Leisure and Recreation

1. The fifty-plus age groups will be recognized as growing markets for recreation goods and services, especially as the boomer generation moves into this age.

2. Leisure opportunities for women, both married and single, will be more diverse and less tied to the family.

3. The increasing size of the "new class" with discretionary income and more education will attract disproportionate attention from those planning for recreation programs and provisions, especially in the market sector.

4. Major attention will have to be given to "off hour" employment and the potential for recreation participation during weekdays and at odd times, especially by those employed in the service sector of the economy.

5. Sunset or declining activities will balance sunrise recreation. For example, the basis of hunting seems to be shrinking at the same time that backpacking is growing. Again, education levels as well as urbanization are factors in such changing tastes.

6. More and more adults at any one time are either single or in a period of transition. Leisure settings and opportunities will increase for those who do not come in couples or families. Singleness will be accepted as a more common and less extraordinary mode of life, whether temporary or relatively permanent. Diversity in sexuality and households will become more accepted.

7. The business sector will become more central to recreation provisions. And the complementary nature of market and public sector resources and programs will become increasingly significant. Market-sector recreation provisions will gain greater recognition as a major sector of the economy.

8. Space scarcities will become more acute, especially in prime environments such as national parks, major museums, and urban facilities. The urban space crunch will be intensified by more multiple-unit housing and the decline of the private residential yard.

9. Home electronic entertainments will become more diverse and less costly. Those technologies that are compatible with current life styles will gain enormous markets and increase the attraction of at-home entertainment.

10. The diversity in life and leisure styles will continue despite the power of mass marketing. In fact, many market segments will be identified more by their leisure styles than by economic factors.

11. Concentration on the "high end" for leisure businesses will saturate the market and cause business failures. Middle mass markets may become recognized for more kinds of businesses. In the meantime, however, the imbalance of opportunities for the affluent will intensify.

12. Reduced public subsidies in areas such as the arts and outdoor resources will open many possible markets for businesses and diversify programs for the public resources. Reliance on cost recovery will tend to raise user fees for public provisions even further.

13. The higher activity levels and greater financial resources of the retired will bring increased attention to the "active old" as recreation participants.

14. New technologies will impact on particular activities much as fiberglass did on boating and skiing. Such technologies are extremely important when they lower the costs or reduce the pain of acquiring enough skill to gain satisfaction from the activity.

15. Nonfamily leisure settings and organization will become more and more important due to demographic changes and the long postparental period of the family life cycle.

16. Health concerns and motivations will be significant in the leisure styles of more adults in their forties, fifties, and sixties.

17. Travel provisions will become more varied to accommodate various styles. Packages will be more diverse and almost any amenity will be available for rent.

18. "Big toys" will be purchased by some. At the same time, however, some highly educated adults will avoid being tied down to particular locales or equipment. They will seek variety by refusing the big-ticket purchases. The "special use" car as a personal expression will become increasingly common with its allure of possession and symbol of individuality.

19. The skills associated with recreation will become more important as more individuals define themselves and their competence in terms of what they can do and accomplish off the job. As a result, provisions for enhancing skills at levels above "beginner" will grow in public and market sector programs. At the same time, gains in skills will create new demand for programs and resources.

20. Employed women will be recognized as a market opportunity almost equal to men. Over time the established bias toward male programs and provisions will almost disappear.

How will all these continuities and changes meld into a varied but integrated whole? There are too many dimensions of change to produce a neat picture of the future. No single direction seems likely to mold leisure into a monolithic and undifferentiated set of meanings or activities. Diversity will continue to characterize leisure as people seek to incorporate different kinds of experiences and meanings in their leisure. One further change may be a heightened awareness of the potential of leisure for human fulfillment and an insistence that every person has a right to his or her share of its freedom and community.

HIGHLIGHTS

1. Technology is one factor in social change, but is tempered by other factors, including the world economy, value systems, and critical resource limitations.
2. Economic factors such as work schedule diversity, technological development, and energy and materials restrictions along with population aging, smaller families with less investment in child rearing, increased women's employment, housing and travel cost increases, and value shifts toward self-development and expression may all reshape the forms of leisure and require new provisions and programs.
3. Diversity in leisure styles, a social consensus on the legitimacy and even importance of leisure, a gradual extension of resources to currently deprived groups, and some reorientation due to the costs of distance and space are changes in leisure itself that will have consequences for the economy and other social institutions.

Discussion Questions

1. What would be your scenario of the best possible leisure in the future? What factors make it likely or unlikely to be realized?

2. How may changes in leisure alter the economy?

3. What are implications of a more varied workweek schedule for public and commercial recreation providers?

4. Is leisure likely to be more or less tied to the family in the future? How and why?

5. What are likely implications of women having more resources, opportunities, and self-determination in both work and leisure? Will the constraints of the "second shift" be reduced?

6. What are probable consequences of an expanded investment in leisure businesses in the next decade?

7. How will higher energy costs affect public recreation? Commercial recreation? Family and community recreation?

8. Are there other scarcities probable in the future that will have an impact on leisure? Give examples.

9. Is the acceptance of a new "leisure ethic" likely to become common in Western societies? Why or why not?

10. What are the implications of "time scarcity" for leisure providers, both public and market sectors?

11. Which are more significant, the continuities or the changes? Why?

12. Which trends offer the greatest opportunity for innovative leisure programs and businesses?

Bibliography

Brinton, Crane, *The Anatomy of Revolution.* Englewood Cliffs, NJ: Prentice-Hall, 1965.

Fuchs, Victor, *How We Live: An Economic Perspective on Americans from Birth to Death.* Cambridge, MA: Harvard University Press, 1983.

Godbey, Geoffrey C., *The Future of Leisure Services: Thriving on Change.* State College, PA: Venture, 1988.

Kelly, John R., *Recreation Trends toward the Year 2000.* Champaign, IL: Management Learning Laboratories, 1987.

Veal, Anthony J., *Leisure and the Future.* London: Allen and Unwin, 1987.

Forms of Leisure and Recreation

What do people do as leisure and recreation? From one perspective, the answer is almost everything. All sorts of action and interaction are leisure in some times and places. Conversation in the kitchen, joking in the workplace, daydreaming on the sidewalk, contemplation in the car, planting seeds, running, flying, and countless other kinds of activity may be leisure.

There are, however, certain forms of activity that have a special place in the spectrum of leisure activity. They may not occupy the most time. Nor are they necessarily the most common activities. As suggested in Section I, the core of activity tends to center around the residence and usual associations with others who are important to us. We talk and walk, watch television and read, putter around the house and yard, and engage in varieties of interaction. Most leisure is not special or specialized activity.

Nonetheless, there are a number of particular forms of activity that have distinct places in the contemporary range of activities. Because of their forms, they make different demands and offer satisfactions and meanings different from the ordinary round of activity. In this section, five kinds of activity are given attention because they have special places in leisure. They have histories of development and participation. Each is connected to environments, built and natural, that are an integral part of the experience.

Like all leisure activity, they vary through the life course, are based in sets of resources and histories, and have changed as cultures and social contexts have changed through the centuries. But most important, they are not all alike.

Sport, resource-based outdoor recreation, the arts, popular culture, and travel—each has unique as well as common elements. The forms and environments of activities do make a difference in the nature of the participation experience. The basic question for each of the next five chapters is "What is special about this kind of activity?"

C h a p t e r *13*

Sport and Exercise

No activity is more demanding and exacting than sport participation at a high level of skill. The complete and intense concentration of the Olympic gymnast or the professional basketball player in the final minutes of a crucial playoff game is unsurpassed in human endeavor. Even less arduous levels of sport competition usually require countless hours of disciplined preparation and rigorous physical and mental effort. In this sense, sport does not seem very leisurely.

However, if one aim of leisure is to provide opportunity for an investment of the self that yields the fullest satisfaction in the experience of participation, then sport may be one mountaintop of leisure amid a full range of activities. Sport is one kind of leisure that may become so completely self-contained in its meaning that the rest of the world seems to disappear. The union of mind and body in coordinated movement, the rhythm and grace of developed skill, and the drama of structure and uncertainty make sport a very special kind of experience—at least on some occasions.

Then there are the spectators—sitting, complaining, and eating as well as leaping, yelling, and letting themselves go. As many as 100,000 onlookers in a stadium may be joined by several million more who watch via television. As a consequence, sport is more a spectacle and a business product for most people than an experience of physical effort and skill mastery. And yet some of the same engrossing drama of participation is shared by those who watch. They identify with the players, become caught up in the emotion of the drama, and vicariously win or lose when the outcome is no longer in doubt.

Just how is sport a part of the panoply of leisure in our society? Just as important, what is the place of sport in the leisure of men, women, and children who work and play out their lives in this culture?

One aspect of sport is its component of physical exertion. This element connects sport to health and physical fitness. All sport is not healthful exercise, nor is all exercise sport. There is, however, a consistent relationship between the two. Increased attention is being given to health in the culture at this time. As a consequence, the exercise element of sport as well as other kinds of physical exercise are becoming significant in the leisure styles of many men and women.

ISSUES

Is sport a major element in American leisure?

What has television meant to sport?

Is sport with its rules and high levels of exertion and discipline really leisure?

How does sport participation change through the life course?

How are health and exercise becoming important dimensions of contemporary leisure?

From the perspective of total numbers, sport participation appears to be a major element in American leisure. Add the numbers who watch others participate directly or on television and it would seem that sport is a central element of the culture. For example, total attendance at professional and college sports events in 1991 has been estimated to exceed 300 million. Other estimates are that more than 44 million persons swam in 1990, 30 million bowled, and 13 million ran or jogged. These are impressive figures.

However, from another perspective, sport seems inconsequential to most American adults. The International Time Budget studies found that North American males average twelve minutes a day in sport participation and females only five minutes a day, about 20 percent as much as men and women in the Federal Republic of Germany.[1] All active sport and outdoor recreation together amount to about 1 percent of the average North American adult's use of time. Put in another way, more than 90 percent of American adults did nothing in sport or organized recreation yesterday.

How can these two perspectives be reconciled? Is someone "lying with statistics" again? To some extent, yes.

Aggregate Participation in Sport

"How many" totals are gathered from a number of sources. Even those made available through government agencies are often industry self-reports. Others are based on national recreation surveys that are of uneven quality. A few totals come from the market surveys of commercial research organizations. Therefore, to begin with, it is not possible to make close comparisons of numbers that are derived from so many different sources in so many different ways.

Also, the totals for some kinds of participation are not total numbers of people who did the activity once or more in the year but the total numbers of those who passed through the gate. For example, if almost 64 million attended thoroughbred racing in 1990, the figure does not represent 64 million different people. Rather, some people attended 10, 50, or 150 times

---

[1] A. Szalai and others, eds., *The Use of Time: Daily Activities of Urban and Suburban Populations in Twelve Countries* (The Hague: Mouton, 1972).

while most people never saw a racehorse in the flesh all year. Spectator totals have to be interpreted in light of percentages of habituees, season-ticket holders, and other repeaters. Also, horseracing is not the attraction for those who spend their time with the racing forms and at the pari-mutuel windows and seldom see the races; gambling is their participant sport.

Along with skepticism about some of the totals and the problem of repeaters, there is the issue of frequency. Most of the participation totals include all who did the activity once during the year. Some of the 44 million swimmers or 19 million golfers may have done it only once while others were in the water or on the course fifty or more times a year. Does one game of table tennis or handball make one a participant? According to most aggregate listings, yes.

Finally, there is the problem of intensity. Even if we know the proportions of participants and spectators who engaged in the activity once, infrequently, or regularly, we do not know anything about the level of their engagement. Playing at a sport may be a purely social event for some and an intense experience for others. Some go to a football game though they neither like nor understand it because they were invited by someone they enjoy. The sport is irrelevant, but the ticket is recorded in attendance figures.

Nevertheless, despite all these warnings and inadequacies, such aggregates give some idea of the scale of sport in the economy and the society. Even granting a 20 percent error in the totals, the comparisons are worth noting (see Table 13–1).

Attendance figures given in Table 13–1 are totals that do not account for repeating. Such aggregate statistics tell us nothing about average time per occasion, frequency, or the importance of the sport to the participant or the spectator. However, the totals do give an indication of the importance of sport as a commercial enterprise and as an element in the public leisure of the society. Reports of household surveys indicate that about 18 percent of the adult population ever attended a baseball game in a year. The percentages are 11 percent for professional football, 10 percent for college football, 8 percent for auto racing, 6 percent for college and professional basketball, 4.5 percent for hockey, 4 percent for horse racing, and 2 percent for boxing.

Disaggregated Sport Statistics

When approached from the perspective of the importance of sport to individuals, the picture is drastically altered. Participation in active or outdoor sports barely makes it onto any

TABLE 13–1   1990 Total Attendance at Selected Spectator Sports

Thoroughbred horseracing	63,803,000
Major league baseball	55,512,000
College football	36,627,000
College basketball	33,660,000
Greyhound racing	28,660,000
National Basketball Association	18,586,000
National Football League	17,666,000
National Hockey League	12,578,000

Source: Statistical Abstract of the United States, 1993.

list of ways in which adults employ time. Despite all the attention given to the growth of participation in sports such as tennis and other racquet sports, the emphasis on sport in school programs, the use of sport celebrities in advertising, the media attention given to the Super Bowl and the Olympic Games, and the increased interest in natural environments, most adult Americans would not have to change their schedules at all if every field, gym, court, pool, bowling alley, and stadium in the land closed for a week.

The average of 1 percent of the week's time given to sport does not accurately represent those who engage in such activity regularly and "religiously." We know that sport is quite important to many adults and even more to youths and children. However, even in terms of relative importance to individuals, sport participation is surprisingly marginal. In a three-community study of adults, pair and individual outdoor sports, spectator sports, and pair and individual indoor sports ranked between fifteenth and twenty-fifth in frequency of selection as among the five or ten "most important" kinds of leisure activities[2] (See Table 13–2). Far

TABLE 13–2 Sports and Fitness Participation, 1990

	Total (millions)	Total percent	Percent male	Percent female	Percent 10 or more per year
Fitness walking	46	25.2	19.8	30.2	21.4
Swimming	44	24.1	24.0	24.1	12.6
Bowling	30	16.8	17.6	16.0	6.0
Fitness programs (twice per week)					
at home	27	15.0	13.0	16.9	
at a club	7	3.7	3.3	4.0	
Bicycling	20	11.1	11.6	10.8	7.0
Golf	19	10.6	14.6	7.0	4.7
Jogging/running	13	7.1	9.4	5.0	5.4
Tennis	12	6.7	7.5	6.1	2.6
Softball/baseball	12	6.4	9.1	4.0	
Aerobics	12	6.4	2.1	10.5	5.2
Volleyball	11	6.0	6.5	5.5	
Weight training					
dumbbells	10	5.3	7.7	3.2	4.5
machines	7	3.9	3.9	3.9	3.3
Basketball	8	4.7	7.7	1.9	
Downhill skiing	8	4.2	5.5	3.0	1.1
Racquetball	7	4.0	5.3	2.8	2.0
Football	4	2.4	4.4	0.6	
Cross country skiing	4	2.2	2.0	2.4	0.5

Other sports (percent of population age 18 and over who played at least once in 1990): rollerskating 3.6, water-skiing 3.2, ice skating 2.2; archery 1.8; snorkeling/scuba 1.7; motorcycling (dirt, trail) 1.5; karate/martial arts 1.2; rowing (outdoor) 1.1; soccer 0.9; airplane flying 0.7; handball 0.6.

Source: Simmons Market Research Bureau, 1990. Study of Media and Markets. National sample of 19,874 adults.

[2] John R. Kelly, "Leisure Styles and Choices in Three Environments," *Pacific Sociological Review,* 21 (1978), 187–207.

ahead were informal, available, and family kinds of activity and home activities such as reading, listening to music, and watching television.

To some extent, we are caught between the impressive aggregate totals and the low rankings in individual schedules and among leisure priorities. More than $3.7 billion a year is spent gaining admission to spectator sports, while less than 10 percent of the adult population either did or directly watched a sport activity on any weekday. Both perspectives are worth considering, but probably neither is complete without the other. They are complementary. The picture is further complicated by that accessible secondhand sport attraction, television, and by the greater importance of sport for younger segments of the population.

Sport and Television

Not that many years ago the radio broadcasts of Joe Louis's fights and the baseball World Series were major cultural events. It was important and exciting to know and imagine what was happening at the moment of occurrence. There was an interaction between experience and observation of a sport and the verbal description that made an imaginative participation possible.

Now with television, sight and sound are united in a new immediacy that has become a major aspect of sport participation. It used to be possible to divide participants and spectators into two neat categories of sport contact. Now there is a new method of consumption of sport-related time, in which the amount of time involved dwarfs that of both playing and on-site watching. Sport is a mass media product of staggering proportions (see Table 13–3).

The average professional football game draws 10 percent of the national audience with more than 40 percent watching the Super Bowl and special local audiences exceeding 50 percent. More than 20 percent watch the daytime World Series games of American professional baseball. Between 100 and 500 people will be watching a nationally televised game for every one person there in person.

TABLE 13–3   Percent of Adults Who Watch Sports on Television

Sport	Watch occasionally	Watch frequently	Total
Baseball	20.6	12.1	32.7
Basketball, professional	15.0	8.0	23.0
Basketball, college	12.1	7.9	20.0
Football, professional	18.0	21.3	39.3
Football, college	14.5	10.7	25.2
Boxing	12.7	5.5	18.2
Wrestling	11.0	6.4	17.4
Golf	10.3	4.4	14.7
Stock car racing	9.5	3.3	12.8
Tennis	10.4	2.5	12.9

Other totals: fishing 15.6; ice hockey 9.1; rodeo 9.0; soccer 4.5.

Source: Simmons Market Research Bureau, 1990. Volume 10.

Television has made the business of sport a growth industry. Franchises valued at a few hundred thousand dollars before television are now sold for $20 to $50 million. Expansion franchises are allocated taking the projected television market more into account than the projected actual attendance. Every owner gets a share of the television proceeds and these proceeds undergird the finances of the operation even when attendance is low. For team owners television revenue combines with tax advantages (such as being able to depreciate the purchase price of a player) to make the business aspects of professional sport both complex and potentially rewarding.

However, amateur sport is big business as well. Television contracts have made post-season bowl appearances so lucrative for university football teams that a coach's failure to obtain a bowl bid for several years is considered adequate grounds for dismissal. On the other hand, a football team that consistently receives such television-augmented postseason income as well as the receipts from occasional network coverage of regular-season games can support vast multi-sport athletic programs. To meet television requirements for commercials, time-outs are called in football and basketball games that are unrelated to the flow of the game, and schedules are rearranged to accommodate the viewing markets. Uniforms are designed for color cameras and even styles of play are altered to be more entertaining.

Remember that sport hardly appears in the time diaries of most North American adults. Television viewing, however, is found to consume close to one-third of all nonobligated time. Although the national urban time diary study reports less time spent watching television than is reported by the rating services—between two and two and a half hours per day,[3]—nothing approaches television in absorbing nonwork waking hours. Further, that time seems to have increased since 1965.

In short, the most common sport contact for American adults is on the screen right in their living room or den. Whatever impact sport may have on American life must take into account this third sport arena. The three worlds of sport are participation (which falls off drastically with age), firsthand watching, and in-home viewing. While participation may be very important to those who do it and on-site spectators may have considerable investment in being there, it is televised sport that touches directly the greatest number of lives.

The results of having the sport right there at home have only begun to be measured. One result is that previously exclusive sports such as golf have increased their participation base. Televised Olympic events have given great impetus to participation by children and youths in competitive swimming, figure skating, and gymnastics. Models of performance on the highest levels are immediately available for the young performers to watch and emulate. Both a breadth of contact and a depth of sophistication have been produced by this mass medium that is in 95 percent of North American homes. Although televised sport may keep some adults home to watch in comfort, its consequences for the young have included a greater diversity of possibility and desire for participation.

Televised sport is a business that has transformed many aspects of the games and has increased the financial rewards for a few. However, it is also a socialization medium that has opened new worlds of participation and achievement to countless children and youth. It has both capitalized on and democratized sports.

---

[3] John Robinson, Americans' Use of Time Project. In B. Butler, "Where Does the Free Time Go?" *American Demographics* (November, 1990).

Sport and Leisure

Having introduced something of the scope and impact of the activities we call sport, it is necessary to be more precise as to what we mean by the term *sport*. What is the relationship between leisure and sport? Is all sport leisure? If not, when and for whom is sport leisure? More important, what is the place of sport in our leisure careers?

Defining Sport

Listing sports is easy. Classifying sports as indoor and outdoor, professional and amateur, and formal and informal is only slightly more difficult. However, a definition that draws parameters around sport that clearly include and exclude agreed-on kinds of activity is less simple. As with leisure, there is the issue of preferring an inclusive or exclusive definition. If organized and competitive games such as basketball and gymnastics are clearly to be included, what about noncompetitive activities such as fishing and jogging? Does sport include watching as well as playing, learning and practicing as well as competing, body-control exercise as well as head-to-head contest? And does it also include cheerleading, physical development disciplines, martial arts, and such mental contests as chess?

Sociologist Harry Edwards gives a relatively narrow definition that excludes many games and considerable play by stressing physical effort and competition. Sport involves "activities having formally recorded histories and traditions, stressing physical exertion through competition within limits set in explicit and formal rules governing role and position relationships, and carried out by actors who represent or who are part of formally organized associations having the goal of achieving valued tangibles or intangibles though defeating opposing groups."[4] Edwards refers primarily to competitive, institutionalized sports. Sport should include not only accepted rules and forms but also physical effort and goals of rewards through competition. He would, then, exclude purely mental contests and playful "new games" that stress making up new rules and savoring the experience rather than the score.

Most scholars would be more inclusive. Gunther Lüschen stresses institutionalization and physical activity with competition as a common goal, but would include more individual and informal activity than does Edwards.[5] John Loy is perhaps most comprehensive, when he lists a series of dimensions of sport without drawing strict boundaries as to just exactly what may be included.[6] He proposes game, institutional, social organization, and social situation dimensions of sport. Sport as game may be playful in the sense of being free, unproductive, uncertain, and even make-believe. The game also includes the structure of rules, competition, physical and mental skills, and physical mastery.

There are certain persistent themes among all these definitions. Physical activity and effort and a degree of regularity in form are central to every definition. The regularity may be expressed in rules, forms, development of specific skills, and social organization of role expectations and authority patterns. Further, the dimension of some kind of relative measurement according to competition, performance standards, outcomes, and judgment is part

---

[4] Harry Edwards, *Sociology of Sport* (Homewood, IL: Dorsey, 1973), pp. 52–58.

[5] Gunther Lüschen, *The Sociology of Sport* (Paris: Mouton, 1968).

[6] John Loy, "The Nature of Sport: A Definitional Effort," in J. Loy and G. Kenyon, eds., *Sport, Culture, and Society* (New York: Macmillan, 1969).

of every definition. While the motivation for participating in a sport may be intrinsic to the experience, the sport itself is a measured activity. Usually present is some element of play in the sense of uncertainty of outcomes and freedom of participation. The three central elements of sport seem to be physical effort, regularity, and measurement.

Therefore, an inclusive definition would be: *Sport is organized activity in which physical effort is related to that of others in some relative measurement of outcomes with accepted regularities and forms.*

As a consequence, sport would include relatively informal and spontaneous games without spectators or a larger context of recorded results and rankings. It would include the adapted forms that children play and skill acquisition sessions without competition for which the measurement goal is delayed until a later event.

Sport as Leisure

If leisure is defined in terms of relative freedom, action, and intrinsic satisfactions, then much sport is certainly leisure for the participant. The organized and goal-oriented physical exertion of sport is chosen by participants because that form of activity produces for them particular outcomes that are found satisfying. On the other hand, for some participants, sport is surely not leisure.

There are obvious examples. Sport participation may be employment for some professionals who demonstrate or teach skills in some contractual arrangement for financial reward. Whatever the satisfactions, the rigorous and demanding schedule of a National Basketball Association player is hardly leisure; playing through pain night after night on the road becomes very much a meeting of employment obligations.

The same might be said for others who have little or no choice about their participation: those in required physical education classes or who believe that they have to play in the company golf tournament to provide a supervisor with a partner. A sport is hardly leisure when the athlete has engaged a lawyer to represent his interests, when it is required for graduation, or when one's employment is contingent on playing.

Certain role expectations may reduce the freedom of choice in some sport participation to the point that it is hardly leisure. When peer and parental expectations are overpowering, a student may join a team primarily as a duty. Institutional constraints may make real choice and the question of personal satisfactions irrelevant. In other cases, requirements for gaining or maintaining a necessary level of health or fitness may motivate participation in a sport that is not enjoyed for any reasons related to the experience of doing it. Some sport may not be free enough to be leisure.

However, the spontaneous games of children and the noninstitutionalized sports of adults may be among the least constrained of human activities. The sheer joy of combining the effort and the structure of the sport obliterates consciousness of the evaluation of others and any winning-losing goals. Being fully caught up in the exercise of the skills of a sport can be as fully its own reward and justification as anything people do. Sport may be as free as any leisure can be.

Social Meanings of Sport

Sport has long been a center of excitement and attention in Western societies. Whether the national sport is the soccer version of football, the collegiate-professional form of the

United States, another variety, or another sport entirely, the packed stadiums and large television audiences testify to the attraction of spectator sports. The significance of sport participation in school status hierarchies and in social identities makes sport more than an adult pastime. Sport is integrally related to self-images, sex roles and identities, and societal identification and mass culture. As a consequence, sport has been both exalted and attacked by social philosophers and critics with diverse backgrounds. Theologians, philosophical ethicists, journalists, literature professors, and athletes themselves have joined in the critical and sometimes strident analysis of sport.

Christopher Lasch is a historian who has reflected on both the corruption and the contributions of sport in contemporary society.[7] He begins with the intrinsic satisfaction of sport participation. The intensity of concentration in sport participation is a pure form of engagement without side effects or external consequences. The "ideal conditions" of the game contrast with the moral confusion of most of life. The game begins new and fresh in conditions of temporary equality, the action is self-contained, and the outcome uncertain. The very "futility" of play partly explains its appeal. The meaning that is so hard to find in the routinized world of work is clear and immediate in the artificiality of the game.

Lasch argues that there is nothing inherently evil about the spectator element of sport. On the contrary, the spectator participates in the drama of the contest through an identification with the players and the action. This vicarious participation yields some of the same sense of meaning and engagement as actually playing the sport. Further, being part of a collectivity of spectators with a sense of community and purpose augments feelings of social solidarity as a counter to estrangement and alienation. The spectator is part of the drama giving fuller meaning to the contest for players as well as watchers.

However, mass spectator sports and their television marketing have created a problem. The problem is not a new one, but was known in Greece and Rome as well. As the crowd grows larger and therefore more distant, how can the intensity of emotion and identification carry to the back row of the Circus Maximus or the Los Angeles Coliseum? How can the drama be so stark and gripping that it commands the attention, and even loyalty, of someone sitting alone in a soft chair before a screen about two feet wide with the action interrupted by commercials every few minutes?

When the roles, format, and pacing of the sport are altered to heighten that attraction and intensity, then the clear and self-contained nature of the sport experience is changed. When the Roman gladiatorial combats became bloodier and the games more violent to extend the range of appeal, then what had been exciting but not "serious" became overserious. Today the direct nature of the sport is profaned as the media-transmitted impact becomes the new end of the drama. The contest is manipulated to grip spectators who are defined as a market rather than a community.

One essential element of sport includes a sharing of virtuosity with onlookers. Play leads to display. The extraordinary level of control, grace, and even risk demonstrated by those most adept does heighten the meaning and satisfaction of those who engage in the sport at a lower level. Sport is consequential in its own realm, and much of its meaning lies in ascribing importance to the contest in that set-apart time and place. However, enlarging the audience may alter that meaning as the game becomes primarily a spectacle. The sport becomes first of all entertainment. The players, then, may come to find their motivation in

---

[7] Christopher Lasch, "The Corruption of Sport," *New York Review,* April 28, 1977.

the size and enthusiasm of the watchers and in the financial rewards that result from the enlarged crowd.

Sport may become too serious in different kinds of societies. The spectacle of the ancient Greek Olympics became entertainment rather than a peak demonstration of athletic achievement by citizens. The modern Olympics has become a political arena, in which national identities and even economic systems are represented in the contest. The mass media keep national totals of medals in what was to have been a series of contests among individuals. While capitalist interests have made sport a profit-seeking product for mass consumption, socialist interests have organized sport even among children as a national movement.

It is true that, historically, sport has often been linked with warfare and preparation for combat. Some of the fiercely violent games of social groups with regular territorial conflicts are directly and deliberately war preparation and testing. More recently we have had Walter Camp proclaim the grand do-or-die spirit of football that held the line in World War I and General Douglas MacArthur's more eloquent "Upon the fields of friendly strife are sown the seeds which, on other days, on other fields, will bear the fruits of victory."[8] While such references to war may be outmoded, the purpose of *character building* is still extolled as a major value of sport.

Actually, even character building is one element of the secularization of sport. Sport is supported and redesigned to be good for something else: war, learning, developing moral values, physical health, social cohesion, revenue production, or escape from routinization. Lasch argues that whatever the extrinsic purpose, sport is transformed by this imposition of "serious" aim. It is the unrelatedness of the drama and the contest that characterizes real sport and gives it special meaning.

Other changes within sport have also vitiated its special character. The linking of university prestige and alumni pride to football victories requires an elaborately organized program with explicit means and ends. The addition of the importance of the income through increasing the gate receipts and television revenues has intensified the extrinsic goals of winning and entertaining. The proliferation of statistical records in all sports has led to various kinds of *scientific training* to reach new levels of performance. Such sports as swimming and track are measured by milliseconds with elaborate and punishing training schedules.

Some who would restore a clean and uncorrupted kind of sport in which the intrinsic joy of participation is regained call for an insulation of sport from business, politics, and entertainment. However, the history of sport is against this hope for purification. While the satisfaction and even thrill of participation may call for such separation and nonseriousness, the political and economic institutions cannot be sealed off from a phenomenon of such mobilizing power. As a result, the history of sport will probably continue to be a dialectic between the preservation and reinstitution of games and play for their own sake and the functional organization of sport for institutional gain.

Nevertheless, the nature of sport may reemerge among those who recognize that the basic appeal of the spectacle is in personal or vicarious participation in the high level of skill and attainment and in the self-contained drama of the contest. They find that the meaning of the sport experience is in the exercise of special skills in a special world with its own satisfactions and rewards.

---

[8] Ibid.

Personal Meanings of Sport

The meanings of sport may be found in the experience of the player and the onlooker, in the developmental outcomes of participation, and in the social institutions that provide for sport participation. Here we will look at reports of personal satisfactions before going on to social contexts and meanings.

Satisfactions in Adult Sport

The previous discussion of sport in modern societies implies that the personal meaning is found in direct or vicarious participation in the contest-drama of the sport world-of-its-own. The experience of engagement in this realm of fresh beginnings and nonserious outcomes is its own reward. Such experiential satisfaction would seem to be directly related to the nature of sport as structured physical activity with some measurement and uncertainty of outcomes.

Direct inquiry into the satisfactions that adult sport participants perceive supports both the philosophy and definitions. In general, intrinsic and relational satisfactions outweigh those of recuperation and response to role obligations. However, there is a strong self-enhancement element of the retention and improvement of personal health and fitness. Some sport participation, however attractive the experience and the companions, is chosen with physical and emotional health as one extrinsic goal. In general, the aims of adult sport are more directed toward the self than toward social ends.

Not only is sport highly important to those who especially value its rewards, but there is some evidence of increasing importance of physical activity, especially for women. Further, the greater inclination of younger people to choose activity for quite personal reasons and without extrinsic justification along with a greater emphasis on health and fitness suggests that sport may take a more prominent place in adult leisure as those now in their twenties and thirties move through their life careers. Also, the greater stress on introducing "lifetime sports" in school programs may encourage adult participation.

Sport participation has its own career for many participants. It begins with neighborhood engagement, moves to school and other organized contexts, and then tends to be reduced in post-school years. However, not only the contexts and rates but also the meanings of sport change through the life course. For adults, especially those in sedentary occupations, sport may be seen as an important way to engage in regular physical exertion. The benefits for health, physical fitness, and appearance become a significant element in participation motivations.

The reasons for choosing to engage in a sport vary with the nature of the activity. The degree of skill required, the number of joint participants, the locale and form, and the social context partly determine the kinds of satisfactions that predominate. Also, some categories of activity may be done in quite different ways though the differences are obscured by a general label such as *walking* or *swimming*. In the sports for which enough data were obtained to give indications, the following satisfactions were reported:

Tennis: active exercise and skill mastery

Golf: skill mastery

Indoor pair sports: active exercise, enjoyable companions, and excitement

Team sports: exercise and companionship

Motorized sports: excitement

Swimming: exercise, enhancement of health and fitness, and relaxation

Swimming may be the best example of variations in mode of participation. Some of those interviewed regularly visit a pool for the purpose of swimming twenty to two hundred lengths. They are actually swimming and claim beneficial outcomes related to the physical exertion and conditioning. On the other hand, most who visit a pool regularly actually do little swimming. They enjoy the water in modes of play rather than disciplined effort, enjoy being with others who come to the pool, and find the experience relaxing. They contrast with adults in competitive *masters'* swimming programs who receive coaching, keep careful records, and find the competition exciting. Unless visiting lake and ocean beaches is separated from swimming as an activity, time spent on the sand with little contact with the water may also be listed as "swimming" even though the satisfactions may be much like those of going with friends to a shopping center. The rigor and discipline of one kind of swimming contrast with the freedom and relaxation of another to suggest that our approach to an activity may be more significant that the label.

Mihaly Csikszentmihalyi investigated the peak "flow" experiences that are the heart of activities with essentially intrinsic meaning.[9] Sport is one kind of activity in which this kind of personal involvement seems most likely to occur. The conditions of flow are related both to the preparation of the participant and the nature of the activity. Flow requires familiarity with the structure of the sport, the investment of the self in the effort, a level of skill mastery, and concentration on the act itself. In sport there are self-transcendent moments when everything seems to disappear except grace and performance in a union of mind, body, and emotion. These occur when the difficulty of the performance is matched with the skill level in such a way that the participant is conscious of nothing but the action. The consequent "high" of flow is its own reward and a central incentive to continuation of the activity.

Sport Socialization

The life career approach as learning leisure and the relationship of sport to personal and social identity have been introduced in Chapter 6. However, there are a number of issues specific to sport that merit attention. Among them are these:

What is the *carryover* from physical education programs to adult participation?

How does age affect sport participation?

What kind of role socialization takes place in youth sports?

Does sport promote sexism?

Is there negative learning in sports?

[9] Mihaly Csikszentmihalyi, *Beyond Boredom and Anxiety* (San Francisco: Jossey-Bass, 1975).

How is sport related to school status? To community identity?

What changes are developing in patterns and meanings of sport participation?

School, Physical Education, and Sport

The histories of recreation and physical education are closely intertwined. Luther Gulick and the institution that became Springfield College in Massachusetts were central to the development of both the recreation movement and the training of leaders in physical education. Basketball has become highly technological and professionalized sport, but it began in Springfield as an informal winter game. Sport was central to most early urban recreation programs. People whose preparation was largely in physical education have now been employed in public recreation for almost a century. Further, college and university departments of recreation have generally been the offspring of existing physical education programs. Sport may be only one kind of recreation, but it has taken a central place in recreation programs and provisions.

There is remarkably little published research on the carryover from school physical education into adult participation in games and sport. One reason is that it is difficult to sort out the influences of a school program from those of family and peers. We know that sports begun in school programs are seldom played by adults.[10] Since the most common sports are introduced by other family members or by age-peer friends, the effects of school training would generally be additive. Further, support to continue a sport into postsecondary school years tends to come from immediate communities rather than required courses of instruction. Interests in sport seem to be brought to school rather than begun in school.

However, the influence of courses and programs that develop skills may be supportive and difficult to measure. Some skill acquisition is general rather than specific. Running, hand-eye coordination, ball manipulation, strength and endurance, and other kinds of general skills may be developed in one kind of activity and then employed in another. "Learning how to learn" may be good education in physical skills as well as mental. Current efforts to teach general skills in physical education programs may be even more difficult to measure in long-term outcomes but may have significant results. Learning how to acquire skills and building a confidence that one *can* learn may be more important than the sport-specific skills imparted.

At the same time, there is more stress on freedom and choice in many high schools and colleges. Recognizing that being *required to play* a game may result in a dislike rather than an interest, educators have tried to allow students to choose from a variety of sports, games, and conditioning activities. When a program is chosen because of prior interest, continuation would appear to be more probable. However, there may be conflict between the basic skill acquisition approach and the attempt to maximize freedom of choice. Another trend is to offer introduction to lifetime sports that can be continued after school years rather than the traditional team sports that require high levels of fitness and organization as well as specialized space. At present, however, much that has been labeled physical education continues to be a period to quiet down students for their return to the classroom.

---

[10] John R. Kelly, "Leisure Socialization: Replication and Extension," *Journal of Leisure Research*, 9 (1977), 121–132.

Age and Sport Participation

No kind of activity participation decreases as drastically with age as sport. With the notable exception of golf, every passing decade of the life journey tends to include less participation in sports. For some sports, there are especially great declines at two times: on leaving school and some time in the forties. The first reflects the loss of the organized and available programs of the school. The second may be more related to physical competence. As indicated in Table 13–4, the variations from sport to sport are relatively minor in relation to the general trend. One interesting question is whether the cohorts now in their twenties, thirties, and forties will be more persistent in their engagement in sport in their adult years than those in their fifties and sixties today.

Some reasons for such a decrease are obvious. Physical condition, strength, and endurance generally decrease with age. Opportunities for team sports diminish after leaving school. The logistics of playing are more complex for those who are employed, caring for a home, and raising a family. And in some cases, active sport participation is not seen as appropriate for older people.

While physical fitness and activity by those in middle years may be more valued now than in previous generations, the "middle-aged athlete" is still the exception. Those engaging in regular sport participation have tended to be people with more education and greater financial resources and who have a history of such activity. It would seem that those whose interests and confidence were enhanced when they *made the team* in earlier years are most likely to persist in sport participation.

Sport and Role Learning

Sport organizations and programs have been accused of fostering both racism and sexism. Actually, criticisms of the values learned in sport often seem contradictory.

TABLE 13–4   Percentage of Sport and Fitness Participation by Age

Activity	18–24	25–34	35–44	45–54	55–64	65+
Fitness walking	24.1	24.7	27.6	28.6	27.6	19.5
Aerobics	9.9	8.7	8.9	3.8	3.0	1.9
Golf	10.3	12.4	11.4	11.3	10.9	6.4
Bowling	25.0	23.3	17.9	14.1	9.4	6.2
Swimming	32.3	32.1	29.1	21.8	14.2	7.8
Jogging/running	13.5	10.3	7.5	4.4	3.8	2.1
Downhill skiing	7.2	6.8	4.4	2.5	1.6	0.7
Tennis	12.3	19.0	7.2	4.4	3.8	2.1
Racquetball	8.3	5.0	4.2	2.7	2.0	1.1
Softball	10.4	11.2	6.4	3.2	2.6	1.4
Volleyball	10.6	9.9	8.7	4.0	2.0	1.0
Basketball	9.8	8.0	3.8	2.4	1.6	0.7
Football	6.0	3.3	1.9	1.1	1.3	0.6

Source: Simmons Market Research Bureau, Inc., 1990

For example, there are a long series of charges that the clear racial discrimination that was practiced until the color barrier began to fall after World War II has now taken more subtle but still vicious forms. Rather than excluding black athletes, universities and professional teams are now accused of exploiting them. The number of college athletes who play four years on scholarships but never graduate is cited as evidence that their programs are designed to keep these athletes eligible to play but not to help them meet graduation requirements. The disproportionate number of black football players in positions such as running and defensive backfield as opposed to the alleged "skill" positions such as quarterback has been explained in interviews by coaches who admit to making decisions according to racial stereotypes. In both university and professional sports, there are still few nonwhite head coaches, athletic directors, general managers, and owners. The power structure of sport is almost entirely white.

The charge is that this kind of structural racism not only limits the opportunities of nonwhite athletes but has negative consequences for their identities and self-esteem. Whenever any group identified by race, sex, religion, or ethnic background is treated as inferior in some dimension critical to selfhood and social position, then members of that group often come to think less of themselves or react to the stereotyping with bitterness and anger or by being cut off through alienation. Social discrimination can do to a group what continual repetition by a parent of "You're not as good as your brother" can do to a child.

Questions have been raised concerning race and personal goals. The fact that black athletes are doing well in professional sports may engender a sense of hope and self-esteem in young athletes. Conversely, it may direct effort away from study and acquiring work skills toward the one-in-a-half-million chance of becoming a professional football or basketball player.

Much the same analysis applies to sexual discrimination. When females are systematically defined as less worthy, less interesting, and less competent in what they do themselves, some may come to believe it. Sport has been one aspect of our society in which sexism has been most clear. Females have received so much less encouragement, coaching, access to facilities, praise and attention for achievement, and financial investment and so many fewer opportunities for participation that it is no wonder that many women have come to agree that demanding physical activity should be reserved for males.

Of course, recent events have shown that female athletes are quite capable of demonstrating strength, endurance, grace, discipline, team dedication, and all the other attributes of athletic ability. World-class gymnasts, swimmers, and runners have led the way for participants in team sports by reaching high standards. Whatever benefits in self-image, self-discipline, physical fitness, and self-esteem have been available to males in the past cannot now be denied—by law or by social conscience—to females. The secondary roles formerly reserved for females in sport mirrored their roles in the larger society. Female roles that have been most rewarded have been those secondary to male achievement. In high school the cheerleader who supports the male athlete has been granted a reflection of his status and rewards. The young woman who preferred to test and develop her own skills was relegated to the old gym, the off-hours, and often had to furnish her own equipment. Federal law and the raised consciousness of both men and women are beginning to challenge this type of discrimination.

There have been other charges against contemporary manifestations of sport. They, too, often seem contradictory. For example, major contact sports such as football and hockey are accused both of concentrating too much on winning at any cost and of being totalitarian in requiring subordination to a single authority. In fact, the same spokesmen for such team sports voice both values at the same time. On the one hand, "Football prepares *men* for the competition of life and separates real winners from lesser beings." On the other hand, "Football teaches that the team comes first and it is in the disciplined subordination of the self that real character is formed."[11]

It might be argued that winning is the goal and that subordination to authority is the means. Both may be necessary to fulfill the ultimate goals of filling the stadiums with paying patrons, gaining television contracts, and enhancing the coaches' reputations. The real issue is to what extent these values are those we desire for people who are maturing in this society. Are competition, winning, and submission to authority values to be fostered at the expense of reflection, sensitivity in personal relations, cooperation, spontaneity, and individual creativity? There are, after all, sports that require somewhat different orientations, even for success. There are also other modes of sport participation. Some would argue that competition and discipline are important values, but that like any aims they can be distorted when they become the *only* values of sport participation.

Is there something about sport itself that inevitably leads to distortion of competition and a single-minded stress on winning? Is the combination of a societal emphasis on *being a man* in a sense of demonstrating power over others and the attention given to competitive sports too much for young athletes to cope with? It may be that it is the social context of school sport more than the nature of the contests themselves that makes being a winner *over* others so important to some.

And there is always the other side of the emphasis on winning. There are also losers. More than those who lose a particular contest, there are those who lose out in the progressive exclusion model of school sport. As more and more are left out of participation and asked to take secondary supporting roles for the few who still play, most young men and women become losers. They are left out and judged unqualified to compete. The consequences of this filtering that begins in elementary school and sport programs for the very young have yet to be measured.

The New Participatory Thrust of Sport

On many campuses there has been an explosion of sport participation. The increase is reflected in many communities as playing fields are overscheduled, courts are filled, pools are crowded, and even jogging paths are busy. Again, although studies of individual participation do not reflect this explosion, the general impression is that more people are doing, as well as watching, sport. Commercial interests have tried to catch this wave by offering racquet sports clubs and retail equipment outlets in greatly increased numbers.

At the same time that many varsity teams are playing to lots of empty seats, intramural programs in a wide variety of sports are expanding. Not only basketball, softball, and touch football, which have been traditionally for men, but soccer, table tennis, rugby, racquetball,

---

[11] Eldon Snyder and E. Spreitzer, *Social Aspects of Sport* (Englewood Cliffs, NJ: Prentice-Hall, 1978).

and lacrosse as well are now being played by both men and women on single-sex and coed teams. League games have had to be compounded with complicated interleague playoff schedules. Much of the increase is a demand on the part of those who have been excluded in the varsity progressive-exclusion process to be able to *do* sports and not just watch. They are returning to sport participation because for all the reasons outlined earlier they find such activity personally rewarding.

The complications for community programs are immense. When a sport requires special and often expensive space and equipment, then the priorities of the community recreation providers are challenged again. Especially women and older people now desire more opportunities to engage in physical activity with the excitement and appeal of sport.

Along with the return to organized sport participation, there are also indications that some prefer self-organized activity. Many who do not want the regularity or pressure of an organized team and league, even an intramural league, still want to play basketball or soccer on their own terms. So a group of players will meet at a gym or on a field and set up their own game. The stress is not so much on winning as on doing it for its own sake. People for whom the traditional years of competition lie far behind find they still enjoy the old sport in a less stressful atmosphere. In a sense, they are returning to their childhood games and for much the same reasons.

New Sports

Some programs designed to increase self-awareness and to develop personal potential in an integrated way have given some attention to sport. There has been both criticism of many current forms of sport and a growing interest in what variations of sport may do to provide experiences of personal and social integration.

One approach retains the old sport forms but alters the definition of the experience. This approach concentrates on sensory awareness, control of one's body, mastery of skills, and the personal expression of participation. The orientation of participation is toward the self rather than to social norms or status. At the same time, the discipline, the testing through competition, the measurement of mastery, and the previous level of competence are incorporated with a new set of purposes. Now the athlete is developing skill and control of the sport forms for their own sake and for the sake of self-development and awareness. The old form is given new meaning rather than being abandoned. Sport becomes more *leisurely*. The experience of doing the sport is the meaning, and the outcome is only one element in the total experience.

Some of the same approach is found in efforts to restructure competitive team sports, especially for children and youth, in order to reduce the competitive motivation. The statistical records of team and individual scoring are not kept; thus each game has its own meaning. All-star teams, awards for scoring the most goals, and other such extrinsic rewards are avoided. Playing time is equalized rather than being dependent on skill. Rules are altered to minimize aggressive behavior against other players. The aim is to retain the drama and the excitement of the sport experience without subjecting the boys and girls to the pressures of overseriousness about outcomes. The hope is that they will find more satisfaction in the sport itself and in relationships with other players when the emphasis on results is reduced.

Sport and Social Status

The importance of sports in high school social hierarchies has been documented in studies that began with research by James Coleman in 1961.[12] The most powerful single factor in high status among the student population is athletic prowess and recognition. However, that connection between sport and peer group status is not limited to high schools. Early physical maturity and athletic prominence are significant factors in esteem and status in the neighborhood, on the playground, and in elementary school as well.

The implications are manifold. First, such status is limited to males in all situations where traditionally male sports are most important. Second, other aspects of development that may be more related to adult achievement are given less attention and reward. Third, development of identity and self-worth is related to this one kind of activity to too great an extent. Fourth, grade-level competition rewards those whose physical maturity is advanced. Fifth, rewards for athletic achievement continue in later phases of the life cycle and are instilled in later generations by parents and school staff.

It is difficult to ignore the fact that sexual attractiveness, headlines, praise from a whole array of significant adults, and overall social importance often result, for men, from sport achievement rather than similar achievement in the arts, scholarship, or some kind of service to others. In the same way, for women it is hard to ignore the fact that more status may accrue to the cheerleader dating the football star than to the soloist with the school orchestra or the scholarship winner.

Reinforcing this status reward of interscholastic competition is the symbolic meaning of school sports in many communities. Just as professional sport stars are celebrities in their own cities, the school hero is a celebrity in his smaller town. The high school football or basketball team is frequently the last remaining symbol of the unity and identity of the community itself. As a consequence, scoring the winning touchdown or sinking the deciding shot has meaning for the entire town. The results of the athletic contests are a symbol of the standing of the town in relation to other towns. The contained drama on the field is more than a contest of players, it is a struggle to *be something* in a world full of communities no one has heard of.

There are indications of change. Stress on opportunities for females has altered the one-sided focus on males. Sports heroes may be more televised professionals than local youth. The place of sports in the social system of the school is placed in question by empty bleachers and general community disinterest.

Sport still, however, may become a focus of meaning for social groups as well as for individuals. In a complex world, sport is a moment in time when something blessedly simple seems to happen. For that moment a straightforwardly consequential event occurs. When that event is endowed with significance by the social group of a school, community, or nation, then the players who make a difference are rewarded with a special place in the collective. The beginning and the end of the sport event allow for agreed-on definitions of exactly *who* has made a difference, a designation difficult to assign in the larger and more complex world. It is no wonder, then, that social rewards become very important to the representative athlete in a sport that symbolizes collective identity and worth.

[12] James Coleman, *The Adolescent Society* (New York: Free Press, 1961).

Exercise and Health

A variety of studies have documented the contribution of regular physical exercise to health. There are many indications of a greater concern for health among American adults—a concern manifested in attention to diet, environmental factors of air and water, restrictions on toxic substances, preventive health-care practices, and physical fitness. More adults are attempting to maintain some level of fitness through a schedule of physical activity. For some, that activity takes the form of sport. For others, there is running, jogging, bicycling, walking, Nordic skiing, hiking, dance, aerobic exercise, weight training, and other forms of physical exertion. The so-called "fitness boom," however, seems to have stalled. Only fitness walking has increased in participation since 1985. Both aerobics and jogging peaked in the 1980s and have declined since.

The aims are not all health-related. Appearance is important to many men and women who desire to gain or maintain certain body shapes and contours. Some are resisting effects of aging. Some are seeking to renew images of attractiveness. Others have come to accept a specific image of what is an admired or acceptable physique. And some simply feel better when they engage in regular exercise. For many, outcomes of health, appearance, and self-appraisal are all involved in participation in sport and exercise.

Many forms of exercise are different from sport in that they do not involve a measured outcome for the experience or a historic set of rules and forms. There is no score, no opponent, and no uncertainty. Exercise and sport share many motivations, but are different in form. For some, sport is a preferable form of exercise because it adds dimensions of interest and excitement to the physical exertion.

Of course, there is a wide variety in the commitment and regularity of those who engage in sport and exercise. Dropout rates tend to be high in many fitness programs outside the home. Trend data indicate that participation in exercise programs may have reached a peak in the mid-1980s, declined slightly, and now is maintaining a more stable level.[13] Media attention to health and fitness has tended to exaggerate the extent of regular participation. Nevertheless, it is clear that exercise programs have grown rapidly to become a major recreation-related activity. National surveys (see Table 13–2) show that about 15 percent of the adult population may engage in fitness activity in the home and 25 percent walk while 13 percent jog or run. Rate of participation in health clubs was less than 4 percent. All such activity is much more common for youth and young adults than for those who are older (see Table 13–4).

One important distinction is between exercise that requires meeting the requirements of a timetable and that which can be done "on demand." A major advantage of activity such as walking, jogging, and at-home exercise is that it can be fit into the schedule of the day and does not require adherence to an external schedule. On the other hand, meeting others in an activity context offers both the incentives and satisfactions of companionship. Persistence in fitness activity is supported by positive feedback and social support.

Jogging and running illustrate how an exercise program can become a sport as participants enter "runs" of a variety of lengths and competitive intensities. Jogging also illustrates that common finding with sport and exercise that only about 20 to 30 percent of those

---

[13] John R. Kelly, *Recreation Trends toward the Year 2000* (Champaign, IL: Management Learning Laboratories, 1987).

who engage in the activity at all do it with great regularity. The market surveys are consistent in their findings that about 30 percent of those who claim to have jogged in a given year have done so as often as once a week all year.

Concern for health and engagement in some regular exercise, through sport or other activity, has been much more common for those in their twenties and thirties, for those with higher levels of education, and for those with incomes that are above average. Closer attention to recent trend data, however, suggests the possibility that there may be significant cohort trends. Those now in their thirties and forties may be more likely to retain a commitment to health-oriented exercise and sport than older cohorts. More adults may have adopted lifestyles in which regular exercise has a consistent place that may be retained through the life course.

Summary of Issues

Sport has a major place in modern society as an element of the economy, a spectacle with symbolic meanings, an arena of development for the young, and in the leisure lives of many individuals. However, there is recurring ambivalence about the meaning of sport in modern society and in the lives of its members.

In a sense, sport is both more and less than leisure. Some sport participation is highly constrained and extrinsically rewarded, and, therefore, not really leisure at all. Further, despite the importance of sport in school years, participation declines with age until it just does not figure at all in the leisure of most people of middle and advanced years. Further, the highly competitive school programs tend to narrow participation down to the very few who have the greatest skill and experience. When various forms of discrimination and exclusion are combined, the beneficial influence of sport on the development of personal and social identities for most people can be held in question.

On the other hand, the special world of sport provides certain satisfactions and meanings not quite like any other kind of activity. The sport occasion with its new beginning, its familiar structure and expectations, its measured outcomes, and its opportunity for physical effort and movement is a critical experience for many. In sport, mind and body are coordinated in a directed effort that has immediate feedback. The results are known in the event, often within split seconds of the effort. There is an engagement and excitement that may capture the attention of the player as no other activity does. The movement, effort, coordination, measurement, and regularity yield a consequential event without extramural significance. Participation may also provide a social context and set of companions that are unrelated to the serious world of work.

Therefore, sport is important as leisure in its unique combination of challenges and experiences. It is also important in the society as a symbolic spectacle in which onlookers identify with the drama and its results. However, that identification has led to the development of sport as a business enterprise ready to alter the game to increase the return on capital and as a political enterprise in which victory is given national importance.

There are many unresolved issues:

What kinds of sport participation provide the greatest satisfaction as leisure?

How can school and community sport programs be directed toward self-development and enhancement?

Can traditional forms and programs be altered to stress the experience and involvement without losing the excitement of competition?

How can understanding life careers of sport contribute to maximizing the value of programs for the young?

HIGHLIGHTS

1. Frequency of sport participation declines drastically with age but may be an intense high-priority activity for the increasing number who continue or reinstitute participation.
2. Television is not only the main contact with sports for most adults, but it has reshaped elements of the sports themselves.
3. The structure, discipline, and problematic outcomes of sport make it especially suited for absorbing participation that leads to "flow," concentration on skill mastery, and the enhancement of personal identities.
4. Programs that provide opportunity for sport for its own sake and for continued growth of mastery seem most likely to lead to later engagement.
5. Despite a variety of social and economic uses and manipulations of sport, it provides a special set-apart world of physical activity, meaning, competence, and uncertain outcomes that may be most "leisurely" in its intrinsic and social experiences.
6. Greater opportunities for females in sport may, in time, change the sexist structure of the focus on male performance and female support.
7. The physical exertion element of sport makes it one context of activity oriented toward health, physical fitness, and appearance.

Discussion Questions

1. What is the place of spectators in the meaning of sport? Are they necessary? How are sport participation and watching related?

2. Is it true that satisfaction in sport participation increases with higher skill levels? Why or why not?

3. Is there something inherently militant and disciplined about sports? If so, how can sport express the freedom of leisure?

4. What are the reasons that sport participation decreases with age? Will this falloff be less for those now in their teens and twenties? Are more females likely to continue sport participation?

5. How has television changed sports on the university and professional levels? Has it also changed sport for children? If so, how?

6. How do the meanings of sport change through the life course? When are elements of play, display, competition, self-testing, health, social solidarity, and intrinsic satisfaction most central? When is sport likely to be most leisurely?

7. How are rules and standards essential to the sport experience? Explain how sport is a "dramatic event with self-contained consequences." Can sport become too serious?

8. Are some kinds of sport more conducive to "flow" experiences than others? Which ones and why?

9. Is sport structurally discriminating rather than inclusive? What are the implications for school and public recreation programs? Who are the usual victims of sport discrimination and what can be done to minimize negative consequences? How is sport racist? Sexist?

10. Does the health and fitness motivation for sport participation change for older adults? How much fitness activity is aimed more toward appearance than health?

11. What would you predict for future female sport participation? Why?

Bibliography

Hoch, Paul, *Rip Off the Big Game.* Garden City, NY: Doubleday, 1972.

Leonard, George, *The Ultimate Athlete.* New York: Viking, 1975.

Michener, James A., *Sports in America.* New York: Random House, 1976.

Novak, Michael, *The Joy of Sports.* New York: Basic Books, 1975.

Orlick, Terry, *Every Kid Can Win.* Chicago: Nelson-Hall, 1975.

Snyder, Eldon, and E. Spreitzer, *Social Aspects of Sport.* Englewood Cliffs, NJ: Prentice-Hall, 1978.

Snyder, Eldon, and E. Spreitzer, "Sociology of Sport: An Overview," *Sociological Quarterly,* 15 (1974), 467–487.

C h a p t e r 14

Outdoor Recreation

There are many issues related to the recreational use of natural environments. One of the most important is access. How can opportunities be provided for those who seek the satisfactions of being in forests, by a flowing stream, at an ocean beach, or on a mountainside without spoiling the experience with crowding? What is the role of government, not only in holding the land and water for public use but in regulating the use to maximize satisfaction and prevent resource deterioration? Other questions include

The right to own and control land has led to private ownership of many scarce outdoor recreation resources including 70 percent of United States shorelines. How can adequate public access be assured?

The same land-use planning that provides the greatest freedom for outdoor recreation will restrict the freedom of private owners to control land for their own uses.

Human beings are purposeful interveners into the natural ecology, not only when they come to cut trees and mine coal but also when they come to hike, ride, camp, and play with their leisure toys. Even appreciation of nature may do irremediable damage to natural resources as roads are built and paths compacted. How can use and preservation be reconciled?

Should those who pay the highest taxes to the government receive the most benefits, or should public provisions increase equality of opportunity?

Why are some outdoor environments so special? What happens there that makes them worth such extraordinary measures of public ownership, control, and management?

ISSUES

How can public agencies manage outdoor recreation resources for both use and preservation?

Why conserve forests, rivers, lakes, shores, and wilderness for the relative few who use them regularly?

Is there something special about outdoor recreation experiences that warrants extraordinary support?

What kinds of outdoor recreation are most popular?

More than 260 million acres of federal land are available for recreation use. States offer another 42 million acres, and local government bodies about 10 million acres. These areas include forests, lakes, rivers, mountains, deserts, beaches, trails, prairies, and other terrains. Of the total about half is forest, 9 percent wilderness, 10 percent fish and game preserves, and 6 percent parks and other designated recreation locales.[1] Federal land in the coastal and mountain West, not including Alaska, makes up about 75 percent of this total.

On these public lands, as well as others that are private, people hike, fish, hunt, climb, sail, canoe, tube, race, run, play games, swim, sun, ski, camp, drive motorized vehicles, soar, and enjoy innumerable other kinds of activity. In some locations, the managing agency offers access, parking, safety protection, facilities, prepared resources such as ski slopes and harbors, and other improvements that make recreation participation possible. At other sites the provider does nothing except permit use.

Along with the public provisions, there are businesses that facilitate recreation activity in such outdoor locales. They provide equipment such as boats, boots, or casting rods. They offer access with boat launching or transportation. There are guide services to the backcountry, rafts and canoes on the rivers, and flights into wilderness lakes. They teach novices how to kayak or boardsail, safety on the sheer rock face, and techniques of underwater swimming. They sell, rent, and repair all kinds of equipment. There is, in fact, a critical complementarity between the public and business providers. Perhaps this relationship is seen most clearly in those resorts that are located in or near attractive public resources such as beaches and the shores of bodies of water.

Many land and water resources provide opportunities for more than one kind of recreation activity. Forest may be the environment for many different kinds of camping and hiking as well as nature study, wilderness survival schools, and hunting. A reservoir will be used for powerboating, waterskiing, sailing, swimming, fishing, canoeing, family picnics, regattas, and amphibious flying—sometimes all at one time. In some cases, the recreation participation may be spread over a considerable area. A major body of water may have many access points, especially for small craft. A forest may be entered from many places on its perimeter with parking being the main constraint. Some sites are near population centers, and others are remote. The patterns of use are usually a combination of the nature of the resource and the size and composition of the user public.

[1] Michael Chubb and Holly Chubb, *One Third of Our Time?* (New York: John Wiley, 1981), p. 417.

What do people do in outdoor recreation resources? National surveys have indicated that the most popular activities are swimming, fishing, camping, hiking, driving various kinds of off-road vehicles, hunting, boating, and skiing. More inclusively, the most common activity is sightseeing while driving, along with picnicking and just visiting. Some use of outdoor recreation resources is directed toward some particular activity, such as fly casting or rockhounding, while other use is more social or just enjoying the different environment. What is special in all cases is the blending of activity and environment. Being outdoors is different. Having access to water and woods, hillsides and deserts, and other environments makes possible kinds of action that do not occur elsewhere.

Lakes, rivers, ocean beaches, forests, and mountains have a special appeal as leisure environments. Certain kinds of activity require such outdoor recreation resources. Fishing, backpacking, water and snow skiing, camping, boating, and just hiking are only a few of the activities that draw people to special sites. However, outdoor recreation is more than the activity. There is something about being *in* the special environment that is central to the meaning of the experience.

The quality of the environment is important. Sailors and waterskiers pull their boats hundreds of miles to a lake they find especially attractive. Campers drive far into the mountain forest on dirt roads to that unique campsite. Families fight the city traffic to get out into the country for a brief weekend.

As a result, supplying such outdoor recreation resources has become a major function of governmental agencies. While many campgrounds, ski slopes, boat marinas, and even fishing lakes are offered commercially, it is the federal government that makes available the largest holdings of recreation land and water.

Federal Recreation Programs

Several agencies share recreation resource management. Among them, the National Park Service and the Forest Service are most prominent. Other agencies that manage vast amounts of land and water used by millions of people for outdoor recreation include the Bureau of Land Management, the Fish and Wildlife Service, the Army Corps of Engineers, and the Bureau of Reclamation.

National Park Service

The National Park Service (NPS) of the Department of the Interior is responsible for the national parks such as Yellowstone, Yosemite, and the Great Smoky Mountains and for battlefields and historic sites in Boston, Philadelphia, and elsewhere, military parks, some national cemeteries, and the National Capital parks. The dominance of the great western parks has been lessened in recent years by development of national seashores. Further, the rural bias has been altered with a national policy giving greater attention to urban areas. The Gateway National Recreation Areas near New York and San Francisco are the first major urban thrusts of the NPS.

Historically, the NPS had a central mission of the preservation of unique resources as well as making them available for use and appreciation. No hunting, commercial development, or harvesting of resources were permitted. National park areas were set apart to be managed in ways that preserve their uniqueness. However, the preservation mission has been balanced by the provision of recreation opportunities. Camping, lodging, educational programs, boating facilities, and other recreation provisions are part of the total management plan for a park. The sheer numbers of visitors has created conflicts between the preservation and recreation goals, requiring considerable management sophistication. Overnight stays alone in all 300-plus national parks totaled more than 17.6 million in 1990. In the same year, there were more than 260 million visits to national parks and other sites. In 1980, there were forty parks, ninety-four national monuments, forty-three seashore and other recreation areas, and seventy-four historic sites administered by the NPS. Twenty-eight of the parks are in the West, but only eleven of the forty-three recreation areas. Growth in the park system was relatively slow from 1958 until 1978, when 56 million acres in Alaska were added.

National Forest Service

The Forest Service of the Department of Agriculture manages more than 200 million acres of forest, grassland, and desert, including mountains in Alaska, ocean coastal property, scrub pine and swamps in the Southeast, and hardwood stands in the Northeast. National forests are to have multiple uses of which recreation is only one. However, greater attention to the recreation and preservation elements of Forest Service management has paralleled planning for sustained yields of timber harvesting. Recreation users are not only at the developed sites such as campgrounds, boat-launching facilities, and trails but also in millions of acres where they find their own sites for camping and hiking. The Forest Service also is responsible for wilderness areas, chiefly in the West. Conflict between development and conservation interests has intensified in the 1990s.

By 1982, there were a total of 155 national forests with more than 187 million acres. With the passage of the Wilderness Act in 1964, significant sections of the forests have been reserved for nonextractive uses and are to be maintained in relatively natural states. On the other hand, other parts of the national forests have been developed for more intensive recreational use by skiers, campers, and others. Sites are leased for recreational development such as ski runs. Camping has been the activity with the greatest participation. Altogether well over 200 million visits are made to national forests each year. Each national forest is required to develop a management plan that incorporates long-term goals for each of the resource elements that are to be kept in ecological as well as economic balance.

Bureau of Land Management

Federal land not designated as national parks, forests, or rangelands is generally supervised by the Bureau of Land Management (BLM) of the Department of the Interior. Although mining and other resource harvesting interests tend to be more active on the acres managed by the BLM, the recreation potential of this land is tremendous. Reallocation of land in Alaska is shifting the responsibilities of the BLM in a process that will take many years to implement. Although the BLM has not developed the comprehensive recreation programs of the National Parks and Forest Services, the deserts, mountains and plateaus, rivers and canyons, and other resources are a major outdoor recreation resource for further development. While recreation use statistics are only approximate for most federal land, the

BLM experienced a growth to about 70 million visits in 1990. In 1982, the addition of land in Alaska almost doubled BLM's holdings to 143 million acres.

Fish and Wildlife Service

Interior's Fish and Wildlife Service manages more than 80 million acres of land that is intended for use as preserves for fish and wildlife. The agency also cooperates with the other land-management agencies in developing programs for species of fish and wildlife protected under the Endangered Species Preservation acts. Two bureaus, one for Commercial Fisheries and the other for Sports Fisheries and Wildlife, support a variety of conservation programs on public land and manage some critical land and water acres.

U.S. Army Corps of Engineers

The civil works division of the Army Corps of Engineers has entered the recreation field due to its construction and operation of waterways and reservoirs. Most such construction has been primarily for purposes of commercial navigation, flood control, and irrigation impoundment. The growth of pleasure boating has added to the traffic in locks, canals, and other waterways. Boating, fishing, swimming, and various recreation uses of water impounded by Corps dams and the land close around the high-water mark has grown so that the Corps has been led into both recreation design and planning and site management. Corps-constructed sites are frequently managed by other federal, state, and local units. However, many water resources are in areas without natural lakes and shorelines and relatively near urban populations. As a result, Corps projects have also had a rapid increase in recreation use. Such water resources are more likely to be primarily for day use with provisions delegated to those who lease land and facilities for food services, marinas, and other support enterprises. Approximately 80 percent of the Corps' multipurpose reservoirs are located within fifty miles of an urban area. As a consequence, day use has increased rapidly, close to 500 million recreation use days annually.[2]

Bureau of Reclamation

Also a Department of the Interior agency, the Bureau of Reclamation has developed a number of major water projects in the West. With irrigation and power production as primary aims, the bureau has generally transferred major recreation sites to the Park Service or other managers. However, in areas where such a shift of responsibility is not feasible, the bureau has developed some basic facilities for access to and use of the water resource.

Other Federal Recreation Programs

There are several other federal agencies with recreation components in their overall mission. These include the Bureau of Indian Affairs, the Soil Conservation Service, and the

---

[2] Sources of statistics in this section are *Statistics on Outdoor Recreation,* edited by Carlton S. Van Doren and published by Resources for the Future of Washington, DC, in 1984, and the *1993 Statistical Abstract of the United States.*

Tennessee Valley Authority. Further, agencies engaged in developments near water such as those for the production of atomic energy and hydroelectric power and mining programs that offer reclamation possibilities for recreation use are also giving some attention to recreation planning and provisions.

It is impossible to keep up with every law, regulation, and program that may have some effect on outdoor recreation. For example, legislation such as the Wilderness Act of 1964 has been amended in ways that have increased opportunities for dispersed recreation. The Wild and Scenic Rivers Act of 1968 has enabled certain waterways to be protected from changes that would have altered their recreation potential. Acts requiring the classification and multiple use of lands have directed that recreation be a use category along with timber protection, grazing, and other commercial uses. The Urban Open Space Land Program was enacted in 1961, the Land and Water Conservation Fund in 1964, a National Trails System in 1968, as were many more. More recently, the National Environmental Policy Act has required that impacts of programs on the ecological and human environments be studied and reported prior to significant action. As a result, not only have land and water resources been protected, but recreation gains and losses are now considered as part of the social impact of governmental programs and policies. All of these laws have been enacted only after considerable political conflict.

State Recreation Provisions

A comparison of the amounts of land managed by federal, state, and local government units for recreation purposes indicates the dominance of the federal level. Federal agencies control more than six times the area managed by the states as parks, forest, wildlife preserves, wilderness, and for other recreation-related uses. Much of the growth in state park provisions since the 1950s was due to funding from the federal Land and Water Conservation Fund. The future of this source of support for land acquisition and facilities is in doubt and subject to considerable political negotiation.

Nevertheless, the states are an important element in the overall public recreation picture. There is considerable variety in programs from state to state. Some have elaborate systems of state parks developed over many decades since their construction during the 1930s. Others have relied on federal provisions for large-tract outdoor recreation and on municipalities and commercial enterprises for less space-intensive provisions. In general, states with the most elaborate education programs have also tended to be most active in developing recreation resources.

The total acreage of state parks almost doubled between 1955 and 1982. Many states now provide a variety of parks for special uses. Along with traditional camping and day-use areas, there are a variety of parks with historical backgrounds, cultural programs, and even resort parks with hotels.

Total attendance at state parks increased four times from the 1950s to the 1990s, topping 700 million visits by 1991. Day visitors are about 90 percent of the total.

In land provisions, the state agencies are a distant second to the federal government, but still provide a significant share of the total for outdoor recreation. State forestry departments as well as conservation and recreation agencies control acreage that is extremely critical in some states due to its proximity to populations not otherwise served or to the uniqueness of the land and water resources.

States also enforce regulations for health and safety in campgrounds and other recreation areas and license various enterprises that provide food and services to those engaged in recreation. A growing interest in many states has been the tourist industry. While out-of-state visitors are generally a primary target of tourist promotion, information and facilities may also enhance the recreation opportunities for residents who are not priced out by affluent tourists or squeezed out by crowding.

In Canada, all provinces have recreation programs with outdoor recreation as a main focus. Some major parks have been established near population centers and even in the cities themselves. Provinces such as Nova Scotia, Ontario, and Alberta have granted funds to municipalities and other local governments for capital additions to public recreation.

Recreation Environment Conflicts

There has been intense conflict over the use of outdoor space. Conflicts have been most acute over land that might be utilized in more than one way. For example, two kinds of development of a forested mountain slope may be combined when timber harvesters and those who want to develop ski runs both want to cut trees. Recreation users who now use the land for hiking or camping would oppose the cutting, but downhill skiers might side with the developers. Preservation groups would combat timber harvesting and the ski runs most fiercely but might also oppose expansion of campground, hiking trails, and horseback trail-riding provisions.

The three interest groups are the developers, recreation users, and preservers. Developers would alter the land so that it can be used in a profit-making enterprise. The enterprise may be a resort area for recreation, timber harvesting, or mineral extraction. In any case, the developer will make major changes in the land. At the other end of the spectrum are the preservation interests. Represented by such organizations as the Sierra Club, preservers take the long view and attempt to prevent action that is irretrievable. They usually oppose development or use that will damage or degrade land of special beauty or ecological importance. Except for organizations of equipment manufacturers, recreation users are the least organized of the three interest groups. Depending on the form of their recreation pursuits, they may support some kinds of development and oppose others. Recreation users may side with preservers to add to wilderness holdings in one case and support programs for outdoor recreation development in others.

While coalitions may form between two of the interest groups over particular interventions, most land-use conflicts are more than a failure to communicate. The interests of the three groups are often fundamentally different. Therefore, one of the tasks of public land management is to plan for the long-term common welfare in ways that take into account the legitimacy of all three claims.

Ideally, cooperative planning that can meet at least some of the needs of each group is possible. Such planning begins with a thorough understanding of the ecology of the land—of just how terrain, water drainage and supplies, tree and plant growth, animal life, soil composition, and all other natural elements of the ecosystem are interrelated and mutually supporting. Any change or intervention should be calculated for its initial and cumulative effects on the ecosystem. The goal-oriented and deliberate interventions of users and developers require integrated and comprehensive plans if the land is to best fulfill its sustaining potential for life.

The aim of land-use planning is not to control and inhibit human freedom. On the contrary, it is to maximize freedom and opportunity in situations where space is scarce and various groups have conflicting interests. Not only is space a context of freedom, but land is a context of opportunity for a variety of life's elements. We live in a socio-ecosystem in which every action has "ripple effects" in the pond of existence. Further, those purposive interveners—human beings—have their specific interests that may foreclose possibilities for the desired actions of others. In the pursuit of our own interests, we may block fulfillment of the interests of others or even eliminate the necessary resources for everyone. Planning is recognition of scarcity and conflict and of the ecological base of human life.

In many cases land is used in several ways. We tend to concentrate only on direct uses by human beings. People enter the forest to cut trees, extract minerals, hike, camp, hunt, fish, ski, ride motorized trail bikes or horses, explore for rocks, take pictures, study flora and fauna, form temporary communities, and combine activities. We live on the land, cultivate it, exploit it, study it, appreciate it, and manage it. Some uses are easily combined and others conflict. Some uses are temporary and others create major impacts that last forever.

While management is in part scientific and based on the best information about short and long-term impacts of actions, public programs are also political. The relative influence and political leverage of various groups of present and potential users cannot be ignored. When interests are in conflict, public management plans are more than a weighing of scientific information about environmental and social consequences. The right of citizens, whatever their interest in the resource, to be not only heard but considered is central to the democratic process. However, those most seriously affected by a management plan may not have the greatest political influence.

Recreation and Ecological Fragility

Compromises must be made in many sites where recreation use threatens the very ecology that has attracted the users. Sometimes, as with ski runs, the natural environment of a limited area is sacrificed to use so that the encompassing area may be preserved. Access to some wilderness areas, river canyons, or campsites may be rationed. Particular kinds of equipment such as motorboats may be prohibited on one lake to conserve a special resource and facilitated on another less fragile body of water. Plans, then, need to be regional rather than local.

Some sites have a considerable "carrying capacity" to accommodate recreation use without serious degradation. Others are especially vulnerable to damage by even the most considerate users. The public management of environmental resources requires the fullest possible knowledge of both the ecosystem and of the behavior patterns of the human users. Then a comprehensive plan can be developed that minimizes environmental loss and maximizes satisfying recreation use.

Just what are the social needs for developed and dispersed outdoor recreation? How important to the regional ecosystem is the retention of forests, deserts, grasslands, and water in something approaching their natural condition? How much should be paid by public agencies for restoration of land now degraded? How rigorous should be the regulation of private land use and conservation? Are the benefits of natural environments and the costs of their loss amenable to dollar calculation at all? Can the risky business of major ecosystem alteration be continued indefinitely without destroying the basis of the system? Could we literally run out of clean air, water, and safe products of the land?

In the whole picture, recreation use is only one factor. Forests are seldom withheld from timber harvesting simply because they are now or may be someday used for recreation. Nevertheless, the probabilities of increased urbanization and less personal space around residences due to construction and land costs suggest that a greater demand may be placed on outdoor recreation resources in the future.

Leisure and Natural Environments

Some have claimed that Americans have a continuing romance with the outdoors. The rural cultural roots, frontier heritage, vast areas of mountains and forests, values of individualism and conquest, nostalgia, escape from urban congestion and stress, and many other factors may be involved in the appeal of natural environments. For many, experiences of walking along an ocean beach, stopping to view a jagged horizon of snowcapped peaks, the reflection of green forests in the mirror of a mountain lake, the fragrance of pine woods, or sitting alongside the rush of white water through a river canyon are self-authenticating. Something happens there that cannot be duplicated in other settings. Even people who have not had such experiences in childhood may respond immediately to the sensations of unique natural environments.

The range of "outdoor recreation" includes not only activities that require a natural resource but also those that take place on city sidewalks, playgrounds, and backyards. Some outdoor activities require special resources such as wilderness backpacking, while others just call for enough space to walk, run, or even sit. Some outdoor recreation is appreciative, some social, some competitive, and some a direct encounter with the resource itself. Table 14–1 gives some indication of the extent of resource-based outdoor recreation.

The kinds of activities that are most common are not those that require vast forests, wilderness areas, or unique resources. Rather they are the ones that are relatively close at hand: picnicking, pleasure driving, pool swimming, and attending community events. Those that require special locales, expensive equipment, high fees or rentals, or considerable travel are done more than five times a year only by 5 to 15 percent of the adult population.

**TABLE 14-1   Percentage of the Adult Population Who Engage
in Various Outdoor Recreation Activities**

Activity	Total	Male	Female
Swimming	24.1%	24.0%	24.1%
Bicycling	11.1	11.6	10.8
Fishing			
Salt water	4.0	5.7	2.4
Fly casting	2.9	4.5	1.5
Other fresh water	12.9	17.5	8.6
Camping	10.5	11.3	9.7
Hiking	6.7	6.7	6.6
Hunting	6.5	11.2	12.2
Powerboating	6.6	7.4	5.9
Downhill skiing	4.2	5.5	3.0
Waterskiing	4.1	5.5	2.8
Horseback riding	3.8	3.5	4.1
Sailing	2.5	3.2	1.9
Cross-country skiing	2.2	2.0	2.4
Snowmobiling	2.0	2.5	1.5
Dirt/trail motorcycling	1.5	2.4	0.6
Skin diving/snorkeling	1.7	2.1	1.4
Backpacking	1.4	2.0	0.8

Source: Simmons Market Research Bureau, Inc., 1990.

Nevertheless, natural-resource-based outdoor recreation is more significant in the leisure scheme of many people than the participation rates suggest. Many who are able to go camping only two or three times a year or backpacking only once still value the experience highly. Even a once-a-year vacation camping trip may be considered the high point of the year's leisure—long anticipated and recollected.

A comparison of results from the 1960 and 1982 National Recreation Surveys[3] reveal that the activities with the greatest rates of growth in participation were canoeing, bicycling, attending outdoor cultural events, sailing, hiking and backpacking, attending outdoor sports events, walking for pleasure, and waterskiing. More recent trend analysis indicates that only walking has increased in the 1990s.

The same surveys, however, found that 50 percent or more of the population twelve years of age or older engaged in the following activities: picnicking, driving for pleasure, swimming, sightseeing, and walking for pleasure.

The 1987 report of the President's Commission on Americans Outdoors included some results from a 1986 market study of participation in outdoor recreation. This national survey, with a sample size of 2,000, yielded a similar set of most frequent activities, as shown in Table 14–2.

---

[3] Report of the President's Commission on Americans Outdoors, *Americans Outdoors: The Legacy, The Challenge* (Washington, DC: Island Press, 1987).

TABLE 14–2   Percentage of Activities Participated in Often or Very Often by Adults

Walking for pleasure	50%
Driving for pleasure	43
Swimming outdoors	43
Sightseeing	34
Picnicking	28
Fishing	25
Camping	21
Bicycling	17
Running or jogging	17
Birdwatching, nature study	15
Motorboating, waterskiing	15
Day hiking	12
Hunting	11
Off-road vehicles, snowmobiles	11
Backpacking	5
Downhill skiing	5
Cross-country skiing	3

Source: Report of the President's Commission on Americans Outdoors, *Americans Outdoors: The Legacy, the Challenge* (Washington, DC: Island Press, 1987).

The Life Course

The life course approach is one useful framework from which to analyze the variation in group composition and orientation. A few suggestions illustrate the possibilities:

A group of students will often see the park as another party environment with activities oriented toward interactive "fun" and many patterns of party behavior simply transferred to the outdoor site.

A couple exploring an intimate relationship may try to do almost everything together and use the site to be "alone together."

Parents of young children may use the resources to maximize doing things together. They are also concerned about safety and may hope for quiet when the children are put to bed.

Parents of older children often seek environments in which shared learning experiences can be alternated with some separation in which children have their own recreational activities, often with peers.

Single parents, usually mothers, may see the outdoor locale as a special opportunity for sharing responsibility with children. They also are concerned about safety. The process of camping itself is intended to facilitate interaction and communication.

Older couples are more likely to plan trips with designated stopover points and to see the trip as just as important as the destinations. They may also be open to interaction with others having similar interests and relaxed timetables.

The point is that the most important factor in what people do is usually whom they are with. Further, the group is more determined by life course sequences than anything else. The same young man who was in the white water at age twenty-three is now walking his two-year-old along the shore at age twenty-five.

One other factor: More often than not, the group originated in an urban area. The natural resource is a change from the concrete, small apartment, telephone, shopping mall, and even from the swimming pool and tennis court. The group seeks change from what has been left behind as well as activity that is based on group composition. Resources tend to be most crowded near urban areas. Rates of back-country use, however, are highest in the West.

Recreation Experiences in Natural Environments

Some write about "*the* wilderness experience" as though it were a singular and undifferentiated entity. Of course, there are innumerable kinds of wilderness experiences as well as sightseeing, escape, social, and learning experiences. The intent of all visitors, however, is to have a good time. They intend to combine the resource opportunities, companions, and their own action into some enjoyable set of experiences. Sometimes they succeed; sometimes they fail.

Considerable research indicates that for most vacationers activities come in bundles or packages. There are clusters of activities that more or less fit the opportunities. The bundles incorporate the group composition as well as their particular personal and social resources. There is a "fit" between the setting and the resources of the participant. Often the family is an imperative that requires some packages or styles and precludes others. In other cases, the site has been selected because it offers particular rather than general opportunities: sheer rock faces, stocks of fish, gradual hiking trails, or beach access.

The context of activity has three dimensions: (1) the social dimension of commitments to companions, (2) the environmental dimension of space and resources, and (3) the time dimension of the articulation of multiple engagements. Further, contingencies such as weather, transportation, and crowding may impact the selection process. Predetermined priority for morning fishing may preclude a long hike, but package well with a lakeside stroll and swimming. A boat may facilitate waterskiing or drinking and locate a party near the water and away from the mountainside. The nature and management of the resource as well as the activity patterns of others open and close access to various bundles of activity. When enjoyment depends on particular combinations, then factors that block one aspect and alter the package may unbalance the enjoyment for some group members.

A Summary of Motivations

Without specifying sources and combinations, the following is an ordinary language list of the multiple dimensions sought in outdoor recreation:

We want to escape. There is a hope for some disengagement from the fullness of day-to-day life. We want out, to get away.

We want to escape together. Most often there is a select number of others with whom we desire the enhanced communication and intimacy fostered by the more general disengagement. We want to be with each other as well as apart from usual demands and limitations.

We want to "let go" in emotional release and expression. So much of life is circumscribed in permissible responses that the different environment may be chosen for its affective opportunities.

We want to "be ourselves." Again, our work and community roles have their pervasive expectations that limit what we do and who we are allowed to be. In the forest or on the water, we may hope to be that "something more" that we believe has been denied in our ordinary routines and missions.

We want an experience that is based on the special environment. It may be difficult to express just what is different about wide vistas, rich colors, powerful natural forces, and open trails. What we know is that we are somehow a part of all this and that an immersion in the natural is a needed balance to our urban built surroundings. Partly it is a matter of space and openness; partly it is scope and variety. Whatever the dimensions, we expect that the environment will provide an experience of immersion that we value, need, and find fulfilling.

What is it that is so special about resource-based recreation experiences? B. L. Driver at the U.S. Forest Service has developed and refined methods of examining and measuring the satisfactions of water- and forest-related leisure. There is a variety of types of such meanings:

1. *Social:* social recognition, family togetherness, being with friends, meeting new people, exercising leadership and sharing skills
2. *Personal expression and development:* achievement, reinforcing self-image, competence testing, discovery and learning of creativity in personal reflection and physical fitness
3. *Experimental (intrinsic):* stimulation, risk taking, tranquillity, using equipment, and nostalgia
4. *Nature appreciation:* enjoyment of scenery, closeness to nature, learning about nature, and seeking open space and privacy
5. *Change:* rest, escape from pressures and routines, avoiding crowds, and getting away from head[4]

In general the appreciation of the environment and the reduction of stress are common themes in outdoor recreation. The forest, river, lake, beach, or mountain is a setting for activity. Much of that activity is social or expressive in content. However, the environment itself is an important part of the meaning of such experiences.

Summary of Issues

The geographic imbalance between population and outdoor recreation resources has intensified both the importance of travel costs and time in screening participants and the problem of crowding at sites near cities. Especially in the Northeast, recent policies of the major provider, the federal government, have been to give greater emphasis to resources accessi-

---

[4] Adapted from reports by B. L. Driver, Rocky Mountain Forest Service Experiment Station.

ble to urban populations. However, the unique attractions—the Grand Canyon, Glacier and Yellowstone National Parks, and great mountain ranges—are in the West.

Some extension of opportunities has been supported by grants to state and local agencies for recreation land acquisition and by exploitation of the recreation potential of second-growth forests, flood reservoirs, and once-polluted waterways. Such development often requires the coordinated planning of several federal, state, and local organizations.

Conflicts over the management of land with recreation use appeal have been between user groups who find that their environmental needs not only differ but are incompatible. Noise from camping groups, beach parties, or motorized off-road vehicles may be perceived to degrade the anticipated experience of backcountry hikers or trail skiers, family groups, or those seeking solitude. Crowding has been found to be a factor in the discontinuation of camping by many families.

Other conflicts occur between those who want to preserve a special area or ecosystem, those who want to use it for their recreation, and those with an interest in commercial development. Courts, legislative bodies, and public management agencies have all become engaged in planning decisions made in the midst of such conflicts. As a result, land-use planning is a political as well as an economic and scientific enterprise.

Nevertheless, there is still something special about natural environments. Careful plans, long trips, and considerable costs may be involved in the realization of a preferred resource-based recreation experience. While the types of satisfaction vary, they are given an added dimension by being in the midst of the forest, on the water, or framed by a dramatic horizon.

HIGHLIGHTS

1. The dominant federal land management agencies are still developing management programs that combine environmental goals with recreation uses.
2. Preservation, development, and use interests when in conflict require careful adjudication as well as long-range foresight.
3. In the interrelated socioecosystem, all interventions, including recreation, have chains of impacts.
4. Natural-resource-based outdoor recreation yields outcomes that depend on the environment as well as social, intrinsic, expressive, and change satisfactions. Not only the unique attractions but more accessible sites are considered special by users who place high value on activity in such settings.

Discussion Questions

1. Is private ownership and control of desirable recreation space, especially land, a serious problem in your region? Are there particular kinds of space that are closed to most of the public?

2. Would you agree that in leisure "space is freedom"? Why or why not?

3. Does planning always lead to control, or may planning sometimes be necessary to ensure freedom? Give examples.

4. Which has the greater value, environmental preservation or recreation use? What are the most important decision criteria when there is a conflict between the two?

5. How can use conflicts be resolved by planning and management? Give examples.

6. How can there be "too much of a good thing" when too many people are attracted to a recreation locale?

7. What is the best way to prevent crowding—raising prices, rationing, use restrictions, or just letting dissatisfaction drive some users out? Why?

8. Which outdoor recreation activities are likely to increase in participation? Decrease? Why?

Bibliography

Burch, W. R., *Daydreams and Nightmares: A Sociological Essay on the American Environment.* New York: Harper & Row, 1971.

Cichetti, C., "A Review of the Empirical Analyses That Have Been Based upon the National Outdoor Recreation Surveys," *Journal of Leisure Research,* 4 (1972), 90–107.

Clawson, M., and J. Knetsch, *Economics of Outdoor Recreation.* Baltimore: Johns Hopkins University Press, 1966.

Kelly, John R., *Recreation Business.* New York: Macmillan, 1985.

Nash, R., *Wilderness and the American Mind.* New Haven, CT: Yale University Press, 1967.

Report of the President's Commission on Americans Outdoors, *Americans Outdoors: The Legacy, the Challenge.* Washington, DC: Island Press, 1987.

Wilderness. Washington, DC: Wilderness Society. Any issue.

Chapter 15

Leisure and the Arts

The arts and leisure have a long association. Fine arts, like popular culture, are expressions of their historical time and place. The great cathedrals of Europe with their Gothic spires reaching heavenward are the products of a profoundly religious and ecclesiastical culture. The Japanese tea ceremony expresses a grace and precision characteristic of classical themes of the Japanese culture. Michelangelo's *David* came out of Renaissance humanism. And the music of Stravinsky or Benjamin Britten blends folk elements with new harmonies and disharmonies. Fine arts may endure, but they are not timeless.

Along with greater variety in the older arts a diversity of artistic forms has emerged. Folk arts such as pottery and woodcarving, folk music of historic authenticity, and many such forms previously excluded from "high culture" and the "fine arts" are now accepted as worthy of inclusion in the best museums and concert halls.

Such diversity has also fostered a second trend of increasing participation in the creation of art by nonprofessionals. Doing art rather than just appreciating art has become more and more important to leisure. As a result, the simple artist-consumer distinction no longer reflects the state of the arts. Rather, professionals and amateurs may both have the highest standards of performance. And learning arts skills has become a major leisure activity employing more and more full- and part-time instructors. The artist may be as central to community recreation programs as the coach and program leader.

Among issues to be addressed in this chapter are the growth of creation in the arts, the special place of the arts in contemporary leisure, social and personal meanings of artistic enterprise, and the relationship of freedom and form in the arts.

ISSUES

Are fine arts and folk arts quite different?
Is appreciation of the performance of others the main leisure engagement with the arts?
Are the arts only for the elite of a society?
Why do some people devote such time and effort to developing skills in the arts?

The fine arts of music, sculpture, painting, dance, and theater have been joined by several relatives who are just now being acknowledged as part of the family. For example, the design and making of fine pottery, metalwork, jewelry, woodcarving, and ceramics are generally accepted as art. Since folk melodies have been incorporated into music by the greatest composers for centuries, it is not that radical to accept some folk music—both recently composed and historically authentic—as significant in the whole spectrum of music. And even the classic ballet companies have incorporated many folk and jazz elements into their repertoires. Arts such as music and dance express a variety of cultures in both ancient and modern forms. The trend in the arts is toward inclusion rather than toward narrowing.

At the same time, there is growth in participation in the arts. However, that growth is not in support of major orchestras or opera companies, but in community orchestras and theater companies, in school and university programs, and in small arts-related businesses. More people are creating art, on some level, rather than being content to support and applaud the work of others. A national Harris poll indicated that as many as 40 percent of American adults are participating in some arts activity.

The Scope of the Arts as Leisure

There are two separable issues here: one is the magnitude of the arts in the society and the other is the significance of the arts in the leisure of Americans. As with sport, some of the indicators seem contradictory.

Table 15–1 indicates the percentages of adults who attended various kinds of cultural events in 1985. In the year, 23 million people attended at least one classical music concert, 30 million a musical play, 21 million a play, and 39 million visited an art museum or gallery.

Education level has more of an effect on arts interest than any other kind of leisure. Baumol and Bowen found a definite relationship between education and attending performing arts events.[1] Those with graduate school education made up more than 50 percent of the male and more than 30 percent of the female performing arts audience although they are less than 5 percent of the population.

Participation in the arts is a major element in the leisure of those who have a college education in the United States. Further, graduate school, the quality of the college or uni-

---

[1] J. Baumol and W. G. Bowen, *Performing Arts—The Economic Dilemma* (New York: Twentieth Century Fund, 1966).

TABLE 15–1   Participation Percentages for Various Arts Activities by Those Age Eighteen and Older*

Activity	Total	Male	Female	High School Graduate	College Graduate
Attend					
Classical music concert	13%	11%	14%	7%	29%
Opera	3	2	3	1	6
Plays	12	11	12	6	26
Ballet	4	3	5	2	9
Jazz concert	10	10	9	7	18
Musical plays	17	15	19	12	34
Visit art museum	22	21	23	14	45
Read book	56	48	63	52	78

*At least once in past twelve months.

Source: Statistical Abstract of the United States, 1988. Based on 1985 national survey conducted by the U.S. Bureau of the Census.

versity, and the opportunities associated with urban centers affect the participation. There appears to be a cosmopolitan life style for educated people with discretionary income that includes going to concerts and the theater and supporting various kinds of performing arts events and organizations. The socialization process of the university develops interests in the arts that are less likely to occur in other social settings.

Unfortunately, reliable figures on engagement in the production of music, ceramics, and other elements of the arts are not available. There is no way of knowing just how many people are taking lessons in pottery in the thousands of college, public school, public recreation, and private programs where such instruction is offered. Even less is it possible to estimate how many people not now in organized programs continue regular or occasional pottery making.

The fine and performing arts, then, are not peripheral to American leisure. Especially for the increasing proportion of the population with some college education, both making art and appreciating artistic production are not only a part of the leisure schedule but a significant element of the personal leisure balance. And for some, participation in the arts is the center of their leisure and their lives.

The Performing Arts

It is difficult to draw lines that categorize the arts. The simple classification into performing arts, graphic arts, and literary arts requires subordination of the graphic and literary elements in theater and dance to a focus on the performer. At the same time the performance elements of painting and poetry reading, the graphic illustration of literature, the wedding of music and literature on the opera stage, and other such combined elements are ignored in the classification. More important than categorization is the understanding that in all the arts there is a blending of imagination and action, form and creation, and materials and symbols that suggests commonality of the arts rather than divisions.

Nevertheless, the performing, graphic, and literary categories give some shape to the wide spectrum of the arts. Performing arts include orchestral, band, and vocal music; dance; opera; theater drama; and some filmwork. Any of these forms can be televised as well as produced for an audience that is present. All can be produced by professionals, amateurs, and students. All involve learning particular skills, often over periods that begin in childhood and continue through most of a lifetime. All, in one context or another, involve those who perform and those who observe.

Again, figures from the *Statistical Abstract of the United States* are only examples that can give an impression of the scope of the performing arts:

In 1991, there were about 1,600 community orchestras in the United States with total budgets of more than $680 million. Of these, thirty-seven are considered major performing units. Half as many people attended their concerts as went to major league baseball games. However, there has been no per capita increase in the paid attendance for most major orchestras since 1980.

Trends in classical music record, cassette, and compact disk sales are difficult to measure due to shifts among the formats. In general, over the past three decades sales have been relatively steady. During the same period the sale of musical instruments has grown, with most sales at the instructional level.

In 1991, more than 1,200 companies were producing opera in the United States. The 200 professional companies had budgets of $400 million. There has been a steady growth in the number of performances to more than 15,000 in 1990.

While the $90 million a year spent for classical recordings has not changed greatly, more than 400 FM radio stations are oriented primarily to presenting programs of classical music.

Dance appears to be a growing area in the performing arts with marked increases in the number of performances by resident companies and touring groups. Regional and urban companies are developing stronger support and are gaining critical acclaim. The basis of support may be younger people now being instructed in dance in the expanding private and community dance programs. Despite this growth, ballet is far behind theater in total attendance.

If more than 20 million people attended at least one play in 1990, then a considerable number were also involved in producing those plays, either as performers or stage and production crew. Commercial theaters on New York's Broadway have declined in number, attendance has shown little increase, and the number of productions has been slightly reduced. On the other hand, amateur theater, school drama, summer theater, and other community groups present a lot of plays. As many as 100 million people attend the half million plays produced by the 5,000 nonprofit theater groups, 5,000 college-affiliated groups, and 15,000 groups related to churches, clubs, and schools. Amateur theater is a major phenomenon.

In general, there is no sign of a boom in attendance or support of the professional levels of the performing arts. While urbanization and higher education levels may suggest gradual gains in attendance at theaters and concerts, there is also evidence suggesting problems. Major performing arts centers in growing cities have had serious financial diffi- culties. Ecological time-cost problems may offset gains in discretionary income and college- induced interests.

Total attendance figures for symphony concerts, theater, and opera indicate steady if gradual increases in the period from 1970 to 1990. A 1988 Harris poll, on the other hand, reports a decline since 1984 of 3 percent for plays, 9 percent for classical music concerts, and 23 percent for opera and musical theater. The increases in the same period were 24 percent for visiting art museums, 9 percent for motion picture attendance, and 2 percent for the purchase of classical music recordings. The conflicting figures result partly from comparing the self-reports of surveys with the total attendance figures compiled by asso- ciations of music and theater companies. One possibility, however, is that those who en- gage in such activities are more regular while at the same time fringe participants are dropping out due to time pressures. Marketing data indicate that about 40 percent of those who attend live performances at all do so four or more times a year.

The Graphic Arts

The 1990 census lists more than 600,000 persons employed as writers, artists, musicians, actors, and other performers, an increase of 25 percent since 1980. Despite relatively high unemployment rates for artists, the proportion of woman sculptors and painters grew about 50 percent. More and more people are trying to earn a living as producing artists. They teach, sell, and usually accept a modest standard of living in their effort to unify their leisure and their work in satisfying activity.

Much art is sold in small shops and street bazaars. The major city galleries with their paintings and crafts by known artists and prices of several hundred dollars for prints and $1,000-plus for paintings are important to the financial structure of the arts, but sell pro- portionately few of the works that pass through the market. The variety of sales contexts makes accurate figures unobtainable. The producing element of the graphic arts over- whelms the capacity of the 600 art museums to show even representative samples of the productive capacity of America.

Perhaps the best reminder of the scope of participation in the graphic and plastic arts would be a trip to the local "Saturday market" or a discussion with the operators of com- munity shops and galleries where art and craft producers display their wares. The enroll- ments in community college courses for art production and in community recreation arts programs give a glimpse of the numbers of people engaged in upgrading their skills or learning new ones.

The 1985 Simmons survey reported that 6.5 percent of the adult population engaged in painting, drawing, or sculpting during the year. More were female than male, 7.7 per- cent versus 5.2 percent. Participation was consistent through all ages except for a higher percentage for those of school age. Those who had attended or graduated from college were twice as likely to engage in the graphic arts as those who had not graduated from high school. Like other arts, painting and sculpting require considerable investment in skill de- velopment. As a consequence, it tends to be more than just one activity out of many for those who do it regularly. It is often very central to the identity of the artist.

The same survey found that 7.3 percent of the adult population played a musical instrument in 1985, 6.8 percent of males and 7.7 percent of females. Again, rates were higher for those with some college education.

The Literary Arts

How many people are producing literature in America today? Again, estimates are difficult to make. Even excluding all the writing done by students for various classes and programs, there is no way of knowing how many people are writing poetry, short stories, essays, autobiographies, novels, and other works. Some writing is personal and private. Some is aimed at commercial publication but will never get to its target. Some writers would like to be published but do not expect to be.

In 1991, about 48,000 new books were published in the United States. Of these, about 2,100 were biography, 5,400 fiction, 5,100 juvenile, 2,000 literature, 900 poetry and drama, and the rest related to a wide variety of fields and interests. This does not include new editions of books previously published, government publications, or books published privately. There has been a steady increase in total books published each year. In 1991, more than 838 million hardbound trade volumes and almost 1.2 billion paperbound were sold, not including textbooks and technical, juvenile, and religious books.

There are countless literary journals, often published by colleges, that print works of poetry, fiction, and imagination. Various popular periodicals include works done by well-known authors. This is just the known literary production and does not include all that is self-published or never published. By some standards most writing is not literature, but is written communication without the creative aims and standards of literature. Nevertheless, much is being written with the intent of bringing an artistic product into being out of the imagination and craft of the author.

Participation Trends in the Arts

Two trends in arts participation seem in opposition to each other. The first is the indication of a short-term decrease in arts participation during the 1980s.[2] Women have been more likely than men to engage in the arts. With a higher proportion of women in the work force, time available for demanding arts disciplines is reduced. The reductions in activities such as painting have been less for men than women so that the gender gap is gradually closing. This loss of the time required for arts engagement is consistent with the Harris survey and other evidence of a compression of time available for leisure. The time factor may be one reason that frequency rates for both men and women are consistent with only about 20 percent of the total participants drawing or painting at least once a week.

The countertrend is based on the consistent relationship between participation in the arts and higher education. Each cohort of men and women in the population has higher rates of having attended college than the older cohorts. As a result, it would be reasonable to project a long-term increase in engagement in the arts.

[2] John R. Kelly, *Recreation Trends toward the Year 2000* (Champaign, IL: Management Learning Laboratories, 1987).

As with any activities that demand high levels of skill for maximum satisfaction, the key is the commitment level. Unless school programs intensify that commitment for those who attend college, increased artistic participation as leisure seems unlikely in this century. On the other hand, the dramatic drop for women may lessen as more leave the demanding parental period of the life course. There may be some resurgence of doing the arts among the large cohort who will be entering the postparental period in the coming decades.

In any case, those whose engagement is primarily in appreciating the performance of others far outnumber those who are engaged as professionals or amateurs in producing works of art (see Table 15–2).

TABLE 15–2   Frequency of Participation in Cultural Activity

	Total	2+ times a week	Once a week	2–3 times a month	Once a month	Less than once a month
			How Often			
Adult education	7.3%	2.3%	2.5%	0.4%	0.3%	1.0%
Attend music/dance	12.4	0.3	0.4	0.8	1.6	7.7
Concerts on radio	5.6	1.6	1.0	0.8	0.5	1.1
Live theater	12.1	0.1	0.2	0.6	1.7	8.0
Go to museums	11.5	0.1	0.1	0.4	1.1	8.4
Paint/draw	6.4	1.6	0.8	1.0	0.5	1.5
Photography	12.5	1.6	1.4	2.7	2.2	2.9
Read books	41.0	22.5	4.5	4.1	2.8	3.2
Woodworking	5.3	1.2	0.4	0.8	0.7	1.3

Source: Mediamark Research, 1990 National Survey, sample of 2,724 households.

The Fine Arts as Leisure

One trend in community public recreation programs in the last decades has been greater interest in programs related to the fine and folk arts. There has been an increase not only in folk guitar classes for teens, leathercraft workshops for all ages, and china painting for retirees but also summer productions of plays and musical comedies, children's classes in stagecraft and scenery design, and a variety of performing music groups. These supplement but do not replace courses in adult education programs, choirs and other arts groups in churches, and established community orchestras, choral groups, art centers, dance academies, and theaters. While each of these programs seeks some group who will act as the appreciators and consumers of the products, the emphasis is on doing rather than appreciating. In a sense, the producers need just enough people to come to legitimate the production. In fact, often the consumers are mostly family and friends of the producers rather than followers of the particular art.

This stress on doing the arts opens a number of issues important to understanding the place of the arts in leisure: How are participants socialized into it? What are the satisfactions of the participation? Are cost and other factors problems in limiting participation? And what are the effects of technologies such as television on the arts as leisure?

Socialization in the Arts

Just as support of performing arts programs has been provided almost entirely by the financial and educational elite, so introduction to participation in the fine arts has been most available to those in families with the interests and the financial resources to pay. While school programs may provide an introduction to painting, vocal music, playing musical instruments, and dance, the development of skills requires more concentrated programs of instruction. For the most part, those programs are open to those who can afford them. Further, in order to have an adequate base of support, the programs are located in areas where people tend to have the income, educational background, and developed interest. As is the case with most types of leisure, opportunities are disproportionately available to those with the greatest resources.

There are exceptions. A New York City public high school has drawn students identified as gifted to one location for concentrated instruction in arts performance. Skilled professionals have gone into Harlem and Watts with special programs for ghetto children and youth. Many kinds of programs have accepted and even recruited with scholarships students unable to meet the costs of their instruction. Musical instruments are available on loan from schools and in some cases may be taken home and used during the summer for a nominal insurance charge.

However, there is more to socialization than access to opportunities to learn skills. The most clearly defined relationship in interest and participation in the arts is with education. School—elementary, secondary, college, university, and graduate—is the most available place where arts are going on. The further we go in school, the more likely we are to be exposed to, interested in, and enticed by one of the arts. Especially in college situations, we may come to know people with a special interest in one of the arts who introduce us to that enthusiasm. In school we have opportunities to try out our aptitudes and interests at minimal cost. Especially in schools where performance education is directed toward non-professional participation, students develop their skills and widen their interests.

As with most socialization, various elements provide reinforcement. Children in schools with the fullest art programs, who are most likely to enter institutions of higher education with even richer opportunities, are most often from homes in which interests in the arts have already been introduced by parents who read, go to the theater, and have art, books, and music in their homes.

Of course, all people with the opportunity to learn to play the cello or sing Bach cantatas do not do so. Some are discouraged by teachers or others who perceive a lack of talent. Others are more strongly pulled toward other kinds of activities that win out in the competition for time and attention. And some find artistic performance more satisfying than do others.

Further, artists tend to form small groups of interaction that shape and support their efforts. These "small worlds" of colleagues are the primary set of critics whose standards are relevant for performance.[3]

[3] Howard Becker, *Art Worlds* (Berkeley, CA: University of California Press, 1982); Pierre Bourdieu, *Distinction: A Social Critique of the Judgment of Taste* (Cambridge, MA: Harvard University Press, 1984).

Satisfactions of Doing the Arts

Generalizations are always somewhat inaccurate when applied to a particular artist. For example, strong identification with a particular artist or teacher may lead a younger performer to reflect the satisfactions and meanings articulated by that role model. And there are differences among the arts. Those whose performance is done as part of a group such as a choir or orchestra may find more satisfaction out of the experience of the shared contribution than those who perform solo. Dancers are more likely to report satisfaction in physical coordination and grace than those who perform seated or standing still. However, there are satisfactions specifically associated with the arts as leisure that are different from playing cards or softball.

Unconditional or intrinsic satisfactions tend to dominate the choice of fine arts leisure more than with family activities, community organizations, travel, or most activity at home. Arts participation tends to have high requirements of intensity, of mental and emotional energy. It is also activity in which there is a product, a performance or created artifact. Creation in the arts combines long-term development of skill with outcomes that are different from any that previously existed. There is an existential "becoming" for the creating self in the act of performance.

While the rest-recuperation element is present in almost all leisure activities, it is least dominant in activities that require a discipline of skill development or include considerable social obligation. Artistic participation ranks with certain sports and activities done alone in having satisfaction most often perceived as intrinsic. And, of course, there are social meanings in doing the arts as leisure. The associations in a choir, orchestra, pottery class, or art center may become quite central to the friendship community of participants. In many cases, the relationships may outweigh the intrinsic satisfaction in maintaining interest in an arts group. Nevertheless, the experiential satisfactions are likely to remain salient. Among them are the following:

Self-Expression. "Painting allows me to begin within my own imagination and put on canvas something that is uniquely mine." "The form of the music is a material into which I put my whole self when singing: mind, body, emotions, everything."

Mastery. "Even though I'm not a Heifitz or Menuhin, the time and concentration I put into the violin does make a difference. When I can play a difficult passage well, there is a special kind of satisfaction for me." "The whole process of developing a characterization from the first read-through to the last performance is one in which there is always something more to master and express."

Skill Development. "I like rehearsals better than performances because we can stop and work on the rough spots. It's in rehearsal that you are learning." "When you are learning to dance, nothing is more exciting than when you say 'I did it' about a movement impossible a month before." "When you know what you have accomplished, how others react to your performance is secondary."

Personal Growth. "All the hard work makes me more of a person when I get through the tough spots and reach a new level of competence." "Even though at the concert no one can hear me sing, I know when I have worked hard enough to make my contribution. It's good to do it without any personal gain or attention."

The Product.   "Whether it's good by some standards or not; it's something that I made out of a piece of wood. It's real and it's finished." "Somehow no one else would have done it just this way. It's mine and it's there to look at and touch and use." "It all comes together at the concert when we actually make a symphony."

Perhaps the most important aspect of doing an art is the experience itself. In doing what may be strenuous, demanding, at times frustrating, and often exhausting, the artist becomes part of a process in which something actually happens that has a grace of shape, a richness of texture, and a newness of actualization. There is uncertainty and risk in the process. There are costs and even failures. But for the artist who goes from the beginning of the process to an end product—even one that will be started over the next day—there is a rise and fall of meaning that becomes a part of the acting, re-creating self.

Appreciation and Creation in the Arts

Focus here has been primarily on the artist, the creator of art. The artist may be a once-a-week baritone, a neophyte nature photographer, or a dancer who has been developing skills for fifteen years under expert tutelage. The premise is that doing and creating in the arts—regardless of skill level—is more important to leisure than being a consumer of the work of others.

Of course, in many cases that is not true. Some travelers build an entire summer around visiting European cities to see certain works of art and architecture. For a music lover in a small town, a fine collection of records and a good stereo system may be a critical element in the total environment of living. Attending plays at large and small theaters may be the central leisure passion of a resident of New York or Los Angeles. Appreciation may be an art, too.

However, there seems to be something special about producing a work of art—on some level of competence—that is different from perceiving the work of others. There is an investment of the self and an identification with the creation that is missing in simple appreciation of the creations of others. This difference may be best illustrated in the engagement of what Robert Stebbins calls "the amateur."[4]

Modern amateurism, according to Stebbins, is not just messing around with an art or an activity. While the amateur is not a professional gaining a substantial part of his livelihood from the craft, neither is the amateur a dilettante or a dabbler. Rather, the modern amateur accepts and strives for the same standards of excellence as the professional. This kind of amateur participates in highly disciplined and systematized ways. If an amateur violinist, he or she practices regularly, seeks help in improving skills, and is a regular member of one or more musical aggregations that practice and perform regularly. Further, the amateur recognizes that this nonprofessional engagement is quite central to his or her pattern of life. The discipline and the participation take precedence in scheduling, allocating scarce

[4] Robert A. Stebbins, *Amateurs: On the Margin between Work and Leisure* (Beverly Hills, CA: Sage Publications, 1979).

resources, and personal identity. While all amateurs are not like the devotee who says that she is a tennis player who practices dentistry rather than a dentist who plays tennis, something of that kind of identification is common. When playing chamber music with other amateurs takes high priority, the person cannot define the self apart from being a musician.

Stebbins adds that there is a public involved in the professional-amateur participation in the arts. Some feedback from those who watch or listen is anticipated and is part of the meaning of doing the art. While practice and rehearsal are satisfying in themselves, there is the public offering in mind and the expectation of some positive evaluation of the performance. Serious artistic endeavor is an offering to others as well as an experience of intrinsic satisfaction. From this perspective, it is impossible to completely separate creation and appreciation in the arts.

Further, the feedback that is most valued by the performer is informed evaluation. For the most part, those best able to appreciate the quality of a work of art are those who have been producers themselves. As only one who has played a sport can really comprehend the intricacies of a well-played game, so it is the pianist who understands the techniques and interpretation of another performer and the dancer who recognizes the burst of grace in the midst of an ordinary ballet. As a consequence there is a symbiosis between doing the arts and appreciating what others do. Empathy with what has gone into a production—in theater, music, or any other art—is most complete when one has had the experience oneself. Of course, the skilled performer may also be most critical and least patient with inept or shoddy work.

Arts in the Community

As suggested earlier, there has been a growth in the number of offerings in the arts on the part of public recreation programs. Some recreation professionals have been reluctant to become involved in the classic arts, but have entered the field through folk arts and crafts. Somehow metalworking and photography seemed less formidable than painting and sculpture, and folk music easier than madrigals. More and more frequently the old barriers and distinctions have been lowered. In some communities a summer program may include an opera workshop as well as swimming lessons and ballet as well as track and field.

However, public programs are only one part of the spectrum of fine arts in the community. Depending on the size and cultural orientation of the community, opportunities in music, graphic arts, theater and the rest may be offered by many kinds of organizations:

Public recreation programs

Nonprofit organizations such as orchestras, opera companies, community theaters, dance companies, and others

Commercial enterprises such as theaters

Educational organizations, both public and private; public and private schools on all levels

Instructional programs in one of the arts operated by one person or a small group

Voluntary organizations made up of the artists such as camera clubs, art guilds, and theater groups

Church organizations both within the church program and sponsored by the church for the community

Some are for children, some for older people, and some open to all. Some present works of "amateur" art on very high levels. Others are open to all who would like to participate and are unable to maintain consistency in quality. Some are aimed at producing a very few performers of high levels of skill and others are more inclusive with a philosophy reflecting a leisure-participation point of view.

One phenomenon is the growth in programs and cultural acceptance of arts once considered as outside the realm of the "real arts." Among these would be photography, ceramics, modern and jazz music, and graphic art employing a variety of instruments and materials. Not only is there a widening of definitions of what is art, but such expansion enlarges the opportunities and interests of those who want to do art in a way satisfying to themselves. Also, while there is no end to the challenge of skills not yet mastered, some media have lower thresholds of satisfying participation than others. Jazz dancing does not require going "on point," and a potter may produce an interesting and graceful bowl on a first or second firing. The delay of several years before "acceptable production" in some arts has been one factor in limiting participation.

Currently there is a growth of interest in a wide range of ethnic artistic expressions. Eastern, African, and Latin art forms have their own special expressions that widen the cultural base of all the arts. They enrich the artistic development of other cultures as well as the celebrations of their own.

Mass Media Availability and the Arts

Television has had some of the same impact on the performing arts as it has had on sports. Now via the screen, videotape, and satellites the great events of the art world may be reproduced in the living room. The finest opera performances, the best Broadway plays, the premier concerts, and even productions of Russia's Bolshoi Ballet and the Edinburgh Festival are available without cost in almost every American home. As the Olympics may inspire young athletes to dreams of excellence, so much reproduction in the arts may inspire young artists to a single-minded climb toward greatness. Even more, a much wider spectrum of young people may be drawn into more modest participation by the excitement of seeing and hearing something very special.

Of course, there is also a negative possibility. The ease of turning on the television and remaining home might divert potential supporters of live performances. Also some might be concerned that the tastes that are developed from constant exposure to television fare will no longer respond to the more demanding presentation of Shakespeare and Beethoven. The key may well be the extent to which television encourages participation. In general, the more that young people participate in doing the arts themselves, the less they will be satisfied with the reduced experience of the electronic media.

Freedom and Form

In an influential essay published in English in 1952, Josef Pieper developed an argument that leisure is the "basis of culture."[5] This European philosopher advanced the concern that in Western civilization we are quite "unleisurely" in order to have leisure. We tend to work very hard and seriously to obtain the opportunity for something far inferior to the real freedom of leisure. Leisure is, according to the philosophers, a "mental and spiritual attitude" rather than spare time or a holiday. It is an inner condition of openness and receptivity. It exists for its own sake rather than as a restoration for anything else.

While all music is not the last movement of Beethoven's Ninth Symphony, it is a means of communication of shared meanings, moods, and memories. Theater not only communicates the language but, in the drama, projects themes that underlie the words themselves. A painting or sculpture makes a statement about nature or people rather than simply reproducing their appearance. The arts are forms of social communication, expressing the meaning, emotion, and coherence of some facet of existence.

In art there is a heightening of meaning. An artistic work expresses something of life that is true to the artist but often hidden beneath the commonplace and trite. As the myth or legend tells of "truth" that is more than history, so art has meaning that is more than nature. It is an occurrence of communication that becomes celebration when received and accepted by a community of people. Art, then, is more than a personal expression. Art may embody meaning essential to the development of a culture. Leisure, as a social space of freedom that may be devoted to art, is essential to the life of the culture.

The Arts as Freedom

Even more central to the nature of leisure is the element of freedom in the arts. Though dance is limited by the capabilities of the body and the forms of music, painting by the dimensions and color of the materials, and theater by language and the stage, there is the freedom to create in the arts. Even within traditional forms, the creating artist produces something that has not existed before, a work not quite like that of any other artist. The freedom to choose and the satisfaction of production are uniquely combined in the arts. Today what is most "modern" in the arts is the inclusion of new media and forms. The traditional limits are being expanded with the freedom of the composer to create new sounds and of the sculpture to incorporate new materials and movement.

In the performing and creative arts, the old forms and molds are always being tested from within and even broken by those whose imaginations cannot be restrained. Fantasy and play are part of the work of the artist as the aim or the communication seems to call for some element that is novel and fresh. A choir makes staccato clicks. A piece of metalwork moves in the breeze. A dancer makes an ungainly move that expresses an emotion unthinkable in traditional ballet. The composer, artist, and performer are creating in the sense of always working toward the future, the "not yet" of life and existence.

[5] Josef Pieper, *Leisure: The Basis of Culture* (New York: New American Library, 1963).

Insofar as the essence of leisure is freedom, then the creative arts are, of all human activities, most "leisurely." Aristotle was not all wrong when he had difficulty thinking of true leisure apart from music and contemplation. The use of human imagination, the exercise of freedom of thought and creation, and the production of something new are the most free of human endeavors.

Form and Discipline in the Arts

Paradoxically, work in the creative arts requires the greatest discipline and mastery of forms and materials. To sing, dance, act, draw, write, or otherwise create well in the arts usually requires a great deal of hard work. While there have been intriguing intuitive or folk artists, for the most part the more imaginative products have come from the minds of those who mastered their craft.

As a result, not only does a high level of creation call for discipline and mastery, but personal satisfaction seems to increase with such mastery. Artists report that the greatest thrill of participation is when the challenge requires every bit of skill that has been painfully acquired. The craftsmanship needed to mold a delicate platter of pottery, to flow through every run in singing a Bach aria, or to communicate new depth in characterization in an O'Neill play may be inexpressibly exciting. These pleasures come after the forms and skills of the craft are well in hand.

Form and discipline are the basis of participation in the arts. There is no art without form and material, no theater without language, and no symphony without notation, instruments, and players. While the end may be the production, the performance, and the finished work of art, part of the meaning is in the preparation. There is satisfaction not only in the end product, but in the engagement in the discipline that makes the product possible.

Doing the arts as leisure, then, is both learning and producing. It is both discipline and freedom. Creation in the arts brings into the world something that is new and expressive of the creator, but that is based on an investment of the self in the craft and an absorption of the work of others.

Summary of Issues

The fine arts have traditionally been identified with major productions of theater, literature, symphony, opera, ballet, painting, sculpture, and the like. However, there are two dimensions of expansion significant for leisure. The first is the widening of diversity in the fine arts. Much that had been considered folk art or crafts is now displayed in major museums or produced in major theaters and halls. The second dimension is the increased importance of participation in the fine arts rather than simply appreciation. More and more there is a widening of the communities of those who produce and create on some level of skill that is found satisfying.

The somewhat lesser skill requirements of folk music and arts in order to produce work satisfying to the artist would appear to be one factor in this emphasis on production. However, both the media and community programs are offering exposure of artistic production to a wider spectrum of the population than before. The greater proportion of the population continuing into higher education has also increased exposure and opportunity to participate.

Participation in the arts as leisure is somewhat like sport in its requirements of discipline and attention. Skill acquisition is demanding and unending. However, it is just this demand and discipline that yields the leisure satisfactions of a sense of mastery and personal development as well as of creation and expression. The fine arts have long been associated with classic leisure just because of the union of freedom and form, of expression and discipline.

HIGHLIGHTS

1. Creation rather than appreciation in the fine and folk arts seems a potential growth area with more and more community programs and opportunities.
2. The performing, graphic, and literary arts are often combined in forms of presentation.
3. While education is associated with the acquisition of many arts skills and interests, participation in low-threshold artistic creation is an important leisure phenomenon.
4. Participation in the arts, while often social, revolves more around motivations of expression, creation, mastery, personal development, and emotional involvement than is the case with less demanding leisure.
5. The arts combine freedom and discipline in ways that call for great investment of the self that may yield proportionate satisfactions.

Discussion Questions

1. Which is more fulfilling—creation in the arts at relatively low skill levels or appreciating the best production of others? Why?

2. Is there evidence of increased public support for the fine arts in North America?

3. What are the special values and limitations of community arts programs? Are they likely to lose or gain support as public stations and cable programs increase the range of drama, music, and dance available in the home?

4. Does art require the feedback of appreciators? Why or why not? Is art always a social offering as well as a personal creation?

5. Should men be given more encouragement to participate in the arts as women are given greater opportunities for sport activity? Why?

6. Can most arts learning programs be left to the schools and private providers rather than supplied by public recreation? Why or why not? Should public programs stress inclusiveness or skill?

7. Viewing the arts as leisure, what is the relationship between creating and appreciating?

8. How can arts participation have both the freedom of leisure and the discipline of art?

9. Is there likely to be an increase in amateur arts engagement? Why?

Bibliography

Arnold, N. D., *The Interrelated Arts in Leisure: Perceiving and Creating.* St. Louis, MO: C. V. Mosby, 1976.

Becker, Howard. *Art Worlds.* Berkeley, CA: University of California Press, 1982.

Hans, James, *The Play of the World.* Amherst, MA: University of Massachusetts Press, 1981.

Hantrais, Linda, and T. Kamphorst, eds., *Trends in the Arts: A Multinational Perspective.* Amersfoort, The Netherlands: Giordano Bruno Press, 1987.

Huizinga, Johan, *Homo Ludens.* Boston: Beacon Press, 1955.

Pieper, Josef, *Leisure: The Basis of Culture.* New York: New American Library, 1963.

Schiller, Friedrick, *On the Aesthetic Education of Man,* trans. R. Snell. New Haven, CT: Yale University Press, 1954.

Stebbins, Robert, *Amateurs: On the Margin between Work and Leisure.* Beverly Hills, CA: Sage Publications, 1979.

Zolberg, Vera. *Constructing a Sociology of the Arts.* New York: Cambridge University Press, 1990.

Chapter *16*

Popular Culture and Mass Media

"Popular" culture is not defined by its form or content. It includes music, literature, drama, and sport. In fact, some people make the designation so inclusive that it takes in almost anything that is popular. However, there is more to popular culture than its popularity. As culture, it reflects and expresses themes of meaning among identifiable groups in the society. Popular culture is commercial, but it is more than a product. Its embeddedness in the culture is more than the result of advertising and mass sales. There is a dialectic between business and an emerging consciousness of the culture that needs to be communicated and made concrete. Its popularity is dependent on its being truly *of* the culture.

This is not to ignore the matter of popularity. Popular culture may take forms that do not last through the centuries, but it is what lots of people are doing now. On a weekday last week no more than 5 percent of the adult population engaged in any sport, but the average American watched more than two hours of television. The most popular cultural medium, television, was available in more than 95 percent of American homes.

Printed media, visual media, music, and other forms of entertainment are common leisure fare for many and are big business for the economy. Popular culture is in the marketplace and is supplied by those who both respond to and attempt to shape consumer choices. And there are all those passing symbols that appear on printed T-shirts and fade in the wash of time. Popular culture is to leisure what the Chevy and Ford are to the auto market, what ABC and NBC are to drama, and what hamburgers are to cuisine. It is what most people do most of the time and yet something more—perhaps conveying the clearest signs of who we are as individuals in a mass society where identities must be overstated to be quickly recognized.

ISSUES

Is popular culture just a product of advertising and mass marketing?

What are the implications for leisure of that culture medium that reaches 95 percent of American households daily?

Why are popular culture items so important to youth?

Is television something less than "real leisure?"

Is popular culture always second-rate and trivial?

If we were to characterize an age in the history of a society, we would probably do it in terms of its popular culture. Some would say that in America the age of the front porch, Chautauqua, and the horse and buggy gave way to radio and the Model T and then to more recent symbols of how we live and move and communicate. If we were to characterize an age group in a society, it might also be in pop culture terms—youth is the age of Saturday night rock and jeans, of cars with their windows rolled down and tape decks alive with sound.

An outline of the centrality of popular culture through the life course would be illustrated by the following summary:

Children—Television and all the clothing, games, and toys modeled on popular television programs; the rise in wartime and fall in peacetime of popularity of war toys, comic books, and uniforms, the use of comic characters to sell vitamins, breakfast food, and shoes. More than in other ages, children seem to be passive recipients of the culture.

Youth—Rock groups and rap, dancing and MTV, concerts and television specials, transistor radios and tape decks, stereo and quadrophonic—nothing characterizes and bonds together teenagers in American culture like popular music. However, teens are less passive than children. They may respond to marketing and promotion, but they also choose what they like. Teens are the largest part of the movie market and a prime target audience for television programming. Identification is important so they gather at the right places, wear the right clothing, and drink the right beverages. In a sense, teens *are* popular culture—in ways that change and yet continue to form a behavior style with independent character.

Adult singles—Most adult singles do not fit the image of the playboy and playgirl with 2,000 CDs and records, a sports car, the latest clothes, and a trip to the sun every other month. Beginning incomes make that level of consumption only a frustrated dream for most. But the transition from teen to established adult includes a period of experimentation and courting of life styles as well as of a marriage partner. Magazines, automobiles, and weekend entertainment are all part of the culture of being adult and single. One aim is to employ the culture symbols that present a self that will be accepted in the social milieu where hoped-for relationships can be formed.

Parents—The more home-centered leisure of parents shifts popular culture interests to "adult" television entertainment, the broad range of couple-group activities in the community, and symbols of social establishment. "Pop" culture tends to be replaced by conventional culture. As a result, longer-term "investments" in leisure skills, facilities, and equipment center around community culture, home opportunities and equipment, and family activity. Popular culture outside the home is more likely to mean McDonalds than a rock festival and Fourth of July fireworks and picnics than the scene "where a lady may buy a gentleman a drink."

Older people—Popular culture may mean becoming reinterested in things that were popular during an earlier period. Popular culture markets may become increasingly turned toward the retained tastes of the "growing older" segment of the population.

The point is that by listening to the music, seeing the clothing styles, classifying the vocabulary, or observing the interests the age cohort can often be identified without ever seeing the people themselves. We can accurately guess ages when we know television program and music preferences and leisure styles. The essence of popular culture is that its forms and expressions are always changing. More than with other leisure, those expressions may distinguish the preteens from the teens, the young adults from those in the midst of parenthood, and even those in their sixties from those in their eighties.

Popular culture is the media—television, music, and reading. As seen in Table 16–1, popular culture is what people do in their everyday lives.

TABLE 16–1   Everyday Participation in Common Activities

Activity	Teens	Singles	Age 65+	Parents, One Income	Dual-Income Parents	Single Parents
Watch television	89%	67%	81%	74%	72%	62%
Read newspaper	49	62	87	65	68	66
Listen to recorded music	78	76	20	42	46	50
Talk on phone	62	50	47	48	40	65
Exercise	54	48	34	35	30	39
Talk with friends	34	32	30	32	29	37
Read books	20	18	35	17	27	25
Read magazines	34	21	20	14	14	12
Hobbies	39	29	39	14	19	13
Gardening	11	6	30	34	24	9

Source: Where Does the Time Go? The United Media Enterprises Report on Leisure in America (New York: Newspaper Enterprise Association, 1983).

The Scope of Popular Culture

The three main categories of popular culture are the printed media, visual media, and audio media. In a broader sense, popular culture is entertainment as well as symbolic social identity and whatever is age-group conventional rather than esoteric. The history of popular culture in America is a vast field of study in itself.

Popular Culture in History

A *History of Recreation* is more a narrative of popular culture than a full history.[1] However, it suggests the variety and change of entertainment important at different times. Just a few items can suggest the kinds of activities that have taken a prominent place in the culture at some time or place:

In the seventeenth century ballads of life and love reflected the more rural dispersed character of settlement. However, there were the recurring popular attractions of sports, shooting matches, and horse races to go along with farm festivals and country dances. The eighteenth century added the first drama in theaters as well as traveling companies, races that were more than local runs of pleasure horses, and even boat races in the East. However, for such entertainment to be "popular culture" there needed to be a crowd and some means of communication.

As the cities began to grow in the nineteenth century, popular culture grew as well. Dulles writes that now the theater came of age with offerings ranging from Shakespeare's tragedies such as *Hamlet* and *Macbeth* to farces like *The Double-Bedded Room* and *High Life Below Stairs.* Before 1840, the Bowery Theatre in New York had opened to seat 3,500 people. Traveling theater included many of the famous English actors of the day, but it was a very American melodrama, *Uncle Tom's Cabin,* that gripped half the nation. When the Swedish singer Jenny Lind made her triumphal tours of the land, pop culture and commercialism joined hands to produce Jenny Lind coats, hats, and food dishes. The identification phenomenon had hit the American market.

The circus provides an example of the rise and fall of a popular phenomenon. At first it was P. T. Barnum with his combination of entertaining acts and "freaks" (who were often manufactured in the makeup room). The tiny General Tom Thumb was real, however, and for some years was the premier attraction in the world. When the circus came to town, whether it was Barnum's three-ring extravaganza or a lesser show, all the town came to attention. The arrival by train, the great parade down Main Street, and all the aura of mystery and even danger made the circus more than entertainment; it was excitement in the midst of life's routines. The circus was more than a fad. It still exists in its theatrical version taken from one indoor arena to another by truck and train. Whatever its appeal for parents and grandparents who take their children, it is no longer the phenomenon it once was. Marcello Truzzi attributes the rise to almost 100 known circuses and menageries in 1900 and fall to about ten in 1960 to railroad problems and the loss of the circus train with its mystique of travel, the decline of the panoramic spectacle and especially the parade, and

---

[1] Foster Rhea Dulles, *A History of Recreation: America Learns to Play,* Second edition. (Englewood Cliffs, NJ: Prentice-Hall, 1965).

the rationalization that has rendered commonplace or trivial attractions once exotic and mysterious.[2] More generally, as the culture changed, the power of the circus to command attention and to be a pivotal element of the social ethos changed as well. New media and new experiences left the circus behind as more nostalgic than contemporary.

In the twentieth century there have been other cultural phenomena. Sports heroes from bare-knuckle boxer John L. Sullivan to the unique Muhammad Ali have sparked responses of adulation and admiration. Ali even became a comic book and television cartoon hero while still boxing. Probably no sport figure was as larger than life than the incomparable Babe Ruth, whose feats on and off the baseball field were legend. In Ruth's day, baseball was in truth the "national pastime" with the newspaper and eventually radio transmitting the latest feats to a waiting world. However, baseball has also lost its special status as television has brought a variety of sports into the home, and baseball was found less exciting on the cool tube than other sports.

Sport figures have had times of special symbolic glory. Notre Dame's "Four Horsemen" ran over Army and became an offensive legend bringing college football to a new level of recognition. However, few players lived in memory as did "The Babe." With all its millions of spectators, modern sport does not seem to meld national spirit as it did in a less diffuse era, despite the promotion of advertising icons on television.

Following World War I, the barnstorming pilot, the first airmail aviators, and the "Lone Eagle" Lindbergh were a cultural phenomenon. At the same time the less dramatic pool room and scattered new "Coney Islands" became something special in the lore of the land. In smaller towns, the Chautauqua circuit with its mixture of "inspiring speakers" and the entertainment of drama and music provided the high point of the summer. In other weeks the church ice-cream social was the big event. The early part of the century saw the rise of the silent films and noisy automobile races. Indoors there were jazz, ragtime, and ballroom dancing.

Popular culture is a combination of participation and symbolism. As the early pilot became a folk hero symbolizing adventure in a new triumphant technology, so popular culture crystallized for a time around a symbolic person, event, or movement. It gives new meaning to the ordinary and heightens the meaning that is already embedded there in the ordinary culture. Popular culture is ever-changing, not because it is necessarily inferior to "high culture" but because it is a phenomenon of a particular time and people. Bach may be almost timeless, but the Beatles were an expression of a time and symbol for a particular set of people within that time. There has been much "classical" music that is inferior and deserves to be forgotten and much pop music that is imaginative and creative. But "popular culture" is more than music or sport or a story. It is *the* music or story of that time in the history of a culture.

The Printed Media

Despite the amounts of time spent watching television, reading is claimed as the most valued nonsocial leisure activity among American adults.[3] Publishing is a major industry that consumes more than 10 million tons of paper a year for newspapers alone. People do read

[2] Marcello Truzzi, "The Decline of the American Circus," in M. Truzzi, ed., *Sociology and Everyday Life,* (Englewood Cliffs, NJ: Prentice-Hall, 1968).

[3] John R. Kelly, "Leisure Styles and Choices in Three Environments," *Pacific Sociological Review, 21* (1978), 187–207.

for pleasure, and with a variety of interests that can only be suggested by the offerings of a bookstore, magazine rack, or newspaper stand.

Of course, many of the books published and sold in any year are not for leisure reading. They are textbooks, standardized tests, reference works, and technical books. However, other categories of books still make up a formidable total. In 1991, over $12 billion was spent on hardcover books, and $7.7 billion on paperbacks. Of this, only 12 percent were college texts; 35 percent were trade books. Total number of books sold increased over 17 percent from 1980 to 1990 with dollar receipts more than doubling in the same period.[4]

Subjects of such books include not only various kinds of fiction but also biography, history, the arts, sports, travel, and many kinds of "how to" books read for reasons related to leisure. A major growth element of the book industry is the popular paperback that is delivered to the local supermarket, drugstore, or discount store by magazine wholesalers. These books are designed to appeal to mass markets and follow sales trends in the proportions delivered. While some are reprints of hardcover books, many are written especially for the mass paperback market according to current formulas.

Important from a leisure perspective are the mixed aims of leisure book reading. Some reading is primarily escape and relaxation. Some is intended to enrich the self through immersion in the story, culture, events, or information presented. And, more than any other major leisure activity, reading is done alone.

However, books are only one kind of reading material. At the other end of the spectrum in terms of frequency of publishing are the daily and weekly newspapers. In 1991, there were 1,586 daily, 8,546 weekly, and 574 semiweekly newspapers in the United States.[5] Of these, those that were published Sunday had a circulation of more than 62 million and those that were published daily had a circulation of about 61 million per day. If most of those papers are read, at least in part, by two or more persons, then newspaper reading would be a daily occurrence for most adult Americans. Even allowing for some inflation of those totals because of bulk deliveries, free copies, and other copies not read, something in excess of 60 million copies are purchased each day. Add an estimated 7,000 weekly and semiweekly papers and the total amount of newsprint available for reading is considerable.

Some newspaper reading is for business purposes and some for pleasure. Some takes place on commuter trains and buses, and some in a soft chair at home. Some is almost a form of study, and some used to fill time during commercials on television. Some people read the financial reports to check their investments, and others begin and end with the sport pages and the comics. Considerable reading of local newspapers may be for leisure when opportunities for an evening out are compared from listings and advertisements. The newspaper may be read for pleasure or may be instrumental toward another end or activity. In any case, more than 60 percent of the adults in the United States read a newspaper every day with more than 75 percent of the college-educated reading at least one paper a day.[6]

The production of periodicals is even more diverse and complex. Magazines include farm journals, specialized journals for technical, business, and professional readers, newsmagazines, women's magazines, comics, and other general entertainment periodicals. And

[4] *Statistical Abstract of the United States,* 1993.

[5] Ibid.

[6] Thomas M. Kando, *Leisure and Popular Culture in Transition* (St. Louis, MO: C. V. Mosby, 1975), p. 142.

then there are all the special-interest publications for rockhounds, antique-car restorers, trailer campers, tennis buffs, and amateur photographers. There are movie star magazines, gossip papers, collections of romance, mystery, and science fiction stories, and quite a variety of explicit sex publications. There are scientific journals and children's playbooks, art catalogs printed carefully on fine paper and sales ads for stamps, airplanes, or boats printed hastily on newsprint. There are magazines on almost every conceivable topic, sometimes sold only to members of a related society or club. There are in-house company magazines for employees and ad-laden glossies given away by airlines.

By any measure, reading periodicals is a common leisure pursuit. The levels and meaning may vary, but the print media are major providers of leisure.

The Visual Media

Television is the major time consumer outside of work and sleep for American adults. Some of the figures are misleading. For example, the estimate that television sets are on for an average of six hours a day does not mean that the entire household is watching all or even half that time. In fact, during a portion of those hours there may be no one watching at all and during another portion the intensity of viewing may be low as the screen is checked occasionally during a conversation or while reading the newspaper. Nevertheless, the per person average from time diaries is high enough—more than two hours a day per person.[7]

Motion pictures, on the other hand, are another story. Although attendance totaled about 1 billion in 1990, the place of films in American popular culture has been on a long-term decline. The effects of television on reading and family interaction are partly speculative, but the impact on in-theater movies is evident. Filmmakers are in an industry that has declined, leveled, and is threatened with further decline due to technological developments. Currently, total motion picture theater attendance has remained at about 1 billion per year. However, with VCRs in 70 percent of American homes, the "aftermarket" for films may equal the theater revenue.

Presentings statistics on television is almost like quantifying the atmosphere; it is there all the time almost to the extent of being taken for granted. One indication of its pervasiveness is the change in the home when the only set is off for repairs. However, that crisis is alleviated in many homes that have bought a second set to reduce conflicts over preferences or to have a small set in the bedroom or in front of the ironing board.

Television is in more than 95 percent of American homes. In some, the set is on whenever anyone is home, while in others, it is reserved for special programs and events. During one fateful period in the fall of 1963, almost the entire nation watched the drama of the burial of an assassinated president in a strange unity of electronic immediacy. More ordinary patterns of television use combine adjustment of family and personal schedules around favorite programs and anticipated specials with some use of the medium—almost regardless of what is on—for relaxation and recuperation. As a consequence, some television watching is chosen and given a high level of attention while other use is of low intensity and becomes almost a sedative. Sometimes a program grips and holds interest while at other times "viewers" are not even sure what is on.

---

[7] John P. Robinson, *Americans Use of Time Project,* University of Maryland, 1990.

On the other hand, there are "media events" that are not only popular but have wide impacts in the culture. In 1978, the eight-day series of Alex Haley's *Roots* had a total of 130 million viewers. It became a common topic of conversation and sparked new interest in family histories. Further, hundreds of thousands of whites had at least this laundered exposure to black history and some of the meanings of the slave experience. The Super Bowl and the World Series, election nights and campaign debates, and other such events are more than popular programs. They focus attention on something going on in a way that provides commonality and a highlighting to the fund of conversation. Television, more than any other medium, has the power to touch the lives of those of different regions, income levels, education, religion, ethnicity, and life styles. Through television there is a common culture experienced simultaneously in a way never before possible.

Movies, on the other hand, have a more segmented and limited clientele. There was a 65 percent decline in motion picture theater attendance since 1950 and a 25 percent drop in the number of theaters. Even the 4,000 drive-in theaters opened between 1950 and 1965 could not offset the closure of 11,000 enclosed theaters. The number of films made in Hollywood declined by about one-half between the end of World War II and 1970.

While some mass-appeal motion pictures have been quite successful financially, the trends are in two directions. One is the made-for-television movie that may be released first in commercial theaters in North America or Europe, but with the major intended audience to be reached through network television. The motion picture industry has joined television so that network production facilities are now found in and around the old movie studios. The second trend is to aim a picture at a particular segment of the market. There are pop movies for teens that are linked to cultural fads and even feature the latest television celebrities. There are the "art" films that are aimed at the urban and cosmopolitan moviegoer who retains an interest in films as "high culture." There are still the family films of the Disney studios and others. Current restrictions on what can be shown on television has kept many theaters open—a situation that may change in time.

Movies are one example of a medium that draws a disproportionate amount of its regular clientele from one end of the age spectrum. In one study, 70 percent of all moviegoers were found to be under thirty and more than 50 percent under twenty. The 50 percent under twenty who attend movies is twice the proportion of those forty to sixty. The greatest interest in the movies is on the part of teens for whom the theater, enclosed or outdoor, provides a place to go, meet, and obtain a measure of privacy. In some cases, the attraction is the darkness and the acceptability of the meeting place rather than the film itself. As a result, it is no wonder that many teen films tend to be produced on low budgets.

The new electronic technology to make a major impact on media use is the videocassette recorder/player. In 1992, 70 percent of homes with television had the VCR as well, double the number in 1986. Not only are television programs recorded, but the movie rental business has become a major enterprise. This aftermarket for movies has provided a greatly expanded source of funds for the industry. The innovation has offered increased choice and variety for home entertainment without requiring any significant change in leisure styles, commitments, or schedules. The most common use of the VCR is to play rental movies rather than recording from television.

This variety in visual formats may produce some conflict in markets. Conventional television, cable television, and videos all compete for the time available for home entertainment. What is a greater set of opportunities for the consumer becomes possible market saturation for the producers. Time scarcity, however, suggests significant markets for the greater choice offered by cable and video formats.

The Auditory Media: Popular Music

More than any other element of popular culture, music is the special mark of the adolescent, the student, and preestablishment adults. Popular music is also the element of popular culture that is most changeable. Examples of types of current popular music would be out of date before this could reach print. Not only musical groups and performers but even their styles change. While it may be possible to trace continuities of rock, country, and folk music from phase to phase, the nature of both the industry and the clientele mandates change. At the heart of the popular music enterprise is the recording industry. The market is based on novelty rather than replacement. The industry is not producing a new washer to replace the old one or a car with only fenders and chrome altered to replace the old high-mileage model. Rather, each musical production is something new. A new album may build on old loyalties to styles and performers, but it is an addition to present holdings and promoted as an experience different enough to warrant the purchase. Once bought, intensive use may prepare the young buyer for another new album followed by yet another.

In 1986, more than $2 billion worth of audio sound equipment was sold along with more than $2 billion in home music components and systems. Total record and cassette sales approached $8 billion in 1991.

Popular music is played on radio stations and performed on television. Major performers and groups travel from one large arena to another giving concerts with formidable ticket prices. Performers not yet established are at work in clubs, bars, and dance emporiums as they are used by promoters to draw a local audience. But the center of it all is the recording—on tape, disc, or videocassette—that may be sold to a million purchasers who rush to get the latest release.

While the youth market is the biggest and most enthusiastic, there are other important segments of the popular music market. Some music is ethnic, some is regional, and some even specific to a religious orientation. The folk themes and mode have been most popular among college students and those with political and cultural ideologies. Western music is distinct from the more general country style that is most popular in the South and Midwest. The Bible belt and rural America tend to be the largest market for pop religious records that are in turn quite different from the gospel music of the black culture. While soul music is sold to white as well as black purchasers, there are types of soul music that have remained largely within the black community.

These segmented markets are large enough to attract literally thousands of record promoters and producers who hope to make it big with the right combination of star and music. At the same time, there is the more general popular music market that draws buyers and listeners from a wide cross section of the population. Themes of romance predominate among these standard offerings that often feature established performers whose wide appeal is enhanced by their television exposure. The romantic ballad is a form of popular music that recurs almost regardless of the rise and fall of other types of music. The beat and the vocabulary may change somewhat, but the industry goes on. Technology and science have produced the transistor that has lowered the cost, size, and weight of radios and tape players and made music the most portable of media.

Popular Culture and Group Identity

Popular culture items are the evident signs that there is something real that can be referred to as a "youth culture." First there is the music, changing from year to year and yet always distinctive. There are always the latest styles, beats, themes, and hot performers. There is always the new album that those who are "in" know and can discuss, pro and con.

Then there is the clothing. While styles may have some continuity, the particularities are subtle signs of knowing what is right for that time and place. Clothes in the youth culture are more than approximations of acceptability. The textures, ornamentation, colors, and cuts are altered enough to be able to distinguish groups within a school. With their clothing, students announce how they hope to be identified. All symbols are not as obvious as sports letters and jackets and shorts emblazoned with Greek letters, but the intent is still there.

Other aspects of popular culture are vocabulary, dances, movies, cars, hairstyles, makeup, and possessions such as radios, jewelry, and reading material. Together they make up a set of activities, symbols, and rituals that indicate to others and assure the self that one is really a part of the chosen youth culture.

These signs and symbols are not accidental or trivial. The need to establish independence from parents and other authority in the process of developing selfhood is facilitated by some social separation. The peer group becomes both a support community and a supplier of new behavioral norms and identities. Within the youth culture there is stress on sensual expression related to the need to come to terms with personal and social sexuality. Ideas and values are expressed in ways that emphasize their difference from adult norms. The youth culture is new and real for each age cohort that passes through this period and yet maintains some of the same functions from generation to generation.

Youth Culture and Mass Marketing

One side of the youth culture phenomenon is the need for a support community and identification in the transition from childhood to adulthood. As such, popular culture elements serve to focus on and identify both independence from childhood roles and the choice of the peer community as primary. The other side of the picture is the marketing aimed toward that segment of the population. Most youths do not save. They tend to spend the money they earn, the money they receive from parents, and any other money that comes along. While there is some saving for education, most is for consumption. Further, the emphasis on what is "in" right at that time keeps youth demand for goods at a high level.

The kinds of goods already mentioned—recordings and videos, video games, movies, clothing, cars, and more transitory interests—are one part of the multi-billion-dollar market. All sorts of items that purport to enhance appearance are a response to the preoccupation with looking acceptable to gatekeepers for social participation and especially those of the other sex. And youth makes up a major part of the sports equipment market. It is no wonder that considerable effort is made to promote particular products and experiences. Advertising is through the radio and television media that are most likely to reach youth. With some radio stations programming almost exclusively for young listeners and some television programs found to have major proportions of the teen viewers, such advertising can be designed for the youth market.

However, there is more to it than sophisticated marketing techniques. Waves of popularity are augmented by carefully orchestrated campaigns promoting the product, whether it is a cult movie or a new rock album. Yet much of the promotion is done by the youths themselves as they respond to what is offered, decide what appeals to them, and develop their own standards of excellence. Fads can be promoted, but the youth market is not entirely passive. Nevertheless, choices must be made from what is available and what is known. There is little attempt to sell to youth products that last, events that can be repeated without payment, or experiences that are cost-free.

Popular Culture and Counterculture

As a result, movements have emerged that reject the dominant youth culture as well as imposition of adult norms and values. A youth culture has distinctive and identifying symbols, language, and behavior. A counterculture is not only distinctive but is set up in opposition to another and dominant culture. Persistent themes are opposition to many of the manifestations of technology, bureaucracy, capitalism, and consumerism.

The variety of countercultural groups precludes any quick generalizations. Some have been highly political with their opposition to war, racism, sexism, and educational authoritarianism. Others have withdrawn from the political scene to concentrate on self-development and inner awareness. Some have been based on a religious ideology, and still others have rejected religion as an instrument of patriarchal authority. Some movements have been ascetic and others have stressed sensuality and sexuality. Some have organized separate communities, and others have remained in the mainstream institutions. The forms and styles that come from and express ethnic cultures have been adopted by youth from majorities to symbolize their discontent with the conventional and accepted.

However, one characteristic that most have had in common is a rejection of conventional leisure—especially leisure that is dependent on the consumption of products of the economy, that exploits rather than appreciates the environment, that reflects competitive values rather than cooperation and community, and that binds participants further into obedience to the social system. Leisure is seen as a means of social control that rewards those who conform to the system rather than as a social space maximizing freedom and creativity. From this perspective, most leisure is seen as something to be bought and possessed or consumed rather than as experience. Perhaps most important, leisure as a commodity is said to separate people and place them in competition for rewards rather than bring them together into communities of mutual understanding and enrichment.

Conventional leisure activity, then, may be replaced by greater emphasis on self-awareness and communication, possession of goods by creation of new experiences, competition by cooperation, sexual exploitation by an acceptance of sensuality and an exploration of feelings, attacks on the natural world by more gentle absorption of its beauties and melodies, and conformity by a relaxed individuality. And countercultural leisure may also employ religious ideas that are outside the cultural heritage, activities that have been considered immoral, and acts that are illegal. Experimentation leads people beyond the usual to try ideas, relationships, and activities condemned by the normative culture. Included in countercultural leisure has been the use of illegal drugs, engagement in illegal acts on public and private land, and attacks on and breaking of the law.

And then there has been the strange response of the market culture. Repression, suppression, and sanctions are expected and sometimes even welcomed as a clear sign that the attacks are being felt. The use of special authority to penalize behavior that is, at least for a time, seen as dangerous to the social order and consensus is predictable. But the appropriation of many of the symbols by the market is more surprising. When the vocabularies of dissent become the lyrics of hit records, they seem less frightening. When the clothing of a counterculture becomes—modified somewhat for mass production—the uniform of the middle-class student, it loses its shock effect as well as its usefulness for social identification. When rap is used to sell cola, its ethnic origin and meanings are just one more advertising gimmick.

What happens is that symbols of rebellion are used to capture the desire of youth to be different and to belong to themselves. When music is still rejected by older generations and yet available to anyone with a radio or a cassette player, then the cost of being part of a distinctive culture is relatively low. When even the law can be broken on a street corner a block from school, then rebellion is convenient if still somewhat risky. When the right clothes can be picked up at Penney's, then no one need feel excluded by a failure to look right. So painfully developed signs of social rebellion and rejection become the commercial products of the market economy. The youth culture is a market response to a social phenomenon as well as a functional transition. And those truly desiring to shape a different cultural context for themselves must find new symbols of their values and identities. After all, when a countercultural symbol becomes a popular culture commodity, then it is time to move on to something new.

Television: The Omnipresent Entertainer

As already suggested, *the* center of popular culture is television. Not only does it hold a central place in the use of time, but it has become the primary means of communicating and validating what is popular. Figures on television use vary, depending on the method and the source. In general, estimates are as follows:[8]

Television sets are turned on an average of six hours a day in a household.

American adults watch television between two and two and one-half hours a day. That amounts to about one-third of time not obligated for work and maintenance.

Those with the most unobligated time tend to watch the most television.

Television is watched chiefly for entertainment rather than for information.

Most regular viewers indicate that they enjoy television; it is not just a way to fill time.

[8] John P. Robinson, *How Americans Use Time* (New York: Holt, Rinehart, & Winston, 1977).

Of course, there are variations by age, employment status, and other factors, as seen in Tables 16–2 and 16–3. Further, these are averages. There are still some who refuse to have a television set in the house, even if their children are continually finding excuses to visit friends in the evenings. There are others who turn the set on early in the morning and live with it all day. Absorption in the lives of daytime serial characters, vicarious participation in games, and arguments with newscasters and public figures may do a great deal to alleviate the loneliness of some who are housebound. The main change in such patterns since 1985 is in the increased use of VCRs.

However, the central fact about television is its availability. It is right there in 95 to 98 percent of American homes. While the initial cost of a color set may be considerable, the long-term cost, including electricity and repairs, is pennies an hour. The rest of the price is paid by yielding about ten minutes of the entertainment hour to commercials. Otherwise, rain or shine, early or late, alone or together, there is always television at the push of a button or turn of a knob. It is no wonder that when it comes to popular culture and nonwork time, this is what people do.

Further, according to John Robinson's time diary studies, those who like television best tend to watch it most.[9] Some television viewing is sheer relaxation, chosen because it is available and demands nothing. It is recreation and rest for the tired. Some television watching, at the other extreme, is almost cultish. Members of particular social groups plan their week so they will not miss episode six of the current miniseries or the year's hit program. The program is a primary topic of conversation at school or work the next day.

However, most viewing is a combination of interest and access. Television is always there when there is nothing better to do, but even within such residual time there is some choice. Alternatives of reading, talking, or some little task around the house are generally available. Television is chosen because there is interest in the program and some memory of past enjoyment of a similar offering. There is still choice, however biased by the low-cost availability of such entertainment.

TABLE 16–2   Hours Watching Television and Hours Available for Leisure

	Average Hours per Day Watching Television	Average Hours Available for Leisure
Teens	3.97	5.85
Age 65 and older	3.50	6.18
Singles	2.89	5.45
Parents, children grown	2.78	4.44
Single parents	2.68	3.64
One-income parents	2.52	3.41
Married, no children	2.42	5.22
Two-income parents	2.24	3.25

Source: Where Does the Time Go? The United Media Enterprises Report on Leisure in America (New York: Newspaper Enterprise Association, 1983). National sample of 1,000+.

[9] Ibid.

TABLE 16–3   Variation in Average Daily Television Viewing (Minutes)

	Men	Women
1. National average (urban)	107	80
2. Age		
18–29	129	91
30–39	97	80
40–49	109	76
50–59	102	72
3. Education		
Grade school	112	112
Some high school	121	97
High school graduate	115	76
Some college	87	63
College graduate	83	55
4. Employment		
Yes	105	62
No	148	96
5. Income		
Under $5,000	133	92
$5,000–$9,999	100	79
$10,000–$14,999	124	76
$15,000 and over	106	71
6. Day of the week		
Weekly	92	77
Saturday	109	80
Sunday	177	99

Source: John Robinson, *How Americans Use Time* (New York: Holt, Rinehart & Winston, 1977).

The Intensity of Television Viewing

Statistics on hours watching television may be misleading. Just how powerful is the impact of television?

Television has transformed nonwork time use in modern Western society. People of all ages have not just added television to their schedules but have continued to give more of their available time to it. The greatest proportion of the increase in nonwork time from 1965 to 1975 was subtracted from family care and added to television.

The immediacy and vividness of the medium may influence people in ways previously unknown. Research on changes in attitudes and actions has not, for the most part, produced clear results. There is, however, some evidence that the thousands of incidents of violence viewed before a person is eighteen may produce a numbing to its reality. The resolution of conflict by violence is the common theme of considerable television fare. The combined visual and auditory stimuli plus the prolonged exposure of an estimated seven of forty-seven waking years in a lifetime suggests that television is a phenomenon with a potential power not yet realized or measured.

In its introductory period, there was a concern that television would obliterate reading, that children would no longer play, and that families would forget how to communicate. The impacts of television have not proven to be that devastating. One reason that the results have not been so powerful may be the intensity of viewing. How many of the fifteen to eighteen hours a week are spent drowsing or in some mode of only partial attention? The 1986 Simmons market research study reported that 60 to 70 percent of television watching involved full attention with the intensity lowest for young adults and those with higher level occupations. Nevertheless, the medium has changed every aspect of time allocation, family patterns, and entertainment for all ages. One study sampled people's time use and the place of television of their lives.[10] There were variations in television use, but a number of findings were general:

1. Most television viewing is passive and relaxing, employing a low level of concentration.
2. Television may increase the time families spend together, but with low levels of attention and communication.
3. Television watching is often an escape from negative feelings such as loneliness.
4. Satisfaction declines the longer television is watched.
5. Those who watch most tend to enjoy it less and be less satisfied with their lives.

In general, watching television is found to be primarily entertainment. It is relaxing rather than challenging, passive rather than active. Insofar as the overall balance of leisure includes relaxation and low intensity in its rhythm, television provides easy, accessible, and enjoyable opportunity. The issue is the extent to which it takes the place of more demanding action and interaction. Is television so easy and pleasant that it replaces activity that is more challenging and developmental?

Along with work, television provides a kind of schedule for life. Now with the VCR and cable, there may be even more variety in that schedule. Favorite programs and events such as sports now add a new structure to the timetable. Further, the images of life presented on the screen tend to reinforce its advertising messages. Enjoyment is found in purchasing the commodities of transportation, home, and entertainment. When that much time, day after day, is devoted to a medium designed to sell products, then some impacts on values and views of life would seem inevitable. Television is not only violent, it is also the great marketplace of the world.

Consequences of Availability

Even time diary research has not carefully examined the question of leisure scheduling and the sequence of events and commitments. What are the effects on other leisure of television's availability? How is family interaction altered by the living room entertainment box? To what extent does television fill in the spaces between events considered more important and to what extent does its convenience discourage commitment to more demanding enterprises?

---

[10] R. Kubey and M. Csikszentmihalyi, *Television and the Quality of Life: How Viewing Shapes Everyday Experience* (Hillsdale, NJ: Erlbaum, 1990).

Television does replace other activity, sometimes because it is defined as more attractive and sometimes just because it's there. A television program may be seen as more interesting than talking over the day with family members, taking a walk, or starting a new book. It may take precedence, especially when there is little to talk about or if it is still hot outdoors. Or it may be chosen because it is totally undemanding. The television set does not monitor our attention, our wakefulness, or our comprehension.

One issue is the extent to which television replaces more active and demanding activity because it is easy. It does not require making appointments with other participants, arranging transportation, out-of-pocket cost, synchronizing schedules with others, or preparation. As a consequence, activity that might be more physically, emotionally, or socially demanding may be postponed for the easier program. If it is true that the costs and disciplines of some kinds of activity are precisely what makes them enriching and satisfying in the end, then the convenience of television may serve to narrow leisure participation and eliminate activity with the highest personal costs and potential rewards.

A related issue stems from the nonsocial character of television. Although television programs provide a major topic for common conversation, watching may involve little interaction with other people even when they are in the same room. If a major portion of time available for leisure is diverted from social interaction to television viewing, then the loss may be more than the mere physical passivity of the medium would suggest. If the argument is valid that leisure is a major opportunity for social bonding, for building and developing relationships, then the immediate communities of family and friendship may suffer. Both communication and common activity are needed to enjoy companionship and develop friendship. Television's easiness may be enjoyed at the cost of community.

Television and Marketing

Public television in the United States provides a variety of programs, not all of which are "educational." The quality of drama, the arts, and special event coverage on public television is frequently quite high. Nevertheless, most sets are tuned to commercial channels most of the time despite the great variety of cable and the VCR. The criterion of programming on commercial television is financial. Commercial television is dominated by the major networks, each of which supplies in some form more than 90 percent of the programming for its own flagship stations and its affiliates. Even the relatively few independent stations depend on network-produced programs for most of their nonlocal offerings.

The networks are supported by the selling of programs to the stations and of advertising time to a wide variety of sponsors. Each local station carries network advertising and then sells more advertising time locally or through a marketing agreement. The income that makes possible the enormous expenses of sending programs without fees into the homes of America is from advertising time sold. The networks are brokers who sell an audience to corporations who have a message—usually a product promotion—to put before that audience.

Marketing research employs several methods, including phone surveys, time diaries, and recording devices on home sets, to estimate how many people watch a program, who they are, and sometimes their response to the advertising. Networks present plans and possibilities to potential sponsors. The item being sold is the audience and advertising time, with the program usually a vehicle to attract that set of viewers. Those with the incomes to purchase Cadillacs and second homes may be more valued to the sponsor than 10 million low-income people. Programs are often aimed at particular sales groups—teens, families making durable goods purchases such as household appliances, or those who buy food and household products. The intent is to reach those whose choices can be directed toward the product.

All of this is hardly startling or new. However, it has considerable influence on the leisure of Americans. When the largest single proportion of time for leisure is devoted to a marketing device, then it would be no surprise if the aims of the medium were of some influence. Not only is the advertising intended to persuade viewers that they will be happier, more potent, more attractive, more valued, or more something if they are able to make the recommended purchase, but the programs themselves tend to be commodity-intensive. People drive new cars, live in gracious homes, fly off on interesting trips, and in general seem to have stimulating social environments. They are seldom alone, and when alone are subject to depression or physical attack. They go to restaurants and nightclubs, but seldom to a quiet spot in the woods where the light would be poor for the camera. They have parties rather than read, drive rather than walk, and change their clothes a lot. Their lives seem to be defined by their possessions.

The image of life presented in most—not all—such programs is complementary to the intent of the sponsors. It is more than a question of wrecking cars built by competitive manufacturers and polishing your own product. It is a view of life and especially of leisure that stresses the consumption of economic goods. It is a commodity culture rather than one that emphasizes self-development, inner richness, and the spontaneity gained in freedom from dependence on the market. Television is much more than a major option for nonwork time; it is an in-home visualization of a way of life only occasionally countered by a splash of realism or introspection.

Television as a Determinative Technology

Technology has reshaped leisure more than once. The three developments that may have done the most to alter the forms of modern Western leisure are printing, the automobile, and now television. Along with major technology advances that reshaped the entire economy, these three have altered the content of leisure. Reading and printed material are now assumed in so much leisure that we are hardly conscious of the medium. The automobile has altered the ecology of leisure. Now television has invaded leisure schedules to the extent that research on time use, family interaction, and mass culture done before the early 1950s is only of historical interest (see Table 16–4).

TABLE 16–4   Television and Radio Use, 1950, 1970, and 1990

Households With	1950	1970	1990
Radio sets (percent)	92.6	98.6	99.0
Average number	2.1	5.1	5.6
Television sets (percent)	9.0	95.3	98.2
Average number	1.01	1.4	2.1
Average viewing per day (hours)	4.6	5.9	7.2
Cable (percent)	0	6.7	58.9
VCRs (percent)	0	0	71.9

Source: Statistical Abstract of the United States, 1993.

Popular Culture as Leisure

Is popular culture something less than "real leisure"? Some comparison of popular culture and "the arts" is inevitable. While today's pop product may be art in the future, the usual fate of popular music, art, drama, and other items is oblivion. As already suggested, the essence of popular culture is that it provides a contemporary means of social identification at the same time that it delivers a commercial message. Does this make pop culture in some sense inferior and unworthy of the time of people who use their leisure well?

If leisure is defined in terms of freedom and then no kind of activity can be ruled out by its content alone. Rather, leisure choices are both personal and social. They are in part related to what Herbert Gans calls a "taste culture."[11] He suggests the obvious—that some culture is popular because people want it. They have learned to enjoy and appreciate particular forms in music and other arts. What will stand the test of time is a question about which we can speculate; however, it is not necessary to wait for the judgment of the ages to know that a sizable taste culture is responding to some aspect of popular culture now. Further, people choose to invest some of their discretionary time and financial resources in that cultural offering. As such, it is a form of leisure for which the types and intensities of satisfaction are varied and may be partly measured. Whatever their merits according to particular standards of the arts, rock music and chamber music may both be played or listened to as leisure.

Summary of Issues

Popular culture includes leisure that might be described as what most people do in most of their leisure. Reading and television are major elements in the leisure of most North Americans. However, popular culture includes special kinds of music, insignia, symbols, clothing, transportation, equipment, and games. Popular culture is generally dependent on the market for availability and distribution, but is more than the concoction of entrepreneurs.

Popular culture is popular not only because of its availability but also because it expresses some developmental reality for a group traveling through its life course. The most dramatic example is the youth cohort with its music that expresses themes of independence, sensuality, sexuality, and belonging. The market may not only supply but promote the latest album and performer, but consumer response requires some contact with authentic meaning for young people and their need to identify with their own group. In less dramatic ways, popular culture changes through the life course and varies according to ethnic and regional identification. Both personal and social identity are tied up in the kinds of popular culture selected as attractive and symbolic of self-definition and presentation.

Television, of course, is the omnipresent entertainer—remarkable in availability and low cost as well as the time devoted to watching. However, the intensity of involvement with television may be quite low in comparison to other kinds of leisure. Its influence as a commercial venture in sales promotion may not be commensurate with the time the set is

---

[11] Herbert J. Gans, *Popular Culture and High Culture* (New York: Basic Books, 1974).

turned on. While some television is given high priority in leisure schedules, other viewing is residual and more a matter of relaxation and the filling of time. Nevertheless, its availability may lessen participation in more demanding forms of activity and communication as well as promote a market-oriented lifestyle.

HIGHLIGHTS

1. Items of popular culture are symbols of social identification through the life course that express changing developmental preoccupations.
2. Visual, printed, and auditory media are major elements in the economy with considerable overlap and reinforcement.
3. The market makes items of popular culture available, but persistent acceptance by an age cohort requires that they be authentic expressions of common goals and concerns.
4. Television is watched with varying intensity due to its easy availability and low cost. It may replace activity that is more costly, difficult to arrange, or personally demanding.
5. The variety of "taste cultures" in our society reflects different backgrounds and associations. Quality is not determined simply by style.

Discussion Questions

1. In what ways may popular culture be something less than leisure?

2. Are there new technologies on the horizon that, like television, may have a great impact on popular leisure?

3. How is television likely to develop as in-home entertainment? Will it become more or less the predominant filler of nonwork time?

4. In what ways does television enrich the lives of many children? In what ways may it limit their leisure? Their social development? Their learning?

5. Do you agree that there are different "taste cultures" but no legitimate value differentiation into "high culture" and "low culture"? Is culture whatever people choose to do?

6. How do the popular culture symbols of a youth cohort change? What evidence is there that music, clothing, and other items are manipulated by their promoters? How do they reflect the fundamental preoccupations of the youth cohort?

7. How have counterculture expressions been adopted by popular culture suppliers? Why is there a market for what were once symbols of protest?

8. Explain why the video technology was such an instant marketing success.

9. What are the impacts of so much television on how we view life?

Bibliography

Bellah, R. N., R. Madsen, W. Sullivan, A. Swiedler, & S. Tipton, *Habits of the Heart.* Berkeley: University of California Press, 1985.

Birenbaum, Arnold, and Edward Sagarin, eds., *People in Places.* New York: Praeger, 1973.

Dulles, Foster R., *A History of Recreation: America Learns to Play,* Second edition. Englewood Cliffs, NJ.: Prentice-Hall, 1965.

Ewen, Stuart, *Captains of Consciousness: Advertising and the Social Roots of the Consumer Culture.* New York: McGraw Hill, 1976.

Gans, Herbert J., *Popular Culture and High Culture.* New York: Basic Books, 1974.

Kando, Thomas M., *Leisure and Popular Culture in Transition,* Second edition. St. Louis, MO: C. V. Mosby, 1980.

Kubey, Robert and M. Csikszentmihalyi, *Television and the Quality of Life: How Viewing Shapes Everyday Experience.* Hillsdale, NJ: L. Erlbaum, 1990.

Lewis, George H., ed., *Side-Saddle on the Golden Calf.* Pacific Palisades, CA: Goodyear, 1972.

Truzzi, Marcello, ed., *Sociology for Pleasure.* Englewood Cliffs, NJ: Prentice-Hall, 1974.

Chapter **17**

═══════════════════════════════

Travel and Tourism

Leisure travel is more than a summer vacation trip or a flight to the ski slopes. Some institutions of "high culture"—museums and concert halls—are still in the central city many miles from most patrons. Outdoor recreation opportunities usually require access to a car for even the least planned family picnic. The scheduling of sports events for children and youths requires transportation within and between communities. The dispersed population makes dropping in on relatives— the equivalent of the old neighborhood kin network—a trip. Travel *to* leisure sites is a daily and weekly matter and not reserved for the "big trip."

However, the vacation trip is still a major factor in leisure patterns. People in the United States took more than 465 million pleasure trips in 1991. Some 42 million visited another country. Despite the growth of air travel and the promotions of travel arrangers, more than 80 percent of those trips were taken by car. The one- to two-week auto trip is still the standard American vacation.

There seems to be something about travel that is appealing. If not, how can we explain the following:

> A couple fight traffic tie-ups for two hours each way to leave their comfortable, air-conditioned home in Los Angeles County and weekend in their little trailer in the desert.

> A family of five squeezes into a compact car for a yearly trip during which six days are spent in the car, four days visiting relatives who are not really very congenial, and four days camping in a national forest.

> A government employee accepts a lateral transfer that is different from her present job only in its requirement that ten days to two weeks of every month be spent in travel around the country.

> A family with young children saves for three years so that accumulated vacation time can be employed in a cross-country trip that will involve driving close

to 10,000 miles. This trip is anticipated as the highlight of the half-decade and a peak experience for the parenting years.

The first thing that the just-retired couple does is take a three-month trip that has been planned for four years to integrate visiting a number of natural wonders, old friends, and long-scattered kin.

Travel to leisure and travel as leisure are central to the plans, hopes, and experiences of most Americans who are not ruled out of travel by poverty. Why do people place such importance on travel? How do they travel? And, what kinds of problems are associated with leisure travel?

ISSUES

Is leisure travel just a matter of getting to a destination, or is the experience of traveling part of the satisfaction?

Do only the wealthy travel for leisure?

How are most leisure trips taken?

How do travel styles change through the life course?

Does modern leisure require private transportation?

Tourism is usually defined as travel requiring an overnight stay or as travel of more than 100 miles. In this chapter, the focus will be on travel for recreation purposes. Of the over 660 million trips made a year in the United States, about two-thirds are for the purpose of visiting family or friends or for leisure (see Table 17–1). Recreation travel is more than just going from one place to another to play. Recreational tourism is leisure on the move, engaging in activity away from home in which travel is at least part of the satisfaction sought. Like other leisure, travel combines a number of motivations and satisfactions. Nevertheless, fundamental to recreation tourism is the premise that people like to travel, to get away and go somewhere.

More than 120 million people in the United States take at least one trip lasting ten days or more each year. The one- to two-week auto trip is still the standard American vacation despite the increase in the number of trips taken by air. There are, however, many kinds of leisure travel. Among the most common are

The multipurpose vacation trip combining destinations

The multipurpose local trip: to the shopping center, to deliver an item to a friend and pause for a chat, and to pick up the kids at the pool

The business trip that includes some leisure opportunities and associations

The weekend trip to a recreation destination

The weekend trip to visit family or friends

The day trip to a recreation destination

The day trip to visit family or friends

The day trip primarily for the drive itself

Local trips to a recreation site or program

Local trips to prepare for leisure: to purchase or repair equipment, make arrangements for a later event, etc.

The trip to the second home or time-share

However, any list is misleading because of the mixture of purposes and motivations for so many trips. Further, the car is more than a means of transportation. Its styles and shapes, equipment and symbols, as well as the sense of power and movement it provides are signs of social identity and a means to freedom. With the automobile, the individual can make a decision and effectuate a result, control power and speed, demonstrate social status in multiple locations, and actually do something that seems to provide an alterative to so many of the limitations of life.

Most recreation-related travel does not require direct support services. The means of transportation is the multipurpose car. Destinations are familiar and nearby. Meals away from home are taken at facilities that combine local and transient trade. Plans and arrangements are simple and made within the household decision modes. Therefore, only recreation travel that is at least over one night and of more than local distance requires the support of special business. For the most part, recreation travel businesses serve trips that encompass at least a weekend and range up to extended travel for vacations or even an entire season. There are a number of statistical indications that such trips provide a number of major markets (see Table 17–2).

TABLE 17–1   Travel by U.S. Residents, 1991

	Trips (in millions)	Person-Trips (in millions)
Total	664	1,306
Purpose		
Visit family, friends	226 (34%)	496
Other pleasure	240 (36%)	496
Business, convention	153 (23%)	209
Other	46 (7%)	104
Mode of transport		
Auto, truck, RV	498 (75%)	1,045
Airplane	133 (20%)	209
Other	33 (5%)	52
Vacation trip	418	901
Weekend trip	392	770

Source: U.S. Travel Data Center, 1991 National Travel Survey, Washington, DC.

TABLE 17–2   Business Receipts and Employment in Travel Industry Sectors

	Receipts ($ million)	Employment
Total	$334,881	10,027,000
Transportation		
Air	$45,324	751,000
Bus	$2,000	
Rail	$888	
Motel, hotel	$60,490	1,595,000
Eating and drinking businesses	$182,044	6,565,000
Amusement and recreation services	$44,135	1,089,000

Source: U.S. Travel Data Center, *The 1990–91 Economic Review of Travel in America* (Washington, DC).

For the traveler, one estimate is that transportation accounts for thirty-five cents of every dollar spent followed by twenty-two cents for food, nineteen cents for lodging, twelve cents for entertainment and recreation, and twelve cents for incidentals.[1]

The Costs of Leisure Travel

The most evident difference setting apart the leisure of the rich is that they go farther to do it. Almost whatever "it" is, the rich either provide private opportunities for themselves with clubs, associations, and private holdings or are able to expand their opportunities by going to the most desirable locations. The rich have their own pools for swimming, their own clubs for gambling, and their own courses for golf. They pay high fees to avoid the crowding that besets most people who must rely on public or commercial provisions. In much the same way, the wealthy may fly to Aspen or Chamonix for skiing rather than join the lines at the bottom of the smaller New Hampshire hill. They fly to London for theater and shopping rather than head back into the city. And even when they shop, they go to the stores where comfort, service, and convenience make purchasing a pleasure.

The leisure of the poor is also characterized by its travel component—or rather by its lack of travel. Even a trip across the city is formidable when you do not have a car. A drive to the beach is problematic on a hot afternoon when the old car has an unreliable cooling system. And visiting relatives 200 miles away is more than a pleasant spin in an old car or on the bus or train. It is no accident that there is a strong correlation between income and travel (see Table 17–3).

For those who are less than wealthy but have reliable incomes, leisure travel emerges in a cost-determined way. The middle-income family has at least one car in condition for a long trip—usually in the summer. However, that trip must be planned in ways that meet

[1] Robert W. McIntosh and C. R. Goeldner, *Tourism: Principles, Practices, and Philosophies,* Fifth edition (New York: John Wiley, 1986), p. 16.

TABLE 17–3   Domestic and International Travel by U.S. Adults

	Domestic		International
	One Last Year	Four or More Last Year	One or More Vacations in Last Three Years
Total	50.3%	16.8%	7.5%
Male	50.6	18.8	3.9
Female	50.0	15.0	4.0
Income			
Under $10,000	25.9	5.6	2.2
$10,000–$19,999	41.8	12.2	4.7
$20,000–$29,999	53.3	17.2	6.7
$30,000–$39,999	60.9	22.5	8.4
$40,000 or more	63.5	23.9	13.4
$50,000 or more	66.2	26.2	15.7

Source: Simmons Market Research Bureau, 1986.

the budget. Some camping may be done along the way to save money. The route may be planned to include stopovers with relatives and friends for financial as well as social reasons. The mode of travel is adjusted to the age and endurance of both children and parents. Unless the trip is the special one for which savings and credit cards allow an extraordinary set of expenditures, the costs are relatively modest and carefully controlled.

Contrast this with the rich on the one hand and with the travel of the poor on the other. When a California or Oregon farm-labor family heads back to Texas and the extended family for Christmas, the aim is just to get there. The entire family is packed into a car of uncertain reliability for a drive that will continue day and night until arrival in a south Texas town forty or sixty hours later. Fast foods are purchased along the road with as few stops as possible. Getting there is not "half the fun" because even the modest costs of middle-class travel are out of the question. If the car breaks down, a tourist cabin on the edge of town will be sought at a minimum cost during the repair period. The aim of the trip is to bring the family together for the holidays and the travel is just a means to that end. More than any other kind of leisure, travel is related to discretionary income.

Who Are the Travelers?

The simplest answer to this question is fundamental to more sophisticated answers. Those who travel, especially for pleasure, are those who can afford it. Granted this basic factor, what are other elements in travel participation?

Age.   Young adults are a major travel-oriented group. However, the forty- to fifty-five age group is also prone to recreation travel, and early-retirement adults are a significant travel market. In general, Americans seem to be more likely to travel for pleasure as each generation moves into adulthood. More and more, travel is an expectation of life styles.

Family Life Cycle.   Young, single adults are more likely to engage in commercial travel than those who are married. Further, young parents, with the constraints of child rearing and values geared toward the establishment of a family, are more likely to stay near home for their leisure. Young parents who are striving to build the basis for a work career are also more likely to invest time in work-oriented activity. However, as children become older and eventually leave home, the parents become better able to travel. Older adults who combine freedom from parenting with adequate incomes often choose to do the traveling that they have postponed. However, we should be careful not to assume that those who are twenty-five to thirty now will, thirty years from now, travel at the same rates as those currently fifty-five to sixty. Rather, most indications are that leisure travel is more an expectation for each cohort entering the life cycle.

Education.   In modern society, education is highly correlated to income. Nevertheless, the interests and values developed in higher education are another factor in propensity to travel. Students in higher education, without high incomes, also tend to travel widely if inexpensively. The interests in other places and cultures that are fostered through education are combined with a greater confidence in coping with different environments and people.

Time.   Too much attention has been given to the presumed reduction in average weekly employment hours. The significant time factor in recreation travel is not the average time spent at work but the blocks of time available. Travel requires more than coming home from a job an hour earlier; it requires the long weekend, the vacation, or the ability to control schedules of work and family. Trends in allocating such blocks of time are not clear. More and more people are employed in services—retailing and health care, for example—that call for varied schedules and some weekends on the job. On the other hand, many corporations are experimenting with greater flexibility in work schedules. Also, the increase in women's employment may complicate the ability of a family to free a common period for travel while adding to the financial resources for travel. In general, however, those with the greatest discretion over their schedules are most likely to be able to travel. These include students and the retired as well as the single and those at higher levels of employment.

Demographic Trends.   The population of the United States is aging. There will be a higher proportion as well as a greater number of retirement-age people. Families are smaller and the child-rearing phase of the life course is compressed into a shorter period. Most women, including mothers, will be employed outside the home. Marriages are increasingly unstable, producing a higher proportion of the adult population in some stage of transition, in or out of a marriage, and at all ages. The travel characteristics of particular age groups may become more varied as income, family context, work situations, and life styles and orientations become more differentiated. The decrease in the young adult population and increase in those approaching and entering retirement will affect travel markets in the coming decades.

Income and other factors are the basis for the *resources* for leisure travel. Travel requires money and time and is directed by interest. However, there is another important aspect of travel: *style.* In order to understand who travels, we need to know more than income and age characteristics. We need to know about the styles of travel of various groups in the society.

Why Choose to Travel?

As traffic jams on the freeways increased in Los Angeles County in the 1960s, many confidently predicted that the future of leisure was at home. People would increasingly seek to provide for themselves in ways that did not require going anywhere. No doubt many have done just this, but the appeal of going somewhere for leisure has been too powerful to turn all Americans into homebodies. It is true that travel takes time and may be reserved for long weekends and vacations, but Americans still take to the roads by the millions when they get the chance. What is the appeal of travel?

No two trips may be quite alike, but reported satisfactions tend to be related to three elements of the trip: (1) the trip itself, including anticipations and recollections, (2) the destinations, and (3) the companions. However, there is also an element of escape in travel that is reported for both short and longer trips.[2] There is something refreshing about getting into a different environment and away from the obligations of work, home, and community. A trip may be described as relaxing and restful for some. Others may describe the escape from the telephone, from unfinished tasks around the house, from too familiar environments, and even from too familiar people. No kind of leisure is as likely to be described in terms of compensation and escape as travel. Only entertainments such as television, movies, or reading are found as restful. The trip is more than a change; it is getting away as well as getting somewhere.

However, that is not all. There are *satisfactions intrinsic to the experience:* "A drive in the country not only gets me outdoors but gives a feeling of freedom from all the restrictions of work and the city." "I like being able to decide spontaneously where we will go and which way we will turn," "It isn't just the fall foliage that is appealing; it is also the openness of the horizon and the road away from everything that reminds me of all the things I have to do."

There are *satisfactions in the companionship:* "The car is the only place our family is really together. It's when we get in touch with the kids and what is going on in their lives." "We always camp and travel with friends and have found that most of our deepest friendships have developed from our summer trips." "We try to renew at least one old relationship on our vacation trips and often find that to be the high point of the trip." "There's nothing like going somewhere together among strangers to bring a couple back together in communication."

There are *satisfactions in the destinations:* "There's something about the ocean that just isn't like anything else. The kids like the sand, my wife likes to relax and sun on the beach, and I like the sound of the surf. Whatever it is, the ocean seems to pull us back every year." "The trip to Disneyland was the high point of those early years with the children."

[2] John R. Kelly, "Situational and Social Factors in Leisure Decisions," *Pacific Sociological Review,* 21 (1978), 313–330.

A Blue-Collar Vacation

Jim Crosby and his family have known all year pretty much what they would be doing the first three weeks in August. Jim has enough seniority at the steel mill to choose his vacation time. For the past six years that time has been in August. Since the last six or seven days of the vacation are devoted to some postponed fix-up projects around the house, the first weeks are for the annual vacation trip. It's a long drive from northern California to the hometown in Nebraska not far from the Wyoming border where Jim's parents still live. Emily's mother is not in good health and her father died a few years ago, so there is considerable pressure on her to get back to the home community in the summer. One summer she flew to Denver in June and stayed through July, but this year she will go both ways in the family car.

Their oldest son is not going this year, but will stay to finish up his baseball season and work at a local fast-food establishment. When he was in a Little League program, their vacation was shifted from July to August to accommodate his season. The summer programs that have attracted the two younger daughters wind down at the end of July so that August remains the vacation time despite the heat. However, the Crosbys have developed a way of coping with the hot weather. They drive to Lake Tahoe in the morning and spend the afternoon on the beach and in the cool gambling casinos. Then, after supper, they start down the mountainside and drive across the hottest parts of Nevada and Utah at night. That way they also cut out a day of driving and have a little longer to visit family and old friends.

The traditional family picnic on their first Sunday in Nebraska enables the Crosbys to see cousins and other more distant relatives whom they might otherwise miss. Also, they have two standing dinner dates with old high school friends. However, most of the eight days in the old hometown are spent with more immediate family—eating, talking, and reestablishing contact.

This year, partly due to illness and consequent pressures to maximize time with family, there will be no detour on the way home. However, they all remember the tour north to Yellowstone Park a few years ago and the year they took an extra week to head south to the Grand Canyon. This summer there will be a second stop at Tahoe and a day of camping in the Rockies on the way home. Also, the whole family will camp while fishing in the Medicine Bow National Forest on the second weekend.

The satisfactions of the trip are many and varied. There has been less and less enthusiasm from the children as they got older and more involved in their local opportunities and later in jobs. However, this renewal of family ties has meant a lot to them all. Jim and Emily feel considerable obligation to return as their parents have gotten older, but they also find great satisfaction in renewing those old relationships. This year, the first time with only four going, they also remember with pleasure the long hours and different experiences of driving and camping as a family unit. Maybe in a few years only the two parents will be heading east, and they may fly. So now they are looking forward to the trip, to being together, to familiar sights and natural beauty, and even to revisiting a couple of restaurants discovered years ago along the way.

"We try to get up to the mountains at least once a month in the summer to camp and hike and just be where the air is clean and the nights are cold." "If I have to work twice as hard for a month to get ready for my winter ski trip, it's worth it. There's just nothing like it!"

And, of course, there are the *obligations:* "My folks expect us to come back every Christmas. Even when the kids would rather have the holiday at home, we feel we have to go."

There are *educational factors:* "We think it's important for the kids to know something about their country, so we aim for the places that are historical like Boston and Williamsburg and the Capitol."

Which reasons for choosing to travel are most important? It depends on the ages of those children, on the opportunities afforded at home and at work, on the quality of companionship experienced, on the weather and natural resources, and on what is anticipated and remembered. Some love the planning. Some love to go back through the slides taken along the way. Some just like the experience of movement and speed. Leisure travel is getting away, going, and arriving. And some say that the best part is getting back home.

There have been a number of speculations about why people like to travel. Lists may combine the attractions of site-specific activities such as gambling, water skiing, or fishing with psychological outcomes such as relaxation, escape, stimulation, change, excitement, and spiritual and intellectual growth. Some travelers seek the new and exotic locale and experience. Others prefer the familiar and secure. Some never repeat a trip and others go the same place every year. Some head for the cities and others for the wilderness. Advertising is found to be a factor in attracting people to tours and commercial destinations. Recollected satisfactions from the past are important to some who develop a travel style much like that remembered from their childhood. Others are drawn into travel by circumstances and find their own set of reasons for continuing.

Among the themes that emerge in studies of travel are a number of dimensions that include both relaxation and activity, familiarity and novelty, dependence and autonomy, and order and disorder.[3] One analysis suggests that the tourist is seeking to renew a relation to the history and meaning of the social world rather than looking for the novel.[4]

A phenomenon of leisure travel that seems paradoxical is that many are attracted to the familiar and predictable rather than to the novel. Not only do many people go to the same place by the same route week after week or year after year, but even in new places some travelers seek out familiar accommodations. The rising phenomenon of the travel business is standardization. Chains of motels and hotels may even have room designs and prices that are the same nationwide. Chains of eating establishments have a single menu printed for the season in every state in the Union. In some, frozen entrees are shipped from central kitchens and cooked in microwave ovens on the site. The visitor knows before entering the restaurant exactly what will be available and at what price.

The packages developed and marketed by many travel agencies also advertise reliability and security. They provide a way of visiting a new place and even a strange culture with predictable provision of rooms, meals, guides, shopping opportunities, and language assistance. It is possible to *see* a new culture without having to experience it and *visit* a famous attraction without becoming lost in it. As one motel chain advertises, there are "no surprises."

Such provisions seem to appeal to seemingly contradictory motivations for travel. People want to feel secure while having a new experience. They like to meet new people without the risk of being left out or alone. They would like to try the water of a different city

---

[3] B. O'Rourke, "Travel in the Recreational Experience," *Journal of Leisure Research,* 6 (1974), 140–156.

[4] Dean McCannell, *The Tourist: A New Theory of the Leisure Class* (New York: Schocken, 1976).

or culture without losing the option of a quick withdrawal into safety. They would like the excitement of travel without the loss of conveniences. They like new places with predictable prices. In short, a form of travel that lies somewhere between repetition and adventure is the package that takes us somewhere new in a plastic bubble. The popularity of such travel is further evidence of the mixed motivations involved in the leisure trip.

Critical Issues

Two critical issues have received considerable attention in recent analyses of tourism. The first is the tendency to produce special worlds for tourists. The "back world" of authentic life is protected by host cultures. The tourist is presented with a fake world that is intended to appeal to travelers who prefer a kind of entertainment to any real encounter the authentic, different, and often challenging cultures. The great destinations are manufactured for the tourist to meet expectations and provide a colorful and safe experience. The ultimate in such created destinations is, of course, Disney World, where the Magic Kingdom is a fake representation of the artificial world of the Disney films. The design of the streets is intended to extract money from the tourist in rows of shops. And there is the World Showcase in which nothing is real and yet everything claims to depict some attractive part of the tourist world. Wherever the tourist goes, there is the contrived show that claims to give a safe taste of another culture, preferable in a glamorous and expurgated form. The tourist sees a show and the authentic culture remains hidden.

The second issue is that of the impacts of tourism on host cultures. It was once assumed that the tourist expenditure was an unmitigated economic gain for the countries being visited. More recent studies have identified costs. In many cases the natural environments are being damaged or destroyed by hordes of tourists. In others, places of natural beauty are closed off to local residents by the development of resorts. Most of the profits go to investors, most often multinational corporations that specialize in mass tourism. Tourism is, after all, very big business designed to maximize a return on investments in the hundreds of millions of dollars. The jobs for locals tend to be low-income services rather than management. In some locales, the natives are even forced out of their environments when prime sites are bought by developers.

These two problems have produced a reaction. There is a new movement of ecotourism or "green" tourism. Some individual tourists arrange their travel to engage authentic cultures most fully and with the least possible negative impacts. They attempt to penetrate the screen of commercial attractions to be with local residents and in the host culture. In response to this different style of travel, some environmental and travel organizations have developed programs for ecotourists that bypass customary attractions to find where people really live and natural environments are relatively unspoiled. The problem, or course is that even ecotourism has impacts, especially in rare and fragile locales and communities. It is clear, however, that despite the enormous growth of commercial tourism that provides a show and minimizes the challenge of the unexpected, there are some travelers who seek more authentic experiences that may even support indigenous cultures and protect special environments.

Styles of Travel

The variety of travel styles has been documented in a number of studies. From a business perspective, these stylistic differences are one approach to identifying and segmenting the tourism market. From a leisure perspective, it is important to recognize the extent to which the recreational dimensions of the trip or vacation are central to the overall style. Economic resources provide a basis for tourism decisions, but cultural values and leisure orientations fill in the content.

One market analysis of tourism was conducted in Canada in the 1970s.[5] The market was divided among four life style groups:

Extravagant consumers (18 percent)—Higher income persons of all age groups who travel distances and expect a high level of service.

Nature people (20 percent)—Young, often single, and with higher education. Go to new and different places to avoid schedules and routines.

Playsters (23 percent)—Young, disproportionately male, who seek pleasure, activity, and fun.

Cautious homebodies (39 percent)—Older, less affluent, and with less education. Want safety, security, and a predictable environment.

A second analysis was carried out on the national sample using adjectives that would describe their ideal vacation. These adjectives clustered into the following ideal vacation types:

Peace and quiet (20 percent)—Middle-age people of less than average discretionary income who want a relaxing setting.

Aesthetic appreciation (22 percent)—Well-educated people who seek an educational experience.

Hot winter (19 percent)—Both luxury- and fun-seekers who want to get out of the cold winter and onto the beach.

Grand hotel (19 percent)—A luxury vacation with service, good food, and entertainment.

Inexpensive active (9 percent)—Low cost and active fun, meeting other younger people.

Relatives and friends (12 percent)—Family-centered vacation with shared experiences for middle-income people of modest incomes.

While the percentages might shift for a different population base, the lifestyle and vacation typologies illustrate the variety in aims and agendas associated with leisure travel. There is no single image of the traveler that fits even half of all those who take trips. There are, however, a number of consistent dimensions. The first is that of companions. The as-

[5] Paul Burak, "Designing Products for the Leisure Travel Market," in Robert C. Mill and A. M. Morrison, *The Tourism System* (Englewood Cliffs, NJ: Prentice-Hall, 1985), pp. 86–87.

sociations of travel are central to the choices of environments and activities. As a consequence, age and place in the family lifecycle are critical to tourism decisions. Second, cost is a major factor for all those with limited discretionary incomes, at least 80 to 90 percent of those who travel. And, third, there would appear to be some consistency between overall leisure styles and vacation styles. Travelers do not become completely different people when they leave home. This consistency with general patterns of values, resources, and activities is demonstrated by another set of vacation types.

Budget Travelers. Almost 28 percent of the sample were interested in travel, but always at a price. They are often campers and seek educational gains in their travel. They tend to be middle-income adults with some college education. They are least likely to use credit for travel. Their occupations are often managerial, and they may have begun families earlier than the rest of the sample.[6]

Adventurers. Those who seek excitement and are willing to pay for it comprise 24 percent of the sample. They like to relate accounts of the challenge and uniqueness of their trips. They are younger, have higher incomes, and are financially optimistic. More sophisticated in their social life, they are least home-oriented, most nontraditional in role expectations, and not involved in community organizations, even cultural ones. They want to "get out and go."

Homebodies. Twenty percent are distinctive in the travel they do not do. They have no travel plans even though they may have enjoyed some vacation travel in the past. Neither camping nor educational tours interest them. They are more withdrawn socially and concentrate their lives on home activities and resources. They are the oldest group, least optimistic financially despite relatively high current incomes, and least interested in the world outside their own households.

Vacationers. This smaller set, 7 percent of the sample, are the opposite of the homebodies. They like to travel, are constantly making plans and changing them, leave home on weekends more frequently, and talk about vacations a lot. They would like to travel first-class, even on credit. They tend to be quite active socially even though their incomes and education levels are the lowest of the five styles.

Moderates. More than 20 percent like to travel, but within limits. They are low in inclinations to camp or engage in sports. They are middle level in income and education and without definitive characteristics in relation to vacations. Vacation travel is just one interest among many. In this analysis, they are the residual category with travel orientations difficult to define as a reachable market.

In general, the variety of travel styles reflects the variety in lifestyles within the culture. Travel takes a place within that overall scheme of leisure and life. For some, it is a

[6] W. D. Perrault, D. K. Darden, and W. R. Darden, "A Psychological Classification of Vacation Life Styles," *Journal of Leisure Research*, 9 (1977), 208–224.

dominant form of leisure. For most, it is one interest among many and restricted by the high costs of time and money. Nevertheless, there are different styles of travel that require different support services and marketing approaches.

A more general and yet useful approach to market segmentation focuses on salient characteristics of the sample. For example, styles of travel vary according to place in the family cycle. Further, the kinds of services and accommodations desired also vary according to the composition and aims of the travel group. Leisure orientations as well as resources and constraints vary through the life course. Therefore, the importance and modes of recreation travel are significantly affected by role changes and transitions. For example

Those who are not married usually hope to travel to environments where they will have opportunities for social interaction with age peers.

Two-career couples may have discretionary income but are limited by the necessity of coordinating two work schedules as well as the aims of establishing and advancing work careers. Time tends to be the scarce resource.

Parents of preschool children most often travel, when they travel at all, in ways that utilize space and services for small children. Unless they leave the children behind for a special trip by air, they most often vacation by car, with distances regulated each day by childcare logistics. However, they also value the opportunities to use the trip as a nurturing and companionship experience for the family.

As children move through the school years, their schedules become a greater determinative factor in travel decisions. Not only the school year but also summer activities may limit the vacation trip to late summer. Again, the orientation of travel tends to be quite familial, with destinations chosen that facilitate common activity and interaction.

Postlaunching adults, whose children live away from home, have a new schedule freedom and often greater financial resources. Travel may be redirected toward the kind of trips that were neither possible nor preferred in the more familial periods. Air travel, urban destinations, historical and cultural attractions, and nonfamilial group travel are often of interest. In a period when the present may be valued because an end is recognized, the possibility of investment in present and postponed experiences may increase the likelihood of more cost-intensive tourism. Also, services sought can be chosen more for convenience and comfort than for price.

Throughout the life course there are the possibilities of a break in the family lifecycle. Death or divorce may end any marriage at any time. Therefore, the market for those undergoing a transition in or out of a marriage and family context is increasing. Singles come in all ages now. Both the hopes and fears of those who make their travel plans alone need to be taken into consideration in providing services.

Problems of Leisure Travel

The most evident problems associated with leisure travel are those of cost, time, and distance. However, there are other issues that reflect the economic system and social styles.

The Costs of Distance

Overcoming distance is costly. Airline fares for long distances run fifteen cents a mile or more. The federal government allows twenty-five cents or more a mile for operating an automobile. On a trip by car added costs include lodging, meals, and other on-the-road expenses. However the cost is calculated, the use of any recreation site is increased greatly by distance from it.

For many leisure travelers, the cost in time is even more significant than the money cost.

The costs of distance filter out the low-income segments of the population from some kinds of leisure taken for granted by most. The first threshold that eliminates some from participation in many kinds of on-site and resource-based activities is the lack of an automobile. Estimates vary from city to city, but somewhere between 10 and 30 percent of urban households do not have a car. Some of those without cars are older citizens living alone, while others are simply unable to afford to keep a car running. As long as amusement parks, public beaches, rivers for fishing, reservoirs for boating, and other such attractions are either inaccessible or expensive to reach by public transportation, then some cannot even consider their use.

However, the cost-distance threshold operates for those with cars as well. The simple "gravity" model of recreation travel assumes that distance and the attractiveness of the resource work to determine use. The greater the distance the less the power of attraction. However, there is some evidence that the model does not operate quite that simply. Rather, there is an "inertia" or start-up factor.[7] It takes some effort just to get moving, to make arrangements for going anywhere with anyone—even a short distance. However, once that inertia is overcome and the auto is under way, a recreation opportunity ten minutes away may be about as attractive as one three minutes away. In fact, on some occasions those leaving home may prefer to go far enough to feel they have actually "been somewhere." Especially if there is any perceived difference in crowding or quality, driving another ten to thirty minutes may have little effect on use. However, the distance effect does take hold at some point perceived as too costly in time or money by the leisure participant.

The Costs of Distance

An Oklahoma contractor closes down his construction site on weekends for many reasons—one being the cost of overtime labor. But he also wants to take his $10,000 fishing boat to a Corps of Engineers reservoir for two days on the water. While there he fishes, skims the water from one spot to another, sleeps in his camper, and drinks a bit. The reservoir is 175 miles from home. Travel costs include more than thirty cents a mile for a rig that gets seven miles to the gallon, plus investment in the boat, trailer, and most of the cost of the pickup and camper. Further, he may be forgoing considerable income by setting aside his business interests for two days. The mileage is only the beginning. The eight hours on the road, the travel equipment, and the possible business loss are the real costs of the distance. Further, if the water were closer, he could run over after work on long summer evenings rather than save it all for weekends.

---

[7] R. I. Wolfe, "The Inertia Model," *Journal of Leisure Research,* 4 (1972), 73–76.

For those with regular incomes one threshold has been lowered in recent years. For those who were paid once or twice a month, there has been a cyclical barrier to some leisure opportunities. On the last weekend before payday, there just might not be enough cash left available to go where people might like to go and do what they would like to do. Eating out, filling the car with gas, and other travel costs would be just enough to keep would-be travelers home. The change has been the ubiquitous credit card. When the expense of meals, transportation, and even equipment can be postponed until the following month by using the appropriate credit cards, then the weekend trip or evening out may be still on. The cash-flow problem is partly eliminated by the piece of plastic.

Credit has also had an impact on longer and more costly trips. The sojourn in Europe and the week at the beach may also be financed on credit plans that allow months and even years to repay. The advertising appeal is "You owe it to yourself to do it now" and little reference is made to what will be owed to others in the months following.

Trade-Offs of Time and Money

Compounding the problem of the general failure of public systems to provide for recreation travel is the problem of time. Despite crowded highways and parking lots, the private car is usually the most time-efficient mode of leisure transportation. There are exceptions when the modern subway train goes near a destination, but for the typical multipurpose family outing, the car seems indispensable. It just takes too long to catch a weekend bus, transfer, wait again, and then still be several blocks from your destination.

For some trips the time may be a benefit. We may enjoy the scenery and the companionship; but for most around-town trips and for many of long distances, time is critical. We just cannot take the time to go by bus to a park or on the thousand-mile journey. So we drive or we fly to save time. The time is more precious than the money that might be saved by the alternative mode of travel.

There are no indications that this current trade-off of travel price for travel time is likely to be reduced. Rather the ecology of leisure suggests quite the contrary. The least energy-efficient and more costly modes of transportation may well increase in their appeal as time becomes more scarce and valued. The time costs of the metropolitan distances and congestion are not being reduced for many leisure resources.

One aspect of this problem is acute for those who cannot continue previous mobility. Older people who can no longer drive themselves wherever they want to go whenever they desire may find the adjustment to less convenient means difficult. In many cases, older people report staying home and even dropping out of valued activities because they have not been able to adapt to the loss of personal transportation.

The Impact of Leisure Schedules

The concentration of public transportation on employment-related travel is only one aspect of a series of interrelated scheduling issues. First, there is the common work schedule of eight to five Monday through Friday. This means that leisure requiring a block of time for travel must take place on weekends. While there may be some increase in retail weekend employment with weekday holidays and in four-day workweeks in a few industries, the Monday through Friday schedule is still normative. Therefore, crowding at leisure sites less than three hours' drive from population centers is acute on weekends.

Second, the three-day weekend for most of those who are employed now yields a longer chunk of time several times a year, but at the same time as most other workers. Therefore, highways and recreation destinations tend to be even more crowded on those special weekends.

The requirement of a block of time for recreational tourism combined with a dissatisfaction with the traditional once-a-year vacation has stimulated a somewhat different approach to travel. The "mini-vacation" is becoming more common according to the 1986 Market Opinion Research Survey conducted for the President's Commission on Americans Outdoors. The new pattern retains the vacations of a week or more, but adds mini-vacations on long weekends. The survey found that 30 percent of adults took six or more such breaks and an additional 20 percent took four or five. Such short trips are one way of coping with the limitations on joint vacation time experienced in many two-income households as well as with the impacts of time pressures during the ordinary workweek.

Third, much recreation is both seasonal and weather-dependent. For the northern two-thirds of the United States and all of Canada, beaches can be used for swimming only for a limited season. Further, some weather during the season is too cold or stormy for beach safety or enjoyment. Therefore, beaches tend to be jammed on summer weekends with good weather—in some areas as few as six to eight times a year. It is no wonder that such locations tend to be crowded. The parking lots at a Jones Beach on Long Island or Zuma near Los Angeles may be full by nine in the morning on a sunny Saturday or Sunday. Further, the time spent in a car in traffic jams does not enhance the freedom and joy of the occasion.

Fourth, within a household or family, there may be considerable conflict over the use of automobiles for leisure transportation. The kind of management, juggling, and compromising described earlier is characteristic of many families with multiple leisure commitments and schedules. As long as most out-of-home leisure events require car transportation and are subject to scheduling outside usual school and employment hours, there will be intrafamilial conflict over leisure-related transportation. As schedules become more and more rigid with golf, tennis, theater, lessons, rehearsals, and games timed to the minute to maximize the use of scarce space, the synchronization of family leisure schedules will be increasingly complex and a potential source of family strife.

Greater flexibility in work schedules, fuller provisions of public transportation to recreation locales, more centralization of multiple recreation provisions, and community planning that maximizes leisure opportunities in the neighborhood could all lessen the conflict and the crowding. However, such provisions would require giving a priority to leisure in community planning that would be a change from most current practices.

Resources and Opportunities

Tourism is more than a business. The resources that make leisure travel possible and attractive involve everything from sewage disposal to guide services. One basic distinction among these resources is between infrastructure and superstructure.

Infrastructure includes all the forms of construction that make integrated life possible in an organized society: transportation projects, such as roads, parking, railway lines, and airport runways, as well as sewage disposal, power and water utilities, and other basic built items. Infrastructure usually also includes the basic institutional structures that operate the constructed items.

Superstructure consists of the built items such as terminals, hotels, restaurants, shopping facilities, and the institutional organization to operate them. The focus of business is generally on the superstructure. Superstructure is more likely in the private sector and in a capitalist or mixed economic system to be provided by profit-seeking firms. However, a breakdown in the infrastructure will bring everything to a halt. Especially in recreation businesses such as resorts, the condition of the regional and local infrastructure is essential to the operation of the business. The public and private sectors are highly interdependent rather than separate or in competition.

Further, tourism frequently is dependent on resources that are *common ground,* available to the general population. Tourism businesses on the Oregon coast depend on public access to the beaches, which have been declared common ground. Much recreation travel is to areas that have access to water resources that are common, open for use to those who want to swim or boat on them. Considerable vacation travel is directed toward the scenic vistas that are available to everyone who travels the public roadway or who flies over. In most countries many of those special resources are held by the state as common ground, with at least regulated access given to visitors in some equitable manner.

Therefore, recreation travel is highly dependent on public action that provides the infrastructure and ensures access and use of common ground for recreation. The access networks of airways, waterways, and highways is essential for travel. A political system that ensures freedom of movement as well as an integrated system of transportation and utilities is a prerequisite of tourism.

Weather: A Fundamental Resource

One final note on tourism is so obvious that it is frequently overlooked. It is, of course, weather. So much recreation travel is dependent on weather that an otherwise viable business can be destroyed by weather conditions in a few years or less. A cold winter week in Florida precipitates cancellations. Any ski-based business must be capitalized to cope with a season without snow in some areas or a season in which too much snow blocks access in others.

Weather is a fundamental factor in recreation travel and in planning a travel-related business. A few examples will illustrate the point:

The states most dependent on tourism income—Florida, Hawaii, and Nevada—are warmweather areas that attract the "snowbirds" fleeing cold climates. However, unseasonable cold can produce millions of dollars of cancellations in a few days.

Destination resorts with a central activity that is weather-dependent, such as skiing, golf, or sailboating, must charge enough in good weather to pay for the cancellations caused by bad weather or provide alternative opportunities that are not closed by thaws, rain, or whatever prevents the primary activity.

There are two interrelated elements: The first is climate, the conditions of seasonality of an area. The second is weather, the day-to-day changes in temperature, precipitation, and winds that are part of the recreational environment. Some resource-based recreation calls for adapting to weather changes as part of the experience—wilderness hiking or competitive sailing, for example—but most resource-drawn tourism is based on climate and highly affected by weather. The marketing of recreation travel support requires inclusion of a variable that is, at least in part, out of control.

Summary of Issues

More than most kinds of leisure, travel is shaped by its costs. Not only the direct costs of transportation but associated costs of maintenance, entertainment, and travel equipment make leisure travel a cost-intensive kind of activity. Further, travel involves time and the opportunity costs of forgone income as well as the price of the trip.

And the traditional vacation trip is only the most obvious kind of leisure travel. The ecology of leisure resources requires travel within the community as well as to more distant destination attractions. As a result, the short car trip is the most common kind of leisure travel. The energy and time costs of leisure travel when resources are not neighborhood-based seem a major planning issue. However, the private automobile provides both a freedom and time efficiency that make it peculiarly central to leisure in North America.

When the various satisfactions of leisure travel are found to include the trip itself as well as the destination, then treating time simply as a price paid to get somewhere is inadequate. The experience of travel includes escape and change, freedom from routines, various meanings intrinsic to the experience, companionship and communication, and the values placed on destination opportunities and environments. Also, there are a variety of styles of leisure travel as well as changes related to the life course.

While major destinations are one element in commercial and public provisions for leisure travel, there are also myriad small businesses that provide travel-related services. These include many kinds of franchises with their standardization as well as local businesses that depend on the trade of those who are away from home.

Tourism is a major world industry. As a consequence, tourist packages and destinations are designed to attract markets, often by offering a contrived entertainment rather than an authentic experience with a different culture. Further, such touristic developments may destroy the very cultures and environments they claim to offer.

HIGHLIGHTS

1. A variety of intrinsic and social reasons for travel are often as important as the destination or environment.
2. Wealth may determine travel styles, but some form of travel is the norm in contemporary culture.
3. In both metropolitan and rural areas, many leisure activities require travel by car to the site or social gathering.
4. Time, forgone income, and competing opportunities as well as direct and indirect costs and investments in transportation make the one-third of auto mileage that is employed for leisure use a major element in the economy of the nation and of the household.
5. The variety of vacation styles and schedules reflects the diversity of resources and cultural backgrounds of those who seek to fit schedules, environments, and companions into a tourism experience of change.
6. Tourism is big business, organized to sell travel experiences to mass and elite markets.

Discussion Questions

1. How does metropolitan sprawl increase the necessity of travel for leisure? Is the time-cost problem likely to increase the amount of leisure that urban residents will seek at home?

2. Is there a possible substitute for the private automobile in vacation travel? For around-town leisure transportation? Is the private car essential to leisure freedom in American society?

3. What are likely impacts on leisure travel of increased energy costs, more people with nontraditional work schedules, and more two-income families?

4. How can leisure travel be both a social experience and one of "getting away"?

5. For what kinds of trips is travel time a cost? For what trips is time a benefit and getting there really half the fun?

6. Which is the central dimension of leisure travel, newness and exploration or familiarity and reassurance? Do most people prefer freedom and independence or prearranged package tours?

7. Which vacation style describes your family? Your friends? Why?

8. How does tourism benefit a host culture? What are possible negative impacts?

9. Describe an "authentic touristic experience."

Bibliography

Kelly, John R., *Recreation Business.* New York: Macmillan, 1985.

Lundberg, Donald, *International Travel and Tourism.* New York: John Wiley, 1985.

McIntosh, Robert W., and Charles Goeldner, *Tourism: Principles, Practices, and Philosophies.* New York: John Wiley, 1986.

Mill, Robert C., and Alastair Morrison, *The Tourism System.* Englewood Cliffs, NJ: Prentice-Hall, 1985.

Pearce, Philip, *The Social Psychology of Tourist Behavior.* New York: Pergamon Press, 1982.

Wahab, Salah, *Tourism Management.* London: Tourism International Press, 1975.

Section IV

Leisure Contexts and Resources

Many resources for leisure are essentially self-supplied. We have gained skills, both activity-specific and social, that enable us to engage in familiar and new leisure events. We have the resources of our homes, families, friends, and social groups. However, there are other kinds of resources that come more directly from the institutions of our society. These resources include designated space, equipment, skill acquisition, programs organized for common participation, places to see, and things to do. They are supplied both by the economic market and by public providers.

Through the market we gain access to destination resorts and sport equipment, to musical instruments and special vehicles, and to all the services and support enterprises related to travel. The market also supplies that omnipresent leisure toy, television, and the rest of the popular culture items. Commercial recreation is very big business even when only items that are manifestly for leisure are counted.

The public sector may be smaller in magnitude than the commercial in relation to leisure, but it still has an essential place in the whole spectrum of leisure. Educational and sport provisions have already been introduced. In the arts, with community programs for all ages and a variety of special opportunities for the vulnerable, public providers do what seems impossible for those seeking an investment return. Especially the preservation and management of natural environments has been a public responsibility since the establishment of Yellowstone as the first national park.

The aim in this book is to approach both market and nonmarket leisure providers from the perspectives of the life course, leisure learning, and social roles and identities already introduced. Such provisions and programs are a significant part of leisure but do not exhaust either the action or the meaning of leisure in our lives.

Chapter *18*

Public Recreation:
An Introduction

A recognition of the human need for leisure does not necessarily lead to an acceptance of the need for public recreation. Many things that humans seem to need are not provided by the state. Many of the more personal aspects of life are reserved for private decision and provision. Leisure with its stress on freedom and personal experience might well be one of those aspects.

The history of public recreation in America began with a recognition of overwhelming deprivation in the industrial cities of the late nineteenth century. The recreation movement was a social protest response to conditions that stunted and crippled lives, especially the lives of children. The problem was simply one of lack of alternatives. In that time and place, workers and their families could not provide for themselves even the most elementary recreation opportunities. They lacked resources of space, time, and economic power.

The fundamental issue concerning public recreation is still that of opportunity. Are there resources and opportunities important to the leisure of children and adults that they cannot provide for themselves?

Leisure provisions may include both natural and constructed recreation environments, programs of instruction and skill acquisition, and a wide variety of participation opportunities. They may be offered by federal, state, and local agencies. In an overview of the public sector of recreation, we can only begin to assess the aims and accomplishments of public recreation in North America.

ISSUES

Are public, tax-supported recreation programs necessary?
How did public recreation develop in North America?
How are government provisions for recreation planned and managed?
What are current trends in public recreation?
Are there employment opportunities in the field of public recreation?

Why Have Public Recreation?

In a society stressing freedom of opportunity and self-reliance, why are government bodies involved in providing recreation resources and opportunities? Is leisure not something that people can better take care of themselves? Most arguments for public recreation are related to scarcity and equity. Some resources cannot be provided by individuals, the family, or the market in ways that make them generally available for current and future users. Some segments of the population cannot provide critical opportunities for themselves. As a consequence of such limitations, public recreation provisions have been developed by local, state, and federal governments.

Special Resources and Space

The first basis of the need for public participation in the provision of recreation opportunities is access to and preservation of resources. Some leisure resources are unique: scenic wonders such as the Grand Canyon of the Colorado and the Snake River Gorge or historical sites such as Independence Hall and Mt. Vernon. Such unique resources should be maintained both for current access and future preservation. Other resources are scarce because of cost and would be unavailable to most of the population unless some public program were developed. Some resources are so fragile that their survival into the next century requires regulation of current use. While space and land are a major element of such scarce recreation resources, there are a variety of opportunities that are neither commercially viable nor abundant enough for private provision.

High-Cost Resources

Some kinds of leisure require more space than most individuals or households can provide for themselves. In urban areas the cost of land is so high that enough space for outdoor sports such as softball and tennis would be out of reach for all but the superrich. Enough space for a game of tag off the dangerous streets would be out of reach for almost all children. Urban land costs are high, even in areas of badly deteriorated housing.

The even larger expanses of land required for resource-based outdoor hiking, camping, backpacking, and other such activities in the forests and mountains are also beyond the reach of most citizens. It would be the rare family that could afford to own a wilderness or even a few hundred acres of timberland. Water resources such as lakes and beaches are also both expensive and inefficient for private ownership. Further, since most recreational users of such outdoor locales are able to be there only for short periods of time, public ownership and provision would appear to be more efficient in land use.

The same argument holds for various kinds of environments built for recreation. Gymnasiums, tennis courts, swimming pools, craft houses, and other such provisions are simply too costly for all but the wealthy to afford. While some relatively compact activities such as racquetball, painting, or dancing may be made available to the upper third of the population in income through profit-making enterprises, very few can afford to rent or purchase enough space for more space-intensive activities.

Another approach to the issue of resource scarcity is that of economic efficiency. It is not efficient for scarce resources such as urban play space to be owned by an individual or household that might use it occasionally and exclude other users. It is more efficient for softball diamonds, basketball courts, and other recreation spaces to be publicly owned and shared among hundreds or thousands of occasional users. This efficiency argument is especially telling when the resource is a distant park that might be visited only once or twice in the lifetimes of millions who value the experience. Scarcity and cost combine with use patterns to support the economic efficiency of many public recreation resources.

Fragile Resources

Other recreational resources must be managed with care if they are to remain available to future generations. Even the grassy area of the city park may have to be roped off for rejuvenation on occasions or else become like tan concrete. The river canyon can accept some boating and hiking, but too much will pollute the water or drive out wildlife. Even with a "carry out everything you carry in" policy, a wilderness area can be badly degraded. Only management for the long-term preservation of such fragile resources can balance present use with future opportunity.

Therefore, unique resources of natural beauty and high fragility require public management. Yellowstone National Park is a clear example of a unique resource that requires very careful management so that the hot pools and geyser areas will not be destroyed by those who appreciate them too much. Wilderness calls for plans that limit the number and types of human incursions as well as protection from enterprises that irretrievably alter the nature of the resource. Such resources must be managed for the common good both now and a hundred years from now.

Special Populations and Equity

Along with high-cost and ecologically fragile resources, the second half of the case for public recreation is based on population differences. There is no question that most individuals and households can provide a considerable range of leisure opportunities for themselves. Further, there are some who can afford to provide for themselves almost any kind of space or facility for a wide range of activities. However, there are more whose range of opportunities is quite limited without some public provisions.

The Constitution of the United States begins, "We, the People of the United States of America, in order to form a more perfect union, establish justice, insure domestic tranquillity, provide for the common defense, promote the general welfare, and secure the blessings of liberty to ourselves and our posterity, do ordain and establish this Constitution for the United States of America." The welfare of the people has come to include not only health, safety, and protection from aggression but also education, environmental protection, and leisure opportunities. The government is to be concerned about the total life context of all people without regard for age, race, sex, religion, or "previous condition of servitude." While that ideal has not been realized, it is still the basis of any public provision of opportunities or services. The issue of equality, then, is central to any public provisions. If the "pursuit of happiness" is a human right and the "common welfare" a public responsibility, then public recreation is involved in issues of relative need and social deprivation as well as of personal fulfillment and development.

People with Acute Limitations

In almost any community some are unable to participate in many kinds of recreation unless special provision is made for them. Those restricted to wheelchair mobility, the blind, and people with a variety of impairments may not even be able to get to some recreation opportunities without special planning and provisions. Usually there are not enough people with such limitations to make the cost of such provisions recoverable in a commercial operation. Special opportunities are necessary if those in wheelchairs are to play basketball or hike in the forest preserve. Such provisions may be mandated by law, but some providing agency must bear the cost. In general, when costs are high, special facilities will be a public offering or not be available at all.

Groups with Limited Resources

There has already been discussion of segments of the American population with very limited financial resources and access to the kinds of recreation opportunities that many take for granted. The poor who live in crowded cities do not have the space at home, the private outdoor space, the closeness to natural outdoor settings, or the money to purchase opportunities for travel. The public recreation movement in America has from the beginning been a response to deprivation of this kind.

The "cumulative deprivation" of families who for generations have had minimal opportunities has created a condition of lack of skills and interests as well as access to opportunities. Making a fuller range of resources available may also need to be coupled with programs of introduction and information before leisure styles now adapted to the deprivation are altered.

There are many such groups in the population. Some are institutionalized in hospitals, prisons, or schools. Some are cut off from normal community opportunities as members of the armed services. Some have unusual schedules and need opportunities at odd hours and on different days. Others are the more invisible poor, scattered through large populations and housed on the fringes of normal community life. Among them would be migratory farm workers, Native Americans living on reservations, the homeless, the rural poor who are often ignored even in their own communities, and inner-city youth.

The issue is one of equity. Public recreation is an attempt to administer justice in the sense of making some opportunities available to those least able to provide them for themselves. Public recreation recognizes the current inequalities in opportunities and gives special attention to those whose deprivation is most acute. No public program or set of programs can do everything desirable for everyone. However, with the premise that leisure is essential to being human, public recreation is an institution organized to mitigate inequity.

A Social Ethic for Recreation

Public recreation, then, is still based on a social ethic of common responsibility for the "life, liberty, and pursuit of happiness" of all members of the community. The common good requires close attention to the conditions and contexts of life for all people. As public recreation began with a social conscience and a humanitarian basis, so it continues to be much more than just something governments do.

Public recreation has a social ethic that rests on the foundation of humanism and community; it attempts to redress inequities that close some lives off from critical opportunities for development and expression. Public recreation planners must discern just where limitations are most acute and institute public remedy. They must take a long view of the resource base for life and leisure, so that consumption today will not destroy the opportunities in coming decades and centuries. In sum, recreation is an institution—social, political, and economic—that exists for people and for the enrichment of their lives.

The Scope of Public Recreation

The recreation movement in America began as a direct response to conditions in the nineteenth-century industrial city. The park movement developed concurrently as a response to the potential loss of outdoor space in cities and irreplaceable resources in the West. Central Park was a design rather than a preservation. Yellowstone Park was established in 1872 as the first national park to preserve a unique resource for future generations. But they had in common the values placed on outdoor experiences and resources.

The mitigation of urban privation and the preservation of unique locales are not complicated aims. However, the public recreation and park provisions that have grown out of these simple beginnings are both vast and complex. Listing the federal agencies that have some recreation or resource mission would fill more than a page. Recreation on the local level includes not only city and county agencies but also private, voluntary, nonprofit, and commercial providers that use public resources or receive tax support. State agencies not only have their own programs but transfer federal funds to local programs. Add to the local, state, and federal provisions all the organizations and programs that offer recreation to the public on a not-for-profit basis and the picture is further obscured.

The aim here will not be to present a complete picture of public recreation but to give an introduction to the overall scene and to suggest certain pervasive issues. Governmental reorganization and changes in tax support, political orientations, and agency policies threaten the details of any description with instant obsolescence. However, the history and overall shape of public recreation have remained relatively stable.

Twentieth-Century Growth in Public Recreation

We have already glanced at the early developments in public recreation: recreation in the city and the leadership of Joseph Lee, Luther Gulick, Jacob Riis, and others; the first urban and destination parks; the combining of urban space and recreation programs in Boston, Chicago, and elsewhere; the formulation of national park and recreation organizations with the support of national leaders; and the rise of voluntary organizations to serve youth, immigrants, and communities with programs of education and recreation. The Boston Sand Garden, New York's Central Park, Chicago's South Parks, Hull House, scouting and the Y's, Yellowstone and Yosemite, and many other names symbolize those early developments.

In the early twentieth century, the continuation of urban growth was met with the expansion of public recreation programs and resources. In 1922, Clarence Rainwater made an early attempt to summarize the development.[1] He outlined a series of transitions in the expansion of public recreation in America in the early twentieth century. These transitions included the change from serving only children to serving all age groups, from summer to year-around and indoor operations, from the urban emphasis to an emphasis on variety of communities, from philanthropic to public financing, from free play for children to a mixture of more organized and scheduled activities, and to standards for programs and the meeting of community needs.

The expansion in numbers alone is indicative of the change. The number of cities with public parks grew from 100 in 1892 to about 800 in 1902 and 1,680 in 1926.[2] At about the same time, the 12 cities reporting recreation programs in 1900 increased to 40 in 1906 and 465 by 1920. Richard Kraus lists more recent developments as follows:[3]

An emerging concern for physical fitness

Increased programs for the disabled

Expansion of outdoor recreation resources following the Outdoor Recreation Resources Review Commission report in 1962

Increased federal participation in public recreation

Further development in the arts through the Arts and Humanities Act of 1965

Expansion of commercial recreation investments and enterprises

Unification of the parks and recreation movements merging into the National Recreation and Parks Association in 1966

Greater concern with the poor and minority groups in response to the civil rights movement of the 1960s

"New challenges" by various groups, especially youth, with life styles that did not fit comfortably into the traditional programs

---

[1] Cited in Martin and Esther Neumeyer, *Leisure and Recreation* (New York: Ronald Press, 1958), p. 73.

[2] Richard Kraus, *Recreation and Leisure in Modern Society* (Englewood Cliffs, NJ: Prentice-Hall, 1971).

[3] Ibid.

Canadian Developments

Endowed with even greater expanses of outdoor recreation resources and a smaller population than its southern neighbor, Canada has developed national and provincial programs that reflect the opportunities of the land. The history of public recreation in Canada begins with the provision for parks in a number of cities such as the Halifax Common in 1763, Gore Park in Hamilton, and public squares in Montreal in the early nineteenth century.[4] Some of the famous city parks in Canada were established in the second half of the nineteenth century. Urban playgrounds developed with a similar basis as in the United States. Concern for the urban poor led to the formation of playground associations in nine cities by 1914, partly due to the urging of women's councils. Voluntary organizations and community groups were formed with special interests in types of recreation opportunities that eventually resulted in more comprehensive municipal programs,

However, with less urban congestion and more available land attractive for outdoor recreation near most of the population, the need for public provisions seemed less acute. Nevertheless, after World War II the various provincial governments along with the Department of National Health and Welfare encouraged and supported a variety of recreation programs. The National Physical Fitness Act of 1943 established a council to disperse funds to the provinces for the arts as well as physical activities and sports. Nine of the provinces began cooperating with the federal government in developing parks and recreation. Provincial organizations in Quebec were established for sport in 1968 and for recreation and tourism in the late 1970s.

An Overview of Public Recreation Programs

Public recreation is a multifaceted set of programs and provisions. It includes outdoor resources such as forests, water, playgrounds, and parks. It includes programs for all age groups and for general populations, for those with special needs and others with special interests. It includes administration, leadership, the management of resources, therapeutic programs, and research. It includes public schools and the free offerings of public utilities and corporations as well as the provisions of federal, state, and community governments. In the brief outline that follows, we will concentrate on the government providers and their central programs. However, a variety of nonprofit programs are offered by voluntary organizations and by organizations cooperating with the government agencies.

National Recreation Programs

Federal agencies such as the National Park Service, Forest Service, Bureau of Land Management, Tennessee Valley Authority, Bureau of Reclamation, Army Corps of Engineers, and others are the major providers of outdoor recreation space. Both natural and constructed resources have been set aside and developed for forest and water-based recreation.

---

[4] Elsie M. McFarland, *The Development of Public Recreation in Canada* (Vanier City, Ontario: Canadian Parks and Recreation Association, 1970).

The federal government supplies about 85 percent of all land resources for recreation. Further, through the Land and Water Conservation Fund, the Department of the Interior has provided major funding for the state, county, and local acquisition of outdoor recreation space.

The federal government not only manages land and develops recreation programs on that land, but it also provides recreation programs in institutions such as Veterans Administration hospitals and for those in the armed services, gives financial assistance to programs for the handicapped and disadvantaged, supports professional education and research, and engages in countless programs such as highway development and transportation subsidies that facilitate various kinds of leisure participation. However, the special function of land management is the first element of the federal presence in recreation.

Land Management

How much land should be preserved in a natural state for long-term environmental purposes and for wilderness-type recreation? What kinds of economic development of renewable resources such as timber, grazing, and recreation can be accommodated in forestland? Where are there unique resources that must be preserved for the enjoyment of future generations as well as managed for current appreciation? How can the economic interests of a land-rich area such as Alaska be balanced by concern for the natural beauty, wildlife, and recreation potential of its mountains, shoreline, and forests? What kinds of development combine benefits in the land management policies of the Departments of Agriculture and the Interior? A fuller discussion of federal and state outdoor recreation programs is found in Chapter 14.

Health, Education, and Welfare

Outdoor education, land-use planning, in-service training, and a wide spectrum of education programs related to recreation have been supported by the federal government through health, education, and welfare agencies. The Bureau of Education for the Handicapped has provided funds for many programs that train professionals to work in rehabilitation and therapeutic recreation as well as more general education for institutional and community programs. The National Institutes of Health engage in both research and service and support research programs in universities, hospitals, and institutes across the country.

Along with the National Institutes of Health (including the National Institute of Mental Health), old and new agencies such as the Public Health Service, the Rehabilitation Services Administration, the Administration on Aging, the Children's Bureau, and many others have inaugurated various programs of education, research, and service that are related to public recreation. Everything from recreation in infant and child-care facilities to volunteer activity of older citizens is being developed and supported by health and education agencies. Special attention has been given to those who are physically, mentally, or emotionally disabled in a series of acts passed in the 1960s and 1970s.

Housing, Community Development, and Poverty

The Department of Housing and Urban Development has had a number of programs that have enlarged recreation opportunities in urban areas. The Housing Act of 1961 provided for open space and outdoor recreation provisions in areas being built or redeveloped with federal support. Urban renewal, mass transit, public housing, subsidized rent, financing of low-income housing, urban planning, planned communities, neighborhood organization and development, and other programs have taken account of the need for public recreation provisions. Small neighborhood parks, play lots, recreation centers, youth facilities, beautification efforts, and land acquisition have all been aided by a variety of programs, frequently with matching grants to local authorities and programs.

The Economic Opportunity Act of 1964 was the basis for a number of programs intended to attack both the causes and effects of poverty. The residential training of the Job Corps had recreation and conservation components. Summer employment for youths in the Neighborhood Youth Corps, recreation efforts led by VISTA volunteer workers, local initiative in Community Action Programs, and other programs included some concern for recreation opportunities and leadership.

The Armed Forces

The Department of Defense began taking an interest in recreation during the two world wars and has carried on a variety of efforts in the succeeding decades. Often in cooperation with the USO (United Service Organization), the Red Cross, and religious programs, recreation for service personnel and their families has offered outdoor activities, sports, education, arts, library, theater, and entertainment programs on and off military bases. Such programs are supported by a comprehensive fee structure as well as by DOD appropriations.

For those who are receiving treatment at the Veterans Administration Hospitals across the country, recreation programs are administered by the Physical Medicine and Rehabilitation Service of the VA in about 170 institutions. A primary aim of such programs is to augment medical treatment and to provide one kind of therapeutic service to those with physical and emotional disabilities.

Federal Recreation: A Complex Provision

Federal provisions of natural resources, programs, and financial support for recreation are not a neat or integrated package. Many of the recreation provisions are incidental to other missions even though significant to those using the opportunities. Some provisions are part of the land management and conservation efforts of agencies. Others are derived from the health, education, and welfare functions of the government. There are direct provisions for federal employees and matching grants to local communities. There are facilities derived from urban renewal efforts and those recovered from the exploitation of mineral resources in mining. There are efforts to preserve natural beauty and wildlife and programs of systematic harvesting of timber, minerals, fish, and wildlife. There is cooperation with commercial interests and protection of resources against such interests. All of this and more is carried on by countless agencies, commissions, and departments that may or may not be coordinated by numerous councils and boards that go in and out of existence. The overall presence of the federal government in recreation is complex and changing with numerous parallel programs quite uncoordinated with the others.

Through the decades of the 1960s and 1970s, there was growth in both the amount and scope of federal recreation programs. Cooperative programs run by both state and local levels of government and the integration of recreation with environmental preservation and long-range planning increased. There was a renewed attention to inequalities in opportunity and a turn back to urban problems in many current federal policies and programs. In the 1980s, the federal government cut back on almost all programs related to recreation and human services. In the 1990s, no concerted program to increase federal support of public recreation has emerged.

Community Recreation: County and Local Provisions

As varied and diverse as are federal recreation provisions, the local level is even more so. Community programs are organized and funded by counties, townships, municipalities, and special districts. They range in scope from a field on the edge of a small town that is provided for local softball or youth baseball and maintained entirely by volunteers to a $100-million-a-year operation of a major city. Programs include some summer-only sports and playground offerings and also elaborate provisions of continuing education, zoos and museums, theaters, symphonies, and acres of underground parking. Some programs are quite professional and independent; others are run on the side by a county official who hires a couple of students for the summer. Even funding levels vary from district budgets of more than $20 per capita to less than $5.

The National Recreation and Park Association has commissioned studies of employment in community programs. In 1977, more than 2,000 municipal agencies were found to employ one or more full-time persons in recreation followed by 1,211 counties and 345 special districts.[5] More than 80 percent of the agencies now combine park and recreation into a single organization. Fifteen percent reported employing at least one person with a primary responsibility toward programs for the handicapped. The 1990 census reported 93,000 workers in recreation, an increase of over 40 percent in one decade. Over 70 percent were female.

A Comprehensive City Program

Major cities such as Chicago, New York, Boston, and Los Angeles have developed vast and complex public recreation programs. Their annual budgets range from $50 million to $100 million a year. Chicago, for example, has more than 500 parks that encompass more than 6,000 acres. They range from the large parks along the lakeshore and large old "south parks" that are now in the midst of low-income areas to tiny lots with basketball hoops and benches. Just a short list of the kinds of facilities provided offers a glimpse of the variety:

Outdoors there are archery ranges, athletic fields, baseball diamonds for adults and children, basketball backboards, beaches, bicycle paths, bowling greens, bridle paths, casting pools, day camps, football and soccer fields, golf courses, handball courts, harbors for yachts and powerboats, harbor facilities such as docks and moorings, launching ramps, horseshoe courts, boccie courts, lagoons, model boat basins, multiuse paved areas, play-

---

[5] G. Godbey and D. Henkel, "The Manpower Study: A Report," *Parks and Recreation* (November 1976), p. 23.

grounds, sandboxes, shuffleboard courts, skating areas, softball diamonds, spray pools, stadiums, swimming lagoons and beaches, swimming pools, tennis courts, tracks, trapshooting ranges, and volleyball courts.

Indoor facilities include archery ranges, arts and crafts workshops, art centers, art galleries, auditoriums, beach houses, boat-building shops, camera clubs, ceramic shops, club rooms, drama instruction locations, enameling shops, fieldhouses, glassblowing shops, gymnasiums, handball courts, kitchens, lapidary shops, model trains, music locations, natatoriums, public baths, libraries, rifle ranges, senior centers, skating rinks, and tennis courts.

More than 100 million visits may be made in a year to such facilities. Some locations have no programs, only maintenance; others operate elaborate programs for various age groups. Some programs are oriented to their neighborhoods, and others draw from across the city. In fact, the budgets for recreation and for park maintenance are about equal.

Recreation from one perspective is a human service, oriented toward the expressed needs and desires of residents. From another perspective, urban recreation is a political operation, responsive to the aims of those with political power and influence. A variety of interests may be brought to bear on the governing boards. The hiring of employees at almost all levels may be influenced by the recommendations and approval of ward politicians. Neighborhood organizations are learning how to organize to gain access to decision making. Particular user groups such as boat owners or sport leagues lobby for greater allocation of resources to their facilities and programs. Real estate interests are always active in promoting park development related to their investment programs. Park and recreation boards and administrators operate in a climate that is thoroughly political.

Currently there has been renewed attention given to the recreation provisions in inner-city and low-income neighborhoods where crime and unemployment rates are high. Any reallocation of resources to such neighborhoods, however, is balanced by other areas and interests. Within a single park and recreation district, there will be boat basins for the wealthy and mini-parks for the poor, large wooded parks with statues of Civil War figures and asphalted lots with backboards and cement walls, wide beaches and portable pools, symphony concerts and rock festivals, dance programs for seniors and for tots, and tournaments for experts and lessons for beginners. The contrasts of the city itself are mirrored in its recreation provisions.

In many cities, ethnic traditions are celebrated in a variety of festivals. The ethnic composition of a neighborhood may shape the program for parks in that area. At the other extreme, a central location may offer extraordinary presentations of classical music or theater or popular performers with a wide appeal. Some programs are very local; others are city-wide. Some are directed toward groups with special interests or needs. Traditionally, special attention has been given to the young and the old. Other programs are focused on particular activities such as sports, the arts, or festivals.

More and more, park and recreation districts are cooperating with businesses or with voluntary organizations to offer programs and opportunities that they would not be equipped to provide themselves. Both arts and sports organizations use public facilities for their offerings. Increasingly, attention is being given to the use of recreation locations for social services in the fields of education, health, and counseling. Recreation is integrated with social services in programs that attempt to reach those with acute needs and problems.

Contrast: Very Small Town, USA

Visit a small town in the Great Plains between the Rocky Mountains and the fertile Midwest. Towns of 800 and 1,500 residents dot the landscape surrounded by expanses of grassland, hay and wheat fields, and even semidesert.

What does public recreation mean in such a town? Most striking is the centrality of voluntary efforts. The one public park may be on city-owned land, but it was often started by the local garden club or a service club. In recent years a combination of donations, fundraising projects, and tax receipts has made possible the construction of a modest swimming pool there. On the edge of town the old baseball diamond has been restored and divided into two smaller fields for softball. The town and county may divide maintenance chores for the park and pool areas, but the ball fields are usually maintained by interested volunteers. The county extension program has an organized 4-H activity for children and youth in the area that culminates at the county fair. During the school year, most public recreation is provided by the school programs in sports and the arts. There is no full-time recreation director and usually no commission with recreation as its sole or main responsibility. On the other hand, there is outdoor space all around and frequently considerable work for young people to do in the summer.

What Is Happening Everywhere Else?

Somewhere between the complexity of the metropolis and the simplicity of the small town lies most of America's local public recreation. There are many urban programs of considerable variety and sophistication. There are suburban programs that augment the personal resources of families with substantial incomes. There are the interrelated town and county programs of the small cities and county-seat towns across the country. And there are the areas so sparsely populated or poor that public recreation is just not a concern. Rather than attempting to outline all these possibilities, what follows is just a series of vignettes that suggest some of the variety, ingenuity, and innovation that characterize the best of public recreation.

Recycling Space

Many abandoned railroad spurs and lines are being transformed into outdoor recreation resources. One of the most common uses is for trail skiing, snowmobiling, bicycling, and other linear activities. When such a spur was abandoned in 1971, citizens of Seattle helped develop plans for a public hiking and biking trail that now stretches from Gas Works Park across Lake Union from the city center twelve and a half miles north through the university to a park at the northern tip of Lake Washington. Gas Works Park, unique and intriguing with its brightly painted reminder of the abandoned gas plant transformed into a play area, is another example of the imaginative use for recreation of facilities no longer in use for their original purpose.

Older Persons Are Special

So many communities have begun to respond to the needs of their older residents that to begin a list would have no end. In a school no longer needed for children, older persons may be potting in one room, discussing legal problems with an attorney in another, singing madrigals upstairs, planning a trip to the city in an office, and in general using the space and resources to develop their own program. Needs and resources differ from one community to another. However, in all there are older people who need opportunity for community, for expression, and to continue to develop their lives.

Other Glimpses

No list can be more than suggestive of the many striking public recreation provisions across North America. Further, focusing on the special may obscure the programs that are commonplace just because they meet people's needs especially well. Nevertheless, the old gym and playground stereotype of public recreation merits expansion.

> In Portland, Oregon, the Parks Art Center and summer outdoor musical production are only one facet of the diverse cultural offerings in which the Bureau of Parks and Public Recreation cooperates with a number of arts organizations.

> In Minneapolis, it tends to snow some in the winter, so there are public opportunities for downhill skiing right in the city. With lights it is possible to go over to the hill after work for a few runs rather than having to reserve skiing for the long and expensive weekend.

> In Boston, sixteen islands in the harbor are now an urban water park. Facilities for picnicking, boat piers, camping, hiking, and swimming are being developed along with access to old fortifications. Concern for the fragile ecosystems limits some kinds of use, but a boat and water taxi service has made the islands available for recreation use.

> Any number of communities have found ways to bring together waste and wasteland with the need for recreation space. Compacted garbage has been employed in flat areas to create artificial hills for sledding or skiing. Filled garbage dumps have been transformed into sports fields or golf courses. Swamps used for dumping for decades are being cleaned and reshaped to create recreation areas that combine an environment for wildlife with developed land for group sports, picnics, or camping.

> A variety of day camps sponsored by park and recreation districts have developed innovative programs to meet particular needs for children. Many are for those with particular limitations. Others are aimed at learning motivation and enrichment for children identified as needing such summer assistance. Other day camps are designed to further social and racial integration, to provide for children whose parents are employed, to foster environmental awareness, and to develop particular skills.

> Arts programs with a quality emphasis have been developed in many communities, including ballet companies, opera workshops, experimental theaters, a full range of crafts and folk art, and mobile presentations that move from park to park. In some communities, park and recreation commissions have entered into contracts with local theater and dance groups, art centers, and artisans in a variety of crafts to provide programs of introduction and instruction in park facilities that may eventually feed new advanced students and artists into nonpublic centers and programs.

> Public schools in more than 500 districts operate "community school" programs that employ the school facilities for various forms of recreation and learning in afternoons,

evenings, and weekends. Coordination with the community recreation programs reduces duplication and offers a wide range of new opportunities to the recreation agencies.

There is no end to the innovative and creative programs being offered on small and large scales by community providers. Combining imagination and leadership with a keen awareness of the needs of community residents leads to variations on old ideas and the creation of new possibilities in programs that never stop changing and adapting to newly discovered needs. However, there are a number of trends in community recreation that are found in a high proportion of municipal and county programs.

Trends in Community Recreation

Eight trends in program development are common to community recreation in North America.

Comprehensive Planning.   Increasingly, recreation administrators are expected to be part of the community planning efforts. As land-use planning is required and encouraged, the long-range recreation needs of the community have to be considered in planning for space, access, and demographic change. Will there be more older citizens in the future? Will a proposed highway cut off too many children from a critical recreation resource? Will a housing development alter the drainage into a natural area now used for hiking and informal activities? What will be needed in ten years? Twenty? Fifty? Long-range community planning is now a major function of those responsible for public recreation.

Special Populations.   The reduction of barriers, special programs, and adjustments that enable those with special needs to participate in programs for the general population are major changes in community recreation.

Cooperation.   Programs that combine the resources of a number of recreation agencies, recreation programs with public school efforts, and public with private programs are on the increase. The broader scope of activities and concern with groups previously ignored in programs stressing summer sports and children's playgrounds have opened the public agencies to more cooperation. At the same time, common financial problems have required the greatest cost efficiency, especially for new programs. Working with schools, voluntary organizations, industrial recreation, and the market sector minimizes duplication and allows for public resources to be directed toward those not served in other ways.

Volunteerism.   No recreation program can enlist a professional staff to do everything possible in every setting or with every group calling for service. Further, public expenditures on recreation have been pinched in most communities by the combination of inflation and efforts to limit taxation. The enlistment of volunteer leadership, then, becomes a necessity. The work of the professional staff becomes increasingly the coordination of programs, planning and need assessment, general administration, and the training of volunteers who will then provide the direct leadership of programs.

Environmental Concern.   More outdoor recreation programs are conceived to have an educational component that promises an awareness and understanding of the natural environment. Not just nature walks, but programs that enlist assistance in the preservation and enhancement of natural areas have become regular parts of many programs.

Program Diversity.   Community recreation has gone far beyond the old sports and crafts models of yesteryear. Now many communities have full-time coordinators of programs in the fine arts who develop opportunities for learning and demonstration of skills. Health and "wellness" emphases combine activity with educational efforts.

Participatory Programming.   More and more of those who have been defined as the "clients" of the professional recreation directors are now redefined as "colleagues" who have a major part in planning and directing the programs. From various community organization efforts, recreation providers have learned how to engage community groups in every stage of program development and implementation. The phrase "delivery of services" expresses a handing-down mode of operation that is now often being replaced with the fullest possible participation of the community to be served in the development of the service.

Cost Recovery.   As tax support is restricted, "public" recreation programs are relying more on participation fees. Many programs are expected to at least break even. In some public agencies, as much as 80 percent of offerings pay their own way with tax revenue going primarily for facilities and administration.

The Politics of Local Recreation

In any community, there are many different groups with their own ideas of what should be provided in public recreation resources. These groups may be represented in a number of different ways. Some are organized so that they can quickly mobilize pressure on park and recreation boards and staff to respond to their wishes. Others are not organized and have no easy access to decision makers.

For example, organized sports groups such as Little League baseball and age-group swimming have organizations with officers and funds. They can represent their needs for space, facilities, and financial support simply by sending representatives. Their needs are usually quite specific. Further, they have access to local news media and can claim to represent a large group of present and future participants. On the other hand, the mothers of preschool children are not organized. They do not know each other or have access to attention-getting devices. Their recreational needs for both themselves and their children may be both diffuse and localized. In rare instances they can organize to protest a park closing but seldom to influence its design.

Further, there are other community interests that know what they want from park and recreation departments. Realtors and developers want parks to make new neighborhoods attractive to buyers without infringing on the prime stock of housing property. Major business interests are concerned about tax rates and can effectively promote those interests at the highest levels. On occasion, other special-interest groups can organize around a single issue such as bicycle trails or a sport stadium on park property.

It may be that only the alert and observant recreation professional is on the spot to represent the needs of the unorganized. The location of neighborhood parks requires knowledge of patterns of park use and of the demography and geography of the neighborhoods. Advisory committees may include those with special and useful knowledge as well as those representing organized power in the community. In many cases, the knowledge acquired by the staff and competent advisors may be the main defense against a program unbalanced by the pressures of those who are focused and organized.

Not only the older industrial cities but almost all other kinds of communities are under pressure to reduce local taxation levels. When a reduction of services results from a combination of rising costs and lower tax rates, then public recreation is confronted with a double task. The first is to justify an adequate level of support for recreation in the community by identifying who will be denied access and opportunity if the programs are cut back. The second task is to maximize the benefits of the programs that can be supported by developing clear priorities. Significant provisions that cannot be duplicated privately or commercially take priority over those that are or can be provided in other ways. This requires that the recreation administrator be able to document just who are current and potential participants in programs and users of facilities as well as have comprehensive grasp of the total leisure opportunities of the community.

The Recreation Profession

Historically, professionals in recreation were aligned with physical education and social work backgrounds. Public recreation was understood in terms of athletics and physical fitness on the one hand and as one form of attack on the damage being done to people by the industrial city on the other. However, as outlined earlier, in the late nineteenth and early twentieth centuries, increased attention given to public recreation led to the formation of national organizations for recreation workers, park managers, voluntary board and committee members, and those using recreation in therapeutic programs. Eventually those with positions in recreation-related education programs also organized. Finally, all the organizations were brought under the aegis of the National Recreation and Park Association. At the same time, the American Alliance for Health, Physical Education, and Recreation continued its work in recreation based largely on educational affiliations.

In the early decades, the main employment opportunities were in community public recreation and with voluntary organizations. Recreation workers generally had obtained any relevant education in college departments of physical education or social work. Recreation was an educational adjunct to other programs. This has now changed dramatically. According to a survey, the growth in college recreation programs had gone from 63 in 1960 to 227 in 1970 to 345 in 1975.[6] Students are now being prepared for employment in community recreation, planning, natural resource management, voluntary organizations, insti-

---

[6] Ibid.

tutional and community work with special populations, program administration and leadership, outdoor education, and specialized programs.

The 1980s and 1990s have been years of change in programs in preparation for recreation employment. First, there has been a greater recognition of opportunities in the market sector of recreation provisions. The former assumption that students would prefer public sector positions has changed. The lack of growth in public recreation has been only one factor in this shift. Business has been viewed as not only offering more opportunities but also having a great variety of possibilities. Second, there has been a recognition of this variety and change in many of the curricula preparing recreation professionals. This recognition has raised a number of issues:

Should undergraduate curricula provide a more general background in the liberal arts?[7]

How can accreditation requirements be integrated with the increasing variety in recreation employment?

Should recreation curricula prepare more generalists who will have a number of career changes and moves?

What are appropriate means of attracting students in a time of increasing educational costs?

How can recreation curricula be coordinated with other programs such as sport, exercise physiology, business, and urban planning in recognition of the new interests and opportunities?

Change and diversity characterize every level of public recreation. There are more programs in the arts, physical fitness and health, and developmental human services. Many are in cooperation with other providers. The lines between public and market sectors, business and private, school and recreation are becoming blurred. As community populations change, so public agencies will also change in both form and mission.

Voluntary and Private Organization Employment

Voluntary and private organizations have been major providers of recreation opportunities, especially for children and youth, for most of the twentieth century. Many of these organizations have employed recreation workers to manage and administer various aspects of their programs. Most prominent among these organizations are the Boy Scouts, Girl Scouts, Boys' Clubs, Girls' Clubs, Camp Fire Girls, and many youth-serving organizations without national affiliation. Recreation personnel have generally been administrators of programs and are involved in training the local group leaders who actually carry out most of the program.

4-H Clubs are found in metropolitan areas as well as in the agricultural communities where they have their roots. Emphasizing agricultural and homemaking preparation, 4-H is supported by federal and state agriculture extension programs and has a significant recreation component. A broad spectrum of religious organizations has also engaged in recre-

---

[7] Diana R. Dunn, "Professionalism and Human Resources," *Leisure Today* (October 1986).

ation efforts that may include the employment of specialists. Along with the YMCA, YWCA, YMHA, and YWHA, there are the Catholic Youth Organizations and the countless programs sponsored by local and regional religious bodies. While summer camps are the most common efforts, various local congregations have developed extensive programs in the performing arts, sports, fine and folk arts, and social groups for their constituencies. Others have stressed recreation in outreach efforts directed at their neighborhoods or communities. While such programs generally have some religious and institutional aims, their content is recreational in character.

Private enterprises that may employ recreation personnel include country clubs with programs much more diverse than golf and swimming, residential recreation centers attached to large housing developments and to exclusive urban condominiums, homeowners associations in planned communities, and membership-only sports clubs operated on a not-for-profit basis. Such programs increasingly employ recreation directors who are skilled in program development as well as facility maintenance.

Commercial Recreation

Recreation businesses have tended to employ people with a business background and preparation rather than those prepared in recreation. Several academic programs have now been launched that will attempt to alter this pattern by combining business administration courses including personnel management and accounting with background in leisure studies and recreation. At the same time, recreation majors have increasingly found employment as managers of profit-seeking enterprises such as tennis clubs, racquetball clubs, swimming clubs, specialized camps that concentrate on particular skills or population groups, and various kinds of health and fitness facilities. The larger enterprises such as theme parks, outdoor recreation and camping enterprises, winter sports complexes, and urban athletic clubs may also offer vocational opportunities for those with education and experience in recreation. Chapter 20 outlines the scope of opportunities in the market sector of leisure provisions. Chapter 17 introduced the complementarity of the public and market sectors in the tourism industry.

Employee Recreation Programs

More than 800 companies belong to the National Employee Services and Recreation Association, but a variety of estimates suggest that another 30,000 to 50,000 companies have some recreation programs. In most cases it is only an employee-organized softball league and an annual picnic. However, there are also very elaborate programs provided by companies such as IBM, Eastman Kodak, and major chemicals producers. Programs may include expensive facilities such as camping areas, destination resorts, and country clubs. More often they utilize company-owned space for outdoor sports open to the families of workers and even to others in the community. Some are directed toward executives and are a part of the fringe-benefit package for those in upper management. The most prominent trend in employee programs is to unite recreation with health and "wellness" in efforts designed to improve the productivity of workers.

Among the less publicized recreation efforts are those developed by unions. The International Ladies Garment Workers Union and the United Auto Workers are two major unions with recreation programs and vacation opportunities for their members.

Frequently, such programs have found their managers within the personnel programs of the companies. However, as with other recreation programs, specialized preparation is being sought by the more stable and elaborate industrial providers. In some cases, recreation personnel not only manage facilities, direct programs, and train volunteers but also offer "leisure counseling" to those who are seeking more satisfying activities and relationships.

Current Issues in Public Recreation

During the period of the rapid expansion of public recreation programs in the 1960s and 1970s, the future was usually seen in a positive light. There would be more employment opportunities, more public provisions of programs and resources, and more people with the time and income to engage in recreation. These assumptions have now been called into question by reductions in tax support and time scarcities for many. Further, other government programs are in competition for tax dollar support. Very little can be taken for granted in the current political and social climate.

A number of questions have been raised about the future of public recreation and implications for those preparing for work in that field.[8] The following discussion focuses on some of the most provocative.

Seymour Gold argues that the environment of cities will be changing.[9] This change includes more diverse life styles oriented toward human development and expression, a spirit of self-sufficiency, taxpayer frugality, a consolidation of now-fragmented human services, a recognition of the limits of governmental responsibilities and abilities, declining purchasing power for many households and a loss of time discretion for others with dual incomes, and an aging society. These and other changes will require innovative programs by public agencies that are responsive to their publics. Gold expects that the traditional park and recreation districts will be joined by public utilities, franchises on public property, corporation resorts, neighborhood cooperatives, child-care centers with recreation programs, leisure counselors, and community colleges in the total spectrum of recreation opportunities.

Geoffrey Godbey takes a somewhat different approach.[10] In the past, for as little as fifteen dollars per resident, urban recreation agencies have provided a vast range of facilities and services. Now priorities will have to be revised. The city's residents are different, and the age of expansion is over. The central challenge will be to develop a new rationale for leisure services. Amid all the limitations in funding, there is a paradoxical reality. More

---

[8] Thomas L. Goodale and Peter A. Witt, eds., *Recreation and Leisure: Issues in an Era of Change,* Revised edition. (State College, PA: Venture, 1985).

[9] Seymour M. Gold, "Future Environments in Cities," in ibid., pp. 135–151.

[10] Geoffrey Godbey, "Urban Leisure Services: Reshaping a Good Thing," ibid., pp. 152–160.

and more, people believe in the importance of their leisure. They will demand not just more opportunity but also higher quality. In a process of decentralization, professionals will need to join with their constituents in deciding what is really most important and of highest quality.

Finally, Thomas Goodale agrees that the times are different and calls for rethinking the nature of recreation programs.[11] One factor will be the recognition of the needs for other services such as health provisions for the growing older population. Goodale argues that the principle of equity should be reassessed and reasserted, but not just in terms of participation or market demand. Cost reduction and efficiency cannot be the sole criteria for developing priorities. Rather, some measurements of need and of beneficial outcome are required if the welfare of the entire community is to be enhanced by public provisions.

It is not enough simply to attempt to do more of what has been done in the past. Rather, every dimension of public recreation is changing: the populations to be served, the mix of providers, the proportion of public revenues devoted to recreation, and the values that underlie participation. In order to prepare to be a part of this new era in recreation, professionals will be required to know more than programs, budgets, maintenance, and activities, They will need to be able to reassess continually the crucial place of the public sector in the vast and diverse spectrum of leisure and life styles of an ever-changing population and set of resources.

Summary of Issues

Recreation providers include the three levels of government—federal, state, and local—as well as a multitude of commercial, private, industrial, religious, and voluntary organization programs. Each type of provider offers employment opportunities for those with general management, planning, and leadership preparation in recreation and also for those with skills in working with particular activities, age groups, special populations, research, public relations, counseling, and fiscal administration.

Public recreation is based on the management for present and future generations of high-cost and fragile resources and on the need for opportunities directed toward those with acute limitations and inadequate resources. Land management has been the major recreation thrust of the federal government. Government has also provided programs in various institutions such as hospitals, universities and colleges, prisons, and specialized housing. On the local level, municipalities, counties, and special districts offer a wide variety of recreation opportunities intended to meet the particular needs of the population to be served.

Many comprehensive and innovative public recreation programs have been developed by governmental providers in all kinds of communities. Trends identified in public recreation programs include a greater stress on comprehensive long-range planning, serving special populations, cooperation with other types of recreation providers, volunteerism, environmental concern, diverse programs, and user participation in programming and decision making.

[11] Thomas L. Goodale, "Prevailing Winds and Bending Mandates," ibid., pp. 195–206.

Both academic programs and professional organizations are increasingly recognizing the diversity and breadth of employment opportunities in public, private, and commercial recreation and the need to cooperate with many other programs and disciplines.

HIGHLIGHTS

1. Public recreation is based on the need for general access to scarce and costly resources, long-term conservation of special resources, and equity in opportunity for those with acute limitations or deprivations.
2. Public recreation began as a response to urban conditions while the public parks were established to preserve unique sites for use and appreciation.
3. Although federal land management agencies dominate public outdoor recreation programs in size, all levels of federal, state, and local government have a variety of programs, often with a great diversity of activities and resources.
4. Current trends in community recreation include comprehensive planning, concern for special populations, cooperation, volunteerism, environmental concern, the inclusion of participants in planning, and cost recovery.
5. Changes in public recreation are calling for skills and preparation far beyond direct program leadership abilities.

Discussion Questions

1. What is the most persuasive argument for public recreation? What kinds of recreation provisions would be given priority based on this argument?

2. What are the primary criteria for allocating resources in public recreation? Are these the right criteria?

3. If community public recreation provisions were to disappear without warning or notice, what losses would be noticed first by residents? How would different kinds of people in the community be affected first?

4. What evidence is there that "all people need recreation"?

5. How have public parks and public recreation differed historically in their aims and contexts? What factors have tended to bring them together?

6. What would be persuasive arguments for a central coordinating recreation agency or department in the federal government? What might be the critical areas of responsibility for such an agency?

7. Which trends in community recreation are most significant? Which are most likely to continue?

8. How might the planning for community recreation be carried out so that those who are not readily organized politically would have their needs or desires fully considered?

9. How can public recreation programs change to meet the limitations and opportunities of the twenty-first century?

Bibliography

Godbey, Geoffrey. *The Future of Leisure Services: Thriving on Change,* State College, PA: Venture Publishing, 1989.

Goodale, Thomas L., and Peter Witt, eds., *Recreation and Leisure: Issues in an Era of Change,* Revised edition. State College, PA: Venture, 1985.

Knapp, R. F., and Charles Hartsoe, *Play for America: The History of the National Recreation and Park Association: 1906–1965.* Arlington, VA: NRPA, 1979.

Kraus, Richard, *Leisure in a Changing America: Multicultural Perspectives.* New York: Macmillan, 1994.

MacLean, Janet R., James A. Peterson, and W. Donald Martin, *Recreation and Leisure: The Changing Scene,* Fourth edition. New York: John Wiley, 1985.

Sessoms, H. Douglas, H. Meyer, and C. Brightbill, *Leisure Services: The Organized Recreation and Park System,* Fifth edition. Englewood Cliffs, NJ: Prentice-Hall, 1975.

Chapter *19*

Leisure and Education

Educators sometimes have the impression that schools are expected to do just about everything for children and youth. Moreover, some of those expectations appear to be contradictory. For example

Teach basic skills of reading, writing, and arithmetic *and* provide an educational climate in which children develop a love for learning.

Develop a solid set of values in children *and* teach them to have a respect for diversity in religion, culture, and life styles.

Keep youths off the streets and out of trouble *and* prepare them for life in the world as it really is.

Prepare students for the world of work *and* develop them as human beings prepared for citizenship, family life, and the fullest possible personal enrichment.

Meet minimum standards of competence in basic skills *and* start students on the journey of lifelong learning.

Be sure that all students learn agreed-on core material in history and the arts *and* launch them on continuing interests for a lifetime of leisure.

The paradox may be summed up as the twin aims of requirement and freedom. On the one hand, students should be required to grasp basic cultural material and fundamental skills; they should gain a common basis for participation in the society. On the other hand, they should be learning how to exercise freedom in ways that will facilitate learning and self-development when required school days are past; they should not only learn how to learn but come to love to learn.

The issue is much more basic than a conflict between preparation for work and preparation for leisure. Learning is critical to growth and development in the worlds of work and leisure. Basic motor and mental learning capabilities are presupposed in both. Further, there is evidence that freedom is integral to both learning and leisure. We seem to learn best when there is some choice involved in the process and when there is some satisfaction intrinsic to the experience.

Therefore, the real issues are reflected in such questions as

How can we learn to exercise freedom in an institution we are required to attend?

How can we learn the skills required to go on in education and at the same time experience the satisfaction of learning for its own sake?

How can learning be an element of the freedom and intrinsic motivation of leisure when it is identified with minimum standards, evaluation, and credentials for employment?

ISSUES

How is educational experience related to the development of leisure interests and skills?

Can the school be a major contributor to preparation for lifelong satisfying leisure?

What are current problems with organized school recreation?

Which school programs seem to have the greatest carryover to later leisure participation? Why?

Leisure and education are inextricably related. In school we learn basic skills and develop interests that are major factors in our leisure careers. Conversely, recreation is one element of the overall school program in which students are expected to learn to play as well as to study. Further, in a contemporary society overflowing with new knowledge, education is more and more a lifelong process. Continuing education in nonwork hours is sometimes aimed at improving job performance and sometimes at self-development. Lifelong learning appears to mix work and leisure aims in the learning experience. Yet, in the local community, recreation and education may be in competition for public funds.

In this chapter, we begin with evidence of the significance of education for leisure. Level and type of education are good predictors of leisure interests and participation. Further, the essential natures of education and leisure are closely aligned. Then the analysis turns to a series of issues concerning the possibilities of education for leisure.

Education and Leisure Socialization

Education level is generally the best predictor of some kinds of leisure participation. Although increasing age is correlated with decreasing participation in sports and physically demanding outdoor recreation and gender has in the past been related to engagement in contact sports and some social leisure such as bar-visiting, indices of social position have not proved as useful as once was hoped. Occupation, income, and social status are related to the leisure socialization process more in terms of opportunities and limitations than as determining factors in the socialization process.

Education is different. The school is a social and cultural milieu in which many kinds of learning take place. Some learning is part of the institutional program. Formal classes and after-class activities are designed to impart information, develop skills, and induce interest. The structured experience of a chemistry lab is intended to lead the student through a process in which techniques and results are learned and a deeper involvement with the subject is encouraged. Not only basic skills such as reading and computing and content material such as American history or nuclear physics but also cultural and self-development disciplines such as music and gymnastics are introduced. In general, the greater the number of years of education that are experienced, the greater the range of learning.

Education is related to age since it is measured by years of institutionalized affiliation. It is also related to family income and occupation level since higher education requires considerable financial resources. Further, families with a greater educational background tend not only to be able to support more years in school than other families, but they also tend to live in communities with more richly endowed schools and to expose their children to home experiences that aid and encourage learning.

Therefore, it is no surprise that those with more years of education are more likely to engage in a variety of sports and cultural activities, have the resources to travel, have access to leisure opportunities, and be interested in such activity. Family and education have reinforced both the development of interests and expectations and provided a range of opportunities for learning and participation.

In Canada, level of education was found to be more often correlated with both variety and frequency of outdoor recreation participation than was type of occupation, income, family size, city size, or even advancing age.[1] Occupation has little effect apart from education, but income and age each has an independent effect on outdoor recreation participation. As suggested previously, age and income are "filter" variables that represent a lack of physical and financial resources required for participation in some kinds of activity.

Education, on the other hand, is more than a filter. All the experiences related to going through high school, college, and continuing education add to the likelihood of developing interests, skills, and associations for leisure. Even when sports and games are begun with family members and neighborhood groups, there are opportunities in the school to play and raise skill levels. The resources and opportunities for many kinds of music, drama, dance, painting, ceramics, and other arts are a part of many school programs but less likely to be provided in the home. Years in school, in a general way, represent both the quantity and quality of learning opportunities.

Education, then, is both an index of opportunities for leisure socialization and a series of experiences. In the educational process the student is given opportunities to observe, explore, learn about, play with, continue, refine, and master a wide variety of activities. Further, level of education is a reasonably accurate measure of personal and financial resources

---

[1] Terrence H. White, "The Relative Importance of Education and Income as Predictors in Outdoor Recreation Participation," *Journal of Leisure Research,* 7 (1975), 191–199.

necessary for participation in many activities that require special equipment, space, travel, and other costly resources.

This view of education as an entry to skills, interests, and resources for leisure should be balanced by the report that only a small percentage of activities important to adults in one community were begun in school. Only 6 percent of the total and 11 percent of cultural activities had been done first in school.[2] However, these small percentages are probably somewhat misleading. School may provide a significant context of opportunity for learning and practice of activities begun elsewhere. The sports and cultural programs of the school are the main outlet for participation during many of the formative years of childhood.

The Importance of Education for Leisure

Culture is sometimes defined as all that may be learned by those in a society. It includes language as well as art, styles of movement as well as dance, and ways of caring for children as well as literature. In this inclusive sense, all human activity is dependent on the learned culture. Of all kinds of activity, leisure may be most a product of the particular culture—not only learned but learned in ways particular to that culture.

Further, although in contemporary societies most basic learning takes place in the family, the school takes an increasingly large role in the transmission of all that is culture. We learn in school much of what is common to most people in our society. And the farther we go in school, the more we learn that which is uncommon and specialized.

The school has a special place in leisure. Historically, much that has been identified as necessary for leisure has been nurtured in the school. Insofar as leisure is an essential part of full human living, education is a central institutional provider of preparation. Education is more than preparation for employment; it is intended to be preparation for the fullest kind of living.

Charles Brightbill was a forceful proponent of the importance of education for leisure. He believed that leisure and education were inextricably related in a kind of circle in which leisure leads to education and education back to leisure.[3] Both leisure and education are essential to self-development among humans. Both have a core of doing and learning for the sake of satisfaction through experience. Both should be free, open, changing, and universally available. Through education we learn and prepare for the expressions of leisure. We learn by acting in the special world of play. In leisure we both employ the fruits of education and educate ourselves further in leisure's relative freedom and self-determination.

Education is important as preparation for leisure. Much of leisure involves learning. In sport and games we learn physical skills within the contrived context of the activity. Formal education is even more important for cultural leisure expressions. The prerequisites of many games and artistic enterprises are the basic skills of reading and communication. Without language skills, written and oral, many opportunities for leisure are closed. For

---

[2] John R. Kelly, "Leisure Socialization: Replication and Extension," *Journal of Leisure Research,* 9 (1977), 121–132.

[3] Charles K. Brightbill and T. A. Mobley, *Educating for Leisure-Centered Living,* Second edition (New York: John Wiley, 1977).

much leisure a relatively high level of competence in communication is required. There is synergy between learning and leisure. The greater our abilities to learn, communicate, and think, the greater are our leisure opportunities and satisfactions. At the same time, in those leisure experiences in which our skills are exercised and stretched, we augment and refine them for further use in the school as well as in the studio or the playing field.

However, there may be an even deeper connection between leisure and education. Thomas F. Green has argued that the American school system has been geared toward preparation for work.[4] The school is intended to prepare young people for adult roles and to pass on the culture and value systems of the society. In this educational process some social and personal identity should be developed. However, the adult roles that have been primary in the educational design have been work roles. In school the student is prepared for employment in the dominant institutions of the economy—the office and the factory—and to accept the consumer roles in work, government, the community, and in education itself.

In the certification of students for entrance into adult roles through credits, grades, and diplomas, the school accepts a general standardization of requirements and curriculums. State standards for performance in public schools and accreditation of schools and colleges further the standardization. Like a factory, the school is expected to issue a reliable and certified product—in this case, the employable person. However, in the school as in the factory, the loss of autonomy required by this standardization may result for students in loss of a sense of relatedness to the process of learning, to others in the institution, and to their own identity.

But is this education or merely training? If education calls for the development of the self as well as acquisition of skills, for development of thinking and learning abilities as well as accumulating information, and for decisions about the future as well as preparation for preestablished roles, then education must contain a central element of freedom. Training may be totally prescribed when a defined skill is the end. Education includes possibilities of both individual and group decisions on matters concerning the learning process itself.

Many educational philosophers have emphasized freedom as a necessary component of learning. In North America, the work of John Dewey has been most influential in shifting attention from the content of learning to the process. Dewey stressed that some control over the environment by the student enhances learning and that play is learning for the child.[5] Maria Montessori, the Italian innovator, also stressed that development requires freedom and the opportunity for spontaneity.[6] She, in an approach different from Dewey's, developed a program in which the environment is carefully designed to facilitate the choice of activities appropriate to a developmental process of cognitive growth.

Perhaps the most influential current approach is that of Jean Piaget, a Swiss student of the developmental process. Piaget described stages of readiness to learn. Play is a major way in which the child takes in and tries out new experiences. Further, learning from other encounters with the environment may be consolidated in play that represents the stage of

---

[4] Thomas F. Green, *Work, Leisure, and the American Schools* (New York: Random House, 1968).

[5] John Dewey, *Democracy and Education* (New York: Macmillan, 1921).

[6] Maria Montessori, *Spontaneous Activity in Education* (New York: Schocken, 1965).

learning potential of the particular child.[7] Play and learning are not separable, but are united in the developmental process and in their common requirement of freedom.

Education, then, is like leisure in that both require some freedom. Both bring together a set of opportunities with some decision about what is worth time and effort. Both focus on present experience. Education is more than preparation; it is the engagement of the self with the culture in ways that do not allow for premature closure. Education is more than the consumption of *knowledge*. It calls for decisions about the meaning of that knowledge and about the learning process itself. In the end, education is a process that includes both freedom and structure, both self-development and the heritage of the culture. It is no wonder, then, that often in leisure we learn most and in real education we approach the intrinsic meaning of leisure.

Leisure and Education: Current Issues

As outlined, education is important in the development of leisure interests through the provision of opportunities in the school program as well as being important in the acquisition of basic cultural skills. Further, there is an essential union of real education and leisure in the freedom required for both. On a more mundane level, the relationship of education and leisure is problematic. A number of issues are significant in understanding education for leisure and leisure in education, in the present and in the future. The remainder of this chapter will explore several of these issues.

Freedom and the Functions of the School

The educational institution of a society has the recognized aim of preparation for participation in that society. A *function* is defined as the contribution of an institution to the maintenance of the social system. The recognized or *manifest* functions of the school include the teaching of skills required for participation in the economy, government, and other social institutions. Other manifest functions are the transmittal to students of the culture's history, symbol systems, and worldviews. There is also general acceptance of the aim of building character in the sense of imparting the agreed-on moral values of the community.

However, skill development, culture transmission, character building, and even role socialization are not the only functions of the school in American society. These are the manifest functions that are mandated by the society and for the most part accepted by those who direct school programs. There are also unrecognized or *latent* functions that contribute to the maintenance of the social system. Increasingly, analysts of public school systems are finding that these latent functions hold an important place in determining how educational institutions operate. If these functions are not carried out, then disruptions in the society will affect the entire social fabric.

One latent function is *warehousing,* the keeping of the younger population off the job market and, to an extent, off the streets. School is, among other things, a place to put a large proportion of physically and mentally capable youth for whom there is no place in

---

[7] Jean Piaget, *The Moral Judgment of the Child* (New York: Free Press, 1948).

the economy. Unemployment of youth, especially in the inner city, is already a serious problem even with most of those aged fifteen to eighteen in school and out of the job market. The school is a holding tank for this group for whom there is no regular employment available. As a result, many students are in school in order to meet legal and social requirements rather than because they desire to learn.

A second latent function is *sorting.* Increasingly, educational credentials are used as a passport, lack of which prevents portions of the population from even applying for some kinds of employment. A high school diploma, a college degree, or even a graduate degree may have little direct relation to ability to perform the requirements of a particular job. However, calling for an educational credential reduces the task of selection. Further, the school system with its grading, promotion, and eventual weeding-out processes performs as a filter for the economy. Those who leave the system earliest enter the employment market at the lowest levels, while those who continue in school are elevated to more rewarding opportunities. The school is like an elevator letting segments of its human cargo off at various floors of economic opportunity on the way up. While it is possible for some to get back on after once getting off or to sneak up the back stairs, most stay at the general level of their school exit.

Nor is this function entirely inappropriate. Insofar as the school is a miniature of the social system with its rules and roles, its authority and chain of command, and its many ways of rewarding and sanctioning behavior, ability to get along well in school is probably a good measure of ability to get along well in the world of business or government. Further, the less recognized aspects of role socialization in the school may even be designed to prepare students for particular kinds of economic participation. Schools in mill towns may stress rules, order, and discipline more than those in wealthier suburbs that emphasize initiative, the arts, imaginative thinking, and mastery of the more complex symbol systems of language and mathematics. Grades do, in part, measure how well students have met the expectations of the kind of school that fate and parental residence have placed them in.

One other latent function is also related to *socialization.* Through its courses and carefully screened teachers, a common way of viewing the world is imparted. The school not only rewards agreement with the perspectives of teachers, but administrators tend to reward the teachers whose public performance is in line with the value orientations of those representative citizens who make up the local school board. Further, even the basic assumptions of the school strategies and methods transmit implicitly a consensual way of looking at life. For example, the employment of competition and differential rewards almost from the first day of school has convinced many that only by pitting student against student and recording a ranking of their performance can children and other people be induced to perform well. The school system has so completely adopted a system of extrinsic rewards that it is difficult for many to comprehend that cooperation and intrinsic rewards may also be motivations for high effort and achievement.

All this has direct implications for the relationship of education and leisure. First, insofar as leisure is activity that is intrinsically motivated and chosen for anticipated satisfaction in the experience rather than for extrinsic reward, then much of the program of the school has led us away from leisure. Even programs that demonstrate and teach skills in activities of leisure such as sport and the arts may be caught in the external reward system. Motivation to do well may not be in the satisfaction of mastery of the body, the coordination of mind and hand, the good inner feeling that goes with graceful expression, or the thrill of creativity but rather in the ribbon, the trophy, the letter, the public recognition, the praise of the coach or teacher, or higher status in the school society. A school in which almost everything is required, evaluated, and rewarded or penalized is not likely to be good preparation for leisure.

This sorting, grading, and evaluating element of schooling poses a serious problem for those interested in education for leisure. After all, the school is *the* public institution which reaches almost all the population in their more formative years. It is in the school that the hope for the development of interests and skills, the tasting of satisfaction and excitement, and the opening of the wide world of leisure would seem to take place best. No recreation program or institution has the scope or the variety of opportunity that the school has. However, if the functions and the structure of the institution are in contradiction to the basic meanings of leisure as freedom and intrinsic satisfaction, then how can the school educate for leisure? In order for many schools to prepare their students for leisure as well as for employment, greater change may be called for in the institutional aims and premises than is generally expected. It will take more than a new course in *leisure activities 202*.

However, there are also indications that some of the changes necessary may be under way in response to the role requirements of the "postindustrial" economy. Insofar as the economic need for people with creative capacities and interpersonal skills is increasing and the need for those who take orders and repress imagination is diminishing, then the schools would seem likely to alter their programs to encourage and reward a variety of expressions more and conformity less. Even more important, the structure of the school programs may be redesigned to allow for more initiative and cooperative endeavor by the students. Teachers who are already encouraging learning that is more free and satisfying for its own sake may be supported and given greater influence. The competitive system may in time be replaced with one that encourages students to learn together in community. The reward system may be replaced with a process that leads students into the joy and excitement of learning itself. Then the school will be preparation for leisure in the fullest sense.

Second, as long as the functions of warehousing, sorting, and awarding credentials remain central to the school, then there will be a fundamental contradiction between the educational process and leisure. Leisure requires freedom. A school program that is built on interlocking requirements—even when among the requirements are physical education, sport, and music appreciation—will not find it easy to lead children into choosing such activity for its own sake. There is a dilemma here. Without some exposure to a variety of activities, how can students develop interests and even begin to know the satisfaction of participation? Many will not choose such activity without some persuasion or even coercion.

On the other hand, are interests developed by requirement? A program that attracts participation and learning would certainly be preferable to one that makes every student put in a certain number of hours regardless of preference or readiness. Add to this the evidence that often the main function of gym or physical education has been to tire out the students and train them to sit more quietly in the classroom, and the outlook for leisure education becomes even more bleak. When music or art is primarily a coffee break for the classroom teacher, gym a required energy reducer, and sport a battle for ranking, then it is no wonder that the carryover from school to adult participation has not been demonstrated in a measure supporting their expansion.

All this does not suggest that sport and arts programs are without merit. It does suggest that if they are primarily aimed at the future, at lifetime physical activity and artistic enjoyment, they need to be based on some choice and intrinsic satisfaction from the beginning. Just as leading problem readers to discover the excitement of reading seems more effective than tight discipline, so the experience of leisure will be more effective than the requirement of activity in school-based education for leisure. And if such an aim and method conflicts with some of the current functions of the school, then the conflict may be worth following up on.

Six other issues concerning the relationship between leisure and the school will be examined more briefly.

Recreation in the School

As suggested, some recreation within the school program has purposes other than preparation for future participation. Especially physical activity programs may be seen as an energy outlet for the school-bound student, as a means of control, and as moral training. Sometimes just doing the activity for its own sake seems to be the last purpose considered.

Students do get tired of sitting in one place. Buildings with small and crowded classrooms do produce pent-up energy that is expressed in the running, milling, and shouting that often accompany the dash for the playground during recess. Physical activity as well as the period of relative freedom are both desired by most students. However, mere provision for that release serves the purposes of the school first of all. A program aimed toward the future would draw students into testing some of the experiences of a variety of games, sports, and activities that may still be attractive in later years.

Using recreation as a means of control is much more serious. Participation in sport and arts programs is often used as a reward for obedience and cooperation in other aspects of the school program. The class play may be cast in ways that correspond to staff assessment of good citizenship. Coaches sometimes use team positions and playing time to enforce conformity in demeanor, style of appearance, and other nonsport elements of behavior.

Again, introduction to the satisfactions and meanings inherent in the experience of the activity may be obscured by their use for other purposes in the school or other programs. Music or drama participation may be more a reward for meeting expectations—even "time off for good behavior"—than an experience that catches up the whole self in feeling something never felt before. The intrinsic grace of a sport may be lost in the rigid behavioral requirements that accompany participation. No one has followed the consequences for later enjoyment of different modes of introduction of recreation in childhood. What is encouraging is that the intrinsic meaning of many such experiences brings many back to them in later years regardless of the ways they were introduced.

Education and the Arts

The greatest carryover from school to adult years appears to be in the arts. The school not only provides the beginning of experience in music, graphic arts, drama, crafts, and folk arts for many students, but becomes the main context for development and continuation for even more. A career of participation in an expressive art such as music would typically begin with family encouragement through various school opportunities and programs to the choice of one or more postschool affiliations with choirs, orchestras, bands, and musical ensembles.

Such a music career for the nonprofessional also illustrates the symbiosis among the institutional settings related to leisure. While the family is usually the beginning context for activity, the school, community, commercial enterprise, and church provide much of the context for the advancement of skills and the demonstration of the products of skill mastery. Concerts, plays, musicals, entertainment in restaurants and clubs, religious programs and worship, craft fairs, and commercial markets offer opportunities for the presentation of artistic efforts to a wider public. School programs are only a beginning for those who take a lifelong interest in artistic expression.

Suggested by this somewhat higher carryover in arts than in physical activities are two factors. First, the opportunities for artistic expression in the schools are usually elective rather than required. Second, community opportunities for arts and crafts continuation may be available from a wider spectrum of providers than has been the case with physical activity. An increase in public and commercial provisions for sport may alter the continuation patterns for adults.

Leisure and Basic Skills

The attempt to teach basic motor skills such as hand-eye coordination in physical education rather than to stress the sport enterprise with its winners and losers may encourage a greater proportion of students to engage in voluntary physical activity. The problem of possible lack of satisfaction and incentive in such required programs remains to be analyzed. However, such revised programs should not obscure the fact that the school is the primary teacher of several basic skills that are necessary for much leisure participation.

The most important and critical is the ability to read. Such a high proportion of leisure activities presupposes the ability to read on some appropriate level that a lack of reading skill will eliminate consideration of most of the games, cultural enterprises, and even sports that we take for granted. "Read the rules." "Read the signs." "Read the instructions." "Read the cards." "Have you read the book (or newspaper or review) so we can talk about it?" "Here's the menu." "Look in the television program guide." Further, being able to read faster or with greater comprehension gives an edge in many kinds of activity.

Of course, there are many others. Understanding and employing numbers, basic calculation, legible if not always graceful writing, and verbal communication are all basic skills that are taught in the school and required for much leisure. Insofar as meeting and communicating with people assumes not only verbal ability but also a common fund of information, the transmission of the culture in school becomes an assumed base for much conversation and building of relationships.

Education is, ideally, learning how to learn. When we have become familiar and even confident with our competence in learning verbal, cultural, and physical skills, then we are ready to attempt many kinds of activity that are new to us. Reading, writing, counting, coordinating, processing information, decoding language, and other basic competencies are developed in educational institutions and taken for granted by those who provide leisure opportunities. Now there are also computer skills. In this sense, the school is far more fundamental to leisure than carryover from specific programs would even begin to suggest.

The Issue of Finances

In general, interest groups within society are calling on the school to do more and more in preparation of a wider spectrum of people for full social participation. Students with physical, mental, and emotional impairments are being included in school programs from which they had formerly been excluded. New legal requirements tend to be more and more inclusive in defining the mission of the school. Those in the normal range of abilities but with handicaps related to poverty, language differences, and other social background problems are not only required to be included in the public education programs but to receive additional assistance toward reaching expected levels of performance. All of these programs are costly in a time when the overall student population is shrinking and budget increases are difficult to negotiate.

As a consequence, just as there is increased concern that schools should develop programs that prepare students for lifelong leisure expression and satisfaction and that they should endeavor to educate the "whole person," there are also a number of other demands on already tight sources of funding. While financial support for public schools is shared by federal, state, and local governments in varying proportions, each level of government must deal with competing demands on tax revenues. Only when the tax base is rapidly expanding can education count on the funds to expand both the number of groups who are served and the programs needed by the greater range of students. Compounding the problem is that despite some equalization efforts, for the most part the schools with the greatest proportion of special problems are those with the smallest tax base. The concern for leisure as integral to life, and therefore one proper goal of a full leisure program in public education, is not only legitimate but overdue. However, the competitive squeeze on resources does not suggest that implementation will automatically follow presentation. Those concerned about education for leisure will have to enter the political processes prepared for a long and difficult struggle for a place in educational programs.

The School, the Community, and Leisure

Adult and continuing education is one form of adult leisure. About half of the adult community college programs across the country are neither for credit nor applied toward a degree. Some are intended to upgrade employment skills. Some may lead to a change in occupation. But many are taken as leisure.

The greatest change in postsecondary education in the United States is the proliferation of community colleges. These institutions generally combine two-year college programs that lead to associate degrees and often on to four-year programs with vocational programs and opportunities for returning to school. Training for a wide range of occupations, including recreation leadership, is provided in these schools in programs that are usually not intended to lead to further education or to higher-level employment. The vocational programs are designed to prepare students to engage in a wide range of human services and auxiliary occupations.

At the same time, more than half the students enrolled in such institutions do not take part in such programs. At any age and stage in life, adults register at the local college for a course, workshop, one-time program, or series of general interest. Some are taking the opportunity to gain or refine a skill such as television repair primarily for employment. Some are interested only in expanding their leisure by learning how to batik, throw pots, or play computer games. Some combine practical and personal interests by taking courses in weaving, home decorating, or sewing.

Continuing education for some individuals is leisure in its own right. They take courses just because they find them interesting and enjoy meeting a new set of associates. Others have leisure activity in mind when they go to school to begin or hone some skill. In either case, the connection between adult education and adult leisure is evident. Learning itself may become not only one kind of leisure for those who return but for some becomes the center of their leisure life styles. The intrinsic and social satisfactions of learning have been discovered by many who no longer have to go to school.

For more than a hundred years there has been cooperation between public agencies that provide recreational opportunities and those responsible for public education. In some communities recreation is one element of the education program. In most there are separate administrations that seek various kinds of cooperation.

The most common coordination of provisions for education and recreation is the sharing of space. School buildings and gyms are used for evening and weekend programs administered by recreation agencies. Sometimes the space is rented and at other times some exchange is arranged. When communities are planned with foresight, schools and recreation areas may be laid out in coordinated ways. School gymnasiums and craft facilities, outdoor playing fields, swimming facilities, and even classrooms may be accessible to both educational and recreational programs. Coordinated schedules and programs are not only an efficient use of public resources but they also expand the possible offerings of both education and recreation providers.

Leisure Studies

With more than 300 programs for the study of leisure and recreation in existence in 1976, a new area of study and scholarship is emerging. In the beginning it was aimed entirely at the preparation of those who would be employed in various park and recreational programs in communities and by county, state, and federal agencies. The development and leadership of programs and the management of personnel and resources were stressed in such programs. More recently they have been expanded in response to the growing recognition of the importance of leisure and recreation for those in hospitals, prisons, and other residential institutions and for many with impairments that have blocked participation in many kinds of leisure activity. Whether the stress is on the therapeutic values of recreation or on expanding leisure opportunities for the entire population, education in recreation is now preparing many students for work with special populations.

The greatest increases in enrollment in the last few years have been among students who intend to enter recreation businesses. They may be attracted to travel and tourism, to outdoor recreation provisions, to community activity centers, or to employee recreation. As a consequence, academic programs previously oriented entirely to public recreation are developing links with business education. Although the preparation requirements for recreation business opportunities are not yet agreed on, there is agreement that the new entrepreneurs in recreation business should be grounded in both the fundamentals of recreation and business studies.

Another implication of the more inclusive spectrum of work hopes and aims among those studying leisure and recreation is that they need to be prepared to learn new skills, acquire new perspectives, and address new issues after they enter the world of work. No curriculum can provide students with all the knowledge and skills they will need even a few years after leaving school. Rather, the abilities of communication, critical analysis, and problem solving are basic to continued growth in any recreation-based field. Further, courses in recreation may attract more students from other fields such as business, forestry, tourism, and the arts.

Any profession requires continuing education for its members. Recreation is certainly no exception. Not only do specific skills and techniques need to be upgraded and learned, but an understanding of the changing social and economic climates is necessary for programming and planning. Particular provisions for recreation are a part of overall leisure styles that reflect the values, resources, and hopes of people who live in an ever-changing world.

As these programs have developed and grown, the scholarly base of the study of leisure and recreation has grown as well. Research and the dissemination of new concepts and knowledge have taken a larger place in departments specializing in preparation for leisure-related occupations. Faculties with backgrounds in disciplines such as economics, planning, sociology, and psychology are being brought in to broaden and deepen the basis of leisure education. The field has expanded so that universities with graduate programs have often been unable to keep up with the demand for able teachers and scholars.

At the same time, there is evidence that many students who do not plan on careers in recreation would like to know more about leisure. They are concerned about the place of leisure in their own lives. Some simply find leisure a fascinating human phenomenon and want to know more about it. Courses offered by recreation departments are sometimes taken for nonvocational reasons by up to half of those registered for many classes. Leisure has become an area of study as well as a vocational curriculum.

The implications of this change for faculty, course aims and outlines, textbooks, and assignments has only begun to be recognized in many college and university departments. The intentions of various students reading a book such as this one may be quite diverse even when they are enrolled in the same class. The possibilities of developing leisure studies as a subject in its own right are quite exciting for many in the field. However, the adjustments of older curriculums that were designed solely to train recreation leaders will not always be easy. Further, as in programs such as urban planning and medicine, the scholarship and research elements of the total programs will need to be integrated with the elements designed to prepare students to engage in the delivery of leisure services and provisions.

Summary of Issues

The complementarity of education and leisure takes many forms. Insofar as education is viewed as learning how to learn and learning is considered to be a lifetime process most fruitful when freedom is maximized and pursued for its own sake, then education may be one of the more enriching forms of leisure. On the other hand, within the schools, the very lack of freedom and insistence on competition and extrinsic rewards may be a major barrier to the unfolding of a rich life of leisure participation.

Perhaps some of the conflicts can be resolved as both education and leisure concentrate on what is happening to the person in the learning process. The best among current modes of education incorporate autonomy and self-motivation. The fullest kinds of leisure incorporate elements of learning and self-development. Both education and leisure draw on the products of the culture to enhance the total life of the individual. Both may have humanistic purposes as well as social functions.

When education and leisure are understood in this complementary sense and their special relationship is accepted, then they both make the most of choice and the ability to choose. Both are aimed at the unity of the whole person as a learning, deciding, acting, and relating human being. Both anticipate lifelong growth and development. Both require some public provisions in order to begin to achieve equity of opportunity for a diverse population. And both incorporate the experience of learning and living in the actualization of human potential.

HIGHLIGHTS

1. The school is an important context for introduction to a variety of leisure possibilities as well as for the development of both basic and specialized skills.
2. Common functions of educational institutions such as warehousing, sorting, and evaluating are in conflict with the freedom, creativity, and exploration that would prepare one for lifelong leisure.
3. The lack of freedom and choice in many school programs is being mitigated by reorientation toward choices of lifetime activities in school and a variety of opportunities after classes end.
4. The schools remain central to introduction and skill development in the arts; however, financial limitations are a threat to some education for leisure.
5. The study of leisure in colleges and universities is expanding in scope, purposes, knowledge base, and constituencies.

Discussion Questions

1. Why does interest in the arts seem more likely to carry over from school into adult participation than interest in sports?

2. Is learning for its own sake leisure? Can education be more *leisurely?* Should it be?

3. What are the major barriers to the realization of "education for leisure" in public schools? Are there any trends that might make leisure preparation a more central aim of public education?

4. How do children change in school? Do they learn to play?

5. What would be the most important new directions for college and university programs in leisure studies/recreation? Why?

6. How might public school programs be changed to help develop positive attitudes toward leisure? Are such changes possible? What specific new programs would make the greatest contribution to later-life leisure?

7. How are public recreation and public education in conflict? In what ways are they complementary?

Bibliography

Bowles, S., and H. Gintis, *Schooling in Capitalist America.* New York: Basic Books, 1976.

Green, Thomas F., *Work, Leisure, and the American Schools.* New York: Random House, 1968.

Henry, Jules, *Culture against Man.* New York: Vintage Press, 1965.

Kanter, Rosabeth M., *Men and Women of the Corporation.* New York: Basic Books, 1977.

Chapter 20

Recreation Business: The Market Sector

One recurring theme of this book is attention to what people do. Gathered from many sources, reference to actual behavior indicates the major place of commercial provisions for leisure. If commercial recreation is defined as the provisions that are offered for a price with an investment return as one aim for the provider, then the relative importance of leisure as business is evident. For example

Time diary studies show that youths invest large amounts of time and considerable money in their chosen music. Records, tapes, radio, and live concerts are a major leisure interest.

Adults spend far and away the most discretionary time with commercial television. In the three-community study, however, they ranked reading for pleasure as the most important nonsocial activity. Both television and publishing are major industries.

Travel is important to leisure, including family outings, visiting family and friends, short auto trips, and excursions to that new hub of American commercial leisure—the shopping center.

Days go by—and sometimes years—in which most Americans do not visit parks, engage in organized sports, or participate in community recreation programs. However, few days do not include some engagement with market leisure provisions—beginning with television and moving on through social visits to restaurants, reading about or watching professional sport at home, placing a little wager on something, or making a leisure-related purchase.

This is, after all, a market economy in which we negotiate. And this market is a major factor in our leisure as well as in our work.

ISSUES

How important are market provisions for leisure?
Are leisure businesses usually large or small?
How much do we spend for leisure in North America?
Do commercial providers offer a full range of leisure opportunities?
What kinds of recreation are most likely to be offered by for-profit enterprises?
Is the best leisure experience usually the most expensive?

The pervasiveness of market sector leisure offerings raises a number of critical issues. Some are quite practical:

> What are the employment opportunities in recreation business?
>
> What kinds of leisure opportunities can be provided adequately by the market sector of the economy?
>
> Is there needless overlap between commercial and public offerings?
>
> What kinds of recreation provisions can be profitable for the entrepreneur?
>
> How can public and business providers cooperate for the common good?

Other issues are related to the nature of leisure, the society, and the economy:

> Is there an imbalance between investment in provisions that yield high investment return and those that yield a high satisfaction return?
>
> How is commercial leisure related to social status symbolism?
>
> How do people spend money for pleasure? Do they come to equate purchase and possession of goods with leisure?
>
> How is leisure opportunity affected by the distribution of income in a society?

Two major elements in market sector recreation have been dealt with in the chapters on sports and travel. Television and popular culture were introduced in Chapter 16. Therefore, this chapter will concentrate on other kinds of commercial leisure provisions.

The Scope of Recreation Business

The products of recreation businesses are everywhere. In North America they are found on the street and in the playground, in the home and the forest, on the water and in the air, in the sports arena and the school, and even in church and in the shopping center. There are many kinds of equipment that facilitate participation in games, sport, hobbies, the arts, and a variety of social occasions. There are magazines, books, and guides that prepare for and promote participation. There are media that entertain in the home and in public places. There are events that draw us away from home and varieties of entertainment and learning that are delivered into the home. There are all the services that enable us to travel, learn, and recollect.

Recreation business finds its markets with all types of people. Toys for children are hung in the crib, and homebound retirees consume entertainment media and employ equipment to pursue leisure interests. Most gifts to children are related to play in some sense, whether the activity requires disciplined preparation or only a little time and interest. Both the vacation trip and the weekend for the child-rearing family employ countless supplies and services purchased at a price. For most people, there is seldom a day that is untouched by recreation business provisions for some activity, present or anticipated.

Just think about these questions:

How could we travel to visit friends or some attractive environment without the support services that exist?

How would public and school recreation programs continue without the equipment and supplies produced and distributed by recreation businesses?

Where would students gather in our communities if every commercial place providing food, drink, and entertainment closed next weekend?

How would we fill most evenings if all commercial opportunities to watch television, listen to music, and read were taken from us?

How would we plan next year's vacation or remember last year's if there were no travel guides, brochures, motels, near-shore services, agents, picture postcards, or photography supplies?

How would we plan any special evening if all the restaurants, bars, nightclubs, theaters, traveling shows, and other places of entertainment were closed? Or what if they were open but unable to inform us of their offerings through some form of advertising?

How many new residential developments attempt to attract purchasers by promoting their recreation opportunities rather than their floor plans?

Just examine the texture and fabric of ordinary life. It requires no compilation of statistics or testimonies to make clear this simple fact: Our lives have some elements of recreation-related business woven through the timetables and the locales of who we are and what we do.

In general, there are two types of recreation business. The first type is the *direct* supplier of goods and services related to recreation. The second is the *indirect* provider.[1]

Direct suppliers provide the equipment and environments that make recreation activity possible. They include the manufacturers, wholesalers, and retailers of recreation equipment and apparel. They offer campsites for rent, swimming pools and sport clubs for membership or daily fees, resorts at which to stay, athletic contests to watch, concerts to

---

[1] John R. Kelly, *Recreation Business* (New York: Macmillan, 1985).

attend, and tourist attractions to visit. They bring the circus to town, operate the cruise ships, open the racetracks, operate the bowling alleys, and plan the floor shows. They build marinas, organize tours, and offer a week on a ranch, health spa, or tennis camp. They combine lodges with ski tows and parking lots with lift tickets. They rent the raft, provide the guide, and bus clients back to their cars upriver. They are businesses, large and small, that deal directly with the customer.

Indirect suppliers are a step removed from our experience with the recreation occasion. For example, they advertise the products, edit trade periodicals for the business managers, and provide capital for new and expanding businesses. They develop the locales in which the direct providers operate, the shopping malls and centers or the residential locations for the community pool or golf course. They are the businesses that depend on holiday trade for their success—providers of food, drink, lodging, travel by air or rail, car rental, airport specialty shops, and even the supermarket down the road from a public campground. They are all the business services along the highway leading to a national park. They are all the businesses that have viable markets because people are engaged in some kind of leisure.

The financial scope of leisure in the United States is indicated by the current estimate that one dollar out of every eight spent is leisure-related. Up to 10 million jobs are provided in leisure industries and services. In 1983, an estimated $262 billion was spent on leisure in the market sector when all government spending for recreation totaled a little more than $8 billion. Government recreation spending was, therefore, about 3 percent of the total share of leisure and recreation spending. The Office of Management and Budget reports that in 1993 the federal government spent .17 of 1 percent of its budget directly on recreation resources. Estimated total market-sector spending on leisure, however, is as high as $600 billion.

Types of Leisure Providers

The range of kinds of commercial enterprises precludes dealing with any in depth. Many are small: "mom and pop" stores and refreshment stands along the road to a lake or marina, campgrounds on the hilly corner of a farm with four water hookups and two dry toilets, or a fishing concession in the artificial pond scraped out to provide fill for an interstate highway overpass. Others are massive: the billions invested in Walt Disney World, $30 million for even an "ordinary" theme park, at least $1 million for a modern bowling alley, and several hundred million dollars for a sports arena. The mega-malls of Minneapolis and Edmonton combine theme parks with shopping. Further, major recreation enterprises are more and more often part of a business conglomerate. One company's 250 bowling establishments are only one part of its multifaceted leisure-related structure. Another combined food-hotel-amusement park corporation is one segment of a multinational corporation. One trend may be toward *big* so that simple questions such as who owns the television network that owns the publisher that owns the bookstore are hard enough to answer without getting to questions such as the interlocked financing of major banking houses and insurance firms.

There are many types of commercial recreation enterprises. Despite the considerable overlap among the categories, those that follow provide an introduction to the scope of leisure businesses.

Destination Attractions

The traditional destination attractions such as the Grand Canyon or Yellowstone Park are not commercial. However, there are satellite businesses that capitalize on the attraction of these and other federally administered natural wonders.

Some destination attractions are related to seasons and sports such as Sun Valley or Aspen to skiing, Florida's beaches to sun and surf, or the site of the Super Bowl to the big game. Some cities like San Francisco or Las Vegas and multiuse resorts like Hilton Head Island or Lake Tahoe combine attractions. To such destinations, groups are drawn from distant cities by climate, special activities such as gambling, a variety of entertainments, and multiple travel packages combining air travel, hotels, and special opportunities.

All destination attractions are not national in their appeal. Many of the newer theme parks do not expect to draw visitors more than a day's drive away. While the total attendance at the twenty largest theme parks may be more than 50 million a year, most of those people come from within a 200-mile radius. Repeat business is required as the base on which to build a wider "special trip" clientele.

There are also the special commercial attractions. Probably the premier destination single business is Walt Disney World (WDW) near Orlando, Florida. WDW is a magnet that draws people from throughout the eastern half of the United States and Canada. Countless smaller theme parks, shows, and exhibits surround WDW with businesses, hoping to piggyback on the main draw. Travel packages frequently include these satellite enterprises as well as housing and transportation so that the travel entrepreneurs can receive a commission commensurate with their efforts.

The history of the change from amusement parks such as Coney Island that were developed around the turn of the century to the modern theme parks with their franchised and sponsored rides, leased space, and attempts to provide for a wide span of interests and ages is one of gradual change. The opening of Disneyland in California signaled the shift to themes and "experiences" from rides, food, and carnival booths. Current gross receipts approaching $500 million a year testify to the relative success of the shift. However, more recent studies have suggested that parks must either reinvest to maintain their power of attraction or expect a decline in popularity.

There are a number of theme parks that share characteristics. The Six Flags chain probably best exemplifies the genre. This "superpark" chain generally locates its enterprises on the edge of major metropolitan areas near one or more interstate highways. They offer both thrill and nostalgia rides, child- and adult-oriented entertainment on stage and walk-around shows, and a variety of amenities for sitting, climbing, sliding, and other postures. There are many kinds of fast foods and souvenirs. Half the revenue may come from inside expenditures and half from entrance fees. A Six Flags park will have a featured thrill ride, with a new one added often enough to bring back visitors who have "done everything."

The promotion is often directed toward the enjoyment of the varied environment. "Experience and excitement!" is one theme that summarizes what the theme park has to offer. The theme park offers an environment designed to produce an experience of entertainment, physical and sensory excitement, and a change from the usual. For the most part it is a one-day-at-a-time context. Further, it is intended to be a social experience shared with others whose companionship is enjoyed. It is "culture, cuisine, and camaraderie" broadly defined.

From Saturday Afternoon to Disney World

The late Walt Disney was explaining how the world's most popular commercial leisure destinations started:

> It came about when my daughters were very young and Saturday was always Daddy's day with the two daughters. So we'd start out and try to go someplace, and I'd take them to the merry-go-round and I took them different places and as I'd sit while they rode the merry-go-round and did all these things—sit on a bench, you know, eating peanuts—I felt there should be something built where the parents and children could have fun together. So that's how Disneyland started . . . it all started from a daddy with two daughters wondering where he could take them where he could have a little fun with them, too. (From WALT, Walt Disney Productions, 1975.)

From that beginning came Disneyland in California, which has now welcomed more than 300 million daddies, mommies, and children through its turnstiles, has yearly revenues of more than $120 million, and averages more than 10 million paid attendance each year. However, since 1970, the Disney enterprises have concentrated their capital investment on the really big destination park, Walt Disney World, near Orlando, Florida.

There is no way of describing briefly the 2,500 acres of vacation development of the 27,400-acre site. Even the Magic Kingdom's 100 acres of theme park with its six sections, including multifaceted themes of "Main Street" nostalgia, western frontier, patriotic American history, piratical adventure, movie-based attractions such as giant tree houses, river flatboats, and Nemoian submarines, and futuristic technology displays, as well as innumerable shops, fast-food restaurants, and industry-sponsored exhibits, cannot be described in a paragraph. In a phrase, the Magic Kingdom is the model theme park with all the appeal that a $700 million investment can buy.

The key phrases are ones like "destination attraction," "complete vacation package," and even "vacation kingdom." The aim is for entire living units to come for *the* vacation trip and to want to return in three or four years. So the Magic Kingdom theme park is barely the beginning. The Contemporary and Polynesian resort hotels have more than 1,500 rooms with their own pools, beaches, restaurants, shops, and services. The new Lake Buena Vista Village has four high-rise hotels, golf, and a village shopping center featuring international specialty shops. On the same property, the Disney forces have now built EPCOT—the Experimental Prototype Community of Tomorrow, where technology is demonstrated—and the World Showcase as an international theme park to be combined with the drawing power of the Magic Kingdom. Disney has created a world of fantasy, entertainment, and selling the products of the American economy.

To quote Disney again: ". . . there's really no secret to our approach. We're interested in doing things that are fun. . . ." Is it really that simple? Hidden somewhere in the WED think tank in Glendale, California, is there a market research genius who knows what people want better than they know themselves? Is there a computer behind the success story?

Yes and no. The Disney planners do tend to follow the lead of their late founder in deciding for the market what should be attractive rather than trying to respond to the market. They have become the standard for "family entertainment," both on film and in the destination resort, Disney World is *the* place, *the* vacation destination, *the* model of entertainment engineering. In high seasons, they operate at or near capacity.

And what happens when people get to Walt Disney World? An observer sees people in groups—couples, parents with children, students, groups of couples whose children are grown, and various tour groups of relatively uniform ages and often sexes. Generally, these couples and groups are quite busy moving from one attraction to another, checking the A-B-C labels of their tickets against the admission codes, standing in line for the major attractions, eating, shopping, and consulting their guidebooks, while hurrying on to the next line. They seem, for the most part, very busy as they unsmilingly work through the business of spending money at the magnet destination of their big trip.

There are also some things the visitor will not see. Best publicized is the underground network of trash removal tubes and tunnels big enough for trucks so that the above-ground area is clean and uncluttered for the tourist. Disney World may be for all ages, but it is not for those whose childhood experiences and present financial resources are not pretty much middle class. Also not noticed by the one- or two-day visitor is the computerized routinization of personnel, supplies, and schedule. Even the charmingly boisterous parade is timed and programmed to the gesture and the minute. Behind the Mickey and Goofy heads, the people are quite interchangeable.

The most common visitors are families. They include children under twelve and seek some experiences that they can enjoy together. Much of the pleasure of the parents comes from that of the children. In many cases the trip is one that has been planned for more than a year and has involved some saving to cover costs. Many families plan to return to WDW about every three to five years. The most common states of origin are Ohio, Illinois, Pennsylvania, and others in the Northeast and Midwest, as well as Ontario in Canada. The marketing and planning from the very beginning of Disneyland and WDW has been family-oriented. As with Disney films, the intent has been to produce entertainment that can be enjoyed on several levels. The marketing emphasis is on WDW as the complete leisure destination. Most recently, WDW has expanded both its entertainment and its accommodations to the extent that major advertising programs are necessary to fill the rooms and provide a profit on the billions invested. On an international scale, Disney World has been a success in Japan and a failure in France.

Travel Support

Excluding expenditures on the means of private travel, usually the automobile, how is money for a leisure trip spent? One estimate is that lodging, food, and drink are the major costs of travel. From every dollar, twenty-three cents is estimated to be spent on lodging and twenty-seven cents on food and drinks. The remaining fifty cents is divided as follows: recreation and amusement twelve cents, gasoline and auto expense nine cents, clothing and footwear eleven cents, jewelry and souvenirs seven cents, and personal items and miscellaneous eleven cents.[2]

It would be impossible to arrive at an accurate figure for how much of the gross expenditures on hotels and motels, auto service and supplies, food, clothing, and equipment is leisure-based. The specialty shops in hotels and airports sell to many business travelers as well as tourists. The fast-food restaurant near a highway serves travelers, truck drivers, and locals. Further, the 50 percent estimate for food and lodging is probably high

[2] Robert W. McIntosh and Charles Goeldner, *Tourism: Principles, Practices, and Philosophies,* Fifth edition (New York: John Wiley, 1986).

for long camping trips and low for weekends in expensive cities. Nevertheless, it is travel support that may well account for the largest investments in the commercial leisure provisions spectrum.

Community Activity Centers

Almost every community has some recreation businesses that offer participation opportunities. Some provide facilities for particular sports; others are oriented toward the arts, games, social activity, or some combination of activities. The key is participation. The business exists because the activity requires some kind of space or equipment that can be rented for use. Further, there is a demand for use beyond that provided through the public sector. These businesses are community activity centers.

Such businesses can be categorized according to the kind of activity they make possible:

Outdoor sports—Golf, tennis, swimming, fishing, and shooting are some of the activities that may be the basis of a business.

Indoor games—Electronic and mechanical games in arcades, card games, and a variety of gambling games (legal and illegal) are business offerings.

Physical fitness and development—Fitness and exercise programs, development programs employing specialized equipment, and combinations with swimming or sports are offered.

Arts—Painting, ceramics, dance, music, theater, and other arts programs may include both instruction, equipment rental, and opportunity for the exhibition of products.

Motorized activity—Various kinds of motorized carts, small race cars, motorcycles, and winter sport vehicles may be rented and special space or track use offered by the day or hour.

Other outdoor activity—Picnic grounds, horseback riding, gliders, flying, miniature airplanes, and a range of other outdoor activities often require special space and equipment.

Special activity—A variety of opportunities for dancing, special parties, and meeting others at an activity-based event or program can be the basis of a business concept.

New technologies and marketing concepts keep the picture of such community activity-based businesses always changing. New combinations are developed that tie together compatible resources or appeal to the same groups of participants. Some of these businesses demonstrate a short product life cycle with a rapid growth and peak period followed by quick decline. Others build a stable market. Each year or two finds some new "hot item" being promoted as the latest recreation opportunity. These community businesses are based on leisure participation away from the residence. Many kinds of recreation cannot take place—at least for most participants—in private space or with generally accessible equipment. Other kinds of recreation require some period of directed learning.

Bowling is the standard major commercial indoor sport activity. Most bowling alleys are operated for profit, some by major corporations such as AMF's Brunswick division. The size may vary from four to thirty-two lanes with other provisions such as restaurants, snack bars, bars, pool and billiards, and pinball machines frequently on the premises. Bowling centers expanded rapidly during the 1950s and experienced some decline to about 6,000 centers in the 1960s. Estimates of up to 40 million bowlers in the United States would tend to include many who are very occasional bowlers. The basic clientele of a bowling center is the regulars, league and group members who come on a weekly schedule during prime evening hours. Current trends indicate a continued gradual decline in bowling participation.

In the 1970s, racquet sports had a dramatic increase in participation. Indoor facilities for tennis and racquetball were developed in most urban areas. The end of the tennis boom in the 1980s led to a consolidation of the market for profitable indoor centers that was accentuated by the high costs of operating and maintaining such large structures. Racquetball participation reached a peak in the late 1970s and then declined to a plateau.[3] Some businesses failed and others diversified into fitness and sport programs with a broader appeal to women and families. Despite being more space efficient than tennis, as well as easier to learn, racquetball demonstrated that any activity has a life cycle of growth, peak, and some decline that is based on the nature of the activity and the breadth and commitment of its market segments.

Many community activity businesses find themselves in competition with opportunities offered by private clubs and nonprofit organizations such as the Y's. Increasingly, colleges introduce students to indoor sports such as swimming and the racquet sports. This may become a factor in enlarging markets for business enterprises in the future. The major limitation of market provisions for indoor sports is the cost of building and maintenance, which requires either high user fees or a substantial subsidy from a sponsoring organization. One new development is the provision of indoor sport facilities in clustered or high-rise housing for upper-income patrons.

According to a 1987 study,[4] the average indoor racquet club has an operating budget of more than $400,000 and employs seven full-time and ten part-time workers. Health clubs have a mean budget of more than $800,000 and employ about eleven full-time and seventeen part-time workers. The multipurpose health club, often with a targeted market segment, is now the growth area in community activity centers. Participation at such sport and fitness centers, however, seems to have peaked in the mid-1980s and is now stabilizing at lower levels.

Outdoor Sport Provisions

Business provisions for outdoor sports include golf, tennis, pool swimming, skiing, and ice skating—to name only some of the most common. Downhill snow skiing has had a rapid increase in participation with 10 million who may have skied last year. While some cities

---

[3] John R. Kelly, *Recreation Trends toward the Year 2000* (Champaign, IL: Sagamore Press, 1987).

[4] *Managed Recreation Research Report, 1987* (Minneapolis, MN: Lakewood Publications, July/August 1987).

and counties are developing ski areas in or near urban areas, most ski developments are commercial. In the West the land is frequently leased from a federal agency or the state. Along with tows and lifts for which a fee is charged, there are equipment shops, lodging, food concessions, instruction, and often evening entertainment including dancing and music. Major developments such as Vail and Aspen in Colorado, Sun Valley in Idaho, and those near Salt Lake City involve enormous investments and complex provisions. Packages are developed in which airlines, ski operators, and lodging providers work in cooperation. In lower altitudes, small hills and snow-making machines provide a different kind of experience. Skiing in New England is long-established and some enterprises have drawn second and third generations from the seaboard cities. Downhill skiing is expensive in equipment, learning, access to slopes, lodging, and travel. While younger skiers have found many ways to cut corners, regular skiers tend to be at the upper end of the income distribution in North America. The more than 1,000 areas in the United States attract those who can pay for the experience of the rush downhill.

More than half of the nearly 10,000 golf facilities are operated for profit. However, a significant number of the better golf courses are private with title residing in the limited membership. In some cases, land developers have built golf courses and closed them to daily-fee players only when the membership reached a certain level. Such enterprises are commercial not only in their operation but also in their long-range intent. Since the value of a golf course near a population center increases, some courses are not only a short-range business but also a long-range investment that someday may be developed for housing. Although the proportion of adults who play golf is not high—about 20 percent of adult men and 7 percent of women—many who play at all play with regularity. Fees and memberships have increased in price in the past decades, making golf another relatively expensive outdoor sport. The more than 15 million who play are a market not only for the use of the courses but also for affiliated equipment shops, lessons, clothing, and food and drink establishments. Growth in golfing is limited by the scarcity of urban space.

Tennis, on the other hand, is much less a sport for the upper class than it was thirty years ago. Much of its growth in the 1970s was among middle-income and younger segments of the population. Outdoor tennis clubs and commercial facilities are a minor part of the total set of opportunities. Tennis outdoors is most often played on public courts. The major change is the provision of outdoor courts in housing developments where the business aspect is directed toward sales. Business provisions for equipment and apparel expanded during the 1970s, along with special tennis camps where devotees go for a week or more to improve their game in a vacation setting. Current declines in racquet sport participation include all ages.

Spectator Sports

Spectator sports are dealt with in Chapter 13. Total attendance at major league baseball, college and professional football and basketball and hockey together ran over 175 million in 1991. The business aspects of the major sport enterprises have received increased attention in the last few years. Once primarily the playthings of a few rich people, teams have become more and more sophisticated combinations of tax write-offs, capital depreciation, public relations, and investments. They are big business in every sense, with corporate investment for purposes of diversification not unknown.

Skill Acquisition

Teaching skills associated with leisure is one type of small business that requires little capital. As a result, such enterprises go in and out of existence by the thousands every month. The teaching of pottery, drawing, painting, tennis, racquetball, golf, fly casting, Eastern martial arts, astronomy, needlepoint, knitting, dog obedience, dance, yoga, singing, musical instruments, flying, and crewel embroidery is done in homes, public and private schools, community colleges, public recreation programs, private and public clubs, and housing developments.

A large proportion of such instruction is not commercial. It takes place in public programs and schools and in the free exchange of skills among family or friends. However, teaching has become more and more a business in the tennis clubs, martial arts schools, dance academies, gymnastics programs, sewing machine outlets, and guitar stores. For the most part, commercial leisure instruction requires only a small investment of capital. Some instruction may be given for profit on public facilities that are rented. Some requires only the repainting and minor equipping of a rented space such as a vacant store. Basements or garages may be refitted for instruction in some arts. Racquet sports, gymnastics, or golf are usually connected with a major capital investment. Even there, the instructor may work on a lease or commission basis.

The largest investments tend to be in the expanding special interest instruction camps. For children, youth, and adults, there has been an increase in tennis, football, riding, music, climbing, swimming, and other skill development camps. Along with a regular camping program, there is stress on the instruction in a specific skill. For adults, the aim tends to be leisure participation. For youth, the aim may be to raise the level of competitive performance for school or amateur programs. A major tennis camp may employ fifteen to twenty instructors teaching in programs that tend to be quite expensive.

Other skill acquisition camps are designed to teach a group with some learning disability such as a physical handicap, blindness, deafness, or mental impairment. Considerable research now underlies the efforts to teach all kinds of skills to individuals once excluded from physical and cultural expression and development.

Outdoor Resource Sites

Some outdoor resources are required for sports like skiing, as was already discussed. There are other resources that are multiuse or that have a special attraction simply for appreciation. The great spectacles such as the Grand Canyon, Wyoming's Teton mountains, Going-to-the-Sun Highway in Glacier Park, and the perennial Yellowstone geysers and pools are not commercial. They have been set aside by the federal government to be protected and enjoyed. Around such attractions service enterprises cluster on the common approach routes and near the entrances.

Other kinds of sightseeing involve less dramatic but more accessible sights. Two-thirds of the adults in the United States reported taking at least one trip to see special attractions during 1990 and almost 40 percent took five or more such drives. This contrasts with the less than 6 percent who engaged in downhill skiing. Such outdoor sites include flood-control reservoirs, state and national forestland, and even county parks. When at the site, visitors may walk, swim, boat, picnic, view the scenery, play volleyball, or sit around playing cards. In any case, business providers are there. They operate the food, drink, and equipment rental concessions on a lease arrangement with the government managers. They are on the highway nearby to sell the liquor that cannot legally be sold (or often consumed) on the public land. They are the orthopedic surgeons near the Olympic ski training site, the tow service at the local garage, and the campground that takes in the overflow on weekends from the public provisions. They sell climbing gear near Yosemite, skis near Mount Washington, and life preservers near Lake Mead. In some cases, they own the lake and charge for fishing or control access to the water and charge for boat launching.

Mechanized Activities

If 3.5 million people tried snowmobiling or motorcycling last year, their numbers are dwarfed by the 12 million or so whose movement across the water was powered by a gasoline engine. There are high-powered "bass boats" on inland waters and lavish cruisers on the Great Lakes, Puget Sound, or the coastal waterways. Their numbers are smaller, but two-thirds of America's pilots fly primarily for pleasure. Disney World has a scaled-down midget auto racing "speedway," and many local racetracks are being developed across the country, especially in areas with a history of stable industrial employment.

The rise of the snowmobile was the most spectacular development in mechanized leisure in the 1970s. As many as 2 million machines now exist in North America, a jump from less than 25,000 made in a decade. The industry suffered from overproduction and mild winters during the mid-1970s, but may have stabilized since. Snowmobilers require access to miles of trails and seek to have their special space needs met by public land managers. Their clubs have become a political force in some northern states and Canada. Clubs, competitions, and outings are augmented by the commercial provisions of parking space at taverns and motels near choice snow areas. Mechanical service and parts supply are major businesses dependent on mechanized activities.

Off-road vehicles (ORVS) such as trail bikes, four-wheelers, four-wheel-drive cars and trucks, and even amphibious carriers are also a major leisure-related business. ORVs have become a major management concern for those who plan for the use of public land due to the environmental damage and the complaints of nonmotorized users and pose safety problems for many kinds of use.

Popular Culture

The provisions of music, entertainment, and other popular arts opportunities are dealt with in Chapter 16. Here the note that popular culture is the largest single type of market sector leisure provision in investment, return, and participation is inserted as a reminder rather than a summary.

"High" Culture

In the same way, provisions of theater, classical music, and other arts are approached in Chapter 15. The record industry, publishers, manufacturers of instruments and other equipment, sales of art, and all the businesses that provide services such as booking, managing, and financing are included in commercial leisure, whatever their self-definitions of employment.

Equipment and Service Retailers

These enterprises have been mentioned in relation to the types of activities. There are three kinds: (1) the major outlet for equipment such as chains of sporting goods stores that may be integrated with some manufacturers, (2) the local establishment, often specialized, that is incorporated and has several employees and considerable financial stability, and (3) the one-person or "mom and pop" enterprise that tends to serve a very localized or specialized clientele. Some combine sales with rentals, repairs, and even instruction. While the chain operations are little different from other large retail corporations, the smaller local stores often develop their own community image and are integrally a part of the entire leisure provision network of the area.

Some small business owners combine their product or service with personal participation in the activity. Skiers start a repair service or a food shop near the slopes so they can engage in their cherished activity. Cavers open a little store near the caverns, and skydivers pack parachutes to make ends meet. Some of the more expensive activities require services so that more affluent participants can conserve time by purchasing convenience. Such businesses may call for little capital and even lend themselves to seasonal opening and closing. Some who choose life style ahead of stable income may follow the sun or the snow with their service enterprise.

Gambling: Legal and Illegal

Statistics on gambling are closely guarded. Only the tip of the iceberg is sighted in such official reports as those on state lotteries, city or state off-track betting, Nevada tax receipts, and now the "riverboat" and reservation gambling operations. In 1994 an estimated sixty riverboats did a $3 billion business. Estimates are that expenditures in legal and illegal gambling may exceed $100 billion per year in the United States. Whatever the total, it is clear that legal gambling is rapidly increasing.

People gamble on horse races, lotteries, stock exchange "numbers," pinball scores, cards, sports, and almost anything with an element of chance that makes it somewhat unpredictable. The Las Vegas Strip is only the most dramatic visual evidence of the scope of gambling as a leisure business. In one national survey 30 percent of the adults admitted having played cards for money, more than 18 percent betting on sports, and about 25 percent bought state lottery tickets in the past year. The Simmons National Survey found over 125 million adults had visited a gambling casino in 1990, almost half of them more than twice. Along with popular culture, gambling may be the biggest "leisure" business of all.

However, its status as leisure may be questionable, especially for many poor people who really hope to change their lives by winning. Gambling is both big business related to organized crime and very small business in the back rooms of bars and on street corners. It is "hustling" as well as lotteries and traveling poker games as well as the Nevada casino.

Food and Drink Provisions

Food and drink purveyors auxiliary to other recreation—the hot-dog stand across from the local park, the highway restaurant, the ski lodge bar, and all the on- or near-site facilities—are one major kind of leisure business. However, there are more primary kinds of food and drink businesses related to leisure. There is the neighborhood bar. In more urban areas there are specialty bars for working males, various sexual orientations and interests, particular preferences in style and decor, and just for drinking. Restaurants are even more varied according to price, mode of service, type of food, and quality of food and service. More than 30 percent of American males went to a bar or tavern several times a month or more last year. Only 35 percent never entered a bar. Half the adult women went to a bar at least once and 25 percent at least once a month. In the last month 70 percent of American adults ate in a restaurant at least once for pleasure. Going out to eat and/or drink is a major leisure activity. Eating establishments did over $190 billion total business in 1992.

Of course, there are many styles of such leisure outings. A family with several children may go to their favorite fast-food chain on Friday to give both the kids and mother a change. A couple with gourmet tastes and high incomes may fly to another city for a prearranged and very expensive meal at a very special restaurant. In between are all those who eat out for a change, to get out of the house, to celebrate, to enjoy a different style of food, to be with friends, or in a leisure routine. The proliferation of fast-food, pizza, and chicken emporia and microwave-equipped chains with standardized menus suggests that predictable price is a major factor for many who eat out. However, ethnic houses, steak houses, and local fare also have their clienteles. Eating and drinking out is a social kind of leisure, especially on weekends when people find the away-from-home atmosphere symbolizes that food and drink are for pleasure and companionship more than nourishment.

Equipment Manufacturing

One manufacturer has advertised that its firm "makes weekends." That is a bit of an overstatement, but this division of a conglomerate does produce motorcycles, snowmobiles, pool tables, tennis racquets, boats, and a long list of other leisure activity equipment. The old sporting goods firms have expanded their lines to include items that Mr. Spalding and Mr. Wilson never heard of. Some firms have been incorporated into large investment management operations with international connections. That famous old brand may be placed on equipment made anywhere in the world, frequently by people who have never seen the activity. Major purchases such as at-home swimming pools and golf and tennis balls for seventy-five cents are two ends of a wide cost spectrum. Some purchases are primarily for style and status; others are very utilitarian.

The market for leisure goods—powerboats and hammocks, parkas and swimsuits—has grown rapidly. The emphasis is on replacement, upgrading, and new styles. Since so much leisure activity requires standing up and moving, in the local retail outlet the big-profit item is shoes. Dealer networks compete with discount houses. Specialty retailers try to develop a clientele by offering expert advice, and the franchise outlet advertises price and name brands. Mail-order suppliers with their catalogs and advertising in specialty magazines are now a major force in equipment marketing.

How much is spent on leisure-related equipment? Again, it depends on what is included in the category. However, the consumption of equipment, special clothing, and necessary service has created a vast network of marketing, product design, wholesaling, retailing, and service that altogether may be one of North America's five largest product categories in total sales.

No list of all those "things" is possible. They range from special-length shoelaces to $500,000 ocean yachts, from socks to surfboards, and from caps to computers. The classification of types of products in Table 20–1 indicates why product development varies widely in aims and methods.

Any of these can be directed primarily toward the *provider*—the school, public recreation program, activity-oriented business, resort, service, instruction program, or any other agent offering resources for participation. Or the product can be aimed directly at the *user*—the recreation participant who is expected to provide a market for the product because it enables or enhances the recreation experience. Some products will be used by both providers and participants.

Other Support

Without entering an elaborate analysis of business, it should be mentioned that the infrastructure includes many elements hidden from the regular consumer. Among these are the market research enterprises, either in-house or independent contractors. Today, measured by dollars spent, most of the research on leisure in the United States is carried on as investigation of present and potential markets for leisure-related products. This includes everything from a secret study of potential National Football League expansion sites to estimates of the number of women tennis players entering the sportswear market.

Increasingly, major leisure purchases may be financed through banks or other lending agencies. Credit cards are often used for travel and other leisure expenditures at the restaurant and store. And the credit lines of manufacturers and retailers themselves are one element of the total financial structure of commercial recreation.

Advertising enters the commercial leisure scene in two ways. The first is simple: the promotion of leisure goods through the various means of advertising. The second is more subtle. Leisure locales, self-images, relationships, and styles are exploited to promote the sales of other products. Leisure satisfaction, social and personal, is promised to those who wear the right outfit, drink the right drink, or drive the right car. Not only are leisure goods advertised, but leisure satisfactions are used to sell products quite unrelated to freedom, expression, and companionship.

All the activity that is part of the merchandising enterprise is involved in commercial leisure. Recreation goods are sold like others in a complex set of investments, marketing,

TABLE 20–1   Types of Recreation Products

Type	Example
Sports	User equipment: racquets, clubs, balls, etc.
	User apparel, shoes, etc.
	Facility items: surfaces, goals, etc.
	Instructional equipment: from batting cages to fishing lines
	Special facilities: artificial ski slopes, half-size tennis, softball, training apparatus, etc.
Services	Environmental care for grass, surfaces, amenities, etc.
	Safety equipment
	Storage lockers, etc.
	Food preparation equipment
	Maintenance equipment and products
Arts	Instruments and equipment
	Facility design and maintenance
	Amenities
	Auxiliary services and products such as tickets, refreshment dispensers, etc.
	Recording equipment
Technology-based	Fiberglass, epoxy, or other products requiring a materials expertise
	Computer products for management, fitness measurement, or the activity itself
	Plastic parts, products, and other items requiring molding technologies
	Other electronic games and products
Hobby-based	Tools for material shaping, cutting, fastening, etc.
	Storage for collections
	Materials for fashioning products
	Means of distribution or communication
Market-segment-oriented	Playground equipment
	Corporate fitness equipment, guides, and programs
	Amusement park games, rides, prizes, and related items
	Residential pool auxiliary equipment, maintenance, additions, etc.
	Activity-defined products involved in engagement in any recreation activity
	Special population adaptations and aids

manufacturing, delivering, and promoting mechanisms. While many recreation businesses are small, leisure business in general is not.

Specialty Publications

A visit to the magazine rack of a local store gives only an initial glimpse of the vast offering of magazines aimed at specific leisure markets. While the largest circulations are associated with activities with the greatest number of participants, such as boating, spectator sports, stamp collecting, and home crafts, there are probably a thousand more focused periodicals for the followers of rock climbing, embroidery, china painting, or scuba diving.

Advertisements carry the largest share of the publication and distribution costs, and most readers are subscribers. Frequently, the magazine is part of the membership package of an association of breeders of afghans, MG drivers, or amateur archeologists.

Employment Preparation and Services

Most often overlooked is the support industry of preparing and placing employees in recreation businesses. Schools for chefs, motel operators, and golf course managers are now augmented by training opportunities in both public institutions and private trade schools. However, most training is not yet included in college and university programs. Increasingly, however, employment agencies and job counselors are recognizing the importance of commercial leisure in the employment opportunity spectrum.

The question is still where to stop. Why not go on to mention the accounting firms that manage the accounts of leisure businesses, the designers of leisure-oriented housing complexes, the providers of hair shampoos and body massages, and a thousand more variations on things people do largely for pleasure? However, the point may be considered amply illustrated: recreation business is quite a large iceberg in the sea of modern life with its above- and below-surface elements highly significant in both the economy and in the leisure of individuals.

Expenditures on Commercial Recreation

Accurately predicting the future of commercial leisure as a segment of the American economy would require information impossible to acquire. However, there are a number of figures that point to steady but not spectacular growth if present economic trends are continued.

Total spending on leisure is estimated to be more than $600 billion a year. That includes home and transportation expenditures with leisure aims and uses, eating and drinking, travel, and all sorts of gadgets and apparel. The increase is close to 100 percent in ten years, but that figure is not adjusted for inflation. The percentage of incomes being spent directly on leisure has not changed as dramatically. Direct expenditures on recreation have increased from 5 percent in 1970 to 8 percent in 1991. The more inclusive percentage would exceed 15 percent. Further, with housing, health, and other costs increasing faster than most incomes, the squeeze on leisure may counter the trend of increased spending for all but the upper 20 to 30 percent in income levels.

Nevertheless, leisure—directly and indirectly—is a major part of the current economy. The leisure market is gaining increased attention from business and from investors. Especially investments that provide tax shelters through depreciation or hedges against inflation such as land and real estate will probably continue to be attractive. Some of the total expenditures have been gathered by the U.S. government and provide a glimpse of the growth of some leisure-related industries (see Table 20–2).

Three trends appear in such statistics. First, in-home entertainment such as television and reading has increased more rapidly than movies or spectator sports. However, the differences are not so great as to suggest a major loss of markets except in motion pictures.

TABLE 20–2 Consumer Expenditures for Recreational Goods and Services (in billions of 1987 dollars)

	1970	1985	1991
Motion Pictures	4.2	3.6	2.9
Spectator sports	3.8	6.3	7.6
Parimutuel net receipts	2.8	3.2	3.4
Video, audio, and musical instruments	8.8	29.7	56.2
Wheel goods, sports and photographic equipment	10.3	24.4	26.4
Nondurable toys and sports supplies	9.5	22.3	28.4
Books and maps	10.5	11.4	15.4

Sources: U.S. Bureau of Economic Analysis. *1993 Statistical Abstract of the United States.*

Second, while the increases exceed the cost-of-living rise, in general there are no dramatic shifts. It would appear that a somewhat larger portion of total household income is being spent for leisure in a gradually rising curve. Third, expenditures on fees and equipment related to sport and outdoor activity have increased dramatically in the last decade.

Certain other trends do not appear in such statistics. Among them are various new forms of ownership of leisure facilities and new forms of business management. One such form is the franchise business. Campgrounds, racquet clubs, health spas, and equipment retailers as well as the more familiar motel and restaurant chains are opened under a common designation with a franchise. The local operator leases the name, advertising, wholesaling and group buying, and management expertise of the parent company through a contract that calls for either fixed payments, percentage payments of sales, or both. In return, the local operator gains immediate recognition for the business, access to products and services, and a method of operation that has been proven successful elsewhere. In some cases, there is also access to investment capital included. The limitations on local autonomy of operation are offset by the demonstrated methods and economies of advertising and buying.

Another new form of ownership provides for cooperative possession by a group of users. In a sense, it is similar to the private country club or resort with a limited membership and an elected board of directors. For example, the apartments of a beachfront condominium are each owned by different persons or groups of persons with common ownership and control of the overall operation. The owners may use their space for their own leisure and then rent it at other times through a rental service of the corporation. In a more recent variation, a number of owners may share time in one unit by purchasing shares entitling them to two or more weeks of use. Time-sharing ownership is intended to be a safeguard against rising rents for resort opportunities, but has not proven to be a good investment due to limited resale markets. Group ownership is also common for land for hunting or fishing, airplanes and boats, and other leisure items that are both expensive and that require a block of time for use.

It is difficult to designate such leisure provisions as private or commercial. It has been traditional to call such country clubs "private." However, increasingly the ownership of land is retained by a developer who is using the golf course to sell real estate and who considers the land a long-term investment. Condominiums may be purchased as investments with the added attraction of occasional leisure use. Memberships are sold in racquet clubs that are "private" but remain a profit-seeking business for the owners of the property. The trend appears to be away from the old private club in which title is held by the members to the new "private" membership business with ownership and control remaining in the hands of the investment group who may not be users themselves.

A further complication is the simultaneous dependence and competition between market sector leisure provisions and public offerings. For example, a commercial campground may be built near a major public park, beach, or other attraction. Its business depends on the public sector maintaining the attractiveness of the destination provision. However, at the same time, the fee structures for public campgrounds are of concern to the business operator. The commercial campground must either compete in facilities or price or be content with the overflow from the public provisions. In either case, the management policies of the government provider are critical to the business operation. The public resource is the attraction. On the other hand, public planners may assume that secondary services essential to users of their facilities will be provided commercially.

Such business provisions may be off-site on privately owned land or on-site through a lease arrangement. Leases include the operation of boat marinas at lakes, harbors, reservoirs, and rivers and shops for food and equipment. In the case of major facilities such as ski runs and lifts, some long-term assurance that the lease will not be cancelled and the investment in facilities forfeited is required by the commercial provider. As a result, leases include protection to the public concerning the operation of the facility and impacts on the environment and some to the business on renewal of the lease.

The kinds and amounts of expenditures on commercial leisure reinforce the theme of the scope and variety of such provisions. By any definition commercial provisions are a major element of leisure participation. Few days go by in which adult Americans engage in no leisure activity that they have not directly or indirectly paid for through the market. However, it is the scope and variety of commercial leisure that raises a number of issues.

Leisure as Business: Business and Public Policy

Several issues concerning business aims and policy merit discussion. The underlying issue is to what extent do business interests provide an adequate range of leisure opportunities. In a market economy, what kinds of opportunities yield an investment return that will draw enough suppliers to meet demand?

Recreation Business and the Public Sector

An analysis of the relationship of public and business recreation provisions begins with their essential complementarity. Consider some examples:

Equipment for community sports programs is obtained through local retail businesses. However, playing fields and outdoor facilities are public provisions.

Recreation businesses often sponsor special public events such as bicycle races, 10,000-meter runs, and softball tournaments.

For-profit schools and academies take musicians, artists, gymnasts, dancers, and others who began in public programs and train them at higher levels of performance. In turn, graduates of such programs often provide the leadership for the public offerings.

Commercial campgrounds complement public provisions by accommodating overflows, providing special facilities for families or locations where trailers may be left all season, locating along travel routes where no public camping is available, and catering to special groups.

Recreation business provides most of the essential services near remote public attractions such as the Grand Canyon, at Corps of Engineers reservoirs, and historic sites such as Philadelphia's Liberty Square.

Businesses lease sites on public land to build and manage recreation resources such as ski runs and marinas.

Travel services handle the arrangements for many trips that have public destinations.

The point is that supplying recreation resources in North America is not a matter of public versus commercial interests. In a mixed economy and a society that combines the public welfare concerns of the state with market distribution of many goods, public and business recreation are frequently complementary. They depend on each other. However, there may be instances of competition especially in efforts to secure an "up-market" clientele. Certainly there are occasions of friction in which the policies of one sector are seen as a threat by the other. However, current recreation practices require both public and market sectors of resource provision, more often in a complementary than competitive relationship.

Further, it is important for those who will be planning and managing public recreation programs and resources to understand the nature of the market sector. Seeking a profit is not necessarily better or worse, but it is different. Accounting for public responsibility is somewhat different from accounting to meet the requirements of investors, lenders, and the Internal Revenue Service. Planning that has to take into account the interest costs of a line of credit is different from planning from a tax base assured for two or five years. Calculating the potential paying market for a resource is different from evaluating whether populations of special need are being adequately served.

Whatever the philosophical premises or the economic ideology of the recreation provider, ours is a system that combines public and market modes of the production and distribution of goods and services.

Investment Return and the Flow of Capital

Although some market sector leisure enterprises require very little capital when they consist primarily of services and rented facilities, most call for some investment. In general, such investment should yield a return at least as high as a similar allocation of resources to an interest-bearing account. Further, since an interest-bearing investment in savings or bonds involves little or no risk, there needs to be an added return for the risk involved in a business investment. For example, if a guaranteed, fixed-rate placement of capital would return 8 percent and the failure rate of small retail businesses that supply leisure equipment is 40 percent, then a profit rate of no less than 15 percent would seem reasonable to compensate for the risk of such an investment.

There are other factors. An owner-operator of a business must calculate his or her own income at a reasonable salary rate and also make some provision for the generation of further capital for the business. As a result, the factors of interest—either for payment on a loan or as a return on the owner's investment, self-employment income, depreciation of stock and equipment, reinvestment capital, and all the expenses of operation—combine to require a consistent margin of profit if the business is to continue. In a major investment such as a bowling alley, theme park, marina, or new product line, all these factors become quite complex. Careful calculations of potential market, long-term credit, tax factors, depreciation, and possible appreciation of real estate are required before the investment is made.

The point is that in any case of investment in commercial leisure enterprises there is a tendency for capital to flow toward those possibilities of the greatest return on the investment. There are always alternative investment possibilities. While in some cases an individual may choose to invest in a particular business because of the life style it engenders rather than for maximum profit, even then a failure to make a profit will in time close the business. Even those willing to take a low rate of return and income to live near ski slopes or the surf can seldom withstand consistent losses.

Further, there are peculiarities to many leisure businesses. Some are seasonal and require a large market and high rate of profit during that season to compensate for months of little or no income. That is why a fishing resort that can add winter skiing to its offerings becomes a much more viable enterprise. Some leisure businesses are capital-intensive and require a heavy front-end investment in land, facilities, or equipment. Such businesses usually have large loans to pay off each month out of revenues and cannot afford a long delay in revenues. Other businesses are labor-intensive, such as those combining equipment repair and instruction in a sport so that capital return is a minor consideration.

The issue is this: Which opportunities are most likely to receive the investment capital? The answer is a financial one. With few exceptions, return on investment attracts capital. While some leisure providers trade off investment return for the opportunity to live in the woods or to be involved in a favorite activity, most have to consider long-and short-term profits.

Some investments promise a quick return. They are businesses that are responsive to a large and proven market in an area with minimal competition from other suppliers. Such enterprises may combine a rapid amortization of investment with tax advantages so that at the end of a few years the investment is recovered and a further profit may be made either by continuing the business or selling it. Other leisure investments may provide less immediate return but have the added attraction of long-term appreciation of the resources. Such long-term appreciation together with immediate tax write-offs is characteristic of land investments that can be used for sports. Suburban golf courses, seashore motels, and waterfront boat facilities tend to gain in value as well as yield an ongoing income.

In general, leisure business investments tend to flow toward cost-intensive activities with a high market potential. If the activity requires considerable investment in equipment purchases, rental of space or fees for access, and a selection of auxiliary costs such as lodging that can be packaged by the provider, then it is a likely candidate for investment. If such cost-intensive characteristics can be combined with long-term appreciation and tax advantages, then the investment is all the more attractive. Of course, the attractions of such investments often lead to over-supply and market saturation.

On the other hand, activities that have a limited market due to short season, inaccessibility of resources, a high skill acquisition threshold, or select cultural appeal are not likely to attract commercial providers. Also, activities with low start-up costs because they require no equipment or access fees are not likely to gain investment. Capital flows to the large market and high-cost participation activities to gain an investment return. Activities that may be highly satisfying and enriching but are low in economic return potential require provision by public sources or by oneself.

Leisure Resources and Long-Range Planning

When an investment is made in any business, a schedule is projected for the recovery of the investment. Since some of the capital is usually borrowed, that schedule is generally developed by the lending institution. In some cases large corporations have a line of credit with a bank that enables them to meet the ongoing expenses of establishing a new enterprise without having to utilize their own capital resources. Such borrowing requires that the new business return enough income to meet that repayment schedule.

As a result, the leisure business will attempt to maximize the use of its provision and to gain as wide a clientele as possible. Advertising, special rates, group discounts, tour packages, and price leaders will be employed to get as many customers as possible started. The limitation of buyers, renters, and other users will be by price. Prices are set to maximize use at a rate that conforms to the investment and operation cost requirements.

In some cases, such use can result in the destruction of the resource for recreation or for other uses in the long term. In a ten-year period the investor may have recovered capital, interest, and a nice profit in a way that leaves the land or the water in a condition from which no recovery is possible.

As a result, long-term considerations may call for restricted use or limited development of a resource so that future generations may also enjoy it. Such long-range considerations may also call for the setting aside of land—urban or far from the city—in order to preserve it for use decades in the future. Once the land is committed to one kind of use, it may be lost irretrievably for other uses. A growing city may need to hold outlying land for future parks. A state may need to close a seaside marsh to development to preserve the overall ecology of a bay and its tributaries. The federal government may close an area to camping so that a fragile watershed will not be damaged.

Unless this kind of planning for the future and for the common welfare is undertaken by public agencies, the resource base for both public and commercial leisure will be restricted in coming years. When price and the market are in control of resources, long-range considerations usually give way to meeting current obligations.

Status Symbolism and Leisure Consumption

Thorstein Veblen proposed that it is in leisure that the wealthy can most readily demonstrate their ability to rise above the necessities of life.[5] By their "conspicuous waste" they

---

[5] Thorstein Veblen, *The Theory of the Leisure Class,* Second edition (New York: New American Library, 1953).

may provide the symbols of their affluence. They need not invest all their time and income in maintaining themselves. They may elevate their status in the society by showing that they give themselves and their resources to leisure.

When Veblen wrote, the "leisure class" was restricted in size. Discretionary income of any magnitude was enjoyed by less than 5 percent of the American population. Today the middle class is far from having the surplus wealth of the old leisure class, but they do have some money to spend at their discretion. Further, in the new suburb where homes and cars all look much alike and one's type of employment is not immediately visible to friends and neighbors, some new status symbols may be sought. As well as in the "success" of children, status may be sought in leisure consumption. The boat, the trip to Europe, the skiing weekend, the built-in bar and party room, the sports car, the tennis togs, and the club membership may set one apart from others in the community. At least such expenditures are a clear sign that one deserves to be considered well up on whatever status hierarchy is operative in the community. When necessities do not differentiate, then leisure consumption may become a prime element of status symbolism.

The concern is that leisure may become primarily consumption rather than action, a matter of being entertained more than personal involvement. When leisure becomes defined by expenditure rather than experience, it is said to be "commodified." It is measured more by possessions than by relationships, more by price than personal development. There are many indications that for those with discretionary income, leisure expenditures have increased, especially in being entertained. Demanding pursuits, for the most part, are not increasing in participation. At the same time, there is growth in the market provisions of cruise ships and luxury resorts. The great wave of the leisure future is said to be the fiber optic onslaught of electronic entertainment for the home. Even the suppliers of sports equipment and apparel alter their products each year to attract markets on the basis of style rather than use. Business provisions for leisure are designed to create markets for goods and services that maximize a consistent return on investment capital. As a consequence, they direct a high proportion of investment toward leisure that is price-intensive rather than experience-intensive, toward activities that have a direct economic costs to buy locales, environments, services, equipment, and the right things to wear. The alleged freedom of leisure may even come to be defined as market choices, as responses to what is offered at a price.

The problem is equating leisure with the purchase rather than the experience. Possessing leisure equipment, demonstrating leisure skills, displaying symbols of leisure histories, and even equating the satisfaction with buying—all these possibilities suggest that for some leisure may become a commodity rather than an experience. And one cost of the commodity may be the time for an experience.

Public Policy and the World of Business

John Kenneth Galbraith, a revisionist economist, has lamented the imbalance of capital flow in the market economy.[6] His thesis is simply that in a market economy a disproportionate amount of capital is invested in those enterprises that are most likely to produce a profit regardless of social utility or contribution to the common welfare. Investment tends

---

[6] John Kenneth Galbraith, *The Affluent Society* (Boston: Houghton Mifflin, 1958).

to go to products that enhance the appearance rather than the mind, that consume rather than conserve energy, that are glamorous rather than durable, and that provide quick pleasure rather than more permanent development. Most specifically, most investment is not in the public sector of education and services but in the private sector of production of consumer goods. In leisure, great investments are made in elaborate destination resorts and few in quiet places to sit with companions in the neighborhood. Great investments are made in jet planes and motor homes and not in a winding path down to a stream or a gallery for amateur painters.

The issue is that maximizing profit may not maximize leisure. People often go where they are led and do what is suggested. Choices are limited as to what is perceived as possible and available. When resources are directed toward high-return provisions, then leisure may come to be defined as buying what is advertised and doing what is promoted. Millions of dollars are spent on commercial amusements rather than creative arts, self-paced outdoor activity, or places for conversation and quiet partly because people tend to do what is visible and available.

Further, the business interests are well organized to apply pressure for public expenditures that facilitate the purchase and use of their products. There has been great pressure to build interstate highways, but little to provide community walkways. There is pressure to keep radio and television frequencies open for teen music promotion, but little for drop-in centers where the same teens can gather to make music and build community. There are many subsidies of leisure opportunity for those who can spend money to travel, but fewer for those without cars and discretionary incomes. Even a highly productive economy produces limited capital resources. When the distribution is strongly skewed toward the market rather than public services, then profit rather than personal satisfaction and growth becomes the criterion of its use.

Again, there is the problem of equity. With great disparities in income, a market distribution of resources creates enormous inequalities in leisure opportunities. Provisions are there for those who can pay. And those provisions tend to be those for which a price can be charged and a market created.

There is the problem of balance. At the present time, market sector leisure is the giant and public leisure provides the supplement. Measured by time, expenditures, or importance, leisure business is primary. Public provisions are concentrated on outdoor space and programs for those least able to pay.

Summary of Issues

On the one hand, the significance of commercial provisions for leisure can hardly be overestimated. Even the types of leisure businesses listed in this chapter provide only a sketchy framework and omit many major kinds of leisure-related enterprises. The common estimates of what is spent through the market on leisure are incomplete since they do not include either major investments in housing, space, and transportation with leisure purposes and uses or the countless small purchases for common leisure at home. In fact, the market itself in the form of the shopping center is a major leisure locale.

On the other hand, there are significant limits to what is likely to be provided through the market. The requirement that investment capital produce an adequate return excludes a number of costly provisions, especially many land resources, as well as facilities not likely to attract a regular paying clientele. A proper coordination of public and market provisions would take account of the limited resources of many citizens and the kinds of leisure that are not cost-intensive enough to yield a return on the investment. A related issue is the concern that those seeking to create markets define leisure as product consumption rather than as experience and development. The power of media advertising—both direct and indirect—to suggest that leisure satisfaction is proportional to the market cost may divert attention away from the intrinsic and social meanings that are not market-provided or cost-intensive.

HIGHLIGHTS

1. Even excluding television, market provisions of material and equipment used for leisure, travel support, eating and drinking establishments, leisure clothing and facilities, financing, and a wide variety of goods touch most lives daily.
2. Although capital requirements vary widely, leisure provisions through the market must be managed for a net return on the investment.
3. Investments tend to flow toward cost-intensive activities with high market potential. Therefore, many kinds of opportunities will not be promoted or offered through the market.
4. Identifying leisure with the consumption of market goods, promoted through direct advertising and indirect media portrayal, may endanger appreciation of less costly possibilities.

Discussion Questions

1. In what ways do public recreation provisions supplement business enterprises? How does commercial recreation supplement public programs?

2. What would you develop as a profitable leisure business in your community? Identify potential markets and capital requirements. What might be a better commercial recreation investment somewhere else?

3. List some cost-intensive leisure pursuits with high potential as investment opportunities.

4. What kinds of leisure opportunities and resources are least likely to be provided commercially? Why?

5. Is there contemporary evidence of leisure consumption as a symbol of social status? Does such leisure still involve "conspicuous waste"?

6. If investment capital flows toward potential profit and consumers exercise market choices according to what they value, are there any reasons why we cannot rely on the market to meet leisure needs? Are not such market decisions more accurate reflections of what people want than the decisions of professional providers?

7. How is identifying expenditure and consumption with leisure satisfaction a danger in modern societies?

Bibliography

Butsch, Richard, ed., *For Fun and Profit: The Transformation of Leisure into Consumption.* Philadelphia: Temple University Press, 1990.

Ellis, Taylor, and R. L. Norton, *Commercial Recreation.* St. Louis, MO: Times Mirror/Mosby, 1988.

Kelly, John R., *Recreation Business.* New York: Macmillan, 1985.

Kelly, John R., and Geoffrey Godbey. *The Sociology of Leisure.* State College, PA: Venture Publishing, 1993.

Chapter *21*

Leisure Specialization and Subcultures

It is no accident that most of the discussion to this point has been about "ordinary" people. We have given primary attention to those who do the things most people do. They use most of the leisure resources, are the targets of most public and private sector planning, and in general are the norm to whom others are compared. Also, most of the research on leisure behavior and meanings has been on these "normals." When random samples are drawn of a community, state, or the nation, they dominate the statistical categories.

But what about all the others—the unemployed, marginally employed youth, residents of urban ghettos and slums, those in first- or second-generation immigrant cultures, single parents, and unmarried adults? What about the handicapped, the chronically ill, and those with emotional difficulties? What about those of us who are in one of these "other" groups for a period of our lives, but not for most of our life careers?

And then there are those with leisure styles that are not normative and balanced. They may be the single-minded who concentrate all their leisure into one fiercely pursued activity or relationship. They may be dissatisfied with ordinary leisure possibilities and attempt to create a "new leisure" context or orientation. They may become fanatics who have no interest in a balance or mixture of leisure experiences.

All these are members of leisure subcultures—their values, language, and behavior are quite different from the common and the ordinary. They are important not only because they are part of the whole spectrum of leisure but also because in their difference they reveal some new insights into the complex phenomenon we call leisure.

ISSUES

Do some people become single-minded in their leisure instead of seeking a balance of activities and outcomes?

What do we learn about leisure in general from those whose leisure patterns are different from the more common and familiar?

How can leisure become central to the identities of those who focus on a specialized investment?

Some of the leisure groups and styles we examine in this chapter hardly appear in statistical samples at all. For example, in a national sample of adults, all of the following activities were done last year by a part of the population so small as to be recorded as less than half of 1 percent: hang gliding, parachute jumping, rock climbing, scuba diving, and surfing. Yet we know of individuals who center their entire lives around one of these activities. They follow the surf around the world and subsist on part-time jobs that leave them free to watch for the big wave. They take extraordinary risks in order to experience the freedom, excitement, and close community of hang gliding or skydiving. They reject the world of competitive sport to explore possibilities of bodily awareness and integration.

Most of the study of special groups has been in a case study form. Such studies may employ observation and participation in the groups, prolonged and repeated interviews, reliance on insiders who are well informed, and material from contemporary novels and other writings. Such case studies are available from a variety of sources, including many that have not given special attention to leisure at all. Community studies, family research, and investigations of interactional situations or episodes may yield considerable insight into leisure. In this chapter, a number of representative sources give some "snapshots" of leisure subcultures. Many merit treatment that would approximate the length of a feature motion picture if we are to begin to grasp the meanings of such different approaches to leisure.

The Ethnicity of Leisure

As suggested in the historical chapters, leisure is one element of a culture and cannot be understood apart from that cultural context. Value systems, economic stratification, and political structures in Greece all shaped concepts of leisure. Religious changes in Western Europe in the fourteenth and fifteenth centuries were a major factor in changes in leisure. Leisure in America has been regionally and ethnically influenced and has changed from one historical epoch to another. Ethnicity in the sense of cultural, linguistic, religious, historical, and social distinction has always characterized leisure.

Current comparisons between the leisure of one culture or nation and another dramatize the fact that the forms and often the intents of leisure are not the same throughout the world. When research findings are reported in an international forum such as the World Leisure and Recreation Association or the Research Committee on Leisure of the International Sociological Association, differences in both what people do and how they do it are evident. It is evident that we cannot study leisure in one country, region, or social system and then generalize about its place in others. There are differences not only in resources but also in the cultural forms and values that are central elements in leisure.

Leisure is not only shaped by its cultural contexts, but also forms cultures and subcultures. In mass societies, leisure can become the basis of identification with an activity commitment and with a a community formed around such a commitment. Such a community develops its own "small world" of symbols, rituals, vocabularies, and rites of inclusion and exclusion.

Social Identification

The usual concentration on the activities that people engage in obscures a dimension central to the social meanings of leisure. Some subcultures are identified by outsiders according to language, dress, or physical characteristics. We may be placed in the group whether we accept the classification or not. In other cases, we adopt symbols of social identification. We may continue life styles that are different from the mainstream culture.

What is different about a subcultural identification is often expressed primarily in leisure. More and more people are living in urban neighborhoods and suburbs that have no particular ethnic identity. Their homes and cars look alike and their children go to the same schools. As a result, they may seek to express their special social identities through their leisure. Leisure becomes more than just a set of preferred activities. It may be a way of life that announces to others something crucial about how we define ourselves. We may even adopt clothing, "badges," and equipment to announce that we are not just one more homogenized urbanite.

We may wish to be seen by others as a "mighty hunter," and so carry a gun in a rack behind the seat of our pickup even when going to work or shopping. We may prefer the "young and active" image and wear our tennis togs to the supermarket. We may wear bowling jackets to work, fraternity or sorority shirts to class, backpacks to the bookstore, or jogging shoes everywhere. We may drive the camper to the job or ride a cross-country ten-speed bike to church. Some of us may make visible the insignia that says to all who look, "I am one of a special group."

Of course, it is often difficult to distinguish leisure styles that are chosen from opportunities and limitations that are merely accepted. Styles of fishing may be a response to the cost of launching boats rather than to an ethnic preference for old railroad trestles and abandoned piers. The blue-collar bar in a mill town or the working-class pub in England may indeed have a distinctive culture and style, but that style is as much an acceptance of space limitations and a lack of alternative locales for community as it is a reflection of cultural preference. Nevertheless leisure is one critical social arena in which identity is worked out and expressed.

Membership in a leisure group may yield a sense of being "someone," but it also demands precise adherence to the norms and expectations of the group. There have been a number of case studies of such smaller face-to-face leisure groups.

The Social Rules of Poker

Studies of groups that meet regularly for poker have discussed not only the formal rules of the game but also the enforcement of informal conventions of behavior and communication. Three studies of "friendly" poker games provide material for this composite description; two were by students and one by a social psychologist.[1] All three were low-stakes games that took place in a home on a weekly or twice-monthly schedule. All had regular players in a core group, but also engaged in a recruitment process when new players were needed. In each case the new players were "tried out" to see how they would fit. Criteria for membership were both social and technical, with social criteria involving acceptance of informal norms of behavior. Technical criteria involved the ability and experience to play the game on the general level of the core group.

Like other games, poker not only has its written rules of play and scoring but also a vast set of unwritten rules, generally accepted norms or etiquette, and the social conventions of each particular group. It is in these social conventions that the groups differed slightly. For example, although women never played in any of the groups, in one group they were occasionally allowed to observe if they remained quiet and helped with refreshments. Second-level rules also differed in the number and size of raises permitted, the variety of games allowed for the dealer's discretion, and allowable breaks in the action.

In each case, a socialization process occurred in which new players were not only evaluated but also instructed casually in the second-level rules and conventions. These rules and conventions had generally been adopted when difficulties had arisen over such practices as split-pot games or having food on the table. When wide differences in financial resources among players presented a potential problem, the rules on size of bets would be augmented by a tacit understanding that each player would take the stakes with equal seriousness during the game.

The convention forbidding interference and interruption by spectators, distracting noises from television or radios, awkward food or drink, or conversation on serious subjects further intensified the "special-world" character of the game. The game itself was taken seriously and the results were real. The amounts of money were large enough that a series of losing evenings would alter the purchasing power and cash-flow position of a player. However, they were small enough that success or failure was unlikely to affect payment of rents or grocery bills. That is, the stakes were within the "discretionary limits" of the players.

Poker players tend to be caught up in the action and the results sufficiently that considerable emotional control must be exercised. The intensity and sustained concentration, the feedback on decisions to bet or withdraw from a hand, the venture of attempting or dealing with a bluff, and the counting up at the end of the evening provide an engrossing activity and a set of "real but nonsubstantial consequences." As a result, the "friendly game of poker" is a social event in which the self is presented and tested. Especially for male self-images, poker serves as an immediate social context in which the control, skills, and courage of the self are demonstrated and measured. The regularity of play signifies that

---

[1] Louis A. Zurcher, Jr., "The 'Friendly' Poker Game: A Study of an Ephemeral Role," *Social Forces,* 49 (1970), 173–186.

there is more here than just a game; there is a set-apart world of self-affirmation and testing of identities.

Community at a Commuter College

The group seems like nothing more than a bunch of drinking buddies. The fact that there
are both women and men students in the group does not make it essentially a group oriented to sexual interaction. It seems to be nothing more than a group of peers all of whom
enjoy each other's company and have a location and educational affiliation in common.
They meet in some apartment on Saturdays to drink, party, and sometimes dance.

However, a closer analysis reveals that there is more here than is evident to the casual
observer. It is no surprise that marginal members come and go as romantic attachments
wax and wane, that one or two key members have been central to the history of formation
and recruitment, or that there are special dyads and triads in the larger group of ten to fifteen. Nor is it a surprise that the drinking and dancing are sometimes more of an excuse
for getting together than activities that are essential to the evening's interaction.

What is more surprising is that the commonalities among the members run deeper
than paying tuition at the same college office. All have been raised in military families
who moved from place to place. Most were raised as Catholics but no longer participate
in the church. All have found themselves cast loose in a major metropolitan center with
a rapidly shifting population; all take the group much more seriously than the informal
meeting and boozing would suggest. This seemingly casual leisure group, with fringe
members coming and going and little sense of organization and purpose, has become almost a family for its core members. A sense of acceptance and ease of communication, together with some familial trust and openness, have been found in this group. Its meaning
is far more profoundly related to self and social identification than to time, place, or activity. It is, first of all, a primary community, with leisure activity providing the filler but
not the structure.

Scott[2] has demonstrated how "social worlds" form around common participation in
leisure activity. "Serious" bridge players form a subculture around the scheduled tournaments with their gradations of skill, vocabulary, social conventions, and organized activity. Such subcultures may form around activities such as the showing of dogs or cats,
breeding particular kinds of horses, tournament bass fishing, rock climbing, or almost any
kind of activity that combines skill with social organization.

Identification and Differentiation In Leisure Groups

A stress on social identification may lead to neglect of the differentiation within a leisure
group. While there are common symbols, language, and behavioral conventions in a leisure
subculture, there are also signs of individuality and uniqueness. A leisure group may provide a context for acceptance and identification in a mass society that causes us to lose
track of who we are. However, it is also a social space in which we may essay to be someone a little different without cost to income or community position.

---

[2] David Scott, "An Analysis of Adult Play Groups." Unpublished Ph.D. dissertation, The Pennsylvania State University, 1990.

Who Is That Masked Rider?

The motocross rider is quite different from the highway bike rider who expresses his identity through the adornment of his machine with chrome, special paint, high handlebars, and other accessories and by "chopping" and raking modifications. The heavy highway motorcycle requires considerable time and money in an unending pursuit of visible superiority. Also, highway bike riders tend to form clubs with some symbolic name and insignia and to ride in packs.

The motocross bike is seldom impressive in appearance. Rather it is designed and maintained for speed and good handling over a course of assorted hills, bumps, curves, mud. and barriers. The machine is a thing to be used effectively rather than an expressive symbol. The competition is the core of the experience with the bike, the club, and the preparation only instrumental.

The outstanding fact about the clubs studied is that with few exceptions their members are working class in background and occupation.[3] Construction workers, mechanics, factory workers, and other blue-collar men are joined by occasional students, teachers, or clerks who usually come from working-class families. The club maintains a racecourse and sponsors competitive events. How does a person come to choose this demanding and dangerous sport, which requires an investment of $1,000 to $2,000 for a bike and equipment?

Those most likely to choose motocross racing are those for whom it is a natural and attractive possibility. They have grown up with other men who like machinery, speed, and competition. They have learned mechanical skills through early ownership of older cars and cycles. Their older brothers and friends had anticipated the time when they could be licensed to drive and, when they were licensed, experienced highway transportation as a freedom. For them, even the sound of the engine carries feelings of independence, control of power and direction, and motion. At the same time that some youths were camping with their families, going to country club dances, or practicing the French horn, these young men were into engines and transmissions.

After all, used cars and cycles are not only valued in the culture, but are generally available. They may require payments, but not wealth. The knowledge and skills necessary to pursue motorized excitement can be learned in and out of school in any community with no social or cultural exclusion evident. The working-class youth who moves from used cars and cycles to motocross *with* his friends is following a natural bent. The lawyer's son who leaves the country club to follow the dirt track has as many barriers to overcome as there are on the racecourse.

Yet, of all the sports and activities available and common for young men in a blue-collar family, why do some take up that particular demanding activity and most do not? Sometimes it is association with a particular friend or the influence of some special person—a father or brother. Some may just be intrigued after seeing the sport on television or while driving by a track.

However, according to Thomas Martin and Kenneth Berry, it is the experience itself that attracts and holds the commitment of these young men whose work worlds provide little opportunity for demonstrating their manhood, for winning, and for acting out the "aggressive activism" and individualism learned in boyhood:

---

[3] Thomas W. Martin and Kenneth Berry, "Competitive Sport in Postindustrial Society: The Case of the Motocross Racer," paper presented at the Midwest Sociological Society, Milwaukee, WI, 1973.

> To sum up, then, in a very basic way the motocrosser is deeply engaged in and committed to a violent sport; a sport that provides him opportunity to test his physical strength and tactical skills against competent opponents in an arena where total effort is required and success is both elusive and blatantly evident. To the racer, the trophy is more than a badge of courage. It is a symbol of excellence, of manhood, of a clearcut achievement of victory against heavy odds.[4]
>
> While the opportunities and limitations of his social context may lead a working-class youth toward motorcycles, it is the experience of testing and presenting his personal identity as a man that makes all the costs of the sport more than worthwhile.

In a sport-related leisure context, gradations of skill are critical in forming subgroups. We do not climb rocks, play tennis, or go backpacking with just anyone. Some compatibility of skill and experience is required in order that the experience be satisfying. The subtleties of knowing and announcing such differentiation vary from group to group as well as from activity to activity. In some contexts understatement is evidence of the highest levels of participation. Too obvious and blatant use of symbols such as badges, special equipment, or clothing may be interpreted as an attempt to enter a group at too high a level.

The differentiation may not only be by skill and experience, but may also be influenced by background and style. While it is expected that each person in a leisure context will have some distinctive style of participation, there are limits to acceptance. Distinctive styles are valued within those commonly accepted limits, but not outside. For example, a poker player whose financial situation depends on winning will usually be excluded from a friendly game. A newcomer who attempts to exploit a casual group for sexual adventures may be pointedly left out of the next gathering. A climber who takes unnecessary chances may find no one to climb with on the following weekend. The rules, etiquette, and conventions of the subculture of leisure form a social context of inclusion, but also of exclusion.

Personal Identity in Leisure Subcultures

While it is impossible to separate completely personal and social identities, there is a useful distinction between "who we are to ourselves" and "who we are in the world." We know ourselves to be something more and somewhat different from the social self that has been presented and validated in our social roles.

The kinds of leisure relationships to be described are different, in that for many people they are much more than one element in a composite social identity. They do more than provide a balancing element in the social self that incorporates family, work, community, and leisure roles. For some people the leisure role becomes the center of personal identity, the self we believe ourselves to be.

[4] Ibid.

Specialization in an Activity

Participation in a leisure activity may have a career. There is the obvious progression from beginner to learner to increasing levels of competence. Hobson Bryan has studied the careers of those who engage in fishing.[5] His analysis suggests a sequence of stages of specialization. The beginner just wants to try the activity and get some result. It's primarily a matter of catching a fish in any way possible. As the fishing person moves through the various stages, there is more and more discrimination. The environments are evaluated more critically. Equipment becomes of higher quality and is matched with actual or anticipated skills. The exercise of skill becomes more important than the result. At the highest levels, the technology may even be simplified to emphasize skill, and most or all fish are returned to the water. It is the highly specialized exercise of developed skill in special environments that has changed the pond-bank worm dipper to a lake caster and finally to a Salmon River fly caster.

Of course, most participants in any activity do not go that far in a career of engagement in any activity. However, for those who do, the highly specialized blending of skill and technology with environment is crucial. Finding meaning in the activity involves linking the rarefied mode of participation with personal identity. Whether the activity is fly fishing or stamp collecting, the style of engagement progresses to greater discrimination as to techniques, environments, and colleagues. In the process, the person comes to identify him- or herself more and more with that level of skill and specialization.

A High-Risk Enterprise

Surprisingly, when people who choose to jump out of airplanes and land on their feet for leisure explain why they do it, they seldom begin with reference to the risk. Skydiving is explained more often as giving a sense of freedom. Looking down at the earth, controlling one's movements in the free fall, perfecting skill and control, escaping from the ordinary routines of life, and developing companionship with fellow jumpers are the satisfactions most often mentioned. However, there is more to it than that.

For example, while the risk is seldom discussed except in jokes about the results of hitting the earth when chutes don't open, high emotions and trepidation are quite real experiences in the early stages of skydiving. The more experienced jumper has shifted attention to the development of skill in accuracy and group formations and considers safety primarily a technical matter of care with equipment.

A parachuting club has the characteristics of a leisure subculture, with special vocabulary, clothing, insignia, skill-related awards and status, rites of initiation and passage, single-interest literature, and a clear understanding of who is in the group, who is marginal, and who is outside. David Arnold and others have found that the set-apart community of skydivers is a group that provides a major source of social identification and community for regular members.[6]

---

[5] Hobson Bryan, *Conflict in the Great Outdoors* (University, AL: University of Alabama Press, 1979).

[6] David O. Arnold, "The Social Organization of Skydiving: A Study in Vertical Mobility," paper presented at the Pacific Sociological Association, Portland, OR, April 1972.

However, the choice of the activity suggests something more. Among all the possibilities of leisure that also yield community and allow for some insignia of social identification, why this expensive, esoteric, and rather awesome activity? One hint may be in the fact that some individuals prepare and make one jump to prove they can do it and then never jump again. There is an element of demonstrating to the self and others that one is able to cope with one of the universal fears, that of height and falling, and come out with control and mastery. In a world where risks are for the most part small and social, skydiving is a recognized physical and emotional conquest of fear and danger. Although in time the satisfactions may turn to those of freedom and the experience itself, there is also a demonstration of a personal identity that may have been denied in life's ongoing routines. The preponderance of males in the sport may also be due to the old masculine sex-role values of courage and conquest as much as to social discouragement of female participants.

When the activity becomes more than something participants enjoy doing and becomes the hub around which both schedules and self-images revolve, then one's relationship to leisure is the essence of one's personal identity. Skydiving is one example of leisure that can become not only a central life interest but the center of self-definition. Many persons see themselves first of all as rock climbers, builders and pilots of small aircraft, skiers, surfers, or folk singers when their employment is something quite different. For such individuals, the where and what of employment is secondary to the opportunity it affords to *be* what is most important to personal identity—a skydiver, stunt pilot, or cellist.

The True Amateur in Leisure

Robert Stebbins has approached a seeming contradiction in leisure by developing the concept of the "amateur." If leisure is defined primarily by freedom and generally includes some elements of rest and relaxation, how can we explain those people who work so hard and discipline themselves so rigorously in their leisure? Is the musician or actor or athlete who sets high standards for performance and does everything possible to maintain those standards really engaged in something other than leisure?

Stebbins has done participant observation with string musicians and then expanded his study to amateur archaeologists, actors, baseball players, magicians, and others.[7] He distinguishes the true amateur from the ordinary or part-time participant who engages in several activities and may be referred to as a player, dabbler, or dilettante. Most persons who engage in a sport or a cultural activity are not amateurs by this definition. They sing in choirs, play golf, camp in the mountains, or travel as one among the many activities that they enjoy for a variety of reasons. As suggested earlier, they seek a balance of leisure that is satisfying to them in their life career period and that both expresses and develops their personal and social identities.

The amateur is not likely to have much time for any other significant leisure investment. He or she is first of all a cellist in a string quartet, a pitcher on a semipro baseball team, or a rockhound planning vacations and weekends around field trips. Work and this amateur investment may balance each other, or employment may become a means to the

[7] Robert A. Stebbins, *Amateurs: On the Margin between Work and Leisure* (Beverly Hills, CA: Sage Publications, 1979).

primary end of being a true amateur in some area of endeavor. In time the amateur comes to define herself as a *choir director who works in a bank,* a *soccer coach who teaches school,* or a *sculptor who is also a housewife.* In personal and social identification, in meaning and satisfaction, the avocation may take center stage away from the principal employment. We may, indeed, become poets who teach or gourmet cooks who type.

There is no reason why leisure cannot be highly disciplined, require great effort, or become a central life interest. The amateur is, from one perspective, a person who takes a focused leisure interest to its ultimate conclusion. Its intrinsic and social meanings become so powerful that they push other types of leisure into the background.

While there is no kind of activity that a primary leisure community may not develop, there are some requirements. One is that the community be able to gather for a large portion of the year. Those who fly a thousand miles for an annual ski trip may attach great importance to the experience, but usually find their primary social identities back home. On the other hand, parents of competition swimmers may be either working at home meets or out of town at other meets during both summer and winter seasons. In time, they find that others similarly engaged have become their friendship circle and reference group. After all, who else can understand the life-and-death importance of hundredths of a second and 6 A.M. practices? For devotees, whether their activity is duplicate bridge or orienteering in the woods, in time those with a similar depth of enthusiasm and understanding form a cultural unit that may take precedence over all others.

There is increasing evidence that sustained involvement in activities that require a development of skill become more than ways to fill nonwork time. "Amateurs" gain a sense of identity that is based on their commitment to an activity and to gaining a competence in it. This "serious leisure" also produces an ongoing community of those who have made similar commitments and who share in the social organization of the activity. Such an identity of ability may be especially significant for those who do not experience challenge in their work or who are now retired from the workplace.[8] Such activity, often continuing a skill developed earlier in life, yields a sense of competence and worth as well as regular interaction with others who have made the same commitment. Such activity combines commitment, challenge, and community. It is, therefore, a form of "flow"[9] when that concept is expanded beyond the immediate experience. When so much of life is boring routine, then such "high investment" or "serious" leisure concentrates the self on challenge that is developmental and exciting. It can provide a sense of meaning for the self, involvement, and social integration based on common action. It is, then, both existential and social. It involves the active self in the immediate experience of meeting challenge, the longer term outcome of developing competence, and the communicative sharing of common activity.

New Technologies of Leisure

Some leisure styles become focused on particular technologies. In some cases, the technology creates a subculture. For example, the application of weapons-aiming microchip tech-

---

[8] Roger Mannell, "High-investment Activity and Life Satisfaction among Older Adults," in J. Kelly, ed., *Activity and Aging* (Newbury Park, CA: Sage, 1993).

[9] Mihaly Csikszentmihalyi, *Flow: The Psychology of Optimal Experience* (New York: Harper, 1990).

nology to video games produced a cohort of youth who, at least for a time, concentrated their time and financial resources on the particular games promoted by the video arcades. The levels of skill, immediate feedback from the game format, competition with other players, and general excitement of the ambiance combined to create a temporary subculture. While electronic games in separate arcades had a boom period followed by retrenchment and the closing of many businesses, there remain groups of devotees as the games have become more diverse and complex. The technology has continued to develop and to attract the consistent participation of specialized groups, mostly young males in their early teens.

Other subcultures have formed around the development of such apparatus as hang gliders, windsurfing boards, and home computer games. In each case, the activity is developed on the new technology. As with activities such as motocross, specialists may come to build their lifestyles around the activity, its advancing technology, its symbols of identification, and the stable communities of participants. The acquisition of skills, differentiation of levels of ability for competition, literature such as specialized magazines, specialty equipment shops with related instruction programs, clothing and other identifying items, and always staying abreast of the changing technology are elements of the developing subculture. In many cases, the promotion efforts of business interests are critical in the development of such participation groups.

The New Leisure

At the same time that the personal and social identities of some are wrapped up in traditional activities such as competitive sports or water-based activities, others have become dissatisfied with the outcomes of such old-style leisure. Reflecting the countercultural stress on self-development, awareness, sensuality, and the wholeness of mind and body, these people have broken with many traditional forms of leisure to explore new forms and orientations.

There has also been resistance to the commodified forms of leisure. The mere consumption of mass entertainment is seen as dehumanizing and a waste of the potential to add significantly to life's meaning.

Some of the traditional aims of recreation have been related to the moral and physical health of participants and to benefits for the social system. Especially in a society with competition and differential rewards central to its educational, political, and economic institutions, the effort and discipline of many kinds of leisure have been valued because they prepare people for more effective participation in these nonleisure settings.

In the past decade, various groups have emerged to challenge that view of recreation. The new emphasis is on the person rather than on the society; leisure is defined as primarily self-enhancing, without reference to competition as testing and preparation for economic participation. The aims of leisure are more humanistic: expression and community. Expression in leisure is the acting out of freedom and creative capacities. The social element in leisure is redefined as community *with* others rather than as a contest against others. The stress on success, accomplishment, self-evaluation, and extrinsic aims is transformed into stress on expression, fulfillment, individuality, and intrinsic satisfaction.

Leisure for Its Own Sake

Advocates of new perspectives on leisure call for a radical shift from values placed on results to values placed on experience. The outcomes are measured in terms of personal fulfillment and community rather than in scores and victories.

For example, running may be advocated as an experience of self-awareness, body-emotion integration, and even spiritual transcendence rather than as a punishing way of preparing for competition. The experience of making music may be stressed over the acclaim of final performance. The expression and freedom of art may transform the experience when valued over the technical perfection of the product.

In the same way, different forms of games and sport have been developed that are designed to bring people together rather than to separate them. The ball is a tactual means of common endeavor rather than a projectile. Bodily contact is friendly and sensual rather than antagonistic and even violent. In one symbol, balloons can replace balls in a game where some of the separation of the game from the real world is emphasized and contributes to the gaiety.

Others would argue that almost any traditional game can be transformed by a different orientation of participants. There is no inherent reason why a sport need be grim rather than a bit frivolous. Opponents can rejoice in the adept play of others as well as feel satisfaction in their own coordination of mind and body. The expressive components can take precedence over the competitive. Old games can be fun if they are redefined in the minds of the players.

Revised Value Systems

The leisure counterculture attacks any instrumental view of leisure by asserting that leisure is self-justifying because it is human. Insofar as the self alone and in community with others is of worth, then leisure is worthwhile in its own right. Leisure is understood in humanistic terms rather than as a social instrument. It is "good" because human freedom, creativity, expression, development, and relationships are "good" in their own right. Learning, playfulness, celebration, and community are valued as human experiences, not just as preparation for the "real world."

There are many implications for planners and providers of leisure opportunities. First, the worth of a program can be measured in the immediate satisfaction of participants rather than in secondary-level benefits such as increased employment productivity. Second, leisure occasions can be organized and structured to enhance human experiences rather than to prepare for a contest or to meet skill standards. Skill acquisition then becomes appropriate to the desired participation experience rather than to preordained standards. Third, leisure events should remain flexible enough to respond to the developing satisfactions of the participants rather than conform to a rigid schedule. Fourth, leisure education will have to deal as much with attitudes and orientations as with activities and skills. And, finally, leisure is defined in the experience rather than in the activity. Leisure may still be situated in events and particular contexts, but the meaning is in the state of being rather than in long-term outcomes.

Diversity in Leisure

There are a number of implications of this approach to leisure as more than a traditional set of activities. The first is the focus on the experience rather than the outcomes. The second is the significance of challenge in which the development of skill may offer a sense of worthwhile identity. The third is the realization of community that builds on a common commitment to such activity.

There is also a fourth implication. It is that of the diversity of leisure. Such diversity has at least three themes. The first is that the activities that may be done as leisure, even serious leisure, are almost without limit. The critical elements for significant leisure are challenge and social interaction, wherever and whenever they may be chosen. The second is the diversity of leisure styles. Not only are there salient ethnic differences in leisure, but there are a variety of styles of engaging in activity. Some leisure has high levels of commitment and skill development sustained over time. Other leisure is disengaging, a withdrawal from challenge and even from other people. Even for those with a central serious leisure commitment, there is also the side of leisure that takes time out from the serious to become caught up in the frivolous. The third implication is that of the diversity of leisure participants. That diversity may be of culture, age , gender, sexual orientation, personal history, or a number of other factors. There is no one "right" way to do anything in leisure, or perhaps in life. One central dimension of leisure is its openness to diversity, to a variety of styles and levels of involvement, and to rhythms of engagement and disengagement.

HIGHLIGHTS

1. Leisure not only reflects limits on opportunities but also a diversity of ethnic values and life styles.
2. Leisure subcultures provide opportunity both for social identification with the group and differentiation from the remainder of society.
3. The "amateur" demonstrates how leisure may be not only strenuous and challenging, but can provide essential meaning and direction to a life.

Discussion Questions

1. What seem to be the differences between individuals who concentrate so fully on one leisure activity or group and those who have more variety and balance in their leisure?

2. Do activity-centered leisure subcultures such as skydiving and rock climbing provide a social identification substitute similar to that given by ethnic or religious identification for others? How?

3. Give examples of people who demonstrate their leisure identities in nonleisure settings. Why do they do it?

4. How important are second-level rules and conventions in face-to-face leisure group interaction? Give examples other than poker.

5. Can leisure be strenuous and disciplined as with amateur musicians or devotees of a sport as well as relaxed and undemanding as with watching television? Which kind of leisure is closer to your understanding of "true" leisure? Why?

6. Is "new leisure" likely to replace older competitive forms of sport and games for most people? Why or why not?

7. Give examples of new diversity in leisure styles.

Bibliography

Csikszentmihalyi, Mihaly. *Flow: The Psychology of Optimal Experience.* New York: Harper, 1990.

Stebbins, Robert. *Amateurs, Professionals, and Serious Leisure.* Montreal: McGill-Queen's University Press, 1992.

Chapter 22

Sexuality and Leisure

We seldom think of ourselves or of anyone else without the fundamental assumption of sexual identification. In any social situation—leisure, work, school, or family—being male or female makes a difference. Any time there are two or more people, gender is a factor in what happens and the mode of interaction. Most leisure is social, and in any social group the gender composition is important.

Just as important is the fact that we are all sexual beings. Not only our social identification of gender but our own sexuality affects all that we do. What it means to be a woman or a man, how sexuality is demonstrated and expressed, and what is expected because of sexuality is irrelevant to almost nothing we are or do. Sexuality is not only a significant element in leisure—in our associations and performances—but is an essential part of what it means to be human. Now there is also recognition of a greater variety in sexual orientations and relationships than was the case even a decade ago.

Beginning with sexuality and personal identity, we look at the significance of sex roles for leisure, developing sexuality for adolescent life, sex as work, and sex as leisure. Finally, issues for leisure planners and providers will be raised out of new expectations for intimacy, companionship, and enjoyment combined with recognition of the pervasiveness of sexuality and sexual expression in a time when many adults are not married or living in families.

ISSUES

How does gender affect childhood and adult leisure choices and styles?

How does sex-role socialization shape leisure in our culture?

What are the negative consequences of differential opportunities and rewards?

Can sexual activity be leisure?

How are sex-related social changes, including an open diversity in sexual orientation, significant for leisure?

The term *sex* may be used in the sense of gender to refer to being either male or female. That identification shapes everything we do for all our conscious lives. How we walk, talk, gesture, move, dress, interact, and just about everything else is done in ways that are defined by gender as *masculine* or *feminine*. Gender is not only biological, but is a social construction.

Sex roles are the sets of social expectations distinguished by sexual identification. Males and females are not expected to act alike in most social situations, whether on the job or on the playing field. In general, in our culture, males are expected to be more dominant, aggressive, and decisive. Females are expected to be more responsive, passive, and supportive. Behavior that conforms to those expectations tends to be rewarded. On the other hand, there are rather unfriendly names to label those who violate the sex-role norms, or who seek to express their sexuality in ways unacceptable to majority cultures.

Sexuality is that aspect of our selfhood that is related to gender identification, behavior in which gender makes a difference, the biology of sexual relatedness, including reproduction, self-definition as men and women, and self-presentation as a person of one sex rather than the other. In short, we are sexual beings. Our sexuality has meanings that are both biological and social. We are, after all, the social animal who creates a culture and is aware of its creation. In our sexuality, the biological animal and the creature who makes symbolic meanings, identifications, and culture are one being. The interpretations, forms, and expressions of that sexuality vary widely among subcultures as well as between cultures, but sexuality itself is universal.

We are all sexual. We are identified by sex or gender. We do thousands of things with sexual meaning. Therefore, sex is more than something we do.

Sex and Identity

Almost every social setting, every activity, and every relationship is an example of sexuality. Small children know very early whether they are girls or boys. Their first play experiences are shaped by sexual identification. The kinds of toys provided and encouraged are usually sex-linked.

For the adolescent, the development of sexual identity in relation to the other sex becomes a central part of every activity, from grooming in the morning to the last thoughts at night. It is a period in which feedback from the looking glass of significant members of the other sex will alter self-definitions, styles of behavior, and even goals for the future. In later years sexual identity is at the heart of the courtship process, the development of the marriage relationship, and of child rearing. How we see ourselves and present ourselves as men and women is an important element of activities that are as widely separate as conducting a business meeting and warming up on the tennis court.

The teen years are also a time when some recognize that they do not conform to majority norms of sexual orientation. Some explore homosexual relationships. A smaller number come to accept their sexual orientation as gay or lesbian. Personal struggles with the costs of public identification as homosexual are a central preoccupation of the adolescent development of a minority in a society that still exhibits considerable homophobia.

The point is that gender and sexual identities are a part of everything we do. For example, observational research about beach behavior has produced insights on the relevance of sexual identity. Sexual presentation barely begins with what is worn. The carefully acted scene of arrival, choice of a place to spread out the beach towel and stake claim to a small territory, the steps in preparing for the water or sunbathing, the approach to and entry into the water, and emerging with appropriate dignity and style are all elements of playing to others who may or may not be paying attention.[1] For the most part, we do not just come, walk, swim, and leave. We see the beach as a kind of stage on which we construct a scene by which we hope to tell a little something of our story to others.

In a case study of the transition from student to establishment worker of a midwestern man, the story of his leisure was found to be primarily a story of sexual exploration, changing locales and styles, and commitments.[2] He seemed to take on the sexual style of the group with which he identified. When in the service, he engaged in group forays to communities near his station in attempts to contact and form relationships with local girls. When he came to the university, he first took on the trappings and style of the counterculture with the deliberately careless appearance and use of drugs in heterosexual groups. Later, he came under the influence of a more conventional young woman and was led into the beer-drinking, party, and "brotherly" life of a fraternity. His mode of behavior with both male and female friends changed. During all of these periods, sexual activity and relationships with women he considered attractive were very important to him. Now that he is married, sexual interaction with his wife is augmented by the desire to associate with attractive women whenever possible. It is important to him that the females in their couple friendships be sexually appealing. Further, a favorite activity is going with another couple to porno films before going to their separate homes for sexual intercourse stimulated by the film.

Studies of older people demonstrate that sexuality is not just something for the young that is outgrown in maturity. The growth in sexual interest and activity by women in their thirties and forties has been accented and perhaps enhanced by the greater availability of material presenting the meanings of sexuality for women and the increased acceptance of sexual expression. Reports on divorce in the middle years suggest that male uncertainty about sexual identity and attractiveness as a man is one factor in the rejection of former partners and interest in different and younger women by many men in their forties and fifties. For both men and women, there is a relationship between self-perceived physical appearance and sexual attractiveness that may produce an emotional crisis with the first signs of grayness, baldness, extra weight, wrinkles, and other changes associated with aging.

Sexual identity is more than just glandular urges toward activity and explicitly sexual activity such as intercourse, masturbation, and other kinds of physical stimulation. Sexual identity is an inextricable element in who we are to ourselves and with others.

Sexual identity is central to our social participation and social roles. Not only whether we are male or female, but also the kind of man or woman we think we are and would like

---

[1] Erving Goffman, *The Presentation of Self in Everyday Life.* Garden City, NY: Doubleday, 1959.

[2] Shelley H. Washburne, "Leisure and Life Cycle Transition from the Young Adult to the Early Establishment Stage." Unpublished Master's thesis, University of Illinois, Urbana-Champaign, August 1978.

others to believe us to be has a major part in shaping our behavior. It may be that especially in many leisure roles we strive most deliberately to present certain sexual selves. Our masculinity and femininity, the potency and depth of our manhood and womanhood, may be most on display in the game or at the party. The security of well-defined roles may be partly laid aside in the more open leisure situation so that concern with our sexual identity becomes paramount.

Sexual identity is also central to our understanding of ourselves. As suggested before, we seldom if ever even think of ourselves apart from that sexual identity. We know that we are unique selves, but those selves are first of all male or female. That does not mean that gender always implies differences. For the most part, women and men act more alike than different. Social expectations are more similar than contrasting. But the differences in what we have learned about selfhood and social interaction are not to be easily laid aside.

The question "Who are you?" is answered by more than a name. Even the name alone says, "I am man or I am woman." Before we begin to explain or demonstrate what kind of man or woman, we accept and present that primary identification. Then there are all the questions about "What kind of man or woman?" How do we define ourselves and carry out our gender identities in different social contexts? Identification as heterosexual, homosexual, or bisexual is only the beginning in our lifelong development and expression of our sexuality.

Sex Roles and Leisure

There are some evident gender differences in leisure. Clearly, opportunities for certain kinds of sports such as football, baseball, rugby, wrestling, and auto racing are much greater for men than for women. As shown in Table 22-1, large differences in male and female participation are almost entirely limited to team sports, golf, hunting and fishing, and such social behavior as going to bars.

Most of the significant differences are related to sex-role socialization. Most sports that men tend to play more than women are the team sports that they have had more encouragement to begin and continue. On the other hand, where opportunities are fairly equal, participation rates for those seventeen and over show no differences by sex. Males do tend to do more hunting and fishing, while females do more window shopping and reading for pleasure. Males go to bars more; females are more likely to avoid them entirely.

However, sports that females are encouraged to play, cultural events, and most social occasions such as entertaining, neighboring, and eating out show no significant differences in this national sample. Men and women garden, watch television, picnic with their families, and take auto rides at about the same rates. With greater attention being given to equalizing opportunities, especially for children, there are evident increases in female participation in physically demanding activities, especially in team sports.

More important than similarities and differences in the kinds of activities engaged in by men and women are the processes underlying the differences. From childhood on, some kinds of activities are defined as acceptable for one sex rather than the other. The definitions change with age. The onset of puberty and the development of sexual characteristics

TABLE 22–1   Sex Differences in Leisure Participation

Activity	Male Percentage	Female Percentage	Is the Difference Significant?*
Sports			
(participated at least once a year)			
Badminton	18	19	No
Basketball	29	15	Yes
Bowling	28	27	No
Football	23	5	Yes
Golf	19	6	Yes
Racquetball, handball	12	8	No
Softball, baseball	38	24	Yes
Swimming	51	45	No
Tennis	19	19	No
Other leisure			
(participated at least once a month)			
Hunt or fish	32	12	Yes
Walk or hike	59	57	No
Attend school sports	15	9	Yes
Attend a movie	37	36	No
Eat at a restaurant	70	70	No
Window shop	57	67	Yes
Attend theater, concert	21	18	No
Go on a picnic	40	41	No
Read for pleasure	75	87	Yes
Take auto ride for pleasure	72	71	No
Garden for pleasure	52	57	No
Attend civic or religious organization	38	45	Yes
Watch television			
(hours per week)			
None	12	12	No
1–2	55	53	No
3–4	19	18	No
5+	15	17	No
Give a party several times per year	41	43	No
Go to bar or lounge often	52	41	Yes
Never go to a bar or lounge	36	51	Yes
Spend a social evening with relatives often	49	68	Yes
Spend a social evening with neighbors often	41	43	No

*Statistically significant at .01 level.

Source: Author's analysis of 1974 national survey.

of the body has always been the time when it becomes no longer acceptable for "nice girls" to engage in body contact sports with boys. This alleged social danger has usually been obscured by claims of physical danger to less muscular and more fragile females. In general, height and weight differentials have made competition between mates and females in many sports uneven after testosterone production has had its effect on males.

Lowered barriers to female participation in gender-biased activities are a beginning. Legal and financial discrimination policies are being changed. There remain, however, a number of barriers to equality of opportunity in recreation. There are still gender definitions that reward and sanction males and females differently. These are adult roles that give males greater freedom from family and household responsibilities. There are income differentials that especially impact women who are the primary parent after divorce. And there are situations in which women do not feel safe from male coercion and violence. Real equality is far from achieved in a society that still discriminates by gender.

Sex-Role Socialization

Why does it make any difference whether both sexes have opportunities and encouragement to develop a full range of leisure interests and skills?

The first concern is for leisure itself. If physical activity and sport, forest and water resource-based activities, appreciation of and creation in the arts, and other kinds of leisure have particular value for participants, then no group should be systematically excluded from any kind of activity. If males are pushed toward sport and away from arts and crafts, then they lose the satisfactions of immersion in the creation of an artistic product. Moreover, they may not achieve a balance in leisure that gives adequate expression to some aspects of their potential selfhood. In the same way, if females are pushed toward parties and away from sports, they may lose the health benefits as well as the satisfactions of experiencing physical mastery and strenuous coordinated movement. Since there is no evidence that either sex lacks aptitudes in appreciative sense, physical coordination, or creative potential, then a full range of leisure should be experienced by both.

The second concern is for the consequences for human and social development. Any activity has outcomes that reach beyond the particular event. Not only are our self-evaluations altered by the outcomes of what we do and the kind of feedback we receive from others, but experiences accumulate to change what we are. Disciplined physical effort will develop our bodies, our strength and coordination, and our feelings of physical competence. In social enterprises we practice interactional skills, learn to communicate, and organize the activity of others to be able to take roles of leadership and influence. Whatever we do has its consequences for ourselves. When a primary set of opportunities for personal development is closed to us, then we either find another set of opportunities or suffer the results of inequality of access. We become less skilled, less developed, and less confident in that aspect of life than those who have had the opportunities.

In the socialization process of learning what is expected of us in our society, we find ourselves in the midst of a system of reinforcements and rewards. Some kinds of activity are simply prohibited. Transgression of clear social rules may be severely punished, usually by some form of exclusion ranging from discouragement through imprisonment to total banishment or execution. However, for the most part, we learn through this process in which some kinds of behavior are reinforced with rewards and others are disapproved and penalized. On the simplest level, if we play a game well, we are always included or chosen to play again, allowed a role central to the action, and praised for our skill. If we play the game poorly, we may not be chosen to play at all. If we play, we find ourselves on the periphery of the game where we may do the least harm and are either ignored or criticized for our lack of skill.

In any social situation—a game or sport, conversation or group interchange, or institutional episode such as class in school, reinforcement is either offered or withheld. If we do it—whatever it may be—acceptably, then we are drawn into chances to do it again. We come to see ourselves as people who *can do* it and who should do it. We go on to refine our already acceptable skills until we do it well and receive a variety of rewards. In short, in this socialization process we not only learn how to perform in social situations but become somewhat different persons in the process.

When females and males are reinforced and rewarded in different ways, then they become different. Whatever their biological differences, even more they have *learned* to be different. Insofar as those differences simply reflect and are appropriate to the biological differences, then differential socialization may be right and appropriate. Insofar as the socialization differences give advantage to one sex over the other in ways that truncate the lives of the more limited sex, then the differences take on a political cast and are subject to charges of injustice.

If being male or female is defined as being inherently less able and of inferior potential for important aspects of life, then the problem is called *institutional sexism* or discrimination. As such, it is both unjust and, in some nations, unconstitutional.

Men, Women, and Values

Different opportunities for males and females have profoundly affected participation and development. Further, social expectations have been different, so that from childhood on, females and males have generally defined themselves differently. Analysis of such social and psychological differences has more and more often been understood as discrimination, not merely difference.

Differences, however, have frequently been viewed from the perspective of masculine values. Not only physical and social attributes but also personality and value characteristics are distinguished with the presumption of male priority. Most recently there have been telling critiques of such male-oriented perspectives. One psychological study agrees that men and women have learned to view themselves and their worlds somewhat differently but disagrees that one is more valid than the other. Carol Gilligan has found that women tend to view the world in terms of relationships.[3] This ethic of relationships emphasizes caring and responsibility for others. It contrasts with male values on results, principles, and rational rule making. She recognizes considerable overlap between genders but finds significantly different value orientations.

Such value differences are consistent with research suggesting that men and women tend to view the world differently. Men tend to give priority to accomplishment, recogni-

---

[3] Carol Gilligan, *In a Different Voice* (Cambridge, MA: Harvard University Press, 1982).

tion, measured results, and rules. Women are more likely to value nurture, communication, sharing, and other relational aspects of life. Again, these are not dichotomous. Further, there are indications that males become more nurturing in later periods of the life course.

The point is that one is not intrinsically superior to the other. When a society systematically rewards one set of values and priorities over the other, then the bias has consequences for the entire society. It also has consequences for leisure. Opportunities and rewards may be greater for the kinds of activity that foster particular values. When competition and accomplishment are valued over communication and relationships, then leisure reinforces what has traditionally been the male world over that which has been female. Leisure may strengthen the cultural bias toward structured and measured activity and disvalue relational action and interaction. If leisure is to be considered a domain of freedom and openness, then it should be one of diversity as well. There are many ways of being oneself—male or female—in all kinds of leisure contexts. Leisure might even be a part of life in which rigid gender roles are challenged and revised.

Play and Sex Roles

Before going on to examine the crucial period of adolescence more closely, we should note charges that have been lodged concerning alleged sexism in children's play. The complaint is that, from the beginning, females are shunted off into kinds of play activity that reduce their chances of accomplishment in their own society. The games of children are said to be not only sex-differentiated but discriminatory.

One research effort was completed in 1975 by Janet Lever of Northwestern University.[4] She was investigating whether socialization in play for boys gave them an advantage in taking adult roles. She assumes that the peer group—in this case, the play group—is a factor in socialization. Further, some kinds of play give more opportunity to learn valued role skills than others.

She found that boys' games are better preparation for successful performance in the economic sphere, through practice in independence, coordination of activities, and adjudication of disputes in rule-bound events. Experience in controlled competitive games may improve ability to deal with interpersonal competition. On the other hand, the play of girls is more likely to occur in small groups and dyads. It tends to occur in private places and to mimic adult primary relationships. Girls' play is more spontaneous, free of rules, and cooperative.

Play, then, is one aspect of the total socialization process. In play there is a tendency for boys to play games in groups that require organizational skills, competition, and adjustment to structured interaction. They have this opportunity to develop role skills appropriate for the business corporation, public institution, and the world of decision making. Girls tend to play in ways that are appropriate to family interaction and the cooperation of the primary group.

No one would suggest that this tendency is all-encompassing. Many females become quite skilled at group organization, are very independent, and deal with competition quite well. And many males are far more comfortable in smaller and more spontaneous group-

---

[4] Janet Lever, "Sex Differences in the Games Children Play," *Social Problems,* 23 (1976), 479–488.

ings. However, in general, the play of children has been found to be consistent with the socialization prevalent in the home, the school, and other community institutions. From the moment that Dad brings home a football to his very small son and Mom begins to sew doll clothes for her tiny daughter, parental expectations, equipment, and role models all combine to direct the boy toward the world of organized competition and the girl toward the smaller world of the family and intimacy.

The games in which boys are encouraged to participate tend to measure relative strength and skill, to require coordination of one team against that of another, to record the statistical totals of personal output, and to call for both decisiveness and subordination to an appointed leader. They are the team sports for which the social rewards for proficiency are greatest in the school and in the community. They are the sports through which fathers begin teaching skill acquisition to their sons at very early ages.

On the other hand, despite new awareness of the value of self-images of physical competence for girls, sex-role socialization has not only provided scant reward for the strong and aggressive girl but has frequently required her to fight the system for participation opportunities. It is no wonder that identification with same-sex parents and other role models leads many girls to play in ways that imitate adult roles of nurturance and passivity. Games may serve a conservative function in the society by starting children toward traditional gender roles at very tender ages.

There are many indications of change. Opportunities and encouragement for girls to engage in the same kinds of activities that boys do are increasing—partly due to the convictions of providers, partly to the pressure of the parents of girls, and partly by law and court action. As the work force includes more and more mothers, the role models for little girls are changing to include the world of business and government as well as the home. Further, some women, finding themselves at a disadvantage in the economic world, are deliberately altering the socialization of their own children toward more inclusive role socialization. Little boys are learning that cooperative play and caring for others can be rewarding, and little girls are learning that there is satisfaction in making decisions, measuring mastery, and organizing complex goal-oriented groups. More important, males are learning that nurturance is enriching and females that competence is satisfying.

One additional note: The socialization aspect of the play of children is another reminder that asexual activities, events, and locales are difficult to find. Even the absence of the other sex is sexual in the likelihood of exclusion by gender and the consequent role learning denied.

Adolescents: Seeking Personal and Social Identity

The adolescent is engaged in a series of role-testing enterprises. Among the roles being tested are those of what it means to be a man among men, a woman among women, a man with a woman, and a woman with a man. Sport participation for a high school age male is more than exercise, companionship, and group identification. It is a public demonstration of what are considered to be fundamental masculine attributes. As a consequence, what he comes to think of himself and how he is identified in the social context of the school are to a large degree dependent on his measured performance. He is measured by physical strength and agility, by demonstrated success against other males, and by his contribution to the school in these most valued symbols of status.

In much the same way, the female student also learns how she may define herself in the crucible of the high school. However, her testing of roles often takes place in a different arena. Along with the academic part of school life and its reward system, there is the social element. While the male is rewarded socially for his masculine achievement, the female is rewarded for her feminine attributes of attractiveness rather than strength, of agreeableness rather than competitive success, and for her relationship to males who symbolize school status. Her relative worth may be based on attractiveness and relationships to the male status hierarchy. To a large extent, achievement by a female student is rewarded in the overall social scheme only if her competence in sports, the arts, or studies is accompanied by attractiveness to males.

Therefore, the critical arena of testing and the formation of self-images is gender-biased. While most such interaction is not "courting" in the restricted sense of deliberately seeking a marriage partner, it is courting in the broad sense of trying out and establishing ways of relating to the other sex. And it is by sex-specific standards that relative acceptability is rated. The attributes that provoke success in the "courting game" are specific to masculinity and femininity. "Strong" females and "cute" males are seldom at the top of the status hierarchy.

Sexuality is a preoccupation for adolescents. Not just in the simple sense of coping with glandular changes and sexual excitement, but sexuality is central to development of a sense of selfhood that incorporates one's own sexual identity in relation to the sexuality of others. For adolescents, sexual activity itself is a major form of leisure. It plays an important part in walking along the school corridor, meeting after school, dating, parties, movies, dances, concerts, driving, parking, and just being together with someone else. While an increase in sexual intercourse has been found among teens, touching, holding, groping, and varied physical contact producing sexual excitement are hardly new phenomena. Especially since the automobile has lent both mobility and privacy, such contact and sensual exploration has been a major pastime for adolescents.

Some fear sexual interaction and attempt to limit opportunities for such contact. There are even suggestions in the recreation literature that very active sports serve as a drain of sexual tension for young men. Basketball and cold showers have been recommended to keep both males and their potential female companions "out of trouble." Even in a more enlightened era, it would be the bold community or school recreation director who would see heterosexual privacy as a major leisure and developmental need for teenagers and recommend that public programs provide opportunity for such dyadic encounter.

Less commonly discussed is the development of same-sex attachments by adolescents. Both males and females often form very deep attachments to a "best friend" in the younger teen years. For most that special friendship takes the form of prolonged communication and serves to help develop peer trust. The most common pattern is to move from such a concentrated same-sex relationship to a wider circle of friends and to a beginning of other-sex relationships. However, although most adolescents are imbued with the taboo against explicit sexual activity with those of the same sex, in some cases a combination of elements in the personal history and inclusion-exclusion events in the years of intensifying sexuality may lead to homosexual relationships. For some, homosexuality is one experience among many and is discarded for dominant heterosexual expressions in later teen years. In other cases, the same-sex relationships become dominant.

The importance of games and play for children and of sport and social events for teens suggests that the social factors in the development of sexual orientations should be understood in a fuller context than just sex-role socialization and courting. The history of any person's sexuality is intertwined with specific relationships, satisfactions, inclusions, exclusions, image-building experiences, feedback from peers and significant adults, and group identifications. While family elements in socialization toward leisure, work, sexuality, and everything else appear to be most influential, the complex working through of sexual identity is at the center of adolescent life. Any approach to recreation and leisure that ignores this centrality is choosing to avoid conflict and complexity in order to gain irrelevant safety.

Sex as Work

There are many ways in which sex is approached as necessary or with extrinsic motivations. People may define sexual activity as very serious or a means to an end, rather than as having its own meaning and satisfaction. Some, of course, believe that sexual intercourse should be undertaken only for purposes of reproduction. Such an attitude makes sex work in the classic sense of necessary production, however satisfying the experience. Sexual activity may be leisure—freely chosen because it promises a high degree of satisfaction in the experience itself. What may be less self-evident is that some sexual activity may be quite unleisurely.

Sexual Relationships as a Contest

Studies of courtship in the 1950s abound with references to the *double standard*. This concept proposed that gender roles had shaped the sexual orientations of young men and women quite differently. On the one hand, males were expected to be aggressors who would gain as much sexual compliance from females as possible. Males were considered to "score" in the sexual contest if they succeeded in having intercourse with females without making any commitments that might be enforced in court. The wider the sexual experience of the male the higher his alleged masculinity rating.

Females, on the other hand, were expected to be passive defenders. They were responsible for protecting themselves from the aggression of males who were to employ a line to produce female compliance. In this uneven contest, responsibility for the level of activity was to rest with the female since the male was to go as far as allowed. However, in general, females who permitted intercourse were labeled as "easy" and not to be considered as eligible for marriage. As a result, it was found that males were most likely to seek intercourse with females they did not intend to marry, while females were most likely to engage in intercourse with males they did hope to marry. Thus, the contest was a much more serious game for females than for males. Further, the contest was not always equal in social resources allocated to males and females.

In high schools and universities there has been considerable change since the 1950s. Women students have been more decisive about their own lives and about their own sexuality. As they increasingly have lives of their own with life goals that include more than marriage and motherhood, they enter the fray with greater equality in resources. Like men, they do not have to marry. Further, the technology of contraception has permitted women to make decisions about sexual activity with minimal risk of pregnancy. As a result, the contest has some new rules. Nevertheless, there are indications that the game is not obsolete. Despite ideologies of mutual decision, enjoyment, and self-determination, sexual intercourse is still defined as conquest by some. It becomes something less than leisure when the aims are winning, a score, and the social prestige of success. Sexual activity is hardly relational leisure when one person becomes a trophy. From this perspective, sexual activity becomes a "commodity" to be purchased with loans of social status.

Nevertheless, there is a game aspect of much sexual interaction that may be interpreted as play. In the process of exploring relationships, communication, and caring, some nonserious activity such as "flirting" may occur. The little drama of "What if we . . . ?" may be played out—sometimes in moments—with both persons knowing that they do not mean it. As when children play house, there are times that it is enjoyable to play the sexual contest game when it is clear that there will be no winners and losers.

Sex as a Commodity

Whether or not prostitution is the "oldest profession," it does make sexual activity a market commodity. With its illegality raising the price, men and women sell their sexual participation quite directly on the streets of cities and through brokers who provide the services of more expensive call girls and escorts. In some cities in Europe and Asia and near Las Vegas, prostitution is licensed, regulated, and advertised. It may be that the purchase of a period of such activity is commercial leisure for the purchaser. However, it is business for the seller. Reports on prostitution suggest that some purchasers prefer to buy the activity for cash rather than having to pay a price in time or emotional involvement. Others who engage prostitutes prefer kinds of activity outside the range accepted by most people whom they might want as partners. For example, sex tourism in Asia offer young girls for sexual exploitation.

Whether or not prostitution predates the priesthood as the oldest profession, it is probably the oldest "leisure service." Insofar as the activity is engaged in by the buyer for intrinsic satisfaction, then it may be the beginning of commercial leisure provisions. The concern for time efficiency that is appealing in other contemporary commercial leisure packages also characterizes some use of prostitutes.

The same preference to have sexual activity without direct emotional involvement or the cost of ongoing relationships may be one basis for the pornography market. In motion pictures, videos, magazines, books, and some live entertainment, sexual exhibitions serve as entertainment, stimulation of sensations and fantasy, and even a kind of foreplay for viewers. Like prostitution, the provision of both theater and portable visual material has become a major business enterprise. Also, like prostitution, some of the business responds to the market for nonconventional sexual expression.

Whether the use of sexuality in advertising is a business use of a leisure activity depends on one's definitions. However, there is no question that leisure equipment for such activities as skiing and boating is sold with the hint of sexual potential at least implicit in the advertising. Vacation trip packages usually are advertised with attractive young women and men pictured in ways that may suggest that this might happen to any purchaser of the package. Those who would attract purchasers of leisure goods seem to believe that their hoped-for purchasers make a connection between their sexuality and leisure. The commodity they would like us to buy—a tennis outfit, ski jacket, cruise, weekend at the lodge or beach resort, aerobic exercise, or just lessons in the glamorous sport—is connected with how we may appear as women and men. We may become more masculine, more feminine, and more attractive if we pay the price.

Sex as Leisure

If *sex as work* implies that sex be extrinsically motivated and productive and that sexuality may be used for commercial ends, then *sex as leisure* suggests that sexual activity may also be done primarily for its own sake. The meaning of the experience may be its own primary motivation rather than some gain in social status, a victory in a contest, or an increase in product sales.

Recreational Sex

There is one theme of sexual ethics in Western culture that insists that sexual activity be serious. Whatever the sensations that participants may feel in the process, sexual expression should be more than pleasurable. There should be some institutional gain for the family or the society in general.

However, there is another approach to sexual expression that defines it as fundamentally a pleasure medium. Sexual activity, with its intense and varied potential for physical pleasure, is seen as a self-contained type of activity. One plays a sexual game with a partner/opponent much as one plays tennis. While it is possible to "practice" alone according to this view, the game is most satisfying when engaged in with at least one other person. The satisfactions from the sexual encounter, like tennis, combine elements of pleasurable physical sensations, skill mastery, diversion from the required aspects of life, an opportunity to be with and communicate with another person. The satisfactions are both intrinsic and social, but the experience itself is foremost.

Sexual activity may be recreation in the sense that it enables the participant to emerge better fit for other activities and responsibilities. It may reduce tensions through an intense concentration on the activity itself. Like an athletic event, there may be moments of "flow" when the self is merged into the experience. However, sex as leisure returns to the proposition that sexual activity is worth doing for its own sake without reference to its place in building relationships, recuperating for work, replenishing the population supply, or enhancing social status.

Study of sexual patterns since the introduction of oral contraceptives has demonstrated that the introduction of a new technology can change human behavior. While there is still a high value placed on marriage and the role of sexuality in building that relationship, for those who are not married intercourse may be engaged in with little fear of social or biological catastrophe. The high effectiveness of contraceptives has made sexual intercourse less serious in its potential and actual results. The possibility of sex for its own sake is a reality.

Some have argued that a "new hedonism" has emerged as a reigning sexual ethic. Sexual expression may be seen as play, self-contained in its meaning and a particularly intense kind of relational leisure. The meaning of the act is in the experience, sensual and relational, rather than in extrinsic goals or consequences. Sex may be a game with its meanings negotiated in the encounter and with a variety of interactions possible just because the event is nonserious. Sexual encounter is viewed as temporary unless the rules of play are replaced by another set of serious norms, as in marriage.

Recently the spread of the sexually transmitted AIDS-HIV loss of immunological defenses against disease has had a dramatic impact on sexual behavior. At first, the impacts seemed limited primarily to male homosexuals. Then, when communication to heterosexuals through the needles of drug users and through bisexual activity was recognized, the drastic consequences of sexual activity reemerged. The potentially fatal results of forms of sexual activity that had seemed "safe" has placed multiple-partner recreational sex in jeopardy. Sexually transmitted diseases again have become a major barrier to many sexual patterns.

Sexuality has display elements as well as those of play. Not only does every aspect of self-presentation from body language to clothing have some sexual messages, but being seen with another person in certain contexts conveys various meanings to others. Just as wearing a warm-up suit to the grocery store is an announcement of a selfhood, public displays of relationships are a statement of sexual status with meanings intended for the onlookers.

Sex as Relational Leisure

There have been suggestions that sexuality has become a preoccupation in American culture. The attention given to sexual expression has been diagnosed by some as needed emphasis on freedom and self-development and by others as a retreat into self-indulgence by a people less and less concerned about greater issues and about other people. The two opposing camps might be identified as those espousing sex for its own sake and those viewing an increased focus on sexual expression as one aspect of a selfish privatism that threatens to erode the common life of the society. Some stress pleasure and others stress social responsibility.

However, defining sexuality as something more than the search for pleasure does not imply a negative attitude toward sexuality. Sexual expression can be and frequently is pleasurable, fun, and an intensely satisfying experience. Further, our sexuality is a pervasive part of our selfhood that needs to be accepted, understood, and developed along with other elements. We are sexual beings as well as social beings, cultural beings, decisive beings, embodied beings, self-conscious beings, thinking beings, and responsible beings.

Nevertheless, there seem to be some problems with separating our sexuality from the rest of our lives and relationships as a kind of discrete activity. Sexual relationships are different from tennis in more than the amount of space required. Sexual relationships involve two persons, not just two bodies. It is partly for this reason that adults being interviewed about their leisure find the affection and intimacy of a stable relationship most difficult to analyze in terms of satisfactions. Demonstrated intimacy such as sexual intercourse is sensual pleasure enjoyable for its own sake. It is also important to the maintenance and enhancement of a very important relationship. It takes place in the context of a full relationship and is, in part, an expression of the quality of that relationship. And, at least at times, there is some element of meeting the expectation of the partner in a particular sexual occasion.

It would seem to be most accurate, then, to classify most sexual intimacy in stable or growing relationships as *relational.* It is chosen for anticipated satisfactions rather than to meet obligations. It has satisfaction intrinsic to the experience and the occasion. However, its persistent meaning is firmly embedded in the ongoing relationship. The affection and intimacy are part of the bonding of the two individuals in a relationship of communication, trust, interdependence, companionship, common responsibility, commitment, and physical expression. Leisure is an integral part of the total relationship, and sex is central to the relational freedom and meaning of leisure.

Sexual activity, then, from this perspective is more than doing something together. It is a demonstration of relatedness. It is a medium of communication as well as of pleasure. It is social as well as physical. It is integral to the exploring, building, and maintaining of intimate relationships. And in its ongoing nature, sexuality includes pain as well as pleasure and estrangement as well as communion. It is a process with a career for each relationship and a personal career related to each person's journey through life.

Social Change and Sexuality

Some social change seems to come in tides that flood and ebb. Other change is more linear and may be represented by graphic trend lines. Some change is gradual and evolutionary and other change sudden and revolutionary. In a time when changes in sexual behavior are still going on, it is difficult to distinguish the tides from the trends.

For example, a number of evident short-term trends are noted:

There is an increase in the proportion of marriages that end in divorce. Unlike previous postwar divorce increases, this rise in the divorce rate toward one for every two marriages includes a full range of ages, education levels, and family life cycle stages.

There is an increase in singleness, both as a result of terminated marriages and of decisions not to marry. Some singleness is temporary and endured rather than preferred, while other singleness is chosen.

More children are being reared in single-parent families.

There is a greater openness about homosexuality as a sexual orientation and a social identity.

The proportion of adolescents who are active sexually has increased at least twofold since 1950.

There is a greater openness about sexual expressions and relationships between people who are not married.

The media and especially television have been more explicit in depicting sexuality and sexual activity as part of the lives of both single and married people.

Whether all this adds up to a "sexual revolution" is debatable, despite clear trends toward single-head households and greater diversity. However, there is increasing agreement that social change in regard to sexuality is more than a temporary phenomenon, that the change is real and persistent.

The more persistent population trends appear to be toward a reduction of marriage permanence and a higher proportion of singleness.[5] Both of these trends have implications for sexuality and leisure.

Marriage and Divorce Changes

While it is still true that couples who are past their teen years, with a higher education level and more stable economic positions, are much less likely to divorce than the young and the less prepared, divorce rates have been consistently rising. As yet, there is no evidence that prolonged periods of courtship, including living together, and greater economic and social independence for educated women will reverse the trend.

One element in the trend appears to be leisure. Both women and men are less likely than their parents to stay in a marriage in which the breadwinner, homemaker, and parent roles are fulfilled adequately but the role of companion is not. Expectations for friendship, companionship, and intimacy in marriage seem to be rising. Divorce may occur partly because one or both partners expect more from the marriage, not because they take marriage less seriously. At the same time, more alternatives for women, less social disapproval of divorce, smaller families, and many other factors are also related to marriage dissolution.

Both men and women may experience satisfying leisure companionship in their marriage. Both may place a high priority on leisure that expresses and reinforces family relationships. Such activity may, however, have somewhat different meanings for women and men. Most often, events such as picnics and holiday festivals require considerable management and preparation by women. The companionship of family leisure may be purchased with the disproportionate time and effort of a parent. Further, family leisure priorities may reflect the nurturing aims of parents. The ending of a marriage, then, has tremendous impact on the leisure of both parents and children.

First, there are all the social occasions in which people are expected to come as couples. There is a reluctance on the part of many to mix single and married people in social occasions. Whatever the reasons, those whose marriages are ended by separation, divorce, or death find themselves outside of circles important to their leisure routines.

Second, many kinds of activities have been fostered by the interest and availability of the marriage partner. Whenever a couple has usually done something together—whether it is a sport, travel, camping, entertaining, or a club—it is often difficult to establish a new pattern of participation.

Third, the termination of a marriage usually reduces the financial resources available, especially for women. Changes in residence may be required by a decrease in income. Leisure requiring costly investments may have to be discarded. This limit disrupts past leisure patterns.

---

[5] George Masnick and Mary Jo Bane, *The Nation's Families: 1960-1990* (Cambridge, MA: MIT-Harvard Joint Center for Urban Studies, 1980).

Fourth, following a divorce one parent, usually the mother, has a greatly increased responsibility for children and the other loses the routine and companionship of the family. In the first case, leisure with adults outside the home may be restricted. In the second, a major element of everyday and accessible leisure is lost.

The implications for leisure are manifold. The major leisure needs of most people who divorce are social. In response to this need such organizations as "Parents without Partners" provide a multifaceted social program in which meeting others is a major purpose. "Singles" organizations, clubs, and programs catering to the formerly married have been increasing. At the same time, participation in some activity-oriented programs by the newly single may have the primary aim of developing new relationships and alleviating loneliness.

One sexual implication of this change is that more and more people are seeking ways to understand and express their sexuality outside marriage. Even when remarriage is desired, the interim period is one in which the need to rebuild sexual identity may be acutely felt. Sexual activity including intercourse is no longer just premarital, marital, and extramarital. There is an entire range of sexual expression critical to the adjustment and reassessment period that follows a divorce. Feedback from significant others is crucial in this period. And a major social context of this exploration and reassessment is leisure.

Singleness and Targeted Provisions

The entertainment pages of any metropolitan newspaper give signs of the new opportunity for commercial leisure providers. Singles clubs, dances, bars, cruises, weekend trips, summer tours, skiing weeks, and beach breaks—all are advertised to reach those who are single. Housing providers caught the market years ago when they began to design apartment complexes around pools and clubhouses. The critical issue is simple: to meet other singles who are deemed interesting and attractive. Some singles are lonely and want to develop friendships. Some are frightened and want reassurance about their own attractiveness. Some just want an evening or weekend filled with activity—be it athletic, social, or sexual.

Public providers have been less alert to the needs. Especially for those who cannot afford the financial cost of the commercial packages and opportunities, what kinds of programs are available to meet the needs for social reestablishment? What is offered for those who cannot leave for the weekend because of child-care responsibilities? What is available for single mothers still at home with infants and preschool children? There is considerable evidence that leisure and community activities are not all that easy to manage, even for urban singles with some discretionary income. Those who are not urban and affluent are especially limited.

Leisure and Sexual Diversity

The movement advocating greater acceptance of variety in sexual orientations has had significant impacts. More gay, lesbian, and bisexual persons are acknowledging their sexual orientation, forming stable relationships, seeking legal protection, and organizing to promote their full rights of citizenship. In response, there has been organized resistance and attempts to insist on the primacy of "traditional" values. There are many implications of this process for governmental policy, economic opportunity, and family law. There are also impacts on leisure. Sexual orientation has become more openly the basis for leisure associations and styles. For the most part, market sector providers have been the primary source of leisure resources designated by sexual orientation. There are gay and lesbian bars, clubs, tours, and programs. The public sector, for the most part, segregates by age and gender, but not explicitly by race or sexual orientation. Exclusion is more a matter of cultural practices including the threat of violence than of policy or deliberate practices. Nevertheless, it is increasingly recognized that sexual identification is a central factor in the styles and associations developed around leisure activity. Sexual identification can be central to the formation of a variety of leisure subcultures that accept differences and yet focus on particular life styles and interests.

Less recognized are the exclusionary practices associated with HIV infection and consequent AIDS. The incredibly difficult process of accepting and coping with impending death for those diagnosed as HIV-positive calls for all kinds of social and personal support. The recreational needs of those so easily ignored and so conveniently segregated are only beginning to be recognized and met by public agencies that have no difficulty responding to the special requirements of those with physical disabilities. Now that an acknowledgment of the heterosexual transmission of the AIDS virus is increasing, there may be a greater acceptance of AIDS as a worldwide health problem that concerns us all.

Summary of Issues

If sex is not just an activity but is relatedness and identity, then what are liable to be the consequences of the general increase in sexual activity?

Since sexuality is integral to who and what we are, two principles follow:

1. Sexuality is involved in whatever we do and especially in any relationships with other people.
2. Sexual activity has the potential for great meaning and satisfaction as well as for considerable damage to our self-esteem and self-concepts.

Therefore, a definition of sexuality that includes only activity and the pleasure that may be derived from it fails to recognize the potential impacts for those engaged in sexual relationships. A critical issue for those who provide and plan leisure opportunities is facilitation of important sexual expression and its development, without leading people into situations that lie outside the realm of their capacity to cope. To ignore the sexual aspects of leisure is to be blind to an important part of the meaning of most social interaction. To pretend that leisure is asexual is to be irresponsible about the outcomes of programs.

On the other hand, with the recognition that sexuality is part of ourselves and not an occasional activity, how can leisure programs and provisions open needed opportunities for sexual expression and development without leading participants into potentially damaging experiences? Further, since it is precisely those with vulnerable sexual identities whose need for companionship and community is greatest, how can the potential for relationships be maximized and the risks minimized as programs are designed and implemented?

Differences in opportunities and role expectations for males and females remain even in a time of change. Such differences not only yield rewards that are critical to sex-role socialization and concepts of self at the time, but also produce sex-differentiated confidence and competence related to adult work roles. When sex-role stereotypes reduce opportunities for development of potentially enriching experiences and learning for either males or females, then the systematic discrimination leads to reduced humanity for some.

Changed sex-role expectations in the past decade have increased the likelihood that males will develop a fuller set of cultural and aesthetic satisfactions and competencies and females a wider spectrum of physical skills and experiences. Related changes in work, family, and community roles suggest that leisure programs will need to adapt to rather fundamental alterations in the kinds of activities that are available to both sexes throughout the life course.

At the same time, both a greater acceptance of the sexual meanings of leisure activity and the increase in the proportion of adults who do not enter leisure settings and programs as couples suggest that the time, compositions, and orientations of many leisure provisions—both public and commercial—will require revision.

HIGHLIGHTS

1. Although current opportunities for many kinds of leisure are far less sex-differentiated than in the past, significant sex-role expectations and differential reward systems remain factors in leisure choices, opportunities, and anticipations.
2. Not only *what* but *how* differs according to gender in many leisure settings and situations.
3. Sex-role stereotyping cuts both males and females off from satisfactions that might contribute to a full and balanced leisure life as well as from developmental opportunities and preparation for certain rewarded social roles.
4. Throughout the life course, sexual activity and sexual meanings in activity are an important dimension of social leisure.
5. The close ties of leisure to family and to sexual identity mean that changes in marriage, child-rearing, and courtship styles and structures will require adjustment of many leisure provisions and programs to provide for relational leisure.
6. Leisure is a significant arena of expression for those with a variety of sexual orientations and relationships.

Discussion Questions

1. How are games or sports changed when they are engaged in by a both-sex group? Give examples.

2. How is leisure sex-segregated for adults? For children? What are the consequences?

3. What is the most important context for the development and expression of sexual identity for adolescents—the school, leisure, or home and family? Why does sport take a special place in sex-role socialization?

4. How might leisure providers design programs to meet the needs of the formerly married? Adult singles? Single parents? Children in single-parent families?

5. How might variant sexual styles affect leisure behavior, interests, and associations?

6. Other than adolescence, what life cycle period is most critical to sexuality? Are there special vulnerabilities in this period that should be recognized by leisure planners?

7. Are sex differences in leisure participation likely to increase or decrease? Why?

8. What evidence is there that the women's movement will have consequences for leisure as well as for work?

9. Is sexual activity for adults better defined as work or as leisure? If leisure, is it best classified as unconditional, relational, recuperative, or role-determined? Why?

10. How can business and public recreation providers respond to sexual diversity?

Bibliography

Deem, Rosemary. *All Work and No Play: The Sociology of Women and Leisure.* Milton Keynes, United Kingdom: Open University Press, 1988.

Gilligan, Carol, *In a Different Voice.* Cambridge, MA: Harvard University Press, 1982.

Henderson, Karla, D. Bialeschki, S. Shaw, and V. Freysinger, *Leisure of One's Own: A Feminist Perspective on Women's Leisure.* State College, PA.: Venture Publishing, 1989.

Linder, Steffan B., *The Harried Leisure Class.* New York: Columbia University Press, 1969.

Money, John, and Patricia Tucker, *Sexual Signatures: On Being a Man or a Woman.* Boston: Little, Brown, 1975.

Snyder, Eldon, and E. Spreitzer, *Social Aspects of Sport.* Englewood Cliffs, NJ: Prentice-Hall, 1978.

Stockard, Jean, and Miriam M. Johnson, *Sex Roles.* Englewood Cliffs, NJ: Prentice-Hall, 1980.

Chapter 23

Leisure for Everyone

If leisure is a profoundly human phenomenon and not just a trivial option in life, then no person should be arbitrarily cut off from it. No condition of life can be allowed to render impossible anything essential to being human.

Only recently has public recreation in general recognized a responsibility to those who cannot participate unless special provisions are made for them. The blind have been left without transportation. Those in wheelchairs have been blocked by long stairways and narrow doors. The presumptions of skill acquisition have kept away those with physical or mental disabilities that make the learning long and hard.

There have been sport programs for those who can run, arts programs for quick learners, and social programs for those able to meet others easily. Public agencies have usually taken a "most for the least" approach that includes the largest proportion of the population at the lowest cost. Now resources are being adapted to maximize access and use. Further, programs aimed at increasing resourcefulness are opening new possibilities of personal development and enrichment to people formerly unable to participate in many forms of recreation. The 1991 Americans with Disabilities Act has now widened standards of accessibility and inclusion of children and adults in recreational as well as educational and work environments.

ISSUES

What is the difference between providing recreation opportunities for special populations and therapeutic recreation?

Who are those who may require extraordinary programs?

What are common barriers to participation?

Where are those with acute limitations?

Why is leisure important for everyone?

When we refer to special populations, we are identifying groups who do not fully participate in the ongoing set of life chances. Sometimes laws forbid their inclusion; more often they are left out by custom or oversight. Some people are permanently unable to do specific things, some can learn with special provisions, and some are only temporarily disabled. Some have a single disability for which they can learn to compensate, and others have pervasive or multiple limitations that require major changes in the provision.

Opportunity and Therapy

The main issue is that of opportunity: If leisure is the element of life in which unique opportunities for expression, development, and relationships are found, then should not a full range of opportunities be available to everyone? Everyone experiences some resource limitations; everything conceivable or desirable just is not available to us where we are. However, everyone does not have limitations or vulnerabilities that cut them off from opportunities that most people take for granted. When a person's adaptive capacities are not great enough to permit engagement in significant sets of activity, then the alternatives are exclusion or the adaptation of the context or form of the activity.

A second issue is that of therapy. Beginning with evidence that people can learn and develop through their experiences, recreation may be designed to facilitate particular kinds of change. Recreation may be organized to enhance intellectual, physical, or social development for children or adults. Especially in institutions of healing, recreation may be integrated into a total treatment program with the aim of moving a person toward the fullest possible functioning. In recreation therapy, both general well-being and specific treatment goals may be augmented through recreation activity and relationships.

Therapeutic Recreation

Some employ *therapeutic recreation (TR)* as a catch-all term to refer to the provision of leisure experiences for any who has "special impairments." This would include not only programs in which recreation is part of the treatment but all efforts to meet the leisure needs of the so-called special populations for whom opportunities require some adaptation to limitations. Therapeutic recreation, from this inclusive perspective, would include programs designed to increase adaptation to conditions and to overcome the results of illness. TR would also include programs of skill learning, interest development, personal counseling, and general competence building aimed at enabling people to engage in a fuller leisure life. Finally, TR would encompass all programs and plans that facilitate leisure participation by adapting resources and opportunities to the limitations of individuals or groups of potential users. Since World War II, therapeutic recreation in institutions and communities has increased rapidly. In most such programs, both aspects of special recreation—the extension of opportunities and the use of recreation as therapy— are interwoven.

In this chapter, the two aspects are discussed, with attention given first to opportunities for vulnerable groups and second to settings and institutions with therapeutic aims. Although both the opportunity and therapy elements of special recreation have the goal of developing the fullest possible human expression for all people, there is a difference between the two. In general, when the stress is on adapting resources to include those with acute vulnerabilities, the assumption is that the problem to be solved is in the restrictions of access and the structures of the activities and facilities. When the stress is on therapy, the assumption is that the person's disabilities can and should be corrected insofar as possible in order to move to a fuller actualization of all of life's potential. In the first approach the focus is on the opportunities and in the second on the person. Together they have the common goal of maximizing the personal and social development and expressions of all people.

At a White House Conference on Child Health and Protection in 1932, a statement was produced that has become a kind of "Bill of Rights for the Handicapped." It calls for

. . . a life on which his handicap casts no shadow, but which is full day by day with those things that make it worthwhile, with comradeship, love, work, play, laughter and tears—a life in which those things bring increasing growth, richness, a release of energies and joy of achievement.[1]

During the decades of the 1950s, 1960s, and 1970s, thousands of programs in public and private institutions, in public recreation and through voluntary organizations, and in schools and universities have opened new possibilities of moving toward that goal for people previously left with few leisure resources. The trend toward opening opportunities to those formerly barred from access has been supported by significant legislation. The Architectural Barriers Act of 1968 requires access provisions for public buildings with federal financing. Most states now have similar legal provisions: The Rehabilitation Act of 1973 and the Education for All Handicapped Children Act of 1975 are part of the legislative effort to provide the fullest possible set of developmental opportunities for the disabled. The 1991 Americans with Disabilities Act further spells out the requirements for opportunity and inclusion in all major aspects of common life.

Aims in Special Recreation

If the general aims of recreation are expressive and developmental, then the goals of special recreation are the same. Recreation is organized for the personal ends of enjoyment, expression of creativity and selfhood, exercise of freedom, and joy of human relationships. Recreation also encompasses the developmental purposes of increasing personal capacities for expression, relationships, physical mastery and coordination, and learning, as well as social capacities for building and strengthening relationships in both intimate and group contexts. In some cases, recreation may be designed to develop particular physical or social skills or to overcome a particular difficulty; that is, it may be therapeutic.

Then what is "special" about recreation for special populations?

---

[1] *The Handicapped Child,* report of the White House Conference on Child Health and Protection (Englewood Cliffs, NJ: Prentice-Hall, 1933).

Barriers to Participation

Most people take for granted a vast range of capabilities. Occasionally they are reminded that others are limited and must make their way in life without one or more of those capabilities. However, in taking the range of capabilities for granted, we tend to overlook the closed access of other people.

For example, people with hearing impairments cannot respond to the verbal signals and cues that start, stop, and direct most group games. Even whistles and sirens are a void to those with profound hearing loss. Think of all the other vulnerabilities that separate so many people from the possibilities that most take for granted. How do you get from one class to another in the allowed ten minutes if you are paralyzed from the waist down? How do you read your assignments or relate to people you have just met if you cannot see? How can others understand that apart from those very occasional seizures you are no different from them in your hopes and desires and dreams? How can you develop physical skills and a sense of competence when invisible asthma constricts your breathing capacity to one-third of normal?

There are so many kinds of barriers to full physical, emotional, and social participation in leisure. The most obvious are physical, but the social are at least as limiting.

Physical Barriers

The first set of physical barriers prevent access to places and facilities for recreation participation. They are the stairways, doorways, fixed seating, uneven paths, and distances that shut out people with mobility limitations. There are physical barriers to personal maintenance in facilities for personal hygiene and toilets, eating and sleeping provisions, and safety related to traffic or other hazards. Other physical barriers prevent some people from participation in desired activities even when they have access to the site. Some games and activities eliminate possible participants unless modifications are made to the area or equipment.

Social Barriers

In some cases, people with defined conditions are banned from sites, activities, or means of transportation by law or regulation. Those who are blind or in wheelchairs have been denied entrance to some buildings, airplanes, or buses due to the enforcement of safety regulations. Other people have lost certain civil rights due to conviction of crimes or commitment to a mental hospital. However, the most common social barriers are not legal. They lie in the reluctance of many in the society to accept those who are different or adjust to those who are vulnerable. In many cases physical barriers are not removed or ameliorated because many in the population are uncomfortable or emotionally threatened by the presence of persons with disabilities. Especially in their leisure they do not want to be reminded of anyone's problems or have to adjust their behavior for those who are different. Those providing commercial recreation may be especially reluctant to risk losing regular clientele by adapting access and activities to those with evident difficulties. Again, it seems to be a matter of social definition. Where do we draw the line between acceptability and exclusion? Some barriers are social in origin when people want to be screened from the limitations of others.

Cases of Acute Limitation

"Accident" It was one of those slippery-street auto accidents that occur every fall. In this one a car was going too fast and the driver didn't see the stop sign until too late. As often happens, it was the driver of the other car who was injured most severely. He spent more than a year in the hospital and in a rehabilitation center due to severe spinal cord damage. He will spend the rest of his life in special beds and a wheelchair. His legs and lower body are paralyzed and his left side is still somewhat numb and its motor control is reduced. A once-active young man, last year quarterback on his intramural flag football team and a pitcher on his summer ball club, is denied such activity. However, that is the smallest loss. It is the daily and hourly struggle with the simplest tasks—dressing, washing, and getting from one place to another—that has made his life a continual battle. Also, while his friends are more than concerned and sympathetic, the easiness of visiting bars with the fellows and of dating is now lost. And he just isn't quite sure when he is welcome and when his presence may be thought a hindrance to what people really want to do.

"Student" She began to know when she was very young that some how she was very different from all those around her. The drug-induced birth defect left her with no legs, no hands, and no arms below the elbow. Even with the most loving parents and skilled professional programs of independence training, she finds it hard to be accepted as a person. Other students admire her ability to cope and her spirit of cheerfulness, but few feel able to plan an evening in which she can fully participate. As a result, her few social events outside the dorm tend to be with others whose mobility is by motorized or self-propelled wheelchair with carefully selected destinations. And, as a matter of fact, getting to classes and the library is so exhausting that she doesn't have much energy to go out most evenings—even if someone were to ask.

"Invisible" How do you tell those you work with that there is something wrong with you, but that problems that interfere with your work and social life are rare? How do you explain to the woman you have begun dating that, although it is very unlikely, it is possible that some evening you might have to hurry home to prevent a fall and seizure that could be dangerous? After all, that first attack didn't come until you were two years out of high school and into your apprenticeship as a carpenter. When that fall was found to be the first sign of epilepsy, a careful examination and drug treatment program led to almost total control. Your boss knew that it was better that you not work in high places, even though a fall without adequate warning was now almost impossible. But some recreation sites that present the possibility of vertigo are threatening. Some activities are unwise and some events too long and tiring. How do you explain? And what about marriage, children, and all the rest? When you look so healthy and feel so strong, how understanding will others be if you tell them? How accepting? How willing to share your life?

"Temporary" A heart attack is more than an illness for a man in his forties. It is a reminder of mortality, a check on boundless plans, and for a time an incredible loss of energy and stamina. It is also a kind of stigma when you can feel others taking into account your supposed fragility and impermanence. In a few months you may be healthier than ever before. You will know yourself better and be prepared to pay the cost of reasonable self-care. You may feel better and even live longer. However, in the meantime, you have to ease yourself back into work and play, into family and friendships, in ways that aid healing. You need opportunities for expression and companionship that end by 10 P.M. and that have a measured pace. How ready will your friends be to accept this temporary disability and still want you there? Are there any public events and programs that are designed for people who are in the process of healing?

   "A Special World"   This is not a case, but a condition. Perhaps a million people in the United States are blind or seriously impaired in vision. More than half a million have cerebral palsy. At least 200,000 suffer from muscular dystrophy. Deafness is lifelong for many and a progressing impairment for many more. People with single impairments are increasingly being included in the ordinary programs of education, recreation, and work preparation. Yet, no matter how much they are included and accepted in mainstream society, they live partly in a world of their own. Somehow living in two worlds may give a special perspective on each. Nevertheless, the difference is always there to give a particular flavor to relationships, to shade every event and to add a dimension to every definition.

Special Programs

What does it take to include as many as possible in recreation opportunities? In general, there are a series of adaptations that can be made to increase the latitude of participation.

   First, there is the matter of access. In simple situations, the activity or group is not viable for people who cannot get to the site or into the building. Transportation and ease of access are costly in some situations, but are not complicated. When new designs and facilities are being prepared, inclusive access may not even be any more expensive.

   Second, there is the viability of the site. Limitations of sight, mobility, and dexterity may inhibit entry into a program even when access is possible. Unless the living and maintenance facilities are usable, then access to an opportunity may be wasted. This includes necessary movement within the site, seating, rest rooms, eating, functional privacy, occasional specific assistance, and possible readiness to deal with medical emergencies. Further, such facilitation should be regularly advertised so that those with limitations will know that they can be accommodated.

   Third, there is the program itself. The equipment may be altered so that it can be used by those with motor, visual, or other impairments. For example, braille playing cards or a divided card holder can open an ordinary poker or bridge game to people previously excluded. More dramatically, basketball and track events have been altered for those in wheelchairs so that national competitions are available for the highly skilled. People ski without sight or on a prosthesis, swim with spinal damage, and join choirs that sing in sign. Almost any kind of activity can be revised so that some who ordinarily cannot join in can either participate with those already doing it or can learn a special version that is adapted for particular disabilities.

   Fourth, there is the acquisition of skills. Considerable research has been done on learning by those with all kinds and levels of mental limitations. Everyone can acquire skills. There are always recreation possibilities that can be opened by learning something new. At this point, concern with widening opportunities for special groups and therapeutic recreation are joined in a program concentrating on the person. Carefully designed learning programs are combined with access and participation opportunities to enable the vulnerable to gain new leisure satisfactions and experiences.

Social Integration
Recreation is more than playing games, singing rounds, and tooling leather. While the satisfactions are closely tied to the nature of the activity, social meanings can cluster around many kinds of activity. Further, the meaning of the relationships and companionship may be far more central than those related to doing the activity. As a consequence, one major effort for those developing programs is to "mainstream" activities. Insofar as possible, access and activities are adapted and skills acquired that allow the limitations to be overcome and recreation to be desegregated. The aim is the fullest possible integration into ongoing recreation opportunities.

Recreation as Therapy
Learning takes place in all activity. In recreation settings and situations, many kinds of learning take place. In craft and art efforts we may learn dexterity and gain the satisfaction of creation. In games and sports we may learn physical coordination and social adaptation and gain satisfactions of participation and achievement. In organized social activities we may learn something of the complex processes of relationships and gain satisfactions of companionship and confidence. For persons with acute conditions—physical, mental, or emotional—all these skills and satisfactions are significant. Not only increasing abilities to accomplish and interact, but enhancing self-images through recreation can be crucial.

Recreation therapy is also employed in residential institutions to provide some balance to life. When very rigorous programs of physical rehabilitation are the main purpose of an institutional stay, then more relaxed and self-directed activity provides a needed alterative mode of engagement. When the main schedule of an institution is very goal-oriented and directive, then recreation may balance the rigor.

Recreation therapy also enhances competence in social interaction. Insofar as the aim of institutional life is to enable people to cope well with the tasks and opportunities of life in integrated communities, then recreation is a context for learning and trying out ways of working and playing with other people.

Who Are the Vulnerable?

It is possible to give estimates of how many are impaired in certain ways. For the most part, the estimates are based on government regulations that define just what degree of disability places a person in a specific classification. Since the laws and regulations may differ from state to state, the estimates are only approximate even if we agree with the criteria.

Special recreation programs have been designed for those who are mentally retarded, those with disabling mental illness, those recovering from alcoholism or substance addiction, those with physical disabilities and sensory impairments, and those in a variety of institutions. The usual numbers are subject to question, but they do give some idea of the scope of the need. For example, it is estimated that there are 1 million blind persons in the United States and another 8 million with visual impairments, more than 2 million deaf with another 11 million with hearing impairment, 12 million who are physically disabled, and 7 million learning disabled. The point is that those requiring consideration for access and activity are not as exceptional or rare as might be assumed.

Usually, standards of disability are functional. The question is what a person can do. This means that disability may be altered by learning. Whenever training or experience can increase ability to function in movement, communication, or social interaction, then the classification may be temporary. A functional basis recognizes that there is a wide variation in abilities to perform particular activities by those with the same condition or disease. Further, those severely limited in one kind of function may be quite able in another. Most important, it does away with the general category of "handicapped," which may be employed to rule large groups of people out of many kinds of opportunities that would be most enriching for them.

Special Recreation: Two Lines of Approach

Public recreation providers may respond to the special conditions of people with such a variety of vulnerabilities by augmenting the resources available to them. The aim will be to generalize, insofar as possible, the opportunities available in the community or institution. Resources will be planned and adapted to enable as many as possible in the population to participate in the programs.

However, there is a second line of approach. Rather than concentrate on the resources, the focus is on personal resourcefulness. Programs not only adapt to broaden inclusiveness but also seek to develop the abilities of people to engage in leisure. The aim is to enhance the capabilities for creative activity of those whose limitations are currently closing off opportunities. In the past, emphasis has been on introduction to activities and on skill acquisition. A newer approach is through counseling and the educational development of social competence. In some cases, quite specific learning may be required to cope with an impairment or overcome inhibitions. For others, growth in leisure resourcefulness will be the result of a series of participation experiences. In either case, the chief aim is to increase a person's store of interests and satisfactions so that leisure may be chosen from a wide and varied range of possibilities.

The first issue is access. Until access to facilities, environments, and programs is established, no other provision can be effective. The second issue is acceptance. Even the common designations of people in terms of their conditions set them apart from the ordinary realms of life that most take for granted. The third issue, however, is facilitation. It requires making the changes that attract participation. Facilitation may also include elements of leisure education that prepare individuals and groups for engagement. The hope is for more than special programs; it is that the entire society will move from labeling to enabling.

Special Recreation Settings and Institutions

Where are those with acute impairments and disabilities? A government study found that no more than 7 percent of those with severe impairments are residents of long-term care facilities such as hospitals, homes, or special schools. The implication is that most recreation programs for persons with physical, mental, or emotional vulnerabilities will have to be in the communities where they live. Institutional programs will be only for the small fraction who spend a major part of their lives there and for those who are institutionalized for rehabilitation or some other short-term program.

Nevertheless, a high proportion of the positions in therapeutic recreation is in such institutions. The concentration of severely limited people in hospitals and special schools has made evident the need for special recreation opportunities as well as recreation with therapeutic goals. However, new legislation requiring equal access and programs for the specifically challenged and calling for their integration in as many programs as possible has begun to expand the possibilities for professional positions in community recreation, government agencies, and even in education.

In-Community Programs

The new attention being given to those with limited resources in community recreation is partly a response to law and partly a recognition of the inadequacy of past efforts. Various estimates range as low as 1 percent of public recreation involvement of people with acute impairments. Even communities that have developed programs of adaptation may serve only 10 or 20 percent of those for whom the programs are designed. More in-depth study of the inhibiting factors, many of which are social and psychological rather than physical, is needed. In 1971, a team from New York University published the results of a three-year study of recreation services for disabled children.[2] While almost 90 percent of the 616 agencies studied provided some programs for such children, the need for greater integration with nondisabled, further elimination of architectural barriers, and more specialized institutional programs suggest the common inadequacy of most efforts. The estimate that in California only 3,000 of the state's 130,000 disabled children were being served by special programs in public park and recreation departments is a sign of the general failure of communities to develop the needed programs.

Insofar as the trend is to help those with such challenges to move back to their communities and to participate as fully as possible in ongoing work and leisure with their neighbors, then community programs will be more and more important to special recreation. Both adapted programs and facilities and efforts to help the vulnerable adapt to inclusive programs will require a higher priority in the planning and budgeting processes.

In the past, many of the recreation programs for those with physical and mental disabilities have been part of more comprehensive programs of voluntary organizations. Schools and sheltered workshops for children and adults with mental conditions have frequently also provided recreation. Not only playgrounds at schools and training centers, but parties, excursions, sport programs, and opportunities in the arts have been developed in some of the larger communities.

There are three general styles of programs for special populations in communities. Sheltered programs are segregated and offer opportunities for recreational, educational, and

---

[2] Doris Berryman, A. Logan, and D. Lander, *Enhancement of Recreation Service to Disabled Children,* report of Children's Bureau Project (New York: New York University School of Education, 1971).

economic activity in settings that enable the impaired to participate in specially designed circumstances. Institutional programs are in the same settings as opportunities for general populations but are oriented toward those with limitations that require some special facilitation. Integrated programs unite the impaired with other participants in common activity. One aim can be to move those with acute limitations along this spectrum toward integration whenever possible.

The best known special program is the Special Olympics, which provides a wide range of competitive sports opportunities. Inclusive community programs, however, do not allow this one set of opportunities to overshadow those for summer camps, aquatics, outdoor experiences, social events and organizations, special events, and a wide range of skill development programs. Further, the most complete programs always include some elements that integrate activity across a range of abilities and conditions. Inclusive programs may include activities in the arts, such as drama, music, and dance, physical fitness, a variety of games, cooking, outdoor adventure, a range of both competitive and noncompetitive sports, swimming, boating, sewing and crafts, discussion groups, individualized skill development, and a variety of social events and informal occasions. The social dimensions of all kinds of activity may be as important as the activities themselves.

One of the most inclusive programs that has become a model of an urban center is in San Francisco. The Fleishhacker Pool Building was converted to provide large halls, craft and music rooms, a library, several multipurpose rooms, activity rooms, a gymnasium, and an indoor pool. The original private funding that enabled the demonstration project to begin in 1952 has been augmented by city recreation, mental health, and social service funds and a series of federal grants. The program, developed by founder Janet Pomeroy and her staff, includes transportation in specially equipped buses that run six days a week. Volunteers assist in the transportation and in the program at the center, where more than 500 people are served. The fulltime staff of twenty and more than 200 volunteers provide over 15,000 hours of programming each month for children, youth, and adults, most of whom have severe conditions. The program includes efforts to prepare children to participate in city schools with programs adapted for the mentally impaired and to enable youths and adults to join in community social and recreation programs. Camping and environmental education have taken a significant place in the overall schedule of crafts, arts, sports, games, drama, music, and excursions.

While a center of this magnitude may seem like too lofty a dream for most communities, the basic aims and structure are possible for communities large enough for some diversification in human services. An accessible place, transportation, program variety, and skilled therapy are the basis of a program that will generally receive considerable public support in funding and in volunteer leadership. One key is the integration of the therapeutic recreation program with other human services and educational institutions that can cooperate in many crucial ways. Federal and state assistance in making architectural changes, adapting buses for people with mobility difficulties, and educational efforts can augment the potential of the program begun with community initiative.

Programs for the Aging

Since everyone is aging and there is only one alternative to growing old, older persons are not a special population. They are like special populations in that relatively few are in institutions; less than 5 percent of those over sixty-five are in hospitals or care facilities. Most older persons are in the community and living in relative independence. In fact, the central aim of most current programs for older persons is to support them in independent living in the community.

Age is, however, accompanied by a higher incidence of many limiting conditions as well as more frequent sensory impairments of hearing and sight. Further, the proportion of the population expected to live into their eighties and nineties is increasing. It is those later years that are most often marked by frailty, greater dependence on others, and the likelihood of institutionalization. Those age eighty-five and above now have the fastest rate of increase of any age segment of the population.

People over sixty-five are no more likely to be poor than any other age segment of the population. Most older persons have established patterns, sets of relationships, and activities. Their later years are marked by continuity until they encounter a major disabling health condition or loss of mental faculties. Only a minority, less than 15 percent of those over 65, join in special age-segregated programs. Most of the "active old" continue the activities and relationships already central to their lives. In the next three decades, however, more and more older persons will be entering those later years of vulnerability in which they will need support to live in the community and eventually institutional care. Both the economic and social requirements to cope with this trend are only beginning to be recognized. Strategies to develop the highest possible quality of life for the "frail elderly" will become a priority for every modern society.

Institutional Programs

Institutions with special recreation programs include schools for special populations, correctional institutions for juveniles and adults, hospitals, nursing homes, rehabilitation centers, colleges and universities, and a variety of special camps. In some, recreation is essentially a diversion while in others recreation is integrated with an overall treatment program.

In the many kinds of institutions with special recreation programs, recreation staff members work under the direction of those responsible for the central treatment program. Therefore, it is important to be able to understand the aims and vocabularies of medical, correctional, and administrative personnel and to interpret the values and opportunities of recreation to them. Since the aim is no less than to enable people to move as far as possible toward wholeness in all aspects of their lives, recreation must be seen as more than "time out" from the real business of the institution. Further, the importance of leisure for all people requires that those in institutions have opportunities for expression, creativity, development, mastery, excitement, companionship, and change whether or not they contribute directly to a treatment program.

Summary of Issues

People with special limitations like to be free to choose, to say yes or no to all of life's possibilities. They have the same needs as others for expression, experiences of joy and self-transcendence, and the fullness of human relationships of trust, communication, and love.

What they want may be expressed in very specific terms. Programs of rehabilitation and the development of competence often have quite specific and concrete step-by-step goals. Those who are adapting to and coping with disabilities and creating new abilities tend to have clear and proximate goals. Goals for mobility, communication, or community may be specific rather than general: "I want to walk one hundred feet without aid." "I want to be able to complete a sentence without hesitation." "I want to make my own way around the block." "I want to make one new friend."

Those proximate goals are steps on a journey toward the fullest possible functioning. Everyone does not care about sports, the arts, or church suppers. No one kind of activity is appealing to every person with a particular type of limitation. Everyone in a wheelchair does not want to play basketball, nor does everyone who is blind want to play the piano. But everyone directed toward the future wants the fullest possible life, a self-actualization that is real and right for that individual.

The fundamental aim of public recreation provisions for the acutely vulnerable is facilitation. It is not to provide for such people, deliver to them, or develop programs for them. It is to provide the opportunities for them to develop their own lives and leisure. It is to facilitate leisure with all the personal freedom and variety that is possible. This means that "enabling" rather than "delivery" is the central concept. Sometimes people can be assisted in gaining the skills to join in ongoing leisure that is attractive to them. Sometimes access to that ongoing leisure can be made more inclusive. Sometimes special provisions can be made for facilities and reconstituted activities to permit participation. But the essence of the enabling approach is in developing the autonomy of the individual whose real options are increased in the process.

Providing the opportunities for others through public programs is based on the concept of equity. Insofar as possible, responsibility for the common welfare mandates that life's chances will not be abridged by any unnecessary factor. This means that any viable means should be employed to increase the leisure opportunities of those with special limitations. No removable barrier should be left intact, be it physical, legal, or social. When people are needlessly or arbitrarily barred from a full set of social opportunities, then they are the victims of discrimination. A facilitating approach to special public recreation attacks discrimination that is built into the structures of our buildings, programs, activities, and social groupings.

Facilitating leisure begins with social acceptance and adaptation of opportunities. It should also include new designs, ability-developing equipment and activities, programs that stress both inclusiveness and learning, and personal counseling to help cope with the barriers in the mind of the vulnerable person. Just as leisure involves the whole person and is part of a full view of life, so special facilitation of leisure is a full and comprehensive approach. It is inclusive and including.

Leisure is expressive and free; realization of freedom requires opportunities that are accessible and attractive. Leisure is also developmental, an opportunity to grow and to prepare for new roles and relationships in the journey of life. Finally, leisure is social—the reality of communication, caring, and the discovery of self in relation to other persons. Leisure, then, is for everyone.

HIGHLIGHTS

1. Programs to maximize leisure access in community settings and uses of recreation in institutional therapy are recognitions of the significance of leisure in the whole of life.
2. Differences in functional abilities in a population frequently require adaptations of activities or facilities and programs of skill acquisition. Both access to resources and personal resourcefulness may be increased through well-designed programs.
3. Social meanings as well as social barriers are critical in providing leisure opportunities for the vulnerable in any community.
4. The importance of institutional programs should not obscure the fact that most of the vulnerable are living in ordinary communities.
5. No one should be needlessly excluded from opportunities to grow, develop, express selfhood, make friends, and create—that is, from the fullness of leisure.

Discussion Questions

1. Are special populations best described from a perspective of exclusion or of personal limitation? Why?

2. Why is recreation especially valuable for some kinds of therapy? Give examples.

3. Are there any barrier-free environments? What common leisure opportunities tend to exclude many potential participants? How?

4. How would you begin to adapt a community recreation program to more inclusive participation? What are critical barriers in many programs?

5. Which is more important in adapted recreation, the activities themselves or the related social interaction? Why? What does your answer imply for mainstreaming?

6. What, if any, is the best way to distinguish vulnerable groups in the population?

7. Which is the better approach to developing recreation for all—attention to increasing resources or resourcefulness? Why?

8. What will be the implications of aging trends for recreation providers?

Bibliography

Kelly, John R., ed., *Activity and Aging: Staying Involved in Later Life.* Newbury Park, CA: Sage, 1993.

Kennedy, Dan W., David R. Austin, and Ralph W. Smith, *Special Recreation: Opportunities for Persons with Disabilities.* Philadelphia: Saunders, 1987.

Kraus, Richard, *Therapeutic Recreation,* Second edition. Philadelphia: Saunders, 1978.

Peterson, Carol A., and Scout Gunn, *Therapeutic Recreation Program Design: Principles and Procedures.* Englewood Cliffs, NJ: Prentice-Hall, 1984.

Rapoport, Rhona, and Robert Rapoport, *Leisure and the Family Life Cycle.* London: Routledge and Kegan Paul, 1975.

Chapter *24*

Theories of Leisure: Freedom and Meaning

Leisure is not simple. It cannot be defined clearly and comprehensively by any single concept or dimension. It involves freedom, but in the sense of action rather than lack of constraint. It includes decision, but always in a social as well as time and space context. It is focused on the experience, but with a history and future orientation. It is motivated intrinsically, but not without long-term meanings and intentions. It is existential and social, immediate and processual, personal and political.

Most definitions and perspectives are limited to a single set of premises about how leisure should be explained. They presuppose a single view of the world and focus on a single dimension. Some are based on a concept of time that is determined by the industrial economic structure. Some concentrate on feelings or emotions within the experience. Others tie leisure to a dominant social institution: the economy and work or the family and social bonding. Some begin with the premise that leisure is an individual matter, and others are based on the meaning of leisure for the society.

Underlying the descriptions and analyses of leisure in this book is the assumption that leisure is complex and multidimensional. Leisure is not just personal experience or social control or creative action or anything else. It is not either/or: either individual or social, either free or controlled, either existential or social, either continuity or contrast.

No one who has flown the length of the Grand Canyon would argue that such an aerial view is superior to that seen by rafters or hikers. Rather each is different, exciting, and often breathtaking. In each mode of approach, the variety of shapes and colors is seen in ways not fully experienced by those who stand only at a single viewpoint. This metaphor of perspectives is intended to suggest a way of understanding theories. They highlight some aspects of the whole and obscure others.

This chapter is based on the idea that theories are like viewpoints that reveal certain aspects of the whole and deny others. In fact, theories are metaphors that begin by stating that "leisure (or whatever is being explained) is something like this." The theory then goes on to draw out the implications: "if we view leisure from this viewpoint, then it may be understood and explained in this way."

Theory is communicated explanation. It is systematic, open to critical analysis, and explanatory. No theory is complete. Rather, each reveals some of the limitations of the others. From its own viewpoint, each is "true" in the sense of pointing to some valid modes of explanation. Leisure is experience, decision, development, identity, interaction, institutional, political, and human. Whether or not it is possible to combine these viewpoints into a coherent whole, our understanding is enriched by each of the eight metaphors. None is "wrong" even when we prefer some over others.

The overall approach to the eight theoretical metaphors is called "dialectical." In this context, it means that there is a countertheory that reveals some of the limitations of each approach. What is not explained by any one theory leads us to another, which in turn is found to be both valuable and incomplete. In such a dialectic we will zigzag our way through eight metaphors that claim that "leisure is something like this." In the end, there is no final claim that closes debate or reveals the previously hidden truth.

In our attempt to explore this dialectic, we begin with the most fundamental view of leisure as immediate experience and move through more inclusive levels of analysis to political and cultural contexts of meaning. This progression stresses the contribution of each metaphor, but also includes the limitations that lead to other theories.

ISSUES

What are the perspectives that illuminate the crucial dimensions of leisure?

Is there a single defining theme for leisure, or is it basically multidimensional?

How can leisure be both existential and social?

Is leisure a social construction or profoundly human, fundamental to being and becoming?

Leisure as Immediate Experience

Experience is self-conscious living. We do more than act and react. We are constantly perceiving, assimilating, processing, storing, and interpreting information. That information is about our environment and our interaction with that environment. Our interaction is mental, physical, and emotional. We feel as well as think, act as well as interpret. We employ our linguistic categories and symbols to make sense of what we do and what is going on around us. We remember, respond, and act toward the future. Experience, then, is our interpretive consciousness of an event or action.

Up to 1980, most investigations of leisure were of forms of behavior, usually called activities. The focus was on what people did: play golf or read, attend concerts or hike. The major exception was the Kansas City Study of Adult Life in which questions of the meanings of activity were raised.[1] In this study, leisure activity was found to have several meanings, including relaxation, social engagement, and self-expression. Later research included resource-based as well as community activity in a design that combined patterns of activity with combinations of meaning.[2]

Three themes of the meaning of activity were consistent in this earlier set of studies: (1) the importance of social relationships, especially family and friends, (2) involvement and expression within the activity itself, and (3) a measure of relaxation and withdrawal from routines and obligations. Such research required those being studied to recall their participation in types of activity and sum up the persistent meanings or reasons for participation.

In such research, there is the assumption that such meaning can be abstracted from an event or series of events. All the times that a person has played basketball or the piano are compiled in memory, and general meanings such as excitement, challenge, and involvement are identified for all or most of those times and events. This is, of course, very different from the immediate experience at the singular time of doing the activity. The dominant elements of the experience on one day may be different from those of other days when there are different companions, outcomes, feelings, and evaluations.

Further, playing basketball or the piano is a process. How one feels changes moment by moment as a shot swishes or rims out or fingers master a chord or hit a clinker. Immediate means right now; and as soon as we pause to evaluate or interpret, that moment is already past. Experience is "going through" an action or interaction, not analyzing it later. In our research, we reduce the process and variety of immediate experience to a recollective abstracting system of interpretation.

Nevertheless, even though our studies and explanations are only generalizations about that immediacy, the experience itself may be identified as the real substance of leisure. Leisure is the experience, the process, the action. Our interpretations, however, are after the fact, abstracted from the process.

For example, Neulinger focuses on perception, the state of consciousness of the experience, when he defines the distinctive elements of leisure.[3] Leisure is the perception of freedom, the orientation of intrinsic motivation, and the meaning of final rather than instrumental goals. Leisure is defined in terms of what is perceived in the experience itself.

Csikszentmihalyi identifies certain environmental conditions under which a heightened experience of involvement may occur.[4] Such "flow" activity incorporates the men-

---

[1] Robert Havighurst, "The Leisure Activities of the Middle Aged," *American Journal of Sociology,* 63 (1957), 162–182.

[2] John R. Kelly, "Situational and Social Factors in Leisure Decisions," *Pacific Sociological Review,* 21 (1978), 187–207.

[3] John Neulinger, *The Psychology of Leisure* (Springfield, IL: Chas. C Thomas, 1974).

[4] Mihaly Csikszentmihalyi, *Beyond Boredom and Anxiety* (San Francisco: Jossey-Bass, 1975).

tal state of freedom and being done for its own sake with environments that engage the actor rather than simply stimulate the senses. In a context of either work or leisure, the focus is on the action context in which ability is matched with challenge. Flow is the experience, at least for the moment, in which the actor is "wholly into" the immediate action.

One dimension of an experience, then, is intensity. Flow is of high intensity. Other action, such as much television watching, is often of low intensity. Leisure would seem to include experience that cannot be identified by any single element. It may, for example, vary in intensity from flow to moderate involvement to relaxation to detached time-filling.[5] There is no one leisure experience; rather, there are leisure experiences.

One model of leisure dimensions includes choice, self-containment, intense enjoyment and involvement, timelessness, fantasy, creativity, spontaneity, and sense of exploration.[6] Each, however, may be found in a greater or lesser degree in any specific experience. The dimensions are pointers or possible marks of leisure rather than defining qualities.

Psychological models incorporate three elements of immediate experience: the environment or stimulus, attitudes or mental states, and behaviors. The stimulus and behavior may be simple or complex. The mental states, however, involve reception, cognition, and evaluation. They are never simple. The term *experience,* then, connotes that mental process rather than a simple state of mind.

A U.S. Forest Service line of research led by B. L. Driver and his colleagues identified seventeen types of experiential outcomes for resource-based recreation such as wilderness backpacking, hiking, camping, fishing, and trail skiing.[7] They include being with others, escaping physical and social pressures, learning and exploring, exercising, and relating to the natural environment. Meanings specific to only some kinds of activity were found to be achievement and challenge, independence, reflection, recollection, risk taking, excitement, meeting other people, family togetherness, privacy, using equipment and skills, and security. It is evident that the form and context of the activity make a difference in the nature of the experience.

Such elements of experience, however, are not unique to leisure. Companionship, emotional release, excitement, and deep involvement may be found in work activity and settings, in goal-directed tasks, as well as in the more self-contained experiences called leisure. Further, any experience has some limiting or structural factors: time, space, the forms of the activity, a history of meaning, a social context with norms and expectations, and situational conditions. There is no "pure freedom," and the perception of such would be an illusion. Also, immediate experience, by definition, is transitory. An event is experienced moment by moment, in a process.

Leisure, then, *is* experience, but in real contexts of action. It is doing, not classifying attitudes at a later time. Leisure is meaningful experience, not in an unconnected state of

---

[5] John R. Kelly, *Leisure Identities and Interaction* (London and Boston: Allen and Unwin, 1983).

[6] B. J. Gunter and Nancy Gunter, "Leisure Styles: A Conceptual Framework," *Sociological Quarterly,* 21 (1980), 361–374.

[7] B. L. Driver and Perry Brown, "The Opportunity Spectrum Concept and Behavioral Information in Outdoor Recreation Resource Supply Inventories," Rocky Mountain Forest and Experiment Station, Ft. Collins, Colorado, 1978.

mind but in real action and interaction. Leisure experience may include a number of elements of meaning of intention, immediacy, and recollection. It is an inclusive process that is always more than any attempt to compress it into a few adjectives or adverbs, to a scale or typology. In all further discussion of leisure, however, the fundamental substance of what is being analyzed is that complex and real experience. On the most basic level, leisure is real lived experience.

Leisure as Existential Action

Leisure is experience. Then what are the elements of that experience? Are there dimensions that are central to leisure? Even if they are also found in other kinds of experience, are there elements that are fundamental to experiences of leisure?

Another perspective is that leisure is meaningful action. It is more than perception. Leisure involves doing, not just being done to. Leisure, at the very least, is the response rather than the stimulus. It is the action rather than the recognition. Historically, every approach to defining leisure incorporates some element of decision or freedom. Leisure is, in some sense, what we choose to do rather than what we have to do. Freedom, from this perspective, is the possibility of action. Decision is the mental act that begins that action.

From an existential perspective, freedom is more than freedom *from* necessity or requirement. It is also more than a mental state. It is freedom *for* action. It stresses decision and action rather than conditions or mental states. There are three central themes of the existential metaphor:

1. Decision and action create meaning.[8]
2. Decision is not necessarily solitary. Rather, it may create community.[9]
3. Decision is an act of creation in which what did not exist comes into being.

Further, the existential metaphor is inclusive of experience. It encompasses the full experience of everyday life in all its actualities. It is not simply rational but is made up of emotions, feelings, and uncertainties. It is unspoken as well as communicated, fragmented as well as articulated. Life is constructed out of countless bits of reality that are both material and immaterial.

For example, the structure or institutions of a social system are in reality a constructed interaction process in which we take for granted the common symbols of communication and action. Actors use those symbols to build regularities of action and interaction. There is a shared universe of meaning, the "consensus" or common sense, that becomes the basis for common action.[10] Even the most routine individual action, then, has the possibility of being decisively something else.

As a part of daily life, leisure is also constructed out of everyday experience. It involves decision, communication, action, and interpretation. And from this existen-

[8] Jean-Paul Sartre, *L'Etre et le Neant* (Paris: Gallimard, 1943).

[9] Martin Buber, *I and Thou,* trans. R. G. Smith (Edinburgh: T. and T. Clark, 1937).

[10] Peter Berger and Thomas Luckman, *The Social Construction of Reality* (New York: Penguin, 1966).

tial perspective, it is not determined. It could have been something else. Leisure, then, is

Decision, an act as well as a state

Creation, a product of decision and action

Process, developed and created in its time and place

Situated in a real social context

Production in its ever-new outcomes

Act, with its history, emotions, interpretations, and intentions

Another term for leisure as action is "play." The term *play* stresses the action dimension of leisure with its openness and lack of predetermined outcomes. Play is action in which the actor becomes absorbed in the process of the activity. In play, the forms of the activity are recognized as constructed rather than fixed. Such play is noninstrumental, yet it can be used to test and produce meaning.[11] Play is the existential side of leisure in its stress on openness, action, and the possibility of creation. Play is free, not as a static state of freedom from necessity but as the exercise of possibility. Play redefines the world through its action.

From this perspective, leisure is meaning-producing action. It cannot be reduced to any single dimension of existence. It is emotion, will, physiology, value, culture, and all that make up action in the everyday world. It is more than either feeling or thought. It is the *act*ualization of possibility in a world that is perceived to be both open and closed, possible and yet limiting.

Leisure is dialectical: experience and context, action and outcomes. It may be referred to as "encounter," "exchange," "conversation," or "play." Leisure involves decision toward action. It is act as well as experience.

Developmental Theory

Leisure is act. It is, however, more than the instant of decision or the immediacy of the moment. Its meanings include long-term outcomes for the self and for relationships. In the action of leisure, we may become something more than we were before. We may develop.

Two questions suggest the developmental dimensions of leisure:

1. What personal change do we anticipate in leisure experiences?
2. What do we hope to become in and through leisure?

Leisure may involve the acquisition of skills. We may engage in activity designed to make us better at the activity. Or we may exercise to become better able to do something else. For example, a skier may run in the summer to maintain or improve physical condition or competence. In the process, however, something more may occur. There may also be a gain in our sense of physical ability. In leisure activity, we may increase our sense of development, not only physical but also social or personal. We may gain in ability to take risks, develop interests, or acquire new skills.

[11] James Hans, *The Play of the World* (Amherst: University of Massachusetts Press, 1981).

Some of the continuities and changes in leisure through the life course have been outlined in Chapter 6. There is considerable evidence that the learning that takes place in leisure is cumulative. A sense of competence or the ability to learn that is experienced in one activity may well provide the basis for a similar or new engagement in later years. A sense of physical, mental, artistic, or social competence that is learned in one context may carry over into others.

Much of life is concentrated on products and outcomes. Leisure may be somewhat different in its focus on the experience and the action. The relative noninstrumentality of leisure contrasts with most roles that are largely product-oriented. Csikszentmihalyi argues that we may be most likely to develop in leisure just because of that concentration.[12] Further, in such experience we are most likely to develop criteria for what is satisfying in the rest of life. For example, the risk, uncertainty, and immediacy of many games and sports make them more exciting and involving than activities that are routinized, predetermined, or lack feedback. Further, the high energy and attention that may be required in such activity along with the discrete and immediate outcomes may contrast with activity that is required in other roles.

Leisure is most likely to be action we choose with companions we prefer and in locales that we select. The skills that are demanded are ones that we are willing to exercise and even have evaluated. How well we have done is seen by others who are important to us. Further, in some leisure, unlike considerable work, initiative is both possible and rewarded. The teenager who is engaged in special activity—dancing or sport or just partying—with a significant peer group is most likely to take the outcomes, positive or negative, very seriously. In leisure we may try out for all kinds of parts in the drama of life with others.

Learning interpersonal skills is enhanced in leisure where the rules may be less prescribed than in more institutionalized life. Leisure may offer opportunities to take some risks, to try out presentations and identities, to become something more or different from what we are. Life is, however, more than our roles, our social designations. It also is our identities, who we are and whom we hope to become in those roles.

Rhona and Robert Rapoport place leisure in the context of the changing roles of family, work, education, and community.[13] They analyze leisure as one arena for working out developmental life tasks. For example, for most, the shift from exploration to commitment in intimate relationships and eventually to the establishment of a new family unit takes place largely in leisure contexts. In fact, a large proportion of the expression and development of significant and intimate relationships takes place in leisure. Developing who we are as sexual beings is at least as much a matter of leisure experience as anything else.

Further, roles have careers. Not only work but also family and leisure roles have both continuities and change. How we enact the roles and what is expected of us change as well. The life course has many predictable transitions such as those from student to worker to retiree. It also has unpredictable disruptive events such as health problems, the death of intimates, or the loss of employment. In this career of intersecting consistencies and changes, we are the same persons and yet also changing. In some ways we are expected to change, in others we have to change, and sometimes we seek to change.

[12] Mihaly Csikszentmihalyi, "Leisure and Socialization," *Social Forces,* 60 (1981), 332–340.

[13] Rhona Rapoport and Robert Rapoport, *Leisure and the Family Life Cycle* (London: Routledge and Kegan Paul, 1975).

In the early years of life, the infant and young child try out many of the possibilities of life in play. While play may become more structured as we grow older, it remains an important kind of action that leads to learning. If life is divided into the major periods of preparation, establishment, and culmination, then the specifics of playful or leisure activity may change in intention as well as form. But relative freedom or openness remains an element in personal development. The play of childhood, the exploration of adolescence, the intimacy building of young adulthood, the competence and personal expression of the middle years, and the social integration of later life are central themes of a developmental perspective on leisure.

The metaphor of a journey provides an approach to the personal openness that may be sought in leisure. Life is seen as a dynamic process with leisure as a significant dimension of becoming. This developmental approach focuses on the individual, but in a social context. We learn and develop with and among others. We relate and connect with the life journeys of others in ways that have consequences for the kind of persons we become as well as for the future role relationships in which we invest. Our journeys are tied to others in sequences that involve both bonding and loss.

This life journey is not made by a static self, unchanging from some point in the earliest years. Rather, we build on what we have become to become something more. This developmental perspective is that the self has to cope with sequences of dilemmas in each period. Just as there are sequences of roles, so there are sequential changes in who we are in those roles. In the ongoing process, leisure is not separate but is often quite central. What we do, what we want to do, whom we want to be with, and how we want others to see us in our leisure are always connected to who we are and want to be in the rest of life. Leisure is one set of resources and opportunities along with others. In some periods of the life journey, it may be quite central to our development as persons of ability.

We are always learning, always developing, always becoming. We learn from and with others—in family, school, work, and play. We see ourselves and who we are in the mirror of how others respond to us. As children and youth, we discover and work out who we are in family and in play as well as in school. There is no separate or leftover segment of life that makes no difference to the rest. As a consequence, to understand leisure, we need to include the longer-term meanings of experiences and actions. Who we are and whom we seek to become are part of the immediate experience of leisure action. The outcomes may not all be positive, as we are excluded as well as included, fail as well as succeed, and develop fears as well as a sense of competence. There are distortions and limitations in our developmental journeys. Nevertheless, leisure has meanings and consequences that are a significant element in the process of becoming that we call life.

Social Identity Theory

"Who am I?" is a question that can be answered in many ways. I am a student or teacher, father or daughter or son, a skier or cellist. Others identify us in those roles and have certain expectations as to how we will act. The developmental metaphor is based on the life-long sequences of such social identities.

There is, however, a more personal way of answering the question. I am this particular person in my role as teacher or mother or even skier. I am not quite like anyone else in those roles. How I play the role, how I define myself in the role is unique to me. I may accept the social identity of how others designate my roles, but I also develop a personal identity of how I define myself in those roles. Through the life course, both social identities and personal identities have continuities and changes.

Identity is one approach to understanding what it is we are becoming in our life journeys. "Who am I?" I am this particular person with my own history, my own set of roles, and my own hopes for the future. I am this person not quite like any other even as I move through a sequence of roles similar to most of my peers. In fact, the similarities are so pervasive that we often refer to transitions such as marriage, employment, parenthood, and retirement as being "on time."

From this perspective, we are constantly developing new attitudes, skills, and self-definitions in the "becoming" process of life. These elements of who we are may be found in our leisure as well as in other engagements. For example, we recognize the adjustments required of the former athlete who no longer commands the playing field or court, the parent whose children are now independent and distant, or the professional whose working days are over. Can identities be transferred from school to work, from work to leisure, or from leisure to the family? Or is it often necessary to create new identities to replace those that are lost? Tennis may replace basketball, but can golf replace parenting or travel replace a marriage?

The metaphor of the looking-glass self proposes that we learn who we are by seeing and interpreting the definitions and responses of others.[14] Especially those who are important to us are very influential in how we define ourselves. We learn who we are and whom we might become among others. From this perspective, development is a process of communication that takes place in community. *Community* is the set of ongoing relationships in which there is reciprocal interaction, communication, sharing of tasks or regular activities, and a history of common enterprise.

We do not do anything quite the same way as anyone else, even when we try. Our *role identity* refers to how we enact a role. My style of being a father or welder, coach or performer, is my own—even though I have learned it from others. The metaphor of the theater is useful again. We "play" our roles rather than simply conform to a rigid set of expectations. There may be a stage and a script, but we enact our parts in ways that are at least somewhat our own. We direct our performances toward securing the responses we want from others.[15]

In all our settings, we identify ourselves through the symbols of clothing, language, and manner of self-presentation. We announce who we would like others to take us to be. Usually we attempt to establish social identities that are consistent with our personal identities. Such action is not just at a single time, but takes place over time. When we initiate a line of action, we have to deal with the outcomes. How others respond makes a difference to what we do next. We may withdraw as well as persist. Not only in that setting but in the longer term, the outcomes have impacts on how we define and evaluate ourselves.

---

[14] Charles H. Cooley, *Human Nature and the Social Order* (New York: Scribner's, 1902).

[15] Kelly, *Leisure Identities and Interactions*.

One paradox of leisure is that it has structure despite being defined in terms of relative freedom. Activities have rules. Events have roles. In a game or at a party, we take roles that have accompanying expectations. At the same time, we have expectations of ourselves. These expectations or identities have histories that stem from other times and places. They are built up over time. We enter any action sequence with a preformed identity as well as with some anticipated outcome. There is a continual dialectic between meeting role expectations and re-forming who we are as women and men in those roles.

At the center of life are the primary relationships with those who are significant through at least major segments of the life course—parents, brothers and sisters, friends, lovers, teachers, spouses, workmates, and children. According to Cheek and Burch, one reason that leisure takes such an important place in values and priorities is because it is a social space in which those relationships are developed, expressed, and enhanced.[16] Social bonding comes from what people do together, in expressive play as well as in the necessary tasks of life.

The expressive elements of intimacy—affection, humor, self-disclosure, and playfulness—require some openness for mutual action. So we travel together, walk and talk, and play games together in modes of interaction that develop and express relationships. Leisure, then, is not a separate set of activities but is closely tied to our central relationships.

This does not mean that all life becomes directed at how we are defined by others. Rather, there is a continual dialectic between how we define ourselves and how others define us. Our personal identities are developed in relationships with others and yet have their own integrity. We seek to establish who we are and want to be, not just respond to others.

Leisure events often provide immediate results that make a difference in self-evaluation. Unlike the bureaucracy in which behaviors are more prescribed, the leisure setting may offer the possibility of novelty or the exploration of a new or altered identity. Events may be designed to be problematic, uncertain in outcome. Therefore, leisure affords opportunity for *becoming,* for essaying some change.

In a mass culture in which so much is standardized, the particularities of selfhood may become buried in the anonymity of the social system. In the midst of this sameness, leisure commitments can offer a set of identities that are special and chosen. Leisure contexts may be a place in which the individual is recognized. Leisure identities, then, may be central to the uniqueness of the self.

The concept of identity may focus on the self, but can be understood only in the context of the society. We learn as well as develop identities. We are and become who we are with others, especially in ongoing communities. The individual is social, in leisure as well as in family, school, and work. The dialectic of self and society is joined in the metaphor of identity that is both personal and social.

Interaction Theory

Identities are developed in the process of social interaction. We learn and become who we are in interaction with others. Social interaction, however, may also itself be leisure. When

---

[16] Neil Cheek and William Burch, *The Social Organization of Leisure in Human Society* (New York: Harper & Row, 1976).

the central meaning of the experience is the process of communication and sharing, then interaction is the action of the episode or event.

Leisure episodes may occur in the midst of any engagement—at the workplace as well as the playground. Playful exchange that is off-task and primarily for its own sake is common on the factory floor and in the office corridor as well as the family room and street corner. In fact, it may be such playful communication that enables people to get through the otherwise routinized day. Social interaction that is nonserious, intrinsic rather than extrinsic in aim, expressive rather than product-oriented, may occur any time and anywhere. Leisure is not only for set-apart times and places. Its action may be developed in family, work, community, political, or religious settings.

Leisure may take place totally in the imagination and the mind. Most leisure, however, literally takes time and place. It is in a physical and social environment and has duration over time. Moments of play are created in the midst of the most goal-oriented exchanges. Flights of fancy may happen despite the agendas and schedules of a meeting or event. Often such moments are bits of social interaction, playful behavior, or conversation. Individuals not only act; they interact to form episodes of leisure.

Face-to-face interaction, however playful. has its implicit rules as well as emergent action.[17] We have expectations for the behavior and communication of others. Sometimes it is the violation of such expectations that makes the interaction play. Further, an activity may be only the setting for the communicative encounter that is the real action. People play games with each other. They create lines of communication or action with uncertain outcomes. Such outcomes are playful or nonserious when they are confined to the social space of the event.[18] Simmel called such interaction with the primary aim of mutual pleasure "sociability."[19]

Some events such as parties or gatherings in public places are essentially times of sociability. The process of interaction is the action. In such events, the expectation is that there will be communication for its own sake. People will tell stories, respond, joke, play with words, and generally seek to enjoy what is said and done. Such social settings are explicitly leisure-oriented.

We can, however, create temporary verbal worlds of play by signaling the beginning of a nonserious communication. Such leisure interaction may be interstitial, created in the midst of otherwise serious exchange. Such deliberate misdirection of the flow of communication provides a lightening of task-directed behavior. The contrast provides emotional release. In order to create play in the midst of action directed toward a product, however, it is necessary to signal a break in the action. By word or gesture, we invite others to share, if only for a moment, the shift off-task to play. By signal or sign we may even pause to make light of the serious process in which we are engaged.

Interaction as leisure ranges from the intimacy of two who know each other well to the "fancy milling"[20] of a large group. It may involve the exploration and development of new relationships or the familiar communication of intimates with a long history that has

---

[17] Erving Goffman, *Interaction Ritual* (New York: Anchor Books, 1967).

[18] Johan Huizinga, *Homo Ludens* (Boston: Beacon Press, 1955).

[19] Georg Simmel, *The Sociology of George Simmel,* trans. and ed. Kurt Wolf (New York: Free Press, 1950).

[20] Goffman, *Interactional Ritual.*

been shared. It may be highly structured as at a formal banquet or constructed moment by moment as a series of surprises. It may occur in the midst of a structured event such as a sport contest or in a chance meeting at the intersection of a shopping mall. It may be among family or relative strangers, The variety of social interaction as leisure is almost limitless. What is evident is that it is common, at the very center of the ordinary round of life. Such leisure is not special and set apart. Rather, it is like bright threads woven through the entire fabric of life.

Leisure as interaction is both an occurrence and a process. It may be identified as having a beginning and an end. It may have a kind of story line in which there is an inauguration, a development of the theme, and a conclusion. This occurrence is a process, however long or brief, in which two or more people take action with and toward others. Such action creates its own meaning of the moment. It is for fun, with its meaning largely contained in the experience.

This does not mean that who we are is irrelevant. Rather, we come into any social setting with some identification, with social identities that are known or may be discovered by others. We also come with our personal identities that we select and put on display in the situation. In some cases such as in a family or long-term friendship, there are an infinite number of shared meanings that are implicit in the exchange. Nevertheless, as leisure the episode is not designed to get anything done except carry out its own meaning. When one or more participants in the interaction use it to further their own ends, to manipulate others for their own purposes, then the play ends. When the episode becomes directed toward the predetermined ends of any of the actors, then the nonserious meaning that makes play possible is destroyed.

Social interaction as leisure reveals its own constructed nature, its self-containment, in its mixture of openness and rules. It may occur just about any time or any place. It is existential, the creation of actors who venture to do something new. It is also social, requiring the shared meanings of those actors who direct what they do toward each other. There is no one kind of action that is necessarily "most leisurely." Playful social interaction, however, may well be the most common form of leisure in our world that is profoundly shared with others.

Institutional Theory

Leisure is social in being of the culture, learned from others. It is also frequently social in the form of interaction and communication. The focus has been on leisure as action that creates its meaning, on the freedom of leisure. Leisure, however, is also social in being related to the institutions of the social system.

Leisure is not separate from the rest of life, detached from the world of rules and roles. Rather, leisure is connected with the institutions of the society—family, work, education, religion, government, and the organizational life of the community. Leisure, after all, requires resources—always time and often money, space, and other aspects of opportunity. These resources are provided or denied for the most part by the institutional structure of the society.

In this metaphor, society is viewed as a system in which the institutions are interrelated to provide what is needed for the continuation of the system. Individuals take and are assigned roles in those institutions. They respond to the expectations and requirements associated with the roles. In general, there is considerable consensus as to what is expected of those in the roles of student, mother, foreman, secretary, senator, priest, and PTA president. Further, these roles intersect so that we carry the identification and expectations from one institutional setting to another.

In most societies, economic roles are basic to the allocation of resources. The family is central to everyday living as well as the primary locus of the nurture of children. The government has the functions of protection as well as some other responsibilities for the common welfare. The church reinforces values. The school passes on skills and the cultural heritage.

In these institutions, individuals take roles that change through the life course. For most, the dependence of being a daughter or son moves into relative independence and often to a final period of caring for a dependent parent. The student becomes a worker who becomes a retiree. The beginner becomes a performer who becomes a teacher. In the sequence of life course roles, not only do opportunities and resources change, but also there are changes in what is expected of us in our roles.

These institutional roles are somewhat separated, but are not fully segregated. The roles of parent and child are carried from the family into leisure. Economic roles may confer prestige or power in a leisure setting at the club or playing field. The intersections of roles are multidimensional involving resources, goals, and relationships.

As discussed in Chapter 7, work and leisure are related, but not with work determining leisure. Yet much of the social system is ordered by the economy. Schedules are designed around economic organization. The status of work roles is carried into nonwork settings. Most important, economic roles generally determine ability to command resources in the distribution systems of a society.

Family interaction is itself a major form of leisure. It also illustrates how the expressive openness of leisure and role expectations are intertwined. Parents do not cease their protective and nurturing roles on a picnic. Mothers do not abandon their caretaking and planning functions on a vacation trip. Fathers do not drop all authority when playing games with children. Leisure is central to the expression and development of family relationships, of intimacy and love. It is a social space for developmental activity for children. As a consequence, role expectations permeate family leisure and reduce the dimension of freedom to one theme among many.

The expression and development of primary relationships is itself a central aim of considerable leisure. The leisure that is most important to most people involves those other persons who are central to their lives. As a result, all the history of those relationships as well as their future orientations is brought into the leisure occurrence. The leisure event, however self-contained and for its own sake, is also embedded in a context of regular and agreed-on habits and expectations. Any leisure occurrence, then, can be analyzed from the perspective of role-related rules and regularities as well as from the perspective of an emergent process.

Through the life course, work, leisure, and family have careers that intersect. Who we are in our leisure, our leisure identities, is related to who we are in our other social roles. Leisure, however existential and open, is also the action of persons with well-recognized social identities tied to their institutional roles. Our life conditions include the specifics of who we are as gendered beings of a particular age and social status.

Leisure is also ethnic, of the culture. The forms and values of leisure are developed in particular cultures. Not only the details of what people do, but also the aims and meanings of activity, differ from one culture to another. This implies not only that leisure is learned behavior but also that it is always subject to change. Conversely, leisure is also a major context for the development and expression of a culture.[21] Especially in the social celebrations of leisure, in the holidays or "holy days" of a culture, the deeper meanings of a social history are remembered and celebrated.

As outlined in Chapter 3, the sources of leisure styles are social as well as personal. Age and gender differences, education-based interests, the economic determination of access to resources—all demonstrate that leisure is thoroughly connected with every institution of the social system. From this perspective, the "freedom" of leisure is always relative, always tied to the interrelated roles of the individual.

Again, any explanation of leisure as decision or action is dialectical. It takes account of the contextual social structure and of the existential becoming of social action and interaction. Further, at a deeper level, even what we mean by leisure is learned through our lifelong socialization within the institutional contexts of a particular society at a given time in its history. Leisure, then, is action, but is never asocial, apart from its social and cultural context.

As action and interaction, leisure takes place throughout the institutional contexts of a society—in the kitchen as well as the family room, in the school corridor as well as the gym or theater.

To summarize, leisure is based in the culture of its time and place. Leisure is complementary to the functioning social system.

Yet leisure still has its other side. Its elements of openness allow actors to construct special worlds of becoming in its times and places. Leisure, then, is expressive activity even though it occurs in and through social institutions and employs institutional resources.

Conflict Theory

Institutional theory is premised on a model of society that is integrated and articulated. Conflict theory is premised on a different model of society. Any society is held to be divided among segments with conflicting interests. The themes of such political theory are conflict, control, and power.

A divided society may be held together by the direct exercise of power, by coercion. The interests of those without fundamental economic and political power are subordinated to those of the ruling elite. Failure to submit is punished. In many societies, however, control is exercised by persuasion. In what is called "false consciousness," the subordinate classes come to believe that it is in their interest to assent to the institutional structure controlled by the ruling class.

Leisure, in this model, becomes one means of social control. How? When leisure is identified with what can be purchased in the market, it becomes a primary reward for eco-

[21] Josef Pieper, *Leisure: The Basis of Culture,* trans. Alexander Dru (New York: Random House, 1963).

nomic and political cooperation. Even the most routine and demeaning job is considered worthwhile if it provides for the purchase and rent of leisure goods and services. Leisure, then, is not viewed as existential action but as participation in the marketplace. It is purchasing travel, toys, and entertainment. A good time becomes identified with spending money, opportunity with purchasing access, and activity with being entertained. Leisure is being in the right place in the right clothes doing the right thing. Buying or renting leisure commodities is the special reward for contributing labor to the economic system. Leisure, then, is not a human right or a basic human action; it is a reward.

In a socialist system the economy is designed to support the state and its ruling elites. Worker ownership through the state is the ideology that tends to obscure the concentration of political power. In a capitalist system the economy is constructed to give control and primary rewards to investment capital. Workers are instrumental, a cost of production. Their labor is purchased at a price that keeps them maintained in a standard of living defined as adequate. Work for most is extrinsic, not satisfying productive engagement but a means to other ends. Economic cooperation is rewarded with purchasing power to maintain the self, family, and home along with the possibility of purchasing leisure. Leisure is that something more, the purchase of pleasure.

In such a system, how is leisure identified? Not by self-determination, development, or building community. Leisure is defined by where you go, what you wear, and what you do. The signs of leisure are distributed by the economic market at prices accessible to the mass of households. The rewards for cooperative acquiescence are more than survival and shelter. Leisure is the bonus, the arena of life that gives the appearance of choice. Wages are believed to buy pleasure. In a system in which the greatest returns go to investment capital and in which labor is instrumental, leisure becomes part of the reward system. Workers deserve "free time" and earn market participation through their instrumental activity in the workplace.

The economic system requires a stratified set of employees. Some are specially prepared and costly to replace. Others perform necessary tasks, but can be replaced by almost anyone else at low cost. Therefore, the reward system discriminates to attract and hold workers in the high-cost positions. Gender, race, and ethnicity are employed to close opportunities to those who are directed into the low-cost and low-reward positions of the replaceable. Research and development technicians are given more money and security than those who clean up after them. Leisure is a part of the clear hierarchy of rewards related to the scarcity, cost, and economic value of workers. At the top, a wide range of resources can be purchased with price assumed to index quality.

Public provisions for recreation are justified as supporting the health and productivity of workers at various levels. Leisure, then, is both part of the reward system and an economically useful behavior. Recreation provisions such as open spaces and parks are not a right of all citizens but a means of keeping people fit to work. Public recreation provisions are allocated by an economic efficiency standard of measured return on the investment. Parks are justified by how many tourists they attract. Children's programs are supported insofar as they contribute to the development of useful workers. There is some equity for the poor and dispossessed, enough space and opportunity to minimize their potential to disrupt the lives of others. Targeted groups such as the young unemployed are given special consideration to segregate them from the more privileged.

Thorstein Veblen analyzed the leisure of a century ago as a symbol of social differentiation.[22] The higher classes used leisure to demonstrate that they had transcended ordinary necessity. Contemporary critical analysis goes further to argue that leisure is one dimension of the control of the working classes by the economic and political elites. As in Rome, entertainment is provided to quiet the masses.

The central issue is how to produce a social consensus among those who lack the power to determine their own lives. The preferred approach in almost any society, totalitarian or democratic, capitalist or socialist, is to persuade rather than coerce. In capitalist systems and increasingly in socialist as well, that persuasion is in terms of the distribution of purchasing power and the support of desired life styles. The sanction or penalty for the failure to cooperate is the withdrawal of purchasing power in the market. And increasingly, leisure is a significant part of that market.

What is freedom in this context? It is the ability of make market choices. What is leisure? It is the exercise of that freedom, buying and using those market-provided goods and services. For some, shopping itself comes to be identified as the most pleasurable leisure activity.

Employment is not satisfying productive activity; it is renting the self to others. It is justified by the market activity it supports rather than by any sense of purpose or self-development. Humans are units in a process, alienated from their own natures, from others, and from a sense of worth. At the same time, leisure is alienated into "commodity fetishism."[23] It is not an action of becoming, but is defined in terms of what can be possessed and utilized, consumed and displayed.

Herbert Marcuse argued that alienated individuals have surrendered their freedom and sensuality to commodification.[24] The control and ownership of *things* has become the prime symbol of existence that replaces action with and for others. Self-determination and community are lost to the focus on possession. The standard of value becomes price rather than use. Along with the rest of life, leisure is seen as alienated in its loss of community. Leisure styles become concentrated on privatized individual and personal satisfaction.

To summarize the argument:

1. Leisure is a reward for acquiescence in the economy.
2. Leisure is commodified so that styles are reduced to market choices that symbolize social status.
3. Wages provide markets for the "leisure sector" of the economy.
4. Recreation is supported in terms of preparing current and future workers to be more productive.
5. The media reinforce this picture of the "good life" that is defined by possessions, especially in the home and in leisure.

The fundamental issue is whether we come to believe the package, the social construction that this is indeed right and good. Do we believe that leisure is really best for

---

[22] Thornstein Veblen, *The Theory of the Leisure Class,* Second edition (New York: New American Library, 1953[1899]).

[23] Karl Marx, *Capital,* ed. Frederick Engels (New York: International Publishers, 1967[1867]).

[24] Herbert Marcuse, *One-Dimensional Man* (Boston: Beacon Press, 1964).

those with the most money to spend on it? Do we equate satisfaction with spending, action with possession, and meaning with things? Is freedom as self-determining and community-building action lost in this system? And what are the ideologies that work to keep women and men in their social "place"?

There is, of course, another possibility. Distortions may be found in any social system. But despite limitations, does a society provide opportunities for real action? If leisure is creative action, then it cannot be the gift of any social system. Rather, the society can only minimize limitations and provide adequate opportunities for leisure. As action, leisure may always be more of a struggle than a gift, more of a possibility than a provision.

Conflict theory leads to questions of value as well as to social analysis. Is life measured by achievement, status, reward symbols, and market choices? Or is leisure one element in the "natural balance" of life,[25] a balance of productive activity and a place for personal development and building community? Is so much of the routine and outcome-specification of economic roles inevitable that leisure is a balancing realm of relative freedom, even when limited by market choice and time scarcities?

The fundamental issue is whether there is freedom adequate for self-developing action. If so, what is the place of leisure in providing such opportunity? Is leisure deeply alienated or a possibility for humanizing action? Freedom is, after all, a process rather than a state. It is created and re-created in authentic action. Leisure should, at least, be a domain of life in which such action is both possible and fostered.

Humanist Theory

Leisure is part of being human, not leftover time or a reward for doing something else. It is an openness to seek and create the "not yet," including the developing self. Creative activity is directed toward a realization of the potential in the creator as well as in what is being created. There, leisure and creation are both acts of becoming.

What does the actor become? There may be no final goal or achievement, but the direction is toward becoming human, toward a realization of one's nature. How does this happen? In both work and play, there may be action that creates and that is developmental. Both are "ex-static" in the sense of bringing the "not yet" into being.

In classical Greek terms, leisure is to provide time for exploration and development, for becoming human and creating humanizing opportunities for others. Being human is, from this perspective, not a given. It is a process, not a final state. We become human. The issue is how. This final metaphor is not a behavioral approach but a philosophical one.

On an individual level, leisure has been identified with the "freedom to become." It is also a context for action, for creation. According to Aristotle in the *Politics,* the separation of leisure from the world of necessity is a context for self-directed action. Johan Huizinga argued that play is voluntary, free, bounded in time and space, and creates its own order.[26] Play is doing something, usually performing with and for others. It is productive in bring-

[25] Herbert Marcuse, *Eros and Civilization* (Boston: Beacon Press, 1966).

[26] Huizinga, *Homo Ludens.*

ing into being what does not yet exist.[27] The openness of leisure, then, is a context for the creation of play. Thus, leisure is not added on to life as a leftover or reward. As Schiller proposed in the eighteenth century, it is at the center of what it means to be human.[28]

Pieper argues that leisure is the basis of culture.[29] It is the context of creation of the ideas, representations, and the forms that celebrate the past and present of civilization and move it forward. Leisure, according to this view, is a condition of the mind that is free from necessity and open to novelty.

As in leisure, creation is composed of a series of dialectical elements:

Creation is at the same time free in its act and constrained in its form.

It is open to the imagination and composed of the forms and materials of the world.

It is always new and yet communicated in ways familiar to others.

It is based in the perceived world and yet has dimensions that heighten or re-form that world.

It is self-contained in playful action and yet involves others.

It is paradoxical: for itself and yet the basis of all that moves life forward in experience and understanding.

It is freedom that is necessary.

Common play such as festival is a ritual of celebration. It dramatizes the themes and historical basis of a society. Yet it also reveals that the culture is the creation of its people and subject to their intervention.

Defining leisure is not the central issue. Leisure is more a dimension of life than a discrete entity with boundaries. The real question is what happens in times and places that are relatively free from necessity and are oriented primarily toward the experience. The fundamental negation of leisure is not external constraint. It is the failure to act. Leisure is the possibility of self-determined action in a structured world. The actualization of leisure is authentic action. Alienation, on the other hand, is the denial of freedom and of community. Alienation, in work or leisure, in family or solitude, is the failure to take humanizing action.

Authentic action in leisure may be negated by false consciousness that substitutes slogans for action. Leisure may also be negated by an elitism that limits such action to a few of the privileged at the expense of the masses. Leisure as self-determining action requires a space—freedom of environment as well as of consciousness. It is political and social as well as existential and philosophical.

The aim of life and of leisure as a part of life is not self-expression but self-creation. It is not simply to be but to become. Leisure is, then, both action and environment in which such creation is possible. It is freedom not from, but for, others. It is human.

---

[27] Hans, *The Play of the World.*

[28] Friedrich Schiller, *On the Aesthetic Education of Man,* trans. R. Snell (New Haven, CT: Yale University Press, 1954).

[29] Pieper, *Leisure.*

There is, however, no perfect environment. Rather, existential action takes place in the struggle and confusion of ordinary life. And leisure may be the context we create in order to act. Leisure is not separation, but possibility; it is not finality, but activity.

As activity, life is a becoming—a process. In this process, leisure is a special place of freedom for action. As action, leisure is the freedom to become. As environment, it is the possibility of becoming.

Finally, leisure is both existential and social.[30] It is a social creation, of its culture and yet re-creating the culture. From a dialectical perspective, it is creative: existentially creative of the self and socially creative of the culture. It is both being and becoming.

HIGHLIGHTS

1. Each of the eight theoretical perspectives draws our attention to elements of leisure that are both real and contemporary.
2. Freedom is not a simple absence of constraint, but is self-determined action that is possible in environments that are always limited.
3. Leisure is dialectical with its essential dimensions of action and of social context.
4. Leisure is more than a historical phenomenon. It is being and becoming, a possibility of creative action.

Discussion Questions

1. Is there one of the eight approaches to leisure that might be considered basic to all the others?

2. Give examples from your own experience of how leisure is at the same time existential and social, action and learned behavior?

3. Can leisure be defined at all? Are there concepts that differentiate it clearly from other kinds of attitudes, actions, or social behaviors? If so, what are they?

4. Is leisure the creation of industrial society, a kind of time, or a fundamental theme of human life?

5. Is leisure a reward or a right? Is it freedom or a struggle?

6. What is the most significant barrier to the realization of leisure in contemporary Western societies? In developing nations?

7. What are the ideologies and value systems that cut men and women off from action that is truly creative and liberating?

---

[30] John R. Kelly, *Freedom to Be: A New Sociology of Leisure* (New York: Macmillan, 1987).

Index